CARICOM INTEGRATION
PROGRESS AND HURDLES

– A EUROPEAN VIEW –

CARICOM INTEGRATION

PROGRESS AND HURDLES

A EUROPEAN VIEW

CHRISTOPH MÜLLERLEILE

LMH Publishing Limited

First Edition 1996
Second Edition 2003

Translated by *Fitzroy Fraser*
Cover designed by Robert Harris
Cover redesigned by Lee-Quee Design
Typeset by Zamal's Software Company, 6 Dowding St. Kitty, Georgetown, Guyana

Published by: LMH Publishing Limited
7 Norman Road,
LOJ Industrial Complex
Building 10
Kingston C.S.O., Jamaica
Tel: 876-938-0005; 938-0712
Fax: 876-759-8752
Email: lmhbookpublishing@cwjamaica.com
Website: www.lmhpublishingjamaica.com

Printed in the U.S.A.

ISBN 976-8184-61-2

CONTENTS

PUBLISHERS NOTE

The importance and extent of the scope of this book, coming out of the European perspective, has demanded a careful approach to the recording of the dynamics of a geographical and political area still searching for its integration

With such ever-changing dynamics it is almost inevitable that, in a book of this nature, certain facts recorded therein will be overtaken by current developments between the time of writing and the time of publication.

Just prior to the publication of this book, in July 1996, a CARICOM Heads of Government meeting was held in Barbados. At that conference agriculture, and in particular banana production, was high on the agenda. The Heads of Government agreed to a New Vision for Agriculture focusing on agriculture as a business and making it more internationally competitive.

Further discussions took place regarding the CARICOM Single Market and Economy (CSME); with the Heads of Government endorsing recommendations to allow artistes, musicians, sportsmen and media personnel to move and work throughout the region – an addition to the provisions already existing in six Member States for the free movement of University Graduates.

The next meeting will be held in Jamaica in 1997, and we look forward to further developments along the road to Caribbean integration.

The publishers regret the untimely death of the book's translator, Dr. Fitzroy Fraser, in early 1996. His passing was a sad loss to the Caribbean academic and intellectual world.

FOREWORD

by Professor Rex Nettleford

This extensive investigation into Caribbean integration — the process, the institutional manifestations over time and the possibilities of achieving it in the foreseeable future — appears at an auspicious time when fourteen states that have gone to form the Caribbean Community (CARICOM) are psychologically attuned to a "new beginning".

This itself follows on years of reflection on the performance of that body which is universally acknowledged to have been long on decisions, but short on implementation. It was an admission, by CARICOM States themselves, of the weaknesses of the regional system of collaboration that led to the establishment of an independent West Indian Commission in 1990. It was that "independence" which drove the Commissioners to a full and frank report entitled ***Time For Action***, so designated to send a clear message that Caribbean integration needed less talk and more action.

Much thought, much talk and some action had admittedly gone into designing the institutional framework for such integration as this volume clearly indicates, drawing, as it does, on an impressive array of authorities ranging from academics and technocrats to politicians and journalists, who have all been challenged by the elusive prize of integration, especially after the break-up of the short-lived West Indies Federation which lasted from 1958 to 1961.

The author Christoph Müllerleile, himself a native witness to Europe's contemporary efforts to integrate, speculates on the future of similar efforts in the Caribbean. He understandably shares a former CARICOM Secretary General's hope that "the self-dynamism of the integration process" will provide "a spillover effect" — in other words, the hope of an "effective political and functional psychological environment, which would maintain that process of economic collaboration".

That hope was equally shared by the West Indian Commission which half-way in its existence sought to accelerate that process by recommending, "for immediate action", some six steps towards early integration. These covered (i) freedom of movement of nationals within the Region; (ii) free movement of skilled people starting with West Indian graduates of the University of the West Indies, as an aid to economic development and growth; (iii) work towards establishing a common currency; (iv) launching of a Regional Investment Fund to invest in the Region's stock market; (v) completion, "**as a matter of urgency**", of the CARICOM Single Market with its three principal instruments — the Common External Tariff, the Harmonised Scheme of Fiscal Incentives and the Rules of Origin; and (vi) mobilisation of "CARICOM to have a single voice for international negotiations vital to the common interest".

The final Report of the Commission went beyond these as this volume helpfully outlines in its final chapter. But the Commission also elaborated on the interim recommendations since they remained in the Commissioners' minds essential tasks "on the way to effective regional integration".

One of the most significant developments out of the continuing process is the establishment of the Association of Caribbean States (ACS) following on the Commissioners' considered view that regionalism in CARICOM terms alone is no longer enough. There is need for the expansion of the existing CARICOM market of 5.5 million souls to one with a population of 200 million including Cuba in the North, Suriname in the South and countries like Venezuela, Colombia, Central America and Mexico, all of which are washed by the Caribbean Sea.

By the time this book is published initial meetings of that new grouping will have been held in Trinidad, the headquarters of the ACS. CARICOM, ***per se***, would have admitted Suriname as a full-fledged member; and the author's eleven well argued points, which he feels should be on the region's agenda of concerns, would have been tabled for action.

Meanwhile, the people of the Commonwealth Caribbean will continue to "integrate" after their fashion via cricket, carnival and other such popular artistic endeavours, as well as through the intellectual activities carried out in the University of the West Indies. "We in the Caribbean are already integrated. It is only the Governments who didn't know". This view once expressed by the West Indian economist and former public scholar, the late George Beckford, is aptly quoted by Dr. Müllerleile, if only by way of reassurance that all is not lost since the possibility for such integration is, after all, very much in place.

December, 1995

Preface

In September, 1983, delegates of political organisations from sixteen English-speaking Caribbean countries met in Kingston, Jamaica, where they founded the *Caribbean Youth Conference.* The author, as the representative of a German Foundation, had the privilege of sitting at the head table.

Quite abruptly, he received a note, which bore the signature of one of the organisers of the gathering. 'Please do not interfere in this, no matter what mistakes we make,' it read.

That was good advice which, during his stint of several years in the Caribbean, he often pondered over. Social scientists are among the many people who have 'interfered' in Caribbean affairs. The number of scholarly studies dealing with every aspect of Caribbean life has increased sharply in the last two decades. Sociologists, political scientists, economists, ethnologists and geographers especially in the USA, Canada and the United Kingdom have focused on the Caribbean in large numbers. The reason for this is surely not because, as Trinidad and Tobago's Prime Minister, Eric Williams, who died in 1981, once remarked, 'They had nothing to write about at home' (1973a, p.14).

Generally, the judgements of social scientists of non-Caribbean origin or 'roots' are more independent in their judgement and free from the need to pay attention to the possible negative impact their views may have on their jobs and careers, personal safety and friendships. Indigenous experts, on the other hand, can hardly free themselves from these considerations in their own countries or territories. In small island societies, everybody knows everybody else. Impartiality in any field is almost impossible. Moreover, it should be noted that foreign social scientists in several cases have easier access to local sources and contacts than do their native counterparts. To the former, many things are new and pertinent which locals would simply overlook or regard as run-of-the-mill.

For the study, a whole raft of books, essays and speeches by foreign experts on the Caribbean have, therefore, been relied on. This has been done especially because some of them contain the most thoroughly documented summaries of the development of Caribbean integration[1]. Nevertheless, there is validity to Axline's (1979, p.xiii) finding that no non-Caribbean academic can write about Caribbean politics and culture with the depth of understanding and feeling of a West Indian. Indeed, the late Carl Stone (1984)[2] warned even about the 'intellectual imperialism' of foreign academic authors, who hardly had more

---

[1] E g . Preiswerk (1969), Crassweller (1972), Axline (1979), Payne (1980), Freymond (1980), Woehlcke (1982), Serbín (1987), Gewecke (1988), and Lennert (1991)

[2] The work of Stone, a Jamaican social scientist and journalist who died (aged 52 years) in February 1993, is often quoted in this book. He was one of the best known and most independent analysts of Caribbean affairs The author obtained valuable insights from discussions with Stone and reading his numerous books, essays and newspaper columns.

knowledge of the Caribbean than a tourist, but who exerted influence on thinking in, and about, the Caribbean.

Caribbean authors and sources have been preferred, where available. Numerous newspaper and magazine sources are, therefore, quoted although their scientific rigour and impartiality are not equal to those of other publications.

Hence, this study makes an attempt to give the appropriate classification and weight to the sources.

In this connection, it may be advantageous that the author, with his family, lived and worked in the Caribbean from October, 1981 to the end of 1985, and visited all States and territories of the Commonwealth Caribbean and some of the non-Commonwealth.

The knowledge of the situation facilitated the contextual evaluation of persons and sources as well as the recognition of intentions and allusions behind statements and mannerisms, which would have remained hidden from the unwary or uninitiated observer. Out of the numerous discussions with politicians, academics, trade unionists, business people, journalists, artists and ministers of religion of the countries and territories, the author was able to come to the opinions expressed in this book. Wherever such opinions are given without supporting source, then they should be seen as his.

I wish, in particular to express my thanks to Professor Manfred Mols of the Institute of Political Science at the Johannes Gutenberg University, Mainz/Germany, who suggested and supervised this study, and strongly recommended that it be translated into English. I also wish to express my gratitude to Manzoor Nadir in Guyana, Dr. Fitzroy Fraser and Joseph McPherson in Jamaica, Alvin Knight in Dominica, Dr. Gernot Lennert in Mainz/Germany and Michael Abend, then in Barbados, for their numerous suggestions and critical assessment. The study does not necessarily express their opinions, but they helped me to avoid many errors.

July, 1995

Abbreviations Frequently Used in This Book[3]

AIFLD American Institute for Free Labor Development

ACP African, Caribbean and Pacific Countries with special Link to the European Union (EU)

ALADI *Asociación Latinoamericana de Integración* (Latin American Integration Association)

AMP Agricultural Marketing Protocol

ANC African National Congress

ante Above (Latin)

AP Associated Press

APEC Asia-Pacific Economic Cooperation

ASEAN Association of South-East Asian Nations

BBC British Broadcasting Corporation

BVI British Virgin Islands

BWI British West Indies

BWIA British West Indian Airways

CA *Caribbean Affairs*, Port-of-Spain, Trinidad and Tobago

CADORIT Caribbean Area Division of ORIT

CAIC Caribbean Association of Industry and Commerce

CANA Caribbean News Agency

CARIBCAN Caribbean and Canada Trade Agreement

CARICOM Caribbean Community and Common Market

CARIFTA Caribbean Free Trade Association

CARIMAC Caribbean Institute of Mass Communication, of the University of The West Indies

CBI Caribbean Basin Initiative

CC *Caribbean Contact*, Bridgetown, Barbados

CCC Caribbean Conference of Churches

CCM Caribbean Common Market

CCL Caribbean Congress of Labour

CDB Caribbean Development Bank

CDCC Caribbean Development and Cooperation Committee (a Sub-Committee of ECLAC)

CDU Caribbean Defnocrat [*sic*] Union

CEDP CARICOM Export Development Project

CER CARICOM Enterprise Regime

Cf Compare (*Confer* Latin)

CET Common External Tariff

CFC Caribbean Food Corporation

CFNI Caribbean Food and Nutrition Institute

---

[3] Not a complete list of all abbreviations used.

CI *Caribbean Insight,* London, UK
CIPS CARICOM Industrial Programming Scheme
CLC Caribbean Labour Congress
CMC (CARICOM) Common Market Council
CMCF CARICOM Multilateral Clearing Facility
COC Commonwealth Caribbean
CP *Caricom Perspective,* Georgetown, Guyana
CPUSTAL Congreso Permanente de Unidad de los Trabajadores de America Latina
CR *Caribbean Report*—Latin American Regional Reports (London)
CXC Caribbean Examinations Council
CU *Caribbean Update,* Maplewood, N.J., USA
CYC Caribbean Youth Conference
DG *The Daily Gleaner,* Kingston, Jamaica
EAI Enterprise for the Americas Initiative
ECCA East Caribbean Currency Authority
ECCM East Caribbean Common Market
ECEDA East Caribbean Economic Development Agency
ECLAC Economic Commission for Latin America and the Caribbean of the United Nations
ECOSOC Economic and Social Council of the United Nations
EFTA European Free Trade Association
EC European Community
EEC European Economic Community
et al. and others (*et alii* Latin)
EU European Union
GCE General Certificate of Education (Examination)
GNP Gross National Product
ICFTU International Confederation of Free Trade Unions
IDA International Development Agency
IDB Inter-American Development Bank
IMF International Monetary Fund
Intra Below (Latin)
IPPF International Planned Parenthood Federation
JLP Jamaica Labour Party
JTEC Joint Trade and Economic Co-operation Committee
LDC Less Developed Country
MDC More Developed Country
NAFTA North American Free Trade Agreement
NATO North Atlantic Treaty Organization
n.d. No data on year or place of publication, or page no., etc.
NGO Non-governmental Organisation
OAS Organization of American States *(Organisación de los Estados Americanos)* = OEA

Abbreviations Frequently Used In This Book

ODCA *Organisación Demócrata Cristiana de América* (Christian Democratic Organization of America)

OECS Organisation of Eastern Caribbean States

OLADE *Organisación Latinoamericana de Energía* (Latin American Energy Organisation)

ORIT *Organisación de los Trabajadores* (Inter-American Organisation of Workers)

PNP People's National Party

q.v. Refer to (*quod vide* Latin)

RCA Regional Constituent Assembly

REC Regional Economic Committee

RSS Regional Defence and Security System

SCOPE Standing Conference of Popular Democratic Parties in East Caribbean States[4]

SELA *Sistema Económico Latinoamericano* (Latin American Economic System)

SG *The Sunday Gleaner*, Kingston, Jamaica

TUCCW Trade Union Council of Caribbean Workers

UN The United Nations

UNDP The United Nations Development Programme

UNCTAD The United Nations Conference on Trade and Development

UNESCO The United Nations Educational Scientific and Cultural Organisation

UNFPA The United Nations Fund for Population Activities

USVI The US Virgin Islands

UWI University of the West Indies

WG *The Weekly Gleaner*, London, UK

WISA [*sic*] West Indies Associated States

WISCO West Indies Shipping Corporation

---

[4]Originally: Standing Committee of Opposition Parties of the Eastern Caribbean States.

CARICOM INTEGRATION

PROGRESS AND HURDLES

- A EUROPEAN VIEW -

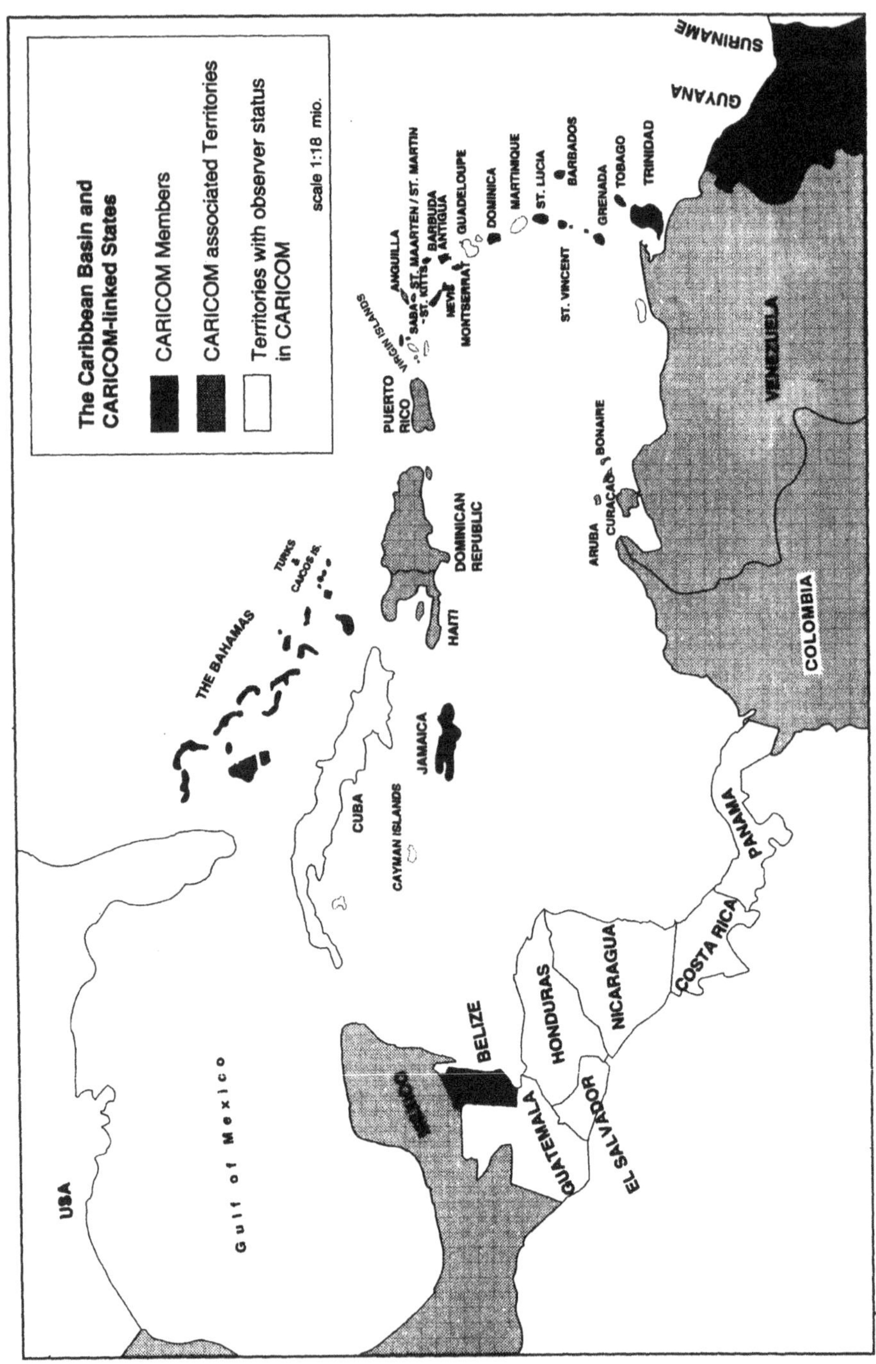

The Caribbean Basin and CARICOM-linked States
CARICOM Members
CARICOM associated Territories
Territories with observer status in CARICOM
scale 1:18 mio.
USA
Gulf of Mexico
BELIZE
GUATEMALA
HONDURAS
EL SALVADOR
NICARAGUA
COSTA RICA
PANAMA
COLOMBIA
VENEZUELA
GUYANA
SURINAME
CUBA
CAYMAN ISLANDS
JAMAICA
THE BAHAMAS
TURKS & CAICOS IS.
HAITI
DOMINICAN REPUBLIC
PUERTO RICO
VIRGIN ISLANDS
ANGUILLA
SABA
ST. MAARTEN / ST. MARTIN
ST. KITTS
NEVIS
BARBUDA
ANTIGUA
MONTSERRAT
GUADELOUPE
DOMINICA
MARTINIQUE
ST. LUCIA
ST. VINCENT
BARBADOS
GRENADA
TOBAGO
TRINIDAD
ARUBA
CURAÇAO
BONAIRE

Introduction

Islands are particularly ideal research objects for integration studies. Their geographic delimitations are quite precise. Statistically, inter-action between islands is more easily established and measured than is the case in mainland countries with artificially determined borders. Being enclosed by water reduces the frequency of inter-action with the outside world and enables the local actors to regulate access — even between archipelagic islands separated by only a few kilometres. Moreover, external influences can be isolated, and their effect, evaluated.

Small islands, unlike larger ones, are less able to dispense with inter-action and co-operation with the outside world. This is because, once they have attained a certain demographic density and/or their population has developed a certain need structure, they lose the capacity for autarky.

Population exchange between neighbouring islands stimulates integration. Family relationships and the cultivation of consciousness of one's origins help to prevent the breaking-off of links to one's native land (Wiltshire-Brodber, 1984, pp. 192-197). A long distance, however, separates this view of a limited island area from social, economic or political integration.

'Integration' in this connection may be defined as the process of the transfer of loyalty, whereby a new single body results from two (*cf.* Bellers, 1986, p.201). The former is marked by increasing coherence through common positions and actions. Either step by step or by leaps and bounds, it passes from smaller to the larger organisational stages, from the individual stage through state or private sector institutions to huge bodies of a more complex nature. A stable political union may come into being at the end of the process. Internal and external influences may either accelerate or decelerate the integration process. But stabilisation can occur only after completing the integration stages which had been overleapt.

The stabilisation of each integration level requires that the participants are both ready and able to continue the integration process. Internal and external factors favouring integration must be stronger than the factors leading to disintegration and the stagnation of integration. The most important motives behind Caribbean integration are as follows: The linking of resources, production and markets to attain 'self-sufficiency', and [5] the achievement of 'effective', as opposed to merely 'formal', sovereignty (Demas, 1975, p. 53), the creation and maintenance of a Caribbean identity offering protection against non-Caribbean influences.

Up to at least the 1980s, the main focus of academic studies on Caribbean integration was on politics and economics. But a proper examination of this subject cannot be so reduced, since it neglects territories which reject political and economic integration in the Caribbean Community (i.e. CARICOM) or, for certain reasons, cannot achieve it — although their populations belong

---

[5]Please see Axline (1986, p.6, note 6) for a definition of *collective self-reliance* for the Caribbean

ethnically and socioculturally to the Commonwealth Caribbean and consider this characteristic as part of its identity.

Nor does it suffice, in this connection, to limit oneself merely to the behaviour of the *élite* and governments. Regional integration without the broad participation of both the population and NGOs as their special interest groups (Kirton, 1983) would hardly last. Or as an Antiguan weekly put it:

> 'It is clear that the people are not being reached by all this talk of regional integration, something more needs to be done. The region's musicians and calypsonians have managed to unite us in sound, the same goes for the rockermen from Jamaica and Guyana but that has not been enough. Barbadians and Dominicans are not supposed to get along, the same goes for Antiguans and people from St. Kitts. Guyanese and Trinidadians have, from time to time immemorial, had a running feud. Caribbean people cannot justify irritation with those outside the region who mistake Guyana for Ghana, Dominica for the Dominican Republic, the Grenadines for Grenada or Barbuda for Bermuda when we know little more than the names ourselves. The need now is for an effort to introduce one end of the Caribbean to the other by exchange of films, visits for students and parents alike, much lower airfares and the discouragement of petty jealousies' (Osborn, 1985).

The necessity of the participation of the *masses* was, however, hardly considered by both theoreticians and practitioners of Caribbean integration. According to Wiltshire-Brodber (1984, p.199), integration attempts are more likely to be successful, if

1. The institutional linkages coincide with strong informal economic, political and social linkages among the units;
2. Power at the core outweighs power at the periphery.

Vaughan Lewis (1984, p. 38) has adduced a similar line of reasoning: If integration proposals are to be convincing, then the system sought after must be viable within its borders, so that it provides a sufficiently strong countervailing force through stimuli and resources, that can outweigh the advantages suggested by the international environment of a continuation of segmented integration.

Vaughan Lewis's thesis, cited above, should be examined. According to this thesis, the integration space is more stable, if a leading state exists within the proposed system, and has enough capital and other resources to extend its internal system as a type of seed capital to the other States. The leading State will then also have enough capacity to stabilise the integration area in the course of time.

In keeping with this thesis, the working hypothesis is proposed that the absence of such a leading State in the Commonwealth Caribbean has rendered political and economic integration more difficult. The polarity, caused by rival and unrealised leadership claims, between Jamaica and Trinidad and Tobago, runs through the entire recent history of integration of the Commonwealth Caribbean region. It contributed to the destruction of the West Indies Federation (1958-62) and has several times brought CARICOM to the brink of collapse.

According to Lewis (1984a), the basic condition for the creation of an integrated system as per the aforementioned model is this: The geographical area to which it belongs, and which had been recognised either previously or simultaneously as a relatively stable 'diplomatic zone' or 'theatre', must not be exposed to undesirable influences on its integration process, either automatically or unpredictably. The geographical area in question Lewis defines as a geopolitically delimited region characterised by certain behavioural norms, strengthened by the extensive autonomy of the integration area. In conflict definition and resolution, those norms must be accepted.

The absence in the Caribbean of such a clearly definable 'diplomatic zone' leads, in Lewis's view, to the incapacity shown by these countries hitherto to solve their common problems. The US-led military intervention in Grenada in October, 1983, for example, must therefore be examined as to whether the Commonwealth Caribbean has since developed into being a 'diplomatic zone'. In this regard, autonomy of action plays a decisive role.

Wiltshire-Brodber (1984) uses a holistic model. She lists the informal links, with the institutional ones, of the various countries and territories. Those links condition each other and determine the stage of maturity of the integration process. Mols (1982) has a similar point of view. His eight integration stages in Latin America are applied and tested in this book.

It is difficult to determine the attitude of the masses objectively towards integration. Representative, Caribbean-wide public opinion studies which could provide information on this attitude are unknown. Even the 1961 referendum in Jamaica — the only one dealing *prima facie* with integration questions — was rather a plebiscite over personalities and parties. Elections, the results of which are determined by statements by the competing political parties on integration, were rare in the Commonwealth Caribbean.

An attempt to obtain a comprehensive view of the posture to integration of leading representatives of population was made by the West Indian Commission under University of the West Indies (UWI) Chancellor, Sir Shridath Ramphal, which was set up in 1989 and reported some two years later, after holding hearings in all CARICOM Member States and the United Kingdom as well as visiting some non-Anglophone Caribbean countries[6]. This commission attached importance to hearing a broad spectrum of opinion. It was the first time since the Moyne Commission in the 1930s, that the people of the Region had been consulted in this manner (Caribbean Community, 1993, p. 79).

The 1983 US-led Grenada intervention — one of the most significant events in recent Commonwealth Caribbean history — must be studied also for its effect on Caribbean integration. Ideological coherence, one of the integration factors paid little attention in non-Marxist integration research, has to be assessed.

The main aims of this study are as follows:

— to demonstrate the specific internal and external profederal factors concerning the Commonwealth Caribbean, to assess their significance and prognosis with regard to regional integration, as well as,

[6]Please see Chapter 2.2 10 for more detailed information

— to draw general inferences concerning the possibilities for integration of mini-States, and, in particular, those which are islands in the 'Third World'; and

— to point out further research areas.

1. The Commonwealth Caribbean

1.1 The Area around the Commonwealth Caribbean

The Caribbean Basin, excluding the United States of America, includes a total of twenty-six independent countries including the Central American States as well as Colombia, Guyana, Panama, Suriname, Mexico and Venezuela and twelve dependent territories, with a total of 197 million inhabitants (1991)[7].

The islands of the Basin range in size from Cuba (the largest, with some 10.7 million inhabitants and 114,524 square kilometres, or as big as Belgium, Denmark, and the Netherlands together) to inhabited land surfaces of only a few hundred square metres.

The total population stood at about 32 million in 1991, with a total GDP of over US$79.5 billion (1991)[8].

Geo-strategically, the Caribbean Basin can be regarded as an entity, which the United States of America, owing to its significance for her own security, considers to be within her traditional sphere of influence. For only three decades, starting with the 1959 Cuban Revolution under Fidel Castro, did the ex-USSR mount a challenge to US hegemony in the region.

The Caribbean Basin is characterised by cultural, linguistic, racial and ethnic differences among the various independent States and the dependent territories. Common to all of them is a history of colonial domination, albeit of varying duration and intensity. The region has been the subject of competing colonial interests since the first documented arrival of the Europeans there, near the end of the fifteenth century. Spaniards, British, French, Dutch, Danes and Swedes claimed land there for economic exploitation.

Ethnically, the Caribbean has become the most multi-faceted region in the world. Today it is mainly peopled by the descendants of slaves from Africa, of indentured labourers from China and India, transported convicts from England, as well as others from France, Java, the Netherlands, Portugal, Spain and the United States of America — in addition to the descendants of the various long-resident Amerindian peoples who survived subjection and escaped almost total extermination in the islands. Out of the mixing of these groups have arisen new ethnic groups: The best-known are the *mulattoes*, the offspring of unions of blacks with whites, and the *mestizos*, descendants of unions between Amerindians and whites. *Black Caribs*, the results of unions between Africans and Caribs are the minorities in St. Vincent and Belize — in the latter they are known as *Garifuna*. The multi-faceted ethnic picture corresponds to the linguistic situation. English, Spanish, Dutch and French are both the principal languages and the components of local dialects, for example, Patois, Creole and Papiamento. On the mainland, languages — or their remnants — of the old-established peoples, have also been able to remain in existence.

[7] The author's own calculations, based on Fischer's Weltalmanach (1994).
[8] The author's own calculations from Fischer's Weltalmanach (1994).

The varieties of religions in the region range from Christian denominations and groups, through Muslims and Hindus, to practitioners of animism. Christian evangelical sects, most of US origin, have been increasing their number of converts.

The cultural richness of the area is in keeping with the ethnic and linguistic situation. The mores and customs of the various countries of origin are mixed with those of the relevant Caribbean states and territories in which the descendants of the immigrants now live. The European colonial masters sought in vain to prevent the independent cultural forms of expression of the African slaves. These forms, despite differing origins, grew extremely swiftly. Over the centuries, three main cultural areas have developed in the Caribbean, corresponding to the English, French and Spanish language areas. The exchange of music, dance and literature occurs largely within each of these language areas. The Dominican Republic and Puerto Rico are culturally closer to Cuba and Colombia than to their closer neighbours — namely, Haiti and Jamaica. This chasm also has political *sequelae*. Thus, for instance, the 1959 Cuban Revolution attracted less support in the English and French-speaking Caribbean areas than it did in Latin America. The political expulsion of the Cubans in Jamaica in 1980 and in Grenada in 1983 was less directed from outside these countries than the proponents of the ubiquitous presence of 'US Imperialism' want to believe.

The life of Caribbean residents has been determined by external economic interests since European colonisation. Only since World War II have independence and self-determination been won, except in Haiti. The main interest of the colonial masters was the growth of agricultural produce highly sought after in Europe, such as sugar, bananas and citrus. This caused a radical restructuring of the hitherto small-holder subsistence economy to a plantation economy, and it was paralleled by the enslavement of the original inhabitants and, then, the importation and enslavement of people from Africa.

With the decline of Spain's world power status in the nineteenth century that country's colonial role also came to an end. France had to cede Haiti in the throes of the French Revolution's turmoil and Napoleon's defeats. The Netherlands and the United Kingdom did not find it difficult to separate themselves from a portion of their Caribbean 'possessions', owing to their decreasing strategic interests in the Caribbean region.

Caribbean states and territories do not, with few exceptions, belong to the category of the poorest countries in the world, when compared in global perspective. Only Haiti is rated as a 'least developed country' (LLDC), whereas most are rated as 'less developed countries' (LDCs), and some are rated as 'more developed countries' (MDCs) in the UN classification. Almost all of them, however, have increasing economic problems, which endanger their economic and political status and may have consequences, above all, on their internal security.

The economic problems are essentially determined by the following two factors:

1. The fall in the demand for commodities, especially bauxite and oil, and agricultural produce, or the fall in earnings of such exports, despite un-

changed or even increased demand, owing to increased competition in the world market, and

2. Lack of competitiveness of their goods and services.

Most Caribbean states and territories receive US economic aid. The Caribbean islands, apart from Cuba, the US Virgin Islands and Puerto Rico, enjoy Lomé Treaties' benefits as ACP Member States.

Illegal narcotics, especially cocaine and marijuana, known as 'ganja' locally or 'ganga', constitute two of the few agricultural and trading products in which the Caribbean is really competitive in the world market. Moreover, proximity to both the United States of America and Canada gives the region an advantage based on its location. Big profits from their planting, distribution and sale present most Caribbean authorities with problems they can hardly solve. Only under US pressure have they been ready to take visible counter-measures. They open the door to corruption and the violent confrontations of criminal groups. Increasing domestic use endangers the health of the local population and also exerts a negative socio-economic influence.

The high population growth has rendered the economic problems more acute. 'Babies are one of the main products of the region,' found the British geographer, David Lowenthal, back in 1961, during the short-lived West Indies Federation. Restrictive immigration laws in Canada, the United Kingdom and the United States of America in the last few years have blocked the traditional ways of holding overpopulation in check. These restrictions affect mainly the population strata, due to deficient professional qualifications, have only limited employment opportunities.

On the other hand, such emigration possibilities as exist, now as previously, for trained Caribbean personnel are leading to the feared 'brain drain'. Hence, education and training costs of Caribbean experts are off-loaded onto their less developed homelands, whereas the highly developed host countries benefit from their education and training. Plans to motivate Caribbean nationals in heavily populated islands to relocate to thinly populated countries such as Belize or Guyana by means of special attractions were abandoned, for, even when Guyana was better off economically, only few Caribbean nationals wanted to take advantage of that opportunity.

The internal state structure of Caribbean countries and territories is oriented towards the model of the respective influencing power as well as of the historically developed structure. Pluralistic democracy produced less sturdy roots in Caribbean states belonging to the Spanish colonial tradition — except in Costa Rica and Puerto Rico — than in the ex-British colonies. Oligarchy, military dictatorship and clientelism play a greater political and economic role in the former than in the latter.

In the former Spanish colonies, greater class differences developed, a small land-owing class stood at the opposite pole from the mass of poverty-stricken peasants, only a relatively small middle-class could develop, and the literacy rate was generally low. But a different development occurred in the Anglophone Caribbean (*cf.* 'Western Interests', p.3). Cuba played a particular role. While its political system for a time was oriented towards ex-Soviet Union models, it nonetheless stood firmly in the traditional line of the Latin American State and a culture marked by Iberian Catholicism (Krämer, 1991, p.20). The vast majority of the Commonwealth Caribbean states are governed along the Westminster Model handed down by the United Kingdom. Most other Caribbean states with a pluralistic democratic system of governance have a Presidential system with a limited period of office and proportional representation.

The political status of the individual Caribbean countries and territories is as varied as is the number of governmental systems in the region. Formally, most of them have been politically independent for varyingly long periods of time. Haiti (1804) was, after the United States of America, the first to declare itself an independent Republic. The last to date is St. Kitts (or St. Christopher) and Nevis (September,1983). Several Commonwealth Caribbean islands are colonies with differing dependence status and internal self-government. Puerto Rico has Commonwealth status as a US dependent territory; the US Virgin Islands are an 'unincorporated territory'[9].

Territorial conflicts exist between some states in the region. The entering into force of the new International Law of the Sea will increase the number of such conflicts. Particularly striking is the Guyana-Venezuela dispute in which Venezuela claims the mineral-rich Essequibo region, almost two-thirds the territory of Guyana. So is the Belize-Guatemala dispute, in which the latter still claims the total territory of Belize — even though it has since diplomatically recognised Belize, which has been independent from UK rule since 1981.

---

[9]In both cases, discussion had been taking place about their future status In Puerto Rico, the New Progressive Party (NPP) won a landslide victory for its platform of Puerto Rico becoming a state of the United States of America in the November, 1992 Governor's Congressional elections (*CI* December 1992, 10f). In both territories *referenda* took place in 1993 in which the people voted for the *status quo*, in Puerto Rico with 48%, in the USVI with 80% of the votes polled. The referendum in the USVI, however, is not valid since the minimum turn out could not be achieved (*CI* December 1993, p 5)

1.2 Geopolitical Definition of the Commonwealth Caribbean

The 'Commonwealth of Nations' is a group of autonomous communities within the former British Empire, which, with each having equal status and without mutual subordination, have freely associated and recognise the British Monarch as a symbol of the free association of the Member States and as Head of the Commonwealth (Paxton, 1981, p. 31).

TABLE 1 - GEOPOLITICAL DATA[10]

Table 1a—Independent States

State	Area (sq. km)	Population	Capital	Date of Independence
Antigua and Barbuda	440	63,880[11]	St. John's	Nov. 1, 1981
The Commonwealth of the Bahamas	13,942	264,400	Nassau	July 10, 1973
Barbados	432	258,800	Bridgetown	Nov. 30, 1966
Belize	22,960	199,500	Belmopan	Sept. 21, 1981
Commonwealth of Dominica	750	71,900	Roseau	Nov. 3, 1978
State of Grenada	345	95,400	St. George's	Feb. 7, 1974
Co-operative Republic of Guyana	214,970	723,800[12]	Georgetown	May 26, 1966
Jamaica	11,424	2,448,200	Kingston	Aug. 6, 1962
Federation of St. Kitts and Nevis	269	42,000	Basseterre	Sept. 19, 1983
St. Lucia	616	135,200	Castries	Feb. 22, 1979
St. Vincent and the Grenadines	388	109,000	Kingstown	Oct. 27, 1979
Republic of Trinidad and Tobago	5,128	1,241,600	Port-of-Spain	Aug. 31, 1962
TOTAL	272,688	5,653,680		

[10] Figures from Caribbean Developlnent Bank (*Annual Report 1993*, p. 15).

[11] 1991 Census (*CI* March, 1992, p 6).

[12] Population estimate of 1991 (*CI* October 1994, p 9).

Table 1b — UK-Dependent States[13]

Name of Territory	Area (Sq. Km)	Population	Capital
Anguilla	91	9,700	The Valley
The British Virgin Islands	150	17,000	Roadtown
The Cayman Islands	264	27,400	George Town
Montserrat	102	10,600	Plymouth
The Turks and Caicos Islands	417	12,600	Cockburntown
	1,024	77,300	

The Commonwealth Caribbean[14],which, up to the 1960s, was generally termed the 'British West Indies' by the British generally, is not a geographical entity. It is defined as countries in the Caribbean Basin which belong directly to the Commonwealth as independent states or indirectly as UK-dependent territories.

The term, 'Commonwealth Caribbean', covers several hundred islands spread over the entire Caribbean Sea, plus Guyana in the extreme southeastern corner, the Bahamas to the north and Belize to the west. The distance from Belmopan (the capital of Belize) to Georgetown (the capital of Guyana) is 3,600 kilometres; Belmopan to Nassau (the capital of Bahamas), 1,400; and Nassau to Georgetown, 2,700.

The Commonwealth Caribbean consists of seventeen political entities, including twelve former and five current British colonies. The surface area of the Commonwealth Caribbean totals 272,688 km^2, the island states and territories accounting for 12.7 % that is, 34,758 km^2; and Guyana, for almost 80%.

Numerous initiatives and institutions are called 'Caribbean', but refer only to a part of the region. Demas (1990, p.15) has proposed, from the viewpoint of the English-speaking Caribbean, a three-circle division, as follows:

- *The West Indies*, which includes the Commonwealth Caribbean islands;
- *The Caribbean Archipelago*, which includes the other islands, Guyana, French Guyana and Suriname as well as Belize;
- *The Caribbean Basin*, which includes all the remaining Caribbean Basin mainland states.

[13]Some authors include Bermuda, which however, lies geographically apart from the Caribbean (that is, in the Atlantic) and, owing to its formally dependent status and limited inter-action with Commonwealth Caribbean States, plays no significant role in the Caribbean integration process.

[14]The term, 'Commonwealth Caribbean countries' was first used at the First Conference of Commonwealth Countries (CCC) in July, 1963, in Trinidad, according to former diplomat, J. O'Neil Lewis (1989b, p. 58). That conference was chaired by Dr. Eric Williams, the Prime Minister of Trinidad and Tobago, and was attended by the Prime Minister of Jamaica, the Premier of Barbados of and the Premier of British Guiana.

1.3 Demographic Structure

The Commonwealth Caribbean with its some 5.8 million inhabitants has less than, say, the US State of Massachusetts. The population density varies from 3.4 residents per square kilometre (in Guyana) to 599.1 (in Barbados), and averages 21.1. The population density for the island states and territories (that is, excluding Belize and Guyana) is approximately 139.0 residents per square kilometre. Sixty-four percent of the population live in the islands of Jamaica and Trinidad and Tobago[15].

The Commonwealth Caribbean belongs to the 'more overpopulated' regions of the world, in terms of the relationship between the population and the agriculturally exploitable land surface. The Bahamas, according to the UN Fund for Population Activities (UNFPA), had the highest population land density of 1,468 residents per square kilometre of agrarian land, followed by Trinidad and Tobago (702), Grenada (700), Barbados (692), St. Vincent and the Grenadines (626), St. Lucia (610) and Jamaica (463)[16].

The annual rate of population increase for 1989-92 varied between -4.4% (in Guyana) and 6.5% (in Anguilla), with an average of 0.8%[17]. The under-16-year-old population segment in 1980 was highest (44%) in St. Vincent and the Grenadines and lowest (20%) in Barbados (*Caribbean Development to the Year 2000*, pp.130ff)

The CARICOM Member States top the United Nations Crisis Committee's quality of life index among developing countries[18], with an average life expectancy of 71 years. The literacy rate exceeds 90%, except in St. Vincent and the Grenadines (84%). Free health care is of a high standard. Pregnancy-induced maternal mortality is lower than in most other developing countries.

Barbados, among developing countries, was rated first (ahead of Hong Kong) in the 1993 United Nations Development Report rating states according to income and quality of life, Trinidad and Tobago was rated fifth; and the Bahamas, sixth — followed by Dominica (14th), Grenada (21st) and Antigua and Barbuda (22nd)[19].

The per head 1992 GDP, as an indication of potential prosperity, slopes sharply between the different CARICOM Member States[20], with the Cayman Islands[21], at US$30,511, above the United States of America[22], and Guyana, at US$500. The Bahamas (US$11,570), the British Virgin Islands (US$10,882), Anguilla (US$6,834), Antigua and Barbuda (US$6,769), Turks and Caicos Islands (US$6,252), Barbados (US$6,117), Montserrat (US$5,976), Trinidad and Tobago (US$4,383), St. Kitts and Nevis (US$3,990), St. Lucia (US$3,490), Dominica (US$2,636), Belize (US$2,374), Grenada (US$2,244), St. Vincent

[15] All 1992 figures, calculated from the *Caribbean Development Bank* (1994, p. 15).

[16] *Cf.*: India (381) and Haiti (425) — *DG* 11.11.1983, p. 15.

[17] *Caribbean Development Bank*, 1994, p. 15.

[18] Quoted following Tony Best (1992).

[19] *WG* 1.6.93, p. 19, *cf.* South Korea (7th), Costa Rica (9th), Argentina (12th), Venezuela (13th), Kuwait (15th) and Mexico (16th).

[20] Source: Caribbean Development Bank, 1992, p. 15.

[21] The Cayman Islands, as an off-shore banking centre and favoured company headquarters plays a special role, which in far smaller measure, also applies to the other U.K.-dependent territories.

[22] At US$22,203 in 1991 (*Fischer Weltalmanach*, 1994).

and the Grenadines (US$2,078), and Jamaica (US$ 1,291) were between these extremes. Remarkably, all the UK dependent territories are in the top Caribbean group.

The racial and ethnic composition of the population corresponds to pan-Caribbean multi-facetedness. The largest population segments consist of the descendants of slaves from Africa and indentured workers from India as well as the groups' offspring from unions with ethnic minorities. The Indians have largely retained their identity; but 'pure' African ancestry is hardly possible to determine. About 76% of the inhabitants of the Commonwealth Caribbean are classified as being predominantly of African origin, as against some 18% of Indian origin, and 1-2% each as Caucasians from Euro-America and Chinese[23]. The rest of the population consists of the descendants of native born Amerindians in Guyana, the Mayas and other Central American peoples in Belize, the Caribs in the East Caribbean islands, especially in Dominica and St. Vincent, and the Black Caribs (Garifuna) in Belize.

1.4 State and Governance Forms

All the larger Commonwealth Caribbean countries became independent from the United Kingdom in the 1960s. The smaller ones followed in the 1970s and 1980s — the last being St. Christopher (St. Kitts) and Nevis, with only 42,000 inhabitants and roughly one-third of the land area of, say, the city of Hamburg (Germany), in September, 1983, following the end of a territorial dispute with Anguilla. Territorial conflicts with Guatemala caused Belize as well, which is relatively larger in land area but is thinly populated, to put off its independence for a long time. Up to the end of 1994, the British garrison, which had been established there during the colonial period, would have protected Belize against possible attacks from its neighbours.

Independence, for these countries, means that they have become sovereign states after centuries of colonial rule and a short transitional period of internal self-government. During the latter period, the United Kingdom retained co-determination and deciding rights, especially in foreign affairs, external security and financial matters. The links with the United Kingdom have remained close. Nine of these twelve independent States are bi-cameral constitutional monarchies. Under this system, the English monarch is represented by a Governor-General she appoints after consultation with the Prime Minister of the Caribbean country in question. The main official duties of the Governor-General include affixing his or her signature to laws passed by the local Parliament and summoning the Government and naming members of the Senate as well as high Government officials.

Dominica, Guyana and Trinidad and Tobago have all become republics. The Presidents of Dominica and Trinidad and Tobago are elected by Parliament and have functions similar to those of the Governors-General.

In Guyana, an Executive President at the head of a political party's list is elected by the electorate, together with the members of the uni-cameral National Assembly, at least once every five years. National Assembly seats are allocated

[23]The author's own calculations, based on Fischer's Weltalmanach (1988).

by means of proportional representation. The party list does not impose the order in which that allocation is to be done. Indeed, it is the head of the list who, after the election, determines who on it will become members of the National Assembly. Parliament in Guyana consists of elected members as well as those representing local bodies. The President of Guyana, as occurs in neighbouring Latin American Presidential democracies, determines policy; and is eligible for re-election without term limits. Based on his instructions, the Prime Minister conducts governance.

In all Commonwealth Caribbean countries, the majority vote rule obtains in Parliament. Each Prime Minister must, therefore, command the confidence of a majority of the elected members of the House of Representatives. To remain in office, the Prime Minister must retain that confidence.

Constitutionally, there is also in Guyana an official Minority Leader who is that member of the National Assembly who is best able to command the support of a majority of those members who do not support the Government. Alternatively, the Leader of the Opposition is the member of that House who commands the support of the largest single group of such members who are prepared to support one leader.

The people's representation consists, as per their British model, of two chambers constitutionally attributed, whereby the members of the Upper House (Senate) are appointed, by the Governor-General or the President, after some being nominated by the Prime Minister and some by the Leader of the Opposition. The members of the Lower House (House of Representatives or House of Assembly) are elected in constituencies by the enfranchised population. In most countries, the Governor-General, or President, may appoint additional, independent Senators.

Small nations, such as Dominica, St. Kitts and Nevis, and St. Vincent and the Grenadines, have single-chamber Parliaments to which both elected and nominated MPs belong.

In multi-island States with one dominant island the minor islands have been able, in part, to secure special rights. Most strikingly this occurred in St. Kitts and Nevis, the only federal state in the Commonwealth Caribbean.

The Tobagonians, as the Nevisians, have established their own island Parliament, although one with rather limited authority, at the expense of the Trinidadians; and so have the Barbudans from the Antiguans.

The tiniest Commonwealth Caribbean territories — Anguilla, the British Virgin Islands, the Cayman Islands, and the Turks and Caicos Islands — are UK-dependent colonies with, however, internal self-government. In each case, the Crown is here too represented by a Governor. But he is usually a British career official and is delegated independent of the preferences of the local Head of Government. The Parliaments are uni-cameral Parliaments and consist of elected MPs as well as those designated on the proposal of both the Government and the Opposition. In Anguilla, the British Virgin Islands and the Turks and Caicos Islands, the Governor summons the Chief Minister on whose recommendations he also appoints a part of the Cabinet from the ranks of elected and nominated MPs. The Governor, being responsible for Finance and Justice, as a rule appoints external experts from the British Civil Service.

He himself is responsible for External Affairs and Security. In the Cayman Islands, a variant on this system exists, whereby the Governor presides over the Executive Council consisting in part of members appointed by himself and in part of elected members, and is himself quasi-Head of Government.

New elections for the Parliaments in the Commonwealth Caribbean must, following varying rules, take place at the latest after the end of four or five years, on a date determined by the Government.

Among the British colonies in the Caribbean, political self-determination in Montserrat is most advanced. The island is a member of the Caribbean Community and CARICOM Common Market and the OECS. But Montserrat is consulted only indirectly with regard to their decisions on foreign affairs or security policy. Thus, Montserrat is not a member of the Standing Committee of CARICOM Foreign Ministers and the OECS Foreign and Defence Ministers. The island was not allowed to take part in the October, 1983, intervention in Grenada.

The British Government has in the last few years, left clear signs for its colonies that colonial dependence does not exist merely on paper. It promulgated a new Constitution for Montserrat in December, 1989. This followed the Government's allegedly deficient supervision of so-called off-shore banking.

The draft envisaged considerably more rights for the Governor. Supported by protests from the other OECS Heads of Government, Montserrat's Chief Minister travelled to London and was able to obtain a significantly milder version (*Cf. CC* December, 1989, p.2; *CR* 7.12.89, p.6; Fergus, 1990).

Against the opposition of the Government of the Turks and Caicos Islands, the Governor there, in 1984 leased the airport for twenty years to a Texan entrepreneur as well as all other airports which would be constructed in the future in the group of islands. The islands' Government received no support from London in the lawsuit with the Texan. (*CC* July-August, 1990, p.13).

In July, 1986, the Governor temporarily took over the running of the Government. This followed allegations of corruption and abuse of office made against the Government and the opposition in a Report of a Commission of Enquiry. The deployment of British troops was considered to deal with any local resistance to this decision (*CI* August 1986, p.2).

Faced with heavy criticism from the dependent territories, the British Foreign Office established, at the end of 1992, a Ministerial Group on the Dependent Territories with its regional secretariat in Bridgetown, Barbados. This Ministerial Group was supposed to support the Governor in the execution of the decisions of the British Government in the dependent territories. The behaviour of the island Governments with regards to the drug trade and dubious financial institutions was regarded with open mistrust (*CI* September, 1992, pp. 1f; November, 1992, p.2; February 1993, p.2).

In 1994 the British Government considered changing the constitution of the British Virgin Islands and enlarging the Legislative Council with a new category of representatives, against the will of the majority of the Council. The CARICOM Heads of Government backed the then BVI Chief Minister, the late Lavity Stoutt, in his efforts to find a consensus (*CI* August 1994, p. 12).

1.5 The Special Situation of Small States in the International System

The Commonwealth Caribbean States, after obtaining their formal sovereignty, strove to prove that they were fully worth their value as members of the international community. The great expectations, made of the West Indian States exceeded, many times over, however, their political and economic possibilities. Despite their desire to play a leading role among developing countries, they have had to recognise the limits imposed on small island states.

Sovereign states with a population of up to one million inhabitants have been defined as small states in the August, 1985, Report of the Consultative Group on the Special Needs of Small States established by the 1983 Commonwealth Heads of Government Conference in New Delhi. In the Caribbean, in spite of larger populations, Trinidad and Tobago and Jamaica would be counted among them.

Small Island Developing Countries (SIDCs) form a special group among small states. Insularity is assumed if the land is so far away from the continent that it is free from continental influences in terms of physical, human and economic factor[24].

The category, 'Developing Country' is moot. Some island territories, when evaluated by their per head incomes, are rated as areas with high incomes. But, on the other hand, their insular location and small size expose them to dangers, which may impair their development on a more sustained basis than the non-insular small States of a similar stage of development. Blackman (1991, p.7) lists the following:

- Tendency to natural catastrophes such as hurricanes, volcanoes, earthquakes.
- Misuse of remote location for smuggling, illegal fishing, *coups d'état* attempts.
- Damage to the particularly fragile ecological system, coastal pollution.
- Population pressure.
- Extensive specialisation on certain sectors of the economy.
- Foreign influences on culture.
- Loss of competitivity through scientific advances in biotechnology and basic research.
- Dependence on the political decisions of larger states.

The ninth meeting of the Caribbean Development and Co-operation Committee (CDCC) in Port-of-Spain, in June, 1985, provided an opportunity to make clear to the United Nations the problems of smaller developing island states at the international level. Special problems of the island states[25] were named there as follows:

- Inadequate transportation and communication links.
- Proneness to natural disasters.
- Difficulties in the efficient use of water and land.

[24] François Doumenge, quoted according to Blackman, 1991, p 2
[25] *Cf* as well Plieschke, 1977, *Small is Dangerous*

- Extreme susceptibility to external market influences, owing to the domestic markets being too small.
- Limited resources endowment and heavy dependence on external services.
- Brain drain.
- Inadequate and expensive infrastructure and administration (*CP* 31:4).

Fanger (1982, pp. 193-195) has pointed out that the bureaucracy of small States moves in small circles; and that this may inhibit innovation. The lack of anonymity and discretion impairs administrative objectivity and effectiveness.

In April and May 1994 delegates from 120 nations attended the first ever UN Conference[26] on Small Island Developing States (SIDS) in Barbados. However, no specific funds were allocated; the programme of action and the 'Barbados Declaration' endorsed by the conference fell short of expectations. A parallel forum of non-governmental organisations was addressed by Cuba's and Guyana's Presidents, Castro and Jagan (*CI* June 1994, 11).

Objectively, small size is *per se* no obstacle to viability. It is, like sovereignty, a question of definition and claims (*cf.* Woehlcke 1982). The smallest Caribbean territories are almost entirely also the most prosperous. *A priori*, they should also be considered as viable when on their own.

But, since their prosperity and internal stability are closely linked with their quasi-colonial status, they delay their separation from the 'mother country'. The special status as small, insular developing countries could at least help a part of independent Commonwealth Caribbean States to continue being supported by international funding agencies as a priority, after relative prosperity threatened to block their access to particularly favourable credits.

As far back as in 1977, Commonwealth Finance Ministers, at their meeting in Barbados, examined the special characteristic of the economy of small island states. The decision for the setting-up of the Commonwealth group of experts was triggered off through the occurrences in Grenada which, in their Report, they characterised as 'the most dramatic demonstration of the problems inherent in the location of small states near to a dominant power' (*Vulnerability*, p.29)[27].

In order to reduce the endangerment of the small state in all its relevant aspects — military, political, economic, technical, social and cultural — the experts came out in favour of close regional co-operation, which should be seen as a form of self-help. Regional co-operation between states, which are not separated by deep ideological divides, could reduce the need for military protection from major countries. Moreover, positive psychological and political advantages could arise through the pooling of brain power and the enhancing of bargaining power (*Vulnerability*, p. 65).

Small island states, with their penchant for particularism, have, however, a particular psychology. Lowenthal and Clarke (1982, p. 226) have found that the larger islands within an archipelago do not really wish to be responsible for the

[26]United Nations Global Conference on The Sustainable Development of Small Island Developing States.

[27]Such 'demonstrations' also exist in members of the Commonwealth of nations. Three years after the publication of the Report, India played the policeman in internal uprisings in the Maldives and in Sri Lanka, at the invitations of the Heads of State in the two cases.

smaller ones or for them to be left on their own. The latter, conversely, do not wish to be ruled by the larger ones. Through this, a pendulum situation develops between the feeling of belonging together and the wish for independence, which is characteristic of the Commonwealth Caribbean.

2. Internal Factors of Caribbean Integration

2.1 Historical Identity

It is difficult to write the pan-Caribbean history for a region which consists of several sub-regions and diverse societies without a common language or culture, and which exists without a geographical area, that is clearly distinguishable from one another. (*Cf.* 'Problems in Writing').

Nonetheless, the Commonwealth Caribbean does demonstrate, in broad sections, a common or similar historical development. In the course of well-nigh four centuries, there has developed, under the influences and through the miscegenation of Europeans, Africans and Asian forced labourers as well as voluntary immigrants, a society and culture, which, because of its anthropological roots, displays, over political and social barriers, typical traits of a New Antillean World. Common values, attitudes and thought patterns, which can be described as unique, have developed — especially in religion and ideology.

Gordon Lewis[28] (1984, pp. 39-40) has divided the cultural-historical heritage of the entire Caribbean region into the following three epochs:

- The post-Discovery period after 1492, which lasted up to the abolition of slavery and was marked by the sugar plantation economy and imported slave labour;
- The post-Emancipation period from the abolition of slavery in the British possessions (1834) to the abolition in Cuba (1886);
- The post-Independence period, beginning with Haiti (1804), the Dominican Republic (1844) and Cuba (1900), to the post-World War II independence of the British territories.

Sir Philip Sherlock[29] (1985, p. 12) distinguishes four areas of continuity and convergence in West Indian history, as follows:

1. The long struggle for freedom of the African slaves, marked by slave uprisings[30] and other forms of resistance, through Maroon societies; these became established in Hispaniola with the introduction of slavery and spread via Jamaica and Colombia's coastal areas to the *Palmares* Republic in Brazil and the Bush Negroes in Suriname.
2. The fight of the Africans and Indians for social security and justice.

---

[28]A political scientist who, at his death, in 1991, was Director of the Institute of Caribbean Studies at the University of Puerto Rico

[29]Jamaican educator, former Vice-Chancellor of the UWI, now Executive Vice-President of the Caribbean Resources Development Foundation, based in Miami, Fla

[30]The biggest were the Haitian Revolution (the 'Second American War of Independence', the third he describes as Simón Bolivar's in Latin America) and Sam Sharpe's 1831 Baptist revolt in Western Jamaica.

3. The fight for the control of their own affairs, involving two waves of protest — one by the workers for better living conditions; and the other, by a small group of intellectuals for constitutional reform and self-government, whereby the first level of success was the introduction of Universal Adult Suffrage.

4. The creation of a West Indian culture, creole languages, common proverbs, cuisine, music and dances.

Christopher Columbus' arrival in the Caribbean in 1492 changed the world more than any other occurrence in its history (Mitchell, 1987, p.25). When the Spaniards 'discovered' the region for Europe, they found ethnic groups there, who presumably had come from the North of South America — that is, present-day Guyana — peoples such as the Ciboneys, Tainos, Arawaks and Caribs, with a culture that is traced back to the year 2,500 B.C. (*Cf.* Moreno Fraginals, 1981).

The peaceful Arawaks, who dedicated themselves to small farming and livestock rearing, and were held to be little suited for war, were at this time almost completely pushed out of the Eastern Caribbean by the warlike Caribs but remained in the Greater Antilles. The Mayas still remain in the thinly populated area of modern-day Belize.

Under the *conquistadores*, the long-resident Arawak population was swiftly decimated by illness and forced labour. In 1494, Columbus, on Hispaniola[31], selected fifty natives to sell in Spain as slaves. He gradually wanted to make profits from the sale of all natives. As early as in 1508, the hunting down of natives was legally allowed, so that they could be enslaved. Between 1508 and 1513, some 40,000 such persons were taken prisoner and sold to work in the gold mines (Moreno Fraginals, 1981).

Under French and British colonial rule, the Caribs disappeared except for small remnants. They did not submit to slavery and were systematically exterminated or deported. Only in Dominica do the descendants of the Caribs still play a role as a group of people. The British transported thousands of Black Caribs the mixed-race issue of unions between black slaves and the Caribs, to Honduras, whence they migrated to the present day Belize.

After the original inhabitants had been exterminated by genocide, epidemics, destruction of their economic foundations and spiritual shock (Moreno Fraginals, 1981), the colonisers found in Africa cheap and easily available labour who, as slaves, could be put to work on Caribbean plantations. On the depopulated islands there came into being a uniform economic structure, the plantation economy, which should satisfy the increasing European demand for sugar and other tropical agrarian produce.

The Spaniards had supposedly adopted the slave plantation model from Portuguese colonial praxis in Africa and perfected it. Since the sixteenth century, an estimated thirteen million slaves from Africa were shipped to Brazil, the Southern USA and the sugar-producing islands, a great portion of them in the Caribbean (Curtin, 1969). Under the concept of the plantation economy, the Lesser Antilles were transformed almost completely — and the Greater Antilles, to a very great extent — into plantations.

---

[31] The present-day Haiti and Dominican Republic.

2. Internal Factors of Caribbean Integration

After the abolition of slavery, indentured workers from India, China and Europe filled the need for labour. Between 1838 and 1917, some 416,000 such indentured workers from India came to the British Caribbean colonies. The majority of the Chinese indentured workers arrived between 1852 and 1878, roughly 15,000 in Guyana; and a smaller number in Jamaica and Trinidad. Only a portion returned to their native lands after the ends of the contracts (Murray, 1971, pp. 104ff).

The European settlers came mainly from England, Scotland and Ireland ('Irish slaves'). Under Charles I, the English began to send rebellious Irish into slavery[32]. European immigrants came also from Germany and Portugal[33]. But only a few remained in the colonies, if they survived the hardships and tropical illnesses (Murray, 1971, pp. 104-108). The plantation economy, which centred on the profitable sugar industry, marked power relationships for centuries. The military and the colonial administrator protected the interests of the British Crown. Suffrage was granted to the plantocracy and other well-to-do citizens who made use of these rights in Barbados and Jamaica, separate and apart from their rights which were protected by their elected representatives.

In the sixteenth and seventeenth centuries, the English drove the Spaniards out of most of the colonies which now belong to the Commonwealth Caribbean, as well as, in 1797, from Trinidad. The interest of the Spaniards had been limited to the Greater Antilles, which Columbus had at first wrongly believed was India where he hoped to find gold.

In the Eastern Caribbean and North-Eastern South America, the English shared territorial domination with two other sea powers — namely, France and the Netherlands. The power interests of the Monarchs were joined with the commercially motivated thrust for expansion of the trading houses, sales people, ship-owners, landless peasants, adventurers and financiers from the nobility and middle class.

In the Caribbean, they found ideal conditions for the profit-producing cultivation of sugar-cane: Proximity to the sea, favourable air temperature and rainfall levels, forest, adequate livestock supply, excellent shipping links between the European consumer market and labour-providing Africa (Moreno Fraginals, 1981, p.10). The triangular trade between the Caribbean, Europe and Africa made the Caribbean the most-prized colonial territory of the English and the French. From the Caribbean, ships brought sugar, rum and raw materials, such as molasses and indigo, to Europe. These same ships transported finished products from Europe to the west coast of Africa and then, laden with slaves, sailed back to the Caribbean (i.e. called the Triangular Trade).

While England and the Netherlands usually settled their differences peacefully[34], certain conflicts over territory between England and France concerning hegemony in the Eastern Caribbean in the eighteenth century determined the history of the region. Only Barbados, which was 'discovered' by the Portuguese

---

[32]Some 20,000 Irish Roman Catholics were registered in St Kitts and neighbouring islands in 1643, Oliver Cromwell's bloody punitive actions led to the systematic expulsion of ten thousand Irish people, in part via Barbados to the rest of the West Indies, in part to New England in the present-day USA, from 1649 onwards

[33]Here, in particular, from the island of Madeira

[34]England ceded Suriname to the Netherlands in 1667 in exchange for the island of Manhattan (*'Nieuw Amsterdam'*)

in 1536 and settled by the English in 1627, remained British uninterruptedly after that settlement. Trinidad, which was colonised by the Spaniards in 1592 remained from 1797 to 1962 in British hands. Most of the East Caribbean islands changed their colonial masters several times[35].

Up to 1782, almost every island in the British sphere of interest in the Eastern Caribbean belonged to France, excepting Antigua, Barbados and Trinidad. The naval massacre, the *Battle of the Saints* (1782) over Dominica and Guadeloupe, however, saw a change of fortune in favour of the British. By the treaty of Versailles, which followed, Britain obtained Grenada, St. Vincent, St. Kitts, Dominica, Nevis and Montserrat. France, however, kept only St. Lucia and Tobago. St. Lucia finally became a British possession only in 1803; Tobago, in 1814. France retained Martinique, Guadeloupe, Saint Barthélémy and a part of Saint Martin.

The Netherlands, which was rather marginally involved in the changing ownership of colonies in the Eastern Caribbean, kept Aruba, Curaçao, Bonaire, Saint Eustatius, Saba, Sint Maarten[36] and parts of Guyana/Guiana (the present-day Suriname).

The decline of sugar-cane, through the development of beet sugar in Europe, economic mismanagement[37], exhaustion of the soil, competition from produce from other colonies, the ending of the slave trade by Britain in 1808, the abolition of slavery in 1833 with the apprenticeship system of transition to 1838 caused deep cuts into the economic and social fabric of the British West Indies. The settlement of Asians, who, as indentured workers, were supposed to replace the manumitted slaves, again changed — especially in Guyana and Trinidad — the ethnic structure of the population. This laid the groundwork for conflicts, which, up to the present time, have had considerable effect on the political, social and economic life of the countries in question.

The power of the plantocracy had reached its zenith in the middle of the eighteenth century. Their decline then took place gradually and continuously, and was determined jointly by wars, the boycott imposed on the rebellious New England colonies, high tariffs in England with which the English Government wanted to finance the rising war costs, the monoculture which subjected the economic fate of whole countries to the ups-and-downs of the world market, higher production costs following the abolition of slavery as well as natural catastrophes.

With abolition, the small-farming population, which hitherto had consisted of runaway or manumitted slaves, increased sharply. Subsistence as a small farmer was the alternative to the life of dependency as a plantation worker. The latter was now paid a wage, but nonetheless had to work in conditions similar to those of slavery. Gradually, the plantocracy gave way to a new West Indian peasantry (Murray, 1971, pp. 97-99).

Despite abolition, there remained the contrasts of race and skin colour.

---

[35]St Lucia, for instance, fourteen times

[36]The southern section of Saint Martin

[37]Many plantations, in the absence of their owners who lived in Europe, were managed by local overseers who knew little about agriculture and were often dishonest

Moreover, class contrasts became tangible. Black-and-poor, on the one hand, and, on the other, white-and-rich, were, and still are even today, the opposing poles of the rating scale.

The real beneficiaries of Emancipation appeared to be the mulattoes. Previously, they had enjoyed privileged positions, owing to their being house slaves and through their rather close family and ethnic links to the white masters[38].

The British Government used the conflicts between colonial administrations and sections of the plantocracy in the second half of the nineteenth century to abolish the system of representation of the ruling classes. It turned its Caribbean possessions, with the exception of Barbados, into Crown colonies under the direct rule of the Crown. The Governors, as representatives of the monarch, replaced the Parliaments to a great extent through the Executive Councils they nominated[39].

Under Crown Colony status, little changed in the condition of the poorer segments of the population. After Emancipation, the standard of living of most Caribbean residents was not decidedly improved. Economic depression in the importing countries after World War I and over-production caused lower world market prices for agricultural produce. Moreover, these conditions made it easy for the Caribbean employers, supported by the colonial administrations, to fob off workers with low wages and send back the discontented into the army of the unemployed. This led, in the 1930s, to disturbances among agricultural workers and longshoremen, and, in turn, to the establishment of trade unions.

At the head of the protest and strike movements came native personalities as leaders, who prepared the ground for the subsequent independence of the colonies. Stimulated by the fight of the trade unions in the USA for better living and working conditions and the efforts of black leaders — above all, the Jamaican Marcus Garvey — both there and in the Caribbean to raise the feeling of self-worth of the segment of the population which was of African origin, they attacked the colonial power at first with trade union demands and developed their movements into political parties at the start of World War II.

The political parties, as their first step towards independence from the war-weakened and colony-weary British, won Universal Adult Suffrage and the right to internal self-government. The mass base resulting from trade union work brought numerous trade union leaders under the new system to the head of Governments: Bustamante in Jamaica, Price in Belize, Bird in Antigua, Bradshaw in St. Kitts, Adams in Barbados and Gairy in Grenada. The British Government tried to grant its Caribbean colonies Independence as one unit, if possible, thereby obviating individual negotiations and financial settlements. The *Federation of the West Indies*, which it initiated, could not stop the growing nationalism of the territories or the particularism motivated by political power.

This Federation existed only from 1958 to 1962, and broke apart following the secession of Jamaica and Trinidad and Tobago. In the same year (1962)

---

[38] *Cf* Gordon Lewis, 1984, p 45

[39] In Jamaica, the immediate occasion for the dissolution of the *Assembly* was the uprising by black peasants in Morant Bay in 1865 under the leadership of Paul Bogle, in which several white people were killed The Governor reacted with much severity, and had over 400 of the rebels executed, several hundred flogged and a thousand houses destroyed He was then replaced. The land-owning class, which was apparently unable to resolve the conflict, was punished

these two countries became independent. They were followed by the remaining larger territories, and, in the 1970s and up to the start of the 1980s, by most of the smaller ones, which, since 1967, had enjoyed, as Associated States a special status of internal self-government within the British colonial system.

Rigid nationalism with all its symbols and attributes, such as own flags, national anthems, National Heroes, Days of Remembrance and currencies, followed colonialism — despite their common historical legacy and socio-cultural background. It appeared as if the new wielders of power in the Caribbean countries wanted to enjoy the advantages of closer regional co-operation but without surrendering their own personal gains from sovereignty, power, status, position, their own personal financial advantages in favour of an immaterial commonalty resulting from arbitrary behaviour and exploitation by the colonial power.

Such thinking is enhanced by the isolation of the island state imposed by geography. But this is rather anachronistic. For, as Gordon Lewis (1984, 44) has put it:

> 'Economic and political nationalism can only lead to international and regional anarchy (in the political sense) and self-destructive protectionism (in the economic sense)'.

Insular particularism was stimulated by the lack of social, economic and political links between the islands and the orientation towards the colonial power in question. Under British colonial rule, the smaller political units within the British-ruled Leeward and Windward Islands were purely administrative and had no integrative character. The interaction between the populations of individual islands was consciously not encouraged.

Information channels and travel routes went via England. News of slave uprisings in distant territories reached the inhabitants of the islands in a round-about way via the British media. When the Anglican Bishops of the West Indian region wanted to meet, they gathered in England, because intra-regional travel took months.

Through the insular situation, the delimitation of borders was relatively simple. Territories consisting of several islands did, however, themselves have typically insular problems as well as difficulties with national integration. The most outstanding case of this was that of the island grouping, St. Kitts-Nevis-Anguilla, which the British Government wanted to grant Associated Statehood in 1967.

As early as in the nineteenth century, the Anguillans had opposed being ruled by St. Kitts. In May, 1967, they decided, by 1,813 votes to five, in a referendum, and two years later confirmed this in a second vote, to secede from a planned state. Following the failure of a British attempt at mediation, the British Government in May, 1969, despatched paratroops and police to the island, as it saw a danger to law and order there[40].

The Anguillans were, however, unimpressed. The British Government felt obliged in 1971 to pass emergency legislation for the island, to introduce a

[40] *Cf*; *Moko Review* 18 4.1969, p 11, reprinted in Munroe/Lewis, 1971, pp. 222f, and *New World Quarterly* 4 1 (1967) with several articles on Anguilla.

special Constitution for Anguilla in 1976, and, in 1980, to revert the island, at the emphatic request of its inhabitants, to being a British Crown Colony[41]. Even Nevis showed tendencies to secede from St. Kitts. The Nevisians promulgated in 1983 a federal constitution, giving the island with its 9,000 inhabitants its own Parliament, its own Government under the leadership of a Premier, and also giving it the right, through a two-thirds Parliamentary majority, to declare its secession from St. Kitts. Secession did not, however, take place.

Secessionist efforts have been made and are still being made *vis-à-vis* Trinidad[42] by Tobago, against Antigua[43] by Barbuda, and against St. Vincent by the Grenadines. On the other hand, however, Jamaica created no difficulties in 1962, when its hitherto administered dependencies of the Cayman Islands and the Turks and Caicos Islands chose to retain their colonial status and not to become independent together with Jamaica[44].

After the failure of the West Indies Federation in 1962, the individual States tried at first to implement economic and functional co-operation, through the establishment of the Caribbean Free Trade Association (CARIFTA) in 1968. Eleven Commonwealth Caribbean States became members of CARIFTA.

In the same year, seven Commonwealth Eastern Caribbean States founded the East Caribbean Common Market (ECCM). Out of CARIFTA, there came into being in 1973, the Caribbean Community (CARICOM) which now has fourteen[45] Member States and the Caribbean Common Market (CARICOM), with thirteen[46]. In 1981, the Eastern Caribbean States extended their economic and functional co-operation to include foreign affairs and security policy, in the creation of the Organisation of Eastern Caribbean States (OECS), to which seven Eastern Caribbean States belong.

With increasing clarity, the Commonwealth Caribbean developed into an independent sub-system with common historical, cultural, linguistic, economic and political features. The West Indies Cricket Team became the symbol of Caribbean co-operation in sport.

The common features in education, which is so important for building Caribbean consciousness, have found expression in the unified Caribbean examinations of the Caribbean Examinations Council (CXC) and the University of the West Indies (UWI). Reggae, calypso, soca and cadence have achieved prominence Caribbean-wide, against musical influences from the USA and Europe. The region is proud of its artists, artistes and creative writers, who work in native dialects — called 'Creole' in the Eastern Caribbean and 'Patois' in Jamaica — in addition to English.

From points of view of foreign policy and foreign economic policy, a re-orientation from Great Britain to North America — Canada and the USA — took place with the independence of the States in the Region. But, even then,

---

[41]Petty, 1984, contains a comprehensive study. For the background and course of the secession, please see as well the memoirs of the then Governor, Sir Fred Phillips (1991, pp 100-162)

[42]*Cf.*; the debate in Tobago on a constitutional change (*CR* 11.5.89, pp 6-7)

[43]*Cf.*: Lowenthal and Clarke, 1982, pp. 230ff.

[44]*Cf.*: Gordon Lewis, 1968, pp. 333ff.

[45]As of July, 1995.

[46]As of July, 1995

they retained significant elements of the British political system and links to the Commonwealth and the British Crown.

The Caribbean Basin Initiative (CBI) launched in 1982 by then US President, Ronald Reagan, and the US intervention in Grenada in 1983 were results of this development. Political and economic orientation towards the USA has stimulated anew the decades-long debate over the economic course of the Commonwealth Caribbean, over non-alignment, ideological and cultural orientation, as well as security interests.

These were not merely theoretical discussions. That much was clear from the developments in Grenada and Guyana. After Maurice Bishop and his New Jewel Movement seized power in 1979, Grenada proceeded along its own path, patterned on the Cuban model, which was lauded by its advocates as the Socialist developmental model, but condemned by its opponents as the start of totalitarian rule under the superpower influence of the then USSR.

The historical commonalties within the Commonwealth Caribbean — and, in certain conditions, also within the wider Caribbean — were described by Barbadian writer, George Lamming, in the following manner:

> 'Caribbean society historically was never conceived as the coming together of people with any design for social living.... It is a society in which men and women were brought from all corners of the world, and they were brought for one purpose only: Labour, to be transformed from persons into instruments of production'[47].

A complete exchange of a new population took place. A fully new society arose out of the thin minority of plantation owners and managers/administrators and armed services of the Crown, artisans and salesmen, small farmers, manumitted slaves and the mammoth army of slaves and indentured workers.

The ethnic distribution of West Indian society linked certain races with certain professions or occupations: Caucasians produced the Governments; the mulattoes — the teachers, lawyers and doctors; the Chinese dominated the grocery business; the Indians worked in agriculture; the Arabs and Jews — in trade. At the bottom end of the social scale, the Africans sought to raise themselves above the Indians, who had willingly migrated to the region.

Seen in its totality, however, the racial contrast in the Caribbean had, in the opinion of Gordon Lewis, much more peaceful traits than was the case in, for instance, the Southern USA after the American Civil War. By means of education, social position and economic prosperity, Caribbean inhabitants could compensate for racial disadvantage[48].

Black self-consciousness inspired by Marcus Garvey played an important role in preparing for the political protests of the 1930s in Jamaica. But, with the emergence of political parties, Garveyism and black nationalism became multiracialism, non-ethnic territorial nationalism and systematic efforts to purify the State apparatus of the question of race (Carl Stone, 1988, p. 11). No revolution occurred — unlike Haiti in 1791—1804; or Cuba in 1959.

---

[47]Address to the Press Association of Jamaica, printed in *Sunday Sun* (Kingston, Jamaica) 20 12 1981, pp 8-9

[48]Lewis calls this the 'concept of social colour' 'In the American Society, money talks, in the Caribbean Society, money whitens' (1984, p 46)

While slave uprisings occurred in almost all the territories, the former did not lead to upliftment of the entire oppressed majority of the population; nor, as in Cuba in 1959, did it lead to a significant segment of the population turning against a corrupt regime. In the nineteenth century, the slave uprisings, in the wake of the debate in Great Britain over the abolition of slavery, succeeded in sealing the 'Emancipation' of the slaves after opposition for decades from the slave owners[49].

The change from colonial rule to national independence brought about a change of the actors rather than one of socio-cultural relationships and conditions. A new type of indigenous creole politician replaced the old white colonial administration. Critics of present-day West Indian society and its development assert that the spirit of colonialism is still intact there and has been revived by neo-colonialism. The Trinidadian economist Lloyd Best (1968) holds that the basic conditions of the pure plantation economy still exist in the Caribbean, and it operates under the following rules of the game:

- Exclusivity of spheres of influence by different metropolitan powers;
- division of labour between the metropolis and the colony;
- navigation provision;
- metropolitan exchange standard.

The debate as to whether the Commonwealth Caribbean is in the stage of decolonisation[50] or neo-colonisation[51] is part of the ideological discussion in academic and political circles in the region.

In view of the economic problems, many Commonwealth Caribbean nationals have fled to Great Britain, North America and Canada, with a smaller number going to Central America and Panama. The Caribbean region is a 'net exporter of people'. More Caribbean nationals and their descendants live outside the region than in it.[52]

Intra-regional migration from the poorer to the richer Caribbean countries also plays a role[53]. As many Grenadians are estimated to live in Trinidad as the some 100,000 who live in Grenada itself.

The mistaken trip, which created these conditions, namely, the 'discovery' of the Americas by Columbus 500 years ago, was commemorated with little enthusiasm at its quincentenary in 1992.

'Why are you commemorating an event which brought so much wreck and havoc to the people of this part of the world ?'[54] quoted ex-Jamaican Prime Minister Seaga, one of the opponents of the project, simultaneously warning that 'belated bitterness' is 'unproductive and harmful'. One must look for the good which came out of the changes — for instance, the exciting developments, the cultural enrichment, the new peoples, that emerged from the combination of the

[49] *Cf* Murray, 1971, pp 91ff

[50] *Cf* Carl Stone, 1983c, p 38-39.

[51] *Cf inter alia*, Edwin Jones in *The State*, 1986, p 146, Jones sees three stages of historical development colonial-aristocratic, neo-Fabian, and neo-colonial

[52] *cf* Chapter 3 6 Migration

[53] *Cf.* Crassweller, 1972, pp 317-319

[54] Trinidad and Tobago earlier celebrated Discovery Day on July 31 as a National Holiday, but changed that to August 1, as Emancipation Day as from 1985 because Trinidad was already peopled when Columbus 'discovered' it in 1498, and the arrival of the first Europeans led to the extermination of the Amerindian population (*CP* July-October 1985, p 161)

old, new crops, animals, industries, associations, forms of government, ideas and movements and new countries, Seaga said (*DG* 20.9.1983, pp. 1 and 13).

Since December, 1981, a group of Caribbean historians, acting on an initiative of UNESCO, has been writing a *General History of the Caribbean*. Varying linguistic knowledge of the historians — many Commonwealth Caribbean ones have learnt only one language — and the uneven level of historical research on individual territories, have rendered the research project more difficult[55].

Thus, Cuba, Puerto Rico and the vast majority of the Commonwealth Caribbean have been copiously researched — unlike, on the other hand, the Netherlands Antilles, the Bahamas and Belize.

Belize — formerly British Honduras — has had a different course of development from that of the rest of the Commonwealth Caribbean. It is the only English-speaking country in Central America. This sparsely populated strip of land between Mexico, Guatemala and Honduras was at first settled predominantly by British woodcutters and their black slaves. After decades of fighting, they defeated the Spaniards in 1788 at the battle of St. George's Cay. Between slave-owners and slaves, who had fought side by side, there developed a relationship of mutual dependence and co-operation (*Cf.* Murray, p. 56).

---

[55]*Cf.*: 'Problems'.

2.2 The Integration Movement in the Commonwealth Caribbean

2.2.1 The Early Phase of the Integration Movement

'The natural state of our Caribbean is fragmentation', warned Shridath Ramphal (1975, p.7) shortly after the establishment of the Caribbean Community. 'Without constant effort, without unrelenting perseverance and discipline in suppressing instincts born of tradition and environment, it is to our natural state of disunity that we shall return.'

Generations of Caribbean integrationists have tried to overcome the condition of fragmentation. After the futile efforts of the British colonial power, it was politicians of Commonwealth Caribbean States, which had become independent or attained internal self-government, who gave institutional form to the integration process, above all through the creation of CARICOM — the Caribbean Community and the Caribbean Common Market.

The integration movement, which, with varying motivation and intensity, worked at the stronger inter-action and co-operation of the Anglophone Caribbean territories, arose from efforts to put an end to fragmentation. In this context, the 'integration movement' may be defined as the coordinated efforts of persons to further, with the objective of political unity, the cooperation of sovereign states. 'Political unity', in turn, means that sovereign states transfer political values in a certain binding way, to a new political instance or actor — and thereby cede, either temporarily or permanently, a portion of their own sovereignty.

The aim of the integration movement described in this study is the political unity of the Commonwealth Caribbean and, at a later stage, of the larger Caribbean integration area. But, at the time of the establishment of the Caribbean Community, this political unity lay in the far distance. Thus, for instance, William Demas in 1974 (p.10), complained as follows:

> 'As you know, in spite of our achievement in establishing the Caribbean Community, we West Indians are still the laughing-stock of the world, what with our petty insularities and vanities, our tendency to fragmentation, divisiveness and secessionism. We glibly excuse ourselves and blame the state of affairs on the fact that we are all separated by the sea. This, however, is seen to be a very shallow and indeed fallacious line of argument, when we consider that both Indonesia and the Philippines — both of which are Unitary States, and not even Federations — consist of thousands of islands'.

Varying motives guide the integration movement as follows:

- Integration as natural law: Nature requires the joining together of what is split up, in order to avert decline or collapse[56].

[56]Viktor Schoelcher wrote in 1852 that Caribbean unity would come one day for it is 'natural that it be so' (*Les Colonies Françaises*, quoted by Gordon Lewis 1968, p. 415).

- Caribbean identity: Under the pressure of powerful external interests and influences, the ethnic, cultural and religious gains in Caribbean specificity of the last few hundred years risk being lost. Caribbean integration enhances the self-esteem, dignity and human rights of Caribbean peoples.
- Sovereignty: Independent Caribbean states can survive as autonomous territories, only if they unite economically and politically and, hence, thereby surrender national sovereignty in favour of functional or political unity or unities. Only in that way can 'formal' sovereignty replace 'real' sovereignty (Demas, 1987, p. 13).
- Economic Prosperity: Each state or territory of the Commonwealth Caribbean is *per se* too weak to attain the 'critical mass'[57] which enables it to achieve self-reliance, whereby here the following are meant: Satisfying the basic needs of food, clothing and shelter, as well as providing adequate employment and education. Functional co-operation, domestic free trade, protection against the outside world and integration of the means of production, make the participating states and territories more independent of external economic and political influences. It also leads gradually, and on its own, to the economic prosperity of the population.
- Foreign policy and security interests: The wish to 'survive' is put by Hugh Springer[58] (1962, p. 51) at the top of the motives for the cooperation of states or other political units. Even the desire for independence and economic prosperity therefore, in Springer's opinion, are lesser priorities. The Caribbean states, in his view, acting in concert, could better pursue their foreign policy and implement their security policy.
- Quality of the leadership: Public and private sector leaders need 'a wider field for ambition' (Norman Manley, quoted by Demas, 1987, p. 13). This need can be better satisfied by larger political units than by mini-States. The brain drain from small states should be stopped, in order to make available a broader leadership cadre for administrative, technical, political and other professional functions.

In the historical development of the integration of the Commonwealth Caribbean, the following two phases can be distinguished:

1. The efforts from the earliest days of British rule and to 1962, of the British colonial power, concerning the administrative integration of its Caribbean possessions.
2. The efforts of the independent States or half-independent territories to achieve functional and political integration since the end of the West Indies Federation in 1962.

The British colonial power attempted quite early to group its Caribbean possessions into administrative units[59]. Britain's efforts to introduce federal

[57] The term indicates the impossibility of small states, unaided, to produce enough qualified leaders, technical experts, scientists and teachers, etc , in order to become 'competitive' by world standards by themselves The term is also used to describe the process of displacement and domination of Caribbean culture Caribbean artists and artistes, writers and media workers should come together and conduct exchanges among themselves, in order to secure 'cultural survival' of the region (Fergus, 1988, p 18)

[58] Later (that is, 1984-90) Governor-General of Barbados Died in April 1994

[59] For an overview, please see Murray, 1971, pp 165ff, Payne, 1980, pp 1-22, Eric Williams 1973b, Augier, 1989, Appendix 4

structures were intensified in the nineteenth century. But they failed, mainly because of the opposition of the plantocracy.

The Colonial Office had little or nothing at all to contribute, as a means of advancing inter-island co-operation. For hundreds of years, a climate of isolation and resultant petty jealousies between the various islands characterised the political profile (Eric Williams, 1973b, p. 1).

In 1921-22, then Under Secretary of State for the Colonies, Hon. E. F. L. Wood, acting on the directive of the Colonial Office, canvassed the possibilities for political union of the British Caribbean colonies. His finding was that political union, while desirable, was inopportune and impracticable at that time. Nonetheless, he considered a Federation consisting of Trinidad and Tobago and the Windward Islands to be possible, insofar as the local population could be convinced of this (*Cf.* 'Report by the Hon. E. F. L. Wood'. Cmd. 1679).

Functional co-operation worthy of being mentioned within the British West Indian colonies practically first began under the military imperatives of World War II. The United States of America established several military bases[60] in the region. British and American security interests were now united. This found expression in the creation of the Anglo-American Caribbean Commission[61], headquartered in Port-of-Spain, which accompanied the gradual replacement of Britain's hegemonic position in her Caribbean colonies by the United States of America. A Regional Economic Committee (REC) brought together leading regional personalities, but without being able to increase its influence (Payne 1980, p. 11). As long-term functional institutions, there developed merely the anglophone Caribbean University system with the founding of the University College of the West Indies in 1948 as well as the maritime and meteorological services.

Parallel to Britain's efforts at the administrative consolidation of her fragmented Caribbean colonies, pressure intensified on her in the 1920s and 1930s to grant them total or partial independence. Common action was, however, hardly possible, owing to the great distances involved, the resultant communications difficulties and lack of non-colonial leadership cadres. While one anti-colonial disturbance often inspired another disturbance elsewhere, one cannot properly speak of the co-ordinated, pan-Caribbean action of a combined opposition to the ruling minority at that time.

The access of the majority to higher education and the development of urban structures brought forth leadership cadres, who knew how to articulate the discontent of the people, their yearning for freedom, education and equality with the ruling plantocracy, as well as the desire for freedom from the colonial yoke. Some of them founded British-type trade unions from which political parties often emerged later.

Among these personalities were lawyers, journalists, creative writers, preachers, ex-servicemen and money lenders: Personalities such as Cecil Rawle

---

[60]In the 1941 agreements, Great Britain ceded to the United States of America Marine bases in the region for 99 years

[61]Established in 1942; continued as the *Caribbean Organisation* with headquarters in Puerto Rico, in 1961-65, the successor agency has been the *Caribbean Economic Development Corporation* (Crassweller, pp 264 ff , Gordon Lewis, 1968, p. 350)

in Dominica; Albert Marryshow in Grenada; Alexander Bustamante and Norman Manley in Jamaica; Arthur Cipriani, Clement Payne and Uriah Butler in Trinidad; Vere Bird Sr. in Antigua; Grantley Adams in Barbados; A. R. F. Webber and Hubert Critchlow in Guyana; and Robert Bradshaw in St. Kitts. Their aim was, on one hand, to create a mass base for their demands. On the other hand, they sought to work with other like-minded Caribbean personalities. By these means, they aimed at putting pressure directly on the British colonial officials in the respective islands and territories, as well as, indirectly, via links in London.

Caribbean-wide labour laws, which legalised trade union work and improved the social position of wage-earners[62], resulted from the unrest triggered off in the 1930s by trade unions in Jamaica, Trinidad and St. Kitts. The first rather large meeting of the leaders of the workers of the English-speaking Caribbean took place in 1926 on the invitation of Hubert Critchlow in then British Guiana. Similar meetings followed in 1927, 1938, 1944, 1945 and 1947. The 1945 meeting in Barbados led to the establishment of the Caribbean Labour Congress which, in 1960, was re-named the Caribbean Congress of Labour[63].

In 1932, West Indian politicians meeting in Dominica for the Conference of Unofficial Caribbean Leaders[64], recommended the creation of a Federation, with its capital either in Barbados or Trinidad, and consisting of Trinidad, Barbados, the Leeward and the Windward Islands. They also sought, for this Federation, Universal Adult Suffrage and Dominion status[65].

Dominion status was also demanded by the CLC at the 1945 and 1947 meetings, with full internal self-government for a Federation, including the then British Guiana, which they demanded as well.

Norman Manley and Grantley Adams at first supported these demands, but later abandoned them in favour of the British points of view (Gordon Lewis, 1968, p. 361).

2.2.2 The West Indies Federation

Serious steps to prepare for what, between 1958 and 1962, was to exist as the Federation of the West Indies began in 1947. That was when the British Government invited the representatives of all its Caribbean territories, including the then British Honduras and British Guiana, to a conference at Montego Bay (Jamaica). Only the Bahamas did not attend.

Great Britain, weakened by World War II, seemed to regard its Caribbean colonies as a burden (Gordon Lewis, 1968, pp. 344ff), especially since it had ceded to the United States of America the responsibility for taking care of London's security interests in the region. Under British influence and with the help of the representatives of West Indian Governments, which were 'more or less unrepresentative of the West Indian peoples', they laid the foundations of

---

[62] *Cf.*; Nurse, pp. 131ff.

[63] *Cf.*: Caribbean Congress of Labour 1985, pp. 6ff.

[64] *Cf.*: *CP* 38: pp. 40 and 46. This conference was brought into being by Cecil Rawle.

[65] Dominion status, that is, full internal self-government under the British monarch as sovereign, had, up to that time, been granted only to the rather large British ex-colonies, that is, Canada (1867), the earliest, Australia (1901) New Zealand (1907), South Africa (1910), Newfoundland (1917), and Ireland (1921).

the Federation (Eric Williams, 1973b, p. 4). Trinidad and Tobago, Barbados, Jamaica, Antigua, Dominica, Grenada, Montserrat, St. Kitts-Nevis-Anguilla, St. Lucia and St. Vincent were the ten territories scheduled to belong to the new Federation. British Honduras, British Guiana and the British Virgin Islands did not take part in it[66].

The Federal Constitution provided for, as the Government, an Executive Council and, following the British model, two Houses of Parliament. The Governor-General, named by the British monarch, was given absolute authority similar to that of a French President of the Fifth Republic. He could, for example, prorogue the two Houses, dissolve the Lower House, as well as name three members of the Executive Council and three Senators. The position of the Premier was quite weak. Great Britain retained financial control over the Federation. Trinidad was selected, at a preliminary conference in Jamaica in 1957, to be the site of the Federal Government.

The Constitution of the Federation was sharply criticised, especially from the ruling People's National Party (PNP) and People's National Movement(PNM) in Jamaica and Trinidad and Tobago, respectively. Since many politicians in the ten participating territories hoped, however, to obtain independence from the colonial power via the Federation, either together or, after the failure of the Federation as the Heads of Government of individual states, they acquiesced to the disadvantageous clauses of the Constitution.

The 1958 Federal elections were the precursors of the coming debacle of the integration movement. The West Indies Federal Labour Party (WIFLP), led by Jamaica's Chief Minister Norman Manley, who was also the President of the PNP, and supported in Trinidad and Tobago by Dr. Eric Williams, did not secure a clear majority at the polls. Its main opponent was the Democratic Labour Party (DLP) led by integration opponent and JLP Leader, Alexander Bustamante. The WIFLP lost in Jamaica and in Trinidad and Tobago. Thanks to the majority of votes in the Eastern Caribbean, it was able to assume the leadership in the Federal Parliament. But its majority was uncertain.

The Federal Government with Barbadian trade unionist Sir Grantley Adams as Premier was established in April, 1958, under unfavourable conditions. Eric Williams (1973b, p. 6) ridiculed it as follows:

> 'The infant nation was presented to the world in swaddling clothes made in the United States of America and out of the made-in-Britain shroud of colonialism'.

The differences of opinion concerning the authority of the Federal Parliament became increasingly more pronounced. Jamaica fought against the interference of the Federal Government in that territory's internal affairs. But Trinidad and Tobago stood for a strengthening of Federal jurisdiction and the centralisation of economic integration and regional planning[67]. Jamaica was practically isolated and often outvoted 1:9.

The Federal Parliament and Government started making efforts to change the Federal Constitution and institute a new system — instead of trying to

---

[66]British Honduras and British Guiana's rejection was due, in part, to their fear of mass immigration.
[67]*Cf.*: Eric Williams 1969, pp. 187ff.

consolidate the Federation. Secret talks between Norman Manley and Eric Williams in Antigua in August, 1960, did not succeed in ironing out their differences (*cf.* Murray, p. 169). The Federal experiment could hardly be saved. Bustamante prepared to return to power in Jamaica by means of the Federation question. The atmosphere in the Federal Parliament was weighed down at first by misunderstandings, then by differences and finally burdened also by hatred between the antipodes (Hoyos, 1978, p. 232).

Bustamante (1977, p. 61) exploited Manley's and Williams's lack of legitimation and the power vacuum created by their differences in the integration question, to oppose the Federation and seek Jamaica's Independence alone:

'Federation will not solve our problem of poverty, hunger and unemployment ....and if these are not tackled Communism will be rife.'

At public meetings, he accused the small Eastern Caribbean territories of recouping its costs in the Federation at Jamaica's expense. Jamaica and Trinidad and Tobago, which accounted for over 70% of the population in the Federation, received only 27% of the seats in the Federal parliament and had to pay 81% of the Federal expenditure (Murray, 1971, p. 167). In addition, The Federal Premier, Sir Grantley Adams, contributed to the confusion, when, during his first official visit to Jamaica, he indicated the possibility of raising taxes in the various territories of the Federation — and that even retroactively.

Bustamante and the Jamaica Labour Party exploited the prejudice of the Jamaican population to obtain the holding of the referendum on September 19, 1961. Fifty-four percent of the electorate which voted opposed Jamaica's continuing in the Federation[68].

As a result of his defeat in the referendum, Manley called snap general elections in 1962. Bustamante's JLP emerged victorious. Bustamante immediately began Independence negotiations with Great Britain. Trinidad and Tobago also hastened to become independent. Both these countries became independent in August, 1962. Eric Williams (1969, p. 203) claimed to have rebuffed the demarches from Britain and the Eastern Caribbean States for a Federation without Jamaica and with himself as Prime Minister. This was because the smaller neighbours were interested only in freedom of movement into Trinidad and Tobago. In a speech after the Jamaica referendum, his answer was categorical: 'One from ten leaves zero'[69] Efforts of the remaining eight territories (the 'Little Eight') to continue the Federation alone failed[70].

The reasons for the failure of the West Indies Federation are many. Its conception was unclear from the very beginning; the motivation of the participating states, varied.

Vague, romantic feelings may have played a role in the case of some politicians. Trade unionists hoped for a link with the world economy.

The Colonial Office's concern was rather the efficiency of a common Federal Administration. But it also wanted to rid itself, in as simple a way as possible, of its responsibility for these Caribbean colonies, which, from as long

---

[68]To the question, put 'Should Jamaica remain in the Federation of the West Indies, yes or no?', 256, 261 voted 'no' to 217, 319 'yes'

[69]1969, p. 203

[70]Dealt with in detail by Arthur Lewis, 1965

ago as the nineteenth century, no longer played a noteworthy role for the British economy.

Others may well have thought, in the context of the Federation, of functional co-operation as expressed in the establishment of the Caribbean Bar Association, the Imperial College of Tropical Agriculture, the University of the West Indies and the Caribbean Meteorological Service. Businessmen and lawyers could have thought of higher incomes and profits from a larger number of clients and an expanded market (Gordon Lewis 1968, p. 344ff).

The main reason for the collapse of the Federation was its colonial nature[71]. In view of the anti-colonial trends in the world and the growing number of sovereign states following World War II, that colonial character was no longer tenable[72].

Efforts at integration were marked by an absolute lack of enthusiasm or interest of the population for the new creation. Ignorance provided space for demagoguery and misinformation. In Barbados, the planters told the farm workers that Federation meant the re-introduction of slavery. But many Barbadians said that Federation meant that they would get money or land or both (Eric Williams, 1973b, p. 4). Neither the regional Press nor the then University College of the West Indies (later, the University of the West Indies) became the outrider of integration (Payne, 1980, p. 21).

Shortly after the start of the Federal experiment, Caribbean politicians inquired in Great Britain about the possibility of becoming independent, even without the Federation. Soon, therefore, the main arguments of the pro-Federal group lost its validity, whereby the Federation facilitated the swifter achievement of independence together than in individual negotiations (Murray, 1971, p. 170). The shortage, in both the Federal Executive and Legislature, of outstanding leadership material was also quite remarkable.

Neither Norman Manley nor Eric Williams ran for Federal Parliament or concerned themselves with the affairs of the Federal Government (Murray, 1971, p. 168). Personal ambitions prevented the transfer of power from the unit to the whole. Norman Manley lost respect as a Federalist among West Indians, when he refused to exchange the post of Head of Government in Jamaica for that of Head of Government of the Federation. This also cost him his credibility with many local voters, who preferred to vote for Bustamante, the clear opponent of the Federation, than its luke-warm advocate, Manley. If the Federation died, owing to the behaviour of its political personalities, then Manley was the principal perpetrator of this, according to Gordon Lewis (1968, p. 372).

The *Daily Gleaner*, in Jamaica, in its editorial of 18.10.1983 (at p. 10), wrote on the occasion of the twenty-fifth anniversary of the establishment of the Federation:

> 'But there is little doubt that if either Mr. Norman Manley of Jamaica, or Dr. Eric Williams of Trinidad had been able to lead a strong team of party colleagues into the Federal Parliament, the

---

[71] *Cf* Hoyos 1978, p 231, Eric Williams, 1973c, 13, Gordon K Lewis, 1968, pp 354ff and 386
[72] *Cf* as well Payne, 1980, p 16

> experiment might just have had a chance to succeed. But as they left it to the 'Second XI' members, as it were, the people accepted their view, and preferred Bustamante's first teams in Jamaica and Trinidad. Thus the Federal Parliament began with an opposition pulling a much stronger set of parliamentarians who would have made Federation work, if they were in power.'

The capriciousness of Eric Williams contributed to the fact that the Caribbean population did not regard him as a dependable leader and guarantor of a Federation granted Independence. Even later, he repeatedly sent his fellow Caribbean people alternating signals of hope and doubt over the prospects for Caribbean integration. In 1973, in an essay in a London political science journal, which was distributed through his party apparatus, he expressed optimism concerning the creation of a new Federation in the Commonwealth Caribbean (1973b).

But, in September of the very same year, he stated that there was no doubt that Caribbean integration would not happen in the foreseeable future and that disunity would be an ongoing reality, perhaps even the renewal of colonialism.[73].

Shridath Ramphal (1985, pp. 11-13) believes that West Indian history would have taken a different turning, if the Jamaican referendum's results had not been negative. He points out that the Lancaster House Conference of 1961 was in the process of fixing the details for the independence of the Federation, when these efforts were reduced to nothing by the 'No' in Jamaica.

Ramphal also believes that a 'Yes' would have moved Grantley Adams, the then Federal Premier, to let himself be replaced by Manley shortly after the independence of the Federation. Manley's conflict with Eric Williams would have been resolved; then British Guiana and British Honduras, as well as the Bahamas, would have gradually joined the Federation.

The region would have been more stable. In Grenada, neither the 'excesses' of Sir Eric Gairy nor Maurice Bishop's *coup d'état* would have occurred, according to Ramphal. The residents of the Commonwealth Caribbean would have had better possibilities for development. The brain drain — that is, the emigration of Commonwealth Caribbean specialist personnel to Great Britain, Canada and the USA — would have been less severe, because young people would have had more confidence in the future of the West Indies.

Hugh Springer, in an essay published in 1962 (pp. 48-50), regarded the break-up of the Federation, after the Jamaican referendum, as 'unnecessary'. Over time, Springer argued the process of inter-action, co-operation and exchange, 'the constant give and take' between the communities, would have led to the Federation becoming a unit 'emotionally' as well.

The difficulties in the growing together of the Federation, Springer partly ascribes to the fact that the basic conditions for its creation had not been fulfilled. Among these conditions, he counts the hope for economic advantage from union, a desire to be independent and the need for a common defence.

---

[73] *Cf.* Vaughan Lewis, 1974.

These objectives, he argues, however, could be attained even without a Federation.

Economic prosperity occurred in Trinidad and Tobago and Jamaica, thanks to their natural resources. But these were the very territories which were the opponents of the West Indies Federation. All participants would have obtained a certain independence, anyway, through almost complete internal self-government. Common defence, he argued, was guaranteed by the colonial power.

The question of the Federal capital also played a role. Augier (1989, p. 21) holds that the Federation would have survived, if Kingston had been the site of the Federal Government. Port-of-Spain, after Guyana's refusal, lay, according to Augier, too far on the periphery[74].

2.2.3 Political Disintegration and Economic Co-operation

The collapse of the West Indies Federation of 1958-62 led to a change in thinking in the integration movement. After 1962, the integrationists sought to achieve political integration by means of economic co-operation ('form follows fact'). This was in contrast to 'fact follows form' — the predominant view in the 1940s and 1950s whereby the West Indian small states should first become a political unit, after which co-operation in all fields would follow almost automatically.

The late Barbadian Prime Minister, Tom Adams (1984, p. 4), son of the Premier of the failed Federation, termed the idea of a political unit, which should precede the economic as not only wrong, but positively dangerous. Political matters are always considered divisive within itself, whereas 'reasonable men' could always be at one in economic questions, despite their being of varying views in party political and ideological matters.

The model for this was the European Union formerly, of course, the European Community and, before that, the European Economic Community. The view grew that traditional export products could not guarantee jobs and foreign exchange inflows, for the needs and wants of a growing population. Economic experts propagated the concept of 'industrialisation by invitation', inspired by economists, such as St. Lucia-born Nobel Prize winner, Sir Arthur Lewis (1959), whereby foreign investors would be invited to establish labour-intensive and export-oriented industrial plants, on the Puerto Rican model. Under the influence of the United Nations Economic Commission for Latin America (ECLA)[75], concepts were developed for the former British colonies following Latin American and European models.

Schools of economic thought have arisen. One of these (*Cf.* McIntyre 1966) advocated the creation of an EFTA-type Caribbean Free Trade Association for regional trade and, for foreign trade, 'resource combination' as the means against structural dependence. The other school of thought advised against a free trade zone and put the integration of key production sectors in the foreground. The two concepts were not mutually exclusive. But the integration

[74]Similarly, Crassweller, p. 267.
[75]Later with the addition, '*and the Caribbean* (ECLAC)'; in Spanish, CEPALC.

of production by political and administrative means seemed by far more difficult to accomplish than was the creation of a free trade zone. The former requires not only a central, thorough and co-ordinated planning of the siting of production plants but also the waiving by the participating States of their right to have certain industries or production types in favour of other States of the community. The concept runs against market economic order and free trade; and it necessitates dirigiste interventions in the affairs of native, and, more difficult still, foreign and multi-national firms — up to the point of expropriation, closure or forced relocation of businesses.

In 1951, the British colonial power, in order to further the economic co-operation of the British colonies in the Caribbean, established the Regional Economic Committee (REC), which lasted up to the creation of the Federation. The REC consisted of representatives of all British West Indian Governments and maintained a Secretariat in Barbados, in the head office of the regional Colonial Development and Welfare Organisation. But it had only limited jurisdiction and no power of decision.

The West Indies Federation brought little progress in the economic co-operation of the participating countries. A plan for a customs union was indeed drawn up; but the customs union itself was not established. The West Indies Shipping Corporation came into being during the Federation and had two ships, the *Federal Palm* and the *Federal Maple*, donated by the Canadian Government.

A Common Services Conference in Port-of-Spain, under the direction of the administrator appointed by the British Government as the Commissioner of the countries which had participated in the former West Indies Federation, decided, in mid-1962, to maintain both these organisations after the end of the Federation. A Ministerial Council of the participating countries should supervise these common services. In 1962, the Caribbean Meteorological Service was created. It, together with the University which was founded in 1948 and the shipping service, formed the core of the functional co-operation, which was later continued in the common market, CARICOM.

The Government of Trinidad and Tobago, even as it withdrew from the West Indies Federation, had broached the subject of the creation of a Caribbean Economic Community. This new body should consist not only of the ten ex-members of the former Federation, but also of the three Guianas and all islands in the Caribbean sea, independent or dependent. Trinidad and Tobago's Prime Minister, Eric Williams, issued invitations in July, 1963, for the first Heads of Government Conference. The participants spoke out in favour of closer co-operation in the Caribbean region. They wanted to orient themselves on models of regional co-operation in Europe, Africa and Latin America.

The participants in the first three Heads of Government Conferences were only the Heads of the four 'MDCs': Barbados, Jamaica, British Guiana and Trinidad and Tobago. The Heads of Government of the 'LDCs' — that is, Belize, St. Kitts-Nevis-Anguilla, Antigua, Montserrat, Dominica, St. Lucia, St. Vincent and Grenada — came first to the fourth Conference in 1967. So did the Bahamas.

2. Internal Factors of Caribbean Integration

The discrimination between MDCs and LDCs[76] did not remain without psychological influence on the integration movement. That difference led eventually to the eight East Caribbean LDCs later joining together and forming the Organisation of Eastern Caribbean States (OECS). On the other hand, the classification as LDC brought certain favours[77] within the common market and CARICOM-associated bodies, such as the Caribbean Development Bank.

In July, 1965, talks between the Prime Ministers of Barbados (Errol Barrow) and British Guiana (Forbes Burnham) led to the establishment of a free trade zone in the Commonwealth Caribbean. In the same year, the Chief Minister of Antigua, Vere Bird Sr., joined the zone. On December 15, 1965, they signed the Agreement of Dickenson Bay and founded the Caribbean Free Trade Association (CARIFTA). The practical conversion of the Agreement began two years later, however, with the Fourth Heads of Government Conference, when Trinidad and Tobago, Jamaica and the other countries, which had participated in the defunct Federation, formally approved the creation of CARIFTA.

The Agreements became effective for Antigua, Barbados, Guyana and Trinidad and Tobago on May 1, 1968; for Dominica, Grenada, St. Kitts-Nevis-Anguilla, St. Lucia and St. Vincent on July 1, 1968; for Jamaica and Montserrat on August 1, 1968. Belize acceded to the Agreements in May, 1971.

Resulting from the 1967 Conference, the CARIFTA regional Secretariat was established in Georgetown, the capital of Guyana, in 1968. Similarly, the Caribbean Development Bank, with head office in Barbados, was founded in October, 1969.

The CARIFTA Agreements, like the CARICOM Treaty later, contained no pointers on the building of a political unit. The preamble defines as its objectives, full employment and an improved living standard for people in the Commonwealth Caribbean. These objectives should be attained by the broadening of the regional markets and through removing trade barriers between the territories, by creating a customs union and an economic community for all Caribbean territories, which so desired. But initiators, such as Guyana's Head of Government, Burnham, in their speeches and activities, left no doubt that they contemplated political integration over and above economic integration.

In October, 1972, the Seventh Heads of Government Conference decided to convert CARIFTA into the Caribbean Common Market and also establish the Caribbean Community (CARICOM)[78] an integral component of which should be the common market. At the Eighth Heads of Government Conference in Georgetown in April, 1973, the participating countries, except Antigua and Montserrat, signed the Georgetown Accord, which paved the way for the signing of the Caribbean Community Treaty on July 4, 1973, at Chaguaramas in Trinidad and Tobago, the former site of the Government of the West Indies Federation.

---

[76] William Demas (1974, p 12) found the distinction between LDCs and MDCs unfortunate, because all CARICOM member-states are underdeveloped The only difference was one 'of degree'

[77] Articles 51-62 'Special Regime' for the LDCs in the *Treaty Establishing the Caribbean Community*

[78] The acronym, 'CARICOM' stands for both the *Caribbean Community* and the *Caribbean Common Market* — easily leading to confusion of the terms

This Treaty came into force on August 1, 1973, for the independent Member States; namely, Barbados, Guyana, Jamaica, Trinidad and Tobago. For the ten still dependent ex-CARIFTA territories — that is, Antigua, Belize, Dominica, Grenada, Montserrat, St. Kitts-Nevis-Anguilla, St. Lucia and St. Vincent — it became effective on May 1, 1974. At the Fifth CARICOM Summit, in July, 1983, again at Chaguaramas in Trinidad and Tobago, the Bahamas became the thirteenth CARICOM member-State. But it had long worked informally on CARICOM bodies[79].

In February, 1995 the Heads of Government Conference agreed to approve the application by Suriname for membership in the Caribbean Community and Common Market with effect from the 16th Meeting of the Conference on terms and conditions agreed by both sides. Suriname will be the first member from outside the Commonwealth Caribbean. The country has been an observer for a long time, and applied for full membership in May, 1994, because it did not want to be isolated within the trade and power blocs. Suriname, however, was only accepted after it got rid of the military rule that dominated its political decisions until 1993 (*cf. CI* March, 1995, p. 1).

Ratification of the CARICOM Treaty would have been considerably more difficult in the individual Member States, if it had furthered their political integration. Hence, its preamble merely asserted that the Governments of the contracting Member States:

> '*Determined* to consolidate and strengthen the bonds which have historically existed among their peoples;
>
> *Sharing* a common determination to fulfill the hopes and aspirations of their peoples for full employment and improved standards of work and living;
>
> *Conscious* that these objectives can most rapidly be attained by the optimum utilisation of available human and natural resources of the Region by accelerated, co-ordinated and sustained economic development, particularly through the exercise of permanent sovereignty over their natural resources; by the efficient operation of common services and functional co-operation in the social, cultural, educational and technological fields; and by a common front in relation to the external world;
>
> *Convinced* of the need to elaborate an effective regime by establishing and utilising institutions designed to enhance the economic, social and cultural development of their people.'

In practice, these intentions should be realised by the establishment of a common market *régime*, co-ordination of the foreign policies, and functional co-operation (Article 4). An Annex to the Treaty contains details of the Caribbean Common Market. In the preamble of this Appendix, the contracting Member States express the conviction that their economic integration will contribute to the creation of a 'viable economic community' of the countries of the Commonwealth Caribbean.

---

[79] *Cf.*: The speech of the Bahamas' Head of Government, Sir Lynden Oscar Pindling, at the Fourth CARICOM Summit at Chaguaramas, printed in *CP* 20, pp. 8ff.

2. Internal Factors of Caribbean Integration

The Common External Tariff (CET) is an important component of the CARICOM Treaty. The implementation of this Treaty serves as the test of the readiness for integration of the CARICOM Member States, since it is an excellent means for furthering intra-regional trade and its implementation is verifiable. But the harmonisation period laid down in Article 5 of the Treaty for the adjustment of national customs duties to the common tariff was honoured neither by the original signatories nor by the other states, which acceded to the Treaty subsequently.

The shock caused by the failure of the West Indies Federation in 1962 gave the integration movement impulses in several directions. Advocates of political integration regard the economic community as the intermediate stage to political unity. But others — and especially politicians from the Caribbean periphery — can well regard the economic community as the final stage of regional co-operation, the instruments of which need merely to be fine-tuned.

The view that no political unity can come out of CARICOM in the foreseeable future is based on the experience of the failed Federation. As early as in the 1960s, efforts were made to achieve integration solutions for the smaller islands.

When, at the start of 1962, it was established that Trinidad and Tobago would not become part of a truncated Federation, but would instead, like Jamaica, become independent on its own, the Heads of Government of the remaining eight territories in the Federation met in Barbados in February, 1962, and agreed on a new Federal Constitution. But the birth of the planned East Caribbean Federation did not occur[80]. The temptation to join with oil and industry-rich Trinidad and Tobago, instead of with the small Caribbean States, was too great.

This was especially true of Grenada, the classic emigration land for Trinidad, where the August, 1962, elections saw a clash between the idea of a unitary State against a Federal one. The unitary idea, represented by the Grenada National Party of Herbert Blaize emerged victorious over outgoing Gairy's rather pro-Federal Grenada United Labour Party[81]. Grenada then broke off negotiations concerning the truncated Federation and opened talks with Trinidad and Tobago concerning amalgamation.

But the Government in Port-of-Spain dragged out the negotiations so long that the subsequent general elections, five years later, practically solved the problem, in that Gairy returned to power. It was anyway doubtful whether Eric Williams, the Prime Minister of Trinidad and Tobago had ever taken seriously the idea of a unitary State with neighbouring Grenada and St. Vincent. He knew only too well that the adjustment of the living standard and public sector salaries to the levels in Trinidad and Tobago would cost enormous sums; and also that total freedom of movement within the participating islands would lead to uncontrollable mass immigration into Trinidad — where the idea was correspondingly unpopular.

---

[80] *Cf.*: Bahadoorsingh. 1969.

[81] Gairy went weakened into the election race, as the U.K.-designated Lloyd Commission of Enquiry had found him guilty of financial irregularities in office and wastefulness.

Three years after the collapse of the West Indies Federation, thoughts about a federation of the remaining territories were definitely abandoned. On April 29, 1965, the regional Ministerial Council of the remnants of the Federation adjourned *sine die*, after Antigua, Montserrat and St. Lucia had announced their withdrawal (Payne 1980, p. 51).

2.2.4 Political Emancipation of the Sub-Region

In 1967, the British Government granted six East Caribbean territories[82] extended autonomy as West Indies Associated States (WISA)[83], in the expectation that they would become a new Federation. The new Associated States co-ordinated their economic relationship through a Council of Ministers, which, first of all, regulated their functional co-operation. In 1968, these territories founded the East[84] Caribbean Common Market (ECCM). The Agreements for the creation of the common market came into effect on June 15, 1968 — that is, a few days before the CARIFTA Agreements.

The WISA Ministerial Council had no legislative jurisdiction; but it did succeed in creating a series of institutions legitimised by laws in the participating territories. Among these institutions were the East Caribbean Currency Authority (ECCA) for the circulation and supervision of a common currency; the West Indies Associated States Supreme Court with appellate jurisdiction; and the East Caribbean Tourist Association (ECTA) for the co-ordination of regional efforts in tourism.

As, in the course of the 1970s, an increasing number of the Associated States received independence from Great Britain, the six, with Montserrat, decided to create the Organisation of Eastern Caribbean States (OECS), which came into being on June 18, 1981. The creation of a sub-regional unit within — but also in competition with — CARICOM seemed necessary. This was because the initial optimism which had accompanied the founding of the Caribbean Community (1973) had largely disappeared under the weight of the problems of the region. The larger CARICOM Member States, above all, Guyana and Jamaica, which had formerly been relatively prosperous, had run into great difficulties, owing to bad economic management, falling demand for raw materials and the generally poor global economic situation. In the impending atmosphere of protectionism and the contraction of the intra-regional markets, there developed in the LDCs the need to take action to defend their interests (Vaughan Lewis, 1987, p. 5).

One determining factor of OECS co-operation is the effort, despite the waning readiness of international financial agencies to provide international aid, to further the implementation of small projects in small states. The high costs of foreign representation ought to be reduced through common foreign missions.

The OECS Treaty defines the aim of the Organisation in Article 3 as follows:

---

[82] That is, Antigua and Barbuda, Dominica, Grenada, St Kitts-Nevis-Anguilla, St Lucia, St Vincent and the Grenadines

[83] The official acronym does not tally with the initial letters of the words

[84] Currently termed '*Eastern*' usually, as an accommodation with the Organisation of *Eastern* Caribbean States

'(a) to promote co-operation among the Member States and at the regional and international levels having due regard to the Treaty establishing the Caribbean Community and the Charter of the United Nations;

(b) to promote unity and solidarity among the Member States and to defend their sovereignty, territorial integrity and independence;

(c) to assist the Member States in the realisation of their obligations and responsibilities to the international community with due regard to the role of international law as a standard of conduct in their relationship;

(d) to seek to achieve the fullest possible harmonisation of foreign policy among the Member States; to seek to adopt, as far as possible, common positions on international issues and to establish and maintain wherever possible, arrangements for joint overseas representation and/or common services;

(e) to promote economic integration among the Member States through the provisions of the Agreement Establishing the East Caribbean Common Market; and

(f) to pursue the said purposes through its respective institutions by discussion of questions of common concern and by agreement and common action.'

The expectations placed in WISA and later in the OECS went beyond the common market and functional integration. The most concrete plans to bring about Caribbean political unity now emanate from the Eastern Caribbean. Here were the common foreign policy and security interests most clearly formulated, and in the October, 1983 intervention in Grenada, put most spectacularly in practice.

Following the creation of WISA, there were numerous initiatives for bringing about East Caribbean political unity. In May, 1970, the then Minister in St. Vincent and the Grenadines for Trade, Agriculture and Tourism, James Mitchell (1987b, pp. 3-8), in a Labour Day speech, spoke out in favour of ceding the claim of St. Vincent and the Grenadines to separate sovereignty in favour of a sovereign unit of the associated states. Mitchell accepted that this, having regard to the year-long struggle for independence, at first required the renunciation of the prior claim to enjoy to the full the fruits of the struggle. In the long run, according to him, the region would stumble from crisis to crisis, if it did not build political unity.

Mitchell circulated detailed proposals about the territorial co-ordination of the exercise of executive and legislative power: Determination of the capital; the geographical location of Parliament; the site of the annual Throne Speech for the opening of Parliament and the presentation of the national budget. The possibilities for the election of the Head of State, the geographical distribution of the most important executive functions, the appointment of Ambassadors to the United Nations and the common Foreign Minister as well as the role of the regional radio and TV media were all dealt with. His position was that unity should not wait until all Associated States joined the integration movement.

Instead, unity should be undertaken immediately with the nearest neighbours, especially St. Lucia and Grenada. The others would then follow soon enough[85].

Essentially on the initiative of the LDCs and Guyana's then Prime Minister, Linden Forbes Burnham, the Heads of Government of Dominica, Grenada, Guyana, St. Kitts-Nevis-Anguilla, St. Lucia, as well as St. Vincent and the Grenadines met in Grenada in 1971 with the intention 'to seek to establish out of their territories a new State in the Caribbean'. In their Grenada Declaration[86], the way to political unity was laid down through the creation of a Preparatory Commission, the nomination of a Constituent Assembly, the promulgation of a common constitution on April 22, 1973, and the holding of new elections in each participating State by June 30, 1973.

The Governments of Trinidad and Tobago and Barbados participated in the consultation only marginally, and did not sign the Grenada Declaration. Jamaica, Belize and the Bahamas were not involved. The MDCs, with the exception of Guyana, were little interested in the proclaimed political unity. The disinterest of Trinidad and Tobago and Barbados caused the initiative to die, even before a first meeting of the Preparatory Commission. The LDCs which participated made it clear that they wished to build no political unity with Guyana alone, which, since 1970, had been pursuing a self-prescribed policy of Co-operative Socialism'[87].

Doubts about Burnham's sincerity in the integration question have never been silent. He had, through his rigorous style of coming to, and exercising, power in Guyana, discredited himself too much. Thus, the much-read Jamaican columnist, 'Jane Patmos'[88], for instance, declared, in *The Sunday Gleaner* of 17.6.1984, p. 13:

> 'Personally I have never been convinced that Comrade Burnham felt that the Caribbean islands have much to contribute to his destiny.'

On the initiative of the newly-elected Prime Minister of St. Vincent, James Mitchell, the Heads of Government of Grenada, St. Lucia and St. Vincent, at a week-end meeting in St. Vincent, agreed, in June, 1972, to complete freedom of movement and unlimited right of residence for their respective nationals. The Petit St. Vincent Initiative crashed, however, at the very next change of government in St. Vincent[89].

In June, 1972, twenty West Indian technocrats, journalists, lawyers and pedagogues met in Tobago and consulted on West Indian integration. Among them were the then UWI Chancellor and former Chief Justice of Trinidad and Tobago, Sir Hugh Wooding, and the then Governor of the Caribbean Development Bank and Chancellor of the University of Guyana, Arthur Lewis. They published The *Tobago Declaration, 1972*, in which they advocated a new Federation of the Eastern Caribbean States. The doors would be left open for

---

[85] Mitchell's formula was the 'association of any'.
[86] Guyana's then Foreign Minister, Shridath Ramphal, played an important role in its formulation
[87] *Cf.*: Payne, 1980, pp 259-263, and Freymond, 1980, p. 52.
[88] Aimee Webster-Delisser.
[89] *Cf.* Payne, 1980, pp 178 and 191, note 32.

Jamaica and other territories. The participation of Trinidad and Tobago was essential.

A Federation of the Associated States alone was given no chance of success owing to trade, cultural and social links with Barbados and Trinidad and Tobago. Under Federal control should be defence, foreign policy, justice, civic freedoms, customs duties, legislation governing income tax, the Central Bank and the commercial banking system, tertiary education, the public service, civil aviation, shipping, postal and telecommunications services (excepting the telephone) and examination of the public accounts of both local and Federal budgets. The Governments of the territories should keep the initiative for their own industrial and agricultural development; and also finance themselves their social charges. Unlimited freedom of movement and freedom of residence within the region should not exist for the time being. The Federal Government should develop proposals for controlling inter-territorial tourism and creating a customs union. The authors of the document supported a Federation of gradually increasing strength. The Federal capital should be sited in one of the smaller territories; the Federation should bear the name, 'The West Indies'.

The Tobago Initiative remained largely academic and without response. But a portion of the recommendations surfaced in the aforementioned essay, 'A New Federation for the Commonwealth Caribbean', of 1973 by the then Prime Minister of Trinidad and Tobago, Eric Williams. In this essay, he showed understanding for Jamaica's reservations against the Federation. He proposed the creation of a Federation either without Jamaica — at least, at the beginning — or a Federation of the larger, independent Caribbean States with the possibility of the later accession of the smaller islands — in that case, preferably after they have been united politically. Federal MPs would also be simultaneously able to be MPs at national level, unlike the situation in the old Federation. Foreign policy and defence should be the responsibilities of the Federal Government.

A highly mobile and well-equipped police force should be created, in order to maintain internal security. It should also be to fight organised crime, especially the illegal narcotics trade. The Federal Government should have the right, in clearly defined cases (such as the complete breakdown of law and order, the illegal seizing of power or the refusal of the Government of any member-State to obey the directives of the Federal Court) to suspend the constitution of a member-State. The public service should be federalised and put under the control of the Federal Court. But freedom of movement should exist only with limitations.

Williams saw difficulties in economic co-operation being resolved or brought close to solution through the creation of CARICOM. The Federal Government should be responsible for the levying of customs duties. But income tax should initially belong to the Member States, and, in the course of further developments, be also made available to the Federal Government.

In addition, Williams pleaded in his essay for the *economic* integration of the entire Caribbean, including the Spanish, Dutch and French-speaking parts, and explicitly Cuba.

In 1974, the Report of the Caribbean Task Force, established by Williams under the chairmanship of economist, Fitzgerald Francis, dealt with the relationship between Trinidad and Tobago and the other Caribbean countries and made recommendations for the creation of a political union of the seven Associated States with Barbados, Trinidad and Tobago and Guyana.

In the same year, the then CARICOM Secretary-General, William Demas, in an essay, (pp. 55 *et seq*) suggested the creation of political mergers of the Eastern Caribbean English-speaking countries. The Leeward and Windward Islands should each build a political unit. Demas argued that the Caribbean Community in the then constitutional situation of still dependent States could not function effectively. Separate independence of the then Associated States and the colonies, he argued, would lead only to formal but not effective sovereignty.

Demas did not posit the political unity of the Eastern Caribbean States in the form of a 'classical' Federation or a unitary state. Instead, it was seen as a hitherto single division of power between the individual island Governments and a central authority. A central Cabinet consisting of the Heads of Government of the individual territories could exist for a 5-10 year transition period. Foreign policy and foreign trade should fall from the very beginning within the jurisdiction of the Central Government which should gradually receive other functions.

The merger of the Leeward and Windward Islands could build a political unit with the larger territories of the Eastern Caribbean. The latter, as relatively highly-developed States, would have to bear the financial burden which would result from this arrangement. Aid from Great Britain, Canada and international financial agencies could be expected. The new political unit would, together with Belize, Jamaica and the Bahamas, form the Caribbean Community and Common Market, which, up to then, consisted of four members.

Demas later evaluated his above-mentioned proposals rather sceptically. The structure of Eastern Caribbean unity thought out by him, he decided, would have created too weak a central government (Demas, 1987, p. 9).

In 1974, St. Vincent's Premier, James Mitchell, spontaneously agreed with his counterpart from St. Kitts-Nevis-Anguilla, Robert Bradshaw, for their countries to proceed to independence together. This agreement was made on the periphery of joint negotiations with the then European Community in Brussels. But nothing came out of it.

The Prime Minister of Trinidad and Tobago, Eric Williams, provided money for establishing a Constitutional Commission under the leadership of Sir Hugh Wooding, to formulate constitutional proposals for the Independence of Montserrat and the then Associated States. Shortly after the Commission came into being in May 1974, however, Sir Hugh died. In the same year, following elections, James Mitchell lost power as Head of Government. Lawyer and University Professor, Telford Georges, became Chairman of the Commission, which had the assistance of a technical committee headed by Alister McIntyre, that presented its Report in 1975 (Emmanuel *et al.*, 1975).

The total report, which appeared in 1976 (*Report of the Constitutional Commission on the West Indies Associated States and Montserrat*), recommended that the Windward and Leeward Islands should form a single, independent State. The Council of the Heads of Government should be the highest deciding and executive body. Its Chairman should be one of the Heads, each serving a rotating two-year term. The Union House of Assembly — initially nominated then later elected as the controlling body of all officials with the right to allocations from the budget — would be the other main branch of this State.

The Council should not be a Cabinet. Instead, the *Commissioners* consisting of chief officials of the Union Administration, should function as the Cabinet. The Heads of Government should name Ministers for the various Union portfolios which they could represent in the Council. Neither the *Council* nor the *Assembly* should exercise any legislative authority.

The Constitutional Commission declined, therefore, to fix concurrent areas of jurisdiction as between the Union and its Member States. One of the principal aims of integration should be the co-ordination of the foreign and security policies of the participants. Common services for air and sea transportation, as well as for postal and telecommunications traffic, a common currency and banking system and the jurisdiction of the Federal Court should be included in the integration process. A common nationality should be created. But here too, freedom of movement should at first be limited.

The proposals of the Commission received little attention. The territories of the Leeward and Windward Islands sought their independence separately. Alternatively, like Montserrat, Anguilla and the British Virgin Islands, they remained UK-dependent colonies (*Cf.*; Mitchell 1987b, p. 1).

Nonetheless, the Organisation of Eastern Caribbean States (OECS) in 1981 was formed exactly according to the proposed model. But this was done without formally declaring itself a political unit; or providing a common nationality for the nationals of its constituent member-islands; or undertaking the level of functional co-operation recommended by the Commission.

In 1979, the Heads of Government of the Windward islands of Dominica, Grenada and St. Lucia promised, in the *Declaration of St. George's*, freedom of movement for the citizens of the participating countries (*Cf.* Demas 1987, p. 10). The initiative was the expression of ideological commitment. In March, 1979, Maurice Bishop had come to power through a *coup d'état*; in June, in Dominica, Oliver Seraphine had formed an interim coalition; in July, the St. Lucia Labour Party had won a big election victory. George Odlum became Foreign Minister. The three politicians were self-confessed adherents of Socialist policies, albeit of varying manifestations and consistency.

But, shortly thereafter, a change of Government in Dominica made this initiative, too, come to naught.

2.2.5 Ideological Change and Stagnation of the Movement

The significance of the numerous initiatives concerning the political integration of the Commonwealth Caribbean was this: They kept the idea alive and brought new impulses into the discussion. Proposals relating to economic and functional co-operation found their acceptance and implementation in the practical work of CARICOM and the OECS, with the affiliated common markets.

Scientists and technocrats obtained the opportunity to convert theoretical knowledge into praxis. One of the most remarkable personalities in this category was William Arthur Lewis(1915-1991), the St. Lucian Nobel prize-winning economist, who had observed the independence and integration efforts of the Commonwealth Caribbean from the 1950s as University Professor, sometime Chancellor of the University of Guyana and Vice-Chancellor/Principal of the University of the West Indies; as adviser to Trinidad and Tobago's Prime Minister, Eric Williams, and, as the first President of the Caribbean Development Bank. William Demas of Trinidad and Tobago, who in 1965, put out his first great piece on the economic development of small states, should also be mentioned. He was Secretary-General of CARIFTA and CARICOM as already stated, then up to 1992, Governor of the Central Bank of Trinidad and Tobago, after being President of the Caribbean Development Bank.

Other Caribbean intellectuals who have been allowed to put integration theories into political praxis and have reached high technocratic office are: Norman Girvan, adviser for many years of former Jamaican Prime Minister, Michael Manley; Vaughan Lewis, OECS Director-General; Sir Alister McIntyre, Deputy Secretary-General of UNCTAD for many years and now UWI Vice-Chancellor; Patrick Emmanuel, member of the interim Government in Grenada after the October, 1983 intervention; Swinburn Lestrade, former Director of the OECS Secretariat for Economic Affairs; and Eastern Caribbean Central Bank Governor, Dwight Venner.

Vaughan Lewis, Lestrade, Venner and others put out in 1972, a publication on political aspects of the integration of the Windward and Leeward Islands, with detailed proposals for making a federal political unit of the future OECS (Venner *et al.* 1972).

From the end of the 1970s to the mid-1980s, no new proposals or initiatives concerning political integration emanated from Commonwealth Caribbean Governments. Regional co-operation receded to the end of political priorities. The reasons for this are diverse. All CARICOM Member States struggled with increasingly more difficult economic conditions. The latter were linked to the general world economic situation and were partly determined by sharply rising energy costs, falling earnings from primary raw materials such as bauxite (from Guyana and Jamaica), crude oil (Trinidad and Tobago) and agricultural produce, failed industrialisation plans, bad management, the brain drain and political polarisation.

The Common Market was too weak to stave off the economic decline of the CARICOM Member States. The Report, which was published in 1981, of a Group of Caribbean Experts commissioned by the Caribbean Community stated as follows:

> 'It is becoming increasingly recognised that regional integration is not a panacea for the economic ills of the region and that it cannot by itself bring instant prosperity to its Member States. What integration can do is to provide additional development opportunities and increased bargaining power for

Member States as part of their national development effort.' (*Caribbean Community in the 1980s*, p. 2)

The participating Governments, for which economic success was the only means to stabilise their political power, tried in isolation, and often in competition against each other, to get aid from the industrialised countries and international lending agencies. The *Caribbean Basin Initiative*, which was originally hailed in the region as the 'Marshall Plan' for the Commonwealth Caribbean, was typical of this form of selective bilateral aid for the region.

Between 1976 and 1982, no meeting of CARICOM Heads of Government took place. The third CARICOM Summit in Jamaica in November, 1982, reflected the ideological change which had occurred in the interim. Left-wing-rated Governments in Jamaica, St. Lucia and Dominica had been replaced by rather conservative ones. This development continued in all territories, most spectacularly in Grenada, but also in Belize, St. Vincent and the Grenadines and Trinidad and Tobago.

In Guyana, after the death of Burnham in August, 1985, a new political attitude seemed to open up under his successor, Desmond Hoyte. The latter moved away from Burnham's Socialist rhetoric to a more pragmatic consideration of the economic and social problems of the country. This became clear in the posture of the OECS and Barbados to the Hoyte Government, following an informal meeting of the Heads of Government with Hoyte on the island of Mustique in the Grenadines in January, 1986. Whereas Heads of Government, as Dominica's Prime Minister, Eugenia Charles, had wanted to block a CARICOM Summit scheduled to be held in Guyana, their stance changed remarkably, after the discussions with Hoyte (*cf.* Ballantyne, 1986, pp. 10-11).

In the 1980s, the CARICOM Heads of Government manifested a readiness to fine-tune the instruments of economic and functional integration. The euphoria of the 1970s had, however, given way to a rather sober examination of the possibilities and limits of integration. 'Self-reliance', 'independence' and 'sovereignty' disappeared from the vocabulary of the Governments or were interpreted differently. Intra-regional trade fell continuously, because Trinidad and Tobago, as the main importer of CARICOM products up to that time, owing to its own economic difficulties, almost ceased to matter.

Foreign investments, export-enhancing non-traditional products, the stimulation of tourism and the extension of bi-lateral trade relations with industrialised countries, were seen as the ways out of the economic malaise, with its growing unemployment, anxiety about the future, and the brain drain. Under structural adjustment programmes, the Governments made efforts to balance their budgets, to foster labour-intensive industries, reduce their foreign debt and increase their foreign exchange inflows. The adjustment was, however, oriented not towards the needs of the intra-regional market, but towards the markets of the most important importing countries: namely, the USA, Canada and Great Britain. South-South trade, which had been heavily touted in the 1970s, within the framework of the thrust for a new international economic order, weakened considerably.

In Jamaica, the Jamaica Labour Party (JLP) under Edward Seaga replaced the Manley Government in October, 1980, after an election campaign conducted with nationalistic election slogans. A similar strategy had brought the JLP to power in 1962. Seaga explicitly referred to this 'mandate of the Jamaican people', as he, in November 1985, abruptly rebuffed, in the presence of the then Prime Minister of Trinidad and Tobago, George Chambers, the Eastern Caribbean intimations to ponder again on the feasibility of the Federation. The Government and people of Jamaica fully supported the programme of regional co-operation and economic integration, but were not of the view that a federation was in the best interest of the region (*DG* 18.11.1985, pp. 1 and 3).

Chambers himself, who became Prime Minister after the death of Eric Williams in 1981, made no effort to conceal the low priority which regional co-operation had in his governmental policy options. His annoyance at Caribbean participation, against his advice, in the 1983 Grenada intervention and the increasing economic difficulties of his country gave him the opportunity to reduce the role of Trinidad and Tobago as the donor of funds among CARICOM Member States and put a brake on the flood of 'illegal immigrants', especially from Grenada and St. Vincent and the Grenadines. After their rivals in the North Caribbean who had long made 'Jamaica First'[90] into a household term, Chambers now declared that 'Trinidad and Tobago must come first from now' (*Cf.* Deosaran 1984a, p. 7).

Dominica's Prime Minister, Dame Mary Eugenia Charles, repeatedly expressed her scepticism about the political unity of the Commonwealth Caribbean. She played a key role in inner-Caribbean co-operation and also, as the chairwoman of the OECS in 1983, assumed responsibility for the call for US help in the Grenada intervention. She often pointed out that the political unity of the Commonwealth Caribbean was not likely during her lifetime.

In 1971, however, she had been one of the signatories of the 'Joint Opposition Statement' of the Eastern Caribbean Opposition political parties calling for creation of an independent, living and viable Caribbean nation.

Only little progress towards integration resulted from the CARICOM Summits of 1982 (in Jamaica) and 1983 (in Trinidad and Tobago). In the *Nassau Understanding*, issued as a communiqué at the fifth CARICOM Summit in the Bahamas in July, 1984, all participants pledged to introduce the Common External Tariff (CET) and remove the barriers to intra-regional trade.

2.2.6 The Eastern Caribbean on the Way to Political Union

William Demas gave the integration movement a new impulse with his lecture in June, 1986, at the UWI Institute of International Relations in Trinidad. Independence for the small and very small English-speaking Caribbean countries could, in his view, in the true sense of the term, proceed only from political unity. But that unity must include the territories of the former West Indies Federation as well as the mainland state of Guyana.

Demas proposed beginning with the seven-member OECS and then extending unity to the ten Eastern Caribbean CARICOM Member States. This was

---

[90] The slogan was widely distributed as car stickers at the end of the 1979s

because he regarded it as unlikely that all relevant countries would participate in the union.

A West Indian Forum, he went on, consisting of personalities from the individual countries, should work out the modalities for the new union which should not slavishly copy either the orthodox patterns of classical Federations or those of unitary States. The advantages and disadvantages of the union should be laid openly before the people and thoroughly discussed with them.

The Commonwealth Caribbean Heads of Government reacted to Demas' proposals with little enthusiasm. Jamaica's then Prime Minister, Edward Seaga, confirmed the opposition of the Jamaica Labour Party in the following terms:

> 'I do not believe in the integration movement ... I believe that we can have an economic integration, but no political one. And my reasons not to support it are the same as in 1961.'

The Prime Minister of Belize, Manuel Esquivel, expressed doubts that political unity 'would come in our lifetime', a view shared by Dominica's Prime Minister, Eugenia Charles : 'I believe we have missed the boat.' St. Lucia's Deputy Prime Minister, George Mallet, vaguely espied political unity 'not in the immediate future.' It could perhaps come to the entire Caribbean, he held, but would then certainly start with the OECS.

Positive statements were, however, made by both the then Guyana's President Desmond Hoyte, and Barbados' Prime Minister, Errol Barrow[91]. Hoyte called attention to the 1971 *Grenada Declaration*:

'I myself am in favour of a political union. I think it's our destiny...it may be far-fetched and so on, but that's a different matter.'

Barrow wanted to entrust the preparations for political unity not to a task force but rather deal with them at the political level[92].

At an OECS Heads of Government breakfast in September, 1986, during the annual IMF/World Bank meeting, St. Vincent and the Grenadines' Prime Minister, James Mitchell (1987b, p. 9) exhorted his colleagues; that is, Blaize from Grenada and Compton from St. Lucia, 'to explain categorically' their attitude to political association. They made positive statements, according to Mitchell.

OECS Director-General, Vaughan Lewis, suggested that the matter be discussed at the next official OECS Heads of Government meeting in St. Lucia, in October, 1986. For this meeting, Mitchell prepared a paper in which he listed the advantages of political union of the OECS and pointed out that the Governments shared the 'same political philosophy', which — with the exception of Antigua — found expression in the membership of their parties in the Caribbean Democrat Union (CDU)[93]: 'If we do not come together now, it will not happen again.' Mitchell (1987b, p.11) challenged parties of other political colours to unite as well.

In his paper, Mitchell proposed a firm orientation timetable for the introduction of the union and to decide on the areas of responsibility to be left to the

[91] This CARIFTA and CARICOM pioneer died in 1987

[92] All quotations are from *CC* August, 1986, p 9.

[93] *Cf* Chapter 2 7 3.3

local island Governments. He cautioned that terms, such as Federation, should be 'avoided at all costs' as well as disputes over leadership questions and the site of the Government. This was an allusion to the failures of the past.

He dealt individually with the constitutional framework of the future nation, the Eastern Caribbean, whose inhabitants should be known as Caribbean People. This nation should be a Republic with a President — elected on the French-Latin American model and a Parliament elected on the German model. Rather weak island Governments should be subordinate to a strong Central Government (pp. 12-16).

For the preparation of the political union, the Governments should, according to Mitchell's proposals, set up a constitutional committee as well as a committee for functional co-operation. By the end of 1987, all participating territories should hold referenda on the constitutional proposal. By Easter, 1988, they should hold elections under the new constitution. The proposal should have the motto, 'Reuniting the Caribbean'. Mitchell explicitly included Anguilla and the British Virgin Islands, British colonies with only observer status in the OECS.

On October 13, 1986, at their meeting in St. Lucia, the Heads of Government of the OECS[94] agreed 'in principle' to the proposals and decided to set up a 'technical committee' to deal with the implementation. This committee, consisting of William Demas, Alister McIntyre, Vaughan Lewis and Crispin Sorhaindo[95], was briefed by Mitchell on its terms of reference on November 15.

Mitchell stoutly put forward his proposal at the Tortola (British Virgin Islands) OECS Heads of Government's next meeting on May 27, 1987. In a speech (1987d, pp. 16ff) entitled 'To Be or Not To Be a Single Nation: That is the Question', he preempted two reactions to his appeals known from his own sorrowful experience: 'When we the leaders do not discuss Caribbean unification, we are disparaged for not doing so, when we do so, we are criticised for contemplating the idea on our own'. After 'decades of errors' action must now be taken, he argued. History would show who should be condemned for it.

An irresistible momentum for the other OECS members would exist, even if only three of them founded the union at first, he urged further. He was himself prepared, he declared, 'to serve under every other Head of Government' and to launch immediately a campaign in his country for the union. Nonetheless, he could do nothing, he added, unless the Heads of Government and the people were prepared.

Mitchell demanded that, before year's end, the people should be asked in a referendum whether they were in favour of a unified State. If they were in favour, then a Constitution was to be designed. After Parliamentary approval of the Constitution, the people would vote on the latter in a second referendum. All this should occur within two years. To the opponents and procrastinators he said:

> 'Those who will preserve the status quo to satisfy their selfish ambitions with that status quo, or who for whatever political whim

[94] Antigua was absent; but its Foreign Minister, Lester Bird, was officially informed, at the next OECS Heads of Government meeting on November 29 in Antigua, about the initiative.

[95] Then Vice-President of the Caribbean Development Bank.

> would jeopardise our progress to unity, simply categorise themselves as lacking a sense of history of unity in the rest of the world, and do not understand our geography.'

The audience gave Mitchell's speech a standing ovation. The Summit passed a resolution in which the demand for a political union and the need for close consultation with the people was affirmed. The view of a newspaper commentator was that never before had one felt so sincere a wish for Caribbean unity. The Summit could possibly go down in Caribbean history as the 'turning point of our destiny as a Caribbean people' and as a 'milestone' (*The Island Sun* 30.5.1987, p. 19). OECS Chairman and St. Lucia's Prime Minister, John Compton, also ascribed a historical dimension to the Tortola meeting 'as it is at this meeting that the question of OECS unity was removed from realm of rhetoric and pious declaration and placed firmly on the agenda for discussion and decision'(*Youth Link* 2.4, p.2).

A few days after the Tortola Summit, however, the British Virgin Islands' Government declared that its territory did not 'at present' wish to join in a closer union of the OECS. OECS Chairman, John Compton, showed understanding for this position, since the British Virgin Islands had for a long time kept out of the political process of the Caribbean. They were, however, welcome, should they wish to become a member of the 'new nation' (*The Island Sun* 6.6.1987, pp. 1 and 18).

At the following CARICOM Heads of Government meeting in St. Lucia, at the end of June, 1987, James Mitchell (1987b, p. 20) affirmed the 'deep philosophical commitment' of the MDCs' Heads of Government to Caribbean political unity. He showed understanding that this unity was not then on the common or national agenda. But he felt encouraged by Guyana's President Hoyte, Trinídad and Tobago's Prime Minister Robinson, the late Barbadian Prime Minister Barrow and even by Jamaica's Prime Minister Seaga's efforts for the founding of the Caribbean Democrat Union, 'which has not been without significance in bringing our parties together.'

Only on the periphery of their meeting did the CARICOM Heads of Government speak about Caribbean unity. But they again agreed to the removal of all mutual tariff barriers and the imposition of a uniform 15% CET, by, at the latest, September, 1988 (*CC* August 1987, p. 14).

A few days after the Summit, that is, on July 20, 1987, James Mitchell began officially consulting the population of St. Vincent and the Grenadines about Eastern Caribbean political unity. At the installation of the National Advisory Committee, guest speaker, William Demas, (1987, p. 3) warned against blocking further steps to political unity with new scientific studies and reworking old ones. 'We must decisively resist the temptation to study to death' the issues, he said. As previously in his June 10, 1986, speech in Trinidad, Demas made it clear that he regarded OECS unity as the first step to political unity with other CARICOM Member States. The creation of a new nation from the OECS would strengthen the Caribbean Community which would then have to deal with a relatively strong economic and political unit instead of seven relatively weak ones. Conversely, a unified OECS nation would be strengthened by the community, which would lower administrative costs. The LDCs would also have more weight within CARICOM (pp. 48ff).

Demas again decisively moved away from the thesis that political integration would automatically follow economic integration. 'Experience has shown that this is never so. What has emerged from the experience is the conclusion that — particularly in developing countries — political integration, so far from being the end product of successful economic integration, in certain point, is a condition for further deepening of economic, functional and foreign policy integration.' Demas referred to then West European experience, which led to the same conclusion (p. 20). He came down against a Federation — whether with a strong or weak Government — and pleaded for the creation of a unitary Eastern Caribbean State with the transfer of a certain amount of power to the constituent units (pp. 30-31).

As the next step towards OECS political unity, Demas recommended the simplification of tourism travel, customs union, the freedom of movement of capital, management and entrepreneurial activities, the appointment in each case of a common Ambassador to foreign diplomatic posts, common customs services as well as in levying indirect taxes, in statistics, auditing and anti-narcotics operations (pp. 50 ff).

At the next meeting of the East Caribbean Heads of Government, on November 25, 1987, in St. Lucia, OECS Chairman and St. Lucian Prime Minister, John Compton, affirmed the spirit of Tortola and put forward the following as fundamental elements of a future union: A democratic State system; single citizenship; freedom of movement; a Bill of Rights as a component of the Constitution; a Central Government strong enough to guarantee the general welfare of the people and the security of the borders; and the remaining of a substantial portion of power with the constituent units.

Besides, the articles of the constitution should be flexible enough to solve problems which arise and fill any gaps.

> 'The long years of insularity will not disappear overnight. The journey will be long, but for God's sake let us take the first bold step into meaningful nationhood.'

Compton's call received support, especially from St. Vincent and the Grenadines and from Grenada's Prime Minister, Herbert Blaize (*WG* 8.12.1987, p. 18). But the Heads of Government did not wish to tie themselves down to a timetable for the common OECS referendum in each member-State suggested by Mitchell. Instead, they set up several working groups, which should report by the next OECS Summit in St. Vincent. The referenda were scheduled to be held in the third quarter of 1988 (*CI* January, 1988, p. 15).

At the OECS Summit in St. Vincent in June, 1988, however, no decision was reached about a date for the referenda. The new OECS Chairman, James Mitchell, then threatened that the Windward Islands would proceed alone (*CI* July 1988, pp. 14ff). Since the Leeward Islands, in the integration question, kept their cards all too close to their chests, and Antigua's open rejection was obvious, the Heads of Government of the Windward Islands of Dominica, St. Lucia, Grenada and St. Vincent and the Grenadines decided at the next OECS Summit in June, 1989, in Antigua, to hold referenda on political union in their respective countries in the first half of 1990, without waiting on the other three OECS members (*CR* 20.7.1989, p. 4).

2.2.7 James Mitchell's Plan

St. Vincent's Prime Minister, James Mitchell (1987, p. 1) has frankly and drastically described his experience as the Head of Government of a tiny and largely unknown country in the following terms:

'We have to behave like Grenada or Fiji[96] to get attention, and when we stop misbehaving we are left to languish in what a constituent of mine calls 'blissful obscurity.'

And on another occasion in the British Virgin Islands (1987c, p. 11):

> 'I travel around representing independent St. Vincent and the Grenadines, and when I am in an international area or a cocktail party, I meet people whether from the Eastern block or from the Western block, 'Who are you ?' 'I am the Prime Minister of St. Vincent & the Grenadines.' They ask you two questions then. 'Where is that? 'And you get embarrassed. 'How many people you have? 'And when you from the B.V.I. tell them 12.000 even if you've got your vote in the United Nations, nobody will be talking to you again [...] The international community is a power circus! When you go and stand up in the World Bank to address the annual meeting, the place is empty. When President Reagan comes in, the place is full [...] When some of us speak in the United Nations and the World Bank, that's the time when other people have meetings or go to the washroom.'

Like Mitchell, the OECS Secretariat in St. Lucia endeavoured to inform the population about the pre-conditions for political union. It, in a 'discussion paper' (1988a, pp. 22ff) published in April, 1988, adduced varying models of closer political co-operation of independent States and advocated a 'Strong Federation'. In that Federation, the areas of governmental responsibility would be divided between the Federal and State authorities. Compared to loose Federations, a strong Federation's Central Government would, it was argued, be treated by the outside world with 'far greater respect', bringing greater benefits.

If political integration means the transfer of rights hitherto exercised in a sovereign way to a Central Government, then the OECS members have already performed considerable preliminary work, the effect of which has been staring their inhabitants in the face for years. The Central Bank and a single currency have prevented otherwise largely inevitable and differing monetary developments (Vaughan Lewis, 1989, p. 8). A unified justice system with a Court of Appeal common to all the island jurisdictions has enabled the bringing together of scarce legal personnel. A single air transport authority co-ordinates air travel. By means of diplomatic missions in Ottawa, London, Brussels and soon in Washington, sharing the same building or having one common

[96] The May 1987, military coup *d' état* in Fiji and the subsequent suspension of the Constitution of that country led to the expulsion of the country from the Commonwealth.

representative, the OECS' foreign policy has been presented more effectively. Negotiating positions have been strengthened, and costs reduced as well.

The freedom of movement of goods, capital, services and labour within the OECS region has now been largely realised. Most of the trade barriers were removed on July 1, 1988 (*CC* July 1988, pp. 2 and 14ff). The obligation to travel abroad in the OECS region on their passports no longer exists for OECS nationals. Legislation on freedom of residence and the freedom to purchase land by OECS nationals in the OECS region is being prepared.

The advocates of integration have repeatedly demanded that the future Eastern Caribbean Union should have a different character from that of the inherited colonial system. The most detailed presentation of this position has been that by James Mitchell (1987, pp. 9-17), prepared at the end of 1986 in his paper for the OECS Heads of Government. His framework plan for an 'East Caribbean' Republic envisaged, *inter alia*, the following:[97]

- A single Republic with a President elected for a single fixed five year term. The President should be elected on the French Constitutional model with more than 50% of the votes. If not there must be a run-off between the two front-runners. The President shall appoint a Governor on each island. The President should be free to choose his Cabinet from inside or outside the Parliament. The President should have the right to dissolve Parliament and call an election for the remainder of the Parliamentary term.
- There shall be an elected Parliament on the German model — 50% of the votes based on Proportional Representation (Party Vote) and 50% on a Constituency basis. The Parliament or Congress will be legislative. The size of the Parliament should be fifty seats for five States. The whole new country should be treated as one constituency, and a minimum threshold of 5% of votes cast to earn a seat. The Parliament should be able to impeach the President with two-thirds majority, provided the decision is upheld in the Courts.
- The Queen should be retained in her role as Head of the Commonwealth.
- The jurisdiction of the Judicial Committee of the Privy Council should be retained for the time being.

Before Mitchell, no other Commonwealth Caribbean Head of Government, or leading Opposition politician had ever dared to make such far-reaching proposals for a future Constitution. According to his initial proposals, a constitutional commission was now supposed to undertake the working out of details. But Mitchell's proposals were hardly discussed publicly by politically relevant interests, despite having been officially presented to the Heads of Government in November, 1986. At the July, 1988, Conference in St. Vincent under Mitchell's chairmanship, the OECS Heads of Government mutually demanded that still more detailed information over a suitable form of union be provided.

Mitchell was disappointed. 'We can study this and that to death. Some people or countries appear to be dragging their feet indefinitely', he said (*CI* July 1988, p. 14). The consultations, decided upon by the OECS Heads of

[97] *Cf.*: as well, Mitchell's *Thoughts of Some OECS Leaders*, pp. 62-63.

Government at the end of 1986, with all politically relevant groups in their respective territories over the form of a political union, were carried out rather half-heartedly. Only Mitchell had undertaken special efforts and established the aforementioned advisory body consisting of distinguished experts with the political Opposition, in order to build a rather broad consensus.

The procrastinating posture and insecurity with which the OECS Heads of Government approached the question of political union, became especially pronounced in the deficient way in which Opposition parties were brought into the unification process. St. Lucia's Prime Minister, John Compton, openly one of the most articulate advocates of political union, regarded the consultation of the Opposition as unnecessary. This was because, as he said in August, 1988 (p. 19), 'all the Governments have decided that this is not to be a political issue.' Consequently, political parties were not represented in the Independent Committee of St. Lucia, which was supposed to discuss the question of political union. Nor did Compton take particularly seriously the Standing Conference of Popular Democratic Parties in East Caribbean States (SCOPE), which had been founded on an initiative of the Leader of the Opposition in St. Lucia, Julian Hunte. In Compton's view (1988, p. 19), SCOPE had been founded rather on 'opportunistic' grounds; and one did not hear much from it anyway.

In July, 1987, the Co-ordinating Committee of SCOPE, in a letter to Compton, the then Chairman of the OECS Authority, demanded that all future discussions with Opposition parties should be done via SCOPE. The latter also demanded detailed proposals for the parties, 'that we cannot, in all good conscience recommend to our supporters and to the people as a whole unreserved support for an issue about which no details have been provided'. Moreover, the Government should 'create a political climate which will nurture and foster an atmosphere for genuine consultative and democratic participation of the people'. The Heads of Government should, it went on, give an example of the statesmanlike behaviour and political maturity which one so admired elsewhere[98].

The letter received no reply. In view of the disputes between the parties, which have often been conducted with great bitterness, the exclusion of the Opposition from the Government's initiatives is understandable. But that exclusion of political opposition seems to have been at least unwise, within the context of political union. Political integration is not possible without incisive constitutional amendments, which require at least a two-thirds Parliamentary majority[99] and mostly confirmation in a subsequent referendum.

Even holding a referendum to change the national Constitution can be done only after the approval of at least two-thirds, or, in many countries, three-quarters, of the MPs. If this Parliamentary hurdle has been cleared, then the proposed constitutional amendment must, in a referendum, be supported by two-thirds of the votes cast. Without the Opposition's support, these hurdles cannot be cleared (Sanders, 1989, pp. 122ff).

---

[98]Julian Hunte's letter of 15.7.87 to Compton (quoted from the original).

[99]The fact that Commonwealth Caribbean Governments, thanks to the first-past-the-post electoral system, often have enough MPs for such a majority provides no security for advocates of integration. A Parliamentary majority can easily fall apart.

2.2.8 Opposition to Political Union

After Mitchell's May 1987, speech in Tortola, there were signs that the creation of an Eastern Caribbean Union could become a reality in this century. Demas (1987, p. 55) termed the initiative as 'may well be the last opportunity for achieving a Political Union in the West Indies'. Mitchell put his political existence on the line, in order to achieve unity. The first Parliamentary elections in St. Vincent and the Grenadines after his Tortola initiative, however, showed that his plans for union did not have a negative effect on the behaviour of the electorate[100].

Mitchell's pledged common political philosophy of Caribbean Government parties led to prominent opponents of political union, such as Seaga and Charles, at least toning down their external opposition. Jamaica's then Prime Minister, Seaga, merely warned against the identity of the region within the international community being sacrificed on the altar of OECS political union (*Caribbean Democrat [sic] Union Monthly Newsletter* 2.7 (August 1987) p. 3).

With sharp rejection, on the other hand, Antigua's then Prime Minister, Vere Bird Sr., reacted against Mitchell's speech. Bird declared that he would not sacrifice the hard-fought-for Independence[101] of his country (*CC* August 1987, p. 8). The octogenarian was the only remaining Commonwealth Caribbean Head of Government who had been in office during the West Indies Federation. He had been among the initiators of CARIFTA in 1965; but was not present later on at most CARICOM Summits. One of Antigua's main reasons for refusing to participate in political union may well have been the relative economic prosperity of the group of islands of which it is a part. This wealth, however, is only borrowed, making Antigua and Barbuda the country with the highest *per capita* debt[102] in the Americas and, according to the CDB, a lack of creditworthiness[103].

When Bird's son, Lester Bird, took over the office from his father in 1994 he admitted that Antigua and Barbuda's preoccupation with internal problems led to a lowering of regional concern on the national agenda. But under his administration the country would again be active in the councils of the region, making 'full contributions to the strengthening of our institutions' (*The Financial Gleaner* 27.5.1994, p.22).

The most certain indicator of the seriousness of unification efforts in the Eastern Caribbean is the initial opposition of the Opposition parties. As in November, 1971, when the *Grenada Declaration* lay on the table, they came together, in order to discuss counter-measures (*CC* August 1987, p.9). Similar to the leaders of the ten Opposition parties assembled in Castries, the capital of St.

---

[100] Mitchell's *New Democratic Party* won all fifteen parliamentary seats on May 16, 1989 (*CR* 16 5 1989, p 6) But Caribbean integration had not been a controversial election issue, because Mitchell had extensively included the Opposition in the consultations. Mitchell and his party were impressively backed at the next general elections on 21st February 1994, by winning twelve out of fifteen parliamentary seats (*CI* March 1994, p 12).

[101] Antigua and Barbuda became independent only in 1981.

[102] About US$ 5906 at the end of 1993 (*cf Caribbean Development Bank* 1994, p. 26).

[103] *Caribbean Development Bank* 1993, p. 25. See also *Associated Press* in a report from St John's, undated in *WG* 22 3 1994, p 26.

Lucia, in July, 1987, had the Opposition leaders, sixteen years earlier, cavilled at the allegedly over-hasty unification efforts ('Joint Opposition Statement')[104].

The main reproach then, as in 1987, was insufficient consultation with the Opposition by ruling parties in the creation of the proposed political union. Unlike in 1971, the participating parties this time got organised, founding the Standing Conference of Popular Democratic Parties in East Caribbean States (SCOPE). Statements by the initiator and Leader of the St. Lucia Labour Party, Julian Hunte, show that SCOPE was thought of not only as a spontaneous initiative against the unification efforts of the OECS Heads of Government but was planned to last.

Hunte is, with some other party leaders in SCOPE, of the view that the present Federation initiative emanates from the USA and serves, with the help of the CDU, to consolidate the power of US-friendly forces in the region and to oppose the rising sentiment for a change (*CC* August 1987, p. 8). As proof of this was adduced the fact that St. Lucia's Government at first gave only a 24-hour entry visa to an Opposition politician who participated in the creation of SCOPE, and who was classified as 'communist' by the befriended Charles Government in Dominica. The supposition was obvious that SCOPE was founded to rival the CDU. This view was supported by the fact that the working group changed its name to the *Standing Conference of Popular Democratic Parties of the Eastern Caribbean* in February 1988, again in Castries (*WG* 8.3.1988, p.11).

The arguments of SCOPE against the integration proposala — apart from the ideological perspective—moved in the usual framework of the Opposition. Before political union, it demanded questions such as the freedom of movement within the participating countries, the freedom of money transfer, the harmonisation of economic legislation and unified employment conditions for the Civil Service, must be resolved (*WG* 9.2.1988, p. 12).

Within SCOPE, there are opposing currents, which make it rather unlikely that a strong anti-integration movement will come into being. The larger OECS Opposition parties have reservations about political union, because they could, over time, have the possibility of acquiring governmental authority separately. But some smaller, far Left parties sympathise thoroughly with Mitchell's proposal for the introduction of proportional representation. They regard this as an opportunity to enter Parliament and perhaps the Government as well (Sanders, 1989, pp. 118ff).

Opposition to political union in the OECS and in the entire Commonwealth Caribbean comes in the first place from the following two sources: From those who basically support union, but have reservations about individual steps or measures[105]; and from those basically opposed to political integration. The reservations of the former group are as follows:

[104] The then front consisted of six Opposition parties, which, at the invitation of Eugenia Charles, met in Dominica Four of the six are now in power, one no longer exists, and the sixth, the St Lucia Labour Party, was the initiator of the 1987 Opposition meeting

[105] Mitchell (1987d) ridicules them as 'Yes but-ers' and 'Not yet-ers'

1. Political union should be accomplished step by step and without too great a hurry[106]. Demas (1987, p. 32) holds that the complex conditions of the Caribbean Community and other Agreements in 1973 were drafted in a great hurry. The Treaty of Rome, which created the European Economic Community was also drafted in record time and signed.
2. The harmonisation of legislation must precede political union. This, according to Demas (1987, p. 33) is not necessary. Even Great Britain, as a unitary State, has different laws in England and Scotland. The harmonisation of legislation, Demas points out, could quite follow the founding of the union.
3. The risk exists of unequal treatment of parts of the union in the co-ordination of economic development programmes. Demas (1987, p. 33) points out that this problem occurs in all unitary States and must be solved in consensus with all; from politics, business, trade unions, and so on.
4. A development plan, in which foreign financial aid is also factored, must precede political union. The development plan is necessary, according to Demas (1987, p. 39), but not necessarily before political union:

   > 'We should not draw up a Development Plan in order to get aid to entice us to establish Political Union. This approach would be psychologically bad for our people, since it would not constitute a desirable or dignified basis for Political Union'.
5. Freedom of movement parallel with political union would lead to the mass immigration of uneducated or half-educated workers. Demas (1987, pp. 40ff) holds that this concern applies less within the OECS than between the OECS and the MDCs in the Commonwealth Caribbean. Immigration declines only when the host countries become economically worse off, whereby a great excess of labour then exists. The participating States must take this disadvantage in their stride. But a balancing economic and development policy can, Demas argues, reduce the emigration thrust.
6. Political union at present serves the interests of some profit seekers and a certain ideology. The retort to this is this: Political union against the will of the political Opposition can hardly be introduced, even if all current Heads of Governments are ideologically convergent; this is because constitutional amendments in the individual States require either a two-thirds majority in the Parliaments or referenda — or both (Demas 1987, p. 32).

The basic opponents of political union claim that:

1. It suffices to expand the existing OECS and CARICOM institutions. Political union is unnecessary to accomplish economic goals. The supporters' rejoinder is, however, that political union creates a dependable framework for the exchange of goods, services, capital and labour within the Member States. This, they add, is also true for political measures to direct the flow of production, investments, savings and consumption. Political union enables more dependable arrangements for international economic relationships. A full economic union requires political union anyway (Demas 1987, p. 44).

[106]For instance, Grenada's leading weekly, *Grenadian Voice*, cautioned, 'Make haste slowly'; it suggested setting up a 'Committee of Wise Men' to study political structures world-wide and then propose an appropriate system for the OECS (*WG* 14.7.1987, p. 14).

2. Political union would lead to the surrender of bitterly-won sovereignty[107]. Advocates of political union hold, however, the following: When economically diplomatically and militarily weak and extremely foreign-dependent countries come together for political integration, then the peoples make a free choice, collectively to surrender their formal sovereignty, in order to become 'really sovereign' (Demas, 1987, p. 35).
3. As individual sovereign States, the Commonwealth Caribbean has more votes in international organisations[108]. James Mitchell (1987c, p. 11) retorts that the people of his islands seldom gained when he voted in the United Nations on resolutions on South Africa or nuclear waste. The international financial agencies are, he argues, really important. But other voting criteria apply there. Demas (1987, p. 37) calls attention to the West Indies Cricket Team, which is strong only because each West Indian State does not enter the international arena with its own team. The OECS must collectively send their best people to international diplomatic service. The quality of the West Indian representatives at the Lomé-I negotiations in Brussels was more effective than their number. Only in the OAS and SELA does the number of votes make a serious difference.
4. Through a new Central power, which exists parallel to the local administrations, administration becomes more expensive and more ineffective. Dominica's Eugenia Charles as Prime Minister, above all, had this concern. But a unified public service would be probably more cost effective than the OECS public service taken together. Relevant studies have been undertaken since 1963 (Demas, 1987, p. 42).
5. It is too late for political integration. The people in the Commonwealth Caribbean have become so accustomed to their independence that they can no longer come together[109]. The advocates of political union have a different opinion, but find that time is gradually running out for political integration. Demas (1986, p. 30) 'If the 21st century arrives without a Union of the West Indies, we might well by then have no alternative but to abandon the project'.

Under the influence of the Heads of Government of St. Vincent and the Grenadines (Mitchell) and Antigua and Barbuda (Bird), two camps arose in the Eastern Caribbean: The States of the Windward Islands, which aimed at political union; and those of the Leeward Islands, which did not so wish — at least for the time being.

The Vere Bird Government in Antigua in its first official statement after its resounding victory at the polls in March, 1989, made it clear that it at first, sought only a further 'deepening' of functional co-operation within the Caribbean Community and OECS. 'For it is by this method of incremental advance that the ultimate goal of political unity will be achieved' (*CR* 11.5.89, p. 7).

[107] For example, Vere Bird Sr.

[108] Edward Seaga's rejoinder is clear; (*CC* August 1986, p. 9). 'It is a fallacy to believe that the Caribbean would speak with one voice, the same voice, the same intensity, and gain the same respect, if we were speaking as a single voice'.

[109] So e.g. Vere Bird Sr..

Behind the traditional leadership role of Antigua within the Leeward Islands, St. Kitts and Nevis and Montserrat could also hide their reservation. Montserrat's then Chief Minister Osborne stressed that, for his territory, there would be no journey alone without Antigua in the direction of political union. St. Kitts and Nevis' Prime Minister, Dr. Kennedy Simmonds, declared in November, 1988, before OECS Heads of Government that the Consultative Committee appointed by him had come to the conclusion that, in his country, an overwhelming sentiment existed against political union (Sanders, 1989, p, 118). In July, 1991, he confirmed, his country, owing to differing experience of its people and differing views on the integration process, would not participate in a political union of Eastern Caribbean States (*CR* 25.7.91, p. 5).

In the special posture of the Leeward Islands, the economic structure plays a particular role. Economically, the three participating territories are relatively better off than are the Windward Islands. They benefit from tourism more than do the agriculturally-oriented Windward Islands. The future of agriculture is at least not clear, in view of the uncertainty over access to the British market after the introduction of the European Single Market. Any worthwhile industrialisation is hardly to be expected, in view of the small markets and the scant supply of specialist personnel. Moreover, limits exist to the expansion of the tourism industry.

Nonetheless, the political landscape of the Leeward Islands can change swiftly. Simmonds' former coalition partner, the Nevis Reformation Party has a positive attitude to Eastern Caribbean political union. The statement of the then Premier of Nevis, Simeon Daniel, that his country would secede from the Federation with St. Kitts (*CR* 15.6.1989, p. 7) and enter the union as a separate entity shows that the pressure for a political union can become stronger.

It is also unknown whether Vere Bird's successor in Antigua and Barbuda, his son Lester, will maintain the rejection of a political union. Observers are anyway of the view that even Vere Bird, had he been mobilised in time, would not have refused participating in an Eastern Caribbean Federation in which Antigua and Barbuda were left with adequate areas of responsibility (Sanders, 1989, p. 121).

Montserrat's then Chief Minister Osborne declared at the annual Caribbean Youth Conference (CYC) meeting in St. Lucia in August, 1988 that he had intended his statement that Montserrat would enter a political union only when Antigua also did, to be merely 'provocative'. He did not believe, he said, that the majority of the Antiguans shared the rejecting attitude of their Head of Government with regard to political union[11].

2.2.9 Small Solution for the Windward Islands

Disappointment over the development of the Caribbean Community had led to the creation of the smaller OECS. Discontentment with the progress of integration in the OECS made the Windward Islands, nine years later, again seek a smaller unit.

---

[11] The author's own notes

James Mitchell had said quite earlier that a political union would begin with only two parties, in order to convince others of its advantages. In August 1990, the Heads of Government of Dominica, Grenada, St. Lucia and St. Vincent and the Grenadines met on Palm Island in the Grenadines. In September, they met again, this time in Grenada; and decided that all territories should create a Regional Constituent Assembly (RCA) and prepare a referendum for mid-1991. Each country should send delegates — three each from the business sector, trade unions, the churches, women and agricultural interests.

SCOPE decided at first to boycott the RCA. In order to get the SCOPE members to serve on the RCA, however, the first constituent meeting was postponed from November, 1990, to January, 1991. By that time, viewpoints did, in fact, change.

The RCA had its first meeting on January 20, 1991, in Kingstown, the capital of St.Vincent. The assembly decided to ask the Parliaments of the participating States to deliberate on the alternatives; that is, Federation; or a unitary State. Most of those gathered supported political union. SCOPE - affiliated parties — apart from Grenada's ruling New Democratic Party — were not officially represented; but did participate in individual working sessions.

They demanded a separate secretariat for the RCA instead of the OECS Secretariat, which, up to that time, dealt with the administrative matters of the RCA (*CI* February, 1991, p. 12). The holding of the referendum was postponed. In April, 1991, at the next meeting of the RCA in St. Lucia, only the St. Lucia Labour Party was still strictly against political union and was absent (*WG* 23.4.91, p. 16). At the next RCA meeting, in September, 1991, in Dominica, it was decided that the basic agreement of the population to the concept of integration should be obtained by referenda in all four territories. The Parliaments should then vote on the matter. Thereafter, the population should, in a second referendum, decide on a common constitution.

The majority of the delegates, then seemed to prefer a federal structure to a unitary one, in order to do justice to the individual identities of the various participating islands. Parliament should consist of two Chambers, one elected by the first-past-the-post system; the other, by proportional representation, that is, on lists to be voted for. The economic effects of union and the question of the closeness of the politicians of the future State structure to the people seemed to create problems for the RCA delegates.

The RCA, at its fourth session in Grenada, in January 1992 discussed the governmental structure and the distribution of power between the Central Government and the units. Again, the participants spoke out in favour of a Federal Republic (Singh, 1992). The new structure should also offer the possibilities of accession. The majority moreover agreed to the following:

- an Executive President elected by the people for a maximum of two terms;
- a bi-cameral legislature with a five-year term, and the Upper House reflecting the social groups of all the participating States;
- a mixed first-past-the-post and proportional representation for the Lower House and proportional representation for the Upper House; and

- he temporary retention of the UK Privy Council as the final Court of Appeal (*Fourth and Final Report* pp. 6-11).

A final, fifth session in March, 1992, in Castries, St. Lucia, decided that the RCA Secretariat should carry out an information and educational programme for the population of the participating countries, in order to break down the existing mistrust and reservations against an imminent referendum (*cf. Fourth and Final Report*, pp. 14ff).

The results of St. Lucia's elections in May, 1992, in which the decidedly integration supporter, John Compton, faced the equally determined, integration opponent, Julian Hunte, were regarded by political observers as important for the unity efforts. Were Compton defeated, then the union could not be realised with the participation of St. Lucia, owing to the 75% Parliamentary majority in St. Lucia necessary for constitutional changes. A defeat in the Windwards would, however, also have consequences on the integration movement in the entire Commonwealth Caribbean.

Compton, with 56.3% of the popular vote and 11 of 17 seats, won a resounding victory in the elections (*CI* June, 1992, p. 11). He let it be known that he wanted to give up the post of Prime Minister shortly and seek a regional political career (*CC* May-June, 1992, p. 1). Although political union had not been an election theme, it had nonetheless played an important role. In pre-election public opinion polls, 50% of the respondents supported St. Lucia's participation in political union with 29% against, and 21% 'don't knows/won't says' (*CC* May-June, 1992, p. 1).

Compton pressed for the referenda which were now due, to be held within the first three months of 1993, in the four participating States. But, so far no date has been fixed.

2.2.10 New Moves by CARICOM

At the CARICOM Heads of Government Summit in St. Lucia in June, 1987, the then Trinidad and Tobago Prime Minister, A.N.R. Robinson (1988b, p.27) proposed the introduction of a CARICOM nationality for prominent regional personalities[111]. The other Heads of Government were unwilling to accept this suggestion, but decided to honour extraordinary, special accomplishments by CARICOM citizens by means of the special distinction of the *Order of the Caribbean Community* (OCC). The honoured would receive diplomatic status and residence, work and land-owning rights in all CARICOM Member States (*CR* 23.7.92, p.2)[112].

At the 1987 and 1988 CARICOM Summits, the then Barbados Prime Minister, Erskine Sandiford, proposed the creation of an Assembly of Caribbean Community Parliamentarians. His then Jamaican colleague, Seaga, rejected this as an attempt to re-introduce The West Indies Federation 'through the back-door' (*CI* August, 1988, p.2).

---

[111]Robinson repeated his call in a speech in London in October 1988, and named personalities in literature, sport, science and music who should be so honoured (1988c, p. 9)

[112]The July 1991, CARICOM Summit awarded the new Order to its first recipients: William Demas, Sir Shridath Ramphal and the later Nobel Prize-winning poet, Derek Walcott (CP July-December 1991, p. 35). The awards ceremony took place at the CARICOM Summit in Trinidad, in July 1992.

At the 1989 CARICOM Summit in Grenada—with Jamaica's then new Prime Minister, Michael Manley — the proposal was, however, approved by the Heads of Government. Seaga's, now the Opposition, Jamaica Labour Party, announced its opposition. The JLP called back to mind the 1962 Jamaican referendum, which he claimed, was still binding on Jamaican Governments. Instead, the Caribbean group of the Commonwealth Parliamentary Association should be revived (*WG* 18.7.89, p.8).

Sandiford affirmed his proposal, by referring to the European Parliament, at the next (i.e. 1990) CARICOM Summit in Jamaica. In his view, the Assembly of Caribbean Community Parliamentarians could become a 'powerful unifying force'. He asked his procrastinating colleagues, if 'we are really afraid of getting too close together'[113]. In the *Kingston Declaration*, which was adopted at the Summit, the Heads of Government confirmed their intention of establishing the Assembly of Parliamentarians, in order to give the people the possibility of determining their own fate. Moreover, this would deepen the integration movement and create a 'truly authentic Caribbean personality'. The Assembly formally came into being on August 3, 1994, when seven countries of CARICOM had ratified the agreement to establish it (*CI* September 1994, p. 11).

Under the chairmanship of UWI Chancellor, Sir Shridath Ramphal, CARICOM Heads of Government, at their July, 1989, meeting in Grenada, appointed a West Indian Commission for Advancing the Goals of the Treaty of Chaguaramas. The 55-person group held hearings in all CARICOM Member States as well as in the UK In these hearings, teachers, writers, politicians, intellectuals, artists, business people, sportsmen and sportswomen, church people and representatives of local bodies stated their views. At the July, 1991, CARICOM Summit in Basseterre, Ramphal submitted an interim report.

The report

- found that virtual absence of effective machinery for implementation of regional decisions is a major impediment to the progress of the integration movement;
- feared for the future of CARICOM if the Community's governments do not systematically implement the agreements made to transform CARICOM into a single market;
- criticised impediments to free movement and the implications of cultural penetration;
- demanded a common CARICOM currency and the setting up of a special Caribbean Investment Fund (CR 25.7.1991, p.4).

Freedom of movement posed a heavy problem for the Commonwealth Caribbean States. The fear of competition for jobs is too great[114]. While the OECS agreed to remove the passport obligation for travel between their respective countries from December, 1991, the CARICOM Heads of Government could, in August, 1990, struggle only to a new programme with the

---

[113] *CP* 49, Supplement: Communiqué and Addresses 11th Meeting of Heads of Government of the Caribbean Community, p 8

[114] 53% of the respondents to a representative public opinion poll in St. Lucia in early 1992 held that all foreign workers should leave the country (with only 37% against the severe demand) (*CC* May-June 1992, p 2).

acronym, AFFIRM (Arrangement for Free Intra-Region Movement) which was supposed to stimulate the freedom of travel within the region. Artists, sportsmen, sportswomen and media practitioners should no longer need work permits to take part in regional events.

In February, 1992, Grenada, Guyana, Jamaica, St. Kitts and Nevis, St. Lucia and Trinidad and Tobago released CARICOM nationals from the passport-travel obligation. Guyana and Jamaica automatically gave work permits to UWI graduates; Jamaica also included entertainment artists and media workers in this exempt group (*CI* March 1992, p. 4).

The CARICOM Secretariat, together with the Heads of CARICOM Social Security Agencies has finalised a CARICOM Agreement on Social Security that includes provisions for the payment of benefits to insured persons who would have worked in more than one Member State of the Community (Caribbean Community, 1993, p. 60).

The West Indian Commission, in its Final Report, *Time for Action*, of June, 1992, recommended the creation, as of 1.1.1993, of a CARICOM Commission with executive powers and a decentralised Secretariat. The Commission should consist of a President and two other members; the serving CARICOM Secretary-General should also be an *ex officio* member. The Heads of Government Conference should remain the supreme deciding body, followed by a Council of Ministers comprising the Ministers in the national Governments responsible for CARICOM questions. A Federation or political union should not be aimed at. A CARICOM Assembly should be created but rather, as an assembly of the people, consisting of the representatives of different groups and less as a legislative body.

Decisions of the Conference of Heads of Government and of the Council of Ministers should be able to have legal force at national level. A CARICOM Supreme Court should be the regional Appeal Court as well as the Court responsible for CARICOM matters.

To the total of 225 recommendations of the West Indian Commission belong as well:

- The creation of an Association of Caribbean States consisting of all Caribbean Basin countries; and
- The re-organisation and partial relocation of the CARICOM Secretariat[115].

The proposals of the Commission were greeted with reserve, but the Heads of Government accepted most of them. However, the creation of the proposed CARICOM Commission, which was modelled on the Commission of the European Union, was rejected. The main objections, which were heard also in the Barbadian and Jamaican Parliamentary debates, were the absence of democratic legitimation and the cost. A further objection, which was expressed loudly in private, was that the West Indian Commission members were selling new posts for themselves.

Supporters of the CARICOM Commission proposal expressed doubt that the Heads of Government were physically able to share in the executive

[115] *Cf* as well *CI* July 1992, p 3, *CR* 23 7 92, p 3

functions required by the CARICOM Treaties, in addition to their national responsibilities[116].

Instead of creating the CARICOM Commission, the Heads of Government, at a special summit in Port-of-Spain in October, 1992, decided to keep the executive power in their own hands. In January, 1993, a Bureau of Heads of Government came into existence, consisting of the serving, previous and next chairmen of the Heads of Government Conference and the CARICOM Secretary-General. The chairmanship changes every six months. The body should first of all implement the decisions of the CARICOM Summits and adjust these to actual circumstances.

The Summit also decided to strengthen the CARICOM Secretariat the administration of which should make proposals in this regard. The Council of Ministers has been upgraded, to which each member-state should send specifically named Ministers responsible for CARICOM affairs. The readiness to create an Assembly of Caribbean Community Parliamentarians was confirmed.

With the decisions to prepare a CARICOM Charter of Civil Society, and to hold consultations with other Caribbean States on the creation of an Association of Caribbean States, the Heads of Government followed the proposals of the West Indian Commission.

[116]Please see Fergus (1992) for a summary of the reactions to the Commission's proposal

2.3 The Intra-Caribbean System

2.3.1 The Development of the Caribbean Community

In the course of its twenty-two year history, the Caribbean Community, CARICOM, has developed into a significant Caribbean economic system and also into an international sub-system. It embraces all Commonwealth Caribbean territories. The BVI and the Turks and Caicos Islands both have associate status; Anguilla has observer status; and the Cayman Islands participate only in functional co-operation. CARICOM contains perhaps the largest concentration of independent small States in the world (Denis Benn, 1984, p. 27).

The Caribbean Community was created in 1973 by the Treaty of Chaguaramas, in order to achieve two main objectives: To stimulate economic development and also to enhance the 'effective sovereignty' of the Member States and their people (Demas, 1974, p. 43). These main objectives extend beyond those of a purely economic community. The co-operation extends above all to three areas:

- economic integration through the Caribbean Common Market, which replaced the former Caribbean Free Trade Area;
- non-economic fields and common services (e.g. in health, education, school examinations, shipping, air transportation, meteorology, science and research).
- co-ordination of the foreign policies of independent Member States.

As Demas found in 1974, the Caribbean Community represents the highest level of economic integration and general co-operation which has ever been achieved in the English-speaking Caribbean. The Caribbean Community, however, was expressly not planned as a union or Federation (p. 44; *Cf.* Vaughan Lewis, 1974, p. 5). According to Lewis's viewpoint then, it was very much, first of all, a diplomatic institution with a customs union and a mechanism for a common market to stimulate the economic integration of the region.

The supreme body of the Caribbean Community is the Heads of Government Conference. This body determines the guidelines of policy. Committees of CARICOM Ministers for Agriculture, Education, Finance, Foreign Affairs, Health, Labour, Mineral Resources, Industry, Transportation and the Environment are all institutions of CARICOM. They accompany the work of the Caribbean Community Secretariat in the various areas and co-ordinate the work of the Community within their respective areas of competence.

At the head of the Common Market of the Community stands the Common Market Council of Ministers. This is responsible for trade and economic affairs; and as mandated by the Heads of Government, oversees the work of the Secretariat.

Numerous Caribbean institutions are officially associated with CARICOM, but are otherwise autonomous bodies[117]. A Joint Consultative Group includes

[117]Please see Appendix 4.

important regional non-governmental organisations (NGOs) in the deliberations of the Common Market Council of Ministers.

The Caribbean Community does have an international legal personality — that is to say that it can conduct negotiations and conclude contracts and agreements with third countries and groups of third countries as well as international organisations (*cf.* Demas, 1974, p.44). But the decision-making processes hardly confer a supranational character on it, thereby impairing its effectiveness. In order to be effective, decisions must, as a rule, be taken unanimously. This unanimity occurs only on the basis of the lowest common denominator.

The role ascribed to the Caribbean Community Secretariat in Georgetown (Guyana) is, therefore also weak. The Secretariat is hardly comparable to the European Union's Commission in Brussels or the *Junta* of the Common Market of the Andean States, as Demas (1974, p.55) regretted, after ceasing to be the Secretary-General of the Caribbean Community.

The Secretariat, in Demas' opinion, has, in the first place, administrative functions. To a certain extent, Demas believes it plays a role in the discussion of policy and in co-ordination — but not as an executive body. All important decisions of the integration movement depend on the consensus of the constituent national Governments.

The creation of an integrated, protected market, within which goods produced in the region have freedom of movement, is one of the most important objectives of the Caribbean Common Market. The first aim was to overcome the hostility to integration of the colonial system, which regarded the dependencies only as the areas for the cultivation of a limited number of agricultural crops, which were easily sold in Britain and, on the other hand made the dependencies a market for the finished products from there(*Cf.* Denis Benn 1984 pp. 30 -31).

Economically, the Caribbean Common Market came into being at a most unfavourable time, and, not least of that, had an inauspicious debut. The year, 1973, marked the start of the international economic recession caused by markedly rising oil prices. Structural deficits in industrialised countries led to high unemployment levels and strengthened protectionist tendencies among these countries as well as *vis-à-vis* the so-called Third World. The high oil prices hit the territories of the Caribbean Community particularly hard, with the exception of Trinidad and Tobago, because their energy supply was totally generated by using oil.

In 1986, then CARICOM Secretary-General, Roderick Rainford (pp. 14ff) stated that the Commonwealth Caribbean was facing 'the most severe economic blow it had received in the entire period of its independence'. In the 1970s, all CARICOM countries, except Jamaica and St. Lucia, had positive GDP growth rates. In the 1980s, however, these growth rates declined dramatically.

In June, 1988 the Bourne Commission[118], which had been appointed by the CARICOM Heads of Government, found, in its Report, that in seven of the then

[118]Named after its Chairman, the Guyanese economist, Compton Bourne. Ex-CARICOM Secretaries-General, Sir Alister McIntyre and William Demas, as well as CAIC Executive Director, Pat Thompson, collaborated with Bourne in the preparation of this Report on the perspectives of the Caribbean Community up to the year 2000.

thirteen CARICOM Member States, real income was less than it had been in 1980; and that it also fell in the others as well. Instead, annual GNP growth should be at least 6%, in order to counter the unemployment problem rendered acute by the growth of the population. The number of 25 — 49-year-olds, according to the report, would double in some countries up to the year 2000. In all, the growth of the labour force in the CARICOM region would be between 23% and 54%, depending on the country (*Caribbean Development* XV — XIX).

In part, because of the international economic crisis, but also to a great extent owing to the shortage of domestic political consistency in the participating countries, the Caribbean Community has only partially succeeded in attaining its initial objectives. The varying success of the collaboration is mirrored by the decisions taken by the Heads of Government at their ordinary and extraordinary conferences. Most progress has been made in functional co-operation, a certain amount in foreign policy co-ordination, less in the Common Market, and the least progress in the integration of production.

Although the CARICOM Treaties do not define political union as an objective, the hope nonetheless existed that CARICOM would contribute to the region's growing together. This is also expressed in the CARICOM logo, which contains the letter 'C' twice in the blue Caribbean Sea connected like a broken chain as the symbol for the freedom of the fourteen participating States linked by a common history, culture, hopes and their integration movement (*CP* 33, p. 3). Up to the present time, however, only Guyana celebrates CARICOM Day as an official holiday, although the 1974 CARICOM Heads of Government Conference recommended that it should be a holiday for the entire CARICOM region.

Immediately after the founding of CARICOM, the integration process came to a stand-still in almost all areas. Between the second CARICOM Heads of Government Conference (December, 1975, in St. Kitts) and the next summit (in November, 1982, in Jamaica) a hiatus of almost exactly seven years occurred, during which all non-Independent CARICOM Member States, except St. Kitts and Nevis and Montserrat, achieved political independence. The integration movement suffered a significant loss in importance. This was because the ambitious decisions of the summits were seen as not being so swiftly actualised as had been thought; moreover, owing to the absence of a common customs and foreign trade policy, intra-regional trade did not develop as quickly as the smaller CARICOM Member States had hoped.

Additionally, there were the growing ideological tensions within the region. Left-wing parties came to power in Grenada, St. Lucia and Dominica in 1979, thereby bringing to five, including Jamaica and Guyana, the number of self-styled socialist anglophone Caribbean Governments. At the start of the 1980s, however, a reversal occurred in this ideological trend.

Thus, for instance, a mere two Leaders of those socialist parties — namely, the Heads of Government of Grenada and Guyana — were able to take part in the third CARICOM Heads of Government Conference in Ocho Rios, Jamaica, November, 1982.

Only four of the thirteen participating Prime Ministers and Chief Ministers had participated in the previous meeting of the Community in St. Kitts[119].

In the main thrust of the conference[120], Jamaica's Edward Seaga the host, Barbados' Tom Adams and Dominica's Eugenia Charles accused the dictatorship in Grenada of human rights violations, and tried to isolate the regime of Maurice Bishop. The latter countered with a motion seeking to set up, *inter alia*, a multi-disciplinary working group of experts of public opinion and sociologists to examine the attitude of the population in the CARICOM countries to human rights and their violations. This was aimed at Jamaica and Dominica where politically motivated attacks by party supporters and agents of the State repeatedly occurred.

Owing to the overcrowded agenda, and, in order to prevent strife among the conference participants, however, conference host Seaga contented himself, in the *Declaration of Ocho Rios*, with a 'commitment to the political, civil, economic, social and cultural rights of the peoples of the region, in accordance with the Universal Declaration of Human Rights' and other international Agreements (*The Ocho Rios Declaration*, Appendix II, Paragraph 3). At the same time, 'ideological pluralism' in the Caribbean Community was recognised as an 'irreversible trend within the international system', but should 'not impair the integration process' (*ibid.*, Paragraph 4). 'Ideological pluralism' here was not meant to be political pluralism within the individual countries. Rather, it was left to the CARICOM Member States to select for themselves their own state ideologies. With this formula, Jamaica did not recognise the right of the Communists to unlimited freedom of movement inside Jamaica anymore than did Maurice Bishop recognise such a right in Grenada to forces he ascribed as belonging to the 'capitalist system'.

Attacks by Trinidad and Tobago's Prime Minister, George Chambers, before the 1984[121] Bahamas Summit, on the other CARICOM Member States were a reflection of the bewilderment of the Government of a country, which for years, had been able to pump a highly profitable primary raw material out of the earth, but had neglected to take structural precautions for times of crisis. Similarly, Guyana and Jamaica had, for too long, relied on foreign exchange inflows from bauxite and alumina exports.

The *Nassau Understanding*, agreed to at the Nassau Summit by all participating Heads of Government, was dedicated, on the basis of a paper submitted by the Caribbean Development Bank, to the growing structural problems of CARICOM countries and the consequences of integration and development. As the Understanding put it, a swift rise in debt servicing, a sudden and sharp deterioration in the terms of trade, abrupt increases in external debt service, continuing declines in the volume of major agricultural exports and the depletion of a major natural resource could trigger off shocks and lead to a loss of confidence between the government and the population. People and capital

---

[119]They were: Sir Lynden Pindling (The Bahamas), George Price (Belize), Linden Forbes Sampson Burnham (Guyana) and John Compton (St. Lucia)

[120]For a comprehensive report, please see Mullerleile, 1983a.

[121]Chambers (1984, p. 2) defended protectionist measures of his Government against imports from other CARICOM countries and accused critics of ungratefulness, because they had previously benefited from Trinidad and Tobago's economic strength.

would leave the country. Parallel and underground economies would come into existence. The direction of the economy would increasingly be removed from governmental control, with the risk of the collapse of the entire economic and social framework of the state.

The Heads of Government conceded that the *per capita* income of the population in most CARICOM countries seemed to be relatively high. But the economic structure of these countries resided on fairly fragile foundations. Typically a large portion of their income, jobs, revenue and export earnings depends on one or two exports. The manufacturing sector still has no close linkages with the other sectors of the economy; the local entrepreneurs have little breadth; and the export capacity of this sector is still fragmented.

Because the productive sectors as a whole offer only insufficient employment opportunities, unemployment and underemployment exist. This affects especially school-leavers, who, therefore migrate to urban areas and emigrate abroad in search of work. 'Such economic conditions breed chronic discontent, crime, violence and political extremism; putting at risk national cohesion and the democratic process itself ', further stated the Nassau Understanding.

The Heads of Government themselves undertook to prepare national plans for the growth of the productive and private sectors and also to avail themselves of the opportunities for export provided by the Caribbean Common Market. The public sector should be made more efficient and financial and fiscal discipline improved. Education and training should take more into consideration both the professions and other occupations and tertiary education.

Structural adjustment, in the opinions of the Heads of Government, was impossible without external financial aid, which could even take the form of a 'Marshall Plan strategy for reconstruction and development'.

In order for structural adjustment to bear fruit, intra-regional trade should be re-activated, and greater efforts made in the field of production. The precondition for this, the Heads of Government agreed, was that measures, contained in the 1973 Treaty of Chaguaramas, but still not yet implemented, be taken. Topping these measures was the introduction of the Common External Tariff (CET), aimed at removing protectionist barriers in intra-regional trade, while simultaneously erecting barriers to the outside world.

Moreover, the Agreement on the harmonisation of tax concessions for exporting industry should be re-worked; and a CARICOM Enterprise Regime (CER), to facilitate capital movement and the development of entrepreneurial initiatives between the CARICOM Common Market countries, should be established.

The CARICOM Summits following that in Nassau were a reflection of the tussle over the implementation of the 1973 Chaguaramas Treaty. New deadlines for the introduction of the Common External Tariff were constantly set and, therefore, changed — as well as those for the re-activation of the CARICOM Multilateral Clearing Facility (CMCF), which had been closed in 1983, the complete freedom of movement within the CARICOM region of the citizens of CARICOM Member States and the removal of all trade barriers.

The 1989 Grenada Summit saw a new drive to bring about the implementation of agreements. Under the influence of the progress of integration in

Western Europe, a CARICOM Common Market was scheduled to be implemented by January, 1994. A CARICOM Commissioner was also supposed to help the respective Governments in preparing the necessary administrative and legislative measures.

At the July, 1991, Basseterre (St. Kitts) Summit, five of the CARICOM Heads of Government personally assumed responsibility for the following five urgent matters: A common currency; a CARICOM investment fund to support the creation of transnational Caribbean enterprises, freedom for professionals to exercise their professions within CARICOM, freedom for nationals of CARICOM Member States to travel within CARICOM and the creation of a CARICOM Common Market.

As in 1980, when progress towards integration stagnated, a Commission of Experts, this time, the West Indian Commission was now appointed to find out how the basic thoughts of the Caribbean Community could be salvaged into the next millennium.

In February, 1991, a Caribbean Regional Economic Conference took place in Port-of-Spain, the capital of Trinidad and Tobago, on the initiative of that country's then Prime Minister, A.N.R. Robinson. The participants came from all CARICOM countries and formed a broad system of experts from the public and private sectors. Though billed as an economic conference it had far wider scope and was a major consultative meeting of the social partners to exchange views on the dominant social and economic trends (Caribbean Community, 1993, p. 5). The discussion produced the *Port-of-Spain Consensus*[122], containing general recommendations for the development of the Commonwealth Caribbean beyond the year 2000. The conference is supposed to become a fixed component of the Caribbean Community and meet every three years.

2.3.2 The Caribbean Common Market

This Common Market should have become a reality by January 1, 1994 (*CR* 23.7.1992, p. 2) and should strengthen, co-ordinate and regulate the economic and trade relations of the CARICOM Member States, in order to stimulate their accelerated harmonisation and balanced development. The objective is a greater measure of economic independence and effectiveness of the participating States and other entities (*The Caribbean Common Market*, Art. 3). All CARICOM Member States, except the Bahamas, belong to the Common Market. The Government of the Bahamas does not desire membership of the Common Market because a large portion of the national budget is financed from customs revenue[123].

The highest body of the Common Market is the Common Market Council (CMC), in which each member-State is represented by a Minister. The market is administered by a Common Market Secretariat with headquarters in the Caribbean Community Secretariat in Georgetown, Guyana. The CARICOM Heads of Government decisions of July, 1984, in Nassau confirmed once again the agreement contained in the 1973 Treaty: The Liberalisation of intra-regional

[122] Appendix *CP* 50/51 (January-June, 1991).

[123] *Cf.*: Then Prime Minister Pindling *CP* 24 (March-April, 1984) p. 8.

trade; the creation of common external trade barriers; the facilitation of intra-regional capital movement; co-ordination of economic policy and developmental planning as well as the special encouragement of the development of so-called LDCs.

One of the principal components of the Common Market is the introduction of a common external tariff and import quotas[124]. High external barriers, with the simultaneous removal of intra-regional customs barriers, should create the Common Market, which could give price advantages to goods produced in the region as against imported goods and hence bring the Commonwealth Caribbean close to meeting the needs of its people. A protected market for over 5.5 million people could lead, so hoped the Founding Fathers of CARICOM, to industrial development over the longer term, the stronger bonding of qualified Commonwealth Caribbean nationals to the CARICOM region and a more effective integration of the means of production.

From the very beginning, special rules were envisaged for intra-regional trade with the so-called LDCs. Their Heads of Government participated in the signing of the Treaty of Chaguaramas only as observers. The agreement of the MDCs to preferential treatment for the small Eastern Caribbean island states and Belize was supposed to dispel the often-expressed fear of destroying the attempts of industrialisation in the 'Less Developed Countries' by means of the abrupt removal of all the barriers to the more industrialised countries of the Community.

By the same token, opportunities became available to the small agrarian economies in the Community for inverse sales of their produce within the Commonwealth Caribbean region at the expense of farm produce hitherto imported from outside the region.

The agreed rules of exception and protection for the LDCs had to do with practically all areas of the Common Market; customs duties, certificates of origin for finished products and the harmonisation of the financial incentives for industry. Most of these rules have, however, now expired. To a large extent, the LDCs have the same status as the MDCs within the Community.

Originally, the Common External Tariff (CET) and common Import Quota should have been implemented by 1.8.1981 and, for Belize and Montserrat, by 1.8.1985. After several extensions, it took the members of the Common Market until November, 1993, to introduce the CET, the latest being Antigua and Barbuda. In February, 1994, however, Montserrat suspended CET following strong protests over steep rises in the prices of imported goods (*CI* April 1994, p.11).

The opposition of the private sector to the CET, owing to the higher import costs, is considerable. Enterprises in the LDCs are especially affected (*CP* 32:8). Moreover, the tourism sector rejects the customs duties of as high as 45%. The US Government, the IMF and the World Bank have all intervened[125].

---

[124]Given in detail in *CA* 4.3 (July-September, 1991) pp 73-84

[125]*Cf*· *CP* 52 and 53 (July-December, 1991), p 59, then U S Ambassador in Port-of-Spain, Sally Cowal, has warned that the CET could push CARICOM to the edge of the world economy, because other trading blocks have lowered their customs duties

A special CARICOM Heads of Government Summit agreed, in October, 1992, to a 5-20% Common External Tariff as of 1.1.1998. The LDCs are permitted to fall below the 5% level. In the first half of 1993, the 45% top rate should be reduced to 30-35%; and, from 1995, by a further 25-30%. Belize was given a special time-frame to reduce its tariff (*CI* December 1992, p. 3).

The Common Market made less progress in another area. In 1983, agreements of the participating countries over the intra-regional trade with agricultural produce collapsed. The Agricultural Marketing Protocol (AMP), which had existed up to that time, was supposed to contain, over and above the targeted intra-regional free trade, surpluses and deficits of twenty-two basic foodstuff items. These items should be imported from outside the Commonwealth Caribbean, only if they could not be supplied from within the region. Nonetheless, recording the produce and exchange of the information needed turned out to be too difficult (*CP* 24, p.18).

The CARICOM Multilateral Clearing Facility (CMCF), which had been established by the CARICOM Heads of Government at the end of 1975, and started operations in June, 1976, as the common accounting and clearing house for intra-regional trade, collapsed as well. It was supposed to enhance intra-regional trade by facilitating the payments mechanism. It enabled balance of payments settlement with local currencies within the Caribbean Community and provided members with short-term credits with which they could overcome temporary balance of payments difficulties (*Cf.* Emtage 1984, pp. 133ff).

The US$110 million credit ceiling was reached in March, 1983, because Guyana delayed a payment settlement of US$70 million of which US$65 million was owed to Barbados. Guyana sought in vain to get credit from Trinidad and Tobago to cover the debt.

The CMCF was subsequently suspended. Since then, its resuscitation has been discussed. Guyana agreed in 1989 with the creditor countries on repayment of the debts over thirty years, after a ten-year moratorium, in order to satisfy the conditions for IMF loans (*CU* July 1989, p. 11). Notwithstanding numerous attempts, the CMCF was not resuscitated up to 1994, nor was a substitute found (*CI* March 1992, p. 4).

In 1991, intra-regional trade accounted for only 7.7% of the trade volume of all CARICOM Member States, 6.5 % of the imports came from and 10.8% of the exports went into CARICOM countries (*Caribbean Development Bank*, 1994, p. 18). The position of intra-regional trade is significantly higher in other economic communities (*Cf.* McIntyre, 1984b, pp. 20ff). In the consideration of official figures, it should not be overlooked that an active informal trade exists between Commonwealth Caribbean countries, which can hardly be included in the official statistics (*Cf.* Wiltshire-Brodber 1984, p. 196).

From 1971 to 1976, intra-regional trade attained annual growth rates in volume averaging 27%; from 1976 to 1981, 11% (*Cf.* Watson 1990, pp. 53ff). Between 1981 and 1986, however, trade volume fell dramatically[126]. This was linked to the collapse of the market in Trinidad and Tobago; which had hitherto been the largest purchaser of CARICOM goods. Between 1982 and 1984,

[126] I e. from EC $ 1.6 billion to EC $ 796.4 million (EC $1 0 equals US $ 0.37).

Trinidad and Tobago absorbed 50% of all non-oil intra-regional CARICOM exports. This fell to 42% in 1985, however, and to 29% in 1986.

The collapse of crude oil prices and the fall in the demand for oil were responsible for this situation, which caused great economic problems for Trinidad and Tobago, then the only oil-producing country in the Commonwealth Caribbean.

The oil trade between Trinidad and the rest of this region fell in 1986, as against the previous year, by 57.4 % (to EC$233 million). One of the reasons for that was the cessation of oil deliveries to Guyana, owing to its inability to pay. Guyana obtained oil from Venezuela by means of a barter trade (*CI* July 1982, p. 1).

Despite the brake on imports, though, Trinidad and Tobago's deficit in its balance of trade rose in 1986 to about US$556 million (*CC* July 1987, p. 1).

After the 1984 CARICOM Summit, Trinidad and Tobago's then Prime Minister, George Chambers, declared that the only real market in the Community was that of his country. He complained that the other CARICOM countries, apart from buying oil, did not buy any of his country's other products, and apart from the Jamaicans, who anyway didn't buy any — could not afford to buy the motor vehicles assembled in Trinidad. Chambers made it clear that he had no intention of implementing the agreements made in Nassau — that is, uniform external trade barriers and removal of restriction on intra-regional imports. He had, he also pointed out, agreed to the Nassau Understanding, only because of the necessary unanimity rule governing the decision-making process in the deliberations. He answered the direct questions, as to why he did not wish to respect that rule, at least for the sake of Caribbean unity, as follows: 'If they find me nine hundred million dollars, I will do it' (*CC* November 1984, p. 1).

In the course of 1985, Trinidad and Tobago tightened its import restrictions *vis-à-vis* the other CARICOM Member States, although the CARICOM Common Market Treaty expressly forbids quantitative restrictions of the imports of such states[127]. Barbados' foreign trade deficit with Trinidad and Tobago almost doubled. In January 1986, the Barbadian Government erected import barriers against Trinidad's goods. Barbados' then Minister of Commerce, Industry and Consumer Affairs, Louis Tull, declared:

> 'We're not playing games, Barbados has a long tradition of playing by the rules, and we have done our best to live up to the provisions of all the agreements and accords which we have entered. But there comes a time when we have to look after our own interest in a more definite way' (*CI* February 1986, p. 15).

Three years earlier, on the occasion of the tenth anniversary of CARICOM, then Barbadian Prime Minister, Tom Adams, (1984, pp. 4ff) had termed, as the greatest threat for the continuation of CARICOM, the protectionism spreading within the Community. Unfair practices and an increasing tendency to help oneself at one's neighbour's expense, undermined the very foundations on which the entire building of CARICOM rested, he declared.

---

[127]At Article 21 *Cf.*: also CP 38:46. But Articles 28 and 29 allow under certain circumstances, the temporary introduction of import restriction e.g. during acute balance of payments difficulties or if a certain branch of industry falls into serious difficulties, owing to the substantial loss of demand in the domestic market.

In order to restore the price competitivity of Trinidadian industry and also of tourism as well as to attract foreign investors, Trinidad and Tobago, in December 1985, devalued its currency — one of the most stable in CARICOM — by 33.3% (*Barbados Advocate* 18.12.1985, p. 1). At the same time, the Trinidadian Government announced its implementation on 1.1.1986, of the Nassau Understanding. The Trinidad and Tobago market was re-opened to CARICOM goods. But the devaluation made those goods considerably more expensive for the people, whereby locally produced goods had better sales opportunities.

Nonetheless, the re-opening of the Trinidadian market led to a growth in intra-regional trade for the first time since 1981. In 1987, the financial volume of imports of CARICOM countries of the Common market among themselves increased by 7.8%, as against that of the previous year. In 1986, in contrast, it had fallen by 32.9% *vis-à-vis* 1985[128] (*CR* 21.7.1986, p. 6). Official statistics put intra-regional trade in 1987 at EC$858 million compared to EC$796.4 million in 1986. A further increase occurred 1988 as against 1987 of 14.6% to approximately EC$983 million.

In 1989, intra-regional trade, measured by imports, reached its highest growth rate since 1981 of 23.9% (MDCs, 27.3%; LDCs, 18.7%). This was because an increasing number of regional Governments honoured the agreements for removing trade barriers. The volume, however, was not half as high as the volume of imported food and drink alone in the region (Singh 1990, p. 22 and *CP* 48, p. 45).

The 1981-86 fall in intra-regional trade was not compensated for by a corresponding growth in extra-regional exports. Parallel to intra-regional imports, the extra-regional exports of the CARICOM countries had fallen between 1980 and '84 from EC$15.5 billion to EC$ 9.6 billion.

In 1986, public and private sector experts in exports decided to establish the CARICOM Export Development Council (CEDC) as a means of furthering exports, as an advisory body for the Ministerial Council of the Common Market (*CP* 34, p. 9). The CEDC, which started operations in November 1989, and the CARICOM Export Development Project (CEDP), which it supervised, are supposed to help in the removal of several obstacles to free trade within the region. The CEDP is based in Barbados and consists of representatives of export development agencies of the twelve Member States of the Common Market (or the Government officials responsible for trade) plus representatives of the private sector and trade unions.

The CEDP aids CARICOM Governments in their plans for the growth and development of exports. The private sector, as already stated, is a participant. The measures the CEDP has taken include the creation of a marketing information pool and a directory of exporters from the region. Regional trade fairs for exports should serve to stimulate sales (*CR* 7.12.1989, p. 7). Regional Standards have been developed by the Caribbean Common Market Standards Council (CCMSC). A CARICOM Standard Mark Logo will be utilised on goods which keep to that CARICOM standard (Caribbean Community, 1992, pp. 24f).

[128] Or 11 5%, after subtracting oil exports.

Within the CEDP, the Caribbean Trade Information System (CARTIS) with a network of national trade information centres in the Commonwealth Caribbean was cut over into service, for the computer-supported exchange of trade information world-wide (*CP* 44 and 45, p. 60).

The CARICOM Member States wanted to establish, in January 1988, an export credit bank which should offer pre-delivery and post-delivery financing for exports from the region (*CI* June 1987, p. 13). But the 1988 CARICOM Summit postponed the plan, owing to the shortage of the necessary seed capital. Instead, the CDB was asked to offer export credit to 'important sectors'(*CI* August 1988, p. 1; *CR* 25.8.1981, p. 7).

In order to bring together those offering CARICOM goods and services and the users, its secretariat organised, in 1985, in Barbados, together with the Caribbean Association of Industry and Commerce (CAIC), the Barbados Manufacturers Association (BMA) and the Government of Barbados a trade fair, namely, 'CARIMEX' 85'.

This fair was supposed to fill the information gap within the Community concerning what was really produced and offered as goods and services there. CARIMEX' 85 was accompanied by a 'Buy Caribbean' campaign, which should increase the reputation of Caribbean products with Caribbean consumers (*CP* 31, CARIMEX' 85 Supplement, p. 1). In 1990, 'Expo 90' in Trinidad was the next and 'greatest trade fair ever held in the Caribbean' (*CP* 48, p. 59). *Furniture Focus '91*, staged in 1991 in Jamaica with assistance of the CEDP, was the first-ever furniture exhibition in the Region. CEDP co-ordinated the joint participation of Caribbean companies in international fairs and exhibitions, such as the International Food and Drink Exhibition in 1991 in London.

A consensus on the matter of a common regional tax for cruise ship passengers seemed to be near. St. Lucia's Prime Minister, John Compton, termed the CARICOM Heads of Government agreement on a US$6.00 — 10.00 per head minimum tax for cruise line ship passengers at a special Summit in June 1993, in his country as a 'landmark for the regional integration movement'. The Heads of Government thereby seemed to withstand the temptation to outplay each other in getting the desired cruise ships to visit their shores. They also demanded that the cruise shipping lines purchase more provisions in the region than previously as well as pay more attention to the environment.

The higher per head visitor tax should also have improved the competitiveness of the hotels and restaurants, which were taxed more highly by the governments and were starting to feel the pressure of the growing competition of the cruise ships (*CI* July 1993, p. 5; and August 1993, p. 5). Following the pressure of the cruise line companies the Heads of Government at another Special Summit in March, 1994, gave up trying to adjust and raise the taxes.

2.3.3 The Integration of Production

The integration of production[129] is one of the more delicate chapters of Caribbean integration. This is so, because it puts regional self-supply above the

[129] *Cf*: *The Caribbean Common Market*, Chapter VI.

national one; and also requires a transfer of sovereignty to the Community — quite unlike the integration of the markets by means of free trade.

Critics of the free trade agreements go so far as to term the integration of production the only meaningful form of economic integration in the Commonwealth Caribbean. The integration of the markets, they claim, does not function, for they are too small. The integration of resources and production, however, raises the question of distribution, they add, and, at the end of the day, can be attained only through the creation of political unity (Farrell 1986, p. 126).

The region as a whole has an extremely valuable base in natural resources — fruitful agricultural land and pasture, suitable climate, rich fishing banks, aqua culture, forests, oil and natural gas, bauxite, other forms of similar minerals and wealth and a huge hydro-electric potential. Moreover, its natural beauty with sea, sun and sand and its geographical location makes it suitable for tourism. The geographical location also favours trade. There is good labour potential, which only needs to be appropriately trained (*The Barbados Consensus*, p. 3).

The integration of production means that several countries, or firms, in whole or in part, are subjected to common control over their manufacture of certain products. The units manufacture components of a product; alternatively, they divide among themselves the complete production of certain goods. The process is comparable to the decision-making procedures in multi-national enterprises, which, by their very nature, seek to optimise their activities. Decisions concerning the location of production plants must be made by weighing all production factors and — in the case of CARICOM — the justice of allocation among the various Member States.

Joint ventures between extra-regional and local firms have been the most usual forms of production in CARICOM. Units independent of each other work together in certain areas, in order to manufacture and market their products. Common research, quality control, use of means of production and common marketing all belong to this. This form of collaboration does not necessitate large units, insofar as similar conditions exist in the infrastructure of the partners, and it clearly has some advantages.

When, however, it comes to economic co-operation between countries with differing structure, political orientation and public participation in political decisions, better economic results are likely by the integration of production. This is quite apart from the fact that it is also easier to find intra-regional and extra-regional investors for such projects (Byron W. Blake 1984, pp. 119-121).

The history of the integration of production in CARICOM has been accompanied by spectacular failures. Thus, the 1974 agreement between Jamaica, Trinidad and Tobago and Guyana for the establishment of aluminium smelters in the two latter countries collapsed a year later, because the Trinidad and Tobago Head of Government felt cheated by his Jamaican counterpart[130].

[130] Jamaica's then Prime Minister, Michael Manley, had agreed with Venezuela to supply Jamaican bauxite for Venezuela's aluminium smelter. Trinidad and Tobago's Head of Government, Dr Eric Williams, feared Venezuelan aluminium, produced with Jamaican help, would impair sales prospects of aluminium produced in his country (*Cf:* Payne 1980, pp 185 and 215-216)

According to the agreement, Jamaica and Guyana had been supposed to supply bauxite, the primary raw material in aluminium, whereas Trinidad and Tobago and Guyana would contribute their own natural gas and hydro-electric power, respectively. In 1989, the old proposal was, on the initiative of Jamaica, dusted off and put forward again. But, it has not proceeded beyond the determination of the framework conditions for a feasibility study (*CI* March 1992, p. 12).

Trinidad and Tobago has also had bad experiences with the downstream processing of crude oil. The oil refineries in Trinidad were supposed to meet the needs of the entire CARICOM region. But other refineries were established, with the help of multi-national firms, in Barbados, Antigua and Jamaica (*Cf.* Farrell 1988).

Similar difficulties in the realisation of the integration of production occurred with fishing and the manufacture of cement.

The integration of agricultural production offers greater chances of success. In seven member states of CARICOM, agricultural commodities contributed the largest single share of merchandise exports in 1988: Belize, St. Kitts and Nevis, Saint Lucia, St. Vincent and the Grenadines, Dominica, Grenada and Barbados (*Time for Action*, p. 161). Owing to the traditional monoculture, even agrarian states have to import large quantities of foodstuff. Integrated agricultural production could, however, lessen their dependence on foreign food imports, without the Caribbean States waiving the cultivation of certain produce destined for extra-regional export (Alister McIntyre 1984b, p. 24)[131].

In 1974, the CARICOM Heads of Government decided to reduce the quantities of imported food. The Standing Ministerial Committee for Agriculture agreed on a Regional Food and Nutrition Strategy (RFNS). In 1976, to this end, the Caribbean Food Corporation (CFC) was established, which was supposed to drive forward the creation of regional integration of Agricultural Projects. The CFC's brief is to produce, process, pack, store, transport, deal in and market foodstuff — either alone or through public or private sector partners. The Caribbean Agricultural Trading Company (CATCO), provides valuable information to assist farmers, exporters, co-operatives, agricultural research organisations, extension services, marketing boards and others involved in agricultural export marketing. In 1986, the Standing Committee of Ministers responsible for Agriculture decided to modify the approach to development of the Region's agriculture and formulated the Caribbean Community Programme for Agricultural Development (CCPAD). Its main objective is to foster the revitalisation of regional agriculture through enlarging trade opportunities within the Caribbean Community (*cf. Time for Action*, p. 167). The first International Conference in Financing Caribbean Agricultural Development, Agrocarib 2000, in June, 1991, in Castries/St. Lucia was co-sponsored by the CARICOM Secretariat, the CDB and the OECS, and attended by several major traditional donors (*cf.* Caribbean Community, 1992, pp.19f).

The RFNS is perceived as a multi-disciplinary plan for the food and agricultural sector of the Community. It is supposed to support national efforts in

[131] Given in detail also in Axline 1986.

fishing, livestock rearing, oils and fats production, fruits and vegetables, pulses, spices, fertilisers and seed-corn. The aims are economic independence and the better health of the people (*CP* 20, pp. 14-15).

The strategy was developed because 60% of the food consumed in the region is still imported from abroad, whereas agricultural production continues to fall as a percentage of GDP, especially in the MDCs. The RFNS is supposed to be implemented by the Intersectoral Committee (ISC), which was founded in 1979 and consists of representatives of the CARICOM Secretariat, the UWI and the Caribbean Food and Nutrition Institute (CFNI). But the ISC, which meets triennially and should prepare an action plan, does not have any executive powers. Manifest success of the strategy, especially in the diversification and intensification of cultivation is yet to occur.

The lack of freedom of movement between the various CARICOM countries constitutes an obstacle to the integration of production. In order to facilitate the movement of labour, goods and capital for joint ventures within the Common Market the CARICOM Heads of Government agreed, in 1987, on establishing a CARICOM Enterprise Regime (CER). This enables the founding of regional, state-run and private sector firms. The agreement was signed by all CARICOM Member States most of which have since ratified it. Despite being, therefore, in force, the CER is not effective in all of the countries (*CI* March 1992, p. 4).

The CER is supposed to accomplish one of the principal objectives of the Economic Community — namely, the utilisation of the scant resources of the CARICOM Member States for a broadly laid-out and strongly diversified production, and to stimulate exports within the region.

Moreover, the CER should provide the framework for the common exploration of the region's natural resources in agriculture, industry, minerals and the processing of timber; as well as for providing in common, certain services such as financing, insurance, consultancy and construction. CARICOM Enterprises, which are to be founded, should be treated like national firms of the individual Member States. The Registration takes place, in each case, through the member-country in which the relevant firm has its registered head office (*CP* 37, p. 3).

Guyana's then President Hoyte had hoped to pay a portion of its debt to neighbouring Trinidad and Tobago, which had been estimated at over US$632 million, by means of the CER. Trinidadian entrepreneurs should, on this scenario, install factories in Guyana and then export the finished products. The foreign exchange emanating from such sales would then be paid into the Central Bank of Trinidad and Tobago for the amortisation of Guyana's debt. Guyana would have used up its free capacity and create jobs; Trinidad and Tobago would have gotten its money back — and its entrepreneurs would have had the opportunity to exploit, together with Guyanese partners, the quite considerable mineral wealth of Guyana (*WG* 14.7.1987, p. 14).

Hoyte's predecessor, Burnham, had also been a convinced advocate of the integration of production. This earned the latter the reproach of his opponents that he had sacrificed the industrialisation of Guyana to the CARIFTA-imposed role of supplier of agricultural produce to the Community (*Cf.* Cheddi Jagan 1980, pp. 382ff). Guyana is the rice cultivation area of the Caribbean

Community. Burnham prevented the establishment of further banana plantations, because he did not wish to compete with other CARICOM Member States (e.g. Dominica and St. Lucia) whose main produce is the banana (*CP* 33, p. 19). He fixed, as the objective of his agricultural policy, the self-supplying of the region with food[132].

Burnham announced that Guyana would not wish to install its own refinery, should oil be discovered in his country, so long as Trinidad and Tobago had reserve capacity[133]. Clearly, this was a sarcastic gibe against Antigua and Jamaica, both of which had allowed oil refineries to be installed on their soil — even though neither was an oil-producing country.

All integrating communities have, as Alister McIntyre found (1984b, p. 21ff), difficulties with the integration of production. One of the reasons, he argued, lies in deficient entrepreneurial abilities to launch and implement multinational projects. A further reason, he added, was the claim of the participants that the integration of production requires large enterprises. In reality, however, small and medium-sized firms are just as relevant and fit into this pattern just as well.

In 1988, the Common Market Council approved the creation of a CARICOM Industrial Programming Scheme (CIPS) for the stimulation and integration of co-operative industrial development in the region. In view of the decline in foreign investment in the region there, the CARICOM Heads of Government decided in 1991, at the Basseterre/St. Kitts Summit, on the creation of a Caribbean Investment Fund, which should help indigenous firms to expand within the CARICOM area, with special attention to agriculture, tourism, construction, consultancy and financial services (*CI* September 1991, p. 53).

The integration of production has so far not been able to achieve its full potential, owing to national particularism. Shortly after the signing of the Georgetown Declaration in 1987 it became known that Dominica had allowed a Puerto Rican firm to establish in Dominica a plant to make boxes for transporting bananas. This factory provides 60-90 jobs and brings certain tax-advantages to the US investors[134]. It offers competition, however, to a cardboard-box factory in St. Lucia, which had been erected jointly by the Windward Islands and Venezuela (*CI* November 1987, p. 11).

2.3.4 Transnational Functional Relationships

Functional co-operation has been by far the most successful of the types of integrative co-operation contained in the CARICOM Treaty. It does not oblige the contracting Member States to transfer sovereignty to units set above them and often extends beyond the CARICOM region. It is undertaken by a large number of state, quasi-state, private, international and national institutions and

[132] That went so far that he forbade the importation of wheat flour, which was not produced in the region, and thereby made the Indian Community, for whom wheat flour is a food staple, turn even more against him

[133] *Cf* Burnham's speech at the Fourth CARICOM Heads of Government Summit (1983) in Port-of-Spain (*CP* 20, p 9)

[134] According to Title 936 of the US Tax Code which favours American investments in Puerto Rico and their twinned companies outside Puerto Rico

bodies whose responsibilities partly overlap. St. Vincent and the Grenadines' Prime Minister, Mitchell (1987a, p.8) has made the following criticism:

> 'Every week we spawn a new regional organisation, more and more umbrella outfits, integrating more and more activities, be they in sport, disaster attention, women's affairs, customs administration. On and on the list grows. But in all these efforts to bring Caribbean people together we are still avoiding the basic theme, unity. Co-operation is fine, but the goal of unity seems to be avoided. We slip away from it. We spend more time quarrelling about the pot holes in the streets than the constraints of meaningful development.'

On the other hand, functional co-operation is, 'probably one of the reasons why we still have an integration movement', as the former Barbadian Prime Minister, Bernard St. John, put it on one occasion (*CP* 31, p. 39).

In the Treaty of Chaguaramas[135], the following fifteen areas of functional co-operation are listed, which, since 1973, have been carried out with varying success: Shipping, aviation, meteorological services and hurricane insurance, health, intra-regional technical assistance, intra-regional agreements on the public service, education and health, radio and information, culture, harmonisation of the laws and legal systems of the Member States, the role and place of women in Commonwealth Caribbean society, travel within the region, labour matters and employer-employee relationships, research in science and technology and social security.

This can — with some caution — be expanded by including human rights and constitutional systems. Foreign policy co-ordination belongs partly to functional co-operation, but was defined by the CARICOM founding fathers as a special area.

Originally, functional co-operation was accorded merely second-class significance; and was the least publicised form of co-operation within the Community towards the outside world. That changed, however, with the growing success achieved, especially in education and health.

The Caribbean Community practices it on different levels. At the public level, it takes place through the Committees of the Ministers having portfolio responsibility for the relevant subject areas and who meet at varying intervals. Their decisions are taken unanimously but nonetheless are mostly recommendations. Binding decisions can be taken only at the CARICOM Heads of Government Summits.

Further instances of functional co-operation are institutes and organisations founded as a result of decisions taken by CARICOM bodies and which are either administered directly by the CARICOM Secretariat or co-ordinated by it as autonomous organisations. Over and above this, there are special time-limited projects co-ordinated by the CARICOM Secretariat.

Organisations and institutions of varying legal types constitute yet another form of functional co-operation in which the CARICOM Secretariat as well as private and/or public organisations and private firms participate.

---

[135]In the 'Schedule to the Treaty'

Finally, there are regional initiatives, organisations and institutions, which are not linked with CARICOM and do not seek any closer co-operation, because their concerns are only marginally included in the responsibilities of the Community and the Common Market. They are overwhelmingly to be found in the ideological, artistic and religious areas. For this reason and because they fall outside the framework of functional co-operation, owing to the backgrounds of their world views, socio-cultural co-operation is discussed in Chapter 2.7.

The General Secretary of the Caribbean Conference of Churches, Rev. Allan Kirton, in 1985, proposed the holding of an annual regional conference of regional NGOs. But this has not yet taken place. The advantage of such a conference, according to Kirton, would be that 'there becomes available to the integration movement a cadre of interpreters and 'evangelists' who are engaged and committed since they have an investment in it' (*CC* August 1985, p. 3).

2.3.4.1 Education and Training

The close co-operation in education and training is most manifest at the University of the West Indies (UWI) and in the Caribbean Examinations Council (CXC). The idea for the founding of the two institutions dates back to the 1940s (*Cf. CP* 25, p. 17). They both have associate status in CARICOM.

The University of the West Indies has proved to be one of the most dynamic and longest-living elements enhancing and stimulating regional integration (Wiltshire-Brodber 1984, p. 191). It was founded at Mona in Jamaica in 1948, as the University College of the West Indies, as part of the University in London. In 1960 and 1963, respectively, external sites were added at St. Augustine (Trinidad) and Cave Hill (Barbados). The elevation to being an autonomous University took place in the same year as the collapse of the West Indies Federation (i.e. 1962). Three theological seminaries as well as the Institute of International Relations (Trinidad) and the Caribbean Meteorological Institute (Barbados) are all affiliated to it.

Only Guyana of all the Commonwealth Caribbean States and territories went on her own and established the University of Guyana, in 1963.

The UWI is financed by the sixteen participating States and territories of the Commonwealth Caribbean (twelve CARICOM Member States, plus Anguilla, the BVI, the Cayman Islands and the Turks and Caicos Islands)[136]. In the main, however, it is financed by that country where each respective campus is located.

In 1992, the student population was 14,800 (*CC* May-June 1992, p. 16), some 50% of whom studied at Mona. The number of students is, however, considerably higher, if University and pre-University courses, which are taught off campus, are included. Thus, in each participating territory, opportunities exist for studying at University (Extra-Mural) Centres, and doing advanced popular courses.

Many territories maintain Community Colleges, which, in part, lead to university studies. By means of the special Challenge Examination Programme, it is possible to study off-campus. Moreover, the University is experimenting

[136] A comprehensive account of the history and structure is given by Sherlock and Nettleford (1990).

with a programme, UWIDITE[137], which transmits lectures by satellite, radio and cable direct to other territories. The teaching material is complemented by videotapes and printed material. The system is also used for conferences by University bodies[138].

The West Indian University was first oriented on British patterns. Gradually, however, it developed into a West Indian institution, which, through the inter-action of students and staff-members from all the territories and the orientation of the curriculum of studies to West Indian matters, has played a significant role in the development of a regional perspective (Pereira 1984, p. 5).

John Hearne (1990) the late Jamaican novelist held that the University of the West Indies is the 'most successful regional institution'. The untrammelled and trouble-free working-together on the UWI campuses is, he declared, a 'constant surprise.'

Moreover, the UWI enhances integration by giving it the brains to research Caribbean reality, e.g. Alister McIntyre, Clive Y. Thomas and Norman Girvan (Nettleford 1987a, p. 36). These brains include Nettleford himself, the Nobel laureate Sir Arthur Lewis and the economist Lloyd D. Best. The rising generation of UWI integration experts includes Anthony Gonzales, Neville Duncan, Dwight Venner, Vaughan Lewis and Patrick Emmanuel.

From the beginning, the UWI has had unified academic leadership, under a University Council headed by a Chancellor. But efforts have been made to bring it under national responsibility and, therefore, control. Thoroughly differing views exist among the various Caribbean Governments concerning University training: Some place more weight on the expansion of technical courses of study, aimed, in a practical way, at professions and occupations. Others give the arts subjects equal — or, indeed higher — priority.

University bodies have no mass basis, and can do little against the incursions of the Governments in academic affairs. The UWI was, for a long time, seen as the place for training a few privileged persons — and, therefore, not as an institution, which serves everybody (*Cf.* Gordon Lewis 1984b, p. 52). With a long-term re-organisation, the Governments of Jamaica and Trinidad and Tobago desired to obtain greater influence on academic affairs, while the Government of Barbados and the OECS sought, with the majority of the academic staff, to maintain the University as a closed, regional institution[139]. The then Barbadian Prime Minister, Errol Barrow, demanded that the West Indian University must at any price keep its regional character, while moving from the closed campus more into the heart of the communities which make up the region (*CC* July 1987, p. 8).

The advocates of regional unity and the OECS, with Barbados, were victorious in the structural reform, which came into force on October 1, 1984. Since then, in addition to a central University Council, there exists a Council for each campus, which deals particularly with Administration. Academic Boards after consultation with those of the other campuses, decide on courses of study.

[137]The acronym of *University of the West Indies Distance Teaching Experiment.*
[138]*Cf.*: 'UWIDITE' ; Sherlock and Nettleford, pp. 228-236.
[139] See Kathleen Drayton's detailed presentation.

Campus Appointments Committees can make up to middle-level appointments. But the academic career paths as a whole, remain in the hands of a common Senate; and leading academic personnel are appointed by a central committee.

At the head of the University is, now as previously, a Chancellor common to all the campuses, as the ceremonial head. The Vice-Chancellor is, however, the *de facto* head; and his representatives are the Pro-Vice-Chancellors (*Cf.* 'UWI Under New Management'). Offices in Cave Hill and Mona deal with the affairs of non-campus territories.

The present UWI Chancellor, Sir Shridath Ramphal of Guyana, on taking office in October 1989, emphatically supported a unified University system in the Commonwealth Caribbean as well as close co-operation with other Universities in the area. The University of the West Indies won, he argued, the most pronounced confirmation of the fact that the 'West Indies is West Indian' (*WG* 17.10.1989, p. 19). Caribbean Studies is a compulsory subject for all UWI students, except those studying medicine, in order to deal with the 'phenomenal ignorance about the region'[140], which, according to Sherlock and Nettleford (1990, p. 287), 'persists among the adult population who have been accredited by the UWI'.

Thanks to the Commonwealth Caribbean University system, students from the region wishing to have an internationally recognised University degree and promising employment prospects, no longer have to struggle to be admitted to US, Canadian or British Universities. Nonetheless, for less financially well-off students, the UWI has the disadvantage that, without scholarships or bursaries, they are hardly able to finance their studies. Unlike University cities in industrialised countries, the locations of the University campuses in the Commonwealth Caribbean hardly provide University students with opportunities to finance their studies (Pereira 1984, p. 9). Indeed, an increasing number of such students experience difficulties in meeting the rising costs of accommodation, food, transportation, books and fees[141].

Numerous University institutes and special research areas take steps to ensure that work on the campuses continues throughout the calendar year. The Institute of International Relations, on the St. Augustine campus, which is financed largely by Trinidad and Tobago, trains diplomats; the Trade Union Education Institute, at Mona, trade unionists; the Caribbean Institute of Mass Communication (CARIMAC), also at Mona, journalists and other media specialists; the Caribbean Agricultural Research and Development Institute (CARDI) and the Caribbean Agricultural and Rural Development Advisory and Training Service (CARDATS), in St. Augustine, which is attached to its campus, experts in agriculture, within and outside the formal academic curricula, respectively; and the Caribbean Food and Nutrition Institute (CFNI), in St. Augustine, nutritionists. Since 1984, the Consortium Graduate School has

[140]Blackman (1989b, pp 107ff) goes further in his plan to top up the 1984 structural reform and make the various campuses independent of the financial power of the campus territories Besides, he pleads for the 're-integration' of the University of Guyana to the UWI system

[141]Please see, for instance, Keith Bishop's report on the situation on the Mona UWI campus before the start of the 1989-1990 academic year, in October 1989

trained gifted students in the applied social sciences to be professional researchers in the social sciences (*CP* 36, p. 30).

The University of Guyana is linked to the UWI through close co-operation. A commission headed by William Demas is examining the possibilities of a merger between the two. UWI Chancellor, Ramphal, himself a Guyanese, as stated previously, advocates a unified Commonwealth Caribbean University system and networks with Universities in the non-Anglophone Caribbean (1990, p. 11).

A number of associations with special interests have come into existence around the University, e.g., a regional committee of Caribbean Cultural and Intellectual Workers under the Barbadian novelist, George Lamming, a Caribbean Association of Political Economists (CAPE) founded in 1981 under the leadership of the Jamaican economist, Dr. Norman Girvan, and which embraces the entire Caribbean; as well as trade unions, such as the West Indies Group of University Teachers (WIGUT).

The advocates of these mergers are among the critics of the 'traditional' system of university education with high entrance barriers and an elitist selection process. The criticism focuses on the colonial origin of West Indian University education, which, according to them, is excessively oriented towards the hegemonic powers and their 'capitalist' economic system. Their demands, for the unity of the working 'masses' with the intellectuals and dropping the barriers posed by matriculation requirements for those members of the 'working class' (Pereira) willing to study, were partly oriented on the Cuban-Soviet model.

Other Caribbean initiatives surrounding the sciences — such as the Caribbean Academy of Sciences — deal with the advancement and co-ordination of science and learning in specific areas (*CP* 43, p. 23).

The tertiary educational institutions, initially oriented on the UK model, also play a significant role in the teaching system of the Commonwealth Caribbean. They have formed the Association of Caribbean Tertiary Level Institutions (ACTI). The OECS Governments have established a Council of Tertiary Education (CTE), co-ordinated by a high official in the OECS Secretariat who is also responsible for OECS co-ordination with the UWI (*CC* August 1993, p. 9).

In the non-campus territories, the tertiary colleges carry out University-type tasks in the training of technical and teaching personnel. Moreover, they offer courses in the most varied fields, which replace the first year at the UWI courses. They constitute a first challenge to maintaining the regional character of the University (Nettleford 1989, p. 30).

Compared with other regions of the Third World, the ability to read and write is very highly developed in the Commonwealth Caribbean. Almost 100% of the children aged 5-14 years are enrolled in school (*CP* 32, Supplement, p. 2). Higher school and University education have made great progress. Nonetheless, there is a shortage of numerous technical personnel, e.g. trained engineers, technicians, laboratory assistants, medical and scientific assistants, book-keepers, teachers and computer programmers — especially at the middle level.

Farmers with higher educational (or special) training are also in short supply. The CARICOM Heads of Government, at their 1985 Summit, demanded that science, mathematics, economics and EDP applications be included in the educational and training curricula. Education and training, they maintained, should aim at better preparing school-leavers for the world of work — and thereby involve them in the swift technological change taking place in the world (*CP* 32, Supplement, p. 2). The precondition for this is, however, transnational co-operation within the Caribbean Community, because the system can otherwise hardly produce the experts necessary for building an economy less dependent on the outside world (*Cf.* P.A. Thompson 1984, p. 153).

The Caribbean CXC Examinations play a special role in raising and stabilising educational levels and in tailoring education to the needs of the region. The further use of British exams would have perpetuated British-type curricula in the post-colonial period. In 1973, fifteen Caribbean countries signed an agreement for creating the Caribbean Examinations Council (CXC). Study plans for twenty-eight subjects were developed.

Thus, for instance, the guidelines for Caribbean History state that the students should acquire knowledge and understanding of the common historical experiences of people in the Caribbean; understanding and appreciation of the creative contribution of each individual and also of the groups in their own territories and other territories of the Caribbean and a feel for the social, economic and political questions and conflicts in West Indian everyday life. The syllabus for social studies declares that the students should become familiar with the social reality of the Caribbean, so that they can become active members of society in the Caribbean Community.

The aim of the Caribbean examinations is — as then CARIFTA Secretary-General William Demas, put it in 1973 — to replace a system imposed on the region since colonial times from abroad, and which was developed abroad and had syllabuses prescribed abroad and was under the control of foreign examination authorities, with a system which corresponds to West Indian cultural and intellectual independence (*Cf.* Hurley 1988, p. 8).

In keeping with this, the CXC should primarily replace the British GCE 'O' level examinations and be geared more towards being a simple school-leaving examination than towards University studies. The CXC examinations should provide a greater area of knowledge and capability as was usual hitherto and also be more firmly oriented towards technical and job-creating subjects. The Caribbean examinations are predicated on the introduction (or changing of the contents) of certain subjects taught, such as Caribbean History, Integrated Science and Social Studies.

The number of candidates for the CXC Examinations has consistently increased, since they were first held in 1979. Former CARICOM Secretary-General, Kurleigh King, described the CXC as 'one of the success stories of regional integration' (Husbands 1985, p. 42). But the new Caribbean examinations were at first only hesitantly given accreditation outside the Caribbean, as Hurley (1988) reports. It was even more difficult, however, for them to find acceptance in the Caribbean, for Caribbean people always tend to rate foreign systems above their own.

A pilot study in 1984 on the attitude of Guyanese student teachers to regional integration revealed that, despite the CXC, only 50% of the respondents believed that the integration efforts in education had brought progress in the individual CARICOM territories (Grant and Paul 1985, p. 16).

Adult literacy programmes play an important role in Caribbean education. Despite a relatively high school attendance rate, the number of functionally illiterate school-leavers is also high. The Caribbean Centre for Adult Education (CARCAE) is co-ordinating with the CARICOM Secretariat a literacy campaign for the region (*CP* 36, p. 17).

2.3.4.2 Health, Anti-narcotics Action, Environment and Nature

The population of the Commonwealth Caribbean belongs to the healthiest populations in developing countries, with a life expectancy markedly higher, and an infant mortality rate lower, than those on the Latin American mainland[142]. The increased inter-country contact and travel, and self-interest to avoid communicable disease, like yellow fever and cholera, made health an item of interest to all countries. Moreover, 'the positive or negative health image of one country can have implications for the region as a whole, as the Caribbean is still strongly perceived by other nations as a single geographical or ecological entity' (*Whither Caribbean Health,*, p. 59). This image is of special importance for tourism.

Despite its importance, health did not figure prominently among the integration factors mentioned by Caribbean integrationists. 'Health was seen as a purely internal domestic affair and thus not something meriting a Caribbean approach', as the authors of *Whither Caribbean Health* (p.58) confirm. However, that changed. Health matters were included in the Treaty of Chaguaramas. The Ministers of Health of the Caribbean have had regular meetings since 1969. In 1986 they approved the initiative, Caribbean Co-operation in Health (CCH), as a means of assisting governments in improving Caribbean health. Under the supervision of the Conference of CARICOM Ministers of Health, a number of centres and institutes concern themselves in the field of health, with prevention, the fighting of epidemics and contagious diseases, like AIDS; the approval of medication for local use; and the influences of the environment on health. The Caribbean Epidemiology Centre (CAREC), in Port-of-Spain, which was founded in 1975, with twenty Caribbean States and territories as members, and which works closely with the World Health Organisation (WHO) and its regional organisation, the Pan-American Health Organisation (PAHO), headed by Jamaican Sir George Alleyne, is one of these centres (Debbie Jacob 1991, pp. 162ff). It assists Caribbean governments in the surveillance and control of diseases and other problems of public health importance. Among the others are the Caribbean Food and Nutrition Institute (CFNI), in St. Augustine/Trinidad, founded in 1967 to provide practical solutions to the Caribbean's nutrition problems; the Regional Drug Testing Laboratory (RDTL), which tests pharmaceuticals before they are officially allowed on the market; and the Caribbean Environmental Health Institute

[142] *Cf.*: *Whither Caribbean Health* (992, pp. 4ff).

(CEHI), in St. Lucia, which was founded to implement the Environmental Health Strategy, approved by the Ministers of Health in 1979 (*Whither Caribbean Health* p.61). The Faculty of Medicine of the UWI trains doctors and provides advanced training for nurses (*Cf.* Alleyne and Dyer 1990, p. 190).

There are numerous associations of professional health specialists. In 1988, the Caribbean Public Health Association was founded by health departments' employees for promoting the public health service and technical co-operation in this field. The Regional Nursing Body (RNB) wishes, in conjunction with the CARICOM Secretariat, to register nurses and introduce regional nursing examinations (*Annual Report*). There also exist Associations of cardiologists, nephrologists, urologists and surgeons and a College of General Practitioners. The oldest body is the Commonwealth Caribbean Medical Council, which replaced, in 1969, the Caribbean Council of the British Medical Association (*cf. Whither Caribbean Health* p. 65).

The cultivation of, and trade in, narcotics seemed for a long time to be more of a US problem. So long as the Caribbean nations believed that they could profit either directly or indirectly, the implications for domestic policy would be passed over in silence; or would be largely ignored. Today, however, all CARICOM Governments have realised that drug problems, in the long run, can bring only disadvantages. They endanger internal security, because the drug dealers become a state within a state (Vitalis 1988). They endanger, through threats and corruption, the integrity of the public service. They pose a threat to agriculture, since the cultivation of drugs is more lucrative than is the cultivation of traditional agricultural produce[143]. The economies of the small islands are also endangered, as the drug trade makes the banking system and economic development dependent on drug money. Lastly, a danger is posed also to integration, for the drug problems hinder the structural adjustment of the various Commonwealth Caribbean economies and their orientation on production and trade in the region.

Antigua and Barbuda's then Foreign Minister, Lester Bird[144], pointed out that, in view of the attraction of 'big money' in an otherwise desperate economic situation, in which jobs are scarce and the prospects of a comfortable life are limited, no collaboration, no matter how close, with the US Drug Enforcement Administration (DEA) can end the drug trade. Indeed, the latter can be stopped, only by means of effective US assistance (1985, p. 2).

The endangerment of the health of the very people of the Commonwealth Caribbean through drug abuse weighs, however, in the balance. In the Bahamas, serious drug problems exist in state bodies, hospitals, the larger hotels, many banks, restaurants and in industry. Indeed on Bimini Island in the Bahamas, 80% of the 18 to 20-year-olds regularly take drugs. At least 56% of the students attending institutions of further education in the Bahamas regularly consume alcohol or other drugs (Singh 1985d, p. 8).

---

[143]James Mitchell, himself an agriculturist, points out that it is well known that the drug trade means the absolute ruin of agriculture Drug plants are exempt from phytopathology and are much easier to plant than one winter vegetable (1987f, p 2)

[144]Since March 1994, Prime Minister.

In Jamaica, in 1990, 9.6% of the population regularly smoked ganja; and 0.9%, hard drugs (Stone 1991c, p. 151f)[145]. Seventy-two percent of the pupils in schools of further studies in Trinidad and Tobago consumed alcohol or other drugs (Singh, 1985d, p.8). In that country, where, earlier, the drug trade had been regarded rather as a minor offence, high ranking police officers and judges had to leave office, following investigations. In June, 1989, then Prime Minister, A.N.R. Robinson, named in Parliament five former Ministers in the previous Government alleged to have either used, or traded in, drugs.

Under pressure from the US Government, the First Drug Demand Reduction Conference took place in Belize in April, 1987. Experts from most Caribbean States discussed concrete measures to reduce the domestic demand, especially for cocaine and marijuana. Further conferences against the importation of, and trade in, illegal narcotis took place in Barbados and Jamaica, respectively, in 1988 and 1989. Participants included the Caribbean countries, Canada, France, the USA and international organisations. These conferences were supposed to give pointers for national anti-narcotics legislation and its implementation (*WG* 17.10.1989, p. 8). A Regional Programme for Drug Abuse Abatement and Control of the Caribbean Community should, with the support of the European Union and various aid organisations, stem domestic drug consumption (*CP* 43, Supplement, p. 15).

In 1989, Jamaica's then Prime Minister, Michael Manley, strongly advocated and lobbied internationally for the creation of a special UN force to help countries in fighting against illegal narcotics. The Government of Trinidad and Tobago argued the establishment of an international Court for pre-trial and conviction of drug dealers. The two proposals were, albeit in vain, supported by the 1989 CARICOM Summit (*CI* August 1989, p. 3).

CARICOM co-operation in the fields of the environment and protection against natural catastrophe, is increasingly closer. Preventive measures against natural catastrophes were among the earliest activities of functional co-operation. The Caribbean Meteorological Organisation (CMO), which was founded in 1960, with its head office in Port-of-Spain, Trinidad and Tobago, falls under the CARICOM Secretariat and co-ordinates regional weather forecasts. Its special significance lies in providing hurricane warning. The Barbados-based Caribbean Meteorological Institute (CMI) and the Caribbean Operational Hydrology Institute (COHI) within the CMO train personnel and deal with the technical equipment for regional weather observation. The supervisory body of the CMO is a Council consisting of governmental representatives of the countries linked in the programme, i.e. the CARICOM Member States as well as the BVI and the Cayman Islands (*CP* 32, pp. 31-32; 43, p. 45).

Demands for institutionalised diaster relief became louder, following the disastrous hurricanes, 'Gilbert' (1988) and 'Hugo' (1989)[146]. The CARICOM

[145] The proportion of ganja smokers corresponds to that in the USA, in the field of hard drugs it is higher (2%) in the USA (Stone, 1991c, p 151)

[146] In 1988, 'Gilbert' caused great damage in Jamaica, in 1989 'Hugo' raged especially over Antigua, the BVI, Dominica, Montserrat and St Kitts and Nevis Dominica lost 70-80% of its banana crop, although only rather marginally affected.

Disaster Relief Unit (CDRU), based in Antigua, should, in co-operation with the Regional Defence and Security System (RSS's) troops, organise help in cases of catastrophe (Caribbean Community, 1990, p. 8). In August, 1992, it, with a Jamaican contingent, successfully provided help, following a storm in the Bahamas (*CI* October 1992, p. 3). But, even without institutional ties, troops from the Caribbean States provided help in Jamaica after 'Gilbert' and in Montserrat after 'Hugo', in a way which exceeded merely symbolic gestures.

More for the institutionalisation and streamlining of the Regional emergency relief efforts in response to disasters, was done with the establishment of the Caribbean Disaster Emergency Response Agency (CDERA) with headquarters in Barbados, in September 1991 (Caribbean Community, 1992, p.7). It is meant to mobilise emergency response to a Participating State or States in the event of a disaster (Caribbean Community, 1992, p. 58).

Caribbean Oceanic Resources Exploration (CORE), financed jointly by the Indian Government, the Commonwealth Secretariat and the participating countries, collects data from the Caribbean Sea.

The thought of the protection of the natural environment in the Commonwealth Caribbean penetrates even greater into the consciousness of those bearing responsibility for economic and political affairs. Even those who had hitherto opted for economic growth at almost any price, have now become aware of the connection between development and the protection of the environment. The consequences of the policy of blinkered and myopic economic growth are complete deforestation, soil erosion, oil pollution of land and sea, the filling of rivers and sea bays with mud; contamination of potable water through the excessive use of fertiliser and the lack of purification plants; the drying up of river beds; and the despoliation of the landscape by over-development.

An increasing number of development agencies tie their project assistance to environmental questions[147]. The influx of tourists increases foreign exchange inflows; but also contributes to the destruction of the sensitive ecological systems of the islands. CDB President, Sir Neville Nicholls, has therefore warned that high consequential costs stood against the foreign exchange inflows from tourism. Physical barriers existed, therefore, against which, he argued, tourism in the Commonwealth Caribbean could be driven.

Within the CARICOM Ministers' Standing Committees, environmental protection was predominantly the portfolio responsibility of the Ministers of Health, who sought, with the Ministers of Agriculture and Foreign Affairs, to set up regional programmes. Since 1988, a Regional Environment Programme has existed, which is supposed to co-ordinate the relevant programmes and plans on a regional basis (*Caribbean Community* 1988, p. 46). In June, 1989, the newly formed CARICOM Ministerial Conference on the Environment, at a meeting in Port-of-Spain, signed an Accord on the Management and Conservation of the Caribbean Environment, which lays down the priorities and strategies for the solution of Caribbean environmental problems and elucidates the institutional advisory and co-ordination needs involved. In 1992 the Ministers developed a

[147] *Cf.*: Hoyte (1989b, pp. 66ff) who, as President of Guyana, regarded the rider as justified, but considered the consequential checks by ecological specialists as 'speculative' and often inhibiting development.

Caribbean position for the UN Conference on Environment and Development (UNCED), and took an active role in the negotiations of the Climate Change and Biodiversity Conventions, signed by eight CARICOM members in June, 1992, in Rio de Janeiro, Brazil. Among the agreements at the UNCED was the decision to hold periodic regional and global meetings on the Sustainable Development of Small Island Developing States. The first conference was convened in April, 1994, in Barbados.

In March 1983, representatives of thirty Caribbean Governments signed the Caribbean Action Plan for the promotion of integrated development on the basis of rational use of environmental resources. The plan, which had been in preparation since 1973, envisages measures to prevent oil pollution in the Caribbean Sea and to supervise shipping. The protection of plants and animals alongside rivers; the development and strengthening of national health services and water quality control; the promotion in schools of teaching about the environment; the training of managers in industry; and measures for the broad inculcation of awareness by the population about environmental protection, are further objectives (*cf.* 'Caribbean Governments'). The United Nations Environmental Programme (UNEP) is the executing agency of the *Caribbean Action Plan*. Among the signatories are the former colonial powers (i.e. France, The Netherlands and The UK).

NGOs, such as the Barbados-based Caribbean Conservation Association (CCA), which was founded in 1967, participate in environmental protection and the preservation of the natural surroundings in the Caribbean. The organisation, to which Governments, firms, institutions and private individuals from the entire Caribbean Basin belong, has assigned itself the mission of preserving the natural heritage of the region, in addition to the conservation of the natural resources.

The CCA supports regional and national organisations in their work, conducts investigations, formulates developmental objectives and helps in implementing them. In all this, it also works with the Centre for Resource Management and Environmental Studies (CERMES) of the UWI and supports the latter's collaboration with similar institutions of other Universities in the Caribbean (*Action Programme*, p. 11).

2.3.4.3 Sports

Cricket has become the most important binding element of the types of sport played in the Commonwealth Caribbean. The West Indian Cricket Team is the only institution, which appears under a common West Indian flag both abroad and at home (Hector 1987, p. 47).

Cricket, more than any other form of sport, has put the ex-British West Indies on the international stage. Many Caribbean inhabitants — except those in Belize and the Bahamas, where baseball, the US game related to cricket, is played more — know the rest of the region, mainly because of the top cricketers living there.

It is hardly imaginable that a national cricket team from anywhere within the West Indies would play against a national team from abroad — a matter reserved to the West Indies team (*Cf.* Wiltshire-Brodber 1984, p. 191). Barbados, Guyana, Jamaica, Trinidad and Tobago and more recently Antigua, are the main cricketing centres. Since 1927, the West Indies Cricket Board of Control has supervised and co-ordinated the selection of the cricketers and the observation of the rules of the game in the region.

In the OECS, a Combined Islands Cricket Team had been formed to play in the annual intra-regional championship competition, initially known as the *Shell Shield*. This team simultaneously served to promote cricketing talent in the OECS and benefited the promotion of the next generation of players for the West Indies Cricket Team. They now play seperately as the Leeward Islands and Windwards Islands, in what is the current *Red Stripe* competition.

In many Commonwealth Caribbean countries, cricket was the first organised game in which broad population segments could participate (*Cf. inter alia*: Goodwin; Cummings; Manley, 1988). It is practically the only team sport played together by Commonwealth Caribbean countries.

The 'Achilles heel' of Caribbean cricket is, however, the economic poverty of the region. Many West Indian cricketers, in order to play as full professionals, go to England, Australia or New Zealand (Goodwin 1986, p. 183). Many top-class and second-level cricketers could not resist the enticements of South African Clubs in the 1980s to play for large sums, while being upgraded by the authorities there to the status of honorary whites. In their West Indian homeland, however, they thereby risked being banned for life from playing for the West Indies (Goodwin 1986, pp. 173ff).

For the 'West Indian personality', cricket has developed into the perfect sport, which required body co-ordination, benefited from an instinctive sense of relaxation in physical performance, put a premium on humour and individuality, yet required team discipline and steadfastness in application (Manley 1988, p. 383).

West Indian cricket has been a term worth mentioning since the 1920s. Since 1928, Caribbean cricketers have played Test Matches. Outstanding cricketers, such as George Challenor (of Barbados), Learie Constantine (of Trinidad and Tobago) and George Headley (of Jamaica) were known all over the British Empire. In 1975 and 1979, the West Indian cricket team won the first two World Cups in cricket.

The Caribbean cricket grounds on which test matches are played — Sabina Park in Jamaica, Bourda in Guyana, Queens Park Oval in Trinidad and Kensington Oval in Barbados, the Recreation Grounds in Antigua and the Arnos Vale Grounds in St. Vincent are better known than the centuries-old territories in which they are situated.

Additionally, there were cricketing stars, such as Clive Lloyd and Rohan Kanhai from Guyana, Gary Sobers and Mike Worrell from Barbados, Viv Richards from Antigua and the adopted Jamaican, Frank Worrell who, as one of the celebrated 'Three W's ', with Everton Weekes and Clyde Walcott[148], was originally from Barbados, and many others. World-wide success turned the Calypso Cricketers (or Collapso Cricketers, as the West Indian players were, with more than a trace of malice and wit, also called) into internationally

[148] Sir Clyde Walcott formerly President of the *West Indies Cricket Board of Control* and is now the Chairman of the *International Cricket Council*.

acclaimed sports personalities. Their former colonial masters honoured some of them with knighthood or other titles. At home, they were the only heroes in a land almost barren of hèroes or heroic tradition, as the Jamaican writer, Orlando Patterson (1983), observes.

Cricketing ability also overcame racial barriers. From the 1960s, the team has had black captains, starting with Sir Frank Worrell. 'Gentlemen' amateurs were replaced by paid professionals on the cricket field (L.O'Brien Thompson 1983). The intra-Caribbean tournaments, most sponsored by large, regional firms, play a significant role in promoting quality cricket in the Commonwealth Caribbean. The *Shell Shield Tournament* in the mid-1960s was the first successful attempt to bring the four larger Caribbean cricketing nations — namely, Trinidad and Tobago, Guyana, Barbados and Jamaica — together with the smaller islands into regular competition. Numerous cricket clubs exist in the individual countries and territories. The biggest club, in each case, is in the relevant capital and attracts cricketing talent from the rural areas (Goodwin 1986, p. 11).

Why is cricket so popular in the Commonwealth Caribbean? The children are literally born into this game (Goodwin 1986, p. 15). They develop their interest for cricket in an on-going process with their play-mates before the house-door and in their own matches, occasionally led by experienced cricketers. They have great role models to whom cricket has brought high social status and prosperity.

Cricket does not require a large expanse of land for match practice. Talent comes to light individually and does not need to be honed as is the case with football, by selection in numerous matches in competitions from bottom to the top.

As is the case in England, cricket was originally purely a game for men, although the entire family participated in training sessions, and girls actively learnt the game. In the matrifocal Caribbean society, mothers often exert a stronger influence than that of fathers on the development of the cricketing skill of their sons (Goodwin 1986, p. 22). For more than twenty years national females cricket teams and the West Indies Ladies Team play test matches and participate in females World Cup competitions (Beckles 1993). They are organised in the Confederation of West Indies Women's Cricketers.

The WICBC has not yet shown interest in women's cricket, as its President Sir Clyde Walcott (1993, p. 59) admitted.

It is difficult for an outsider to explain the enthusiasm of the Caribbean population for cricket. The larger cricket grounds hold thousands of spectators and are full, during Test Matches, which may last for days. During the radio broadcasts of ball-by-ball commentary, entire nations seem to hold their breath in the region, in the course of important West Indian elimination matches. Even the radio commentators achieve personal prominence as a result of their cricket commentaries.

A host of interpretations exist concerning the significance of cricket for West Indians. The Trinidadian writer, C.L.R. James, who devoted a great part of his literary work to cricket[149], has summarised them as follows:

'West Indians crowding to Tests bring with them the whole past history and future hopes of the islands' (*CP* 24, p. 2).

Patterson put it this way:

> 'How better to express our pent-up rage, our agonising self-contradiction, than to acquire and master this culture, then use it to beat the groups that forced us into acquiring it? This is precisely what Cricket has done for the West Indian.'

The game, which initially was a confrontation with the dominant English culture, now has more the role of a proxy war in the class struggle (of the 'us' versus 'them'). An antagonism results from the fact that the middle and upper classes also have nationalistic feelings for their own team and experience as much joy over a defeat of the English team as do the lower classes. 'Us' and 'them' then melt into a uniform feeling of 'us' (Patterson 1985).

No West Indian team exists in other types of sport, in which no regional teams compete officially. Thus, a regional feeling of togetherness hardly exists in football (soccer) which, however, is just as widespread and, like cricket, also has deep English roots, or in all other types of sport. Here, the CARICOM Member States are in competition against each other. International success strengthens national consciousness.

Football in the region is co-ordinated by the Caribbean Football Union. Some national football associations are members of the FIFA[150] and, therefore, entitled to participate in the World Cup elimination matches. But no national football team has so far managed to triumph over their rivals in Latin America or the USA.

Athletics play a role in all Commonwealth Caribbean states and territories as a school and competitive sport. Jamaica has produced the most successful of these athletes: Herb McKinley, Arthur Wint, Don Quarrie, and Merlene Ottey. Even the former Canadian sprinter, Ben Johnson, was born in Jamaica. Jamaican aspirants of Olympic medals train, however, in the USA. Boxing, though, has a tradition in Jamaica. One of the Jamaican boxers currently most successful internationally is the light heavy-weight fighter, Michael McCallum.

A common British West Indies Olympic Association existed only during the short-lived West Indies Federation. But it was under its flag that, on a single occasion, a common West Indian team took part in 1960 in the Summer Olympics in Rome.

Since 1972, Junior CARIFTA Games take place annually and also include participants from outside the Commonwealth Caribbean. Track and field events, as well as swimming, tennis and shooting are among the disciplines in which they compete. Over 800 athletes from twenty-three States and territories took

[149]The former Jamaican Prime Minister, Michael Manley, is one of the better-known authors on cricket. His *A History of West Indian Cricket* (1988) is a standard work of the genre.

[150]*Fédération Internationale de Football Associations* (International Federation of Football Associations).

part, for instance, in the 1987 Junior CARIFTA Games in Trinidad (*CP* 37, pp. 38ff).

A Youth and Sports Desk, fully staffed, had existed in the CARICOM Secretariat since 1975 to 1985. It promoted sport in the region, in collaboration with the governmental officials responsible for sports and sport education. To this end, an Organisation of Commonwealth Caribbean Sports and Physical-Education Administrators (OCCSPA) was founded in 1983, and comprises of sports persons from within and outside the Governments. Training possibilities for athletes from the region are offered in collaboration with the G.C. Foster [Sports] College in Jamaica. The OCCSPA makes suitable literature and films and also prepares other audio-visual material (*CP* 19, p. 21).

In 1984, the OECS Secretariat established its own Sports Desk, which dedicates itself to the promotion, in the Eastern Caribbean, of those types of sport which are practised there less intensively, such as boxing, volleyball, football, squash, and the organisation of competition in these and other popular types of sport (*CP* 36, pp. 28ff).

2.3.4.4 Women, Youth and Family

Matrifocality is among the most outstanding characteristics of the Family in the Commonwealth Caribbean. The mother — not the father — is predominantly the centre of the family and provides its food (Messiah1983; Goetz 1986; Edith Clarke 1979; *inter multissimas alias*).

The behavioural patterns of individual ethnic groups do, however, vary. Academics from within and outside the Caribbean have thoroughly examined the phenomenon of 'fatherless families' and their effects on the role of both male and female within society. Concern about the 'incomplete' family and reflections on its direct influence on the family structure remained rather the province of the churches and religious bodies, which have sought to reconcile their family ideal with concepts of the family marked with African traits (Hodge 1985, p. 17f).

Ongoing regional co-operation exists especially in family planning. The insular geographical location, limited emigration possibilities and a very slow rise in the number of jobs have led the Caribbean States to work together towards stopping the 'popular explosion'. In 1971, the Caribbean Family Planning Affiliation (CFPA) came into being as the biggest family planning organisation in the region. An NGO, it is a member of the International Planned Parenthood Federation (IPPF), has twenty-one members in the Anglophone, Francophone and Dutch-speaking Caribbean and, since 1981, has had its office, which is staffed with full-time experts, in Antigua.

The task of the CFPA is to advise its member organisations in the various states and territories concerning the setting up and implementation of family planning programmes. To this end, it offers training, technical assistance and equipment; radio programmes, films and other audio-visual material serve to train family planners and to disseminate knowledge of family planning in the entire region (Newell 1982). Since 1985, the CFPA has organised the Caribbean Family Planning Day, in order to call attention to its objectives. In 1985, the Inter-American Parliamentary Group for Population and Growth (IAPG) met in

Barbados, to deal with population development in the Caribbean — a especially teenage pregnancy. On the average, 10% of babies (or over 30% the first born) in the Caribbean are born to mothers under twenty-years old, l by St. Lucia with 14.4% of all babies. The young mothers come mainly fro poor families, and can least afford to have children. As a rule, these youi mothers themselves grew up without their fathers; and they lack, as tl anthropologist, Trirbani Jagdeo, stated at the IAPG conference, a stab authority and a moral point of reference (*DG* 23.5.1985, p. 13).

In *Teenage Pregnancy in the Caribbean* (1984, p. 142), Jagdeo analyses tł effect of previous pregnancies on the health of the mother and the children; o the education and life prospects of the youth; as well as the link betwee population growth and economic development.

Despite their dominant role for the Caribbean family structure, women – apart from a few exceptions — played rather a subordinate role in public life u| to the 1970s. Several associations of women at national and inter-Caribbeai level, have tried to make up for this lag. The oldest such body, which is stil active, is the YWCA[151]. Other church-oriented women's organisation: concerned themselves early on with the education and training of women, a: well as with their management training (*CP* 22, p. 4).

Conferences, seminars and working groups discussed programmes and policies for women. Radio and TV programmes, videos, papers, books, brochures and fliers, dealing with women in the Caribbean, are produced increasingly. Even the arts deal with the subject. Thus, SISTREN, the Jamaican women's theatre, has presented women's themes both within and outside the Caribbean. Some calypsos have dealt with the subject from the viewpoint of the equality of woman in society. The particular role of men and women in Caribbean society and the relationship of the two genders to one another have been the subjects of numerous studies by institutes and individual researchers whose findings underline the congruity of the problems in the entire Commonwealth Caribbean (Shorey-Bryan 1985, pp. 34ff).

The Caribbean Women's Association (CARIWA), an NGO providing technical assistance and training for women's projects and which has national member organisations in numerous territories, came into existence in the 1970s. A Caribbean-wide conference takes place every two years (*CP* 33, p.22).

The women's movement in the Caribbean received a special drive from the UN's proclamation, in 1975, of the Decade of Women. Numerous regional institutions came into existence. The UWI, in 1978, began a women's development programme, Women and Development (WAND)[152];a research programme of the UWI's Institute of Social and Economic Research, on the role of the women in the region and a continuing studies programme for women, in conjunction with the Trade Union Institute of the University. In 1980, the CARICOM Secretariat established a Women's Desk (*CP* 19, pp. 18 and 23).

Similar bodies were created in almost all the Governments of the Member States. In Grenada, during the Maurice Bishop regime, there was even an entire

[151] *Young Women's Christian Association.*

[152] See subject catalogue (*Caribbean Quarterly* 35.1 and 2 (March-June 1989) on the tenth anniversary of WAND.

Ministry. In the region a network of women of all classes both within, and among, the territories, and borne by national and regional institutions, was formed. (Messiah 1985, p. 4).

A rather large delegation of Caribbean women participated in the UN's First World Conference of Women, in Nairobi, in 1985. In the same year, Caribbean women met in Barbados and, in the framework of a Caribbean Association for Feminist Research and Action, examined the results of women's activities, including feminism, in the Region, in the previous decade. Thereupon, the Caribbean Association for Feminist Research and Action (CAFRA) was founded as a regional network of feminists, individual researchers, activists and women's organisations to initiate research projects and to influence policy both within and outside the Caribbean.

A Youth Desk has also existed in the CARICOM Secretariat in Georgetown, but has been unmanned for some time; it observed and co-ordinated diverse regional youth initiatives. It co-operated closely with the Commonwealth Youth Programme Secretariat in Georgetown/Guyana in regional programme activities. The Year of Youth, unlike the UN's Women's Decade, produced no special push for integration among Caribbean youth. An International Youth Conference organised by the then JLP Jamaican Government in April 1985, was dismissed as a JLP event by the then PNP Opposition and boycotted by some political youth organisations in the Caribbean.[153]

Attempts to create regional institutions for young people were undertaken quite early. Only a few of them lasted for rather long, however, if they were not borne by regional or international organisations placed above them. Young people lack the resources for planned travel, which is quite indispensable for maintaining regional institutions in the Caribbean.

Among the 'dependent' organisations with a leading role in youth activities are religious bodies; such as the YMCA; regional religious and sport youth groups; agriculturally-oriented associations, such as the 4-H Clubs; and the youth affiliates of the Service Clubs[154]. The West Indies Jaycees, an organisation of young executives in the private sector, obtained liaison status with the CARICOM Secretariat in 1988[155].

Initiatives to give a regional superstructure to the Youth Councils established by the individual Commonwealth Caribbean Governments were only short-lived. A new attempt to bring national Youth Councils together, in order to promote integration through educational, social, cultural and other measures, which are necessary for the development of Caribbean youth, was made in Barbados in October, 1987, under the designation Caribbean Federation of Youth (CFY) (*The Voice*, Castries, St. Lucia, 2.7.1986, p. 2). On the initiative of the Barbados' Youth Council, national youth councils from St. Kitts and Nevis, Anguilla, Montserrat, Grenada, St. Martin, Trinidad and Tobago, St. Vincent and the Grenadines, St. Lucia and Antigua met for the launching (*Barbados Advocate*, 29.10.1987).

[153]Comprehensive information on this conference and national youth activities in the Caribbean in the Year of Youth is contained in Ajit Jain (1984)

[154]E.g.: Rotary, Lions, Kiwanis, *inter alia*

[155]This status confers consultative rights concerning local programmes.

The highly regarded Caribbean Conference of Churches (CCC) upvalued the CFY, by inviting its President to be a member of an international observer delegation for the Presidential elections in Haiti in 1987 (*Barbados Advocate* 24.11.1987, p. 2).

The National Youth Councils are co-ordinating bodies of different youth groups in the individual Commonwealth Caribbean nations. In part, they work with full-time personnel paid by Governments or development agencies. The lack of a united structure of the Youth Councils makes them susceptible to influences motivated by party political considerations. Party political polarisation is the greater danger to a stable structure of the CFY.

The attempts of private organisations, such as the Bustamante Institute of Public and International Affairs (BIPIA), to hold youth conferences annually on questions of regional interests, were more successful. At one such Conference in Kingston in November, 1989, 150 delegates from the Caribbean and Central America discussed, in the style of the UN General Assembly, the role of the two genders as well as racism.

The participants came from the youth organisations of political parties as well as from the schools, Police Youth Clubs, the Red Cross and other organisations (*Democracy Today* November-December 1989, p. 1f). Subsequent conferences were held in 1990 (in Antigua), 1991 (in St. Kitts) and 1992 (in Belize) with student Parliaments on the well-known Westminster model.

The aforementioned regional youth activities do not explicitly, as an aim, include the political integration of the Commonwealth Caribbean among their objectives. Nonetheless, in the 1980s, regional youth organisations came into existence with the political unity of the Commonwealth Caribbean as their stated objective. The Caribbean Youth Conference (CYC), with its head office in Castries, St. Lucia, and founded in Jamaica in 1983, was one of these. Twenty-seven youth organisations of political parties from sixteen States and territories of the Anglophone Caribbean, and one from the Netherlands Antilles, belonged to it[156]. Membership was restricted to the youth organisations of political parties with the approval of their 'mother' parties.

The CYC members pledged themselves to support 'freedom and parliamentary democracy in the Caribbean', 'to defend the independence and territorial integrity of each Caribbean country and the region as a whole'. Their main objective was, however, the 'furtherance of Caribbean Integration and Unity' (*Constitution*, Articles 1 and 2). The delegates of the member organisations met, apart from their annual general meeting, more often at seminars and events in the four 'zones' into which the Member States and territories were divided. The meetings dealt with problems of regional and extra-regional politics, in each case always from the viewpoint of a common solution to problems and the furtherance of political unity.

The youth conference obtained its stability from different circumstances and factors, as follows:

- A clear membership structure — since only the official youth organisations of political parties were admitted as ordinary members;

[156] That was in 1990. The number has since fallen, owing to withdrawals. Newer figures are not known.

- High hurdles for new members — requiring the approval of two-thirds of existing members;
- Prominent status of delegates and executives (young ministers of Government, Parliamentary Secretaries, Senators and M.P.s, *inter alia*) with both role-model and leadership functions;
- Efforts at political pluralism by involving the youth organisations of both the ruling party and the opposition of the states and territories;
- Intensive acquaintanceship efforts at each five-day annual conference;
- Favourable constellation of the posts of Chairman and General Secretary in the first years;
- Location of the headquarters in a politically and economically stable OECS member-State, which is not dominant; and
- Financing by a political foundation independent of, and not led by, regional power interests (*Cf.* Müllerleile, 1989, pp. 22ff).

The public evaluation of the conference was seen in the very part of the high- level speakers from the fields of politics and learning and also in the media reaction. The Caribbean Youth Conference worked with BIPIA in Jamaica and other institutions for political education both within and outside the region. In 1990, the CYC, supported by business and the Commonwealth Parliamentary Association, organised, in the course of the debate over the unity of the Leeward and Windward Islands, a Windward Islands Youth Parliament in which the youth organisations of nine political parties participated (*The Voice* 21.11.1990).

In 1991 the CYC collapsed due to leadership struggles and the subsequent withdrawal of external financial support.

The Caribbean Youth Movement (CYM), in competition with the Caribbean Youth Conference, came into being in September, 1986, during a conference of the youth organisations of Guyanese People's National Congress. Youth organisations of left-wing Caribbean political parties belong to it. But not much was heard of it.

The Caribbean Youth Institute (CYI), based in Georgetown (Guyana) and emanating from the CYC, supports the political education of the next generation of politicians in the region.[157] Since 1990 it organises the annual Caribbean Youth Festival, the sixth being held in August, 1995, in the B.V.I. The event draws delegates from Guyana, Jamaica, Trinidad and Tobago, St. Kitts and Nevis, Dominica, British Virgin Islands, St. Lucia, the Bahamas, Belize and Suriname. The programme included debates in a mock Parliament, and a festival pageant. The Festival is supported by governments and the German Konrad-Adenauer-Stiftung.

In 1993 students from the region met in St. Lucia at a Regional Youth Conference to celebrate the 20th Anniversary of the signing of the Treaty of Chaguaramas. Young people were there invested as Regional Youth Ambassadors.

---

[157] *cf* Konrad-Adenauer-Stiftung 1993, pp. 11 — 16.

2.3.4.5 Justice and Human Rights

Among the tasks which the small island states and territories of the Commonwealth Caribbean can perform, only on a regional basis, is the creation of the total sovereignty of the legal system. Up to the present time, all of them, except Guyana, recognise the Judicial Committee of the UK Privy Council as their Court of last instance.

But Demas (*CC* March, 1988, p. 5) has bluntly taken issue with this: 'An independent country cannot place final judgements in legal matters in the hands of another country.'

Nonetheless efforts for the re-establishment of the West Indian Court of Appeal, which was dissolved with the 1958-62 Federation, have so far failed, owing to the lack of confidence of the population in the independence and quality of their own system of justice. The 1988 CARICOM Summit entrusted to the Ministers of Justice of the participants, the task of preparing proposals for establishing a Commonwealth Caribbean Court of Appeal (Supreme Court) (*CI* August, 1988, p. 2).

Then, as previously, however, opinions on the subject were divided. The Governments of the MDCs are in favour; on the other hand, the OECS Governments consider the Eastern Caribbean Court of Appeal, which already exists for their area, to be sufficient. Costs are one reason. Additionally, the creation of a Caribbean Appeal Court requires constitutional amendments needing a two-thirds or three-quarters Parliamentary majority plus popular approval in a referendum (*CC* September, 1988, p. 7). Up to now, appeals can be made from the Eastern Caribbean Court of Appeal to, as the highest judicial body, the Judicial Committee of the UK Privy Council.

Human rights protection enjoys high status in the Commonwealth Caribbean. International human rights organisations do criticise the retention of the death penalty in most of these States and territories, as well as the poor conditions of incarceration of convicts, attacks of the security forces on disliked minorities and political opponents, electoral fraud and restrictions on the freedom of expression and opinion. However, this criticism does not apply equally to all of these states and territories. Thus, for instance, Guyana and Jamaica are rated lower than the other Anglophone states or territories by *Freedom House* or *America's Watch* generally.

The creation of a Caribbean Commission on Human Rights was proposed by the Government of Trinidad and Tobago at the June, 1986, CARICOM Heads of Government Conference in Georgetown/Guyana as, indeed, had been done by the Prime Minister of St. Vincent and the Grenadines, James Mitchell, at the 1985 Summit (*DG* 2.7.1985, p. 3). The Commission, it was proposed as per Euro-American models, should draft a Human Rights Convention, in order to guarantee the fundamental rights of the individual *vis-à-vis* the States. National Caribbean Courts had previously displayed little penchant to support the constitutional rights of the citizens against the State — thereby following British common law — whereby the Crown cannot be forced to correct wrong done to the subjects (Trotman 1989, p. 49).

The initiative of Trinidad and Tobago found little support with the other CARICOM Governments. Before that, they had by no means shirked from demanding respect for human rights, when that was politically convenient. The demand to South Africa to abolish apartheid is contained in all the minutes of CARICOM Heads of Government Summits. At the 1982 Ocho Rios Summit, the Heads of Government of Barbados and Jamaica pushed their colleagues to make respect for human rights and the holding of free and fair elections — with their eyes on Grenada and Guyana — the conditions for CARICOM membership (Müllerleile, 1983a).

In the view of the CARICOM Governments, however, the international human rights conventions and the already existing inter-American conventions and commissions for the implementation of human rights do suffice. No particular human rights conventions or jurisdiction in the CARICOM area was needed for this, in their view. Moreover, national legislation should be examined for possible infringements of constitutional rights — a task which could fall to the appeal courts (*Cf.* Trotman, 1989, p. 146).

The highly regarded Guyanese journalist, Rickey Singh, accuses Caribbean Governments of using two different yardsticks in human rights questions. He demands the creation of a Caribbean Electoral Commission to supervise elections, a Caribbean Court of Appeal and the already mentioned Caribbean Human Rights Commission. The people in the region should, he argues, have the possibility of obtaining justice at the regional level, if they cannot do so at home. 'Their faith in regionalism will deepen, leading, ultimately, to new forms of unity and enhancing the whole concept of the people of One Caribbean,' he adds (Singh, 1985e, p. 8).

These recommendations are convergent with those of the Commonwealth consultative group. It had pointed to the dangers to democratic development in small states, in its report on their endangerment in the global society. The 'lack of anonymity, the absence of a range of strong private countervailing sectors and pressure groups, and the lack of varied levels of non-governmental institutional activity' he holds, control all areas of life and erect 'petty tyrannies', which 'place undue pressure on public and judicial officials' (*Vulnerability*, p. 61).

At the non-governmental level in almost all Caribbean States and territories, human rights commissions and organisations have been founded, which make an effort to stand by the people against the over-powerful State apparatus and mobilise international support for their concerns. In 1986 the Caribbean Institute for the Promotion of Human Rights (CARICARE), based in Trinidad and Tobago, was founded. The Institute organises seminars on human rights questions and deals with human rights questions in symposia involving highly-regarded researchers.

In 1987, six national Caribbean human rights organisations formed the Caribbean Human Rights Network (abbreviated to Caribbean Rights) (CC December, 1987, p. 3). Based in Barbados its tasks include *making* human rights questions a general concern of the people (*Working for Justice*, p. 35). In this context, Caribbean Rights has, in particular, proposed the abolition of the death penalty and the improvement of the condition in prisons.

The Caribbean Conference of Churches (CCC) is one of the institutions which have fought particularly intensively against the violation of human rights.

Beyond the confines of the Commonwealth Caribbean, it has concerned itself actively with developments in Haiti; it has sent several special delegations there and kept the public consistently aware with reports on the human rights situation in Haiti. The CCC, through the national Councils of Churches, also works with Caribbean Rights and the latter's national members.

2.3.4.6 The Economy, Trade and Commerce

If the trade unions had earlier been at the vanguard of the integration movement, it was rather the Caribbean employers' associations, which, in the 1970s and 1980s, led the way as the promoters of economic and political unity. The view that political integration can be achieved only through economic integration contributed to this. The increases in production and trade and the creation of jobs were more sought after than the growth in power of the workers *vis-à-vis* management. On the other hand, the trade unions weakened their regional and national effectiveness through their dependence on parties of which they were often degraded to being mere strategic instruments.

The Caribbean Association of Industry and Commerce (CAIC), which is based in Barbados and has official consultative status with the Caribbean Community, has developed into the most important employer organisation of the Commonwealth Caribbean. Most Chambers of Commerce and manufacturers' associations in the Anglophone, Francophone and Dutch-speaking Caribbean belong to it.

Since being re-launched in 1981, following its first launching in 1955 and its temporary decline, it has become increasingly more significant. The CAIC sees itself as the training and co-ordination centre of the private sector, with special emphasis on CARICOM. Since 1985, the association has achieved significant public success by organising several large exhibitions of producers and products both within and outside the Caribbean.

One of the CAIC's services, especially for small to medium-sized firms is the fund for technical assistance, which finances short-term experts and technical training within the enterprise. The CAIC helps regional manufacturers' associations, and exerts influence on political decisions in the region, in order to:

> 'seek to influence public policy, especially regional policy, in ways that help to build an environment favourable to the growth and development of private enterprise, the improvement of regional and intra-regional trade, and the region's social and economic integration.'

The CAIC wishes:

> to help create that kind of climate in the region's economies in which private business may expand and prosper, thus promoting the region's economic development'.

The Caribbean Manufacturers Council (CMC), also based in Barbados, has existed since 1983, as an extension of the CAIC. The CMC is a forum of national manufacturers' associations for advising on common problems and representing manufacturers *vis-à-vis* institutions and authorities on national, regional and international levels (CARIMEX '85).

The Eastern Caribbean Manufacturers Council (ECMC) was formed in 1985, as a sub-group of CAIC and CMC, with the task of promoting the manufacturing industry in the OECS Member States and intra-regional trade in the sub-region.

In 1988, which was declared the Year of Small Business, the first in a series of consultations took place leading to the Fifth Regional Small Business Consultation in 1991 in Trinidad and Tobago (*cf.* Caribbean Community, 1992, p.26). The meeting agreed that the consultation process should continue through regional biennial meetings, but no meeting was held in 1993. The establishment of a Caribbean Small Business Association is planned.

Several institutions, loosely linked to the Community, deal with promoting regional tourism. These include the Caribbean Tourism Organisation (CTO) and the Caribbean Tourism Research and Development Centre (CTRDC) in Barbados, which bring together the tourism public and private sectors. Political implementation of the initiatives should proceed from the Governments of the Community and from the Council of Caribbean Tourism Ministers (*Cf.* Poon 1989). In February, 1992, the First CARICOM Summit Meeting on Tourism in Jamaica was attended by representatives from the wider Caribbean, the leading regional organisations on tourism and related public and private sector regional institutions. The Summit made decisions on regional tourism marketing, cruise ship tourism, tourism product development, financial and investment policies, and regional air transportation. Alerted by sinking market shares in the North American tourism market, the CARICOM Heads of Government decided to establish a Regional Tourism Marketing Programme for North America. It started one year later with the participation of all major tourism organisations and institutions for tourism in the region (*Caribbean Handbook 1993/94*, 12).

2.3.4.7 Transnational Corporations

Transnational enterprises, led by US firms, have penetrated the Caribbean more than other regions of the world. Foreign capital dominates all leading sectors of the economy in the region: Banking; tourism; mining; finished goods; oil production and agriculture. Canadian branches and subsidiaries as well as those from the former colonial powers of France, the Netherlands and the UK are also well represented[158].

On the other hand, transnational corporations with their head offices in the English-speaking Caribbean are in the majority. Most of those which do have their head offices there are located in Trinidad or Jamaica. The biggest transnational corporation with head offices in the CARICOM area is Neal and Massy Ltd. (Trinidad)[159]. By acquiring 93.3% of the regional firm, T. Geddes Grant, it became the regional transnational firm with the largest turnover, namely, US$423 million in September, 1992 calculated for 1991) (*WG* 29.9.1992, p. 23).

Another company, Grace, Kennedy and Company Ltd. (Jamaica), with a turnover of US$ 255.9 in 1989[160], has over seventy affiliated Companies in nine

[158]For an impressive presentation, please see Barry, *inter alias* (pp. 13-26).
[159]Please also see Sandoval, 1984, p.262.
[160]A CANA survey (*WG* 18.9.90).

Caribbean countries and the USA, spanning a broad range of sectors ranging from car assembly and the production of drinks, to car rental and financial operations.

Neal and Massy, with its operations limited to the Caribbean, suffered in the 1980s from the economic decline of Trinidad and Tobago. But remaining in Guyana has paid off for the group, since it benefited from the new entrepreneurial policy of the Hoyte Government. The main problems for Neal and Massy are the small size of the intra-Caribbean market and limited export possibilities outside the Caribbean[161].

Another transnational firm with head offices in the Commonwealth Caribbean and predominantly owned indigenously is Desnoes and Geddes in Jamaica.

McEnearney-Alstons[162], a group consisting of twenty-seven Companies with main offices in Trinidad, Barbados and Miami; manufactures pharmaceuticals, food and beer; assembles vehicles; publishes newspapers and owns a radio station. Transnational initiatives also exist in tourism, especially from the eponymous Issa group and the Sandals chain, under Chairmen, Joseph Issa and Gordon 'Butch' Stewart, respectively — both Jamaicans.

Hardly any direct and immediate effect on Caribbean integration results from the transnational corporations. The head offices and subsidiaries essentially pursue their economic interests, irrespective of their location. But the economic strength of the individual firms does exert great influence there[163].

Similarly, the representatives of non-Caribbean transnational corporations play hardly any part in regional institutions for industry, trade and commerce. Their great significance for the national economies and their only slight inclination to participate in regional integration weaken regional industrial planning and the integration of the productive sector[164].

Plans, aided by the Caribbean Enterprise Regime[165], to promote the creation of transnational Caribbean firms are stuck at their beginning phases. The successful establishment of regional firms requires at least a free, intra-regional market as a pre-condition, possibly including the Spanish-speaking, Francophone and Dutch-speaking parts of the Caribbean, the free movement of goods, capital and labour and the freedom of residence within the region for Caribbean nationals and firms. Additionally, in the privatisation of state enterprises, Caribbean entrepreneurs should be given preferential treatment.

2.3.4.8 Currencies, Finance and Banks

The freedom of movement of wealth and money is the pre-condition for economic integration. But the two need not occur simultaneously. According to Terrence Farrell (1991, p. 23) 'financial integration', i.e. the uniform conditions

---

[161]*Cf.*: the interview with Neal and Massy Holdings Ltd. Chairman, Sidney Knox, in Neal & Massy Holdings Limited 1989, p. 5.

[162]About McEnearney-Alstons and Geddes Grant please also see Sandoval, 1984, pp.262-263

[163]*Cf.*: the examples in Jamaica and Trinidad in Paul Ashley, 1983.

[164]Thus, the oil-producing firms, EXXON, Mobiloil, Shell and Texaco, supported by the relevant CARICOM Governments, share the internal CARICOM market among themselves — although Trinidad and Tobago could meet the entire CARICOM oil demand (Farrell, 1988).

[165]*Cf.*: Chapter 2.3.3.

for the transfer and taxation of wealth, can easily precede 'financial monetary integration'. The necessary pre-condition is merely the standardisation of all relevant material and legal matters.

A significant obstacle to the economic integration of the Commonwealth Caribbean is absence of a common currency. The WISA had a common currency and a *de facto* Central Bank since the 1960s. But the introduction of a common Commonwealth Caribbean currency in the other CARICOM Member States appears rather unlikely, owing to the varying levels of economic stability obtaining in these countries. At the end of the 1970s, CARICOM Travellers' Cheques were introduced, based on the then strongest regional currency, the Trinidad-and-Tobago dollar. Owing to the lack of confidence in the stability of the currency, however, only modest success was obtained (*Time for Action*, p. 37). Since the end of 1993, CARICOM Travellers Cheques have been withdrawn from circulation.

A common currency would, in the opinion of Deputy Bank of Barbados Governor, Delisle Worrell (1992, p. 6), have numerous advantages — such as faster economic growth, through the acceleration of investments in goods and services; the reduction of capital flight and greater incentives for significant foreign exchange inflows, compared with the inflows from non-commercial activities.

Nonetheless, the currencies of all CARICOM Member States are now pegged to the US dollar. Up to 1976, the pound sterling had been their currency of reference (*Cf.* Emtage, 1984, p. 135). Since the switch to the US dollar, the rate of exchange has remained stable for the Barbados dollar as well as for that in the Bahamas, Belize and the OECS. But Jamaica, Guyana and Trinidad and Tobago have devalued their dollar currencies several times. Capital flight and weak export performance inhibit the Governments of Guyana and Jamaica and, to a less extent, Trinidad and Tobago, from braking the slide of their currencies and achieving balance of payments equilibrium. Guyana's foreign exchange reserves have been so low, and its foreign debt so high especially on a per head basis that other CARICOM countries as well as private sector firms have in part made deliveries of exports only against cash settlement in hard currency.

At every devaluation, other CARICOM Member States complain about inadequate prior consultation. They also accuse the Governments in question of desiring to obtain trading benefits through the reduced prices for their goods and cash services. It is hardly to be reasonably expected, however, that the CARICOM countries will discuss decisions on internal monetary policy with each other in advance. The reason for this lack of prior discussion is the secrecy necessarily involved in such matters. The still small proportion of intra-regional trade as a proportion of the total trade of the Member States of the community is another reason (Emtage, 1984, p. 136).

In July, 1991, CARICOM Finance Ministers decided that the intra-regional trading settlements should be made in local currencies (i.e. the US dollar would no longer be used as their trading currency (*WG* 16.7.1991, p. 39). Worrell (1992), at a hearing of the West Indian Commission in 1991, made detailed proposals for creating a common regional currency — to be known as the Caribbean Dollar — pegged to the US dollar. A Central Bank, free from political influences, should be given the responsibility for the stability of the currency. The CARICOM Heads of Government Conference in July 1991 agreed that Monetary Union would be institutionalised through the formation of a Council of Central Bank Governors, charged with establishing a Caribbean Monetary Authority.

At the 1992 CARICOM Summit, the CARICOM Heads of Government discussed the step-by-step implementation of a unified currency up to the year 2000 (*CR* 23.7.1992, p. 3). Barbados, Trinidad and Tobago and the OECS should introduce the unlimited convertibility of capital and the integration of their currencies. Guyana and Jamaica should later be included in the process. The establishment of a Caribbean Central Bank is also aimed at (*CC* July-August, 1992, p. 10).

Following an agreement in April, 1989, between the Heads of Government of Jamaica and Trinidad and Tobago (*CP* 50/51, pp. 3ff), and subsequent decisions at the 1989 and 1990 CARICOM Summits, the stock exchanges in Barbados, Jamaica and Trinidad and Tobago, under the name, Regional Stock Exchange, since April 1991 carried out common trading in securities, with a unified system of quotations of the stocks traded. Cross-border trading among the three participating countries, however, remained minimal.

The Caribbean Development Bank (CDB), with Headquarters at Wildey/Barbados, is the most significant regional development bank in the Commonwealth Caribbean and probably the strongest of all institutions in the CARICOM area (Samuel, 1989, p. 234). The CDB entered into force on January 26, 1970, after seven years of preliminary planning, and was originally intended to provide capital for the development of a Federation consisting of the last eight former members of the defunct West Indies Federation. Moreover, it was intended to lessen the dependence on the World Bank whose credit policy did not seem to be sufficiently adjusted to the needs of small states (Francis, 1969).

The aim of the CDB, as per Article 1 of its founding document, is to enhance economic co-operation and integration of the Member States of the Caribbean region and, in the process, take an interest, in particular, in its least developed members. In 1994, there were twenty regional members, that is, all seventeen States and territories of the Commonwealth Caribbean as well as Colombia, Mexico and Venezuela and five extra-regional ones, namely, Canada, France, the Federal Republic of Germany, Italy and the UK.

The CDB helps regional members by co-ordinating their development programmes for the better utilisation of their resources; for mutually complementing their political economies; and for the expansion of international — and especially intra-regional — trade. (*The Caribbean Development Bank* p. 3).

This Bank finances both public and private sector projects, which are directly connected with the economic development of the regional Member States. Value is attached to the paradigmatic nature of projects for national development, their influence on the reduction of imports and on the inflow of foreign exchange, and also on techniques to raise productivity and create new jobs. The contribution made by their projects to economic co-operation and integration is also ascribed importance. Production-oriented firms are given priority ('Financial Policies', pp. 1ff).

Reference is given among private sector applicants, to citizens of Commonwealth Caribbean Member States or to firms controlled by such persons. Within the Caribbean Community, the CDB has the status of an Associate Institution and promotes projects with a direct integrative effect, especially in agriculture, transportation and industry (*The Caribbean Development Bank*, p. 11).

The CDB is as independent as is possible from Member States. The voting rights in the decision-making body (i.e. the Board of Governors) are determined as a function of the *quantum* of each member's financial contribution. But it remains certain that the Commonwealth Caribbean members constantly have the majority of the votes.

The Bank's financial resources are derived from ordinary capital contributions of the Member States as well as from the special fund to which non-members also make contributions. In 1993, the CDB provided US$48.3 million in credit for the region (*Caribbean Development Bank* 1994, p. 42). From 1970 to 1993, it disbursed US$848.8 million (*ibid.*, pp. 56f), trained thousands of West Indians and gave them reason to remain in the region, ('A Bank for all Seasons' p. 8). Fifty-eight percent of all funds loaned out by the CDB in 1970-93 went to the LDCs, which also received 69.4% of all sums from the particularly favourable *Special Development Funds* (*ibid.*, p. 57).

Among the projects particularly viewed by the CDB as promoting economic co-operation and integration were the intra-regional shipping line, WISCO, and the regional airline for the Eastern Caribbean, LIAT. The latter, in 1975, was saved from collapse only through a generous CDB loan. CARICOM has been aided by the participation of CDB experts at numerous meetings at technical and ministerial levels and also by studies in various fields.

The CDB was less active in fulfilling the mandate contained in its statutes of helping its regional members in the co-ordination of their developmental programmes. In view of the tendency to economic fragmentation and wasteful, uneconomic parallelism of economic activities, developmental institutions and administrative services, and having regard to the strict honouring of the doctrine of 'formal' (instead of 'effective') sovereignty, this is also, according to former CDB President, William Demas (1983, pp. 7ff), a task which almost exceeds the possibilities of the CDB.

This task would be more likely to be performed, if all bilateral and multilateral donors of development aid were to place the promotion of national development in the framework of the efforts of the Caribbean Community for economic integration — and co-ordinate their aid very closely with one another.

The Caribbean Association of Indigenous Banks (CAIB), which was founded in 1974, and to which in 1992 thirty-four local banks belonged, tries to strengthen the Caribbean element in the regional banking system (*CP* 52 and 53, p. 97)[166]. It places emphasis on training and technical equipment for the member-banks.

[166] *Cf.*: the speech of the then Prime Minister of Jamaica at the twelfth meeting of the CAIB in Kingston (A CANA report in: *Sunday Advocate* 1.12.1985, p. 5.

Credit Unions have been established in all States and territories of the region and receive their push-start financing mostly from religious or other financial agencies outside the Caribbean. They play their own specific role in the financing of private sector development projects and small businesses. In 1988, four hundred and forty-nine credit unions, with 756,000 members, in eighteen countries, were members of the Caribbean Confederation of Credit Unions (CCCU) in Barbados (McClean, 1990, p. 139).

2.3.4.9 Trade Unions

The Barbadian novelist, George Lamming has written (in *CC* December, 1987, pp. 14ff) as follows:

> 'It is organised labour that has really democratised Caribbean society. Until 1935 or 1936, there really wasn't much difference between the way most people lived in the 1920s and how they lived just after emancipation a hundred odd years or so before. And it was the eruption of labour, coming into direct confrontation with the colonial power, that created the new political directorates which we now see.'

Lamming also credits the trade union movement with eliminating racism in the region.

Most political parties in the pre-Independent Caribbean founded, or were based on, trade unions. If an ideology of West Indian unity existed during colonial times, then this was due largely to the influence of the trade unions (Demas, 1975, p. 34).

At the end of the 1930s and in the 1940s, West Indian trade unions sought to convert the thought of political unity into practical political reality — which later led to the founding of the West Indian Federation. The trade unions availed themselves of the opportunity to make their large following aware of the thoughts of unity and to press on, with the aid of the population, to implement it against national political currents and populist, territorially-oriented power politics[167].

The link of the trade unions to the political parties proved to be their strength during the anti-colonial struggle. Later, however, it led to their being placed politically below the ambitious objectives of parties and their middle-class leaders — and, therefore, to their fragmentation and weakening. Caribbean trade unions were modelled on English ones. Nonetheless, they were established otherwise than in Europe in a non-industrialised society, based on a plantation economy.

The permanent economic problems of the Commonwealth Caribbean States and territories force their trade unions to fight simultaneously on several fronts: Labour against capital; the employed versus the jobless; and poor developing countries against rich industrialised nations (Demas, 1975, p. 46).

Their political orientation imposes caution on them in representing the interests of their members, when the party they are close to forms the Government of the day.

---

[167]For the history of the workers' movement in the Caribbean, please see W A Lewis (1977)

Hence, little strength remains to represent interests at international level, even though it would be clearly necessary — owing to the claims of the trade unions — to protect the workers from international exploitation, especially by multi-national enterprises. UWI economics lecturer, Karl Theodore (1988, p. 29) put forward the following view: 'If labour is for integration within the region then labour must first be for integration within labour'.

The Barbados-based Caribbean Congress of Labour (CCL) is far and away the most significant regional trade union alliance. It has advisory and observer status with the Caribbean Community as well as in various CARICOM bodies, especially in the Standing Committee of the CARICOM Ministers responsible for Labour Questions. Predecessor of the CCL are the Caribbean Labour Congress, founded in 1945, and the CADORIT[168], which is the sub-regional organisation of the International Confederation of Free Trade Unions (ICFTU). The CCL's member bodies consist of individual trade unions and national trade union councils of the Commonwealth Caribbean and Suriname.

The beginning of the Caribbean trade union movement after World War II was marked by the Cold War and the East-West ideological confrontation, in the wake of which the world trade union movement was split. The larger number of Commonwealth Caribbean trade unions became affiliated to the strongly anti-Communist ICFTU and its regional organisation, ORIT. The smaller number of these unions, on the other hand, sought affiliation with the Communist-influenced World Federation of Trade Unions (WFTU) and its regional body, CPUSTAL[169].

The Christian-oriented World Confederation of Labour (WCL), with its regional organisation, CLAT[170], like ORIT, follows an anti-Communist line. It has also in the past, however, condemned anti-Communist dictators more decisively than ORIT has done. CLAT is oriented to Latin America, whereas ORIT, through the US trade union body, AFL-CIO[171], is also closely linked to the US trade union movement. Following the 1968 CLAT-CPUSTAL signed agreement for promoting unity in the trade union movement, CLAT representatives, in the years after that, repeatedly criticised US foreign economic policy — but also condemned as strongly the imperialism of the then USSR.

Only a few Anglophone Caribbean trade unions are members of the Consejo Sindical de Trabajadores del Carîbe (CSTC), Trade Union Council of Caribbean Workers (TUCCW), the Caribbean CLAT organisation, which was founded in 1970, with head office at first in Willemstad/Curaçao, and now in Caracas, Venezuela. The strong geographical areas of the TUCCW/CSTC are in the Dominican Republic, Haiti, Puerto Rico, Suriname and the Netherlands Antilles. The TUCCW/CSTC could become more significant for the integration movement of the CARICOM countries, only if the Caribbean Community expanded or the CCL were to fragment.

---

[168] i.e., the Caribbean Area Division of ORIT(*Organisación Interamericana de Trabajadores* — The Inter-American Organisation of Workers)

[169] i.e., *Congreso Permanente de Unidad Sindical de los Trabajadores de America Latina* (the Permanent Congress of Trade Union Unity of Latin American Workers).

[170] Central Latinoamericana de Trabajadores — Latin American Centre of Workers.

[171] The American Federation of Labour/Congress of Industrial Organisations

The WFTU has been able to gain only a few Anglophone Caribbean members-mainly trade unions such as the University and Allied Workers Unions (UAWU) in Jamaica, and the Guyana Agricultural and General Workers Union (GAWU), formerly affiliated to Communist Parties. Simultaneous membership of the Guyanese Trade Union Congress, to which most Guyanese trade unions belong, in both the ICFTU and the WFTU remained an episode in the 1970s.

The ICFTU-affiliated CCL, which, as already stated, was created out of CADORIT, had the following objective: To provide an adequate labour movement for the 'Caribbean nationalism' and 'Caribbean identity' promoted by the West Indies Federation[172]. The CCL was supposed to establish relationships to the then new West Indies Federal Government and provide commensurate status and power to the trade union movement[173]. These tasks, according to the statutes of the CCL, include the following:

- the full organisation of workers in the Caribbean
- to fight for the recognition of trade unions
- to secure educational, social, cultural, economic and other benefits for the workers,
- to support other aims in conformity with democratic principles of Free Unionism.

The CCL is supposed to promote the formation of national groupings and centres, establish and strengthen links with other free trade unions in the Caribbean and in the entire world; and also serve as the clearing house for information and researching problems of trade union organisations (*Caribbean Congress of Labour*, 1985, p. 26).

From the very beginning, the CCL tried to overcome the fragmentation of the Commonwealth Caribbean trade union system. To this end, national trade union organisations and centres were supposed to serve, according to the model of the Trade Union Congress (TUC) in the UK. Nevertheless, political party affiliations, power interests and ideological differences prevented the Commonwealth Caribbean version of the TUC from really becoming a powerful mouthpiece for national worker interests. On the other hand, however, the national trade unions were so strong that hardly a Government could afford not to have trade unionists in its Cabinet — or act against the whole trade union movement.

The CCL has exerted the greatest influence in the Commonwealth Caribbean trade union movement through its education programme. In 1981-85 alone, thanks to massive assistance from foreign agencies and friendly organisations, it trained over 2,600 trade unionists in all areas of effective representation of worker interests (*Caribbean Congress of Labour*, 1985, p. 35). Through the participation of worker representatives from various Commonwealth Caribbean States and territories, there has come into being, during the seminars, a network of personal relationships. This is facilitated by the absence of any language problems within the CCL. The rival TUCCW, on the other hand, has to work in at least three languages.

---

[172]Please see the contribution by CCL co-founder, Joseph Pollydore, in: *Caribbean Congress of Labour*, 1985, p 58

The CCL and its member trade unions are, however, examples of the high level of foreign dependence of Commonwealth Caribbean organisations, which are important for integration. Indeed, they have benefited more than most such rather large institutions, from the East-West conflict and US hegemony in the region. From the very beginning, the anti-Communist posture of the CCL ensured for it large financial contributions from the American Institute for Free Labour Development (AIFLD) as well as from ORIT, which stood under heavy US influence.

The AIFLD was founded in 1962 within the framework of then President John F. Kennedy's 'Alliance for Progress', at the behest of the AFL-CIO, with the participation of leading US multi-national enterprises. Its objectives have been to break down the traditional tensions between employers and employees in Latin America and also to counter radical left-wing tendencies in the trade unions and politics (Coldrick and Jones, 1979, p. 1039). It has so far financed the training of thousands of trade union leaders from Latin America and the Caribbean either *in situ* or in its own US training centres. In this context, it links closely with ORIT which has long had the reputation of being the tool of the US State Department and the CIA[174].

George Lamming (*CC* December, 1987, p. 15) quotes AIFLD Director, Frank McDonald, who, in 1971, reportedly made the following statement about the trade union education programmes in the Caribbean:

> 'Its purpose is the organised Americanisation of the Caribbean trade union role in Caribbean politics. Most major political parties are rooted in Labour union. Thus the axiom holds that the politics or ideology of the trade union movement will affect the policies of the regional government, and the more receptive the Caribbean labor is to the presence of American investment and management patterns, the more so will be regional politicians'.

From the very beginning, both ORIT and, later, the AIFLD were among the principal financial backers of the CCL[175]. Thus, for instance, in 1963-66, 85% of the expenditure of the CCL was paid by ORIT. In the mid-1970s, the AIFLD paid the salaries of all full-time CCL staff-members, except the Secretary-General's, as well as the rental for the premises occupied by the organisation. Indeed, so close was the link that the CCL relocated its head office, from Trinidad to Barbados, simply because, two years earlier, the Government of Trinidad and Tobago had expelled the then AIFLD representative. It was only in 1977 that the financial basis of the CCL was broadened, with the resumption of ICFTU assistance and subsidies from the International Labour Organization ILO, the Friedrich-Ebert-Stiftung, the Canadian Labour Congress and other donors[176].

The original hope that the CCL could finance itself out of its members' contributions up to 1966, was swiftly buried. Indeed, it has had difficulty in collecting even the rather modest contribution of 25 cents per member from its

[173] According to Frank Walcott, CCL Founding President, in: *Caribbean Congress of Labour*, 1985, p 55

[174] *Vide* Coldrick and Jones, pp 1026-28, and also the account of the role of the AIFLD and AFL-CIO in Burnham's coming to power in Guyana (Jagan, 1980, p. 355)

[175] *Cf.*: The account in *Caribbean Congress of Labour*, pp 19-22

[176] Ibid.

member trade unions. Usually, the member trade unions are in arrears, and often request waivers — with the exception of a few, which feel themselves particularly closely linked to the regional trade union movement. Hence, they cement the dependence of the regional trade union movement on foreign support, although this contradicts the often trumpeted self-reliance[177]. At the annual CCL meeting in 1988, in Trinidad, a call was made to CARICOM Governments to grant the CCL a yearly subvention (*WG* 2.8.1988, p. 16).

2.3.4.10 Professional Bodies and Service Clubs

In almost all Commonwealth Caribbean states, there exist, at the national level, well-functioning employers' associations, which bind together their negotiating power against the trade unions and work as a lobby group against both the Government and the authorities. Nonetheless, Caribbean-wide alliances, such as the Caribbean Employers Confederation, have rather a shadowy existence, for they may serve at most as an information base. Regional wages and salaries negotiations do not exist. The interests of the private sector are, however, already effectively represented by the CAIC.

Various professional bodies have been founded to limit entry into their professions to qualified personnel. Among these bodies are, for example, the Caribbean Union of Teachers (CUT), which concerns itself with educational standards within the Community, and the Regional Nursing Body (RNB), which, as mentioned previously, registers nurses and wants to introduce a regional nursing examination (Caribbean Community, 1990, p. 52).

While national agricultural societies exist everywhere, regional ones are rare or less active. Windward Island farmers have formed the Windward Islands Farmers Association (WINFA), as a result of their particular interest — which is especially their representation in banana cultivation and marketing[178].

The Caribbean Media Workers Association, which was founded in 1982, seeks to protect media workers from reprisals and restrictions on Press Freedom. It is the opposite number of the Caribbean Publishing and Broadcasting Association (CPBA), the publishers' association, which has existed since the 1960s.

At University level, many professional bodies have been formed, which, in the first place, deal with the exchange of scientific data and ideas in the Caribbean. One of these is the Association of Caribbean Economists (ACE). Its members include UWI scholars and numerous UWI graduates, who, in part, occupy high positions in Governments and regional organisations.

Similarly, in November, 1982, in Grenada, during the People's Revolutionary Government (PRG), a Regional Committee of Cultural and Intellectual Workers was formed, consisting of scholars, artists, journalists and others from the entire West Indian region.

The aim of the organisation was to close the gap existing between the majority of the population and the small group of intellectuals, and also to make available the body of intellectual ideas to the entire region. Conversely, the

[177] Ibid.
[178] *Cf*: Lebourne (1992).

intellectuals should actively participate in the work of the 'mass organisations' of workers, farmers, women and youth groups. They should also help the unemployed to awaken their political interests and deepen their cultural consciousness[179]. The regional Committee received support from the Cuban State publishing house, *Casa de las Américas*.

An extra-ordinarily thick network of contacts exists through the service clubs, especially those started in the USA, namely: Rotary, Lions and Kiwanis — these regularly bring together self-employed professionals, as well as middle and senior employees at the local, national and regional levels. The Jaycees exist for younger professionals and conduct regional competitions (e.g. on free speech) which are open to non-members as well.

The clubs are parts of international organisations. But they are so autonomous at the regional and local levels that they themselves seek out, within the framework of their prescribed rules, their new members — originally only men, but also women for some time now[180] — and autonomously choose their leadership.

2.3.4.11 Media, Postal Service and Telecommunications

An on-going exchange of information has taken place between the various West Indian islands at least since their settlement by Europeans. Trading ships transmitted information. Courier boats took strategically important information from the metropole direct to the colonies. Information concerning slave revolts was quickly known to the oppressed majority on the plantations in the entire region and led to further enquiries.

The exchange of information between the Windward and the Leeward Islands, which are located nearer to each other, was particularly close, especially since they, from time to time, were administrated in common.

It was, however, only with the arrival of the mass media — and especially of the radio in the 1930s — that the network of regional information became more dense and quickly available for everyone. The labour unrest in the late 1930s spread almost simultaneously everywhere. Similarly, Universal Adult Suffrage almost simultaneously became everywhere, the basis of demands for more democracy in the English-speaking Caribbean. But the information available over other parts of the region did not suffice to break down pre-existing prejudices. The West Indies Federation floundered not least on the rocks of an information deficit, which facilitated the stocking up of prejudices and accelerated the premature termination of pro-federal efforts. At the present time, the most important task of the Caribbean media includes helping people to better understand the region and each other (Basdeo, 1989, p. 51).

Newspapers have existed in the Commonwealth Caribbean since the eighteenth century. Indeed, some newspapers — such as the *Gleaner*, founded in Jamaica in 1834 and the *Advocate*, founded in Barbados in 1895 — are still being published.

---

[179] Self-description in loose-leaf supplement to the publications of the Committee

[180] Service clubs exclusively for women have been less established in the Commonwealth Caribbean

Nonetheless, the print media became the mass media only with the increasing expansion of the school system, the active participation of the majority of the population in politics and the rise of the black or coloured middle class to leading positions in the economy. Apart from school books, however, the use of printed media still remains limited to a relatively small section of the population. The total daily sales of the largest newspapers in the region — the *Gleaner* (Jamaica); *Nation* and *Advocate* (Barbados); *Express* and *Guardian* (Trinidad and Tobago) — amount to only 250,000 copies. Actual studies of the level of regional news in each newspaper are unknown. And it is hardly possible to evaluate its influence on regional integration.

Even so, the larger newspapers from Barbados and Trinidad are distributed in the neighbouring East Caribbean islands. The Barbadian Nation Publishing Company published, in 1987, the first East Caribbean daily paper, the *EC News*, which, however, had soon to be given up for economic reasons.

A simple visual examination suggests that the position of regional news is higher in Barbadian and Trinidadian daily papers than 10% — 20% of the total editorial content — a percentage not exceeded, on the other hand, in the daily papers in Jamaica, the Bahamas and Guyana. This percentage of regional news should be even less in the weekly newspapers which, in the Eastern Caribbean LDCs, fill the gap of non-existent daily newspapers. As a rule, regional events are reported upon only when a regional meeting takes place there or a member of Government speaks about regional matters.

Moreover, reading most daily and weekly newspapers gives the impression that regional news is considered less as on-going information, than as fillers. Thus, pre-election confrontations in other Caribbean states are reported — but not the election results; or the formation of a Government — nor the elections itself which led to it. Press announcements of important up-coming regional conferences are not followed by any reports about the proceedings of such conferences.

Alternatively, a report is published about the opening session — but not about the results of the conference. CANA despatches are often so published as they had been prepared, with Reuters clients outside the region in mind, that is, with professional distance, as though the events reported on had occurred in far distant places, without reference to the region in which the Caribbean people live.

School books have made the greatest progress in the direction of the regionalisation of the mass media. Since the school system has been increasingly switched to Caribbean exams, the CXC, and the examinations' syllabuses in all areas require knowledge of the geography, economy, society, history, political development and culture of the Caribbean, the school books have lost their Anglocentricity — although the largest Caribbean school books publishers are still subsidiaries of UK firms.

Outside of the school-room, the significance of Caribbean books as mass media is limited. The Caribbean is a small market. External publishers hardly concern themselves with promoting new indigenous *literati*. The publishers of Caribbean books have scarcely any links between themselves. A Caribbean publishers distribution system does not exist. High interest rates make it difficult for the publishers to pay advance royalties and to commission books. The CARICOM book market could absorb a good 5-10 new titles monthly (Mike Henry; Kamau Brathwaite). The CARICOM Secretariat administers the International Standard Book Numbers (ISBN) for the Caribbean regional publishing trade. In 1991 a total of 126 publishers were registered and 126 new titles allocated to ISBNs (Caribbean Community, 1992, pp. 38f).

Almost all significant creative writers in the region have preferred to seek their professional future in the UK, the USA or Canada, where they publish for the big English-speaking market and, therefore, also for the Caribbean. Most books by Caribbean scholars are published by North American or English publishers. For Caribbean authors, the world-wide distribution possibilities for their writings by powerful publishing houses offers not only financial advantages. Additionally, there is also, with corresponding qualification, world-wide renown as well, which, in turn, cements their position in the Caribbean. Their ideas flow into numerous publications of non-Caribbean authors, who write about the region.

The radio is the most significant mass medium in the Caribbean. It fits in with the oral tradition of information transmission; and has been, since the introduction of the transistor, available to practically everybody. Every third person in the Commonwealth Caribbean has been estimated to have a radio receiver (Nettleford, 1987b, p. 7). Rex Nettleford[181] has termed the radio as probably one of the greatest hopes for Caribbean identity (*ibid.*).

Following the failure of the 1958-62 West Indies Federation, individual radio personalities seized the initiative to fill the lack of information with the aid of the radio, at least between neighbouring Anglophone Caribbean states.

Thus, in the 1960s, radio stations in Guyana, Trinidad and Barbados recorded each other's medium wave programmes, which they transmitted either live or in delayed broadcasts. Out of this, there developed in 1970 a common Sunday radio magazine programme for all three radio stations, that is, the *Guyana Broadcasting Service*, *610 Radio Trinidad* and *Caribbean Broadcasting Corporation* (Barbados).

This programme was put together with the help of tapes flown in and, therefore, had a significantly better acoustic quality. The success of the programme, 'Horizons', proved that its producers were right. Using the same format, the state radio stations in the Leeward Islands produced a weekly, half-hour news programme, 'Cross Roads'.

In 1970, fourteen state-owned radio stations of thirteen countries and territories of the Anglophone Caribbean founded the Caribbean Broadcasting Union (CBU) in Georgetown, Guyana. From 1975, private and state-owned radio stations — including stations in the Dutch and French-speaking Antilles, Bermuda, Cuba, Canada, Germany, the Netherlands, United Kingdom, and the USA — joined them. In 1992, the CBU, now based in Barbados, had 36 full and 20 associate members in 22 countries and territories (Abend, 1992, p.15).

[181] Professor for Continuing Studies at UWI, Mona, Pro-Vice Chancellor of the UWI, choreographer with the *Jamaica National Dance Theatre*, head of the *Trade Union Education Institute* at Mona, lecturer at the *Caribbean Institute of Mass Communication (CARIMAC)*, Mona.

From its stated objectives, the CBU is a voluntary organisation of radio stations in the countries of the Caribbean and neighbouring territories. According to its statutes, its tasks include the 'furtherance and development of programmes relevant to the social, economic and cultural well-being of the countries represented within the Union'. Its other responsibilities include staff training; to maintain professional standards and ethics; to represent its members externally; and to collect and disseminate within the Union, information on all aspects of broadcasting (*CBU Constitution*, 2.4.1979).

The CBU, at the very start of its existence, attempted, in its 'Project One', to close the knowledge gap of the Anglophone Caribbean States about each other. A team of producers visited all CARIFTA States as well as the Bahamas and Belize and put together material recorded there over each country in two thirty-minute documentaries dealing with their historical, social, cultural, political and economic development. Thirteen local radio stations subsequently transmitted the programmes for thirteen weeks in each case.

High points of CBU co-operation in radio have been the larger sporting events (especially cricket), the Commonwealth Games, the Pan-American Games, and Caribbean Tennis and Netball Championships to which the CBU members send common teams of commentators and share the transmission costs.

In the political sphere, the CBU has sought to set up the common reporting of CARICOM Heads of Government Conferences, national elections and other rather important political events. In the field of culture, it co-ordinates the common reporting of festivals, carnivals and similar events of Caribbean-wide interest. In 1984, it started its own annual song festival.

The high share of music in the radio programmes — put at an average of 55% in a 1982 UNESCO study ('Rickey Singh and the Caribbean Media', p. 12-13) — offers local musicians and record producers the opportunity to make their products known and sold on a Caribbean-wide basis. Reggae, Calypso and steel bands and their interpreters include compositions from other parts of the region in their repertoire, resulting in a brisk exchange.

Extra regional musical influences do not impair regional musical production, but give it a variety unequalled in the world (Sealy and Malm, 1982, p. 2).

In Montserrat, the Antilles Radio Corporation (ARC) came into existence as the only regionally operating Caribbean radio station in April, 1963. It transmitted at first on a purely commercial basis, as a private sector entity, in English, French, Spanish and Portuguese. With its 200 kW transmitter — the second most powerful in the Eastern Caribbean[182] — it reached the entire Eastern Caribbean, between Guyana and the USVI, during the day-time; and, at night, the Eastern Coast of Mexico and Central America as well as Colombia, Venezuela, the Bahamas and Cuba.

ARC/BBC audience analysis in 1986 estimated the number of regular listeners at 1.9 million, 63% of them being under 25 years old; and 70% having higher school education.

[182] The most powerful being the 500 kW religious transmitter, *Trans World Radio*

The station had a dense network of correspondents in the entire Caribbean as well as in important world capitals. Owing to its impartiality, comprehensive and topical information, it was the top information radio station in the Caribbean. Its information on the economy, special programmes for certain target groups such as the youth and senior citizens, its musical programmes, which catered for the Caribbean-wide distribution of all greatly demanded forms of Caribbean music, as well as regional and international sports events, were highly valued. Call-in programmes were loved. In them, the radio audience from the entire Eastern Caribbean discussed their personal problems and sent greetings to friends and relatives in other parts of the Caribbean.

Radio Antilles won special significance for its bulletins on natural disasters, especially hurricanes. When, in 1979, hurricane 'David' largely devastated Dominica and paralysed the radio station there, Radio Antilles was for days well-nigh the only source of information for the population from and to the outside world. The station was itself severely damaged by hurricane 'Hugo', which devastated Montserrat. The loss of the main antenna accelerated the termination of its programming. The substantial investment needed prevented the re-opening planned for 1990.

While Radio Antilles ceased its Spanish and Portuguese programming shortly after first going on the air, its French programming survived up to the time of its closure. In 1983, the station tried to tear down language barriers by switching to a completely bi-lingual programming. Nevertheless, this led to a dramatic fall in its audience, which made the ARC change back to separate English and French programming, two years later. Moreover, it invited Radio Canada International, the Voice of America and the British Broadcasting Corporation to broadcast their programming daily, at certain times, over its facilities.

In 1972, the *Deutsche Welle* became part-owner of the station — and, later, sole owner. The purchase had been initially made, merely to obtain a relay station for its North American and South American programming. Although the relay station was subsequently relocated to neighbouring Antigua[183], the *Deutsche Welle* continued its ownership of the ARC, until press exposures made it leave the station in 1989[184].

Radio Antilles was the place of training for numerous Caribbean journalists. It had already had concrete plans to construct a radio training centre in Montserrat for the Caribbean Broadcasting Union (CBU) as well as a Caribbean radio and TV production centre, with the half-regional Montserrat-based Antilles Television (Radio Antilles, 1988, p. 38-39).

Owing to the great importance of the station for the region, the OECS Heads of Government decided, in July, 1989, to buy it in order to prevent its closure (*CI* August, 1989, pp. 15ff). But the negotiations, led by the Government of Montserrat, lasted so long that the station provisionally ceased operations on December 29, 1989 (*CI* February, 1990, p. 11).

---

[183]Together with the BBC.

[184]Especially *Der Spiegel* 1989, No.6, pp. 49ff; No 17 p 266, 1990, p.21, p. 16 Auditors reportedly found that DM 60-70 million of German 'taxpayers' money had flowed into the station in 1971-88, without being covered by the legal programming mission of the *Deutsche Welle*

The OECS Heads of Government at their next meeting, in May, 1990, advocated a joint venture with the *BBC* and the Voice of America for re-opening the station (*CI* July 1990, p. 14). The *Deutsche Welle* sold the ARC to the Government of Montserrat, which, together with the BBC, formed a Management Company. Late in 1993 Radio Antilles resumed transmission.

Up to now, the foreign portion of the texts of the programming of radio stations in the region has been small, ranging between 2.3% and 9% of total hours of programming in six stations, according to a 1987 CBU survey. The most-used foreign material came from the BBC, the *Deutsche Welle*, the Voice of America, UN Radio and the OAS (Knaack 1987, 14A-15A).

In the USVI and Montserrat, radio stations have been set up, which serve merely as relay stations for US audio programmes received from satellites. During the last few years, about one-third of the transmission time of the English-language programme of Radio Antilles has come from programmes from the BBC, the *Deutsche Welle*, Voice of America and the Canadian Broadcasting Corporation. Knaack (*ibid.*) predicts that, in view of the high production costs of the stations' own programmes and small cost of using North American satellite radio programmes, the trend will be towards using imported programming here as well.

This already occurs through seven radio stations of religious organisations located in the English-speaking Caribbean. Among them is Trans World Radio, located in Bonaire and as already mentioned, possessing the most powerful transmitter, one of 500 kW, in the region. Its programmes are produced by numerous different organisations and churches; and are co-ordinated from the headquarters of the sponsoring society in Chatham/USA (Knaack, 1988, p. 20A).

The lucrative offer of the Californian Protestant radio station, Trinity Broadcasting Network, to the Government of St. Lucia to install a television station there with a twenty-four hour programme, which should also reach viewers in St. Vincent and the Grenadines as well as Barbados, was rejected. The local Roman Catholic Archbishop called to mind experiences with televangelists in the USA and announced intensive opposition. Jamaica's High Commissioner in Trinidad had, in this context, pointed to the threat of political interference. Some foreign evangelists had a tendency to presume to pass judgements on non-religious matters on which they had no information and even less knowledge (*CC* December, 1987, p. 12; January, 1988, p.13).

While radio can build on the oral tradition of Caribbean residents, Nascimento (1981, p. 52) acknowledges, as the foundation for television in the Caribbean, a visual literacy, which could make the medium into an important promoter of developmental interests. In his view, television is the most effective mass media tool for formal education supporting national development; it is rather more able than are other media technologies to make people aware of their own natural environment — with the hinterland, the traditional cultural forms, the creation of culture, sports activities, political events and developmental projects.

Television, he holds, can become an important instrument of national unity, in that it arouses in people the illusion of closeness to the scene of the action (*ibid.* p. 54).

TV programming at the start of the 1960s was rather modest. In Trinidad and Tobago, Barbados and Jamaica, local TV programmes were transmitted — originally in black-and-white, but later in colour — on an hourly basis. The residents of neighbouring islands could also watch the programmes, if they had viable TV antennae on their TV sets. In some cases, collective antennae were installed and used commercially. In the Bahamas, several US TV programmes could be viewed. With the increasing number of TV sets and also, in part, owing to the poor attractiveness of the State-monopolised TV programming (Brown, 1990), the pressure to have alternative programmes grew much faster than programmes could be produced locally. The need therefore arose for the importation of foreign programmes, which were obtainable at a low cost and were attractive for the advertising sectors of the economy. There began a form of cultural invasion and Americanisation (Nettleford, 1987b) which were aided by the English language shared by the USA and the Anglophone Caribbean, and the NTSC colour TV system used in the two areas.

With the appearance of directly receivable satelite programmes, Caribbean owners of satellite dishes were able to choose between hundreds of US and Canadian TV programmes and those transmitted by the local TV station. By the end of 1989, in Jamaica alone, the number of such satellite dishes had risen to almost 14,000 (*CU* December 1989, pp. 13-14).

The competition led to local TV stations significantly increasing their portion of foreign programming. Moreover, they adopted the production style of the locally-produced programmes to that of US and UK ones[185]. Further competition to local TV was provided by the VCR and the swiftly-growing number of video rental outlets[186].

In the nineties, the media scene in the Caribbean has become more complex than ever. New radio and TV stations have been established in large numbers. It is not easy to estimate how such a multiplicity of media can be financed by advertisement, considering the very small domestic markets. In Trinidad and Tobago at the end of 1993, there were three daily newspapers, four weeklies, one newspaper published twice weekly, a dozen radio stations, three TV stations and four cable stations, for 1.2 million inhabitants. Moreover the media compete for qualified personnel.

In 1987, Aggrey Brown[187], commissioned by UNESCO, studied the trends in TV programming in the Anglophone Caribbean. He found that the imported portion of TV programmes had risen by an average of 10% — that is 1% *per annum* — in 1976-1986 in Jamaica (JBC-TV), Barbados (CBC), Trinidad and Tobago (TTT) and Antigua (ABS), in each case. Barbados (92%) had the

[185]Thus, the Atlanta-based CNN has become the role model for local news presentation, where whole CNN news clips are now used directly.

[186]Already in 1984, over 129,000 VCRs were counted in Jamaica, i.e one per four households on average Almost 56% of Jamaican households had TV sets, averaging 1.3 TV sets per household. Almost 96% of Jamaican households had a radio in 1984, with an average of almost 1.8 radio sets per household (*Jamaica All-Media Survey* 1984, p. 85).

[187]Director of the UWI's Caribbean Institute of Mass Communication.

highest amount of foreign programming, followed by Antigua (91%); Trinidad and Tobago (89%) and Jamaica (76%) (*CI* May, 1988, p. 15; and Knaack 1987, p. 22A).

The portion of foreign TV programming is even higher in other parts of the Caribbean. On the smaller Anglophone Caribbean islands, satellite programmes, received locally via collective antennae, are made available, via cable or radio, to paying subscribers. The local promoters do not always honour their obligation to produce a certain portion of their programming locally, or regularly to make time available to the Government Information Service.

Having regard to the fact that local TV systems transmit programmes for only 10-15 hours daily, but the TV cable systems, with 6-13 different channels, do so round the clock, Knaack estimates the portion of foreign TV programming appearing on Caribbean TV screens at over 95%. With Aggrey Brown, he is, based on another 1983 UNESCO study, of the view that the Caribbean is the region in the world most penetrated by foreign TV programmes.

The single exception in the region was Guyana. It refused for a long time to introduce television, because the Government feared not being able to control the growing programming needs — thereby exposing the country to 'communication imperialism' (Nascimento 1981, p. 49). In the course of the last few years, foreign hard currency shortage has become so acute that the Government has continued to decline to introduce this medium. This has been despite the fact — as Nascimento found, back in 1981 — that enough foreign programmes would have existed to have satisfied the Government's requirements for a development-promoting news-reporting policy. The Government has not been able to prevent the massive importation of VCRs and video-cassettes (Lent, 1989, pp. 175-76) and the establishment of several pirate stations. Since 1988 there exists a state-owned TV station (*The Caribbean Handbook 1993/94*, p.132). Over the past four years Guyana has rapidly caught up with the other Caribbean territories. It now has more than ten TV stations beaming about 24hrs of American TV to households.

The criticism of the overloading of Caribbean TV screens with foreign media programming has been general. Thus, Demas has found that most foreign electronic media were 'irrelevant' and 'actually harmful', through the contents of their programming, in that they created false values[188] and perceptions.

This programming introduced, Demas has held, North American consumption standards and aspirations in the Commonwealth Caribbean, which owing to the economic plight of the region, cannot be met for 'hundreds of years' (1975, pp. 20-21).

Often, the advertisement in the US TV programmes, directly down-loaded via satellite and cable, refer to products not obtainable locally. A demand is therefore created, the satisfaction of which runs counter to the import-substitution policy of the Caribbean Community. Customs barriers no longer protect local products from remaining[189] unused in cupboards.

---

[188]Please see, in this context, Lashley's study (1991) of school children in Trinidad and Tobago

[189]E g the sales difficulties of 'Bata' shoes and 'Zenith' TV sets. Production has had to be terminated

Anglophone Caribbean television stations find it difficult to increase their portion of local programme content, despite the existence of a significant demand for locally produced series, such as Jamaica's 'Oliver at Large', and 'No Boundaries' and 'Gayelle' from Trinidad and Tobago. Most of these stations are funded entirely by advertising income. Given the small size of the domestic markets from which this income is derived, these stations quickly reach the limit of their financial possibilities — especially since they have to compete with other forms of advertising (Wint 1987).

Discussions over a New International Communication Order serve no purpose, if the developing countries do not have access to the technology which enables them to disseminate information. That is why they wish to be in control of media technology, and especially the use of satellites, themselves (Aggrey Brown, 1983). The efforts of the CBU to promote the exchange of programmes between Caribbean countries — and, in this way, to increase the portion of domestically-produced programmes at an acceptable cost — must be strengthened. The pre-condition for this is, however, that the CBU be given greater support within the region[190].

With regard to television, the CBU, from the very beginning had endeavoured to increase the portion of locally-produced programmes, *vis-à-vis* the overwhelming supply of US programmes. The CBU tried at first to gain influence through a series of annual Caribbean film trade fairs and the common negotiation of TV rights for sport events.

But it failed, finally, owing to the varying demands of the participating TV stations (Rudder 1985). Technical limitations are more noticeable in TV than radio, with regard to the exchange and dissemination of programmes and the incomparably higher production costs. Owing to their small incomes, however, most Commonwealth Caribbean television stations are not in a position to significantly increase the locally-produced portion of their programmes with the same production standards as those of their rivals in the industrialised countries. Nonetheless, the CBU wishes to prove that a higher portion of local programme is possible by pooling the resources of its members — and that regional TV programmes can even become pronounced public favourites. Moreover, the CBU wishes to contribute to resuscitating Caribbean identity, to promote regional integration and put a brake on the one-sided flow of information (Abend 1989a).

Providing the rest of the world with reports on Caribbean developments from a Caribbean point of view should be a further aim (Abend 1989b). As with CANA, these objectives were achieved with German assistance. The Friedrich-Ebert-Stiftung, long linked to the CBU through an advisory relationship and the financing of training and seminar programmes, sent an adviser and provided financial help in the creation of the Caribbean Television Exchange. After only eight months of such work, it succeeded, in 1989, in:

[190] This has to do with the payment pattern of the affiliated stations for the programmes received and their readiness to participate voluntarily in the exchange of programmes.

- creating a daily TV news exchange programme, *Caribvision*, from Mondays to Fridays, with between five and nine news segments, which is sent to four countries via satellite and a further four by courier service;
- establishing a weekly, half-hour, courier-delivered TV magazine (i.e. *Caribscope*) transmitted in eighteen countries of the region and which, within a few months, became one of the most popular television programmes, consisting of items from the participating countries collated in the CBU-co-ordination centre in Barbados, whence it is sent by courier to the recipients;
- developing a CBU technical staff, which takes over the reporting of rather large regional events that cannot be adequately serviced by individual TV stations;
- making efforts to establish a Caribbean-wide, satellite-supported system of programming exchange;
- making preparations for a link with African TV stations; and
- improving generally, the regional TV infrastructure (Abend 1989b).

The CBU TV programmes exchange system experienced its 'baptism of fire' at the July, 1989, CARICOM Summit in Grenada. For the first time in the history of CARICOM, did the effort succeed in providing television stations in all thirteen CARICOM Member States with comprehensive preliminary coverage and daily reports of the Conference. The CBU also provided comprehensive reports of the 1989 ACP/EC Conference in Barbados and dealt primarily with Lomé Treaty projects in different Caribbean countries. Special programmes featured the Week of the Handicapped, International Women's Day and Adult Literacy Day. Thanks to the new transmission opportunities, the 1989 Caribbean Football Championships also became a special event.

In 1989 the CBU team was one of the first to report on the devastation by hurricane 'Hugo' in Montserrat. In 1990 CBU kept the Caribbean up-to-date with the attempted *coup d'état* in Trinidad. 'To this day, Caribscope remains one of the best-produced, most popular regional programmes ever to be broadcast on TV screens around the region,' Debra Johnson, former programme editor, wrote (*M&K forum* (Bonn, Germany), June 1993, p.6).

Bermuda, Curacao, Aruba and Suriname are among the countries in which Caribscope is transmitted regularly. Since mid-1993 Curaçao has also been participating. The exchange with non-Anglophone countries is hampered by language barriers — and, in the case of the Francophone areas, by the additional problem of the incompatibility of the technical i.e. the two colour TV systems involved.

In the Eastern Caribbean, CBU together with the private station Helen Television St. Lucia (HTS) — the first station to be connected with a US Domestic Satellite — established the Eastern Caribbean Television Network (ECTN) comprising the TV stations in six OECS States and Saint Maarten. Via the moderately-priced access to the satellite these TV stations can now broadcast news and features from the sub-region, enriched by material from outside, supplied by the CBU. The Windward Islands Constituent Assembly was broadcast live via this satellite.

The CBU is planning an independent satellite system of its own. This system shall make it possible to directly receive programmes of CBU members within the region and beyond. In this way, the General-Secretary of the CBU, Leo DeLeon, hopes, the integrative effect of broadcasting will be strengthened and cultural penetration virtually reversed. Moreover, Caribbean emigrants should be able to keep in touch with their home region (*DG* 18.6.1993).

CARICOM also makes some efforts to participate in regional Television. At the CARICOM Summit in July 1991, in St. Kitts, the Heads of Government decided on the establishment of a Regional Television Hook-up Facility which would allow the people of the Region to witness events taking place in various Member States. Within less than one year the audiences in all CARICOM States should have had the opportunity to watch the TV programmes of all the other CARICOM countries. However, since the European Union as potential donor preferred to assist the CBU in its efforts, the CARICOM Secretariat for the time being laid aside its own plans (Abend 1993, p.8).

Despite the existence of television, the cinema in the Commonwealth Caribbean still has a large number of patrons. US films are shown there almost exclusively. Regionally produced films, which are also commercially interesting, such as the Jamaican feature film, *The Harder They Come*, are exceptions.[191] Attempts by the Jamaican Government to interest foreign film producers in co-productions in Jamaica by means of a film production programme, were not particularly successful.

The organisation of indigenous news sources is closely linked with the creation of the Caribbean media. Tim Hector, the Antiguan journalist and politician, has found (in: *The Media and the Caribbean State* p. 9) that the American news agencies, Associated Press, and United Press International, the British news agency, Reuters, as well as its French counterparts, Agence France Press, account for a total of 90% of the news distributed by the media in the Caribbean.

The Caribbean News Agency (CANA) was created as an alternative to the dominant news agencies. As early as in 1967, the then CARIFTA Heads of Government Conference had demanded, in a resolution, the creation of a regional news agency, because regional thinking and consciousness are an essential basis for the effective working of regional institutions (Mayers 1985).

The CARIFTA Secretariat requested UNESCO to do a feasibility study for setting up a Caribbean news agency. The UNESCO team of experts recommended that, parallel to the establishment of the free trade zone (i.e. CARIFTA), installations for the development of a regional mass media structure should be created (Mayers 1985; Marlene Cuthbert 1979).

After nine years of preparation and further UNESCO studies, the CANA came into existence on January 7, 1976, with at first fifteen private and public Commonwealth Caribbean media houses as shareholders. The new agency took over the Caribbean office of Reuters in Barbados.

---

[191] *The Harder They Come*, was a cult film of great significance of the late 1970s for the development of the consciousness of the ghetto youth, the spread of Rasta culture and the African identity of young Caribbean intellectuals Extremely expensive one-off marketing was necessary for this film, which was very successful in both the Caribbean and normal cinemas in the industrialised countries, for the producer, Perry Henzell, was left to himself and had made only a few copies available

CANA is a private news agency. Governments are excluded from shareholding. But Governments can exert influence through State-controlled media, which are shareholders in CANA. CANA guarantees its independence by the fact that neither the shareholders nor the Board of Directors of the agency can control its news policy. A supervisory Board, consisting of the UWI Vice-Chancellor, the Secretary-General of the Caribbean Community and the Chief Justice of Barbados, further ensures editorial independence.

The English-language service of CANA at first supplied 5,000-6,000 words of Caribbean news and 15,000 words news from outside the Caribbean daily. With financial assistance from UNESCO and the Government of the Federal Republic of Germany, CANA increased its regional news service daily to 15,000 words by 1991. The agency defined as its principal objective, the preparation of an effective and independent news service through offering fair, comprehensive, accurate and impartial reports on events and developments in the Caribbean, paying particular attention to the public interest (CANA: Self-description).

The network of CANA correspondents extends over all the states and territories of the Anglophone Caribbean, the Netherlands Antilles and Suriname. Almost all print and electronic media in the Caribbean as well as embassies, regional bodies and international organisations in Latin America, are subscribers to the radio and wire services provided by CANA.

In addition to on-going reports and features on political, social and cultural questions, trade, industry, tourism and business, CANA also provides sport reports constantly. Moreover, it offers a special daily international economic service from Reuters for banks and firms. Since 1989, there has existed CANA Business, a monthly CANA circular for the world of finance and business.

In June, 1984, CANA, with German and UNESCO assistance, was able to set up the radio service, CANARADIO, which has since enabled the agency to supply all Radio stations linked to it with news, reports, features and original interviews from the entire region. Since February, 1991, CANA with assistance of CEDP, offers a monthly radio programme *CARICOM Focus* that covers various topics of interest in the area of trade development and promotion.

In February, 1985, CANA relocated to a new building in Barbados. At the opening ceremony, then Barbados' Prime Minister, Tom Adams, declared that, had a news agency like CANA existed at the time of the 1958-62 West Indies Federation, the prejudices and misunderstandings which led to the break-up of the Federation, could possibly have been avoided (CANA Report of 8.2.1985). CANA, owing to its independence and the quality of its journalism, ranks as one of the most successful regional news agencies in the Third World.

CANA is, in the view of Marlene Cuthbert (1981, p. 33) the model of an agency, which writes news from a regional perspective and selects foreign news on the criteria of need and regional interest, whereby it is obliged to maintain objectivity and professionalism. CANA selects news reports out of Reuters' world news offering under 'Caribbean perspective'; and then transmits it to its subscribers in the Caribbean. Conversely, Reuters receives the Caribbean news offered by CANA for it to make selections for its world news service.

The Italian Inter Press Service (IPS) — another news agency with a Third World orientation — maintains a network of correspondents in the Caribbean. IPS was allowed to replace CANA in Guyana, after the Guyanese state party media had 'punished' CANA for several years by withdrawing its subscription, owing to CANA's dissemination of views opposed to the then Burnham Government. For four years now CANA has been back in Guyana.

The most important political monthly publication in the region was *Caribbean Contact*, which had been published from December, 1971 to August, 1994 in Barbados by the *Caribbean Conference of Churches* (CCC). The newsmagazine, which had a newspaper format, and expressly did not regard itself as the mouthpiece of the CCC, had the following editorial policy:

'1. To provide analysis of Caribbean issues, and world issues which have implications for the Caribbean, from the Christian and other perspectives;
2. To stimulate thought and action on issues of development of the Caribbean person;
3. To promote a spirit of Caribbean unity, by fostering among Caribbean people an understanding of the issues that effect them all;
4. To report on the ecumenical scene, raise issues concerning it and, generally, to promote a spirit of Christian unity;
5. To provide its readers regularly with accurate and up-to-date information concerning the Churches' involvement in favour of Caribbean development, especially disseminating available information on programmes of the CCC and on CCC-sponsored projects;
6. To expose Caribbean people, and especially those of the immediate Church constituency, to new perspectives in human development and to sensitise them to participation in experiments which have the all-round development of the Caribbean person in view.'

The publication regarded itself rather as a type of service provider for the Caribbean and entrusted its financing to church agencies abroad[192]. It regarded itself as the single still-surviving 'alternative medium' in the region. Since 1990, it had appeared only bi-monthly (*CC* May-June, 1990, p. 3). In August 1994 *Caribbean Contact* ceased publication due to financial constraints and, as its editor wrote in the last issue, because 'there were too many forces in the Caribbean and in the Caribbean Conference of Churches (CCC) itself which over the years have been mobilised against the publication' (*CC* August 1994, p. 2).

Problems of financing, caused mainly by low circulation, costly operations, different currencies, language difficulties and a limited selection of writers, narrowly limit the multiplicity of regional publications (McDonald, 1990)[193]. Even the official CARICOM publication, *CARICOM Perspective*, appears at

[192] *Inter alia*, the Hamburg-based Evangelische Missionswerk (Germany)

[193] Significant English-language Caribbean journals, in addition to *Caribbean Affairs* and CARICOM PERSPECTIVE, are the culture magazines *Bim* (Barbados); *Kyk-over-al* (Guyana); *The New Voices* (Trinidad); *Journal of West Indian Literature* (Barbados); *Jamaica Journal* (Jamaica); *Banja* (Barbados); *The Caribbean Writers* (St Croix), *Carib* (Jamaica), and the scholarly publications. *Caribbean Quarterly* (Jamaica) and *Archeology and Anthropology* (Guyana) (*Cf*. Ian McDonald, 1990, p. 127)

most two or three times annually instead of six times — contrary to the information on its masthead.

Good conditions for regular publication and international dissemination seem to exist for the bi-monthly journal, *Caribbean Affairs*, which has been published in Port-of-Spain, Trinidad, since 1987, though its publisher Owen Baptiste is lamenting over dwindling advertising support (*CA* 7.2, p.1). The publication is backed mainly by Trinidadian companies, among them the financially strong and regionally committed publishers, Trinidad Express Newspapers Ltd. The journal has an impressive Editorial Board consisting of scholars and other personalities from the public life of the entire Commonwealth Caribbean. Its editorial policy is to publish articles representative of contemporary Caribbean-related thinking. The views published should contribute to informing readers more about the region, which differs as much in its culture and thought as it does in its people and their languages (*Caribbean Affairs* 3:2).

Since 1990 *Caribbean Week* has been published bi-weekly with reports about the whole of the Caribbean. The newspaper is edited in Barbados and printed in Florida/USA.

All significant printed information services on the Caribbean — e.g. *Caribbean Insight* (London), *Caribbean Report,* (Latin American Regional Reports, London), *Caribbean UPDATE,* (Maplewood, N.J., USA), *The Economist Intelligence Unit* (London) appear outside of the region and are oriented towards the piled-up information of foreign persons interested in the Caribbean.

Caribbean Review, a quarterly now published in Miami, Florida, but founded in Puerto Rico in 1969, concerns itself with 'creating greater mutual understanding among the Americas by articulating the culture and ideals of the Caribbean and Latin America and emigrating groups originating therefrom' (16.3-4, p.2). For some time now the magazine has ceased publication — temporarily, as the editors informed their subscribers.

This journal, in collaboration with the Caribbean Studies Association, which is also based in Miami, annually awards a prize to a personality who has contributed to promoting intellectual life in the Caribbean, regardless of the field of activity, ideology, national origin or place of residence of the awardee.

The Caribbean Institute of Mass Communications (CARIMAC) has developed into the most important regional training centre for journalists in the Caribbean outside the workplace (Tracey 1985). The Institute was founded in 1974 as a Department of the Faculty of Arts and General Study of the UWI at its Mona Campus (in Jamaica). Its aim is to give its students the practical and theoretical foundation which should put them in a position — in the words of CARIMAC Director, Aggrey Brown — to play a central role in the development of the region.

CARIMAC offers its female and male students from the Caribbean, depending on their previous education, a one-year or three-year diploma course in mass communication. Technical courses are divided into five-week modules which are open also to media personnel unable to spend a full academic year at the University. Modules are offered in audio-visual production, film production, print journalism, and radio and TV production[194].

With UNESCO support, CARIMAC developed a training programme for national instructors of young talent, who should train upcoming publishers at home. The aim is to promote the publication of all types of printed material at the regional and national level (*CP* 38:33).

The initiative to found CARIMAC came from the Jamaican Government, which financed the building and provided the equipment for the training of print journalists. The German Friedrich-Ebert-Stiftung, UNESCO and USAID, gave essential help in the 'birth' of the Institute.

The UWI has a Printing School to train printing personnel. The Caribbean Publishing and Broadcasting Association (CPBA) and the Caribbean Association of Media Workers (CAMWORK) see themselves as self-protection and lobby organisations. The CPBA was founded in the 1960s to represent the interests of the proprietors of the print media and radio. Natural and legal owners of newspapers, journals, news agencies, radio and television stations or other mass media in the Caribbean belong to it. The task of the CPBA is to promote the exchange of information and experience, with the aim of improving the supply of news, to reduce the costs of collecting and disseminating information and to promote (or hinder) legal and other measures concerning the exchange of information (*CPBA Rules* 1974).

Important impulses to found CANA came from the CPBA. The latter, working closely with the Miami-based Inter-American Press Association (IAPA), came out in favour of Press freedom in the area. The largely privately organised Press — unlike most State-controlled radio and TV stations — sees itself in a watchman's role *vis-à-vis* the Governments. Especially the largest newspapers of the Commonwealth Caribbean i.e. the *Gleaner* in Jamaica, *Advocate* and *Nation* in Barbados, and *Guardian* and *Express* in Trinidad, made their common medium influence felt on several occasions against infringements of Press freedom e.g. through attacks against Maurice Bishop's People's Revolutionary Government (PRG) in Grenada and the People's National Congress (PNC) regime in Guyana (Deosaran 1984b).

The collaboration between newspaper publishing companies went so far that financially strong ones came to the help of those in difficulties in other parts of the Caribbean through advice, financial injections and acquisitions. Model examples of that were the delivery of paper to the weekly, *Catholic Standard*, which was pushed to the wall by the Guyanese Government, and, after the US-Caribbean intervention, to the *Grenadian Voice*, which was banned by Bishop after seizing power[195]. Sometime CPBA and CANA Chairman, Ken Gordon, of the *Trinidad Express*, to name him in particular, successfully helped diverse newspapers, which had got into economic difficulties, by the means of a team of staff-members of the *Express*. He also helped the *Jamaican Daily News*, which had fallen on hard times and was finally closed in 1983, as well as the *Chronicle* (Dominica), *Tobago News*, *The Vincentian* and *Stabroek News* (Guyana). The

[194]CARIMAC self-description in a 1982 brochure.

[195]The then CPBA Chairman called on Caribbean firms to support the *Grenadian Voice* through courtesy ads in its reconstruction (*DG* 15.11.1983, p.1)

Express newspaper group moreover participated in the ownership of the *Voice of St. Lucia*, the *Torchlight* (Grenada), banned under Bishop, the Jamaican daily *Observer*, and the *Nation*. Printeries, radio and television stations, newspapers and periodicals all belong to the Barbadian Nation Group of Companies. After the acquisition of more shares and of TV licenses the *Express* Newspaper Group was renamed *Caribbean Communications Network* (CCN). Together with other Caribbean media houses the combine tries to build its own television network, and secured for itself, among others, the world-wide exclusive rights for the transmission of the Trinidadian Carnival (*cf.* Abend 1993, p.8).

The mixed Trinidadian-Barbadian-US group, McEnearney-Alstons, owns the *Guardian* and the *Evening News* in Trinidad, the *Advocate*, in Barbados and the private *Trinidad Broadcasting Company* (*Cf.* Lent, 1991; and *WG* 11.6.1991, p. 16).

The Caribbean Press Council (CPC) came into being in 1976, at the initiative of the CPBA, with the aim of keeping the character and objectives of the media in the Caribbean in conformity with high professional standards. To this end, it would accept complaints from persons and organisations against the behaviour of the media and make recommendations to settle such matters.

But the CPC lacks the means to enforce the implementation of its recommendations. Its members are representatives of the CPBA and media workers in the Caribbean, under the chairmanship of an acknowledged Caribbean personality from outside the media (*CPC: Articles of Constitution* 1981). In order to be able to process complaints at the national level as well against the behaviour of the media, the CPC founded national committees everywhere in the Commonwealth Caribbean ('Background Paper' 1982).

Increasing pressure of the Governments on the media houses and individual journalists brought journalists from twenty countries in the region, at a meeting in Puerto Rico in 1983, to create their own organisation, the Caribbean Association of Media Workers (CAMWORK). Its primary objectives were supposed to be to hurry to the aid of journalists and their national associations, when necessary; and to promote and 'organise' Caribbean consciousness (*Catholic Standard*, Georgetown, Guyana, 5.6.1983, pp. 1 and 4).

Six national organisations of media workers participated in its official founding in October, 1985, in St. Lucia. In a declaration, they underscored the need to maintain the political and cultural sovereignty of the region and the strengthening of Caribbean unity — given the growing cultural penetration through satellite technology, invasion of the radio waves and also a climate of increasing hostilities against media workers (Rickey Singh, 1985c)[196].

In the field of telecommunications, the Commonwealth Caribbean was almost completely dependent technically on the outside world. The most influential operator in regional telecommunications is the UK multi-national firm Cable & Wireless, with shares in numerous national Commonwealth Caribbean telecommunications companies. The monopoly of the company for the use of satellites was terminated in 1991, when Helen Television St. Lucia

[196]CAMWORK chairman, Rickey Singh, a Guyanese, was Editor-in-chief of *Caribbean Contact* (1974-83) and had his work permit withdrawn in Trinidad and Barbados, owing to unpopular reporting (*Cf.* Lent, 1990, pp 92-96).

(HTS) succeeded in getting a satellite link to a US domestic satellite. Via those links and radio relay the CBU and others want to realise the transmission of events on TV without using the services of *Cable & Wireless* and save money.

Eight such Companies[197] have joined together in the Caribbean Association of National Telecommunications Organisations (CANTO). CANTO meets yearly to consider possibilities for regional co-operation (Lent 1989, pp. 159-160).

The International Telecommunications Union (ITU) has founded in the Caribbean a regional Caribbean Telecommunications Union (CTU) with its head office in Trinidad (Caribbean Community, 1990, p. 56). The founding of the CTU resulted from a meeting of the Standing CARICOM Committee of the Ministers responsible for Transport in February, 1986, in Barbados. The CTU has the task of co-ordinating the exchange of information between the Administrations responsible therefor, in order to harmonise the technical developments and standards and to support its members in the creation of telecommunications industries (Basdeo, 1989, pp. 51ff).

The Caribbean Postal Union (CPU), which facilitates postal services within the Caribbean, arranges the training of post office workers, offers central services and should make possible international collaboration in agreement with the Universal Postal Union in Bern, has long been in preparation. As far back as in 1977, the Postmasters-General of the Anglophone Caribbean, at a meeting in St. Lucia, demanded the creation of the CPU with membership open to both CARICOM Member States and other territories of the Anglophone Caribbean.

2.3.4.12 Transportation and Traffic

CARICOM bodies have intensively concerned themselves with transportation links between the widely scattered islands since the very founding of the Community. In 1961, during the existence of the Federal Government, the West Indies Shipping Corporation (WISCO) took over intra-regional shipping and initially serviced the islands of the Commonwealth Caribbean with two passenger-and-freight ships donated by the Canadian Government. In 1976, a container ship was added.

The two original ships were replaced in 1983, with the help of the then European Community. WISCO served all CARICOM Member States, with the exception of Belize and the Bahamas[198](*CP* 29, p.6).

In January, 1992, WISCO had to cease its operations, owing to its excessive debts (*CI* February, 1992, p. 11). In August, 1992, it was replaced by Carifreight, a joint venture between Caribbean firms and a French shipping line (*CI* July, 1992, p. 11).

Air transportation has been a constant bone of contention among the CARICOM Member States. With the arrival of mass tourism in the Caribbean, arrangements had to be made with the Governments of the tourists' countries and the latters' airlines. Agreements led to mutual landing rights, which the

[197]From Antigua, Bahamas, Barbados, Belize, Guyana, Grenada, Jamaica and Trinidad and Tobago

[198]Belize was linked to the WISCO ships by another shipping line

Caribbean Governments ceded either to their own national airlines or to foreign airlines that they designated for this purpose as national carriers.

In 1961, the Government of Trinidad and Tobago bought from British Overseas Airways Corporation (BOAC) the regional subsidiary, British West Indian Airways (BWIA). As this was done without consultation with the other Unit Governments of the then West Indies Federation, the Trinidadians met with great reservations, upon offering to sell them shares in BWIA and wishing to make it the only regional airline (Payne, 1980, p. 114).

Despite the recommendations of a working committee of the conference of West Indian Heads of Government to make BWIA, the passenger airline, and Guyana Airways Corporation, the freight airline, no agreement was reached. Governments of the larger Commonwealth Caribbean States established airlines on paper, which did not even have a single aeroplane of their own and, therefore, had to lease planes from other airlines.

Jamaica founded Air Jamaica, which plied the lucrative routes between the islands and the USA in leased planes. In 1976, Jamaica used funds from Trinidad, earmarked as development aid, to purchase an expensive building in London, for its High Commission — and also to purchase the first aeroplanes for Air Jamaica, which, in the following years offered serious competition to BWIA (*cf.* 'Troubles in a Paper Paradise'). The two airlines suffered heavy losses. Barbados' national airline, Caribbean Airways, also made no profits. Since 1991, the Government of Jamaica has attempted to privatise Air Jamaica and was successful only in October 1994. The Caribbean Air Cargo Company (CariCargo), which was jointly owned by Barbados and Trinidad and Tobago, was so heavy indebted that one of its two planes had to be auctioned in October, 1989 (*CI* November, 1989, p. 8). It was wound up in 1993 with heavy losses for the two countries involved.

The third CARICOM Summit in Ocho Rios, Jamaica, requested its Member States to strike agreements over air transport collaboration and gather their thoughts over all aspects of the nationalisation of passenger and freight transport in the region (*CP* 16, p.15). The reason for the clashes over air transportation is the increasing dependence of Caribbean States on tourism. Of prime importance is attracting a flood of tourists through reasonably-priced direct flights. In tourism, almost all Commonwealth Caribbean States rival each other with similar offers to the same clientele.

Together, the CARICOM countries succeeded in changing an International Civil Aviation Organisation (ICAO) rule and obtaining acceptance of the principle of designated carrier. By this means, BWIA has been able to become the national airline for several Eastern Caribbean States, thereby acquiring lucrative flying routes to the USA, Canada and Europe (*Time for Action*, p. 43). At the 14th CARICOM Summit in July, 1993, in the Bahamas, the Heads of Government agreed on the fundamental principle that the five national airlines of the Community should be converted into one private airline (*CI* August, 1993, p. 5).

Collaboration in air transport within the smaller Eastern Caribbean territories has been particularly problematic. In August, 1974, the British airline, Court Lines, failed with its Leeward Islands Air Transport Company (LIAT), which had almost monopolised the air routes between them. Only a bridging loan from the Venezuelan Government prevented the total collapse of air traffic. LIAT became the property of the Governments of the Eastern Caribbean CARICOM members (with the exception of Trinidad and Tobago), Jamaica and Guyana (Payne, 1980, pp. 197-198), and served twenty-two Caribbean islands in 1985, partly competing against other airlines (*CP* 29, p.7). In 1988, after two years of heavy losses, it allegedly made a profit for the first time, with its eighteen planes and a total passenger load of 610,000 (*CU* July, 1989, pp. 4ff). Other reports speak of profits in 1981-84, and of losses in 1985-90, which constantly-changed managements tried to stop (Espeut 1991).

In July, 1992, the CARICOM Heads of Government decided to privatise LIAT (*CI* August, 1992, p. 4). One year later, in July 1993, they received proposals by James Mitchell on the privatisation. They agreed to the formation of a Regional Air Carrier by January 1995 comprising existing national airlines of the Community and an appropriate foreign air carrier.

On 1st August, 1994, after another decision of the CARICOM Heads of Government, the governments of Antigua and Barbuda and of Trinidad and Tobago took over the management of LIAT until its privatisation could be finalised (*CI* August 1994, p. 2). The operations of LIAT and BWIA were to be integrated with the intention to make it the common regional carrier. At their Inter-Sessional meeting in February, 1995, in Belize the Heads of Government agreed in principle to a joint proposal of the governments of Antigua and Barbuda and Trinidad and Tobago for the privatisation of LIAT on the basis of majority ownership by regional investors including employees, and the forgiveness by the airline of the subventions owed by the shareholder governments in exchange for the assumption of the liabilities of the airline by the shareholder governments.

However, five governments, Barbados, Dominica, Grenada, St. Lucia and St.Vincent and the Grenadines, supported the launching of a new airline, named Carib Express, backed by regional private investors and British Airways (*CI* October, 1994, p. 11; November 1994, p. 11). This caused strong opposition by some member parties of SCOPE and by the Antiguan government who have insisted that BWIA and LIAT should be made viable instead (Doyle-Marshall 1994, p. 11).

2.4 Sub-regional Co-operation

2.4.1 The Organisation of Eastern Caribbean States (OECS)

Sub-regional co-operation at State level within the Commonwealth Caribbean takes place both bilaterally and in the Organisation of Eastern Caribbean States (OECS). Sub-regional co-operation within the OECS is conditioned by:

1. *Limited size*: 528,000 inhabitants and 2,910 km^{2}, or half the population and less than half the land mass of Trinidad or 25% of Jamaica's[199].
2. *High population growth*, unmatched by similar growth in the number of jobs and/or cultivated land, which could mean a further 150,000 adults by the year 2000 and a 100% increase in the 25-49 year-old — necessitating average annual GNP growth considerably above that given in the 1988 study by Professor Compton Bourne[200]; or a 2% average annual per head GNP growth in real terms (Palmer, 1984, pp. 49ff), which has rarely been reached in the OECS; moreover, there is only a limited probability of a uniform distribution of the growth in income on the entire population.
3. *Limited natural resources*, that consist essentially of their landscape, geographical location and climate which are most suitable for the very fragile economic sector that is tourism, apart from cultivable land and fishing grounds; and hardly have more to offer in terms of natural resources.
4. *Susceptibility to natural disasters*, which have constantly hit the territories as a whole, owing to their limited size, such as hurricanes and earthquakes in the entire region and volcanoes in St. Vincent — with hurricanes, after directly hitting an island, paralysing agriculture and tourism for a certain time and considerably impairing the infrastructure; tropical rainfall increases soil erosion.
5. *Susceptibility to man-made threats*, at relatively little cost, of attacks on islands and *coups d'état.*
6. *Tiny domestic markets* for national production.
7. *Lack of 'critical mass'* (Demas, 1982, p. 5) in the public service and in economic and social capital overheads, thereby resulting in high per head costs for the infrastructure on both these parameters.
8. *Little choice of human resources*; shortage of skilled personnel, owing to limited chances of promotion and pay.
9. *Insufficient national savings*; no popular tendency to save; with national consumption often higher than the GDP.
10. *Extreme external economic and financial dependence*; with the normal national budgets being balanced, in some cases, with subsidies from abroad (Demas, 1982, p. 5).

Essentially, the OECS came into existence owing to the discontentment of these States with the slow pace of the progress of integration of the Caribbean Community (*Cf.* Bryan, 1984, p. 86). The similarity of the economic and social

---

[199] The author's own calculations (*Vide* Cap. 1.3).

[200] *Caribbean Development to the Year 2000*, p. 53

problems, geographical proximity, common foreign policy and security interests favour closer co-operation, which, from the beginning, was not limited only to the economic sector, but which also did not exclude political union. The OECS, discriminated against by the larger CARICOM Member States as Less Developed Countries (LDCs), developed into a sub-system of the inner-Caribbean system and achieved such progress in integration that could lead to the creation of a new East Caribbean State.

Historically, the OECS developed out of several Federations of the Leeward and Windward Islands, which the UK Colonial Office had established essentially for administrative reasons. In 1956, the Leeward Islands Federation ended, thereby making way for the short-lived Federation of the West Indies.

In the aftermath, following the failure of the East Caribbean Federation to materialise, only a few years elapsed before the creation of new regional structures. Within this framework, it had been planned from the very beginning to include the small Commonwealth Caribbean States, as an economic and, perhaps, also a political unit.

The founding of the East Caribbean Currency Authority (ECCA) 1965 and the establishment of a common currency surpassed a pure free trade concept. In 1967, the West Indies Associated States (WISA) [*sic*] Council of Ministers was constituted as an advisory body for the economic and functional co-operation of, at first, five British colonies in the Eastern Caribbean: Antigua and Barbuda; Dominica; Grenada; St. Kitts-Nevis-Anguilla; and St. Lucia — as well as, from 1969, St. Vincent and the Grenadines. Montserrat was not granted Associated Statehood status and kept in both CARICOM and the OECS its status as a colony. The East Caribbean Common Market (ECCM) came into existence in 1968. With the Treaty of Basseterre, seven Eastern Caribbean territories entered into an alliance and became the OECS on June 18, 1981.

The BVI and Anguilla were granted Associated State status. The USVI has shown interest in an association (*CI* March, 1990, p. 15). Of the three, only Anguilla belongs to the Eastern Caribbean monetary system.

Article 3 of the Treaty establishing the OECS lists the tasks of the organisation as follows: Co-operation among the Member States; the promotion of unity and solidarity; the defence of their sovereignty, territorial integrity and independence; common representation *vis-à-vis* the international community, e.g. through the harmonisation of foreign policy, joint overseas representation abroad; and the promotion of economic integration.

Article 5 names the necessary institutions, which give the OECS its organisational backbone as follows: The Authority is the highest decision-making body of the organisation and lays down general policy guidelines. Decisions are effective only when taken unanimously. The body meets at least twice yearly. The chairmanship rotates yearly in alphabetical order of the participating countries.

The *Foreign Affairs Committe* is responsible to the Authority for the development and control of foreign policy. Their decisions and directives are binding on all subordinate bodies of the OECS (Article 7).

The *Defence and Security Committee* consists of the relevant portfolio-holding Ministers of the participating Governments and is responsible for the co-ordination of the collective defence of the Member States, expressly against the activities of those in revolt — whether or not they operate with the support of external or domestic elements (Article 8).

The *Economic Affairs Committes* (EAC) (Article 9) consists of Ministers despatched by the Heads of Government and has succeeded the Council of Ministers of the ECCM. It supervises the Economic Affairs Division, which, as a part of the *Central Secretariat* and also as the successor body of the ECCM Secretariat, has its head office in Antigua.

The *Economic Policy Review Committee* (EPRC) gathers together, as the EAC Sub-Committee, at least twice yearly, higher finance and planning officials of the OECS Governments, in order to discuss important economic and financial questions and provide the OECS Member States with proposals and advice through the authority.

The OECS *Central Secretariat*, with its offices in St. Lucia, is the administrative centre of the organisation; and is headed by a Director General [201], who, like the staff receives instructions directly from the relevant institutions of the OECS and hence, not from the Governments of the Member States. The Central Secretariat is financed from the membership contributions of the affiliated states and territories; but the punctuality of the payment of the contributions leaves much to be desired (*Cf.* OECS in Perspective, 1987, p. 11).

Almost all of the work load of the Secretariat is divided into individual projects, which are financed fully or jointly by a number of international agencies. In this way, a strong dependence exists on foreign sources of finance. But they are so dispersed over numerous donor countries and international agencies that no one of their donors has a dominant position.

Important sources of funds of the Central Secretariat of the OECS are as follows: The Development Fund of the European Union; the UNDP; the International Bank for Reconstruction and Development (i.e. the World Bank); the OAS; as well as Development Funds of the USA, Canada, the UK, the Federal Republic of Germany and other countries. The Society for Technical Co-operation of the German Federal Republic sponsors the *Natural Resource Management Project* of the OECS, which advises the Member States in the use of their natural resources.

Diverse administrative bodies have been created to carry out the collective responsibilities involved. The most important of these bodies is the *Eastern Caribbean Central Bank* which is located in Basseterre, St. Kitts and which was established in 1983 from the ECCA ('*A Profile*' 1985)[202]. The first Governor of the Central Bank, Cecil A. Jacobs, declared that they had undertaken something quite unique, in the sense that it involved so many independent and sovereign states (*ibid*).

The conversion of the Eastern Caribbean Currency Authority, which had existed up to then, into the Central Bank meant, in the view of William Demas, a considerable transfer of sovereignty from the participating Member States to a

---

[201] Dr. Vaughan Lewis has occupied this post from the beginning.

[202] The Treaty establishing this Central Bank was signed at the 1983 CARICOM Summit in Port-of-Spain, Trinidad, which, as the '10th Jubilee Anniversary Summit' of the Community, was particularly significant.

regional authority. This, at the same time, also meant waiving their individual rights to having their own Central Banks — and, therefore, to financial instruments, which are misused almost everywhere in the Third World by Governments which have fallen into financial difficulties (Demas, 1982, p. 20). The Central Bank regulates the money supply in circulation, pools foreign exchange reserves, and serves as the banker and supervisor of the commercial banks in the OECS and regulates their credit policy. In addition, it is the banker to, and adviser of, the participating Governments. It ensures generally that monetary policy is consistent with balanced economics growth and appropriate development of the economies of the participating countries.

The role of the Central Bank in the Eastern Caribbean territories and States must, according to Jacobs (1987, pp. 37ff) be considered in a broader perspective than is the case in a traditional Central Bank. This applies to both the formulation of monetary policy and the objectives of promoting economic growth. This Central Bank recognises its unique position as a regional institution in this context; and makes an effort, whenever possible, in Jacobs' view, to support the promotion and development of the integration movement.

The *Eastern Caribbean Supreme Court* in Castries, St. Lucia, is the successor institution to the West Indian Associated States Supreme Court, which had been established in 1967; and it serves as the Court of Appeal for decisions and verdicts handed down by the courts in the Member States.

2.4.2 Economic Relations in the Sub-region

2.4.2.1 The East Caribbean Common Market (ECCM)

The East Caribbean Common Market (ECCM), which was founded in 1968, has the same mission as the Common Market of the Caribbean Community (CARICOM), which was established five years later. The ECCM was founded in order to promote increasing economic stability in the Member States as well as an accelerated improvement of the standard of living and the facilitation of the exchange of goods and services (Article 2: 'Agreement Establishing the East Caribbean Common Market').

In order to attain these goals, the following are envisaged:

- the elimination between Member States, of customs duties and of quantitative restrictions on the importation and exportation of goods, as well as of all other measures with equivalent effect;
- subject to Article 22, the establishment of common customs tariffs and common commercial policies towards countries and territories, not parties to this Agreement;
- the abolition, as between Member States, of the obstacles to the free movement of persons, services and capital;
- the progressive harmonisation of investment and development policies, including industrial development, treatment of non-resident business establishments and development planning;
- the co-ordination of currency and financial policies;

- the progressive harmonisation of taxation policies and incentive legislation in order to promote the equitable distribution of industries among Member States;
- a co-operative approach to infra-structural development especially in the fields of transport and communication;
- a common policy to agricultural development.

2.4.2.2 Integration of Production in the OECS

Common strategies for the development of agriculture, industry and the services sector are a prerequisite for the OECS Member States growing together to an economic unit. At the present time, the integration of agriculture can exist only in their optimally cultivating the agriculturally usable land and thereby producing as much as possible for both the export market and domestic consumption.

The OECS can try to sell their products by their common marketing efforts and negotiations with purchasing States or regions at advantageous conditions. The *Natural Resource Management Project* of the OECS Secretariat is supposed to advise the Member States on the optimal exploitation of their natural resources. Within the Framework of the *Common Protective Policy for Agriculture*, the OECS develops measures which should ensure the guaranteed sale of OECS agricultural produce. The OECS' *Agricultural Diversification Programme* concerns itself with the division of cultivable regions suitable for agricultural produce.

The OECS' *Fisheries Unit*, located in St. Vincent and the Grenadines, is supposed to advise the OECS Member States on the exploration and protection of fishing grounds. The territorial waters of the Eastern Caribbean islands will be considerably increased, with the entering into force of the International Law of the Sea Convention. Within this context, an important foreign policy responsibility will fall to the OECS in the delimitation negotiations with non-OECS States for the use of the economic zones[203]. In January, 1991, the OECS Heads of Government decided to establish a common fishing surveillance zone.

The industrial sector is little developed in the OECS Member States. Integrated industries are difficult to establish. In view of the great excess of labour, the individual states are also trying, in competition with one another, to acquire as many labour-intensive industries as possible for themselves (*Cf. CU* May, 1989, p. 9).

An *Industrial Allocation Scheme*, which had been set up well before the founding of the OECS, and which is supposed to find optimal locations for the siting of industry in the Eastern Caribbean, has hardly made any progress (*OECS in Perspective*, 1987, p. 10). The Caribbean Investment Corporation, that had been established in 1972 and had its head office in St. Lucia, and which, in collaboration with the private sector and Governments, was supposed to provide

---

[203]Thus, the Aves Islands, some 230 km West of Dominica, belong to Venezuela (*Cf*· Lennert 1991, p 317) Venezuelan fishing boats have been repeatedly caught by the OECS member-States' Coast Guard in their territorial waters Anguilla and Barbados must also reach territorial settlements with France over Martinique and Guadeloupe. Agreements must also include quantities of catch and keeping the sea clean (*OECS in Perspective*, 1987, p. 32).

risk capital for the LDCs in the OECS, failed, as a result of limited marketing possibilities and management mistakes (*Cf.* Emtage 1984, p. 140). Currently, the promotion of investments takes place especially directly through the Caribbean Development Bank, *via* associations and chambers of the private sector (e.g. the Eastern Caribbean Manufacturers Council).

2.4.2.3 Special Status of 'Less Developed Countries'

The July 4, 1973, Treaty for creating the Caribbean Community divided the CARICOM Member States into two groups; namely the less developed countries (LDCs) and the more developed countries (MDCs). Article three of the *Treaty Establishing the Caribbean Community* defines, as LDCs, the present seven OECS Member States and Belize.

For them, special *régimes* are envisaged, which provide them with more flexible terms in the rules of origin for finished products and the harmonisation of the Common External Tariff. They are supposed to promote especially industrial development in the LDCs and prescribe MDCs' aid for the LDCs (Articles 51-62).

While the LDCs, on the one hand, regard their classification as discriminatory, it, on the other hand, may bring them advantages, if the terms of the Treaty are respected by the other CARICOM Member States. This is, however, not always the case (*Cf.* Lestrade 1986). The prosperity gradient between LDCs and MDCs in the Community is no longer so jarring.

In fact, development has made some MDCs into LDCs and vice versa. Within the OECS Member States, one remembers, not without gloating that Jamaica's then Leader of the Opposition, Alexander Bustamante, had demanded the secession of Jamaica from the West Indies Federation, because, *inter alia*, prosperous Jamaica would otherwise have had to feed the then poverty-stricken Eastern Caribbean territories.

Similarly, the economic decline of Trinidad and Tobago is commented on by the OECS Member States not without malicious pleasure. Thus, St. Lucia's Prime Minister, John Compton, said, after the second devaluation of the Trinidad and Tobago dollar in August, 1988, that that country was no longer rich and powerful (*Weekend Voice*, St. Lucia 20.8.1988, p. 3). The difference between the smaller and the larger CARICOM Member States and territories exists, above all, in the potential for industrial development and also in the possibility of self-sustained economic progress. In this, the MDCs, left to themselves, have better developmental prospects (Lestrade 1986).

The LDCs, pointing to their constant external dependence due to their small size, strive to get favourable credits from agencies, although most of them, for a long time now, have no longer been in the category of the developing countries with the lowest incomes[204]. The dichotomy, between on the one hand, wishing to appear particularly poor in order to get more favourable conditions both within CARICOM and through international financial agencies and, on the other, to be accepted as an equal partner and not as the poor houses of the

[204] The IDA's condition an average per head income of under US $ 411 per year

Caribbean, renders the efforts of these OECS Member States and territories to obtain preferential credits, difficult.

The OECS Member States, through collective action within the international community of the donor countries, have succeeded in preventing some of their number from graduating, — that is, being classified in a higher developmental category and, hence, the loss of special advantages[205]. Thanks to collective action of the OECS Member States, they and Belize have also been able to get, with the approval of other CARICOM Member States, a larger share of the funds provided by the European Union for the region under the Lomé Treaty (*Economic Integration*, 1988, p.7). As small island developing countries, the OECS Member States hope to be able to keep the lucrative status of the 'most seriously affected' territories even after future 'graduations'.

2.4.2.4 Intra-regional Trade of the OECS Member States

The OECS Member States wanted to remove, on January 1, 1988, the import restrictions hitherto existing among themselves, as decided at the November, 1987, meeting of the OECS Authority. This decision was implemented in part on July 1, 1988[206]. The Governments wish to get domestic manufacturers to produce higher quality goods in order to make their hitherto protected goods, which from then on were exposed to competition, more competitive (*WG* 12.1.1988, p. 16).

The exchange of goods within the sub-region is, however, relatively small. In 1990, only 3.4% of the imports into the OECS Member States came from their own sub-region and 10.7% from the rest of CARICOM (*WG* 2.10.1990, p. 18). Effective competition cannot exist either, in the absence of customs union, which was supposed to be implemented (*OECS in Perspective* 1987, p. 42).

Manufacturers within the OECS welcome the freeing up of trade, because it enlarges the markets[207]. The larger CARICOM countries are still the principal purchasers of the products manufactured in the OECS Member States, who imported by far more CARICOM products than they could export to the rest of CARICOM. A high foreign trade deficit results.

In order to wipe out the losses, the OECS Member States together with the Council of Eastern Caribbean Manufacturers (CECM), developed export strategies, which were supposed to be realised by the East Caribbean States Development Agency (ECSDA), that came into being in Dominica, with the help of the European Development Fund. At the World Exhibition, EXPO '86, in Vancouver (Canada), there was an OECS pavilion promoting sales of OECS industrial products and agriculture produce as well as tourism (*Cf. OECS in Perspective* 1987, p. 3). The OECS High Commissioner to Ottawa and the OECS Secretariat co-ordinated the exhibition.

---

[205] In the 1960s, the creation of the Caribbean Development Bank was given the objective of getting credits at favourable conditions, despite threatening graduation (*Cf.*: Fitzgerald, 1969).

[206] Only the importation of beer into St Kitts and Nevis and of grain into Grenada remain on the list of goods still under import licence.

[207] *Cf.*: Harker 1987. Peter Harker was President of the Council of Eastern Caribbean Manufacturers (CECM).

Within the region, the OECS Member States organised in September, 1988, in Antigua and in May, 1991, in St. Lucia, an OECS Trade and Investment Exposition patterned after CARIMEX '85 of CARICOM. It was supposed to promote the sales of OECS products and interest European investors in the OECS region; and should be repeated and be complemented through displays of certain industrial products, such as furniture, textiles and shoes. The investors are supposed to be advised by the Eastern Caribbean Investment Promotion Service (ECIPS), which is affiliated to the OECS *Economic Affairs Division* and has an office in Washington, D.C. (*WG* 21.7.1992, p. 26).

The marketing of so-called traditional agricultural exports, such as bananas, citrus, or special island produce, such as arrowroot (mainly from St. Vincent) or nutmeg (principally from Grenada) is regulated either in the collective OECS country agreements or, through sales quotas of the European Union, in the Lomé Treaty.

The co-ordination of tourism, the top foreign exchange earner for most OECS Member States and a particularly competitive service, is still not sufficient. A Central Tourist Authority with state-of-the-art communications for one-stop centralised reservations, and immediate and comprehensive information about accommodation and activities within the region does not exist. There are only common information offices connected to the OECS High Commission in London and Ottawa (Palmer, 1984, pp. 64ff).

2.4.3 Functional Co-operation in the OECS Region

Apart from trade and production, numerous State and parastatal organisations, institutions and authorities exist which perform functional tasks for the OECS Member States and territories. In part, their tasks are convergent with corresponding institutions for the entire CARICOM area. But their collaboration, conditioned by geographical proximity and similarity in the structure of the participating territories, is closer; and the use of the relevant institutions by the participating States and territories is more intense.

In many instances, they have waived working with their own institutions and transferred functional responsibilities to central institutions. Among such institutions within the OECS Secretariat are the *Eastern Caribbean Drug Services Project*, the *National Resource Management Project* and the *Fisheries Unit*. The *Legal Unit* in the OECS Secretariat in St. Lucia deals with the harmonisation of legislation in the Member States (*OECS in Perspective* 1987, pp. 31ff). The authorities, following the example of some African States and Barbados, are revising the international treaties of the OECS Member States inherited from the previous colonial power, Great Britain. Some 400 multilateral and bilateral treaties are involved, which were not yet adapted to the needs and changed realities of the OECS Member States.

In education, the *Eastern Caribbean Text Book Project* is supposed to promote the production of schoolbooks which meet the needs of the sub-region. Other projects are the improvement in the education of teachers of technical subjects and agriculture as well as in pre-University education (*OECS in Perspective*, pp. 31ff).

Sports has particular significance for the spirit of regional integration (*ibid* 29). An OECS Sports Desk, which was established in 1984 in the OECS Secretariat in St. Lucia, co-ordinates regional sports activities, competitions and the information for trainers and the managers of clubs. In sports activities, the priority concern is, according to then OECS sports organiser, Joseph Pereira, to improve the health of the people in the participating nations and give them the opportunity 'to express themselves as nationals and develop their personality' (*CP* 36, p. 28). At the same time, however, the OECS Member States should be put in the position to attain the standard in sports reached in the MDCs namely Jamaica, Barbados and Trinidad and Tobago and collectively perform well in competition. As Pereira puts it: 'People are beginning to take pride in being champions. On the whole, I think there have been some significant achievements with marvellous teamwork by Caribbean people' (*CP* 36, p. 29).

The Eastern Caribbean Popular Theatre Organisation, which developed in 1982 out of the Windward Drama and Development Project (WINDAD), is still in its initial stages. The impulse for this came from the Jamaican School of Drama. Appearance of the popular theatre at the Canadian Popular Theatre Festival in 1985 gave the members further drive.

The Directorate of Civil Aviation for Eastern Caribbean States, which is subordinate to the OECS Secretariat in St. Lucia, regulates the surveillance of the security of air transport, the training of ground staff and advising OECS member-Governments in civil aviation matters. A collectively drafted Civil Aviation Act should make possible the supervision and control of civil aviation in the OECS Member States. The Administration also undertakes negotiations with non-OECS countries over mutual landing and overflight rights (*OECS in Perspective* 1987, pp. 37ff).

2.4.4 OECS Foreign and Security Policy Co-operation

The collaboration of the OECS Member States in the field of foreign policy is based on Article 3.1 (d) of the OECS Treaty. Among the main purposes of the organisation stated there is: 'to seek to achieve the fullest possible harmonisation of foreign policy among the Member States'.

Article 3, Section 2, includes in the 'joint policies', which they would 'endeavour to co-ordinate, harmonise and pursue', the following: 'overseas representation' (Article 3.2 (a)); 'international trade agreements and other external economic relations' (Article 3.2 (b)); and 'mutual defence and security' (Article 3.2 (q)). A 'Foreign Affairs Committee' was established by (Article 5 (b)); and a 'Defence and Security Committee' by Article 5.1 (c).

The *Foreign Affairs Committee*, consisting of the foreign Ministers of the Member States or their representatives (Article 7.1) is responsible for the 'progressive development of the foreign policy of the Organisation and for the general direction and control of the performance of the executive functions of the Organisation in relation to its foreign affairs' (Article 7.4).

The *Defence and Security Committee* also consists of the Ministers with the relevant portfolio responsibility and 'shall take appropriate action on any matters referred to it by the Authority' (Article 8.3). This Committee is responsible 'for co-ordinating the efforts of Member States for collective defence and the preservation of peace and security against external aggression and for the development of close ties among the Member States of the Organisation in matters of external defence and security, including measures to combat the activities of mercenaries, operating with or without the support of internal or national elements' (Article 8.4).

For these two committees, as also for the other OECS committees, the founding Treaty has the significant reservation limiting participation 'in the deliberations' of the Authority (Article 6.3) or the relevant committees (e.g. Articles 7.2 and 8.2, *inter alia*) to 'Member States possessing the necessary competence in respect of matters under consideration from time to time'. Thus, for instance, Montserrat was excluded from the deliberations over the October, 1983, intervention in Grenada. Nonetheless, the treaty gives the colonies which are OECS members, the opportunity to be active in foreign policy — and even to have consulates abroad within the framework of the foreign missions. All independent OECS members have a common High Commissioner in Ottawa and a common Ambassador in Brussels.

The High Commissions of the OECS-States in London should have been converted into a common representation. Similar common representations were also under consideration for New York and Washington, D.C. (*OECS in Perspective 1987*, p. 30). Today, three countries of the OECS, St. Kitts and Nevis, St. Lucia and St. Vincent and the Grenadines, have a joint High Commission in London. The representation in New York, Washington and elsewhere is still separate.

In the common security policy, the OECS Member States push at the frontiers of their personal and material possibilities. Long, unprotected coastlines render them susceptible to interlopers of all sorts: smugglers, criminals, adventurers, and subversives. Additionally, it is difficult for the OECS Member States to enforce their maritime claims (to territorial waters) according to the new international Law of the Sea (*Cf. Vulnerability*, pp. 58-60).

The Governments of Antigua and Barbuda, Barbados, Dominica, St. Lucia and St. Vincent and the Grenadines signed, in 1982, in the capital of Dominica, the *Roseau Security Memorandum* for the creation of a *Regional Defence and Security System* (RSS). A regional defence force is supposed to take over the defence of the participating States and also prevent the overthrow of Governments[208].

In the October, 1983, intervention in Grenada, the regional security agreements and the OECS Treaty were tested, with the involvement of Jamaica. Since then, the USA and the UK have equipped the OECS security forces, have trained military and para-military forces, and annually tested the collaboration in the exercise, 'Trade Wind', in which British, Jamaican, Bahamian and (since 1991) Guyanese units also participate.

---

[208] *The Star*, St Vincent, 12 11 1982, p 2, *CC* April, 1983, p 13 *Vide etiam* Chapters 2 6 2 and 2 6 5 as well as the *Bulletin of Eastern Caribbean Affairs* 11.6 (Jan -Feb , 1986)

2.5 Bilateral Relations of Caribbean States

Thanks to geographical proximity, ideological convergence, family links and personal relationships, close bilateral relationships exist among Eastern Caribbean territories, which are stronger than the links to the rest of the region. Geographically and ethnically, close relationships exist from Trinidad to Guyana, from Grenada to Trinidad, and to St. Vincent and the Grenadines. Large East Indian communities exist in Trinidad which is also a classical 'immigration land' for people from Grenada and St. Vincent and the Grenadines, and Guyana.

Between St. Lucia and St. Vincent, there exist, in turn, close relationships, as a result of the small distance separating these two islands, and family links[209]. Dominica and St. Lucia cultivate closer links to the French Departments of Martinique and Guadeloupe, for both of the former islands had been French possessions, and cultivate common *Créole* traditions, cuisine and speech. Montserrat is closely linked to Antigua. These two islands are also close to St. Kitts and Nevis with which they had formed the Leeward Islands Federation as British colonies. Anguilla, in turn, although a British colony, is closer to the Dutch-French possession of St. Maarten/St. Martin than to St. Kitts, with which it was territorially linked initially.

The BVI maintain close relationships with the USVI and Puerto Rico. Numerous Puerto Ricans live in the island chain. The USVI, with one of the highest per head incomes in the Caribbean, attract in droves immigrants from the Eastern Caribbean, which, in 1980, accounted for 28.8% of the population (Leary and Albuquerque, 1989, pp. 51ff).

Jamaica has rather close links with the Cayman Islands and the Turks and Caicos Islands, which it had previously administered. Belize has closer links with Jamaica than with the other Commonwealth Caribbean States, for the two are geographically closer together than either is to any of the other states and were earlier linked administratively. However, the direct air link has long been abandoned.

The frequency of the inter-action between the various populations manifests itself in the pattern of transportation links. Thus, for instance, the Turks and Caicos Islands are better linked to Florida, the Dominican Republic and Jamaica than to their immediate neighbour, the Bahamas. Belize maintains direct shipping links with Jamaica, whereas flights between the two countries go via Miami. The larger Commonwealth Caribbean airlines, BWIA, and, occasionally, Air Jamaica have provided on-going air links between the MDCs. Guyana has better air links with Trinidad and Barbados than with its immediate neighbours, namely: Venezuela, Brazil and Suriname.

Good personal relationships between Heads of Government may lead to special relationships of a temporary nature between states. In 1979, then Prime Minister of St. Vincent and the Grenadines, Milton Cato, availed himself of his good relationship with his Barbadian counterpart, Tom Adams, to call for Barbadian troops to help against secessionist activities in the Union Islands.

---

[209]Thus, St Lucian Prime Minister, John Compton, comes from the island of Bequia in the Grenadines and is related to Prime Minister James Mitchell of St. Vincent and the Grenadines, who is also from Bequia

The collective experience of the intervention in Grenada led to links between the Governments of Edward Seaga (Jamaica), Tom Adams (Barbados), Vere Bird (Antigua), Dame Eugenia Charles (Dominica), Dr. Kennedy Simmonds (St. Kitts and Nevis) and John Compton (St. Lucia). The common origin in the Grenadines of the Prime Ministers of St. Lucia, and St. Vincent and the Grenadines facilitates their working in agreement in trying to establish the Union of the Windward Islands.

Bilateral understanding between Errol Barrow of Barbados and Forbes Burnham of Guyana led to the creation of CARIFTA. This initiative led to the founding of the Caribbean Community (CARICOM) a few years later.

Bilateral agreements have proved to be useful for both economic and political integration. St. Vincent and the Grenadines' Prime Minister, James Mitchell, uses a bilateral and trilateral strategy to achieve political integration. He recalls how he, peripherally to Lomé-I Treaty negotiations with the then European Community in Brussels, suggested in a *tête-à-tête* with the then Premier of St. Kitts-Nevis-Anguilla, Robert Bradshaw, that their two countries should become independent together. A commission, he suggested further, should work out the formalities in greater detail. St. Lucia's Premier, John Compton, also accepted the proposal for his own country.

The sudden death of the Chairman of the Commission, Sir Hugh Wooding, prevented the implementation of the plan (Mitchell, 1987b, p. 2). Compton and Mitchell are currently again the driving forces behind a political union of the Eastern Caribbean.

In May, 1992, Trinidad and Tobago's Prime Minister, Patrick Manning, a few months after taking office, suggested union between Trinidad and Tobago, Barbados and Guyana (*CC* May-June, 1992, pp. 1ff). In October, 1992, he met Barbados' then Prime Minister Sandiford and Guyana's President Jagan in Port-of-Spain, in order to discuss concrete steps. The three countries want to work closer together especially in functional areas (*CC* Dec., 1992 — Jan., 1993, p. 7)[210]. At the CARICOM Summit in July, 1993, Sandiford proposed a Confederation of the three countries, and was asked by Jagan and Manning to detail his proposals.

Further recent bilateral examples are as follows: Jamaica and Trinidad and Tobago have reviewed discussion about the creation of a joint aluminium complex in Trinidad — a project which had long seemed to have been buried (*CI* March 1992, p. 12). Barbados and Trinidad and Tobago jointly operate a cement factory. BWIA, the state airline of Trinidad and Tobago took over in 1987, the European routes of Caribbean Airways, the failed state airline of Barbados (*CC* May 1987, p. 5).

Services and experiences available in one CARICOM country, but absent in others, have also been made available to the latter, along with the necessary personnel. After hurricanes 'Gilbert' (1988) and 'Hugo' (1989), the CARICOM Member States provided their affected sister countries with exemplary assistance.

[210]Please see also Manning's speech at a February, 1993 Caribbean Youth Institute conference dealing with his initiative, printed in Manning, 1993.

All independent CARICOM Member States maintain diplomatic relations with each other. But only the MDCs have High Commissions — and that, with limitations. Thus, Guyana has an Embassy in Suriname and had to close its High Commissions[211] in Jamaica, Barbados and Trinidad and Tobago, owing to economic difficulties. Jamaica has a High Commission in Trinidad, which, in turn, has High Commissions in both Jamaica and Barbados. Trinidad and Tobago closed its High Commission in Guyana on June 30, 1989, however, after twenty years of existence. The main reasons were Guyana's chronic economic problems, but the closure was certainly also due to the economic downturn in Trinidad and Tobago as well (*CU* August 1989, p. 10).

In 1992, Barbados closed its only High Commission in a CARICOM country — namely, in Trinidad — as an economic measure (*CI* April 1992, p. 6). The *Stabroek News*, the independent Guyanese daily newspaper, has termed the small number of diplomatic missions of CARICOM Member States within the Caribbean Community as one of the weaknesses in the regional integration process (*WG* 18.7.1989, p. 20).

Guyana, Jamaica and especially Trinidad and Tobago, while their economies flourished, were able to afford to undertake rigorous bilateral activities, in which they were patrons rather than partners. Sahadeo Basdeo, formerly External Affairs Minister of Trinidad and Tobago, speaks of the 'obsession' of that country's Prime Minister, Dr. Eric Williams, to turn it into the 'Toronto of the Commonwealth Caribbean' (*Forging a New Democracy*, p. 103).

In the 1970s, Trinidad and Tobago behaved like a highly industrialised country and granted credits to the poorer CARICOM Member States. This was despite the fact that it derived its prosperity from practically one raw material — namely, oil. Indeed, at the start of the 1970s, the country had been virtually almost bankrupt. Through the 1973-74 OPEC oil price rise, however, it was able to receive substantial foreign currency inflows.

The Group of Caribbean Experts, which, under the chairmanship of then CDB President, William Demas, at the start of 1981 presented its report on the development of Caribbean integration and made recommendations for the 1980s, came to the conclusion that bilateral, trilateral or quadrilateral links within the Community were entirely possible in matters not simultaneously affecting all its members (*The Caribbean Community in the 1980s*, pp. 70ff). The group demanded that for such agreements, the following three basic conditions be met:

1. Before such agreements are made, the participating Governments should, as far as possible, inform the other member-Governments and, after the completion of the agreements, supply them, at any rate, with copies of the complete texts of such agreements.

[211]Members of the Commonwealth term as *High Commissions* their highest diplomatic offices in other Commonwealth member-States

2. Where necessary, the agreements should contain a limiting clause reading 'subject to the provisions of the Treaty of Chaguaramas'.

3. If possible, the agreements should expressly offer other CARICOM Member States the opportunity of participation in them (*ibid.* p. 77).

2.6 External Representation and the Limits of Caribbean Interests in the International System

2.6.1 Foreign Policy and Integration

In Article 17 of the Treaty establishing the Caribbean Community, the Member States expressed their intention to co-ordinate their foreign policy and, as far as possible, to adopt common positions on important international questions. To this end, they established a Standing Committee of Ministers Responsible for Foreign Affairs, which should make corresponding recommendations to the Governments of the participating Member States. The recommendations of this committee, which, as a rule, meets twice yearly, must be unanimous.

While the Standing Committee can make only recommendations, which, however, have considerable weight, the important decisions are reserved fòr the Conference of Heads of Government — especially agreements of the Community with other states and/or international organisations.

In view of the threatening marginalization, the CARICOM Member States attach importance to being represented by at least one person in all regions of the world as well as in international fora. In 1991, the Foreign Ministers agreed to have common diplomatic missions in the Far East as well as on twenty-two international bodies (*CR* 20.6.1991, p. 1). Moreover, participation in all important conferences should be ensured. As in the ACP/EU negotiations, common negotiating teams should be formed (Caribbean Community, 1990, pp.33-35).

Numerous contacts with other States and regional associations take place at the level of the CARICOM Secretariat in Georgetown. Official visitors on State visits to Guyana also pay official visits, as a rule, to this Secretariat, which is responsible for the contacts of CARICOM to regional organisations.

In such organisations, the CARICOM Member States often have individual seats — especially in the OAS, ECLAC, the CDCC and to the Council of Ministers of SELA. Contacts at the level of the Secretariat exist as well to the Andean Group, the South African Development and Co-ordinating Conference (SADCC), the Economic Community of West African States (ECOWAS) and to the South Pacific Economic Co-operation Forum (SPEC). The CARICOM Secretariat has observer status with the UN and is a member of UNCTAD and an informal contact group of integration secretariats, which meets annually. The CARICOM Secretariat maintains contacts to all rather large financial and aid agencies working in the region[212].

The Member States, in Article 34 of the Appendix to the CARICOM Treaty, commit themselves gradually to co-ordinate their trade relationships with third countries (or groups thereof) and also to inform the CARICOM Secretariat on the details of every single trade or aid agreement. In 1975, the Heads of Government decided that, in addition, the Member States should hold

---

[212] All dates are from *CP* 24, p 4 and 9

discussions with each other, before concluding economic agreements with third countries (*The Caribbean Community in the 1980s*, p. 85).

The co-ordination of foreign policy alone is in itself not an integrative process, according to Searwar[213]. Nonetheless, this co-ordination has strengthened the integration process in the course of the years. Indeed, it is to be counted among the internal pro-federal factors, insofar as it does not merely react to external influences, but serves for the collective formulation and implementation of the interests of CARICOM Member States *vis-à-vis* other States. Searwar lists the following as elements of this process:

- the cultivation of the habit of intimate consultations; CARICOM Member States' Foreign Ministers hold regular consultations at international conferences as well as at the UN;
- the increasing co-operation and linkage in the area of foreign policy among the key institutions of the Community; the Common Market Council of Ministers consults the Standing Committee of Ministers Responsible for Foreign Affairs, before establishing contacts with larger States or international institutions; the Foreign Ministers routinely meet before every Heads of Government Conference, in order to have a preliminary discussion of the relevant subjects;
- the expansion of the role of the Standing Committee to settle intra-regional political differences, which derive from ideological pluralism[214];
- the perception that the co-ordinated action in foreign policy could enhance the security of the individual Member States and serve as protection against the pretensions of stronger external powers — especially, as in the cases of Guyana and Belize, the territorial claims of neighbouring States;
- the identification of mechanisms for the co-ordination of foreign policy, e.g. the naming of a Standing Foreign Affairs Committee Chairman, who — unlike the customary practice of the other standing committees — is not the host country's Foreign Minister; the regular meetings of the diplomatic representatives of CARICOM Member States accredited abroad; the exchanging of important reports and documents among themselves by the delegations of CARICOM Member States at international conferences; and the dissemination of common positions on international events (Searwar, 1984, pp. 162-166).

In 1989, the then Prime Minister of Trinidad and Tobago, A.N.R. Robinson, suggested that the MDCs should, like the LDCs, establish a closer political association and that all CARICOM Member States should have common diplomatic representations abroad. In London, he demanded the necessary 'quantum leap' in the direction of Caribbean integration; and Guyana's President, Desmond Hoyte, essentially associated himself with these proposals during his January, 1989, visit to Trinidad (Hoyte, 1989a, p. 62). Only the OECS Member States have made progress in these matters. These countries, however, also have special problems of finding qualified personnel for the large

[213] Lloyd Searwar headed the foreign affairs desk in the CARICOM Secretariat for a great many years

[214] Meant here are e.g., the controversies within the Community concerning the intervention in Grenada.

number of international bodies, sub-committees and important diplomatic posts in the world[215].

The Caribbean Community, with its self-commitment to a co-ordinated foreign policy for its sovereign Member States, has gone further than comparable integration associations. Even during the existence of CARIFTA, the independent Member States had agreed on foreign policy measures. In October, 1972, for example, Barbados, Guyana, Jamaica and Trinidad and Tobago had simultaneously established diplomatic relations with Cuba.

After the entry of the UK in the then European Community in 1973, the closed ranks of the Caribbean territories in negotiations concerning the inclusion of the Commonwealth States in agreements with the Community made themselves positively remarked upon. The Caribbean States decided upon a collective approach together with African and Pacific Governments, although they could have negotiated a special contract. In the Lomé-I Treaty preliminary negotiations, they were so markedly a closed lobby group against the European negotiations that they were occasionally regarded as trouble-makers. Jamaica hosted an important ACP/EC round of Ministerial negotiations at which both its then Prime Minister, Manley, and his counterpart from Trinidad and Tobago, Williams, were present (Carrington, 1984, p. 178).

The CARICOM countries successfully took a common stand as well in the Law of the Sea negotiations, which lasted over many years. The preparatory conferences alternated between Kingston (Jamaica) and New York. Jamaica will house the headquarters of the International Seabed Authority. (*CC* August 1994, p.12).

This success ensured the Community a place in the diplomatic arena. 'The Caribbean region has often been simplistically regarded as an historical backwater, a mere tourist destination whose main offerings are sea, sun and sand', said A.N.R. Robinson, then Prime Minister of Trinidad and Tobago, in 1987, at the UN General Assembly in New York. 'Yet the reality is that geographically, historically and culturally, the region constitutes a link between North and South and East and West and has played a part in world affairs and continues to do so out of all proportion to our size and population' (*International Relations*, p.11).

Robinson's Jamaican counterpart, Edward Seaga, stated that the Caribbean, despite its special location and interests, had been previously seen merely as a part of Latin America by the international community. In view of the large number of independent States, which now speak with one voice in a sovereign way, the region, he declared, has become known as 'Latin America and the Caribbean' (*Caribbean Democrat Union Monthly Newsletter* 2.7, p. 3).

Bryan (1984, p. 87) terms the co-ordination of foreign policies of the CARICOM countries as 'probably the most important aspect of the Caribbean Community'. In the first years after the founding of CARICOM, however, foreign policy co-ordination was one of the least successful aspects of regional integration in the Commonwealth Caribbean (Payne, 1984a, p. 139). In the early

---

[215] *Cf.*: the particularly colourful descriptions of St Vincent's Prime Minister, James Mitchell, in *Thoughts of Some OECS Leaders*, 1988, pp 48ff.

days of the Community, the Standing Committee met rarely. The number of members was small, because the dependent Member States were excluded from participation.

Foreign policy was essentially determined by the Governments bilaterally and in meetings on the sidelines of conferences. The Committee became more active at the end of the 1970s, when the number of its members increased to eight. Subjects of common interest were as follows: The situation in Africa — especially South Africa; security problems of the Caribbean in the East-West conflict; the proposals of the US Government for the Caribbean Basin Initiative(CBI); mutual assistance in defence matters; Guyana's territorial dispute with Venezuela and that of Belize with Guatemala (Searwar, 1984, pp. 159-162).

The 1982 Falklands War tested the capacity for consensus of the CARICOM Member States in the field of foreign affairs. Against the pressure of most neighbouring Latin American countries — including some important donors to the Caribbean Community — the CARICOM Member States, together with the USA, supported the UK. Only Grenada, probably acting under their influence of Cuba, broke ranks.

Within the OAS and UN agencies, the CARICOM Member States came down firmly against the invasion by Argentina — a position which was only logical, in view of the territorial threats to both Belize and Guyana. Nonetheless, this foreign policy consensus received its most severe test in the October, 1983, intervention in Grenada. In this, Jamaica and Barbados with the OECS Member States stood firmly in the front-line, as against Guyana, Trinidad and Tobago, the Bahamas and Belize. Guyana, which at that time, was a close ally of Cuba, adopted a particularly vehement line against the undertaking.

The deficient diplomatic coherence of the Caribbean Community in the security field furthered separate efforts of the OECS Member States, together with Barbados, to construct a Regional Defence and Security System (RSS) and use the much more extensive opportunities for foreign policy co-operation, e.g. as stated in Article 8 of the OECS Treaty (Vaughan Lewis, 1989, p. 8).

The intervention in Grenada led to all parties again examining in a special way and discussing the principles of foreign policy adopted by the United Nations, namely non-interference in the internal affairs of States; collective security against aggression; self-determination of people; anti-racism and anti-imperialism.

On several occasions, CARICOM institutions had approved the idea of declaring the Caribbean a 'Zone of Peace'. The Caribbean States, as members of the Non-Aligned Movement, considered themselves to be a strong moral force in international politics, which could dissolve international tension by their 'independence of judgement'[216].

On the other hand, the CARICOM countries remained disunited in their views on Haiti. The 1988 attempt to withdraw Haiti's observer status in CARICOM institutions, owing to electoral malpractices and the inability to

[216]Basdeo the then External Affairs Minister of Trinidad and Tobago, in *Forging a New Democracy* (1985, p. 105); this position also applied, in principle, to the other CARICOM Member States.

introduce a democratic State and governmental system, failed, especially because of Jamaica's firm opposition. The September, 1991, ouster of President Aristide strengthened the position of those demanding Haiti's exclusion.

The CARICOM Member States were divided during the UN General Assembly debate on the condemnation of US invasion of Panama in December, 1989. Thus, Dominica opposed the condemnation; Antigua, Grenada, St. Lucia and St. Vincent abstained; the Bahamas and St. Kitts and Nevis were absent from the session.

Supporting the condemnation were the representatives of Barbados, Belize, Guyana, Jamaica and Trinidad and Tobago. But Jamaica and most of the OECS Member States did not support Mexico's draft motion condemning the forced entry of US soldiers into the residence of the Nicaraguan Ambassador in Panama City (*CC* February, 1990, p. 4).

The UN military action against Iraq in early 1991 was basically approved by the Community. The CARICOM Heads of Government, in Kingston in August, 1990, condemned Iraq's invasion of Kuwait. Trinidad and Tobago offered aid to the other CARICOM Member States to off-set rising oil prices. Its then Prime Minister, A.N.R. Robinson, in January, 1991, arranged an extraordinary crisis Summit with his Jamaican counterpart, Michael Manley, and Venezuelan President, Carlos Andrés Pérez (*CI* 22.1.1991, p. 1).

Despite the close, in part, co-operation of the CARICOM countries to achieve certain results in their common interest in negotiations, the Community, since signing the Treaty of Chaguaramas has not succeeded in becoming an identifiable negotiating international force (Vaughan Lewis, 1989, p. 9); (Searwar, 1990, p. 25). Initially successful initiatives — such as the Lomé-I Treaty. CBI-I and Caribbean and Canada Trade Agreement (CARIBCAN) negotiations — were not followed up collectively.

The co-ordination of the foreign economic relationships of the CARICOM countries was by and large less successful than the co-ordination of those in external political matters. Only a few of these countries — contrary to their Treaty obligations — regard it as necessary to inform the Community, in good time and comprehensively, of economic agreements with Foreign Governments or international agencies.

Only partly successful were the efforts of the CARICOM Member States in their negotiations with the International Development Agency (IDA) to prevent the economic graduation of some of their number — and, hence, the loss of particularly favourable credit terms and conditions (*Cf. Caribbean Community* 1985, p. 29).

Under the leadership of Jamaica's then Prime Minister, Edward Seaga, the CARICOM countries, in 1987, circulated a proposal to overcome the foreign debt problem, which, within Commonwealth diplomatic circles, was described as much more comprehensive than the proposals of Western Governments (*CR* 5.11.1987, p. 6).

McIntyre demands that future Caribbean diplomats must be not only in a position to exercise their functions as representatives of their Governments, but should also have a thorough understanding of trade, finance, investment and technology, in order to be able to promote exports, tourism and investment, including the opening up of new markets and sources of funds as well as the acquisition of new technologies (1984, p.15).

The UWI's Institute of International Relations which, as stated previously, is located on the St. Augustine (Trinidad) campus of the University, developed, as commissioned by CARICOM and with Swiss help, a comprehensive training programme for future diplomats, which pays particular attention to the particular needs and priorities of the Member States (*Caribbean Community* 1986, p. 40).

The training programme which, at times, brings the trainee diplomats together at St. Augustine, Trinidad, helps the foreign affairs experts of CARICOM Member States to get to know each other quite early in their careers — thereby satisfying one of the conditions for the close collaboration expected from them later on.

In view of the fact that about one third of West Indians live abroad, an opportunity would seem to present itself for Caribbean Member States to set up 'West Indian Houses' in metropolitan countries. In such centres, collective pan-CARICOM cultural facilities, legal advisory services, Embassies/High Commissions and Consulates, a West Indian bank, outreach centres of the UWI, a lobbying centre and other institutions for collective representation could all be accommodated (Dennis Pantin, 1987, p. 12). Owing to the high cost of land, the purchase of buildings for common Embassies/High Commissions and office space for CARICOM Member States has been under examination for quite a long time.

2.6.2 Co-operation in Security Policy

From the viewpoint of security, a politically integrated region is less exposed to fear or the direct experience of intervention than are politically divided regions. Commonwealth experts have ascribed responsibility for the Grenada crisis of 1983 to the lack of unity in the region. A closely integrated region would, in their view, make it easier, 'both constitutionally and morally' for a regional power to stand militarily by the side of a member-island affected by revolts (*Vulnerability*, p. 65).

The common security policy of the CARICOM Member States and territories — or better said, the discussion about this — was constantly a fixed item on the foreign and security agenda of meetings of CARICOM bodies. The security threats to the region are multi-faceted. They range from direct military threats, through the permission granted by individual small States to larger countries and, therefore, possibly the involvement of the entire region in military actions, to the secessionist attempts by force of individual islands in multi-island States.

During the 1958-62 West Indies Federation, a regional force, namely the West India Regiment, had existed in Jamaica. It was relatively small and little trained; and was demobilised after the end of the Federation. Duncan (1984, p. 5) believes that, had the West India Regiment remained in existence, then Guyana would perhaps not have built up the most powerful army in the Anglophone Caribbean, with all its political and economic consequences. Belize would have probably become independent sooner. US influence and the type and equipment of the RSS would have been reduced.

Belize and Guyana, above all, have been exposed to military threats from abroad since their formal independence. In 1981, the Bahamas, Barbados, Guyana, Jamaica, Trinidad and Tobago, the UK and Canada signed a Commonwealth Pact for joint action in the case of a threat being made against Belize. This Pact was, however, never activated. As far back as in 1973, at diplomatic level, a Scheme for Mutual Assistance of some future CARICOM States was prepared — but not followed up (Granger, 1992, p. 76).

The sovereignty of small Caribbean States can be violently infringed by illegal immigration in droves, the narcotics trade, piracy, smuggling, illegal fishing in foreign waters, pollution of the environment and through the penetration of foreign forces in pursuit of criminals — in the case of the Caribbean, especially in the course of the fight against drug trafficking, through attempts of extra-territorial jurisdiction and the violation of bankers' discretion. Groups of dissidents living abroad or in hiding at home can be de-stabilising, especially if they are furnished with weapons (*Cf. Vulnerability*, pp. 24-29).

Uprisings, there were many. In 1967, an uprising of Anguillans brought about the secession of Anguilla from St. Kitts and Nevis. In 1969, a rebellion broke out in the Rupununi Savannah against the Government of Guyana. The rebels attempted in vain to incite the Amerindians against the Government. Swiftly, however, Guyanese troops put an end to the rebellion, which was allegedly supported by Venezuela. In 1970, at the peak of the Black Power movement, an attempted *coups d'état* almost brought down the Government of Trinidad and Tobago. Trinidadian security forces were, however, in a position to crush the uprising.

In March, 1979, rebels led by Maurice Bishop, overthrew the regime of Sir Eric Gairy, who had been governing quite dictatorially. Four and a half years later, the 'Revolutionary Government' was, in turn, overthrown by a US-Caribbean intervention. In December, 1979, militant Rastafarians[217] tried to separate Union Island, in the Grenadines, from St. Vincent and the Grenadines. This uprising was put down with the help of soldiers from Barbados.

Groups of Opposition politicians and discontented members of the armed forces tried twice in 1981 to topple the Government of Dominica. Both these revolts were crushed by local police forces. Smaller occurrences of a similar nature have also taken place in other CARICOM States in the course of their independence, but without bringing the relevant Governments seriously in danger.

In July, 1990, the Republic of Trinidad and Tobago was again the scene of an attempted overthrow of the Government — this time, by a radical Muslim sect, whose members occupied the House of Parliament, taking the Prime Minister and several other Ministers as hostages. Public order collapsed. Buildings went up in flames. Looters rampaged through Port-of-Spain. Twenty-six persons died. One hundred and fifty soldiers and police from Barbados, Guyana, Jamaica and the Eastern Caribbean helped with the maintenance of law and order, after the ending of the attempted coup (*Cf.* Griffith, 1992, p. 186).

[217]Adherents of the Rastafarian movement, which began in Jamaica (Please see Chapter 2.7.3.4).

In November, 1994 a 45-strong contingent from the Regional Defence and Security System (RSS) assisted the 300 policemen of St. Kitts and Nevis in crushing the rebellion of 150 prison inmates in St. Kitts (*AP* 13.11.94 from Basseterre).

The OECS, owing to the susceptibility of its members to external and internal threats adopted a security policy in which the harmonisation of foreign policy and of security matters was explicitly included. Protection of coastal waters was one particular concern. But so was the protection of democratically elected Governments against coups d'état. With Barbados, three of the then five independent OECS members, Antigua and Barbuda, Dominica and St. Vincent and the Grenadines, on October 29, 1982 at Roseau, in Dominica, signed a Memorandum of Understanding on Security and Military Co-operation. St. Lucia followed a few days later; St. Kitts and Nevis, officially in February, 1984; and Grenada, in January 1985.

The participants agreed to prepare contingency plans for mutual assistance in the following areas: on request, national states of emergency; the ending of smuggling; surveillance of territorial waters; the protection of installations beyond the coast; pollution control; natural and other catastrophes and threats to national security. Planning is to be co-ordinated by the armed forces of Barbados.

In 1983, the Understanding took form in the decision to equip a 1,000-man strong regional defence force within the framework of the Regional Defence and Security System (RSS) emanating from this agreement. In February, 1984, some Caribbean Heads of Government discussed this in Barbados with then US Secretary of State, George Shultz (*Cf.* Frank Taylor, 1984, p. 16).

In July, 1984, at the first CARICOM Summit after the Grenada intervention, Barbados' then Prime Minister, Tom Adams, demanded measures for collective regional security to protect and not destroy their sovereign independence and territorial integrity (*DG* 6.7.1984, p. 7). He added that the creation of any security mechanism should not serve to prop up discredited regimes in putting down legitimate protests.

The mechanism, he went on, should protect both conformists and deviants from threats, especially external ones, to their freedom. With Grenada clearly in mind, Adams declared that protection against illegitimate internal disorders should, in future, not depend only on intervention by the superpowers or extra-regional states. On the other hand, he added, one should not burden each state with its own individual costs for arms and ammunition and thereby exacerbate the already parlous economic situation of the CARICOM Member States and territories involved.

The regional force seemed at first to fail, owing to the opposition of Adams' successor, Errol Barrow, and of the Prime Minister of St.Vincent and the Grenadines, James Mitchell, whose predecessor, Milton Cato, had been one of the signatories of the 1982 Memorandum of Understanding. Both Barrow and Mitchell also opposed making this memorandum into an official treaty, which would confer on the RSS a personality in international law. Barrow, who died in 1986, in his last speech at a CARICOM Summit (at Georgetown Guyana, in July, 1986) again came out in favour of the Caribbean as a Zone of Peace. As long as he was Prime Minister of Barbados, he declared, his country would n allow itself to be misused to threaten neighbours — whether they be Cuba or t USA (*CC* July, 1987, p. 9).

Mitchell declared that his Government did not intend to waste the sca finances. Even Dominica's Prime Minister, Eugenia Charles, who had played key role in the 1983 Grenada intervention, wanted to limit co-operation with the Eastern Caribbean at first merely to training and military manœuvres - especially coast guard exercises — and mutual exchanges of visits of t existing forces (*DG* 12.6.1985, p. 7).

Mitchell later withdrew his opposition against the RSS and permitt manœuvres on the territory of his country (*CI* January 1990, p. 15).

Antigua's then Foreign Minister, Lester Bird, in November, 1985, e pressed the hope that the remaining independent CARICOM nations would jo the regional security system. The distrust caused by the East-West conflict ha he argued, prevented this up to then. Moreover, the superpowers had, l continued, a firm interest in maintaining conditions of insecurity, in order keep their influence over the CARICOM countries. Despite external milita help, the Caribbean nations prefer real independence in their relationship wi the superpowers. At the same time, the Government represented by Bird made known that the US sea base in Antigua would incorporate a training centre f Caribbean troops (Barbados Advocate 15.11.85, p. 5).

The Council of Defence Ministers stands at the head of the RSS. Tl common forces operate under a Central Liaison Officer (CLO) headed by Regional Security Co-ordinator (RSC) named by the Council of Ministers.

The regional security forces are 40% financed by Barbados and 10% ea by the other members of the RSS. But payment discipline is not the be (Griffith, 1992, p. 181). The RSS receives support from Canada, the UK and t USA.

Armies and police from Antigua and Barbuda and Barbados (as well police from the remaining states without armies[218]) participate in the RSS. Par military units with light weapons, or Special Support Units (SSU), were creat in the four States without armies. The regional forces consisted, in 1990, of tw SSU each of forty men from Dominica, Grenada, St. Lucia and St.Vincent, o of which is linked to the police.

Additionally, there is a Special Patrol Group of eighty men on Antigua, 150-man *task force* on Barbados and 540 troops from all the countries station in Barbados (*Cf.* Maingot, 1990, pp. 73-77).

Regularly, since Operation Exotic Palm in September, 1985, RS manœuvres have taken place, in which troops from the UK, the USA ar CARICOM States participate on a rotating basis. Attempts to extend the RS officially to other CARICOM States were at first a failure.

In 1985, Jamaica did pledge its support for equipment and technologic matters, but feared that its own further engagement could be too costl Barbados' Prime Minister Erskine Sandiford, at the CARICOM Summit short

[218]St. Kitts and Nevis, Dominica and Grenada, which originally had small armies, had demobilized them different reasons

after the 1990 attempted *coup d'état* in Trinidad, pushed other CARICOM States to join the RSS. The tasks of the security system should be extended, he argued, to all forms of security: To the smashing of the illegal drug trade; mutual assistance after natural disasters; defence against threats by criminals to constitutional democracy or by terrorists, subversives or enemies of democracy (Hasters, 1990, p. 15). Barbados (as chairman), Belize, Dominica, Guyana, St. Kitts and Nevis and Trinidad and Tobago set up a committee to examine the possibilities of extending the RSS (Griffith, 1992, p.184).

Outside the RSS, for all CARICOM Member States and territories, there exists a Regional Police Training Centre (RPTC) in Barbados.

Since 1985, the OECS States have maintained an OECS Cadet Camp, which, in 1989, was widened to become an OECS/Caribbean Cadet Camp (Griffith, 1992, pp. 179ff), established in Barbados.

2.6.3 The Intervention in Grenada

The joint intervention in Grenada of US troops and troops and police units of Caribbean States in October, 1983, was, in several ways, a turning point in the history of the Commonwealth Caribbean:

1. For the first time, Commonwealth Caribbean States called on a friendly superpower to intervene militarily in a CARICOM member-country, thereby creating a precedent. Basically, they therefore left the line of non-alignment and peaceful conflict resolution, in order to stave off the acute threat, in their own eyes, to the security of the region.

2. For the first time, the majority of CARICOM decided on joint military action, with great personal risk for all involved. The resulting polarisation temporarily divided the Commonwealth Caribbean into two camps.

3. The Regional Defence and Security System (RSS) of the Eastern Caribbean experienced its 'baptism by fire'[219].

Maurice Bishop on toppling the dictatorially ruling Sir Eric Gairy in a bloodless *coup d' état* in Grenada, in March, 1979, met overwhelming approval not only there but in the entire Commonwealth Caribbean. Gairy had thoroughly discredited himself through oppressing the Opposition at home, electoral fraud and stupid appearances before international bodies. The view arose that a change-over of power with the aid of democratic elections was hardly possible anymore (*Cf.* Manley, 1983, p. 9). Efforts by Gairy, who had been abroad during the coup, to return to Grenada were foiled by CARICOM Governments.

At the time of the *coup*, Bishop was the Leader of the Opposition. Unlike some of his fellow comrade-in-arms in the New Jewel Movement, he was by no means a pronounced socialist. During the revolt, he announced early elections, but immediately suspended parts of the Constitution; and thereafter ruled by decree. Bishop first sought help from the traditional 'protecting powers' — namely Canada, the UK and the USA — for the building-up of the economy of the island state plagued with a 50% unemployment rate. After their rejection, however, he rapidly turned to new partners, especially Cuba and the then USSR.

---

[219]In reality, the Caribbean troops hardly did any fighting. However, they were assigned to watching POWs and later to occupation and law-and-order duties (*Cf.*: Griffith, 1992, pp. 184ff).

Within the Caribbean Community, Maurice Bishop had hardly any difficulty in being recognised as the legal Head of the Government of Grenada. The then left-wing Governments of Guyana, Jamaica, St. Lucia and Dominica ensured that Grenada remained integrated in the Caribbean Community. Bishop participated in all CARICOM Conferences and repeatedly affirmed the 'firm and abiding commitment to Caribbean regionalism, to the Caribbean integration process, and to CARICOM as our region's foremost integration institution' (1983, p. 167)[220].

When Grenada, under the influence of Bishop's deputy, Bernard Coard, seemed to be developing for a long time into a Socialist State in the Third World with a Marxist-Leninist one-party rule, well-meaning observers began to wonder how the regime's autonomous anti-imperialistic developmental strategy could be reconciled with CARICOM (Ambursley, 1984, p. 219). The CARICOM States agreed to the formula of ideological pluralism, i.e. the tolerance of different concepts of the State among its members. But massive criticism was made of human rights violations in Grenada.

Especially on the periphery of the 1982 CARICOM Summit in Ocho Rios, the suppression of the Opposition and of basic rights in Grenada played an important role. The campaign, emanating especially from Jamaica and Barbados, served in the first place to push back the ideological influence of the Bishop regime to the Commonwealth Caribbean. A direct threat to their own security was at first not perceived by the Eastern Caribbean States which were neighbours of Grenada (*Cf.* Payne, 1984, p. 147).

The relatively good relationship which the CARICOM States had with Grenada, was closely linked to Maurice Bishop as a person and the line followed by the moderate wing of his party of a rather Social Democratic orientation.

Mistrust developed when a split occurred in the ruling party between a moderate wing under Bishop and a Marxist-Leninist wing under his deputy, Bernard Coard, for whom the transformation of Grenada and the ruling party to Marxism-Leninism was not progressing fast enough[221].

While Bishop largely left trade and commerce in Grenada in private hands[222], he wished to boost tourism and sought an accommodation with the USA, the Coard wing pleaded for the sustained implementation of the 'Revolution', with nationalisation of private property, strengthening of 'mass organisations', close integration in the Socialist camp led by the then Soviet Union and its Caribbean ally, Cuba.

The USA expressed fears about the construction of the Point Salines International Airport in the South of the island, the location and equipment of which pointed to its projected military use. Then US President, Ronald Reagan, in a March, 1983, TV speech, described the airport as a possible military threat to the USA; but the Bishop Government underscored its significance for promoting tourism.

---

[220]Speech before the CARICOM Foreign Ministers' Standing Committee in Grenada on 29 6 1981

[221]*Cf*, *inter alia*, the New Jewel Movement's Central Committee's minutes in the *Grenada Papers*

[222]Trade and industry had supported the Opposition during Gairy's stint of power. whereas Gairy depended on the rural small farmers

In 1983, Bishop set up a committee to draw up a new Constitution. The Coard faction in the Central Committee of the New Jewel Movement accused Bishop with increasing vehemence of failure in leading the party and consequently switching the Marxist-Leninist course. The attempt to have Bishop share leadership with Coard failed.

When Bishop, on October 13, 1983, was, at the behest of the Central Committee, placed under house arrest, and was killed after being freed on October 19, the OECS Governments regarded this as a case of defence. Whereas consideration had been initially given to freeing Bishop from the hands of his opponents, intervention, with the aim of eliminating the Revolutionary Military Council (RMC), which had since seized power, was now the clear intention. Faced with the new rulers, the OECS Governments gave up all their restraint.

In the resultant intervention, several areas of interest met. The US Government saw in an attack on Grenada the possibility, after all the rhetoric about the Communist threat in the Caribbean and Central America, to make an example. At the same time, it would make amends for its failed involvement in the Lebanon.

Grenada seemed particularly suitable for this, since it was a small island about which US citizens did not know a lot. They would, therefore, be obliged to conclude, based on declarations of their Government, that a blood-smeared, left-wing regime, with Cuban and Soviet help, had taken over the Government and allowed its allies to build a military airport and possibly also naval bases. With the help of these installations, the then Soviet Union wanted to threaten the Southern Caribbean, with the important oil-producing countries of Venezuela and Trinidad. The airport would, according to Washington, also serve as a stop-over for Soviet and Cuban planes flying between Africa and the Caribbean.

The intervention in Grenada — in the manifest calculation of the US Government — could produce military successes without great military efforts or a large number of casualties. Other US opponents in the region, especially Cuba and Nicaragua, would be cowed (*Cf.*, too, Payne, 1984, p. 165). The occasion was particularly favourable, because practically all Caribbean left-wing parties and groups severely condemned Bishop's murder — and, therefore, could not reject measures against the murderers with the same firmness.

CARICOM Member States which participated in the intervention, had a unique opportunity to follow their years of anti-Socialist rhetoric with action. The effect of their common action was not impaired by the fact that it was possible only with US help. They had no need to fear the expected condemnation in academic circles, so long as they would have the support of the majority of the population.

It had been supposed that the US forces had contingency plans ready for their invasion of Grenada. But these plans had to be legitimised by the OECS Member States, whose Heads of Government — except that of Grenada — met in Barbados on October 21 for a special meeting as the Authority, including Montserrat; then excluding Montserrat as the Defence and Security Committee, the Committee responsible as per Article 8 of the OECS Treaty requiring unanimous decisions, following directives of the Authority, for the co-ordination of their collective defence against external attacks. Since Grenada had not been invited, however, the legality of the decision has been consistently questioned (Manley, 1983, p. 46).

The Authority decided that the Chairman, Eugenia Charles, should call on the USA for a joint intervention in Grenada. At the same time, it imposed sanctions on Grenada in the form of a flight ban from their respective States and territories as well as stopping the supply of currency from the ECCA[223].

Barbados' then Prime Minister, Tom Adams, joined the OECS Heads of Governments, thereby making the meeting into a sitting of the RSS, to which Grenada did not belong.

As a result of the events in Grenada, the Prime Minister of Trinidad and Tobago, George Chambers, as the then Chairman of the CARICOM Heads of Government Conference, summoned a conference, on October 22-23, in Port-of-Spain. The new holders of power in Grenada were not invited to this conference, either. Hence, the body could not reach any binding decisions in the sense of the CARICOM Treaty. On the other hand, it would hardly have been possible to bring from Grenada to the venue of the meeting, in these circumstances, the only legal representative of State power in Grenada, the Governor-General, Sir Paul Scoon.

A controversy over possible measures ensued among the CARICOM Heads of Government. Agreement was finally reached that Scoon should be requested to come out in favour of a broad-based Government of National Reconciliation and for early elections. A CARICOM Commission should conduct a fact-finding mission at the *locus in quo*. The Grenadians should, moreover, accept in their country the presence of a peace-keeping force of the CARICOM countries. But Grenada's CARICOM membership should lie dormant. Sanctions as per the OECS decisions were advocated.

The question of the use of military force against the military council in Grenada triggered off vehement discussions. The Heads of Government of the Bahamas, Belize, Guyana and Trinidad and Tobago were firmly opposed; the others of those present were in favour.

In the meantime, the secret preparations for the intervention, in which Jamaica participated actively, progressed intensively. Sub-units of Caribbean troops and police assembled at the Grantley Adams International Airport in Bridgetown, Barbados, for action. US warships steamed towards Grenada. The Grenadian Military Council, which observed the troop movements, tried in vain, through appeals for help to Great Britain and attempts of appeasement to the USA, to avert the military action. The approximately 1000 Americans in Grenada, mainly medical students at an extra-territorial Medical School, received security guarantees.

The US Government expressly insisted on a written invitation to intervene from the OECS Heads of Government, and received it. In the early morning hours of October 25, 1983, 6,000 US Marines and Army Rangers, together with 300 soldiers and police from six CARICOM nations began the invasion of Grenada. Units from Montserrat did not participate, owing to the specific instructions of the British Government (O'Shaughnessy, 1984, p. 169). Then

[223] *Cf.* Hugh O'Shaughnessy's comprehensive description of the intervention

British Prime Minister, Margaret Thatcher, opposed the military action and rejected requests for help.

OECS Chairwoman, Eugenia Charles, at a press conference with President Reagan in Washington, D.C. on the first day of the invasion, confirmed the OECS' request for help to the USA, Barbados and Jamaica. She attested to the fact that the murdered Prime Minister of Grenada had wanted, under pressure from the OECS Member States, to hold free elections and, therefore, had to die. The military action, she declared, was not an invasion, but rather the reply to a call for help to give back to the Grenadians their freedom and the right to elect their own Government (*Barbados Advocate* 26.10.83).

In a statement published on October 26, the participating OECS Governments again made it clear that the armaments in Grenada during the last years had reached a disproportionate military strength *vis-à-vis* the other OECS Member States and territories, which, in the hands of the current power-holders, presented a serious threat to the security of the OECS Member States and territories as well as to other neighbouring States. As soon as that threat was eliminated, Grenada's Governor-General would be asked to form a broad-based interim Government under the 1973 Constitution and arrange for general elections to be held (*CANA* Report, 26.10.83).

In the West Indian population, the arbitrary use of force against unarmed civilians had created a 'psychology of all-pervasive dread' (Lloyd Taylor, 1985, p. 77). The direct reaction to the intervention was enthusiastic rather than reserved. The broad support for the intervention showed the great extent to which socio-political links had already developed beyond geographical borders.

Eugenia Charles, on returning from the USA to her native Dominica where she was Prime Minister (in addition to being the current OECS chairwoman) was feted like a National Heroine. In Barbados, Tom Adams declared on the radio that he had rarely seen in those islands such unanimous support of the media, politically and in the population for a course of action, which was potentially so controversial (*Barbados Advocate*, 28.10.1983). In Jamaica, the social scientist, Carl Stone, in a public opinion poll conducted on the first week-end following the intervention, found overwhelming support for it[224]. Most Jamaicans saw it as a rescue mission[225] in which the Communist activists were given a political lesson (Stone, 1983a, p. 61).

Public opinion polls in Trinidad and Tobago also revealed that a considerable portion of the local population was not in agreement with the rejectionist stand of the Government. External Affairs Minister, Basil Ince, deplored that his fellow citizens had 'not yet fully developed a sense of nationalism' (*Express* 22.2.1984, p. 64). Barbadian novelist, George Lamming, termed it a 'shameful lack of this genuine regional patriotism' that most people in the Caribbean had welcomed the 'invasion' of Grenada (Lamming, 1984, p. 45).

---

[224]58% of the adult Jamaicans in a representative sample of unstated size on October 29-30, 1983, supported the invasion (or 76% of the then Government's supporters, and 38% of the then Opposition), 34% were against it (or 18% and 55% respectively); with the 'don't knows/won't says at 8% (Mullerleile, 1983b, p.3)

[225]Describing the occurrence variously as an *invasion*, *intervention* (the most neutral position) or *rescue mission* indicates the position of the commentators.

The positive reaction of the population had a direct impact on their voting behaviour. In Jamaica, the swing in attitudes led then Head of Government, Seaga, to hold snap elections in December 1983. Public opinion polls had suggested that his party would be returned to power, owing to the swing in the electorate caused by the events in Grenada (Stone 1983a, p. 60ff; 1989f, pp. 44f.). The then Opposition, using a pretext, declined totally to participate in the elections.

The Grenadian population itself seemed in its vast majority, to approve of the intervention. In a public opinion poll in nine of the fifteen constituencies, a year after the intervention, 88% of those questioned judged positively the landing of the US troops (Emmanuel, Brathwaite and Barriteau, 1986, pp. 44-48). Two and a half years later, then US President Reagan was greeted as a liberator by a massive crowd on the island, whereas, at a counter-demonstration, US TV cameras exceeded the number of demonstrators (*Frankfurter Allgemeine Zeitung*, 22.2.1986, p. 3).

The parties, which took a positive view of the intervention, won with overwhelming majority the first free elections in Grenada after the intervention, in December, 1984. The Chairman, Nicholas Braithwaite, of the Interim Government, established at the behest of the intervention forces, became Prime Minister in 1990.

Massive opposition to the intervention came from the founders of the Caribbean Community. Barbados' Errol Barrow accused Adams of being a victim of the Monroe Doctrine (1983, p. 3). Jamaica's Michael Manley opposed it, because there was 'not either a legal, moral or genuine political basis'. Indeed, 'a very important precedent' had been thereby set; and 'history will judge what the consequences of that will be' (1983, p. 47).

Guyana's Linden Forbes Burnham claimed that the real threat was that other countries had joined the successful 'Socialist' conversion of the Grenadian economy. Nothing in international law would justify this as the reason for an invasion (*DG* 26.11.1983, p.22). Burnham spoke of a secret plot of some groups within the region with the 'Big Brother' of the hemisphere, which had now hit Grenada, would hit Guyana tomorrow and, thereafter, some other country[226].

CARICOM Chairman, George Chambers, in his October 26 speech in Parliament, regretted the use of force, and called attention to 1982 CARICOM Heads of Government decision at the Ocho Rios Summit and renewed at the July, 1983, Port-of-Spain Summit. Chambers suggested — as the Heads of Government had decided — the sending of CARICOM peace-keeping troops, including from Trinidad and Tobago, to Grenada; but who should not have the character of a force of occupation (*Caribbean Monthly Bulletin*, October 1983, pp. 29-80).

Prime Minister George Price of Belize, itself threatened with invasion by Guatemala, continuously called to mind the principles hitherto followed by Commonwealth Caribbean States and territories of non-interference in the internal affairs of other States, the abstention from the use of force; and the

[226]Address to the nation on 25.10.1983, reprinted in: *Caribbean Monthly Bulletin*, Supplement No 1 (October, 1983), pp 63-65.

respect of the right to self-determination as per the UN Charter, which was recognised by all participants (Müllerleile, 1983b, p. 7).

During the intervention, and the days thereafter, the future of the Caribbean Community was at stake. Trinidad and Tobago and Barbados broke off current trading affairs. Barbados' Prime Minister, Tom Adams, reported on the radio on October 27 that the Heads of Government, at their meeting in Port-of-Spain on October 22, had spoken of a new order for the Community. This would take into consideration more stringently, respect for human rights and the democratic qualifications of the member-countries; it would also contain the removal of the strict unanimity rule in some areas. Adams spoke in this context about 'CARICOM-II', in which only Guyana did not wish to participate (*Barbados Advocate*, 28.10.1983). Circles in Guyana's capital, Georgetown, suggested the dissolution of the Caribbean Community and the establishment of a new body, which could replace the intervention States with the Dominican Republic and Haiti (*DG* 26.11.1983, p. 22).

Guyana sharply distanced itself in international fora from the intervention. In the UN Security Council, its draft resolution, which termed the intervention a flagrant violation of international law and of the independence, sovereignty and territorial integrity of Grenada, floundered on the US veto (*New York Times* 29.10.1983). The UN General Assembly, on the motion of Nicaragua and Zimbabwe, voted on November 2, 1983, on whether the military action should be 'regretted'. This draft resolution was adopted (108 votes in favour; nine against; and 27 abstentions).

Six CARICOM Member States — namely, Antigua and Barbuda, Barbados, Dominica, Jamaica, St. Lucia and St. Vincent and the Grenadines — were among those voting against. St. Kitts and Nevis, which had only just become a UN member, did not take part in the vote. The Bahamas, the delegate of Grenada, whose legal position was contested, Guyana and Trinidad and Tobago were the four CARICOM Member States voting in favour of the resolution. Belize abstained (Müllerleile, 1983b, p. 8).

Vehement discussions about the intervention also erupted behind the scenes of the Commonwealth Heads of Government Conference in New Delhi in November, 1983 (*Cf.* Barrow, 1983, p. 4). In a communiqué, they spoke of their 'deep disquiet' and recalled the principles of independence, sovereignty and territorial integrity. Emphasis should, however, they declared, be on 'reconstruction, not recrimination'. They promised to devote particular attention to the special situation of small states and directed the Secretary-General of the Commonwealth — himself a Guyanese — to prepare a study on the particular needs of such States in the protection of their right to sovereignty and territorial integrity ('Documents of the Invasion of Grenada', pp. 89ff).

The events in Grenada triggered off nostalgic speculations, which represented the intervention and its circumstances as the belated consequence of the failure of the 1958-62 West Indies Federation. Ramphal (1985, p. 12), an opponent of the intervention, declared that a Federal Government would have limited Gairy's 'excesses' or at least crushed 'the Maurice Bishop *coup d' état*'. Ramphal had himself been the Attorney-General of the Federal Government, and, in 1983, Secretary-General of the Commonwealth. Gordon Lewis saw in the 'invasion' the sequelae of a 'fatal absence of any effective Federal or regional authority'. Grenada in 1983 was, in Lewis' view, the 'aborted child of that dying Federation of 1962' (*CC* November 1987, p. 5). Lloyd Taylor saw in these events a 'crisis of self-determination' of Caribbean people which could be overcome by an intra-regional defence pact, the integration of production and by political integration (1985, pp. 75-83)[227].

The first stage in the restoration of constitutional rule in Grenada was the formation of an interim Government to which Governor-General, Sir Paul Scoon, appointed technocrats from the region. In the meantime, the 'peace-keeping forces' from the USA and participating Caribbean States dealt with the maintenance of law and order. New Grenadian police units were trained in other CARICOM countries. A para-military Special Security Unit (SSU) replaced the army and the militia, which had been demobilised.

Within the Caribbean Community, the new interim Government had hardly any difficulty in being recognised. Even President Burnham of Guyana fell in line. At the first CARICOM Summit after the intervention in July, 1984 in Nassau, in the Bahamas, the topic of Grenada was largely left out. Barbados' Prime Minister, Tom Adams, merely called for the breaches to be healed and the creation of an atmosphere of reconstruction (*CP* 26, Supplement, p. 14).

But the test of democracy came in the first free general elections after the intervention in December, 1984. The OECS Governments, in its statement of 26th October, 1983, had already made it clear that former Prime Minister Gairy and other undesirable political elements would not be welcome in Grenada. An electoral victory by Gairy's Grenada United Labour Party (GULP) would have discredited the whole 'rescue mission' of the USA and the participating Caribbean States. The OECS Government therefore, took steps to prevent this.

Nonetheless, within the first months after the intervention, no democratic political force had developed in Grenada, which could be expected definitely to defeat the GULP. 'After the intervention, the USA found itself in a humpty-dumpty position where all the King's horses and all the King's men did not know how to put democracy together again', recalled James Mitchell, Prime Minister of St. Vincent and the Grenadines, in an interview. 'But those of us close to the problem — John, Tom and I — were able to do it' (Brana-Shute, 1985, p. 29).

In August, 1984, Mitchell, after a mere month in office, invited John Compton and 'Tom' Adams — his St. Lucian and Barbadian counterparts, respectively — as well as Dominica's Prime Minister, Eugenia Charles, to Union Island in the Grenadines. The objective was to convince the leaders of four Grenadian parties of the necessity to merge their respective parties into a common party. This was achieved within five hours; only one of the four broke away two days later. The other three became the New National Party (NNP).

The NNP won 58.8% of the votes and fourteen of the fifteen seats in Parliament in the December, 1984, elections. Gairy did not seek election personally. As to whether the elections results were really so greatly influenced by

[227]Criticism and defence of the intervention produced an avalanche of publications (e.g Payne, Sutton and Thorndike, 1984, Gordon K Lewis, 1987; Mandle, 1985, Jan Carew, 1986, Woehlcke, 1984, and MacDonald, Sandstrom and Goodwin, 1988, Robert J Beck, 1993) in addition to those quoted

massive US aid to the NNP (*Cf.* Singh, 1985), as opponents of the US engagement suppose, is an open question[228].

Later developments revealed, however, that Head of Government, Herbert Blaize, could not control the centrifugal forces in the artificially melded party. Deputy NNP Leaders, George Brizan and Francis Alexis, in strife with the sickly Blaize, left the party, became the Parliamentary Opposition and took other NNP MPs with them.

In June, 1989, the Heads of Government of Dominica, St. Lucia and St. Vincent and the Grenadines met together, in order to discuss with Blaize the early holding of elections. St. Lucia's Prime Minister, Compton, stated that general elections in Grenada and other OECS Member States were no longer only a national question (*CI* July 1989, p. 14). He and others feared Gairy's GULP and the Maurice Bishop Patriotic Movement (MBPM), which had been founded by supporters of the murdered, last Prime Minister of Grenada, could benefit from the strife of the moderate parties (*Cf. CP* 29:29).

But the efforts of neither the Heads of Government nor of the Caribbean Democrat Union could cement the estranged situation. Gairy's GULP did not come into its own, however; and the MBPM sank into insignificance, when in March, 1990 — four months after Blaize's death — elections were held. The National Democratic Congress, founded by Brizan and Alexis with the former Head of the Interim Government, Nicholas Brathwaite, at the head, won a narrow victory.

2.6.4 Relations to Other Caribbean States

2.6.4.1 The Expansion of the Caribbean Community

The Treaty of Chaguaramas makes possible the following six types of membership of CARICOM:

1. Membership of the Community and Common Market;
2. Associate membership of the above;
3. Membership of the Community alone;
4. Associate membership of the Community alone;
5. Membership of the Common Market alone;
6. Associate membership of the Common Market alone.

Additionally, the possibility exists for countries to be granted observer status and/or formal agreements over collaboration to be made in various areas.

In 1991, the BVI and the Turks and Caicos Islands both received Associate Membership in the Community. They attend the Heads of Government Conference as observers, are members of all Standing Committees except that for Foreign Affairs, share the benefits of all relevant CARICOM regional programmes and measures, except the CARICOM travel documents, and pay an appropriate contribution to the budget of CARICOM (*cf. Caribbean Community,* 1992, pp. 29f). Anguilla, Aruba, Bermuda, the Cayman Islands,

[228] Bob Woodward, of Watergate fame, has claimed (1987, p. 383) that the CIA paid US $ 675,000 for opinion moulding and mobilizing the voters The NNP and its party allies did not gainsay external aid, which, however, they did not regard as immoral, either.

Colombia, the Dominican Republic, Haiti, Mexico, Puerto Rico, the Federation of the Netherlands Antilles and Venezuela, all have observer status in some CARICOM Committees.

Venezuela, the Dominican Republic and Haiti have shown interest in full membership. Between the existing CARICOM Member States, however, agreements exist that the integration process should be first of all deepened within that membership, before additional members are admitted, or even agreements concerning economic co-operation with particular obligations are entered into. The recommendation of the Group of Caribbean Experts (*The Caribbean Community in the 1980s*, p. 89) had, in fact, been similar in nature. The West Indian Commission, however, in its final report, proposed the creation of an Association of Caribbean States open to all Caribbean Basin countries (*CR* 23.7.92, p. 3).

At the October, 1993, CARICOM Special Summit in Port-of-Spain, in which State and Government Leaders from Colombia, Mexico, Venezuela and Suriname participated, an action plan was agreed on for closer economic co-operation (*CI* November, 1993, p. 1).

The Association of Caribbean States (ACS)[229], proposed by the West Indian Commission, came into existence on the 24th July, 1994, in Cartagena/Colombia. The ACS according to its Convention is intended to boost economic and political co-operation among the island countries of the Caribbean, the countries in South and Central America bordering the Caribbean Sea, and Guyana, Suriname and French Guiana. Leaders and Senior Ministers of 25 Caribbean and Latin American countries took part, among them Antigua and Barbuda, the Bahamas, Barbados, Belize, Colombia, Costa Rica, Cuba, Dominica, the Dominican Republic, Grenada, Guatemala, Guyana, Haiti, Honduras, Jamaica, Nicaragua, Panama, St. Kitts and Nevis, St. Lucia, St. Vincent and the Grenadines, Suriname, Trinidad and Tobago, Mexico and Venezuela took part in the signing. France signed for its Caribbean *départments*. The British, Dutch and US dependencies will get observer status. The site of the headquarters will be Trinidad and Tobago. The first summit was to be held there in August, 1995.

The Convention by which the Association will be governed was finalised in Caracas in June 1994. It can take effect when two thirds of the 25 states eligible for full membership deposit instruments of ratification with the Government of Colombia. The ACS Convention provides for two permanent organs , the Ministerial Council and the Secretariat. The Council will comprise ministerial representatives of member states and will be the principal organ for policy making and direction of the Association. The Secretariat will be headed by a Secretary General as the chief administrative officer.

The ACS, declared the host of the meeting, Colombia's then President Cesar Gaviria Trujillo[230], presented an opportunity to 'initiate a permanent dialogue to discuss our mutual co-operation in many areas, fostering the development of tourism, expanding the use of Spanish, English and French, increasing

[229] Asociación de Estados del Caribe (AEC)

[230] Now Secretary-General of the Organisation of American States, OAS

transportation links, diversifying agricultural production, making use of our natural resources through a strategy of sustainable development, and co-operation to overcome natural disasters.' Gaviria also mentioned the fight against narco-trafficking and money laundering.

The acting Chairman of the CARICOM Heads of Government Conference, Barbados' Prime Minister Erskine Sandiford, spoke at the foundation meeting of 'our dream for the integration of the entire Latin American and Caribbean region' (*CANA* report from Cartagena, in: *WG* 2.8.94, p. 10).

The ACS has a potential membership of forty states and territories with a population of almost 198 million, and an area of 5.489.533 km^2 (*CARICOM PERSPECTIVE* 61 and 62, p. 9).

The Dominican Republic intends, with its application for CARICOM membership, to end a long period of isolation in the region. Its full membership would more than double the population of the Common Market at one stroke. The fragility of the Common Market with such disequilibrium is clear from a controversy over banana exports early in 1990. The CARICOM Member States had supported the recognition of the Dominican Republic in 1989 as an ACP country by the then EC, following that country's commitment not to profit from the advantages of the banana, sugar and rum protocols. With these import concessions in the West European market, the Dominican Republic would have become the direct rival of CARICOM-members (*CI* March, 1990, pp.1ff). Specifically at issue were banana exports to the UK which were the main exports of some CARICOM countries. The Dominican Republic announced extensive banana exports to the UK two months after being recognised as an ACP State. Only following violent attacks, especially from the Eastern Caribbean, did it relent. The two sides then agreed that the Dominican Republic could export bananas to the UK — but not under Lomé Treaty conditions (*CI* April, 1990, p. 2). The 1990 and 1992 decisions of the then EC on the duty-free status of banana exports from ACP States subsequently rendered the agreement irrelevant. The Dominican Republic intended to increase its banana exports to the EU to 200,000 tons yearly, from a mere 1,500 tons in 1989 (*CI* October, 1992, p. 11). In March 1994 it was allocated an annual quota of less than 95,000 tons (*CI* May 1994, p.4).

Venezuela officially applied in October, 1991, to join the Caribbean Community. Its membership would increase the population of the Community by a further 18.7 million persons or 450%. The reactions of the CARICOM members indicated as little interest in an early admission of Venezuela as in the case of the Dominican Republic.

Puerto Rico, under the leadership of Governor Rafael Hernández Colón, had increasingly shown interest in regional and local collaboration with the Caribbean Community. Colón's Popular Democratic Party (PDP) had sought greater foreign policy freedom, without change of status, for the island.

Puerto Rico's economic relationship with the Caribbean profits from special tax preferences[231], which US investors enjoy in Puerto Rico. The latter's profits

[231] Title 936 of the US Federal Tax Code exempts U.S firms in Puerto Rico from taxes on a considerable portion of their profits re-invested to a given extent in the island or in certain Caribbean States — thereby costing

have been increased by the siting of 'twinned factories' and the relocation of parts of the production process elsewhere in the Caribbean with an even more favourable wage structure.

While some Eastern Caribbean countries test this possibility intensively, critical voices accuse Puerto Rico of having no real interest in the region and of using the small Caribbean states only as a lobby with the US Government to secure the continuation of the tax preferences[232]. The privileges are endangered in view of the tight budgetary situation of the USA. In May, 1993, Puerto Rico's Governor sought support from eleven Caribbean countries against the modification of the preferences. At the same time, he informed them of the discontinuation of credit payments from 936 funds (*WG* 1.6.1993, p. 19).

Puerto Rico seemed for some time to be on the way to becoming a US State. Tax privileges[233] and the form of collaboration with CARICOM States available up to now, in that case, would no longer have been possible. In the November, 1992, Gubernatorial and Congressional elections, the victors were the New Progressive Party (NPP), which had campaigned the most decisively for political integration in the USA.

In December, 1991, the Puerto Ricans, in a referendum, had rejected a law seeking political and cultural independence from the USA (*AP* Report from San Juan dd. 9.12.91). Since February, 1993, English has again become an official language on the island, in addition to Spanish (*CI* March, 1993, p. 11).

In November, 1993, Puerto Rico's voters decided narrowly in a referendum to keep the lucrative Commonwealth status and not become the 51st US State (*CI* December, 1993, p. 5). Puerto Rico did not take part in the establishment of the Association of Caribbean States (ACS) in July, 1994.

2.6.4.2 The Problem of Haiti

CARICOM Member States have more sympathy for Haiti[234], the neighbour of the Dominican Republic, than for the latter State. Despite the Duvalier dictatorship, the CARICOM Heads of Government avoided isolating Haiti, within the Caribbean, and in 1974, that nation applied for membership and received observer status. This secured a regional platform for the regime, but also gave the CARICOM countries the possible scope to obtain more detailed knowledge of the internal situation of that country.

The Government of Jamaica was particularly active in this. In February, 1986, it accelerated Duvalier's departure (*Frankfurter Allgemeine Zeitung*, 10.2.1986, p. 5). Peripherally to a Miami Conference, a Group of Concerned Caribbean Leaders formed around Seaga, then Jamaica's Prime Minister, in November, 1987, and desired to help restore 'normality' in Haiti. In December, the group consisting of the Heads of Government of Jamaica, St. Lucia, St. Vincent and the Grenadines, the Netherlands Antilles and Aruba, travelled to

---

the IRS US $ 2 6 billion yearly, but providing 300,000 jobs, directly and indirectly, in Puerto Rico (*CI* March, 1993, p. 11, April, 1993, pp. 2ff).

[232] *Cf.*: Errol Barrow's criticism in the *Daily Nation* (Barbados) 26.11.1985, p. 2.

[233] *Cf. CI* May, 1993, p. 2.

[234] *Cf.*: Mirlande Manigat, 1988, pp. 102ff.

Haiti, in order to demand the guarantee of free elections from the chairman of the ruling council, General Namphy (*WG* 12.12.1987, p. 4).

When the November, 1987, attempt to hold general elections ended in a blood-bath, critical voices accused the Caribbean Community of not having involved itself energetically enough. The then CARICOM chairman, John Compton, labelled the reproach as absurd. 'What could the Caribbean Community do except to go there and observe, and if we did observe on a government level, we would have to be pointing fingers at who was wrong and who was not'. Hence, CARICOM had sent only an unofficial observer (*WG* 15.12.1987, p. 19).

In January, 1988, the CARICOM Heads of Government met for a day in Barbados, in order to discuss the Haitian situation. The differences of opinion remained. A majority of the participants were clearly in favour of postponing the January 17, 1989, elections and condemning the ruling junta for its role in the failed attempt to hold elections two months previously. Prime Minister Erskine Sandiford, after the meeting, conceded that the CARICOM Treaty pushed the members to harmonise their foreign policy; but this harmonisation had been achieved very rarely. Expectations from the meeting had, he claimed, been too high, so that the results had necessarily been disappointing (*WG* 26.1.1988, p. 12).

In a resolution, the CARICOM Heads of Government regretted the election day occurrences on November 29 and criticised the fact that the newly-created Electoral Committee was not independent of the Government; and that the new electoral decree ran counter to some important democratic electoral practices. The national ruling council should, therefore, up to the elections, restore the credibility of the electoral process, and guarantee that it be conducted peacefully. It should also ensure that all voters should be able to exercise their constitutional franchise and that a transfer of power took place, which would promote the democratic process, strengthen the economy and improve the quality of life of the people in Haiti (*CP* 46 and 47; pp. 42 and 51).

Opposition to a tougher condemnation of the Haitian power-holders came especially from Jamaica's then Prime Minister, Seaga. Delegated by his CARICOM colleagues in July, 1987, and, three months later, by the party leaders of the International Democrat Union (IDU) in Berlin, to observe developments in Haiti, be harboured no illusions about the second attempt at holding elections, scheduled for January 17, 1988. His election observer, Dr. Neville Gallimore, spoke equivocally of a fair electoral process in the traditional Haitian manner (*CC* February 1988, pp. 1-2). The hopes of Seaga and the Caribbean Democrat Union (CDU), which he headed up to 1991, rested rather on the new Presidential candidate, Leslie Manigat, a Haitian social scientist who was highly regarded in the CARICOM region[235]. Before becoming a candidate, he had secured in Caracas the support of the regional organisation of the Christian Democrats (i.e. the ODCA).

Circles within the Christian Democrats and the IDU apparently hypothesised that fair and free elections in Haiti would hardly be possible under current

[235]Manigat had been for a time the Director of the semi-official Institute of International Relations of the UWI in St. Augustine, Trinidad, and, most recently, Professor at the Simón Bolivar University, Caracas.

conditions, given the country's undemocratic tradition and the authoritarian structure of the totally poverty-stricken country. With a functioning civilian Government, however, a certain educational process would be initiated, which, with the help of the USA, Canada and Western European countries, could lead to the gradual raising of the standard of living and start the process of democratisation[236].

After the elections, the Manigat Government was recognised by Jamaica, Dominica and Grenada, whereas Barbados, St. Kitts and Nevis and St. Lucia refused so to do. Barbados demanded the revocation of Haiti's observer status with the Caribbean Community (*CI* March, 1988, p. 10), and felt confirmed in its viewpoint by Manigat's ouster in June, 1988 (*CI* July, 1988, p. 2).

At the following CARICOM Summit in July, 1988, in Antigua, Barbados and Trinidad and Tobago demanded that Haiti's observer status be rescinded. Other participants, however, especially Jamaica, Dominica and Antigua and Barbuda, were opposed to this. Jamaica's then Prime Minister, Seaga, argued that it would be illogical now to punish Haiti, which had received observer status under Duvalier. Moreover, Seaga pointed out, Suriname was granted that status only after its 1980 military *coup d'état*; conversely, Grenada remained a CARICOM member-State, even after the 1979 bloodless coup there (*CI* August, 1988, p. 2). In June, 1989, the Caribbean Community again despatched to Haiti a group of experts who were to report back at the following CARICOM Summit (*CI* July, 1989, p. 12).

When, in November, 1989, then Haitian Foreign Minister, Ivor Perrier, requested financial assistance and debt forgiveness at the 44th Session of the UN General Assembly, he was supported by delegates from various CARICOM Governments, including Trinidad and Tobago, St. Lucia and the Bahamas, relying on statements by then Haitian President, Prosper Avril, on the holding of free and fair elections (*CR* 7.12.1989, p. 5).

The September 1991, military ouster of President Aristide, who was elected in December, 1990, was unanimously condemned by CARICOM Governments. Indeed, the Government of Trinidad and Tobago even offered to participate in a military intervention against the new military junta (*WG* 15.10.1991, p. 17).

Aristide was received as a Head of State while visiting CARICOM countries (*CI* December 1991, p. 3). Indeed, he participated in the July, 1992, CARICOM Summit in Port-of-Spain (*CI* August 1992, p. 3; *CC* July/August 1992, p. 10). The CARICOM Member States participated totally in the OAS economic boycott of Haiti. They also supported plans for military intervention if authorised by a UN Security Council resolution. In July, 1994, Antigua and Barbuda, Dominica and St. Lucia, pressed hard by US authorities, agreed to give Haitian refugees to the USA a temporary 'safe heaven' (*CI* August 1994, p. 3).

Pressured again by the US authorities, Antigua and Barbuda, Barbados, Belize, Guyana, Jamaica and Trinidad and Tobago in September declared their readiness to take part in a US-led Multinational Force (MNF) to restore peace and democracy in Haiti, albeit not as combatants, but as peace-keeping forces

[236] IDU members are Christian Democratic, Liberal and Conservative Parties on five continents

after the intervention. The so-called CARICOM contingent or CARICOM battalion took part in the collective training of the MNF in Puerto Rico, and entered Haiti as part of a 24-nation occupation force in October.[237]

2.6.4.3 Relations with Cuba

Official relations between Cuba and the CARICOM Member States began in 1972 with the establishment of diplomatic relations by Trinidad and Tobago, Guyana, Barbados and Jamaica. These four Governments, headed respectively by Dr. Eric Williams, Linden Forbes Burnham, Errol Barrow and Michael Manley, did not stand all that far away from Castro. They at least shared his views on Non-alignment, closer South-South co-operation and a New International Economic Order.

Nonetheless, Ramphal (1985, pp. 14ff) holds that the establishment of diplomatic relations was 'an act rooted not in ideology but in practical regional considerations and the refusal of Caribbean countries to be pawns in a super-power game.' Cuba's Foreign Minister had, in 1972, at a meeting of Non-aligned Foreign Ministers in Georgetown, Guyana, offered the Guyanese Government the formal establishment of diplomatic relations. Guyana reacted positively, but waited until Barbados, Jamaica and Trinidad and Tobago joined with it in this matter. With that, declares Ramphal, 'Latin American participation in the embargo against Cuba was over.'

The diplomatic recognition of Cuba met the wish of Havana to end its isolation in the region and bring Cuba's significant political and military strength to bear there (Bryan, 1985, p. 339). Thereafter, Havana established much closer relations with some Commonwealth Caribbean Governments than with Spanish-speaking Caribbean countries. Cuba provided substantial technical, economic and military assistance, in part in direct competition with the USA and also with the declared intention of bringing about the Socialist transformation of the region.

The relations between Cuba and the Commonwealth Caribbean States developed bilaterally. The collective decision to establish diplomatic relations with Cuba was not the start of a common policy towards this country (Bryan, 1985, p. 339). But it did introduce a phase of ideological pluralism in the Commonwealth Caribbean, which ended only with the October, 1983, events in Grenada.

The relations of Trinidad and Tobago with Cuba were rather pragmatic, whereas those with Barbados were marked by 'consistent nervousness' (Bryan, 1989a, p. 100). Guyana, Jamaica in 1972-80, and Grenada, after 1979, collaborated closely in technical, economic and military matters with Cuba. In Grenada, Cuban technicians and construction workers started building an international airport, the possible military use of which significantly contributed to the US-Caribbean intervention in 1983. In 1979, newly-elected Governments

[237] Jamaica's Leader of the Opposition, Edward Seaga, and JLP Member of Parliament Dr Neville Gallimore after secret negotiations with the military leaders in Haiti were able to alert the US government that there was still a diplomatic door open for negotiation which could possibly avoid an aggressive military invasion. This helped to convince President Clinton to send a high-level dilpomatic mission to Haiti for talks that turned out successfully (WG 4.10 1994, p 10)

in Dominica and St. Lucia, although short-lived, also established close links with Cuba.

At the start of the 1980s, anti-Cuban resentment accelerated the swing to conservative Governments within the Commonwealth Caribbean. The 'Cuban card' was played ruthlessly and often manipulatively, in order to keep, or win, political power. One part of the political spectrum used the Cuban influence for the revolutionary legitimisation of its power and to suppress the Opposition (*Cf.* Maingot, 1983a, p. 22; Stone, 1983a). The other part warned constantly of the dire consequences of Socialism. Elections in Jamaica, Dominica and St. Lucia brought decidedly anti-Cuban parties to power. The Reagan Administration in the USA supported this course with aid for the region.

In 1981, Jamaica broke off diplomatic relations with Cuba, which became increasingly isolated from the Commonwealth Caribbean. After the intervention in Grenada, Guyana remained the only Commonwealth Caribbean country with rather close links with Cuba, whence some technical and medical assistance was provided. The Cubans tried in vain to reconcile the two socialist parties in Guyana — namely, the then ruling People's National Congress and the People's Progressive Party, then in the Opposition.

Almost no further official relations existed between the OECS Member States and Cuba, following the Grenada intervention. Only St. Lucia at first still had diplomatic relations with Cuba, and these were without resident ambassadors. Cuban offers of scholarships were, however, rejected.

Historically, Cuba has exerted far greater political and ideological influence on the Caribbean and Latin America than has the ex-Soviet Union. In this area, one could really speak of Cuba as a surrogate of Moscow (Bryan, 1989, p. 103). Castro has successfully understood how to present himself to Caribbean people as the advocate of the Non-Aligned Movement and champion of anti-Imperialism and racism. Nelson Mandela, then ANC President, during his July, 1991, visit to Cuba, praised the heroic struggle of the Cuban people for independence, which is, he stated, a model for the fight of black South Africans. He also praised the deployment of the Cuban soldiers for the African people, especially in Angola (*Frankfurter Allgemeine Zeitung*, 29.7.1991, p. 3). Thousands of Caribbean youth have become familiar with the land, people and ideology, through Cuba's scholarship programme. But not all of them returned home as convinced proponents of the Castro regime[238].

The ideological turnaround in the ex-Soviet Union and Cuba's other East European allies has led to a change in Cuba's relationship with the Caribbean Community countries. Growing economic difficulties could lead to unrest, if the Castro regime does not succeed in finding new trading partners. But this almost unavoidably requires accommodation with the USA, whose political and economic boycott against Cuba is still effective. From the relationship with the USA depends the development of Cuba's relationship with the Commonwealth Caribbean.

Michael Manley, once a close ally of Castro's and who, in 1980-89, while out of office, visited Cuba several times, sought to improve his relationship with

[238]*Cf.*, for instance, the portrayal of the reluctant brigadista, Colin Dennis, in his book, *The Road Not Taken* (1985)

the USA at first, on returning to power in February, 1989, as well as with the US-dependent international financial agencies. Only in 1990 were diplomatic relations resumed with Cuba, as had been announced before the elections. The new foreign and domestic policy of the People's National Party Government is free of Cuban influence. Other parties in the region which have not turned away like this, have practically no likelihood of being returned to power.

In July, 1991, a technical CARICOM delegation travelled to Cuba, in order to examine the possibilities of co-operation in tourism, agriculture and hi-tech. At first, however, Cuba's refusal to recognise the current Government of Grenada stood in the way of closer relations with CARICOM. (*WG* 16.7.1991). In October, 1993, ten years after the intervention, the first official Cuban delegation visited Grenada, and had talks among others with then Prime Minister Brathwaite. The Cubans shared interest in the development of trade relations.

After Cuba had normalised its relations with Grenada, the 1992 CARICOM Summit in Port-of-Spain agreed in principle to the creation of a CARICOM/Cuba Joint Commission (*CC* July/August, 1992, p. 19). Cuba was not granted observer status in the Ministerial Committees of CARICOM, despite being invited to CARICOM Summits (*CI* February, 1993, p. 7). In July, 1993, the CARICOM Heads of Government confirmed their decision, in the teeth of US objections, to form the aforementioned Joint Commission (*CI* August, 1993, p. 5). In December 1993 the joint commission was signed into being at the CARICOM Headquarters in Georgetown/Guyana (*CI* January 1994, p.6). Cuba should — according to the wish of the CARICOM Heads of Government — also become a founding member of the *Association of Caribbean States* (*CI* November 1993, p.1).

Former Castro opponents made the running in the rapprochement to Cuba. The Leader of the Opposition in Jamaica, Edward Seaga (1991), has seen Jamaica's future market in the eleven million population of Cuba, which is twice as large as that of the Community — but also Jamaica's greatest rival in the fields of tourism and agriculture. Returning Cuban exiles could contribute their profound knowledge of the US market.

At the end of 1991, several high Caribbean Government and private sector representatives came out in favour of lifting the US economic blockade against Cuba (*CI* November, 1991, pp. 1ff). Dominica's Prime Minister, Dame Eugenia Charles, thinks that Castro would have no difficulty at all in being 'elected handsomely' in a free poll. The USA should lift the embargo, for Cuba, she holds, has 'a leader that the people want' (*CI* March, 1993, p. 8). Trinidad and Tobago's former External Affairs Minister, Sahadeo Basdeo (1992, p. 116) holds that lifting the blockade would strengthen the role of the USA in the region and create new investment markets. Castro would be forced to liberalise the system. In October, 1993, the CARICOM States, with Antigua and Barbuda abstaining and Grenada being absent, agreed to a resolution of the UN General Assembly asking the USA to lift their blockade on Cuba. In October, 1994, nine CARICOM members voted for a UN resolution calling for an end to the economic embargo; Dominica, Grenada and St. Kitts and Nevis did not vote (*CI* November 1994, p. 7).

St. Vincent and the Grenadines established diplomatic relations with Cuba at the end of May, 1992. Decisive here, too, was the hope for new trading relationships (*CI* July, 1992, p. 10).

2.6.5. Foreign Policy in the Americas

2.6.5.1 Relations with the USA

The Caribbean is of great geo-strategic and psychological significance to the USA. American political leaders, therefore, display unusual sensitivity about the region[239]. The foreign policy relationships of the Commonwealth Caribbean to the USA, and conversely, are marked by different interests, which converge only partially and for certain periods of time. Over time, US interests in the region have changed several times; and are defined and assessed differently by different groups in the USA.

The countries of the Commonwealth Caribbean have acknowledged their interdependence with the USA, while keeping a certain degree of autonomy and selling their solidarity as dear as possible (Maingot, 1990). But they have not succeeded, according to Searwar (1990, p. 5), in finding a common answer to the challenge of the hegemonial power, which would leave them with the possibility of the self-determination of their foreign-policy strategy.

The 1823 Monroe Doctrine declared North, Central and South America to be the US sphere of interest and was directed against Western European colonial powers. Up to the late nineteenth century, the USA actively tried to push back European influence in the Caribbean and built bases which were supposed to make possible the free flow of international trade through the Panama Canal. During the Second World War, the USA constructed numerous naval bases against the German Navy and kept some of them after the end of the war.

Today, the Caribbean is the strategic underbelly of the USA and the Achilles heel of NATO (Carlucci 1982). During peacetime, 44% of all imports by sea and 45% of the total US crude oil travel through the Caribbean. Sixty-six percent of the oil destined for Western Europe travels through the Southern Atlantic. In times of war, 50% of the supplies for NATO and the largest portion of oil supplies and the reinforcement for the US forces would come from the US Gulf ports and must travel through the Florida Straits (Carlucci, 1982, p. 4).

In addition to military interests, free access to trade and financial markets of the region plays an important role (Greene and Scowcroft, 1984, pp. 9ff); so do oil production in Mexico and Venezuela, the vulnerability of the oil refineries in the Caribbean, a great number of Caribbean emigrants flooding the USA, the repayment of large debts by the region to US banks and the protection of US investments in the formulation of US interests.

Between 1898 and 1983, the USA intervened sixteen times[240] militarily in the Caribbean Sea. The October, 1983, intervention in Grenada was the first in the Commonwealth Caribbean. Military manœuvres — *Ocean Venture '82*, with 45,000 soldiers, the largest manœuvre undertaken in peace-time by the USA up

---

[239] *Cf.* Crassweller, 1972, pp 41ff, *Russia in the Caribbean*, p 5

[240] Other sources speak of thirty such military interventions between 1900 and 1965 (*Cf* Dymally, 1985)

to that time—have underscored the firm US control of the region (Barry *inter alia*; 1984, p. 196). The Commonwealth Caribbean was involved in these manoeuvres both as their location and through the participation in them of Caribbean troops. Five hundred soldiers and security personnel from Antigua and Barbuda, Barbados, Dominica, Grenada, St. Lucia and St. Kitts and Nevis took part in *Operation Exotic Palm* in St. Lucia in September, 1985. In this military exercise, which was led by UK and US military, the deployment of Coast Guards and the repelling of invaders were practised. The USA, which bore the costs of the manoeuvre (*CI* October 1985, p. 1) also helps to train Commonwealth Caribbean troops and Police.

Complete assistance in creating jobs and achieving balance of payments equilibrium should come from a type of Marshall Plan. This idea was adduced in January, 1981, during the visit by then Jamaican Prime Minister, Edward Seaga, to the White House in Washington, DC.[241]

The original plan was that the USA, together with Venezuela, Mexico and Canada, should reflect on a Caribbean Basin Plan for the region. Despite preparatory discussions (Seaga, 1981, p. 7) the common initiative did not come into existence. On February 24, 1982, US President Reagan announced, at the OAS Conference in Washington, D.C., his own plan, which became known as the Caribbean Basin Initiative (CBI). Reagan left open the participation of Mexico, Canada and Venezuela. With the justification that the prosperity and security of the neighbours of the USA were also in the direct interests of the USA, he announced a 12-year programme for 27 countries of the region. The duty-free importation into the USA of most goods, produced in these countries, tax incentives for investments in the Caribbean Basin, technical assistance, tax concessions for participants at conferences held in the Caribbean and direct financial aid towards achieving balance of payments equilibrium, were included in the CBI[242].

It entered into force in watered-down form early in 1984 and caused extremely diverse reactions. Prime Minister Seaga supported it enthusiastically. Grenada and Guyana, excluded initially from its provisions, rejected it flatly. Venezuela's former President, Carlos Andrés Pérez, feared a division of the Central American and Caribbean countries (*CC* April, 1982, pp. 7-10).

Critics pointed out particularly that the plan hardly sufficed really to help the entire region along the lines of the original Marshall Plan. Moreover, good quality finished products manufactured in the region, (e.g. textiles, clothing and leather goods) were specifically excluded from duty-free status. Critics also argued that, with the CBI, the USA merely wished to reward compliant Caribbean Governments, while punishing less compliant ones—such as Grenada and Guyana (as already mentioned) in addition to Nicaragua. Former US Ambassador in the Eastern Caribbean, Sally Shelton, warned a House of Representatives Committee against isolating Grenada (*'Testimony'*, p. 17).

American trade unions expressed concern. The private sector was largely sceptical over the investment incentives and tax concessions ascribed to the

---

[241] Seaga was the first Head of Government received by the U.S. President, Ronald Reagan, after taking office.

[242] For the text of speech, please see *The Sunday Gleaner* of 28.2.1982, p.11. *bulletin of Eastern Caribbean Affairs*, (Cave Hill/Barbados), 1.8, pp. 23-30.

CBI. Sugar planters, textile and shoe manufacturers, church and development-aid organisations, thrifty citizens and Congressmen for differing motives, all had reservations. In Jamaica, representatives of twelve nations complained that only US firms and, therefore, not local interests would benefit from the CBI (Feinberg *et al.*, 1983, p. 47).

After it entered into effect, the hitherto US trade deficit with the twenty-two favoured Caribbean countries paradoxically changed to a surplus! Indeed, the CBI carefully excluded all Caribbean products which were really competitive from being imported at favourable rates into the USA (J. O'Neil Lewis, 1989b, p. 57).

CBI exports to the USA fell to US$6.499 billion (1986) and US$6.64 billion (1988) from US$9.24 billion (1983) and US$9.134 billion (1984). Sugar exports from 1984 to 1988 fell in value to US$259 million from US$499 million; oil exports to US$1.44 billion from US$4.3 billion. Only the exports of coffee, fruits, vegetables, fish, beef and textiles increased (*CI* November, 1987, p. 15; Thorndike, 1990, p. 38). US exports to the thirteen CARICOM Member States in 1992 showed a trade surplus in value of US$431 million, on a volume of US$2.749 billion (*WG* 1.6.1993, p. 19).

The failure of the CBI was due to the new sugar import quotas introduced in 1981. Between 1982 and 1989, the region lost US$1.8 billion in earnings and 400,000 jobs in sugar — as against creating 136,000 new jobs in the production of finished goods between 1983 and 1988. During the same time-frame, labour supply in the region increased by 2.3 million persons[243]. In 1992 and 1993, the quotas for duty-free and duty-reduced Caribbean sugar imports in the USA were further reduced by 11.75% (*CI* October, 1992, p. 11).

The CBI was successful only for six Central American States whose exports in volume increased by 43% between 1983 and September, 1990. US Commerce Department's figures indicated a 36% decline for the other eighteen CBI beneficiary countries (*CR* 20.6.1991, p. 7).

The USA declined responsibility for its possible failure. Both Reagan and his Vice-President, George Bush, called attention to the fact that its success depended on both sides. Nonetheless, Reagan, in Grenada in February, 1986, announced the duty-free access of Caribbean textiles to the US market, without quota restrictions. Jamaica's then Prime Minister, Seaga, rejoiced that thousands of new jobs would be thereby created in Jamaica and the rest of the Caribbean (*DG* 21.2.1986, pp. 1 and 25).

CARICOM Heads of Government and Ministers with portfolio responsibility dealt with the CBI rather often in common meetings, although the CBI was thought of as a bilateral plan. Previous attempts to convert it into a multilateral aid plan — e.g. via the CDB — foundered on the resistance of the US Administration. In August, 1990, President Bush signed CBI-II, as the new law is known generally, which expanded the original legislation and eased some of the restrictions complained about.

A month later, Bush forwarded to the US Congress draft legislation for the Enterprise for the Americas Initiative (EAI), which envisages free trade agreements, the promotion of investment aid and the reduction of foreign debt

[243] Data according to Pastor and Fletcher, 1992, p 78ff.

for the Western Hemisphere. Free trade treaties are supposed to be able to be signed bilaterally as well as with communities such as CARICOM (Whitney, 1990, p. 70). At the start of 1991, the then Jamaica Prime Minister, Michael Manley, was delegated by his CARICOM counterparts to represent the CARICOM Member States in the relevant negotiations. In May, 1991, he discussed the matter with then President Bush and Vice-President Dan Quayle at the White House (*CR* 20.6.1991, p. 8).

In July, 1991, then CARICOM Secretary-General, Roderick Rainford , and a US Trade Representative, Carla Hill, signed an agreement between the Caribbean Community and the USA concerning the implementation of the EAI. A CARICOM/US Trade and Investment Council was formed as the first institution of this kind to discuss details. It consisted of one representative each from the Bahamas, Barbados, Belize, Guyana, Jamaica and Trinidad and Tobago, two representatives of the OECS Member States and one each from the CARICOM and OECS Secretariats (*CI* August, 1991, p. 1). This agreement, which was made following the approval by the CARICOM Heads of Government, signifies an enhancement of the status of the Secretariat of the Community and is a further step towards common external representation.

The EAI is closely linked with the comprehensive North American Free Trade Agreement (NAFTA), which began at the start of 1994 and aims firstly at removing barriers from US-Canada-Mexico trade relations. It and further trade agreements, are supposed to create a countervailing force to the European Union and the economic power of ASEAN[244]. In view of the tight budgetary situation of the US Government, CARICOM member States feared a limitation of the CBI in favour of trade preferences for Mexico (*CI* April, 1993, p. 1).

Even without restrictions to the CBI, NAFTA could seriously affect the export prospects of Caribbean goods to the USA and Canada. This follows from Mexico being able freely to export sensitive items to the USA, prohibited to other CBI countries by law[245].

NAFTA has at first also triggered off discussions as to whether the CARICOM Member States should not rather try to join the large free trade area, instead of creating their own, tiny one. Trinidad and Tobago's Leader of the Opposition, Basdeo Panday, expressed considerable doubt as to whether, given NAFTA, further pursuing the CARICOM idea still made sense (*WG* 17.11.1992, p. 27). Havelock Brewster (1993), one of the pioneer thinkers of Caribbean economic integration, does not believe that a CARICOM domestic market would bring about additional productive activity. The region should better orient itself to world markets, such as NAFTA, the EU and APEC (Asia-Pacific Economic Cooperation).

The CARICOM Heads of Government seemed, however, sceptical as to whether small states can survive the economic competition of a huge, open market. Guyana's President Cheddi Jagan (1994, p. 27), warned that there was a tendency to rush headlong into new relationships, 'with promises exaggerated to the point where some individual CARICOM States seemed willing to entertain unilateral actions that are at cross purposes with our Community'. The NAFTA

[244] *Cf.* David Lewis, 1991, p. 66; Borchard, 1992.
[245] *Cf.* Anthony Gonzales, 1992.

'mega-trade bloc' did not offer the safety net as the other mega-trade bloc, the EEC. The NAFTA planners needed to examine the EEC's model of regional integration and free trade, especially since the disparities in development and income levels were far wider in the Western Hemisphere than in Europe (*ibid.* p.35).

Prime Minister Lester Bird of Antigua and Barbuda warned his colleagues at the OECS Heads of Government summit not to hurry into NAFTA: 'Free trade goods from NAFTA would cripple, if not kill, many of our industrial enterprises, whose production could not match their cheaper prices.' Instead, he recommended that OECS and Caribbean Community states form an alliance with other Caribbean Basin countries to promote their interests and seek parity with Mexico for Caribbean goods that now enter the US market under the CBI, without the effects of reciprocal trade (*The Financial Gleaner* 27.5.1994, p.22).

At their inter-sessional meeting in St.Vincent in March 1994 the Heads of Government decided, however, that CARICOM should seek early inclusion in the list of countries eligible for negotiating early entry to the NAFTA. Instead of CARICOM, however, individual member countries, Trinidad and Tobago, Jamaica and Barbados, became the first to apply successfully for eligibility. Subsequently Dominica's Prime Minister, Dame Eugenia Charles, renewed her doubts about a political union in the Caribbean. In an interview with a Trinidadian radio station she confessed:

'I always thought it would happen because our own interests are so diverse. Small islands we are, close together, but we do not have identical interests'. One reason why the Windward Islands have been able to work collectively was because of their common interests. 'But I'm one who always felt that CARICOM should stick strictly to matters that deal with trade and industry and should not even try to have joint foreign ideas. I do not think you can get that unity and I don't see any chance for the CARICOM area to become a country' (*CANA* report in: *WG* 24.5.1994, p. 24).

The US has consistently tied its aid closely to the "good behaviour" of the recipient countries (Anduze, 1990, p. 185f). In 1983, the US Government was obliged by law to publish an annual report on the level of approval bestowed on US foreign policy by UN member-Sates. The intention behind the initiative was to show recipient countries that the support also depends on their voting patterns in international forums.

In ten UN General Assembly resolutions in 1983 dealing with US foreign and security policy, St. Lucia in the category 70-90% voting convergence topped the list of the closest Caribbean friends of the USA. With 50-60%, Haiti, Antigua and Barbuda, Jamaica, Dominica, Costa Rica, St. Vincent and the Grenadines, Belize, the Bahamas and the Dominican Republic came next. Venezuela, Trinidad and Tobago and Barbados stood at 40%. In 1983, Panama, Mexico and Guyana voted more often against, than with, the USA. Nicaragua, Cuba and Grenada (before the 1983 intervention) voted consistently against the USA (Stone, 1987a, p.18).

The increasing significance of the drug trade and smuggling has given a new dimension to US-CARICOM relations. In May, 1989, the US Senate voted 57:40 against a motion to strike the Bahamas from the list of countries receiving

US financial aid. The justification given for the motion was unsatisfactory co-operation (*CI* July, 1989, p. 8). The then Prime Minister of the Bahamas, Sir Lynden Pindling, who was suspected by the US authorities of aiding and abetting drug dealers, was moved to speak accusingly at the July 1988 Summit in Antigua of an 'ideologically-motivated, interventionist policy' conducted by the USA through its diplomatic representatives and 'gun-slinging loyalists' (*CP* 43, Supplement, pp. 6ff). The weakness of small Caribbean States, he claimed, was exploited to seek scapegoats for their inability to deal with internal problems, such as drug cultivation, drug dealing and drug taking. In 1984, Pindling had not escaped unscathed from the inquiry of an independent Commission on his relationships with international money launderers and drug barons. Nonetheless, he won the following elections (in 1987) with a large majority. At that time, it was estimated that 40% of the cocaine reaching Florida was smuggled there through the Bahamas from South America and that drug money accounted for some 10% of the national income of the Bahamas (*WG* 30.6.1987, p. 18).

Originally, marijuana, grown especially in the Caribbean, was sent in large quantities to the USA. Today, hard drugs, such as cocaine and heroin, which originate from South America — and, in particular, from Colombia — also reach the USA via the Caribbean islands. Enormous sums of money change hands in local drug cultivation and the intermediate trade in drugs through middle-men. In Caribbean politics, the drug problem was, for a long time, not taken seriously — so long as marijuana was regarded as a rather harmless stimulant and foreign currency earnings from its cultivation and trade provided an extremely welcome relief for the chronic shortage of foreign currency of CARICOM countries. Marijuana cultivation provided a better livelihood for many small farmers. Hence, it was with mixed feelings that the CARICOM countries viewed the massive action of the US anti-drug warriors, especially those from the US Drug Enforcement Administration (DEA), in their sovereign territory against drug traffickers, corrupt officials, Police, Customs officers and even politicians.

Occasionally, US agents lure real or imagined drug smugglers onto US territory, in order to be able to hand them over to US jurisdiction. Thus, in September, 1985, the then Chief Minister of the Turks and Caicos Islands, Norman Saunders, and his Minister for Development, Stafford Missick, were sentenced to eight and ten years, respectively, by a US Federal Court for collusion in drug trading.

The former Deputy Minister of Public Works, Aulden Smith, was sentenced to five years' imprisonment in connection with the same matter in December, 1985 (*CI* February, 1986, p. 14). The three were entrapped in an undercover agents' sting operation. In September, 1985, too, a North Carolina Court sentenced former Energy and Communications Minister of Belize, Elijio Briceño, to seven years' imprisonment and fined him US$50,000 for conspiracy to smuggle drugs (*CI* October, 1985, p. 4).

In April, 1987, William Herbert, then Ambassador of St. Kitts and Nevis in Washington, D.C., resigned as Ambassador to the USA[246] after accusations appeared in the London *Daily Telegraph* that he served as a money launderer for drug business. He categorically rejected the accusations and supposed that US IRS officials and the DEA were the source (*CI* June, 1987, p. 10).

The judgement of the US Supreme Court of June 15, 1992, means that suspects in CARICOM countries run the risk of being abducted henceforth to the USA (*CI* July, 1992, p. 11)[247]. The CARICOM Heads of Government, at their July, 1992, Summit in Port-of-Spain, emphatically rejected all attempts of foreign powers to enforce their laws by kidnapping persons from the territories of sovereign States (*WG* 14.7.1992, p. 28).

In order to bring the drug smugglers under control, the US authorities often operate on Caribbean soil with the approval of CARICOM Governments and have access to bank documents in order to uncover money launderers, in Barbados and the British Caribbean colonies. The Cayman Islands' Government signed the relevant agreements in July, 1984; that of the Turks and Caicos Islands in September, 1986, followed by Anguilla, the BVI, Barbados and Montserrat (*CI* July, 1987, p. 13). Mutual Legal Assistance Treaties enable US officials to pursue their criminal quarry into the territorial waters of Antigua and Barbuda, the Bahamas and Grenada as well (Sanders, 1990, p. 88).

In 1989, the FBI with Scotland Yard and local police undertook action against off-shore banks in Montserrat, which led to several of these banks losing their licences (*CI* July, 1989, p. 12). The US officials are concerned about closing the money-laundering institutions of earnings from drug trafficking and being able to examine the bank accounts of possible tax evaders. Similar suggestions for the Bahamas have repeatedly produced tough reactions from its Government. Bahamian banks have profited from their proximity to the USA and bank secrecy.

CARICOM Heads of Government, as early as after their July, 1988, meeting in Antigua, expressed, in a letter to then US President, Ronald Reagan, their concern over the increasing incidence of interference in the internal affairs of the CARICOM Member States by US authorities. Their letter mentioned the attempts made to extend the State power of the USA on neighbouring powers of the region without regard for their sovereignty and the independent legal system of these countries (Milne, 1989, p. 66). At the same time, they announced their readiness, with other countries, to work together in the creation of an internationally acceptable procedure with the help of which drug dealers can be brought to justice (*CP* 43, Supplement, p. 15).

One can properly speak of a CARICOM policy *vis-à-vis* the USA, only from the end of the 1980s. But, prior to that, below the level of the Summit of CARICOM Heads of Government, there had been common initiatives for fashioning foreign policy co-operation with the USA at the highest level. The most spectacular such action was the collective intervention with seven

[246]But remained Permanent Representative to the OAS. In June 1994 he and family members did not return from a fishing trip and are missing. Herbert was a founder of the Kittitian People's Action Movement

[247]The judges by a 6-3 vote decided that US agents may abduct criminal suspects from other countries for trial in the US without necessarily violating existing extradition treaties with those governments (United States vs. Alvarez Machain).

CARICOM countries in Grenada in October, 1983. The joint manœuvres, within the framework of the RSS, were discussed in Chapter 2.6.2.

In April, 1982, Ronald Reagan paid a visit to Jamaica, as the first US President so to do. Thereafter, he had a working holiday in Barbados where he discussed CBI details with the Heads of Government of Jamaica, Barbados, Antigua and Barbuda, St. Vincent and the Grenadines and St. Kitts and Nevis. He also was informed about the economic and security problems of the island states. Differing opinions existed clearly then on the influence of the ideological and security-policy concepts of Cuba and Grenada on the region. Barbados' then Prime Minister, Tom Adams, spoke in favour of the restoration of democracy in Grenada — but stated that Barbados did not feel threatened by an island with a per head income a mere 20% of that of his own island (*DG* 12.4.1982, p. 7)

In February, 1986, the Heads of Government of Jamaica, Dominica, Barbados, St. Lucia, St. Kitts and Nevis, St. Vincent and the Grenadines, Antigua and Barbuda and Trinidad and Tobago met in Grenada, at the invitation of the latter's Prime Minister, Herbert Blaize, in order to speak again with then President Reagan. Reagan, in a brief discussion, disclosed improvements in the CBI, which he then announced publicly in a speech to 20,000 Grenadians. He further stated that the US Congress was considering a change in tax legislation, which would allow Puerto Rico's Development Bank to grant credits for investment in other Caribbean states to US firms.

Moreover, the number of scholarships for Caribbean students in the USA would be increased from 500 to 1,500 annually. By this means, especially the scholarships awarded hitherto and still offered by Cuba were supposed to be replaced, although the latter were no longer accepted by Commonwealth Caribbean Governments. Jamaica's then Prime Minister, Edward Seaga, praised the measures and declared that President Reagan had once again proved himself to be an extraordinary friend of the Caribbean who gave to the region more than any other President in the history of the USA (*DG* 21.2.1986, p. 25).

Both Guyana's President, Desmond Hoyte, and Jamaica's later Prime Minister, Michael Manley, were unable to avoid the attractiveness and economic strength of the United States. Hoyte, as Burnham's Vice President, and Manley had originally been both vehement opponents of the influence of the USA and US-supported international financial agencies, especially the IMF, in the region[248]. They had initially played the 'Cuban Card', and advocated a South-South co-operation of the Non-Aligned countries and the New International Economic Order. Representatives of their respective parties — the People's National Congress and the People's National Party — accused delegates of conservative Governments, especially after the intervention in Grenada, as lackeys of US Imperialism.

Nonetheless, the USA remained the paradise for Caribbean people of all classes. Barbadian novelist, George Lamming complained, in an address to journalists in Jamaica, as follows: 'Because we almost imagine ourselves to be in the valley of the moon, it is extremely difficult to get the local population of

[248]Hoyte, on succeeding Burnham as President in 1985, pursued a *rapprochement* with both the USA and the international financial agencies.

the Caribbean to think critically of the United States' (*Sunday Sun*, Jamaica, 20.12.1981, pp. 8ff). Public opinion polls confirmed this view[249].

Caribbean politicians, therefore, have no option. They must woo the great neighbour to the north openly. In Jamaica, the then ruling People's National Party, in the 1980 elections, with its anti-US posture, came to grief. Michael Manley, on returning to power in 1989, took this fact into account by means of particular obsequiousness *vis-à-vis* the US Government. In August, 1992, the then Head of Government of the Bahamas, Sir Lynden Pindling, failed to be re-elected, not least because of his poor relationship with the dominant economic partner. In view of the economic recession and increasing US criticism of the narcotics policy of the Commonwealth of the Bahamas, even the most loyal voters of the black social underclass left him in the lurch (*Cf. CI* September 1992, p. 2).

In the 1983 election campaign in Montserrat, the head of the largest trade union, Dr. George Irish, who was also a candidate, was accused of Communist links. He really performed somersaults in listing the good relationships of his party to the US Government (*The Workers Defence*, Montserrat, February, 1983). In the 1984 elections in Grenada, when former Prime Minister, Sir Eric Gairy, sought to win votes by demanding the long-term stationing of US troops of occupation on that island, his most promising fellow candidates took care, not to oppose this too energetically.

The relationships between the United States and the Commonwealth Caribbean were hitherto determined, in the main, by the East-West conflict — and, in particular, by the tensions between the USA and Cuba, as the surrogate of the ex-Soviet Union in the Caribbean. The increasing or decreasing influence of Cuba on the politics of the region was a parameter of the conduct of the USA to the Caribbean States.

For the United States, Cuba was a constant challenge to regional security and co-operation (*Cf.* Vaughan Lewis, 1984b, p. 70). The Foreign Minister of Antigua and Barbuda, Lester Bird, in a speech in the USVI in November, 1985, complained that the Caribbean Community had become one of the early victims of the East-West confrontation. The turning by Jamaica and Guyana to Socialism had, he argued, dealt a serious blow to the Community and prevented the foreign-policy co-ordination of the Member States from even becoming a reality. The seizing of power by Maurice Bishop in Grenada, with his Marxist positions, had further called this objective into question, Bird continued. The parties in the East-West conflict had exploited the difficult economic condition of the CARICOM countries, in order to wage their ideological conflicts.

Bird warned the United States against continuing this policy. He demanded more economic aid to raise the standard of living, because the US balance of trade surplus in the Caribbean continuously exceeded direct US aid to the

---

[249]In February, 1981, 85% of some 1,000 Jamaicans in a representative sample in a poll by Jamaican social scientist, Carl Stone, said that close friendship between Jamaica's Prime Minister, Seaga, and the new US Government under President Reagan was a good idea; 10% opposed this, and 5% had no views. In July, 1981, 78% thought the US President's help for the Caribbean in his fight against Communism and in support of democracy to be a good thing; 7% opposed this; and 15% had no views. 81% believed Jamaica should accept such help; 12% opposed; and 7% had no opinion. In November,1981, 74% thought Jamaica benefited from US help; 23% said no; and 3% did not know (Müllerleile,1983b, pp. 1ff).

region. If the discontentment of the young people led to an explosion, then the latter would not be limited only to the Eastern Caribbean, but would spread to the USA as well (*Barbados Advocate*, 12.11.1985, p. 2).

In November, 1986, Barbados' then Prime Minister, Errol Barrow, warned against justifying US-Caribbean co-operation and US help to the region with the fear of a Communist seizure of power, an invasion of drug traffickers or mass immigration to the USA. This line of argument painted, he declared, a shocking, derogatory and completely false picture of the Caribbean as a stormy sea with surges of catastrophe. They would disturb the internal peace of the USA, if they were not stopped with a lot of money and perhaps weapons.

Barrow showed understanding that such arguments were addressed to the US electorate, in order thereby to obtain help for the Caribbean. The problem, as he saw it, was that one 'might end up believing such nonsense'. The USA, 'with all its money, all its technology and the best will in the world, could not solve the problems of the Caribbean'. The US could contribute enormously, but only if the people of the Caribbean 'were themselves determined in a spirit of self-reliance to grapple with their problems'. Barrow appealed to the USA to switch to a system of multilateral aid (*CI* December 1986, p. 3).

The collapse of Communism in Eastern Europe in 1989-91, the poor economic situation of Cuba without prospects of economic help from Russia, the fall in the standing of Cuban President, Fidel Castro, in the Socialist and the Third World camp, have defused the East-West conflict in the Caribbean. The 'currency' of speculation on a long-lasting East-West conflict and the unlimited US readiness to buy good behaviour has been now 'devalued', as St. Lucia's Prime Minister, John Compton, put it at the July, 1988, CARICOM Summit in Antigua (*CP* 43, Supplement, p. 12).

CBI II, EAI and debt forgiveness document US efforts to have a good relationship with the Caribbean countries, even after the end of the Cold War. Dr Richard Bernal[250] (1991, p. 57) declaring that the USA could not remain 'an oasis of well-being in a Caribbean Sea of poverty', has, however, demanded more comprehensive debt reduction, conversion and forgiveness as occurred in much of Western Europe after World War I and in the German Federal Republic after World War II.

US President, Bill Clinton's, arrival in the White House, and the subsequent change in the US Government, destroyed many personal channels of communication created by Caribbean politicians, after the Grenada intervention, with first the Reagan and then the Bush Administrations. In February, 1993, Dame Eugenia Charles, as the first CARICOM Head of Government, met both President Clinton and Vice-President Al Gore, on the sidelines of a prayer breakfast in Washington, D.C. In a speech at Brown University, she urged the USA not to neglect the Caribbean (*CI* March, 1993, pp. 2ff). Not before August, 1993, did President Clinton find the time to see the Heads of Government of the Bahamas, Barbados, Guyana, Jamaica and Trinidad and Tobago altogether in the White House. The OECS Heads of Government felt left out and, except for Dame Eugenia Charles, boycotted a lunch with Vice-President Al Gore that was meant as a kind of a compensation.

[250] Ambassador of Jamaica to the USA in the early 1990s

The vanishing importance of the Commonwealth Caribbean for US policy makers became obvious when the US administration decided to close the embassies in Grenada, opened after the 1983 intervention, and Antigua and Barbuda. Following representation by Grenada's Prime Minister Brathwaite and Grenadians in the US the decision for Grenada was reversed, but that for Antigua, however, upheld (*CI* June 1994, P.2).

The annual four-day Miami Conference on the Caribbean, organised by the Americas Society-affiliated Caribbean/Central American Action, has proved to be a useful meeting-place for trade and investment in the Caribbean Basin, since first meeting in 1977. Top-level information and discussions are offered. Regional politicians and economists meet during each conference. At least as important as the formal programmes are the talks held peripherally.

Numerous other organisations, bi-laterally and multi-laterally, deal with US-Caribbean relationships. Trade missions, Congressional Committees, individual Senators, Congressmen, Congresswomen, investors and traders are constantly travelling through the Caribbean. Scientific symposia, conferences and seminars on Caribbean themes are initiated in the USA, literary legion.

2.6.5.2 Relations with Canada

Within the Commonwealth, Canada has discreetly taken over the role of looking after the West Indian Member States (Gehren, 1987, p. 9). It heads regular meetings of the Commonwealth Heads of the Western Hemisphere (Baranyi and Dosman 1990). The Prime Minister of St. Vincent and the Grenadines, James Mitchell, has confirmed the existence of a spiritual link in Canadian-Caribbean relations, which must be cultivated (Brana-Shute, 1985, p. 29). Presumably, because Canada itself has had experience with economic dependence on the USA and the UK, it could have particularly good relationships with developing countries.

Canada is an economic, but not a power factor, in the Caribbean. The Canadian Government was not even informed, in advance, of the intervention in Grenada. Canada's waiving of military protection for its investments in the region is possible, thanks to the military presence of the USA and Great Britain (Barry 1984, pp. 220-225).

Canada has never had colonies in the Caribbean, but has had close trade relationships with the West Indies since the eighteenth century. Salted cod from Newfoundland was imported cheaply by the plantation owners to feed the slaves and is still a part of the national dish in Jamaica. Moreover, Canada supplies product, such as wheat, flour and wood, which essentially were used on the plantations.

Conversely, rum which is made into a widely-distributed drink in Canada, sugar and molasses go in the other direction. Canadian ships helped the Caribbean from the early days to bypass the traditional colonial trade routes.

Shortly after becoming a Dominion in 1867, Canada granted preferential customs tariffs to West Indian produce and obtained for itself the same privilege in the other direction. Canada, in the process, paid attention to the fact that the West Indies remained intact economically. Thus, for example, it bought West

Indian sugar at a higher price in 1898 and 1902, when the world market sugar price fell considerably.

The first formal trade treaty between the British West Indian colonies and Canada from the year 1925 was extended by a protocol in 1966, which established stronger trade relationships between the trading partners. In the meantime, Canada had not only extended considerably its trade in the direction of the Caribbean, thereby achieving strong foreign trade surpluses, it had also increased considerably its direct investment in the Caribbean, especially in banking, insurance and mining.

Canadian banks are among the largest ones in the Commonwealth Caribbean. Tourists from Canada and Canadian hotels are a significant economic factor. Canadian firms in the Caribbean are active in extracting minerals, especially bauxite for the production of aluminium, in agriculture, in insurance and in the shoe industry.

The CARICOM Member States ceased being able to continue granting Canada the agreed preferential tariffs, on the coming into force of the Lomé-I Treaty in 1976, which fixed one-way preferential tariffs for inter-alia, Commonwealth Caribbean countries in the direction of the European Union as it now is. Besides, the CARICOM Member States wanted to move away from limiting their trade relationships with Canada to raw materials and replace these by finished products and non-traditional agricultural produce (*CP* 30, p.4).

In 1979, therefore, the CARICOM Member States signed individually the new Canada/CARICOM Co-operation Agreement, even though they had conducted the relevant negotiations collectively. This Agreement was not limited to trade, but rather included investments as well as technical and financial co-operation. It was based on the principle of one-way trade preferences between developed and developing countries and paid particular attention to the LDCs in the region.

The executing agency for the agreement is the Joint Trade and Economic Co-operation Committee (JTEC), which, on the CARICOM side, consists of representatives of the Member States and a Chairman elected by the Common Market Council of Ministers. Important regional institutions, such as the CDB, OECS, CAIC and others involved in economic co-operation, are also included in the work of the committee.

But the new Agreement did not produce the expected expansion of CARICOM exports to Canada. Thus, in 1981, Canada had a US$368 million trade surplus with these Caribbean States. Particularly blatant was the difference to the CARICOM LDCs. Canada exported to them eighteen times in value what these countries exported to Canada as against four times for Barbados (Barry 1984, p. 220). Caribbean exports, e.g. rum, to Canada were subjected to numerous restrictions. Canada bought sugar, unlike the EU, only at the world price. The importation of industrial goods from the Caribbean was anything, but satisfactory.

In 1981, the Caribbean Community succeeded in binding Canada to a certain aid level for five years, ear-marked for national and regional projects according to regionally-defined priorities. The regional programmes proceed via the JTEC, are overseen by the CARICOM Secretariat and are executed by the regional organisations delegated to do so. The CARICOM members of the JTEC complained, at a JTEC meeting in April, 1985, of being under-informed by Canada and also of not sufficiently participating in project formulation (*CP* 30, p.28).

At the February, 1987, JTEC meeting, the Canadian delegation pointed out that Canadian help to the Commonwealth Caribbean had doubled between 1981 and 1986, to reach CDN$93 million — the figure for the following five years as well (*CP* 37, p.11).

At the February, 1985, Summit in Jamaica of Commonwealth Heads of Government of the Western Hemisphere, the Caribbean participants were extremely keen to obtain from then Canadian Prime Minister, Brian Mulroney, the unilateral duty-free entry of Caribbean goods into Canada as well as investment agreements. CARIBCAN came into force at the start of 1986, guaranteeing the duty-free entry onto the Canadian market for 99.8% of contemporary Commonwealth Caribbean exports. Some finished goods, which were easily manufactured (e.g. textiles, shoes, hand-bags, lubricating oil and methanol), were, however, excluded, out of consideration for Canadian manufacturers.

Canada is relatively unimportant for the international relations of Caribbean States (Levitt, 1988, p. 227). Technical, financial and human resources aid from Canada is, however, noticeable all over the Commonwealth Caribbean. It was agreed with the United States and the United Kingdom that Canada's aid to the Caribbean should concentrate on air transport, supplying drinking water and educational programmes (Barry, 1984, p. 222). Over and above this, Canada is also engaged in security — it equips the coast guard, police, military; disaster relief programmes and anti-narcotics operations (*Cf.* Baranyi and Dosman, 1990). The Canadian International Development Agency (CIDA) the official Canadian aid organisation, has several sub-agencies, e.g. the Canadian Association of Latin America (CALA) through which local private sector organisations and Canadian investors and firms in the Caribbean are helped, directly or indirectly. The Canadian economy is also helped in that Canada ties 80% of its bilateral aid to the purchase of goods and services from that country — one of the highest percentages of tied aid among the larger donor countries (Barry, 1984, p. 224).

At a Caribbean-Canadian Conference in Barbados in March, 1990, Canada's then Prime Minister, Brian Mulroney, surprised the Commonwealth Caribbean States by forgiving over 50% of their debts to Canada. Moreover, he promised an adaptation of CARIBCAN to the wishes, in terms of exports, of the partners, a grant of CDN$10 million to the University of the West Indies, the establishment of an office for industrial co-operation in Ottawa, the Canadian capital, and the development of markets for the goods produced (*CC* April, 1990, p. 1).

2.6.5.3 The Caribbean Community and Latin America

The relationship between the Commonwealth Caribbean States and most Latin American countries is marked by prejudices originating in ethnic, cultural and linguistic differences and not least in their differing sizes and economic power. While the Latin American countries achieved their independence from

Spain and Portugal in the last century, the Commonwealth Caribbean States joined the ranks of sovereign nations only in the 1960s and 1970s and are regarded in Latin America, now as then, as the representatives of British and Anglo-American interests.

Even as they became independent, the Commonwealth Caribbean States of Belize and Guyana were denied entry to the Organisation of American States, owing to their territorial disputes with neighbouring Latin American States. Only in 1991 did they gain that entry. Not unjustly, the Latin American countries, as OAS Member States, feared that the English-speaking Caribbean group would gang up against them in controversial foreign-policy questions[251].

The CARICOM Heads of Government, at their seventh Summit, in Georgetown/Guyana in July, 1986, instructed the CARICOM Secretariat to accelerate a broadly structured co-operation in trade and economy with the Member States of the Andean Pact as well as with Brazil and Mexico ('Georgetown Declaration', para. 9).

Venezuela, Mexico and Colombia belong to the pathfinders of closer co-operation with the Commonwealth Caribbean[252]. In November, 1971, then Venezuelan Foreign Minister, Aristides Calvani, invited his Commonwealth Caribbean colleagues to a consultative meeting in Caracas. Two subsequent meetings dealt with regional transportation questions.

In April, 1973, Venezuela became the first non-Anglophone Caribbean CDB member. It is the only CDB member to have established a Trust Fund providing favourable loans to CARICOM Member States. Venezuela benefited from the sharp rise in crude oil prices in 1973-74 and provided some countries importing Venezuelan oil, *inter alia* Jamaica, with developmental credits under the First Programme of Financial Co-operation of Puerto Ordaz.

In August, 1980, the then Presidents of Venezuela and Mexico signed in San José, the capital of Costa Rica, for the benefit of the oil-importing countries of Central America and the Caribbean, a programme for co-operation in energy policy[253] commonly known as the 'San José Accord'. This Accord automatically grants a five-year import credit, at an interest rate of 4% per annum, on 30% of the selling price, on crude oil from Mexico and Venezuela bought by certain Central American and Caribbean countries, including, in the Commonwealth Caribbean, Barbados and Jamaica at first and, later, Belize as well.

The duration of the credit is extended to twenty years at 2% *per annum*, if it is used for development projects (Grayson, 1983, pp. 19ff). The Mexican and Venezuelan Governments renewed the San José Accord in July, 1989, but reduced the quantum of credit to 20% of the selling price. The interest rate on short-term credit was raised to 6%-8% *per annum*; and the duration of long-term credit was cut to twelve years[254].

---

[251] *Cf.* the comprehensive presentation of the different positions in Andrés Serbín (1989), Head of the Institute for Social and Practical Studies, Caracas, Venezuela.

[252] Please see, on this, Serbín (1991).

[253] *El Programa de Cooperación Enegética para Países de Centroamérica y del Caribe* — Energy Co-operation Programme for Central American and Caribbean Countries.

[254] The daily delivery for either country was fixed at 160 million barrels in 1980 and 130 million in 1989 by the San José Accord

Venezuela's territorial claims against Guyana were regularly the subject of resolutions at CARICOM Summits in which Venezuela was put under pressure to yield. Following mutual Presidential visits in 1986 and 1987, the decades-long disputes over the Essequibo region of Guyana was not really settled, but was not regarded as a priority issue. Then UN Secretary-General, Perez de Cuellar, named UWI Vice-chancellor, Alister McIntyre, in 1990, as his personal representative to deal with the future negotiations for a definitive clarification of the border question.

With Trinidad and Tobago and other Eastern Caribbean States, Venezuela has repeatedly had disputes over the exploitation of maritime resources (*Cf.* Vaughan Lewis, 1984b, pp. 61-62). It is not clear whether Venezuela has the right to extend its sovereign territory as far as to the Aves Islands, which are located West of Dominica (*Cf.* Searwar, 1990, p. 18). In July, 1991, then Venezuelan President, Andrés Pérez, and then Trinidad and Tobago's Prime Minister, A.N.R. Robinson, exchanged the documents of ratification for a marine border treaty, establishing the exclusive economic zone between the two countries.

Venezuela's network of Embassies and other diplomatic missions in the Commonwealth Caribbean is second only to that of Great Britain[255]. Señor Carlos Andrés Pérez, after being re-elected as President of Venezuela, at the end of 1988, continued the commitment to the Commonwealth Caribbean, which had marked his first period as President in 1974-79. In August, 1989, he met the Prime Ministers of Trinidad and Tobago, Jamaica, Barbados, St. Vincent and the Grenadines and Guyana, in Tobago (*CR* 28.9.89, p.4f).

In order to improve the Venezuelans' information on their Caribbean neighbours, *Venpress*, the Venezuelan State news agency, established correspondents' offices in Barbados, Trinidad and Tobago and Guyana in 1990 (*WG* 2.10.1990, p. 19). In October, 1991, Venezuela officially applied for membership in the Caribbean Community (*WG* 29.10.1991, p. 24) but, so far, still has only observer status.

The changed geopolitical situation facilitates new South-South trade accords, such as the framework agreement signed in July, 1991, by then CARICOM Chairman, Dr. Kennedy Simmonds, and Sr. Andrés Pérez, at the CARICOM Summit at Basseterre/St. Kitts, granting CARICOM Member States, as of January, 1993, one-way free trade access to the Venezuelan market for five years[256]. This framework agreement was fleshed out by the CARICOM/Venezuela Trade and Investment Agreement signed in Venezuela in October, 1992, by Mr. Patrick Manning, then Head of Government of Trinidad and Tobago, and Sr. Pérez[257]. A free trade area on a mutual basis between the Community and Venezuela is supposed to come into existence, following the expiry of the treaty. A Joint Commission has taken over the preparations for this.

The then External Affairs Minister of Trinidad and Tobago, Sahadeo Basdeo, voiced the hope that similar agreements would be concluded with

---

[255] Only the Commonwealth of the Bahamas, of all the independent Commonwealth Caribbean States, does not have a Venezuelan Embassy located there.

[256] The text is in *CA* (July-December, 1991), pp. 14-23.

[257] For the text, please see *Caribbean Affairs*, Supplement, 6 1 (March, 1993)

Colombia and Mexico (*CR* 25.7.1991, p. 1). Colombia and CARICOM signed an Agreement on Trade Economic and Technical Co-operation in July, 1994, in Cartagena/Colombia, that should come into force in 1995 (*CC* August, 1994, p.2).

Mexico's interest in the Commonwealth Caribbean has, on the other hand, been constantly rather marginal. In July, 1974, it signed with the Caribbean Community, an agreement to establish a Joint Commission — which, however, first met only over six years later, i.e. in November, 1980; and agreed on a deepening of economic, cultural and other relationships. The involvement remained rather superficial, though. But Mexico became an important source of funding for the Caribbean Development Bank (CP 24, p. 4).

In 1986, Mexico closed its Embassy in Port-of-Spain, its only one in the Southern Caribbean (*The Caribbean Community 1986*, p. 38). The appearance by Mexican President, Salinas de Gortari, before the CARICOM Heads of Government in Jamaica in July, 1990, signalled newly-awakened interest of that big neighbour, in good relationships with the Community. In the same month, bilateral trade-promotion negotiations took place in Jamaica between Mexico's national foreign trade bank, *Bancomex*, and CARICOM (*CDB* 1991, p. 39).

Individual Commonwealth Caribbean Sates have close relationships to Colombia and Brazil. In 1991, CARICOM made an agreement with Brazil on co-operation in technical and professional training (*CDB* 1992, p. 43). Colombia is, like Mexico and Venezuela, a CDB member.

The relationship of the CARICOM member-Sates to Nicaragua was rather ambivalent. On the one hand, they have repeatedly spoken out against foreign interference in Central America. On the other hand, they condemned, depending on ideological posture, repressive measures of the Nicaraguan Government and the *contras* in the same way.

In May, 1985, CARICOM Foreign Ministers' meeting welcomed the dialogue begun by the Contadora gathering in 1983 for the pacification of Central America and spoke out firmly against the US-imposed economic sanctions — albeit without mentioning the USA by name (*CP* 31, p. 30).

In January, 1992, the Foreign Ministers of the CARICOM Member States and the Central American countries met for the first time. A CARICOM/Central America Consultative Forum was set up in San Pedro Sula (Honduras), which is supposed to hold meetings at ministerial, technical and other levels, as soon as the need arises (*CP* 54 and 55 (January-June, 1992), p. 90). In 1993 a Basic Co-operation Agreement was signed between the CARICOM Secretariat and the newly founded Central American Economic Integration Organisation SICA[258], to facilitate more inter-institutional co-operation between the two bodies[259].

The CARICOM Secretariat has succeeded in being recognised at the multilateral level, and now has an on-going dialogue with the Andean Pact. The founding of SELA[260] in 1975 linked CARICOM Member States with the Latin American economic system. Barbados, Belize, Grenada, Guyana, Jamaica and

[258] *Sistema de Integración Centroamericana.*

[259] *cf Caribbean Development Bank* 1994, p. 41.

[260] *El Sistema Económico Latinamericano* — The Latin American Economic System; detailed in Mols (1984)

Trinidad and Tobago are SELA Member States from the Commonwealth Caribbean.

The UN Economic Commission for Latin America and the Caribbean ECLAC/CEPALC[261] is more significant for Caribbean-Latin American economic co-operation. Within ECLAC, an office in Port-of-Spain (Trinidad and Tobago) and a Ministerial Caribbean Development and Co-operation Committee (CDCC) to which all CARICOM Member States belong, have, since 1965 and 1975, respectively, formulated and supervised the implementation of programmes of co-operation among the Caribbean Member States. ECLAC works with regional Governments in the analysis of problems of developmental policy, in giving advice on developmental questions and also in training planning staff for the regional Administrations (CP 24, p. 4; 54 and 55, pp.56ff).

During the 1982 Argentina-UK Falklands War, shadows fell on Caribbean-Latin American relationships. Bearing in mind the smouldering Venezuela-Guyana and Guatemala-Belize territorial conflicts, the Commonwealth Caribbean countries—with the exception of then Socialist-ruled Grenada—supported the UK against the Argentine invasion. A direct Caribbean-Latin American confrontation occurred, when Argentina sought the OAS's condemnation of the UK. The relevant motion was thrown out, with the USA and nine[262] Caribbean States voting against.

The majority in favour, which Argentina wanted, was obtained only at a meeting of the OAS members belonging to the Rio Treaty for mutual assistance, which only Trinidad and Tobago, of the Commonwealth Caribbean States, had signed as well. But, even then, this body did not impose on the UK the economic, diplomatic and military sanctions desired by Argentina.

The defeat of the big Latin American countries against the Caribbean 'dwarfs' strengthened thoughts within the OAS to create a new Community without the Caribbean and the USA. Moreover, the Latin American OAS members displayed no particular hurry to admit Belize and Guyana, which had been kept out because of the territorial conflicts already mentioned (*SG*25.7.1982, pp. 8 and 13). Nonetheless, the Commonwealth Caribbean countries had plausibly demonstrated before the public opinion of the wide world its stance in favour of the self-determination of citizens over their territorial affiliation (Maingot, 1982).

Even so, the Falklands crisis left no lasting scars between the Commonwealth Caribbean and Latin America. But it did prevent the election of the Barbadian, Val McComie, to the post of OAS Secretary-General (Lennert, 1991, p. 333).

The inability of the OAS to influence the settlement of the conflict led, in 1985, at the Fourteenth Session of the General Assembly of the OAS, in Cartagena (Colombia), to far reaching structural changes. After 1990 had passed, Belize and Guyana were able to become OAS members, because of a lifting of the ban against the membership of States with territorial dispute, due to the obstinate pressure of the OAS members from the Caribbean (*Barbados*

[261] *Comisión Económica para América Latina y del Caribe.*

[262] Grendad voted in favour; Belize, Guyana and St. Kitts and Nevis were not yet members.

Advocate 9.12.1985, p. 2). In January, 1991, the OAS General Assembly admitted Guyana on the proposal of Venezuela, and Belize, on the proposal of Colombia, as members. After Guatemala's recognition of Belize, the gate to Latin America was opened for the latter country. Its Prime Minister, in December, 1991, was admitted for the first time to a Summit of Central American Presidents *(Frankfurter Allgemeine Zeitung* 13 .12.1991, p. 6).

Caribbean-Latin American co-operation was overshadowed by controversies between ACP and Non-ACP countries about the European import policy for bananas.[263] The heads of government of Dominica, St. Lucia and St. Vincent and the Grenadines threatened to leave the OAS if Latin-American lobbying against Caribbean banana producers was maintained *(CI* March 1993, p.4). Into the ears of the Presidents of the Group of Three – Colombia, Mexico and Venezuela – James Mitchell, the Prime Minister of St. Vincent and the Grenadines, said in October 1993 at the Summit in Port-of-Spain: 'The very survival of our economies depends on this export trade in bananas which supplies the most significant component of our foreign exchange ... Should our economies be destroyed ... by indiscriminate flooding of the market by supplies from Latin America, then relations between Latin America and the countries of the Windward Islands are quite likely to suffer irreparable damage' ('CARICOM/Suriname/Group of Three', p. 12).

Resistance of Costa Rica against the European Union's banana regime led the governments of the Windward Islands in March 1994 to successfully support Colombia's outgoing President Gaviria for the post of OAS Secretary-General against Costa Rica's Foreign Minister Niehaus, whom CARICOM governments had originally favoured *(CI* May 1994, p. 11).

2.6.6 Relations with Africa

South Africa is an important touchstone of the collective foreign policy of CARICOM Member States. Towards the outside world, the Governments of the Caribbean Community have constantly spoken out unanimously against the *apartheid* policy of the South African Government and complied with the relevant resolutions of the United Nations. CARICOM Heads of Government and Foreign Ministers hardly allowed a meeting to pass, without reinforcing this viewpoint. Representatives of the African National Congress (ANC) and South-West African People's Organisation (SWAPO) could expect to be received even by rather conservative Heads of Government in the Commonwealth Caribbean at any time.

Collective declarations did not always mean, however, collective action. CARICOM Foreign Ministers, at their meeting in St. Kitts in 1985, had supported the Gleneagles Agreement against sporting contacts with South Africa as well as a life-long ban for cricketers infringing this Agreement *(CP* 31, p. 30). Nonetheless, in the February, 1986, MCC vs. Leeward Islands cricket match in Antigua, there were four black players on the MCC (i.e. the English) team, who had previously played cricket in South Africa. A fierce controversy developed between the then Antiguan Foreign Minister, Lester Bird, who

[263] See chapter 2 6 8

became Prime Minister in 1994, and who openly opposed the playing of that match, and his Cabinet colleague, Reuben Harris, who had arranged the game. The Minister of State in Bird's Ministry rushed to help the youths arrested by the Police after anti-match protests (*CC* March, 1986, p. 2).

Commonwealth Caribbean countries had all boycotted the 1986 Commonwealth Games in Edinburgh, owing to the participation of South Africa in those Games. But the Heads of Government of these same countries were not totally united, at the November, 1985, Commonwealth Summit, on the question of comprehensive sanctions against South Africa. The UK balked at such sanctions. Basically, however, the CARICOM Member States did not budge, up to 1991, from their demand that sanctions be maintained, 'until such time as clear and irreversible changes had taken place towards the complete dismantling of the *apartheid* system', as the relevant declaration at the 1990 Kingston Summit put it (*CP* 49, Supplement, p. 20).

The July, 1991, Basseterre (St. Kitts) CARICOM Summit welcomed South Africa's return to international sporting events; but it also opposed the lifting just then of sanctions. The Heads of Government gave Sir Garfield Sobers, the cricketing great, the green light to take part in the creation of a multi-racial cricketing association in South Africa (*WG* 16.7.1991, p. 31). The Government of Jamaica and the Opposition there as well, both reinforced their demand for the retention of sanctions during the one-day visit to that country of ANC-President, Nelson Mandela. The Heads of Government of the Bahamas (Pindling), Trinidad and Tobago (Robinson), St. Kitts and Nevis (Simmonds) as well as President Hoyte of Guyana all hurried there for the occasion. Jamaica's largest stadium, owing to overcrowding, had to be closed. Mandela spoke of the most beautiful day of his life (*WG* 30.7.1991, p.1).

In 1992, the West Indies cricket team started again playing Test matches against South Africa (*CP* 55 + 55 (January-June 1992), p. 88). In 1993 most of the CARICOM States lifted their ban against South Africa. In October, Barbados' Prime Minister Sandiford travelled in an aeroplane of South African Airways to Johannesburg and showed interest in a direct flight connection.

In Africa, the CARICOM Secretariat works with its 'sister organisation', the Economic Community of West African States (ECOWAS) from which CARICOM can learn especially how a multi-lingual integration association functions (*CP* 22, p. 9).

The relationships of the CARICOM countries with Africa are otherwise more of a bilateral nature. Only Nigeria and Libya are still diplomatically active in the Caribbean, apart from occasional State visits from Leaders of other African States. Libya's activities were on several occasions the subject of detailed discussions in CARICOM circles. That country was repeatedly accused of participation in attacks on conservative CARICOM Governments and also of providing aid, in the form of cash and arms, to opposition movements. This conjecture was last uttered, following the failed *coup d' état* of the *Jamaat al Muslimeen* in Port-of-Spain in July, 1990, the leader of which was inspired by the Green Book of Libya's Head of State, Gaddafi (*Cf.* Ryan, 1991). Libya had close ties to the Bishop Government in Grenada as well as to Burnham in Guyana. After the 1983 intervention in Grenada, its Embassy in Grenada was closed. In 1984 the Libyans closed their Embassy in Guyana.

In 1992, on the other hand, Jamaica, as a result of budgetary cuts in its Foreign Service closed its Embassy in Ethiopia, the second to last permanent diplomatic mission of a CARICOM land in Africa. The only remaining being in Nigeria, where Jamaica has had a High Commission, currently headed by Dudley Thompson, since 1990.

The CARICOM countries have thereby taken into account the political and economic marginalization of Black Africa as well as the disillusionment over particular relationships which were supposed to develop between the black populations of the Caribbean and Africa. What remains, however, are the cultural links. But the Caribbean currently transmits more cultural impulses to Africa than it receives from that Continent (Wenzel).

2.6.7. Relations with Asia

A common Asian foreign policy of the States of the Commonwealth Caribbean is not recognisable. Investors from Japan, South Korea, Taiwan and Hong Kong view Caribbean countries as markets for their products as well as a springboard for North and South America. The relationships of the former States to Caribbean countries are rather of a bilateral nature, although a collective economic policy of the CARICOM Member States could produce import and export benefits.

Japan supports some Eastern Caribbean States in fisheries. At the July, 1992, meeting of the International Whaling Commission (IWC) Dominica, St. Kitts, St. Lucia and St. Vincent and the Grenadines voted, with Japan, for the resumption of whaling (*CI* August, 1992, p. 11). In May, 1993, the Windwards voted against the creation of a whale-protection zone in the Antarctic (*CI* June, 1993, p. 11) but resorted to a more cautious attitude at the May 1994 IWC meeting in Mexican Puerto Vallarta after animal protection organisations in the USA had called for a boycott of the Windwards as tourism destinations (*CI* July 1994, p.11). These Governments denied the existence of a link between their votes and Japanese aid.

Most CARICOM Member States have diplomatic relations with India. In countries with a large Indian population, the intensive cultural exchange with the 'mother country' is noticeable. India, as a member of the Commonwealth and pathfinder of the Non-Aligned Movement, has concerned itself particularly at international level with the Anglophone Caribbean States.

The Commonwealth Caribbean is the site of a diplomatic competition between Beijing and Taiwan. Seven of the twenty-four countries world-wide which recognise the latter diplomatically are Commonwealth Caribbean States namely, Belize, The Bahamas, Dominica, Grenada, St. Kitts and Nevis, St. Lucia and St. Vincent and the Grenadines (C.I. Sept 1989, p. 12). Indeed, Taiwanese nationals, investing a certain sum in Dominica become economic citizens of that country and receive a local passport, which facilitates travel (C.I. March, 1992, p. 9).

The June, 1989, crushing of the pro-democracy movement in Tienanmen Square seems to have lessened the influence and prestige of Beijing in the region. By the same token, Taiwan conversely received diplomatic benefits, which it has known how to use. Thus, for instance, the Taiwanese Government financed, in June, 1990, a symposium of the Caribbean Youth Conference on the first anniversary of the Tienanmen Square massacre.

Belize and Grenada established diplomatic ties with Taiwan, only in 1989. For a few weeks, in fact, Grenada had diplomatic relations with both Taiwan and Beijing, until the latter broke them off. (*CI* October, 1989, p. 10). Belize's move, in October, of that year by the George Price Government, was a general surprise, since he thereby gave election ammunition to the local Opposition, owing to Taiwan's links with South Africa. On the other hand Belize simply followed the example of its six Central American neighbours who all have established or re-established diplomatic ties with Taiwan.

The previous UDP Government of Belize had recognised Beijing two years before. Now as the Opposition, it reproached the Price Government with having been bought by Taiwan. The Opposition was irritated because Foreign Minister, Said Musa, whom it had hitherto always labelled disparagingly as a 'Communist', now suddenly opted for the two-Chinas policy (*CI* December, 1989, p. 6).

The following five CARICOM Member States have diplomatic relations with Beijing: Antigua and Barbuda, Barbados, Guyana, Jamaica and Trinidad and Tobago. But Beijing has only two resident Ambassadors in the region, as against four by Taiwan. The latter country and Jamaica, having opened trade representation offices in each other's capitals, have been negotiating over investment possibilities and the transfer of technology (*CI* January, 1993, p. 10). Both Beijing and Taiwan give technical and, in part, also financial aid to Caribbean countries which grant them diplomatic recognition.

South Korea has pulled ahead of its rival, North Korea, in the other diplomatic competition in the region. Even Guyana, Grenada and Jamaica, which, under Socialist Governments, had seemed at least to let North Korea appear to gain ground, now have closer links than ever before with South Korea.[264]

Guyana has been the last to loosen its close ties to North Korea, in favour of Seoul (*CI* October 1989, p. 12). The latter's growth in economic strength and increasing democratisation, as well as, conversely, the growing isolation of North Korea, in view of the opening of the former East Bloc in Europe to reform, have been among the main reasons for this. Additionally, the increasingly tighter links of the CARICOM Member States to the USA leave no space any longer for the involvement of North Korea.

2.6.8 Relations with Europe

London and Brussels are the most important diplomatic postings in Europe for the Commonwealth Caribbean. The ties of this region to London and the UK stem from its history as British colonies, close trading relationships and the existence in Britain of a large Caribbean immigrant community.

The separation of the former British colonies in the Caribbean from their 'mother country' occurred, *pari passu*, with a gradual British disengagement in

---

[264] This did not prevent the Georgetown City Council in 1995 from approving the erection of a statue for North Korea's deceased dictator Kim Il Sung in a city garden of Guyana's capital The idea was abandoned after public pressure.

the region. During World War II, the UK lost the initiative in security policy. Its involvement in diplomacy as well as technical and financial assistance declined, when these colonies became independent. The rather generous immigration policy, which had existed previously, became a restrictive one.

In 1982, the CARICOM Member States had taken the side of the UK against Argentina over the Falklands Islands. Hence, some CARICOM Governments reacted with bitterness to London's initial and marked distancing itself from the October, 1983, intervention in Grenada. Thus at a Conference of the West India Committee in Castries, St. Lucia, in March, 1985, that country's Prime Minister, John Compton, declared: 'That Britain did not stand by us when we were in mortal danger still rankles in the public mind'. Britain, therefore, still had, he claimed, 'fences to mend' in the Caribbean (*DG* 15.3.1985, p. 28). On the other hand, the re-opening of British Council offices in Kingston, Jamaica in 1989 (*CI* July, 1989, p. 2) after a fifteen-year hiatus, possibly indicates growth in renewed British Government interest in the region.

Admittedly, the diplomatic relationships between CARICOM Member States and the UK are bilateral in nature. Nonetheless, close contacts exist in London between CARICOM diplomats. Indeed, come OECS diplomatic missions are housed in the same building, as mentioned earlier in this book.

London, as the headquarters of the Commonwealth of Nations, grouping some forty-nine former British colonies, protectorates and dominions, as well as the UK itself, is of particular significance to CARICOM countries. The Commonwealth Heads of Government meet biennially in a different capital, including London, and take decisions which are recommendatory in character. The annual meeting, usually shortly before that the IMF/World Bank, of the Commonwealth Finance Ministers is also significant.

The Jamaican social scientist, Rex Nettleford, has described the significance of the Commonwealth as on-going, common humanity in the sense of the general good about which all are concerned — even when Westminster no longer holds sway over this 'Family of Nations' and economic need has further divided it into North and South, Third World and the rest (*Commonwealth* 28.2, p 54).

The CARICOM Member States have, from the very beginning had a particular weight in the Commonwealth through common actions and as the voice of the Third World — thanks, not least, to its 1975-89 Secretary-General, Sir Shridath Ramphal of Guyana.

The Commonwealth Caribbean obtained access to the European Union through the 1973 entry of the United Kingdom in the then European Economic Community — the integration model for both CARIFTA and the Caribbean Economic Community[265]. This model contributed to their turning away from the original plan of political integration preceding economic integration. Caribbean advocates of integration rather hoped, based on the EU model, to break down the obstacles to political integration through a step-by-step expansion of economic, functional and foreign-policy co-operation (*Cf.* Demas, 1987, p. 20).

From 1973 to 1975, important negotiations took place between the then EEC and former British colonies over the entry of the latter into the ACP group

[265] Avery (1973) uses the term, 'extra-regional echoing', to describe this function of being a model.

— and, therefore, their participation in the one-way entry for their produce into the EEC. The CARICOM Member States closed ranks and obtained particular concessions in the Lomé-I Treaty of 1975. They obtained for the ACP States the unilateral duty-free importation of ACP produce and products, including certain quantities of rum, sugar and bananas, into these European markets. Besides, this Treaty contains agreements on industrial co-operation and the terms governing capital transfer and residence rights (Carrington, 1984, p. 178).

The CARICOM Secretary-General since 1992, Trinidadian, Edwin Carrington, had for many years been the ACP Group's Deputy Secretary-General and then, up to 1990, Secretary-General. His replacement by Ghebray Berhane of Ethiopia indicates declining CARICOM influence and the consolidation of African dominance in the ACP Group[266], whose countries account for 45 of the 68 ACP States. CARICOM members have themselves become weaker, in that, in Brussels, instead of one they have established separate Embassies, which do not speak with one voice, although they do co-operate. (*Cf.* Carrington, 1984, p. 181). On the other hand, the European Union has delegations accredited in Barbados, Guyana, Jamaica and Trinidad and Tobago.

EU-CARICOM co-operation of a multilateral and bilateral nature is multi-faceted. The most significant multi-lateral agreements are the Lomé Treaties, each for five years, which essentially serve to promote, at stable export prices, investments in the ACP States — and simultaneously to ensure the supply of their products and produce to the European Union countries. Lomé-IV, currently in force, runs to the year 2000.

The Trinidadian social scientist, Anthony Gonzales, sees in the Lomé Treaties the obligation of the ex-colonial powers to return to their erstwhile colonies a portion of what the former had collected by exploitation during the colonial era. In his view, the European Community is itself interested, through the assistance to of the ACP countries, to Mediterranean and to North African States following the historic Franco-German concept of a united Europe, which, in the long-term, are regarded as vitally important for the security and independence of the Community (1984a, p. 11)[267].

Gonzales (1985) views the expectations placed in the various Lomé Treaties as, however, increasingly unsatisfied. This is because these treaties have not altered the *status quo* between donor and recipient nations, with the falling prices for primary products, high foreign debt and considerable foreign trade deficits. Nonetheless, he regards the Lomé Treaties as the only development forum really worth maintaining.

Lomé-IV, which marks the first ever inclusion of the Dominican Republic and Haiti in a Lomé Treaty, contains an involvement in the STABEX System of stable export prices for ACP products and produce to the EU. Moreover, the local country of origin content requirement has been reduced to 45% (from 60%).

Commonwealth Caribbean ACP Member States, with other sugar-producing countries, protested, however, against the 2% reduction in the guaranteed

[266] *Cf.* the commentary in the *Advocate News* (Barbados) quoted in : *WG* 21 11 1989, p. 20.

[267] Similar views are given in Payne and Sutton,1984, at pp. 231ff

sugar price (*CI* January 1990, p. 14). Caribbean sugar export prices, to the European Union in particular, largely exceed those on the world market.

Through SYSMIN, a special fund for mined minerals similar to the STABEX System, Guyana and Jamaica receive stable export prices for bauxite. A protocol guarantees the duty-free entry into the EU of certain quantities of ACP-distilled rum. ACP trade and tourism are supported by the financing of feasibility studies and the promotion of facilities for services and advisory/counselling. The Lomé Treaties, in conclusion, all put a premium on collective negotiations and praxis (Sutton, 1992, p. 57).

Financial and technical assistance flows out of the European Development Fund (EDF) to a whole series of regional institutions e.g. the UWI. Unlike the CBI or other forms of US aid provided during President Reagan's administration or CARIBCAN, EDF credits from the European Investment Bank are geared towards the Caribbean as a regional unit, thereby facilitating and assuring the fact of both formal and functional regional integration. Other favoured recipients of EU assistance, in addition to the UWI have included institutions of functional integration such as LIAT, WISCO, CARDI and ECEDA, the Eastern Caribbean Export Development Agency[268].

The creation of the single European market has considerably inspired the Caribbean debate on the need for promoting Caribbean unity and the coming into existence of a single Caribbean market in the sense of the Treaty of Chaguaramas. In the Caribbean, the Single European market begins with the 'next-door neighbour' to CARICOM — namely, the French 'DOM' overseas departments of French Guyana, Guadeloupe and Martinique.

The CARICOM Heads of Government, at their July, 1988, Antigua Summit, expressed grave concern over the possible effects on their exports, especially bananas (*CP* 43, Supplement, p. 16). The Prime Ministers of Dominica and St. Lucia, Dame Eugenia Charles and John Compton respectively, travelled to several European capitals in mid-1989, in order to examine the possibilities there for retaining their existing trade preferences (*CI* June, 1989, p. 16).

Speed seems to be imperative, when one bears in mind the fact that, in 1988, for instance, more than 32% of the export earnings of the CARICOM Member States came from trade with Western Europe. St. Vincent and the Grenadines (with 60%) topped the list of these exporters (Rainford, 1989/90) Between 25% (in the case of Jamaica) and 75% (for Dominica, St. Vincent and the Grenadines) of the exports of the Caribbean Community go to the European Union member-countries — especially the UK, which receives 99% (Thorndike, 1990) consisting mainly of traditional produce, such as bananas, sugar and rum as well as rice, bauxite, oil, cocoa and spices.

The main problem facing a single CARICOM market, on the model of the single European Union market, becomes clearer, when the single product and produce branches of the individual CARICOM Member States are considered; thus, for example, banana cultivation accounts for up to 20% of the labour force — and 40% of the export earnings — of the Windward Islands and, for instance, in the case of St. Lucia, 96% of all of its exports to the European Union.

[268] Please see data in · 'EEC and the Caribbean', 1981, pp. 6ff; Gonzales, 1988;*CR* 23.2.1989, p. 8.

Bananas, cultivated in the Windwards on small 0.5-4.0 hectare farms averaging 1.6 hectares, many of them accessible only with difficulty, are produced labour-intensively. They are more expensive than similar fruit grown in Central America and non-CARICOM Caribbean countries. Non-Caribbean banana imports by the UK have been restricted so far to approximately 10% of the total imported by that country. Since the January 1, 1993, creation of the single European market, however, the danger has existed of the British market being flooded with the cheaper 'dollar bananas' from non-ACP countries.

In December, 1992, the Agricultural Ministers of the then EEC agreed that ACP bananas should continue being imported duty-free by their countries at a maximum *quantum* of 1990 levels[269]. Special rules exist for Belize, that has invested heavily in banana cultivation in the recent past (*CI* January, 1993, pp. 1ff).

Caribbean sugar now also has competition. The European Union has up to now imported 430,000 tons annually from this source at a guaranteed price. But Caribbean sugar suppliers have had difficulty — unlike banana producers — in meeting their quota (*Cf.* Rainford , 1989/90). The following three options to maintain a Caribbean presence in the European market were discussed at the conference held in Barbados under the theme, '1992 and the Caribbean — the Next Steps', in November, 1989, under the auspices of the West India Committee and the Commonwealth and the CARICOM Secretariats:

1. develop Puerto Rico as the region's investment and promotion centre and link between the USA and Europe, with Puerto Rico inviting European firms and becoming the production site for exports to both Europe and the USA;
2. promote the siting in the Caribbean of production facilities of Asian firms wishing to trade with Europe; and
3. invite US Companies to invest in the Caribbean region and thereby gain access to the European market.

Anglophone, Francophone and Spanish-speaking governmental and private sector representatives from the Caribbean, France, the UK and the USA all participated in this Conference. Indeed, even Cuba through its First Vice-Minister for Foreign Affairs took part.

An accelerated process of regional integration, the development of a unified market of 'all Caribbean nations' and their single representation before the European Union in Brussels were found by the participants to be the preconditions for the options proposed (*CR* 7.12.1989, pp. 4ff; *CI* December, 1989, pp. 1ff).

Most recently, the coming into force of NAFTA on January 1, 1994, uniting Canada, Mexico and the USA as a trading bloc and countervailing force to both ASEAN and the EU has been the cause for concern within the latter concerning its influence in the hemisphere. Integrating NAFTA and the EAI could create a

[269] A roughly 70% value surcharge of 750 ECUS per ton is levied on any excess, as against customs duty of 100 ECUs per ton on up to 2.0 million tons of bananas imported annually and one of 750 ECUS on imports per ton above that level. In February, 1993, following a complaint to the European Court of Justice by the Federal Republic of Germany, alleging an infringement of 1957 Treaties of Rome, the Agricultural Ministers of the then EC modified their previous decision. Henceforth, the 2.0 million tons annual quota would be examined monthly and may be raised, if the ACP supply is short. ACP country quotas were fixed, and any excess would attract full customs duty (*CI* March, 1993, pp. 3ff)

mammoth economic zone, which, in order to avert further marginalization, the Caribbean States would have to join[270].

No unified CARICOM foreign policy to Eastern Europe is evident. Some of the CARICOM Governments established Embassies there in the 1960s and 1970s, on becoming sympathetic to Socialist ideologies or at least to stress the independence from the USA and repay ex-Soviet Union support for the Non-Aligned and Third World liberation movements.

Guyana, Grenada[271] and Jamaica at times developed close relationships with the then USSR and other East European States, which supplied technical, financial and, in part, military assistance to them, as well as sometimes large numbers of advisers. Large arms supplies were reportedly delivered to these CARICOM countries as well. The East European Embassies were over-staffed. In 1982, the then Government of Jamaica directed the then Soviet Embassy in Kingston to reduce its staff, following the alleged attempted assassination of a Jamaican Foreign Affairs Officer. Mutual expulsions of diplomats then occurred in Kingston and Moscow.

The then Soviet Union and its East European allies have constantly made capital of having had no colonial past in the Caribbean. Up to 1960, it had an Embassy only in Mexico for all the Caribbean countries. It was only after the ill-fated US-backed Bay of Pigs invasion of Cuba in the year 1960 that the then USSR extended its relationships with Cuba (*Cf.* Jiri Valenta in: Erisman and Mantz, 1982, pp. 49-51) and established diplomatic missions in Guyana, Jamaica and Grenada, this last-named until 1983. Barter agreements for the supply of bauxite have existed between Moscow and Guyana and Moscow and Jamaica. The collapse of the Soviet Union has accelerated reflections in Jamaica on closing its Embassy in Moscow.

2.6.9 Multilateral Co-operation

Multilateral and bilateral co-operation has stood, in the course of the history of Commonwealth Caribbean integration, repeatedly in competition — the former, rather promoting integration of the Commonwealth Caribbean States played a more important role in the 1960s and 1970s than in the 1980s (*Cf.* Ramphal, 1985). This development ran almost parallel to the economic decline of the Commonwealth Caribbean and the tendency of the economic and military superpowers to tie the Caribbean countries to themselves in bilateral treaties. In the 1990s, the tendency to multilateral action has grown again.

CARICOM Member States became members of all international organisations open to them, at the time they became independent, and which seemed useful to the Governments of the day in each case[272]. Even the remaining colonies in the Commonwealth Caribbean sought the possibilities for co-operation with multilateral organisations within the framework of their own scope for action in both foreign policy and external economic policy.

---

[270] *Cf* Fourth European-Caribbean Conference Communiqué, Brussels, November, 1991 (in. *Courier* 123, pp. 64ff).

[271] *Cf.* Shearman (1985).

[272] *Cf.* overview in Lennert, 1991, p 583

ECLAC/CEPALC, the regional Commission for Latin America and the Caribbean of the UN Economic and Social Council (ECOSOC) keeps an office in Port-of-Spain (Trinidad and Tobago). It serves, under the designation, *Caribbean Development and Co-operation Committee* (CDCC) as the liaison office both between the several Latin American and Caribbean States and also between them and the ECOSOC regional Commissions for Europe, Asia and the Pacific, Africa and Western Asia as well as to UN headquarters in New York[273].

The Washington-based *Caribbean Group for Co-operation and Development*, founded in 1977 within the framework of the World Bank, is another forum for co-ordinating technical and financial assistance for the Caribbean and also for promoting regional integration there. Over twenty international and regional organisations, in addition to approximately forty donor and recipient countries, belong to it (*The EEC and the Caribbean*, 1981, p. 7)[274].

Commonwealth Caribbean States, through their representatives, sit in nearly all main bodies of the United Nations and have been non-permanent members of the UN Security Council on several occasions. They are also members of all special organisations and autonomous agencies of the United Nations[275] and have relationships with UN special agencies relevant to the Caribbean.

Some Commonwealth Caribbean specialists are also employed in the UN But the attempt to elect Dame Nita Barrow, one of the region's leading political personalities, as the 1988-89 UN General Assembly President failed, when that post was available to the Latin American and Caribbean regional group. Five years later, the Guyanese career diplomat Rudy Insanally succeeded in becoming President of the 48th UN General Assembly. He declared that his Presidency was not only a Guyanese, but also a CARICOM one (*WG* 12.10.93, p. 18).

The former Barbados Prime Minister, Erskine Sandiford, declared at the UN General Assembly in October, 1989 that the survival of the international community was due to the small states of the world. Conversely, he declared, these small states have benefited considerably from the United Nation System.

He explicitly spoke out in favour of multilateral diplomacy: Large and powerful states often nurtured the illusion that they could neglect multilateral diplomacy and could give up international co-operation, relying only on the balance of power, spheres of influence and alliances, in order to protect and promote their national interest. Small states, however, could not labour under such self-deception. They must, on the contrary, be active participants in the international community, convinced practitioners of international co-operation, active exponents of multilateral diplomacy and powerful advocates of international organisations (*WG* 13.10.1987, p. 22).

The CARICOM countries work together closely in international organisations even in negotiations for direct financial and technical assistance to individual countries, e.g. with the World Bank group, especially the IMF which, based on the very conditionalities for granting assistance, have a bilateral character almost entirely. The CARICOM Secretariat has close relationships

---

[273] Please see as well Chapter 2.6 5.5.

[274] *Cf* also Pastor and Fletcher, 1992, p. 79

[275] *Cf* the listing given in William Demas, 1987, p. 37.

with other regional integration organisations; but participates at most as an observer in multilateral negotiations of the Commonwealth Caribbean Member States, which could have direct consequences on the sovereign decisions of these States. Alister McIntyre(1984b, pp. 16ff), former CARICOM Secretary-General and Deputy Secretary-General of the UNCTAD for a number of years, has suggested bringing regional groupings, such as CARICOM, more strongly into North-South negotiations.

Developing countries could, for example, make greater efforts to get financial aid for regional clearing houses, that could contribute to the liberalisation of regional trade and which donor countries could find opportune as well. A new South-South interdependence could result from the newly-acquired collective self-reliance and the consequential collective economic security, if the countries of the South succeeded in converting their existing potential as the suppliers of raw materials to the industrialised countries, into performance.

The Law of the Sea Treaty, agreed to by the Third UN Law of the Sea Convention (UNCLOS III) in Jamaica in 1982, signed by 159 States and ratified in 1993 by the sixty[276] of them necessary for the treaty to enter into force in late 1994, is of great interest to Caribbean countries. The latter markedly distanced themselves from the UK-US positions, in their efforts at formulating the convention[277]. The ninth CARICOM Summit, in Antigua in July, 1988, pushed the non-signatories to accession to the convention (*CP* 43, Supplement, p. 17).

With the coming into force of the convention, the Caribbean States are likely to extend their territorial sovereignty and economic zones considerably, as well as securing their financial share from the exploitation of seabed minerals. The headquarters of the UN International Seabed Authority, which is to regulate that exploitation, is to be sited in Jamaica. The inaugural meeting was declared open in November 1994 in Kingston by UN Secretary-General Boutros Boutros-Ghali after 68 countries had ratified the UN Convention on the Law of the Sea (*WG* 29.11.94, p. 12). Certain rules of the new Law of the Sea Convention had already been applied either unilaterally or by invoking customary international law (Kiderlen, 1990, p. 7). This has been so especially in the delimitation of the coastal areas and the economic zones of the island and coastal states in the Caribbean.

CARICOM Member States worked intensively in the 1970s in the Non-Aligned Movement, the Group of 77 and other groups of countries of the so-called Third and Fourth World. Each Commonwealth Caribbean State, on becoming independent and also in the UN speeches of its Head of Government, has declared itself to be Non-Aligned[278]. But it was only in 1979 that St. Lucia joined the Non-Aligned Movement, under a short-lived Socialist Government, and, in 1979, too, Grenada, under Bishop's New Jewel Movement Government. Dominica gained, under a left-wing interim- government, observer status. The successor government, led by Eugenia Charles, refused to apply for full

[276] The sixtieth being Guyana on 16th November 1993.

[277] *Cf.* Dr. Kennedy Simmonds' speech at the Fourth CARICOM Heads of Government Summit in Port-of-Spain (Trinidad and Tobago) in 1983 (*CP* 20, p. 28).

[278] Duncan, 1987, p. 5; the debate over 'non-alignment' spread widely even at the very start of the movement, with its self-proclaimed fight against Imperialism, Colonialism, Neo-colonialism and Racism directed mainly against the West, especially the USA and US allies (Müllerleile, 1985, p. 28-31).

membership. Neither St. Kitts and Nevis nor St. Vincent and the Grenadines is a member of the movement; whereas Antigua and Barbuda is only an observer.

Guyana's then President, Linden Forbes Burnham, belonged among the most resolute advocates and activists of the Non-Aligned Movement. In 1972, he hosted the Foreign Ministers' Conference, which was the first rather large meeting in Central and South America of the Non-Aligned Movement.

The relationship of the CARICOM Member States to this movement essentially followed the ideological preferences of three regional Heads of Government, namely Guyana's Burnham, Grenada's Bishop and Jamaica's Manley (in 1972-80). Burnham was able to focus world public opinion on the then still unresolved territorial conflict with Venezuela (Searwar 1990, p. 17).

Conservative Caribbean Governments turned out rather to be critics of the movement. Their posture was influenced by the rejectionist stance of the USA. Thus, for instance, the Foreign Minister of the conservative Jamaica Labour Party, Hugh Lawson Shearer, complained in New Delhi, in 1981 of the movement's biased stance in face of the Afghanistan conflict (Müllerleile, 1985).

The interest in the movement declined in the 1980s, given the predominance then of conservative, pro-US Governments in the region. This ran parallel to the world-wide waning of such movements, and the trend accelerated with the end of the Cold War. The UN, freed thereby from much pressure, became able to mediate more effectively in North-South conflicts as well, than substitute organisations whose decisions were not binding, owing to the absence of an administrative infrastructure[279].

---

[279] *Cf.* Vaughan Lewis, 1990, pp. 32-34.

2.7 Socio-cultural Links

2.7.1 Caribbean Identity

Hardly another subject has been discussed as extensively in the Commonwealth Caribbean in the past decades by intellectuals as that of 'Caribbean identity', the *differentia* of 'Caribbean Man' — or what distinguishes him from the inhabitants of other regions of the world (Demas, 1974, p. 3; 1975, p. 1). His existence, denied by some, is declared to be the *conditio sine qua non* of West Indian nation-building. In the process, the idea of identity, depending on the viewer's standpoint, is used for different geographical areas.

The Caribbean is no idyllic paradise of happy people, who spend their days with 'Rum and Coca-Cola', ripe bananas, sunshine, surfing, calypso, steel-band music and reggae, as is portrayed on tourism posters. The mixture of peoples according to the Colombian novelist, Gabriel García Márquez, who hails from the Caribbean coastal region of his country, calls to mind the blood of Swedish, Dutch and English pirates, the mentality of mulattoes, of Chinese-Indian half-breeds, Indian ivory sellers, the pre-Columbian, African, Andalusian and Galician cultural forms of his native region (Wentzlaff-Eggebert 1985, pp. 53-56).

Anglophone Caribbean writers continuously examine their identity. V.S. Naipaul, the Trinidad-born novelist, has cynically described, in an exaggerated way, the point of departure of the development of Caribbean territories: 'They are manufactured societies, labour camps, creations of the empire; and for a long time they were dependent on the empire for law, language, institutions, culture, even officials. Nothing was generated locally; dependence became a habit (*CARIFESTA FORUM*, 1976, p. 162).

Rex Nettleford (1987b, p. 4) has found that:

> 'much of this has been achieved by cultural resistance filtered through the sense and sensibility of the majority of transplanted souls who had to come to terms with their new environments; who dominated the production process by the centrality of their labour to that process, and actually shaped the cultural profile, albeit of the 'lower orders', by the sheer superiority of numbers as much as by the ingenuity forged from having to survive.
>
> As with people anywhere, it was the exercise of intellect and imagination which marked off the real parameters of combat and decided who governed and who ruled. If the British imperial power governed for those 300-odd years under colonialism, it was the ordinary people who ruled. Their devices were regarded as 'subcultural'.
>
> But that subculture seeping from underground, or as Edward Kamau Brathwaite would say, seeping from under the sea (submarine), influenced, coerced, teased the ethos into something definably 'Caribbean'. The languages, religious expressions, kinship patterns, artistic expressions — even the indigenous modes of production, distribution and exchange — as well as the native organisation of action groups with recognised leaders, all had their

own intrinsic logic, often forcing the Establishment to either resist or appropriate them. What is certain is that their autonomy and legitimacy were never fully conceded and they were to become rallying points for politicians pleading self-government before independence, only to be abandoned by some, once power was won.'

The leaders of the Independence movement in the region had, according to McIntyre (1984a, p. 11) who is from Grenada, a certain perception of the typical West Indian:

> 'To most of them, the West Indian was conceived to be a pragmatist, eschewing dogma and placing great store upon common sense and the ability to think for oneself; was committed to democratic values, including the accommodation of different points of view — enjoying a measure of amusement from them; fully supported the exercise of human rights, reflecting the strong links that several of them had with the trade union movement; and because of that background, articulated an unambiguous preference for dialogue and negotiation over the use of force'.

The Trinidadian, Anthony Maingot, (1980, p. 3) has singled out the emotional in the nature of the West Indian: 'We might strike out in sudden anger, the explosion of emotions for which the area's people are known, but the cold, rational and systematic physical and psychological tormenting of human beings is not a Caribbean trait'.

Under post-colonial political, social, geographic, climatic and other influences, the 'Caribbean personality' (Williams, 1973b, p. 14) has also developed ways of living and behaving, which may inhibit development and integration. Insularity, in Demas's (1974, p. 25) view, has produced a 'dog-eat-dog' mentality, which can only be explained psychologically as that of the landless; it is also observed in the West Indian backyard, where each hand is raised against that of the respective neighbour. Gordon K. Lewis (1984, pp. 51ff) has found an addiction to consumption, that the prosperous population segments have inherited from the old plantocracy and which exists not only in private affairs but also clearly in the mentality of Caribbean politicians as well.

Carl Stone (1989c) warned of the 'stench of corruption' linked to a get-rich-quick-at-any-price-mentality, which includes both politicians and civil servants in a changing value system.

The psychiatrist, John Royer (1983) who lives in Jamaica, has adduced the following nosology of 'some of the distinctive lifestyles of West Indian society', which he regards as particularly alarming:

1. Hand-to-mouth existence.
2. Powerlessness with extreme dependency and fatalism of the 'What to do?' mentality.
3. An Epicurean philosophy; 'Eat, drink, be merry and die'.
4. Life is a gamble. These people believe in luck, their stars, and that they are underlings. The pools, the horses and other gambling games encourage this lifestyle.

5. 'Get rich fast' syndrome. Here 'riches are placed above righteousness, collateral above conscience, stocks above the soul, money above a mission and a pair of dice above the dedicated will' (Solomon Benn III, 1981, cited by Royer). This syndrome is reflected in the almost daily reporting in the newspapers of increased white collar crimes, especially fraudulent conversion.
6. Anancyism: 'wanting something for nothing'. The number of voluntary idlers, self-appointed beggars and 'small-time mafia and mercenaries' attest to the existence of this lifestyle in the Caribbean.
7. Undisciplined, anarchic behaviour. This is now becoming very rampant in our society. It affects all levels of society, at home, school and work.
8. Ginnalism: The get-away-with-it style.
9. The Abundant Life of Christianity: Love, altruism, unselfishness. I believe that this is hope for the 'broken hedges' (Ps. 80:12) and the 'leaking cisterns' (Jer. 2:13) and for relief in the 'storms and vicissitudes of life'.

Royer sees the reason for this behaviour in the constant struggle which, because of absent alternatives, is fruitless, and also produces a feeling of helplessness and cultural deprivation. Often, the result is the withdrawal of affected individuals from the wider society as well as from other individuals and, indeed, from themselves.

The discussion on work attitudes has been conducted rather reservedly. This is hardly surprising, given the considerable differences between the various ethnic groups and that critics of Caribbean behavioural patterns in the production process can be easily accused of racism.

Nonetheless, Naipaul, himself of Hindu ancestry, is quite clear on this point (1972). His essay, 'Power?', castigates the work attitude of the black majority, who will never succeed in shaking free of foreign control of the local economy, because of their orientation towards consumption and not productive work.

'Identity depends in the end on achievement — that is one of his repeated postulates. He foresees the black population as dependent in the future on foreign books, films and production. In this way, they will continue to be the half-made societies of dependent people, the Third World's third world.

A host of appeals for harder and more disciplined work have been addressed to the Caribbean labour force by representatives from the world of politics, the Church and the private sector[280]. As far back as in 1975 (p. 11), Demas was firmly convinced that the 'central failing' of a great many people in this part of the world has been the 'absence of the right attitude towards work and production. Consciousness, critical awareness and idealism have an important part to play. But the new order will not emerge without hard work and sustained effort — both physical and mental'.

Demas has therefore demanded the breaking down of the old conflict between manual labour and intellectual work. In fact, West Indians have not

[280] E g. Grenada's Government Planner, Arthur Bötswain, has declared that it is a 'gross understatement' to say 'that the work ethic of the average Grenadian is poor. The negative attitude toward work displayed by the average worker is undoubtedly the single most destructive force eating away the society (*CI* April, 1991, p. 2).

experienced the 'fatal split' between brawn and brain in the same measure as most people in the so-called developed countries 'and are in a remarkable degree still able to combine thought and sentiment, seriousness and picong, work and play, art and craft, Mozart and Sparrow, the religious and the festive'.

The Guyanese poet and dramatist, Arthur Seymour, has called to mind the fact that slavery and oppression have produced the symbolic figure of Anancy, 'the spider man' cleverly and quite amorally fighting for its own survival at any price. Seymour has lamented the lack of self-awareness in the Caribbean and the problem posed by selfishness instead of service of one's neighbour — a great and daily fight in this world (*CP* 20, p.17).

The 1982 Carl Stone study on work attitudes in Jamaica, which was commissioned by an eponymous Commission set up by then Prime Minister, Edward Seaga, showed that Jamaican workers clearly saw that their productivity was too low. They ascribed their work-shy attitude to limited promotion prospects and a poor management-worker relationship (Stone, 1982c).

West Indian identity must always be considered under the aspect of external influences. People, culture and language were all imported. The British plantocracy had taken care to extinguish the original name, descent, history and language of the African slaves on the Caribbean plantations. Everything which could lead to the cultural and artistic autonomy of the slaves or their descendants was either banned or tabooed.

Demas (1974, p. 24) had seemed amazed at the totally different attitude to work of the West Indian abroad. The influence of migration on Caribbean identity has been only little researched. It would appear, however, that, abroad, Caribbean people exchange their insular rivalry for a special feeling of togetherness, which manifests itself in common Carnival celebrations and all types of other cultural and political events[281]. Racial and cultural differences between the West Indian emigrants and their host countries, reinforced by historically antagonistic relationships of masters and slaves, colonisers and colonised, hinder the integration of the emigrants in their new countries (Wiltshire-Brodber, 1984, pp. 198f).

The Guyanese writer, Martin Carter, has cast doubt on the very notion of a Caribbean identity. He has warned of the possibility of it being an 'identity of inferiority' out of which grows 'complicity at the expense of co-operation' (*CP* 35, p. 8). The Jamaican writer John Hearne (1984, p. 8) was also of the opinion that much in the discussion of Caribbean intellectuals concerning Caribbean identity bears all the signs of a latent inferiority complex: 'Alas, we are still in this business of trying to justify ourselves as equal human beings with other peoples and other cultures. We are still consuming too much of our mental energy in asking each other anxiously whether we are real people,' he has complained (p. 8).

George Headley, according to Hearne, did not have to specially point out that he was a West Indian batsman — instead, he merely batted as only he could, with outstanding success. Similarly, the great Norman Washington Manley, barrister-at-law, National Hero and Jamaica's First Premier, had never, in appearing before the UK Privy Council, claimed to have a special status,

[281] George Lamming has critically incorporated this in his novel, *The Emigrants* (1954).

merely because he was a Jamaican. Manley, in Hearne's view, had 'simply made some of the magisterial, most objective uses of legal argument, and won.' Nor had Bob Marley sought special understanding or protection for his music, just because it came from Jamaica. Millions have bought his records, precisely because he sang how he was — and lost no time in trying to explain this further.

Nobel Prize laureate, Sir Arthur Lewis, the St. Lucia-born economist, has also held (1983) that a specific West Indian personality and a particular West Indian social system are not possible or desirable. He has, instead, advocated an open, egalitarian race-free society. But he has also admitted the existence of a particular West Indian personality marked by its 'aggressiveness', which has led, on the one hand, to a disproportionately large number of black leaders in the USA being West Indians; on the other hand, however, the West Indies Federation broke up, because the regional and Federal leaders were not on normal speaking terms. The lack of business skills, on the one hand, and, on the other, the addiction to conspicuous consumption of Caribbean people did not make them superior to their African forebears. But, in Lewis' opinion, the West Indian could and should be unique in the fields of music, literature and art.

The Jamaican theologian, Robert Cuthbert (1986, p. 15) has claimed that it is much more important to be a Barbadian or Grenadian than it is to be a Caribbean person or a West Indian. The links between family members in the various islands, especially in the Eastern Caribbean, and the large communities of migrants from other Caribbean territories in Barbados and Trinidad have not led to these nationalities becoming a single society. Despite the insularity, however, there does exist, in Cuthbert's view, a similarity, which is characteristic of Caribbean social structures and basic forms of social organisation throughout the entire region; this similarity also distinguishes Caribbean societies from others on the American continent. McIntyre (1988) has warned against overseeing, in the search for identity, the larger interrelationships. The Caribbean appeared to McIntyre to be more vulnerable currently than had been the case at the time of their independence; little knowledge has been obtained as to its real place in the world: 'In a certain sense, we have also become more inward-looking, preoccupied with immediate local problems, and setting aside the larger picture'.

The influence of racial consciousness on Caribbean integration has so far hardly been researched in both the local and foreign literature on the subject (*Cf.* Kohut, 1989). The idea of an individual West Indian identity is predicated on the assumption that, in the Caribbean, people of different races have together formed a West Indian society in which the question of race does not play a role, but where instead, social norms are set rather by income, class and education (*Cf.* Stone, 1988, p. 34). Racial questions seem externally to concern the demographic majority, at least in Jamaica, only a little[282]. Discussions on racial questions, according to Stone (1987c) pre-occupy in Jamaica only a minority of 'black nationalists'; and interest the majority of black Jamaicans, only when linked with concrete ideas for improving the life of the majority of the people in the country. Stone (1990c) has found that, for at least two decades, the minority

[282] Only 4% according to a June, 1987, Carl Stone poll, listed racial problems among their dislikes in Jamaica

who identify strongly with their African roots have remained constant at 33% of the Jamaican population[283].

These adherents of African identity express themselves in public more forcefully than do the segments of the population who treat the question of race with indifference or with marked contempt for everything African. Marcus Garvey's teachings of the superiority of the black race and against the feeling of inferiority of blacks in the USA and the Caribbean exert currently as previously, an important influence not only in intellectual circles (*Cf.* Sosoe, 1989).

One of Marcus Garvey's sons, Marcus Jr., caused quite a sensation in Jamaica in August, 1987, with his speech in London on the occasion of the centenary of the birth of his father. In this speech, Marcus Garvey, Jr. accused Jamaica of sharing with South Africa the dubious distinction of being one of the only two countries in the world with a black majority but a white Prime Minister[284].

What made the matter so upsetting in Garvey's opinion, was that a change of Government would only produce an 'assistant white man' as the new Prime Minister[285]. Stone (1987d) estimated at 8% the percentage of black Jamaicans sharing this point of view — and at about 30% the percentage of those without any positive feelings to Africa but who still state that economic power in Jamaica should not be in the hands of ethnic minorities.

These population segments do not get enthusiastic about the *Rastafarian* movement; but they do support initiatives to improve the opportunities for the black population and the Black Power movement. Stone (1990c) called them 'black militants'. He supposed that especially the younger generation could again identify more strongly with the racist feelings linked with Garvey, the singer, Bob Marley, and South Africa. Nelson Mandela's 1991 visit to Jamaica had a strong Caribbean-wide echo. The CARICOM Governments by no means hurried to recommend the lifting of the sanctions against South Africa.

The surprisingly wide margin of electoral victory of the Barbadian Democratic Labour Party in May, 1986, over the hitherto long-ruling Barbados Labour Party was seen as a return of the population to consciousness and the necessity of 'social transformation' of Caribbean society for the accomplishment of these values. The BLP, now out of power, was seen, unjustifiably, as the symbol of adjustment to the society of the white people, the minority controlling the country's economy[286]. Subsequently the electoral defeat of the Democratic Labour Party eight years later was seen by C.M. Hope (1994), the editor of now defunct *Caribbean Contact*, as a result of the inability of then Prime Minister Erskine Sandiford to please 'Barbados' dominant economic classes which comprise the country's white merchant and planter groups'.

Racial arguments repeatedly play a role in political confrontations. Dominica's then Leader of the Opposition, Michael Douglas (*CC* December, 1987, p. 13) declared, for instance, in an interview with Radio Antilles, looking back

[283] Stone assumed the existence of at least as large a percentage for those who regarded African influence as inferior and white leadership as essential to a better future for the country

[284] Garvey's Jamaican reference was to the then Prime Minister, Seaga's, Lebanese ancestry.

[285] Garvey meant here the fair-skinned Michael Manley, who is of both African and European ancestry.

[286] The candidacy of a white well-known businessman for the BLP helped not least to bring about this result.

on the 1983 intervention in Grenada, as follows: 'For a black woman to ask the United States to invade a black country...clearly... it is unprecedented! It is unusual! It is one of the weird and funny things that we have never been able to explain'. Montserrat's then Chief Minister, John Osborne, in 1989, termed the British Government's attempt to impose a new,Constitution on the colony immediately after the destructive hurricane Hugo, as a 'callous act aimed at kicking black people while they are down' (CR 7.12.1989, p. 6).

Jamaica's first black Prime Minister, Hugh Lawson Shearer, was heavily criticised in 1992, for opposing the demand for a black JLP Leader by praising the leadership qualities of the 'white' JLP founder, Bustamante; Bustamante's successor as Prime Minister, Sir Donald Sangster; Jamaican and Shearer's own 'white' successor as Party Leader, Seaga (*WG* 4.8.1992, p. 1). Implicit in Shearer's praise was, say his critics, his condemnation of himself and his own accomplishments as Prime Minister and JLP Leader — and, by extension, of all black leaders of the country.

'Black self-consciousness', which has its roots in numerous slave revolts and the 1804 Haitian Revolution, experienced a rebirth under the term, ***négritude***, used by the Martinican poet and politician, Aimé Césaire, and Senegalese poet and statesman Léopold Sédar Senghor in France in the 1930s as well as the Pan-Africanism of Marcus Garvey and the Trinidadian, George Padmore (dePestre, 1976; Grigsby, 1987). The University of the West Indies introduced the study of African Literature in 1968, which, on the observations of the poet and historian, Edward Kamau Brathwaite, had a strong revolutionary effect on the students[287]. The Guyanese Professor of African History, Walter Rodney, who had lectured for some years in Tanzania, exerted great influence on the West Indian students. In his native Guyana, as also in Jamaica, he was slapped with a teaching ban at the University by the Governments[288].

In 1970, the Black Power movement spread to the Caribbean from the United States, and had a particularly strong response in Trinidad[289]. There, the black segment of the population started to discover their own ideal of beauty. In the Cathedral of the Immaculate Conception in Port-of-Spain, white statues were daubed with black paint; in the church in San Fernando, a cross had black colour thrown on it. The black population, as the Roman Catholic priest, Harcourt Blackett, a Barbadian, observed, was no longer a spectator; instead, this population had suddenly jumped on the stage, as a principal actor, of Caribbean History (*CC January*, 1988, p. 16).

In April, 1970, sections of the Trinidad and Tobago Defence Force mutinied. Joining with students and trade unionists, they then tried to topple the Eric Williams' Government. The revolt was, however, swiftly crushed[290].

Fascination with the ideas of the Black Power movement continued and led to the creation of the New Jewel Movement in neighbouring Grenada, which, in

[287]Interview with the journal, *West Africa*, dated 16.3.1987, reprinted in: *CC* April, 1987, p. 13.
[288]Rodney was killed in 1980, reportedly by a Guyanese soldier.
[289]*Black Power* Leader, Stokeley Carmichael, was born there.
[290]Please see the comprehensive account in: Oxaal; Lloyd Best (1971): Rattique Shah; Raoul Pantin; *inter alios*, Trinidian novelist, V.S. Naipaul, dedicated his novel, *Guerrillas*, to the revolt.

1979, brought about the first overthrow by force of a Government in the history of the Commonwealth Caribbean[291].

Voices also existed, however, which warned against making Africanism into an ideology. Even Aimé Césaire himself saw the danger (*Cf.* Moreno Fraginals, 1981, p. 14). The Haitian writer, René dePestre (1981) came out against retaining the reduction of social and cultural conflicts to the racial factor, as had been practised during colonial times. It was that reduction, he thought, which had enabled one to speak of the natural inferiority of black people and the equally natural superiority of white people. Terms, such as black, Negro and coloured, for the people of Africa, remained 'semantic anomalies'.

Rodney (1970, pp. 28-34) tried to neutralise the racist element of the *Black Power* movement, in that he stressed especially its class-struggle character. By this means, Rodney wished to integrate the Indian segment of the population and allay the reservations of the Hindu-centric Communists in Guyana[292]. The mass of the West Indian people, he declared, was either African or Indian — and, therefore, black. He marked off these two ethnic groups against the 'exploitative' white people and, as 'lackeys of capitalism and Imperialism', the Chinese and the majority of the mulattos. He accused the whites of sowing the seeds of discord between Indians and Africans, both of whom were, according to him, equal victims of white slave-owners.

Rodney's attempt to produce an inexorable link between the class struggle and racism has been replicated in numerous writings and speeches of Caribbean scientists, politicians and writers. For example, Trevor Munroe, the Jamaican social scientist and then General Secretary of the Communist Workers' Party of Jamaica has found (1987, pp. 255-270) Jamaican Marxists had analysed the Caribbean all too narrowly from the viewpoint of the class struggle and ignored aspects of racism and racial discrimination. Moreover, they had concerned themselves too little with the positive sides of Garveyism. The political scientist and historian, Gordon K. Lewis (1983, pp. 6-10), acknowledged a 'two-dimensional exploitation' along the racial and economic lines, and spoke of the *pigmentocracy* of the social and ethnic groups. The *social colour*, according to which people were classified in this structure, is determined by skin colour, education and social position.

M.G. Smith (1984, pp. 140ff), the Jamaican sociologist, has adduced rather more complex models in opposition to an all too over-simplified separation of Caribbean — and especially Jamaican — societies according to class and race. The social stratification is determined, in Smith's view, by the distribution of power between institutionally distinguishable groups and categories according to race, size, history, culture, prosperity and future prospects. Such stratification along the lines of economic class and social origins is subordinate to differences of race, culture, history and power.

Smith (1984, p. 141) and Lewis (1983, p. 10), different from the Marxists, have posited pluralism and racial democracy as a recipe for survival for

[291] Toppled Head of Government, Sir Eric Gairy, claimed to have won Black Power for Grenada in 1951 — the demand for more power for blacks was therefore unnecessary (*Cf.* Jacobs and Jacobs, 1980).

[292] But Cheddi Jagan, the Indian General Secretary of the then pro-Communist People's Progressive Party (PPP), remained sceptical (Oxaal, 1971, p 41)

Caribbean society, a peaceful equilibrium between the social groups, while respecting their particular specialities and postures.

The racial contrast in Trinidad and Guyana clashes especially hard. The racial integration of these two countries, with their large East Indian population segments, is one of the preconditions for their integration in the closer political union of Caribbean States. The Indians' scepticism with regard to political integration — which is clear, especially in the opposition to integration of the ruling party in Guyana in the early 1990s, namely, the PPP — is based on the fear of being pushed into a minority position more than hitherto and being politically neutered in a Caribbean State with an African majority. That fear is well-founded.

In these two countries, politicians of African origin have repeatedly played the racial card successfully to the benefit of the black segment of the population[293].

The racial differences are reflected in the election results in these two countries, in that the electorate, in each case, votes along ethnic lines essentially at constituency level. This racial bipolarity has resulted, since the first Eric Williams'-led PNM victory in 1956, in constant electoral victories by the political parties dominated by blacks in Trinidad and Tobago.

In Guyana, however, such a victory occurred only once — in 1964 — in free and fair elections[294]. The UWI lecturer in political science, Ralph Premdass (1993, p. 140) has seen the new Guyanese President, Dr. Cheddi Jagan, himself an East Indian, following the October, 1992, elections, sitting on a 'racial tinder box' and waiting on an incident related to this.

Only few observers see 'very good signs' for a *rapprochement* of the races in Guyana. One such has been the Roman Catholic priest, Patrick Connors (*Sunday Advocate* (Barbados), 12.1.1986, p. 31), who has called attention to the increasing number of marriages between husbands of African origin and Indian brides. He has described the differences in temperament as follows: The African is loud and lively; the Indian, on the other hand, very quiet. The latter can handle money better, enjoys studying scientific subjects and performing professional activities; is reliable and more ambitious, so that, in ten years, all of Guyana has fallen into his hands. Colin Clarke (1985, p. 23) has observed that East Indians in Guyana detest illegitimate births in the creole population as well as their lack of thrift and tendency to live just for a day. Indians, according to Clarke, are also opposed to miscegenation and generally stay away from creole *fêtes*, such as Carnival in Trinidad and Tobago. Moreover, they have successfully defended themselves against being assimilated in the dominant creole culture[295].

East Indians[296], first came to the Caribbean as indentured labourers held in contempt by the then recently-emancipated African ex-slaves and settled mainly in the rural areas. In Trinidad and Guyana where the plantation owners paid

[293] *Cf* (among many others) Jagan, 1980, Anglin 1961 and Yelvington 1987

[294] Here, too, only after changing the electoral law and with the help of a coalition partner led by white business people.

[295] *Cf.* Naipaul's critical comparison of the African and Indian mentality in his essay 'Power' in *The Overcrowded Barracoon*

[296] See Dabydeen and Samaroo (1987) on the Indian's role in the Caribbean.

close attention to keeping the races separate they are still the largest rural population segment. The blacks, however, left the plantations, and as soon as they had enough land to settle on and opportunities for employment; they went to the urban areas (Sanders, 1988).

East Indians were allowed to bring their Hindu priests and Muslim holy men with them; and had permission to practise their religious rites and customs as well as speak their own languages. With improved health facilities, their post-World War II population growth rate outstripped that of the black population segment; and their self-awareness increased, thanks to the success of 'Mother India's' Independence struggle. The black middle class in Guyana and Trinidad observed with discontentment the East Indian strategy of conquest in both politics and the economy— despite, in George Lamming's (1984, p. 44) opinion, not consisting by any means of a monolithic group, as prejudice lags stated.

Polemically, the putative Indian push to expand in the Caribbean has been compared with the policy of New Delhi *vis-à-vis* Sikkim, Bangladesh, Sri Lanka, Pakistan and Goa (Cf. A.J. Rampersad); and a warning has been given against 'Indian Imperialism'. Militant Hindu organisations in the USA, on the other hand, warn their adherents against miscegenation and welcome the refusal of Hindu pandits in Trinidad to perform Hindu marriage ceremonies on couples of mixed religion (Ajit Jain, 1984, p. 8).

2.7.2. Caribbean Culture

'The region has more artists per square inch than is probably good for it,' has declared the Jamaican artist and University Professor, Rex Nettleford (1989, p. 25). 'But this merely speaks of that need to survive with dignity where the creative imagination offers a particular kind of freedom of expression and self-fulfillment on a personal as well as a collective (national?) level.'

Caribbean culture is similar to the ethnic composition of the people of the region in being marked by societies forcibly tossed together like dice. The majority of the black population segment was systematically deprived of its culture, i.e. the culture of a group of people was, for economic reasons, eradicated, in order to be able to put them to work as a cheap and ignorant labour force and get as much work as possible from them (Moreno Fraginals, 1981). The black slaves—brought to the Caribbean, to sire their own offspring for their slave-masters, bereft of their customary diet, clothing and habitation as well as their music, religion and their very mother tongue—were supposed to lose every jot and tittle of self-awareness. The dialectical *a priori* confrontation between the dominant culture, serving as the means of integration and subjugation and the dominated culture, as the assembly point of resistance, became one of the points of departure of Caribbean culture today (Moreno Fraginals, 1981, p. 12). In the course of roughly the last 500 years, there has been a mixture of cultural influences from Europe, Africa, Asia, North America and Latin America as well as the indigenous Caribbean in different manifestations. Differences in geography, ethnic composition and colonial history have imprinted themselves on language, religion and other cultural forms.

On the other hand, through the geopolitical realities, cultural sensibilities developed (Nettleford, 1978, p. 150) bringing more closely together the Anglophone, Hispanic, Francophone and Dutch-speaking sections of the Caribbean in a cultural sense. Literature, the theatre, art, music and the dance cross-fertilised each other — thereby giving birth to a uniquely 'Caribbean product' growing beyond the borders of the previous Empires (Nettleford, 1979, p. 29). High literacy levels and a multitude of public lending libraries have provided all segments of the population with access to indigenous poetry and prose. Countless theatre groups perform almost exclusively plays written in dialect by local playwrights.

The media serve as cultural multipliers — but, from the viewpoint of integration, with varying intensity. While the print media and radio promote Caribbean cultural identity, television rather strengthens external cultural influences on the region, owing to the high level of foreign programming (*cf.* Nettleford, 1989, p. 27).

The exchange of the cultural productions of the television stations in the various Caribbean States and territories is still small, although bodies, such as the Caribbean Broadcasting Union (CBU) centrally produce programmes. Plays, music, creative writing or the dance virtually offer themselves for transmission through the electronic media as powerful creators of culture (Fergus, 1988). The cultural penetration of US television was criticised by then Prime Minister of Grenada, Maurice Bishop (1982, pp. 6ff) as 'cultural imperialism', and the end product, as 'Coca Cola culture.' Hence, in his view, the fact that no Caribbean culture had ever had the possibility of developing into the 'bulwark of our sovereignty'.[297]

The effect of a collective culture in conferring identity and the role of culture in society at all is viewed differently by different authors. Thus, for instance, for the sociologist, Anton L. Allahar (1992) who teaches in Canada, there is no common Caribbean culture, owing to the differences existing between Indian and Afro-Caribbean cultures. For the Guyanese writer, Martin Carter, culture is something embracing and registering all efforts to get society moving. Economic powerlessness of a society transfers itself to that society's culture. As Salkey (1972, p. 346) has put it, the real struggle is, therefore, the one for economic independence. Culture, in this context, is reflected in poverty and is, in this exciting way, an expression of Emancipation as well.

Khafra Kambon (1984, p. 27) sees in 'cultural sovereignty' the target of a revolutionary process in which 'culture is an expression of the people, not an intellectualised gift bestowed on the masses by a few who feel they can determine what is authentic.'

English, as a common language, unites the people of the states and territories of the Anglophone Caribbean and, therefore, separates them at the same time from neighbouring people speaking other languages. This language has been repeatedly dismissed as the tongue of colonisers and 'Imperialism'.[298] But English has nonetheless remained the language of literature and the upper

[297] But Bishop, in an address to Caribbean intellectuals, simultaneously defended the suppression of the 'reactionary Caribbean Press' in Grenada, for it was 'manipulated by powerful foreign interests' (1982, p. 16).

[298] *cf* Devonish, 1986

classes, whereas the lower classes communicate among themselves mainly in the local languages of Creole or Patois. This leads to communication difficulties within the population (*cf.* Mervyn Alleyne, 1987). On many occasions, the demand has been made that Creole should be admitted as a second official language, besides English (*cf.* Mervyn Alleyne, 1987; Hellinger, 1987; *CC* March, 1986, p. 14).

Literati and pedagogues in St. Lucia, Grenada and St. Vincent and the Grenadines have made an effort to make Creole, as a written language, also capable of being used in literature.[299] This elevation in the status of *Créole* (or *kweyol*) would create a common speech zone in the Eastern Caribbean, which would include the Francophone *départments* as well.[300] Former UWI Vice-Chancellor, Sir Philip Sherlock, has seen (1986, p. 12) in the Creole language, dance, cooking and music the coming into existence of a real West Indian culture. The common Creole language could also have the effect of giving an identity to the political union of the Eastern Caribbean.

Since the late 1940s, the Commonwealth Caribbean has produced creative writers of note whose books have been translated into numerous languages. These include Nobel prize-winner, Derek Walcott (of St. Lucia), John Hearne (Jamaica), George Lamming (Barbados), C.L.R. James (Trinidad), V.S. Naipaul (Trinidad), Edward Kamau Brathwaite (Barbados), Edgar Mittelholzer and Jan Carew (Guyana). It is worthy of note that most of them reached the peak of their creative work while living far from the Caribbean — in the UK, the USA or Canada — partly for economic reasons. Their voluntary exile also enabled them, however, to describe their tiny native lands from a perspective of 'alienation' (Cobham, 1979, p. 22) and also to provide a world-wide readership with both a metropolitan and Caribbean perspective. Additionally, Caribbean writers are little regarded at home, unless they have been successful in the metropolitan world abroad.[301]

The CXC has helped to make knowledge of Caribbean literature reach all classes of the population. This is also true of Caribbean drama. The plays of Derek Walcott and the Jamaican, Trevor Rhone, would certainly have meant something only to the educated people of the Commonwealth Caribbean, had these plays not also been setbooks in the school-leaving examinations set and marked by the CXC.[302] This follows from the fact that only a few Caribbean theatre troupes go on tour; moreover, the most popular plays have local references, and their play on words is no longer understood on neighbouring islands, owing to the plays being written in local dialect (*cf.* Corsbie, 1984, p. 48).

Only rarely do fans of free dance and the ballet get to enjoy performances by artistes from other Caribbean States. Television helps little to transmit regionally the high quality of the performances. Efforts have been made to

[299] The most prominent of these authors is the 1992 Nobel laureate for literature, St Lucia-born poet Derek Walcott, who writes, in part, in Creole.

[300] The French *Université des Antilles et de la Guyane* began a three-year week-end diploma course in the Creole language in St Lucia in January, 1990

[301] Walcott once said disparagingly that the Caribbean islands are so small that literally each person who wrote anything could become the poet laureate (Januszczah, 1988, p 2)

[302] Walcott, in establishing the James Rodway Prize for CARICOM poets-named after his Guyanese teacher — has highlighted the literary importance of schools (*CC* March 1993, p 19).

expand the most renowned free-dance group locally, the Jamaica National Dance Theatre, into a West Indies Dance Company (McDonald, 1990, pp. 131-132).

The dance does make quite a unique contribution to the preservation of genuine Caribbean cultural forms of expression. The black slaves had to adopt the language of their oppressors, in order to communicate. But the dance, in contrast, belonged to the people quite by themselves. Indeed, it enabled them to render homage to their ancient Gods — which, officially, was forbidden — giving rise to various religious rites (e.g. *kumina, pukkumina, eto, tambo, gerreh, dinkimini, zion, revivalism* and *Rastafarianism* in Jamaica; *voodoo* in Haiti and the Dominican Republic, *santería* in Cuba; *shango* in Trinidad and Tobago; *comfah* in Guyana; and celebrations of a general nature, such as *Jonkonnu* processions, *burru, dinkimini, brucking* party and pre-Lenten Carnival. Now, as in the past, in Nettleford's (1985) view, the dance is a means for cultural survival for the people in the Caribbean.

The people of the Commonwealth Caribbean are united more closely by music than by literature, the theatre, painting and the dance. By means of the radio, cassette players and records, music of all forms of cultural expression, has succeeded in being disseminated the fastest and most comprehensively in the entire region. Indeed, the large amount of musical talent and good texts thereby ensures a world-wide distribution as well. The *calypso*, influenced by music from Spain, Latin America, France and Africa, came into existence at the end of the eighteenth century as the sung commentary on recent local events, often with a satirical element.[303] Harry Belafonte's modified calypso-style rendition of the *Banana Boat Song, 'Day-O!* ', from Jamaica, and *Island in the Sun*, a Barbadian composition for the film version of Alec Waugh's Grenada-based novel of the same name, became world hits. Calypsonians, such as the Mighty Sparrow, Chalkdust and Lord Kitchener, became famous throughout the region.

Reggae, developing totally and uniquely in Jamaica (Spence, 1978, p. 5) from Ska and Rock Steady since the late 1960s, has found a world-wide following[304], extending well beyond the Caribbean and was made popular especially by Bob Marley and cult films, such as 'The Harder They Come.' This form of music, which has its roots deep in the popular tradition of the island and initially found a response in lower-class Jamaicans, became popular with all Caribbean people because of its world-wide success. Conversely, calypso conquered Jamaica, starting with the upper and middle classes.[305] As a synthesis of Trinidadian calypso, African and East-Indian elements and black US soul music, *soca* music (from *soul calypso*) has become the most successful variant commercially (*cf.* Ahyoung, 1981, pp. 119-120).[306] Despite the relative distance

[303] *cf* Sealey and Malm, 1982, pp. 24-27; *The Roaring Lion* 1987;
[304] *cf* Davis and Simon, 1983.
[305] Byron Lee and the Dragonaires has contributed significantly to this by bringing back to Jamaica (and then other Caribbean regions, as well as the USA, Canada and the UK) each year's Carnival hits from Trinidad, where Lee, himself of Chinese-African-Caribbean origin, spends several weeks in the run-up to that event; he, with others, helped to start an annual post-Easter Carnival in Jamaica in the early 1990s (*WG*, 21 7.1992, p 6).
[306] *Soca* is a typical example of Caribbean music being changed by being exported and then re-imported and adopted in its home country in its modified form from the USA, where market acceptance had necessitated the modification (*cf* Regis).

to Belize, calypso, reggae and soca have had great influence there; and Belizean compositions of these types of music have been made (Colville Young, 1989).

The Caribbean-wide distribution has also occurred of the *steel pan* — according to the Barbadian poet and historian, Edward Kamau Brathwaite, a unique musical instrument created in the twentieth century.[307] *Steel bands* employing *steel drums* are made from empty oil containers used in the Trinidadian petroleum industry, the covers of which are hammered to a variety of depths and sizes, to produce a nice-sounding, multi-faceted instrument constantly refined since the 1940s and, are a fixed part of Carnival in the Caribbean and have even spread to London's Jamaica-influenced Notting Hill Carnival, the largest Caribbean Carnival celebration in Europe, as well as to Jamaica.

From their very beginning, both calypso and reggae have had the function of criticism of society, with the former being oriented locally to daily political and other events. Top-rated calypso, unlike reggae, has repeatedly had lyrics dealing with Caribbean unity. Indeed, the Mighty Sparrow — the best-known calypsonian — mentioned the West Indies Federation in several of his calypsos, and called attention to the resentment of his Trinidadian fellow-citizens *vis-à-vis* the other Caribbean people, especially Jamaicans following the negative result of their 1961 referendum on Jamaica's remaining in the West Indies Federation. The lyrics of his winning 1962 Calypso King Competition entry in his country (Warner, 1982, p. 72) included the following words:

'People want to know why Jamaica run
From the Federation
Yes they want to know why Jamaica run away
From the Federation
Jamaica have a right to speak she mind
That is my opinion And if you believe in democracy
You'll agree with me.
But if they know they didn't want Federation
And they know they didn't want to unite as one
Independence was at the door
Why they didn't speak before
This is no time to say you ain't
Federating no more.'

The calypsonian, 'Black Stalin', won the 1970 Calypso King Competition with his calypso, 'Caribbean Man', lamenting the 'disaster' of Caribbean attempts at integration in the following terms:

'You try with a Federation, the whole thing end in confusion
Caricom and then Carifta, but somehow ah smelling disaster
Mister West Indian Politician, you went to big institution
How come you can't unite seven million?
When a West Indian unity I know is very easy
If you only rap to you people and tell them like me.

---

[307] Brathwaite, in a 16.3.1987 interview with the journal, *West Africa* (reprinted in *Caribbean Contact* April, 1987, p. 13). Then Trinidad and Tobago Prime Minister, A.N.R. Robinson (1988, p. 11) claims the *steel oil drum* is the only twentieth century musical instrument made from a used industrial object.

Is for a better life in de region
For we woman and we children
Dat must be de ambition of the Caribbean Man
De Caribbean Man, De Caribbean Man
A man who don't know his history can't form no unity
How could a man who don't know his history form his own ideology
If the rastafari movement spreading and Carifta dying slow
Den is something dem rastas on dat dem politicians don't know.'

In 1985, Barbadian calypsonian, the 'Mighty Gabby', won his country's competition with his 'Make we one Nation' addressed to Caribbean politicians (Kirton, 1986) the theme of the 1972 dream of the 'Mighty Duke' (Annamunthodo, 1972).

'I had a dream wherein which I see
A United States of the Caribbee
Where all West Indian islands under the sun
Walking hand in hand under one command,
One flag of the Union
Then I awake; my poor heart break
I find it's all a sad mistake;
Though just ah dream
How great it seem
That's why I scream
It's mad, that's bad, so sad.
So West Indian leaders the time is now
Let us try to get together somehow
Petty differences we do have I know
But staying apart is not very smart
Let's build for tomorrow.
We must unite and set things right
Among ourselves why do we fight?
Don't you realise we are too small in size
To do otherwise?
Revise, let's rise, get wise.
Federation gone but oh, what a shame!
Independence yes, but what have we gained
Our leaders now silently confess
Their actions were rash when our dreams were smashed
For singular interest.'

Calypso and reggae stand in mutual and productive competition both in the Caribbean and in Caribbean communities outside the region. Historically, this is not dissimilar to the two antipodes, Trinidad and Tobago and Jamaica, of the West Indies Federation — and also the countries where these two forms of music originated. The claim by Carl Stone (1991a) that reggae has 'taken over' the Eastern Caribbean and overtaken calypso popularity, is hardly shared by East Caribbean calypsonians. Carnival there, by far the biggest annual *fête*, would just not be imaginable without soca and calypso. Even in Jamaica, the cradle of reggae, soca rhythms bring hundreds of thousands of revellers onto the streets for the yearly post-Easter Carnival introduced in 1990.[308]

Carnival Trinidad-style has developed into a unifying force for Caribbean communities abroad, especially in Toronto (*cf.* Olivia Bennett, 1986, pp. 24-31), despite the relatively small number of Trinidadian emigrants. Abroad, a new, pan-Caribbean form of Carnival has developed under the influence of reggae.

Culture plays a rather subordinate role officially in regional co-operation. Within the Caribbean Community, it has low priority. Indeed, the 1972 CARICOM Heads of Governments decision to set up a Culture Desk within the CARICOM Secretariat took four years to implement. Revealingly, CARICOM Education Ministers, mostly also responsible for culture as well, rarely are accompanied by their experts in this field to regional meetings dealing with the subject. Indeed, these experts have an opportunity for an exchange of views essentially at meetings of writers, theatre people and musicians partly financed externally and held outside the region.

Cultural matters were, for the first time, discussed for two days at a meeting in 1985 by the relevant CARICOM Ministers, who decided to set up a Regional Cultural Committee. The then CARICOM Secretary-General, Roderick Rainford (*CP* 32:22) described the objective of governmental cultural initiatives 'for the purpose of creating and nurturing the conditions for individual and collective self-expression on the creative plane' as being 'as vital for the life of man in society as are the requirements for physically sustaining life'.

The Ministers agreed to promote a film biennially, as well as the reprinting of rare and out-of-stock books and the publication of a dictionary of Caribbean speech, in addition to supporting Caribbean publishers, as part of a Caribbean publishing strategy. The Caribbean Film and Video Federation, which links producers from all the Region's language groupings, and maintains contact with several international cultural institutions, was established in 1992 by Latin American and Caribbean Ministers of Culture (Caribbean Community, 1993, p. 58).

At a meeting in 1988, the Ministers proposed the establishment of a CARICOM Foundation for Art and Culture to support through a CARICOM Awards Scheme, artists and other creative workers and promote cultural research of the Caribbean Community 1988 (*Caribbean Community*, 1989, pp. 43ff). The Foundation is yet to be established. Anglophone Caribbean playwrights founded in 1976 a Theatre Information Exchange as a clearing house for information and meeting place for thespians. But meetings take place irregularly (Corsbie, 1984, p. 49). Actors in the region established in 1988 an Association of Caribbean Theatre Artists dedicated to training and promoting artists, producing plays and publishing (*ibid.*, p. 44).

In July, 1991, at the UWI/St. Augustine, there came into existence the Caribbean Inter-Cultural Music Institute (CIMI) which is mandated to preserve, harness and give direction to the music of the Region (Caribbean Community,

[308] Forerunners existed some years earlier in the form of several UWI/Mona *fêtes* and the *Orange Carnival*, originally held at Orange Grove, an upper-class neighbourhood in northern Kingston.

1992, pp. 43f). It will offer on-site courses in music as well as the manufacture and repair of musical instruments for all CARICOM nationals. Initially, this Institute will deal especially with regional research and documentation on the steel band and offer training courses (*CP* 32, p. 23 and 52/53, p. 33). The preservation of the Heritage of the Member States is supported by the Regional Museum Development Project of CARICOM in Jamaica.

The Caribbean Festival of Arts (CARIFESTA), the biggest manifestation of official cultural policy in the Caribbean, was last held in Trinidad in August, 1992, after being postponed several times and an eleven-year hiatus, following the 1981 Festival in Barbados and previous ones in 1971 (the first, in Guyana), in 1976 (in Jamaica) and in 1979 (in Cuba). George Lamming has suggested holding smaller Festivals for individual cultural genres with fewer participants, between the large ones (*CC* August, 1983, p. 6). The 1992 Festival consisted among others of a Regional Art Exhibition, a Regional Film and Video Festival, a Book Fair, a Village Devoted to Indigenous People and a series of Symposia.

The most important cultural pro-federal bodies at regional level are the educational institutions, especially the various campuses of the University (Nettleford, 1978, pp. 157-161) and the Caribbean Examinations Council (CXC), which includes in its syllabuses the most varied expressions of Caribbean culture. The UWI also brings artists and students of the creative arts together, e.g. at the Creative Arts Centre, on its Mona campus. Finally, it contributes to the development of high artistic standards by means of courses of study, seminars, summer schools and symposia.

2.7.3. Caribbean World Views

2.7.3.1 The Influence of Ideological Currents

European world views, ideologies and religions have influenced the thought and action of people in the Caribbean for some five hundred years. As to whether specific Caribbean forms have developed and, if so, their influence, if any, on Caribbean integration, should be examined.

World views and religious beliefs can be meaningfully defined as components of ideology. Ideology is defined here as a body of ideas concerning (human) society in a more or less logical context and with a function similar to that of the belief systems of religious denominations (Heberle, 1967, pp. 11ff). Caribbean political ideology, according to Maingot (1983b) is often an act of political faith of an *élite* usually of foreign origin and kept alive with foreign ideas. The probability that this ideology differs from the convictions of broad population segments exists even when the *élites*, who propagate it, succeed in coming to political power. The *élites*, by believing that their own ideology is accepted by the broad masses, try, often against considerable resistance, to change the economic framework. In the process, they themselves get trapped in one-way programmatic and ideological streets. In order to implement their programmes, they have to use force, which leads to alienation and, in their followers, to lower labour productivity and indifference. Gross capitalistic exploitation and Stalinism in Maingot's view, lead finally to the same result.

No new ideologies have been founded in the Caribbean. But there have been further developments at least for the Third World. In this context, Gordon K. Lewis (1983, p. 329) has named *Négritude*, *Black Power*, *Black Nationalism*, *Creole Marxism* and *Cuban Socialism*. It is noticeable that more than an average number of artists, thinkers and University Lecturers of the region are active as politicians.

The first ideological confrontations in the Caribbean took place, according to the findings of Gordon Lewis (1984, p. 43) between the supporters and opponents of slavery. Both sides, in Lewis' view, had the same basic assumption that the so-called New World was not comparable with the Old World; and that the norms of Europe could not be simply extrapolated to the Caribbean region. The pro-slavery camp had used this argument, Lewis claimed, in order to counter the comparison between the slaves and the industrial proletariat in Europe; the anti-slavery grouping, on the other hand, had seen the slaves as protagonists of a new society Europeans had never known.

Ideological influences made themselves felt in the labour unrest of the 1930s, which led to the creation of trade unions and political parties, the introduction of Universal Adult Suffrage, the phased arrival of self-government and, finally, formal independence from the colonial power (i.e. the UK). In Trinidad, Captain Arthur Andrew Cipriani, with World War I veterans and workers of African and East Indian origin, founded a trade union and published a newspaper named *The Socialist*. He formulated his ideological views along the lines of the British Labour Party and the British trade union movement.

West Indians returned from their studies at Universities in the metropolises of industrialised countries with ideological convictions which they tried to convert into political praxis at home. Most remarkable among these returnees were Dr. Cheddi Jagan and Linden Forbes Burnham in Guyana, Dr. Eric Williams in Trinidad who, however, returned only after working for several years abroad and, a generation later, Maurice Bishop in Grenada. Intellectuals, such as C.L.R. James and Malcolm Nurse in Trinidad, Dr. Frantz Fanon from Martinique and Walter Rodney in Guyana exerted, with their analyses of colonialism and neo-colonialism, great influence on the Marxist Left.

Facing and largely preceding the intellectuals were populist labour leaders such as Uriah Butler in Trinidad and Bustamante in Jamaica, who did not build on a formal ideological concept, but rather on an intuitive anti-colonialism; and they also displayed a feel for understanding the needs of the socially-neglected masses.

Up to the 1970s, only few political parties in the Anglophone Caribbean put ideological points of view in the forefront. Indeed, even some two decades later, only the manifestos of a small number of those parties meet the criteria generally associated with ideology — namely, that theoretical elements play at least an equal role with the practical components; and a corpus of ideas is developed, explaining the state of the world and offering means to changing conditions. Interestingly, the Antigua Labour Party and, in Belize, the People's United Party described their political concepts as 'revolutionary', although the contents of their manifestos are anything but radical — rather like the 'Radical' and 'Liberal' parties in Switzerland, which are really Right-wing. Conversely, the Jamaica Labour Party could hardly be called Left-wing. On the other hand

Maurice Bishop's 'People's Revolutionary Government' was correctly so named.

In view of the differing ideological development of the states of the Commonwealth Caribbean, the founding fathers of the Community agreed on the formula of 'ideological pluralism' in the region. This did not mean that, within individual CARICOM States, political pluralism must rule, however. It was, in fact, an attempt to reconcile growing Socialist governmental forms, which were partly authoritarian, with the formal concepts of liberal, pluralistic democracy in other states of the Community. The CARICOM Treaties contain no conditions laying down a certain state or governmental form for the members. The formula of 'ideological pluralism' should be a shield protecting the Member States 'against enforced sameness' — but, on the other hand, should not be a 'sword against solidarity', as the Group of Caribbean Experts, who examined the development of the Community in the 1980s, expressed it (*The Caribbean Community*, 1981, p. 7).

The Standing Committee of the CARICOM Ministers responsible for Foreign Policy, in St. Lucia in February, 1980, dealt with the effect of the ideological multi-facetedness of CARICOM Member States on the external affairs of the Community. The participants expressed the view that the CARICOM countries should not pursue their relationships with third countries at the expense of the Community. On the other hand, the desired Caribbean unity must be underpinned by mutual respect for the ideologies practised by the Member States. 'Ideological pluralism', stated a communiqué from that conference, 'is an irreversible fact of international relations and should not, therefore, constitute a barrier to the strengthening of the mechanism of CARICOM'.[309]

Not all Heads of Government share the viewpoint that each CARICOM country should be left to become blessed in its own way. Thus, Jamaica's Head of Government in 1980-89, Edward Seaga, stressed that the frontiers of pluralism, so understood, lay at the point where human rights were infringed. No system was, in his view, acceptable, which was not legitimised in 'elections free and fair and free from fear', as he stressed at the Fourth Summit of CARICOM Heads of Government in Port-of-Spain (Trinidad) in 1983 (*CP* 20, p. 7). At the previous CARICOM Heads of Government Summit of Ocho Rios (Jamaica) both he and his Barbadian counterpart, Tom Adams, had failed in their *démarche* to link membership in the Community to the respect for human rights. This initiative was aimed especially at the then Socialist Governments in Grenada and Guyana. The principle of ideological pluralism was expressly recognised, as previously stated, in the *Ocho Rios Declaration*, the final document of the conference (*CP* 22, p. 15).

The principle of 'ideological pluralism' was controversial, from the very beginning, however. The then Prime Minister of Trinidad and Tobago, George Chambers, complained, in July, 1983, that taking that principle into consideration hindered decisions at CARICOM meetings and impaired the viability of the Community. Influential newspapers in Jamaica, Barbados and Trinidad lashed out against the understanding about pluralism, publishing full-

[309] Quoted according to Searwar, 1984, p. 161

page adverts in which they demanded freedom of the Press in both Grenada and Guyana. The Jamaica *Daily Gleaner*, the newspaper with the largest circulation in the CARICOM area, ran an editorial (on 21.7.1983, at page 10) in which it declared that it did not consider ideological pluralism to exist when CARICOM countries whose Governments had come to power with the aid of arms, which also kept them in power, enjoyed the same membership rights as others. Dictators, in its view, had no place in the 'brotherhood of democracies'.

Nor did the concept of 'ideological pluralism' find favour with the United States, which, as OECS Director-General, Dr. Vaughan Lewis, said in the same month, strove after the 'ideological harmonisation' of the region (1984b, p. 60). Consequently, the USA could show no understanding for what would amount to accepting Socialist States in the midst of Western-type democracies.

The October, 1983, intervention in Grenada brought an end to the concept of 'ideological pluralism' within CARICOM. Pressure grew on the then Government of Guyana, which was obliged to make changes constantly in the ideological line of the President, Forbes Burnham. Indeed, his successor, Desmond Hoyte, was able to save the 1986 CARICOM Summit in Guyana, only by making a Canossa-like submission in February of that year on the island of Mustique with the OECS Heads of Government.

With the start of the 1990s, the end of ideology in Commonwealth Caribbean politics seemed to have arrived. Thus, rejection of the 1990 US intervention in Panama did not open a new ideological divide, including against Washington. The new PNP Government was able to re-establish diplomatic relations with Cuba, eight years after they had been broken off by the then JLP, pro-US Government, without giving rise to the suspicion of the creation of a new Socialist alliance. The end of the East-West conflict in the region was favourable to this development.

The view that the exercise of tolerance *vis-à-vis* the concept of 'ideological pluralism' has led from regional harmony to fragmentation, as stated by then Commonwealth Secretary-General, Sir Shridath Ramphal, in a UWI/St. Augustine lecture (1985, p. 16) was not likely to be supported by many Commonwealth Caribbean politicians in the 1990s. Following the 1982 Ocho Rios/Jamaica CARICOM Summit, the Haitian political scientist, Mirlande Hippolyte-Manigat (1983, p. 13)[310], asked 'whether any integration movement can support the corrosive effects of ideological and political diversity, without altering its profile, its orientation, its mechanisms of functioning, thereby putting in jeopardy the results expected out of the experience'. The results expected from the 'integration' experience were thereby endangered, she further argued. Lloyd Searwar (1990, pp. 30ff) for his part, ascribed to the ideological confrontation an important role in distracting attention from national problems. The so-called political non-alignment and ideological pluralism had served, in his opinion, rather as a magic formula than as the guideline for prudent policy.

The ideological rapproachment of CARICOM Governments has led to the extinction of numerous side-war battlefields determined by ideology. Convergence now largely exists in security and foreign policy. In place of

[310] She is the wife of Leslie Manigat, Haitian President for a short time in 1988, and was then Lecturer in International Relations at Simón Bolívar University, Caracas, Venezuela

polarising external pluralism, a new internal pluralism has come to the fore, which makes possible a broad spectrum of practical policy implementation measures, with basically the same definition of democracy.

2.7.3.2 Political Structures

A common definition of democracy and democratic State has developed in the Caribbean, after different preliminary ideological signs, the practical shaping of which differed considerably from one another, from time to time. Carl Stone (1983b, p. 235) defined democracy as 'a process which seeks to redistribute power from centres of power concentration to the majority of citizens in a political system.' The channels through which this process runs, are, according to Stone, 'invariably determined by the cleavages and conflicts between social interests, the competition of power between contending *élites* and counter-*élites*, through which competing interests are articulated, and the institutional forms which govern political life.'

One of the dilemmas of the literature on Third World democracy is that democracy is evaluated in that literature according to either distributive (i.e. economic) or individual political points of view. According to Horowitz (1983, p. 228), this is a crude simplification, because this distribution never refers simply to economic goods, but rather to political power. Democracy, therefore, has actually the same structural characteristics in developed countries, the ex-Socialist bloc and the Third World. The Marxist-class system needed to confirm its development theories is, according to Horowitz, hardly marked in the Caribbean and Latin America. A relatively weak and highly differentiated bourgeoisie faces politically a relatively weak and little-differentiated proletariat, while large segments of the population remain outside the political process.

'Democratic pluralism' for Carl Stone (1986a) stood between authoritarian and popular-dirigistic state forms. All three of these state forms exist in the Caribbean Basin, with authoritarian systems in decline, but the other types remaining very much alive. Thus, Costa Rica and Barbados are seen as the prototypes of the democratic, pluralistic state. Similarly, Cuba is taken to be the paradigm of the populist, dirigistic type of state and governmental form in which power is concentrated in the hands of a few, on behalf of the majority of the population.

According to the view of Jamaica's Prime Minister in 1980-89, Edward Seaga (1981, p. 6), it can be truly said that nowhere else in the world does such a number of Parliamentary democracies exist as in the Caribbean. No other geographical area can, he holds, display so many 'practising democracies' — not even in Western Europe and North America. Thomas D. Anderson (1984, p. 119) also views the Caribbean Basin as one of the most democratically ruled regions of the world. Five centuries after the first documented and surviving arrival of Europeans in the Caribbean, of the twenty-four States and twelve self-administered and dependent territories in the Western Hemisphere located between the USA and Brazil, only Cuba and Haiti were not ruled by freely and directly elected Governments in 1992.

In the Third World including obviously the Caribbean, the idea and reality of democracy often stand in contradiction one to the other. This is especially so when Western ideas of democracy and constitutional praxis emanating from a long history of ideas and now existing currently in mint condition, after centuries of successes and aberrations, are lumped and dumped on Third World states not having this constitutional history. Conflicting ideas develop from a democracy as the proper system to bring about political decisions democratically, determined by pluralism and participation, and by a democracy as a comprehensive social manifestation (*cf.* Nohlen, 1988, pp. 6ff).

In 1987, Michael Manley (pp. 168-71), then the President of the PNP, which was not represented in Parliament, warned against slipping into 'populist democracy' living from promises of rival political forces and demanding no personal involvement of the electorate. Here, according to Manley, the citizen remains almost an uninvolved spectator of a faceless government. As an alternative, he proposed a deeper, functionally-oriented democracy with clearly-determined participation of the population in the institutions.

Dr. Trevor Munroe (1986, p. 85) the Jamaican Marxist University lecturer, for his part, wanted to replace 'bourgeois democracy' with 'people's democracy'. The latter would, he claimed, put an end to the poverty of the masses to whom it would provide economic independence from American Imperialism and give the ordinary people power over their daily lives. But even he doubted if Socialist, revolutionary—or merely just a participatory — democracy, such as he sought to establish, would function in the Caribbean, in view of 'US Imperialism'. Other obstacles standing in the way were the relatively little revolutionary class development, clientelism as defined by Stone (1980) and the tendency of Caribbean intellectuals, hardly excluding Munroe, to be loyal to the letter in their abstract understanding and praxis of Marxism-Leninism .

Marxists and other Socialists in the Caribbean have it difficult, especially because confrontations within the multiracial societies there do not run along racial lines. Instead, these confrontations exist between groups of people, rivalling large and small islands, larger against smaller firms, between artificially polarised and tribalized groups, belonging to the same socio-economic class, and, finally, between political parties, which are discontinuously organised and of sworn loyalty to leading personalities alone.

The Venezuelan Caribbean expert, Andrés Serbín (1989, p. 10) has suggested 'pragmatic democracy' as the solution to the problem posed by the failure of Caribbean Socialism and as a defence against neo-liberal policies as incorporated by the Reagan Administration. Serbin saw 'pragmatic democracy' as a mixture of moderate nationalism and moderate capitalism seeking unity within the *élites*. Party leaderships would have a fore-runner role; Government, political parties and the general population would have a *clientèle* relationship to each other.

The role of this party leadership and the creation of clienteles do belong, however, to the problems of democratic praxis—and that, not merely in Commonwealth Caribbean States. The two-party system, which gives deviants from the party, live and independent candidates hardly a chance at the polls, as well as the party and Parliamentary system inherited from the UK, put the particular party leadership in a strong position. Policy is formulated by party leaders in collaboration with experts from the Civil Service and specialists called advisers. The only role left to Parliament is that of distributing political goodies and mobilising votes for the party leadership. In short, Parliament hardly exerts any influence on the policy of the Government (Stone, 1980, p. 75).

The small size of the Caribbean States facilitates the formation of authoritarian governments. The State is oriented towards development and interferes everywhere. Cabinet decides even on marginal matters. This leads to centralisation. The primacy of party policy in small Caribbean States is enhanced by charismatic leadership as defined by Max Weber, neo-patronage, with the low income levels of the population and constant inter-action of the tiny societies. Governmental power, according to Courtney Blackman[311] (1989, pp. 65-68), means, in poor countries, an opportunity for personal enrichment. Each change of Government leads to personal catastrophes and the collapse of existence for the supporters of the losing party. Official posts become personal sinecures. Subordinates on the job are the personal followers of the boss—not co-workers.

The power struggle leads to Governments behaving like 'constitutional dictators' (Stone, 1990a). Opponents, even in the ranks of one's own party, are pitilessly persecuted and kept under surveillance. A 'syndrome of political backwardness' develops, with the violent persecution of opponents, 'penetration and manipulation of the people's culture (religion, music, etc.)' and 'corrupt winner-take-all electoral politics, rampant tribalism, pork barrel politics and corruption, the promotion of authoritarianism and the political divinity of leaders.'

In Jamaica, this type of dealing with the Opposition led in part in 1980 to the bloodiest electoral campaign in the country's history with at least an estimated 800 deaths. A year earlier, in Grenada, the high-handed Head of Government was toppled. In other Caribbean territories, freedom parties came into existence against too powerful ruling parties. The former sometimes behaved like unarmed freedom movements; and, after long years of confrontation, came to power themselves, e.g. the Dominica Freedom Party; the Free National Movement (in the Bahamas); and the People's Liberation Movement (in Montserrat).

A racial component also exists often, especially in Guyana. There, in 1964-92, the supporters of the then Government and the Opposition were the black and East Indian segments of the population, respectively. The People's National Congress Government developed the system of voter manipulation to a certain perfection, which enabled the black minority in the country to remain in power.[312]

The Commonwealth Consultative Group on the Special Needs of Small States has warned (*Vulnerability*, pp. 61ff) against authoritarian tendencies and the infringement of human rights, precisely in small states. The suppression of the Opposition and the occurrence of clear breaches of the Constitution, e.g. in Grenada, Dominica, St. Lucia and Guyana, have repeatedly led to bloody

[311] Former Governor of the Barbados Central Bank.

[312] *cf.* Deosaran (1983) and many others.

confrontations and as far as attempted *coup d'état*. Neville Duncan has pointed out (C.P. 37, p. 2) that the best security against populist uprising is a just government.

The creation of a Federation, in Courtney Blackman's opinion (1988a, p. 71), would remove charismatic influences from politics, limit the authority of insular politicians and create impersonal relations and greater distance among public servants. He has demanded that the University be freed totally from political influence and financial dependence on governments.

No legacy of the earlier British colonial power has contributed so much to the political stability of the Commonwealth Caribbean as the Westminster Model[313] has done. The British wrote this model, in various modifications, into the constitutions of the then emerging colonies, long before their formal independence, giving their local *élites* practice and experience in the intermediate stages, leading to this from self-administration. The model in its current form dates back to the parliamentary development in England between 1867 and 1914 (Norton, 1983, p. 56).

Essential elements of the Westminster Model, transferred to the Commonwealth Caribbean, include the following:

- Constitutional monarchy, with the British monarch as Head of State and represented locally by the Governor-General;

- the strong position of the Head of Government reposing on an elected Parliamentary majority; and the constitutionally-anchored function of the Leader of the Opposition, as the head of the largest group of MPs not supporting the Government, named, like the Head of Government, by the Governor-General, and, again like the Prime Minister, the Head of his political party; the Prime Minister can cause the Governor-General to dissolve Parliament at any time or to name or dismiss Cabinet members or senior Government officials;

- a bi-cameral Parliamentary system in eight of the independent Commonwealth Caribbean countries, with an elected Lower House and a Senate patterned on the House of Lords at Westminster; with a fixed number of Senators named by the Governor-General on the proposal, respectively, of the Prime Minister and the Leader of the Opposition as well as in his (or her) own discretion; and having the function of debating matters dispassionately and without considering constituency and particular interests as well as introducing motions and non-money Bills on their own;

- first-past-the post election system for MPs;

- weak role of Parliament *vis-à-vis* Cabinet and the governmental bureaucracy; Government's Lower House majority serves an acclamatory function to strengthen the Prime Minister and Cabinet decisions, whereas the Opposition in the Lower House tries, by critical appraisal of Government business, and its contribution to Parliamentary debates, as well as successes in by-elections and Local Government polls, to improve its image.

- the administration of justice and the bases of the legal system on the British model, with the Judicial Committee of the UK Privy Council as the final

---

[313] Named after the Palace of Westminster, the seat of the British Houses of Parliament

Court of Appeal all including even the Republic of Trinidad and Tobago, but with the exception of Guyana.

The high degree of acceptance of the Westminster Model in the region also finds expression in its faithful adoption of British Parliamentary ceremony and customs.

Thus, for instance, the Governor-General, representing the British sovereign, who performs the same function at Westminster, annually opens each session of Parliament with a Throne Speech prepared by the Government and his entrance ceremony and that of the MPs into the Senate, acting as the Upper House; and with the Speaker of the (Lower) House being accorded special high status manifested by the Mace[314] borne by the Sergeant-at-arms to begin each sitting of the House. The Speaker has special powers in presiding over sittings, and allowing and ending contributions to debates and in disciplinary measures against both disobedient MPs and strangers to the House. Members, as in the House of Commons at Westminster, the 'Mother of Parliaments', sit facing each other separated by a narrow passage-way, reportedly three sword-lengths wide, with the frontbenchers on the Government side consisting of the Ministers facing the Opposition MPs with shadow responsibility for the various portfolios, and the backbenchers for each side seated at the rear. Changing of political affiliation involves crossing the floor officially.[315]

Unlike the British constitution, however, the constitution of the Commonwealth Caribbean States is written in one basic document in each case, creating 'constitutional rigidity' (Ghany, 1994, p. 63). There are other deviations from the British system. Hamid Ghany suggests that the model should rather be called the *Whitehall Model*[316]. It was conceived by the Foreign Office in London and shows essential differences to the Parliamentary system in the UK Ghany (*ibid.*) identifies five major tenets that give the Commonwealth Caribbean constitutions their peculiar character, besides the 'written interpretation of unwritten Westminster constitutional conventions', these are:

'- The inclusion of a Bill of Rights in the Constitution that diminishes the legislative supremacy of Parliament and the power of the Executive to act decisively.
- A unique bi-cameral system with no security of tenure.
- A more rigid enforcement of the separation of powers than at Westminster.
- The entrenchment of constitutional provisions that further diminishes the legislative supremacy of Parliament.'

Three of the independent countries — namely, Guyana, Trinidad and Tobago and Dominica — are Republics; but nonetheless recognise the British monarch as Head of the Commonwealth. In others, the replacement of that monarch and the change to a Republic have been discussed for a long time. A 1988 poll of 1.342 Jamaican adults revealed that 46% of them supported (as against 45% in 1983) the retention of the Queen as Queen of Jamaica, whereas

[314] Removal of the Mace interrupts or ends the sitting, and is seldom done by the Opposition

[315] For the British Parliamentary tradition on this point, please see Greenleaf (1983), Jennings and Ritter (1970); Loewenstein (1964), Morrison (1956), Punnett (1984) and Sontheimer (1972)

[316] The title was introduced by Leslie Wolf-Phillips (Ghany, 1994, p 63)

35% were in favour of the Governor-General as the Head of State; 14% opposed both the monarch and the Governor-General, with 5% as 'don't knows'/'won't says'.[317] The retention of the British constitutional monarchy has much to do with the prestige of Queen Elizabeth II, the current monarch. Visits by herself or by members of her family to these former colonies are events at which Republicans do better to keep a low profile.[318]

The Westminster Model of democracy contains both system-stabilising and destabilising factors (Butler, 1983, p. 46). The first-past-the-post electoral system is favourable to the two-party system. As a rule, it creates large Government majorities in Parliament, thereby obviating prolonged negotiations between potential coalition partners and averting the formation of fragile Governments. Simplicity of the electoral system is apparent to even little-informed and educated voters. Elected candidates at the constituency level, even after being elected, must concern themselves intensively with their constituencies. Each vote is at stake here. The system is favourable to candidates of political parties with a broad political base and who are acceptable to middle-of-the-road floating voters (Butler, *op. cit.*, p. 48). It is less favourable for political parties with a marked ideological profile. It is not least for this reason that efforts are repeatedly made to introduce a mixed electoral system, the Mixed Member Proportional System as introduced in the 1993 New Zealand general elections, with both a direct election of candidates and also a list to be voted for.[319]

The Westminster System favours clientelism. The candidate, in order to be elected, must have and keep at least 50% plus one of the actual voters in the constituency on his side. Conversely, the candidate who loses his (or her) constituency runs the risk of falling into an abyss, both politically and socially. The tussle for each voter's support can assure violent manifestations, especially if questions of existence are involved insofar as the *clientèle* of the candidate is concerned. Constituencies in the Commonwealth Caribbean are small: Everybody knows everybody else. The strengths, the weaknesses and private problems of the candidate are known and will be known everywhere, even when he (or she) does not reside in the constituency in question. Transparency creates conditions of dependency, which do not bring only advantages for democratic development.

Additionally, only a few politicians dispose of sufficient funds of their own, in order to bind their *clientèle* to themselves in the way expected. A Ministerial portfolio or the function of Member of Parliament can be properly carried out only at the cost of his (or her) normal professional income. The expense allowance given by the State as compensation is relatively small.[320] Dependence on sources of external financing — state pork-barrel or private — is inescapable. Corruption, however, belongs still to the social taboos in the

---

[317] The question put was published in the *Weekly Gleaner* of 10.5.1988, on page 5.

[318] Sir Ivor Jennings, the British constitutional expert, has described the British monarch as having neither political past nor future — but a family history of several centuries of ruling in London — and, therefore, not needing to pursue any self-serving objectives (Jennings / Ritter, 1970, p. 51)

[319] *cf* Lijpart (1990), Jamadar (1989) and Munroe (1990, p. 252). The Constitutional Commission of Trinidad and Tobago proposed, in 1987, a change from a pure first-past-the-post system (*Thinking Things Over*, 1988)

[320] Jamaica, in increasing Parliamentary allowances sharply in 1990, took this into account

Commonwealth Caribbean. If proved, it leads to the loss of office and one's seat in Parliament.

On the whole, the Westminster System has aided the political stability of the region. Unlike other parts of the Third World, the Caribbean has developed political institutions reflecting the depth of West European influences and at the same time, also their adaptability to Caribbean political culture. Indeed, an interesting political equilibrium has arisen between these influences and those of the Third World, which, according to Carl Stone (1986b, p. 28) has no equal in the modern world.

There have been enough challenges in which the system has had to prove itself: Changes of Government, which suddenly banned to the wretched wilderness of the opposition, political parties which had previously been the Government for long years; attempted *coups d'état*; successful *Putsches*; bloody elections and States of Emergency. The system has survived one-party Parliaments in Jamaica and Belize; and virtually the same situation as well in Antigua and Barbuda, Grenada, Barbados, Dominica, and St. Kitts and Nevis. Significant here is that it is not only the form of British Parliamentarism which has been copied. The unwritten conventions have also been adopted — the silent understanding of using political power, the interplay of Government and Opposition — which have justified this form and made it effective, only in the sense of a liberal democratic political system.

A democratic political culture alone is, however, according to Nohlen (1988, pp. 11ff) no guarantee of the stability of democracy. On the contrary, the development of the economy and society, linked to the social integration of the individual, strengthens loyalty to democracy. Continuity of institutions and governmental policy is also essential for a stable democracy. Underpaid public servants, attractive posts in private industry and abroad for capable ones; the tendency, following a change of Government, to fill leading posts in the public sector with the supporters of the victorious party; and, conversely, to terminate contracts or not finish projects of the previous Government, without paying attention to costs already incurred and the returns expected — all this stands in the way as obstacles to continuity, however.

The opponents of liberal democratic traditions from Socialist countries, who give the preference to participatory democracy, belong to the most severe critics of the Westminster model in the Caribbean. For them, Westminster Parliamentarism is too much oriented towards Capitalism and the Social Market Economy. To them, a state which merely guarantees a stable environment for the private sector, and collaborates with it, is suspect. In Westminster-type democracy, they suspect, the private sector buys the right to be consulted, by paying taxes.[321] Here, critics of the Westminster System divide into those who, with certain reforms, regard it as suitable to secure the functioning of representative democracy, and warn against the elimination of the system (Harris and Harris, 1985, pp. 154-158) and the others, who reject the whole system as a development model for the future.

In the 1970s, the state-*dirigiste* non-capitalist path seemed to be the dominant development model. As far back as in 1953, then Premier of British

[321] *cf* Edwin Jones, 1986, pp. 148-149.

Guiana, Cheddi Jagan, had announced such a model, which was, however, thwarted by the British colonial power.[322] Behind the efforts to modify or get rid of the Westminster Model stood manifestly the desire for greater participation of the 'masses' in the exercise of state power.[323] Hidden behind those efforts was the will to change the entire political system. The model here was the Cuban Revolution since 1959, which helped to shape the political development in Jamaica in 1972-80, in St. Lucia (1979-82) and Grenada (1979-83) as well as influencing in a sustained way, the political thought of the Caribbean left, even near to the mid-1990s — irrespective of developments in Eastern Europe since 1989.

Similar to the collectivist models of Socialist systems external to the Caribbean, commonalties of the non-capitalist path in the region were marked by the postulate of dominating state influence on the economy, the reduction of foreign participation and property ownership, the lessening of the foreign dependence of the economy; the preference for state-state instead of state-private sector economic co-operation; initiatives in the field of culture in favour of indigenous art; the building up of mass organisations; the creation of mass political parties; the strengthening of the communes by means of a certain autonomy; the attempt to implement an independent foreign policy on the principles of non-alignment and non-interference; free education and training along egalitarian lines as well as free education for all.[324]

The models received their Caribbean specificity from externally and internally-directed influences — especially from the East-West conflict, which made Cuba, with then-USSR support, the model of 'anti-Imperialist' and especially anti-American posture in the region; through the common colonial past of the participants, influences from the Black Power movement received from the USA, through their insular location; and small population; which seemed to preordain the tiniest nations to apply participatory models; through a high literacy level and a population segment consisting of intellectual technocrats, who could facilitate the practical implementation of ideological concepts.

Collectivist models are predicated on the existence of a state which is both populist and either *dirigiste* or authoritarian. In the 1970s, in Jamaica, Michael Manley, supported by a large Parliamentary majority and the goodwill of sections of the *élites*, tried to bring about the transformation to Democratic Socialism by means of convincing the population. In the process, he purposely opted for polarisation and suppressing the 'reactionary' Opposition, up to introducing emergency measures.[325]

In an even more sustained way than Michael Manley, Guyana's then Head of state, Linden Forbes Burnham, sought to implement collectivist concepts. The expropriation of foreign business, the introduction of a three-sector economy with private, state and co-operative elements, whereby the last-named was supposed to assume the leading role; *de facto* one-party rule; direct or indirect dependence on the State of 80% of the jobs; 'non-alignment' with

---

[322] *cf.* Gordon K. Lewis, 1986, p. 270, and Jagan, 1980

[323] *cf* from a technocratic viewpoint, e.g. Demas, 1974, pp. 19-20

[324] *cf* Huber Stephens and Stephens, 1986, pp. 3-6 and Stone, 1983b, pp 243-244.

[325] *cf* Huber and Stephens, 1986; Kaufman, 1985; Bosshard, 1987; and W A James, 1982, among many others

strong leaning on communist States, State-steered mass organisations for employees, women and youth; as well as attempts at autarky in agriculture, determined Burnham's concept. To implement these measures, he turned to authoritarian practices such as forcing the media into line, suppression of the opposition, electoral fraud, the raising of a people's militia almost as the private army of the ruling party; infiltrating party members into the regular Army; giving favoured treatment to party adherents and the polarisation of the population along racial lines between Government-friendly Afro-Guyanese and Indo-Guyanese hostile to the Government; as well as manipulation of the trade unions. In this way, a hardly-veiled dictatorship arose (*cf.* Clive Y. Thomas, 1984a, p. 72).

In the 1980s Constitution, Burnham raised 'Socialist Democracy' to the aim of the State, which should increasingly give the citizens the opportunity to participate in the leadership and decision-making processes of the State. Co-operativism, based on self-reliance, was supposed to be the dynamic principle of 'Socialist transformation' and permeate all areas of society (*Constitution of the Co-operative Republic of Guyana*, 1980, Chapter II, Art. 13 and 16).

Burnham's co-operative model has been severely disputed by Caribbean Socialists, owing to the history of its creation[326], his racism, the suppression of the socialist opposition above all, corruption and nepotism.[327]

The State system, which the New Jewel Movement sought to implement between 1979 and 1983, has not lost its fascination among some of its adherents in the Caribbean. On the contrary, the 1983 intervention has strengthened the 'anti-Imperialist forces' in their posture against US hegemony and its Caribbean 'lackeys' from the conservative camp. The economic policy of the NJM Government under Maurice Bishop involved seeking to combine the private sector and collectivism. The Westminster-type Constitution still existed formally; competing parties were banned, however; and only State-controlled media allowed. In foreign policy, Grenada was heavily dependent on Cuba and Eastern Europe. For a small group around Bernard Coard, the revolutionary development was too slow. That group, by the violent elimination of Bishop and other leading politicians and trade unionists, facilitated the intervention by Grenada's Caribbean neighbours and the regional hegemonic power.

Whether Communist, Socialist or collectivist ideologies really have any prospects in the Commonwealth Caribbean of being accepted by the population over time, is a moot point. Indications do suggest rather a negative answer to that, however. Stone (1983a, pp. 60-70) saw anti-Communism as deeply rooted in Jamaica's political culture — and this may be true of others as well. With the exception of the PPP in Guyana, clearly Communist parties have not been able to win any Parliamentary seats in the Commonwealth Caribbean.[328] Socialist-oriented Governments, which came to power in the 1970s, all lost their majorities in free elections at the start of the 1980s.

---

[326] Elimination of the 'Communist', Cheddi Jagan, with British and CIA help, and electoral manipulation

[327] *cf.*, among others, Clive Thomas, 1984a, 1984b, J Edward Greene, 1974, *Guyana, Fraudulent Revolution* 1984

[328] Ratcliff (1982, p. 155) doubts that PPP or PNC adherents in Guyana strongly prefer Socialism, and even less for the Cuban or ex-USSR forms; poverty and race determine preference for either party; both parties he holds, are basically the creation of their leaders.

When, in 1989, the People's National Party under Michael Manley again had the possibility of forming the Government of Jamaica, almost nothing was left of its pristine 'Socialist transformation'. Similarly, in the 1992 elections in Guyana, the once-Socialist cadre parties, the PPP and the PNC, mutually accused each other of their ideological past; and offered themselves to the electorate as reform-friendly advocates of free enterprise.[329] In 1994 the PNC adopted a new constitution omitting references to it as a socialist party. The Women's Revolutionary Socialist Movement was renamed the National Congress of Women.

Critics of Socialism have long recognised that a change in property relationships does not automatically change as well the realities of production, distribution and exchange. 'Imperialism', denounced by the Caribbean Left, lost its agitative appeal, with the post-1989 change in Eastern Europe and the shift in the political and economic interests of the United States. The errors of the Socialists include, according to Maingot (1983b) the assumption that American hegemonic striving was automatically coupled with the readiness to invest by industry. But the industrialised countries offer better opportunities by far to invest capital profitably than do many developing countries. Indeed, in Cuba and Guyana, favourable investment opportunities *per se* could hardly be utilised, owing to the political ideologies obtaining there.

While Socialist ideology still has great fascination for Caribbean intellectuals, liberal ideas on the economy have a much harder time to inspire people's imagination. As the engine of enslavement, capitalism is discredited *a priori*. Additionally, the tried and proved system in the region, according to Carl Stone (1982b), does not support the entrepreneurial impulse, which is predicated on the accumulation of wealth through personal risk-taking. Both rich and poor alike are more occupied with consumption and the display of consumption than with achievements, which have to do with the use of the forces of production and creative development by means of creative activities.

Economic liberalism manifests itself less in theory than in praxis. In party programmes, election manifestos and programmatic declarations of Commonwealth Caribbean political parties, terms such as 'capitalism', 'conservative' and 'liberal' are rarely used in a positive sense. In fact, the ideological trend extends to the democracies oriented towards the political centre, as Jamaica's then Prime Minister, Edward Seaga, recognised in 1984. Only in name did the Jamaica Labour Party orient itself on the model of its British namesake. Instead, from the very beginning it was tailor-made to fit the personality of its founder, Sir Alexander Bustamante, and his pragmatic populism.[330] The JLP's fourth Leader, Seaga, later continued Bustamante's free-enterprise and tough anti-Marxist orientation despite not consistently pursuing the divestment and privatisation of public sector enterprises while Prime Minister and also increasing public sector involvement in the bauxite/alumina industry in the mid-1980s. The political philosophy of the JLP was based on a somewhat nebulous 'nationalism', which, in an allusion to the European origin

[329] *cf.* Premdass, 1993, p. 117.

[330] *cf* the observations of ex-British Labour Party Leader, Michael Foot (*Socialist Affairs*, January 1990, p 18).

of Marxism-Leninism, was defined as a philosophy that promotes Jamaican solutions for problems instead of using antiquated imported ideologies (*cf. JLP* 1978, p.15, and *Labour* (Kingston, Jamaica), September 1979, p.4).

St. Lucia's Prime Minister, John Compton (*CP* 22, p.7f), in 1983 defined his ideological development with similar equivocation as follows:

'I have always been a liberal — a liberal with a small 'l' — what they call a leftist-leaning.[331] I have never changed. Sometimes you have got to tailor your own ideological bent to accommodate certain economic forces. But I have never changed. My whole aim is to develop particularly the small man. When I look back at it, when I retire, I would hope that I have provided the basic things for the poor classes; the education, the health, the water supplies, the basic things for them, see that the farmers who want to farm land have land enough to farm.'

Then Barbadian Prime Minister, Tom Adams, whose party belongs to Socialist International gave no open declaration of belief in 'Democratic Socialism' during his visit to Jamaica in July, 1982 (*SG* 1.8.1982, p. 15). His party, he declared, was Socialist, but rather of a Fabian[332] type. Adam's political opposite number, Errol Barrow, also described himself as a Socialist in the sense of the British Labour Party of which he had been previously a member. But he also suggested that political conviction should be illustrated by examples, and not 'isms' (D.L. Phillips, 1985, p. 4). This was so that he would not be tarred with the same brush as other so-called Socialists — namely in the now ex-USSR, Hitler or Fidel Castro.

A sort of ideological dividing line seems to run between the so-called Left-wingers and the so-called Right-wingers in the Commonwealth Caribbean. This was marked, for instance, by the stances of the different Heads of Government with regard to the developments in Grenada between 1979 and 1983. Critics of the New Jewel Movement Government under Maurice Bishop and supporters of the 1983 intervention are regarded as being Right-wingers. Conversely, sympathisers with that Government and critics of the intervention are put on the Left. Instead of this Right-Left nosology, analysts of the political situation in the Commonwealth Caribbean also elect to use the terms 'conservative', 'progressive' and 'revolutionary'. The Prime Minister of St. Vincent and the Grenadines, James Mitchell (Brana-Shute, 1983, p. 12) regarded as belonging to the conservatives, owing to the membership of his party in the Caribbean Democrat Union, does not hold much for such stereotypes. On many occasions, ideological differences were blown up out of all proportion, in order to denigrate political opponents and drive fear into voters or keep them in one's own political camp. During election campaigns, warnings were repeatedly given against the 'Communist' or 'Imperialist' danger — the former being defamed as the accomplices of Cuba; the latter, as 'lackeys of US Imperialism'.

In the process, the realisation gains in significance that the social, economic and political failures touch Governments of all points on the ideological

---

[331] In 1961 on leaving the St. Lucia Labour Party Compton had been labelled a 'Communist' (DaBreo, 1981, p. 32).

[332] The very name of the Fabian Society founded in 1884 (the year of Bustamante's birth) and affiliated to the British Labour Party, indicated its moderation and commitment to the gradual speed of Socialism, rather like the Roman General, Quintus Fabius Maximus, who, by caution and procrastination, defeated Hannibal in the Second Punic War (218-201 B.C.); please also see Serbín, 1987, p. 316.

spectrum, as, according to Farrell (1986, p.7) the examples of Guyana, Jamaica, Grenada, Dominica and Antigua and Barbuda show. The population's party loyalty is oriented more strongly by far to persons than to ideological postures. The speeches of the party leaders are more important than manifestos and political philosophies, which are useful as emergency aid during political campaigns, if personal attacks are ineffective or inopportune. The more Caribbean parties are fixated on leadership figures, the less easily can their ideological orientation be determined. Thus, for instance, Dr. Eric Williams, after governing Trinidad and Tobago for almost twenty-six years, died, leaving his party without a clear ideological profile. Initially tending to rather the Right-wing and liberal views, Williams switched to the Left-wing at the start of the 1970s, in order to steal the thunder of Left-wing radicals. Indeed, his 'Perspectives For a New Society' borrowed numerous ideas from the Black Power movement (Selwyn Ryan, 1978, p. 32).[333]

The influence of ideological homogeneity on Caribbean integration has so far been hardly the subject of thorough studies. The Trinidadian political scientist, Anthony Maingot, holds that it is their lifestyle, rather than their ideological conversion, which brings Caribbean people together (*Trinidad Express* 26.10.1980, p. 3). Tewarie, too, has observed (1986) at least for Trinidad, Guyana and Suriname, that ethnicity exerts a greater influence on feelings of solidarity than do ideologies. Personal links to certain political leaders can lead to a temporary ideological binding, which, however, disappears with a change in personal preference. To that extent, it is actually questionable, whether ideological convergence of the rulers does, in fact, promote integration at the level of the ruled.

Ideological homogeneity among the *élites* either promotes or hinders integration, depending on the consensus the members of the *élites* have arrived at in this question. Marxist-oriented Commonwealth Caribbean politicians, such as Dr. Cheddi Jagan, or social scientists, such as his fellow national, C. Y. Thomas (1988, pp. 319ff), have long adopted a rejectionist stance to regional political union under the same circumstances of CARICOM. This has been because, in their opinion, it could mean a consolidation of the capitalist system and a corresponding reduction in the likelihood of changing the system. Indeed, according to Thomas (1974, pp. 275-85), only under the conditions of Socialism, could integration contribute to structural transformation. All plans for integration under the existing class relationships, in his view magnified only dependence and hindered development. CARICOM, in its current form, is a creation of the past, according to Thomas (1988, p. 24). Regional religious, professional and party organisations, as well as intra-island migration and culture offer greater possibilities to promote integration.

'Socialist transformation', as proposed, for instance, by the economists, George Beckford and Michael Witter (1980, pp. 110-124) did not explicitly include the political integration of the region. Both Beckford and Witter pleaded

[333] Williams, in his 'Perspectives', distanced himself markedly from Socialism and rejected the nationalization of the flourishing crude oil industry, owing to the cost; but he also turned against liberal Capitalism and repeatedly attacked multinational firms sharply, even though he himself created a bloated, partly ineffective, overcentralized and inflexible State apparatus and established numerous State enterprises, only few of which were profitable.

for 'integral man', who is created by '*collective integrity*', expresses himself collectively and represents the converse of people alienated by capitalistic exploitation in a self-determined society.

On the other hand, middle-of-the road politicians and parties, pursuing internally, market economy and, externally, the strengthening of European influence, in order to counter-balance the manifest dependence of the Commonwealth Caribbean on the USA, belong to the constant promoters of Caribbean integration. James Mitchell has repeatedly called attention to the fact that the collective binding of most ruling parties in the OECS in the political study group, the Caribbean Democrat Union (CDU), is advantageous for the efforts at integration in the sub-system. Three of the four ruling parties in the Windward Islands which have been preparing for political union, belong to the CDU. In Grenada, the ruling National Democratic Congress (NDC) was founded from a CDU-affiliated party. NDC leader, Nicholas Brathwaite, who is also the Prime Minister of Grenada, had made himself available as interim Head of Government, following the 1983 intervention.[334] The Regional Constituent Assembly would hardly have come into existence in January, 1991, had either the New Jewel Movement or Gairy's Grenada United Labour Party still been the Government of that country.

2.7.3.3 Network of Parties and Affiliated Institutions

Together with the trade union movement, there came into being near the end of the 1930s in the Commonwealth Caribbean, the first modern, mass-based political parties in the history of the region, some of which continue to exist. Their first objective was to participate in the exercise of political power at the level of the local Administration under the Governance of the British colonial power.

The British Labour Party, with its strong links to trade unions and its moderate socialist programme, served as the model for many of these parties. Indeed, it was officially represented at the formal founding of the People's National Party in Kingston, Jamaica, by Sir Stafford Cripps, the future Chancellor of the Exchequer of the post-war Labour Government. Quite unsurprisingly, therefore, almost everywhere in the region, parties were named as Labour Parties even when, as in the case of the Jamaica Labour Party, they were conservative in ideology, already mentioned. Conversely, none of them bore the word 'conservative' in their names. This characteristic was logically extended to the pan-Commonwealth Caribbean level in the run-up to the elections for the Parliament of the West Indies Federation, which came into existence in 1958. Thus, there was founded, under the leadership of the Premier of Barbados, Sir Grantley Adams, the federally-oriented West Indies Federal Labour Party. In contrast, the Democratic Labour Party, under the then Leader of the Opposition in Jamaica, Alexander Bustamante, was critical of the political integration of the region. With the dissolution of the Federation in 1962, both these parties also ceased to exist.

---

[334] The NDC, while belonging to SCOPE, the opposition movement critical of integration, has no longer played an active role there since becoming the ruling party

Only in few political parties of the Commonwealth Caribbean did their contact to Labour take on an institutional character. Some of them — including the People's National Party and the Barbados Labour Party — became a part of the international Socialist camp. They both became members of Socialist International (SI) the re-establishment of which in 1951 reposed on preliminary work of the international relations department of the British Labour Party. Within the Commonwealth Caribbean region, the New Jewel Movement (NJM) in Grenada and the Progressive Labour Party (PLP) in St. Lucia, both defunct now, joined the SI at the start of the 1980s. Regionally, Commonwealth Caribbean SI members fall within the Committee for Latin America and the Caribbean, comprising of eighteen members in 1985 (*Global Challenge*, p. 209). Michael Manley has been a SI Vice President and Chairman of its Economic Policy Committee.

Both structure and objectives of the four SI member-parties in the Commonwealth Caribbean practically excluded closer collaboration.[335] The NJM and the PLP stood close to each other ideologically based on their Marxist orientation and following the Cuban model. But the Barbados Labour Party, with its Fabian orientation, was an outsider. The ideological divide was seen most clearly in the differing judgements in the following matters: The 1983 Grenada intervention, the Falklands War and political developments in both Nicaragua and Cuba. Then NJM Leader, Maurice Bishop, saw in the heterogeneity of the SI the possibility to show off Grenada's posture to advantage. The NJM also had good contacts with Communist Parties, especially those in Cuba and the then USSR (Nitoburg, 1987, pp. 122-129).

The People's National Party in Jamaica had the distinction of being the only ruling SI member-party in the Commonwealth Caribbean in the mid-1990s, following the electoral defeat of both the PLP and the Barbados Labour Party and the dissolution, a decade earlier, of the NJM after the intervention in Grenada.

The centre of gravity of the Communist movement in the Caribbean is in Cuba. In the 1970s — long after the models in the Hispanic and Francophone Caribbean — numerous Marxist-oriented workers', revolutionary and Black Power parties and liberation movements came into existence in the Commonwealth Caribbean.[336] Their emergence was enhanced by the decline of the power of the USA, black radicalism, increasing militancy of African liberation movements, consolidation of the Cuban Revolution, superpower *détente* as well as ideological pluralism under then US President, Jimmy Carter (Munroe, 1990, p. 242). Their co-operation within the Commonwealth Caribbean occurred, as it did world-wide, in complex interaction models of multi-faceted contacts between the parties at different levels; in the mutual exchange of delegations at party conferences; in bilateral visits; and discussions, special conferences on certain subjects, regional meetings and actions of solidarity with the participation of forces close to the parties in question. The Commonwealth Caribbean parties which openly termed themselves as

[335] Other Commonwealth Caribbean political parties have attended diverse SI conferences, without desiring or seeking official status.

[336] *cf.* Munroe, 1980, pp. 240ff; *Political Parties of the Americas*, vol. 1, pp. 797ff.

Communist, have included the People's Progressive Party led by Dr. Cheddi Jagan in Guyana, the ex-Workers' Party of Jamaica under Dr. Trevor Munroe, the University lecturer and trade unionist; the Movement for National Liberation and the Workers' Party, both in Barbados; the United People's Movement and the United Liberation Movement of St. Vincent and the Grenadines; the Workers' Revolutionary Movement of St. Lucia; the Dominica Liberation Movement; and, in Trinidad and Tobago, the People's Popular Movement. Close to the movement and with more or less close ties to Cuba and the then USSR stood also the Antigua Caribbean Liberation Movement, the Maurice Bishop Patriotic Movement in Grenada, the Working People's Alliance in Guyana and, in the Bahamas, the Vanguard Nationalist and Socialist Party. Despite being members of the SI, the NJM and PLP also belonged to this group.

The Communist Parties did not succeed in getting noteworthy electoral support in the Protestant-oriented Commonwealth Caribbean — unlike what occurred in the Caribbean States which were mainly Roman Catholic (Munroe, 1990, p. 232; Manigat, 1982, p. 22).

With the exception of the PPP in Guyana, none of them obtained a noteworthy number of votes or seats in Parliament. The local Communist movement exerted its actual influence through its youth, student and women's organisations, as well as by means of special conferences for scientists, intellectuals, media workers and other multipliers. Additionally, they took over leadership posts in key groups, such as State-promoted National Youth Councils, trade unions and media.

The Eleventh *World Festival of Youth and Students* in Havana (1978) mobilised political youth organisations in the region for the 'anti-Imperialists' course of Cuba and the then Soviet Union. It also created links which lasted over several years. The Twelfth World Festival, which was held in Moscow in 1985, the International Year of the Youth, once again provided Communist youth organisations with the opportunity to extend their base within the youth through national preparatory committees, to make clear the lines of confrontation to the ruling parties and to reduce the number of participants at the rival event, namely, the *International Youth Conference* organised by the then JLP Government of Jamaica in April, 1985 (*cf. Unity and Action*, 1985). Political parties, such as the PNP in Jamaica, the PNC in Guyana and the St. Lucia Labour Party before the split of the PLP, first played the Cuban Card, when wishing to obtain revolutionary legitimacy, despite not having come to power through revolutionary means.[337]

In contrast, the efforts of the opponents of the pro-Cuban course to get political power were more successful by far. In this connection, they were able to count on the support of the US Government and the antagonism of the then superpowers in the region. It was also to their advantage that society in the Anglophone Caribbean, while politically complex, constantly in agitation and desiring a better future, is hardly revolutionary. As Anthony Maingot has found (1983a) the English-speaking people in the Caribbean are politically radical, but sociologically conservative.

[337] *cf* Maingot 1983a, p. 22

At the start of the 1970s, the practical implementation of the idea to set up Socialist Republics everywhere in the Caribbean seemed within reach. Following the 1983 Grenada intervention, however, there remained only the example of Guyana, which was sharply disputed even within the Socialist camp. In the Eastern Caribbean, Maurice Bishop, who had come to power through a *coup d' état*, failed in the attempt to get fraternal parties in St. Lucia and Dominica to create a common, Socialist State.[338]

The Marxist movement faced a really critical test, in the wake of the US-Caribbean intervention in Grenada in 1983.[339] While the political parties sympathetic to that movement unanimously condemned the 'invasion', they were not united in their assessment of the internal conflict within the NJM, which led to the murder of Maurice Bishop. Between the parties, too, a split occurred in their evaluation of revolutionary developments in the Caribbean area, with the supporters of Moscow on one side, and, on the other, those parties advocating the Cuban line. The Communist Party of Cuba (CPC), in several meetings at different sites, made efforts to unite its supporters behind it (Tulloch, 1984). Under the designation, 'First consultative meeting of anti-imperialist organisations of the Caribbean and Central America', Cuba succeeded in July, 1984, for the first time since the Grenada intervention, in bringing almost the entire Caribbean left to Havana at one conference table. Violent clashes occurred there between the supporters and the critics of the murdered Prime Minister of Grenada (*Grenadian Voice*, 1.9.1984, pp. 12 and 14).

The biggest challenge for the Communist movement in the region, however, came from the radical changes in the then Soviet Union, the switch of the East European States from the Communist system and the voting out of office of the Sandinista regime in Nicaragua. Cuba, despite growing economic difficulties, nonetheless faced these developments inflexibly. In contrast, the two most significant Communist Parties in the Anglophone Caribbean drew the consequences from them. The Workers' Party of Jamaica (WPJ) on the proposal of its General Secretary, Dr. Trevor Munroe, and owing to deficient support from the electorate, was dissolved (*WG* 7.1.1992, p. 13). The WPJ, following the Grenada intervention, had repeatedly examined its role and separated itself from deviants, who did not wish to follow Munroe's Moscow-loyal course. In Guyana, the People's Progressive Party (PPP) modified its hitherto anti-market economy course. Its 1992 election manifesto supported local and foreign private investment with tax breaks and the free, unhindered repatriation of profits as well as a subsidiary relationship between the public and private sectors (*CI* October, 1992, p. 2). In Dominica, at the end of 1992, Rosie Douglas, who had been ascribed to the Socialist camp, renounced the 'moribund ideas of the past' (*CI* January, 1993, p. 3).

Another international alliance of political parties, the Christian Democratic International (CDI) had only limited success in the Commonwealth Caribbean as well. Founded in 1982 in Quito/Equador as successor of the Christian

---

[338] Please see Chapter 2 2.4.

[339] For a comprehensive account, please see Serbin (1986).

Democratic World Union, the Rome based organisation was meant to counterbalance the growing influence of Socialist International.

Its regional Caracas-based ODCA, i.e. *Organización Democratica Cristiana de America* (the Christian Democratic Organisation of America) has merely four affiliated parties in the Anglophone Caribbean, namely, the Dominica Freedom Party, the People's Action Movement (St. Kitts and Nevis), the United National Congress (Trinidad and Tobago) and the Democratic Labour Movement (Guyana). In other words, it has no full members, thereby indicating another similarity between this region and UK-North American party models, which have no tradition of Christian Democratic political parties. The alliance of Christian Democratic parties was not able to overcome the linguistic and ethnic barriers. The lacuna in the collaboration between the non-Socialist parties of the region was filled by founding the Caribbean Democrat Union (CDU) a working association with nine full members in the English-speaking Caribbean.[340]

The Jamaica Labour Party Leader since the 1970s, Edward Seaga, made proposals in 1980 for the creation of an *Alliance of Solidarity, Co-operation and Mutual Assistance amongst the Parliamentary Democratic Parties in the Caribbean.* He suggested the creation of a solidarity movement consisting, initially, of political parties of the Anglophone Caribbean against growing Marxist influences in the region. The parties in question should profess their belief in 'democracy and the multi-party system, to market economies, realistic social programmes and respect for human rights.' They should also provide mutual support against 'proponents of Democratic Socialism and similar half-way houses to totalitarian communism.' The proposed alliance should, he suggested, have a small headquarters staff providing support for the affiliated parties and carrying out a programme of political education. It should not interfere in the internal affairs of the Caribbean Community (CARICOM) with which, however, as with the CDB, it should seek to collaborate. Externally, this alliance should not establish any international party links. But it should, nevertheless, seek to get support from the Christian Democratic parties of Western Europe as well as from the great US and Canadian parties. [341]

Seaga's proposals initially received little positive response. And the creation of his suggested alliance, which he had envisaged as taking place in 1981, did not occur. In a May, 1981, lecture at the University of Miami, after becoming Prime Minister in late 1980, Seaga modified his original proposals under the headline *Parliamentary Democracy in the Caribbean.* He bemoaned the absence, by and large, of political parties in Parliamentary democracies in planning developmental strategies for countries of the Third World, because many of the latter did not have any Parliamentary democracy. In this, however, the Commonwealth Caribbean, he argued, was fundamentally different. While,

[340] Namely, the United Democratic Party (Belize), the Dominica Freedom Party, the New National Party (Grenada), the People's Action Movement (St. Kitts and Nevis), the United Worker's Party (St. Lucia), the New Democratic Party (St. Vincent and the Grenadines), the Nevis Reformation Party, the Jamaica Labour Party and the Anguilla National Alliance. The United Bermuda Party has observer status

[341] '*Aide-mémoire* on a Proposal for an Alliance of Solidarity, Co-operation and Mutual Assistance amongst the Parliamentary Democratic Parties in the Caribbean', n.d.; unpublished (Kingston, Jamaica).

nevertheless, the larger West European political parties were linked internationally, those in the Commonwealth Caribbean and North America (excepting some SI member-parties) were left to their own devices. The time was, therefore, he declared, as propitious, as never before, for like-minded political parties of the Inter-American system to strengthen the democratic struggle through fraternal relationships and support in solidarity.

Nonetheless, the time did not turn out to be quite as propitious for the creation of such an alliance of political parties as proposed. Paradoxically enough, this situation may well have resulted partly from the fact that most CARICOM Member States were governed by like-minded and rather conservative political parties; moreover, the Leaders of these parties, who were also the Heads of Government of the respective States and territories, had on-going opportunities to meet at different levels and come to political arrangements. [342] The conservative political parties of the Commonwealth Caribbean, oriented more towards acclamation than towards participation, degenerate largely into apparatuses for fighting elections when their Leaders are in power, awaiting merely the signal from the party leadership to open the attack. The party executive, saddled fully with the cares and burdens of governance as well as the stabilisation of their power, reduces the party organisation to the base minimum. International relations of the party, being no top priority task even in industrialised countries, are limited to chance meetings, courtesy visits of constantly changing observers at party conferences and topping-up appointments on the periphery of trips abroad.

Efforts by the ODCA to affiliate the JLP and Eastern Caribbean parties in the 1970s and especially the 1980s remained futile. Only the realisation that friendly relations of government officials may collapse, when governing politicians become the Opposition, necessitated long years in Government by the non-Socialist parties, the collective experience with Grenada and the subsequent confrontations with internal and external critics of the intervention, led some non-socialist parties to join forces. In the wake of the International Youth Conference (IYC) which the then JLP Government under Seaga organised in Jamaica in April, 1985, he established links with the International Democrat Union (IDU) in London, some two months later. This was about two years after the IDU had come into being in London as the working organisation of Christian Democratic and conservative political parties. It served as the umbrella body of the European Democrat Union (EDU) which had been founded in 1978 and the Pacific Democrat Union (PDU) which was created in 1982. On the periphery of the July, 1985, CARICOM Summit in Barbados, the then Jamaican Prime Minister, with other Heads of Government he considered to be like-minded, considered the concept of a regional body for the Caribbean under the umbrella of the IDU and the American Democrat Union, which was still to be founded and that would group like-minded parties in the USA, Canada and Central and South America. Over four years earlier, Seaga, in his lecture at the University of Miami in May, 1981, had already held up the EDU as an

[342] For instance, the preparatory meeting for founding the Caribbean Democrat Union took place on the periphery of a CARICOM Summit. Equally typically, SCOPE, the group of parties planned as a rival body, was initially founded as the group of Eastern Caribbean Opposition parties, as pointed out earlier, see chapter 2.2.8.

example for significant party co-operation. The IDU offered to the small Caribbean parties, which were otherwise hardly noticed internationally, the possibility of moving in the same circles as the then ruling parties in Canada, the UK, the Federal Republic of Germany, Japan and other countries, as well as the party of the then US President despite being the minority party in the US Congress.

At the second conference of IDU party leaders in Washington, at the end of July, 1985, the Jamaica Labour Party and the United Democratic Party of Belize became the first Commonwealth Caribbean members to be directly admitted to that body. The swift admission of these two parties by the IDU was due especially to the JLP Leader's good relationship over several years with the conference host, the Republican Party of then US President, Ronald Reagan, and to the German Christian Democrats, who have played an influential role in the IDU as well as, conceivably and logically, due to the IDU's wish to have affiliated member-parties from the Commonwealth Caribbean as quickly as possible.

Some six months later, eight Commonwealth Caribbean parties, in the presence of IDU Executive Secretary, Scott Hamilton, founded the Caribbean Democratic Union (CDU) and elected Edward Seaga as its Chairman. The Charter of the CDU contains a declaration of belief in the basic civic rights as well as in the market economy.[343] At the time, the new CDU Chairman stressed that he expected additional members from moderate parties of the region, which were not SI members (*DG* 18.1.1986, pp. 1 and 3).

The Antigua Labour Party, although invited, did not join the CDU, however. The two Social Democratically-oriented parties in Barbados, the BLP and the DLP, and the ruling parties in Guyana and Trinidad and Tobago, were not invited. In 1988, the Nevis Reformation Party and the Anguilla National Alliance became members of the CDU.

It officially became the third IDU regional organisation at the Third Party Leaders' Conference of the IDU, which was held in the *Reichstag* Building in Berlin in September, 1987. The CDU member-parties, led by Seaga, who was elected to be an IDU Vice-President, came with a large delegation. The Dominica Freedom Party, the New National Party (Grenada), the People's Action Movement (St. Kitts and Nevis) and the New Democratic Party (St. Vincent and the Grenadines) were all admitted as full members. Two years later, a JLP member, attorney-at-law Harold Brady, became the IDU Executive Secretary. The JLP Leader was returned as an IDU Vice-President at its Tokyo Summit in September, 1989; two years later, he headed an *ad hoc* committee on Africa, and was delegated by the IDU board to undertake a fact-finding mission in South Africa and Namibia (*WG*, 23.7.1991, p. 13).

Organisationally, the CDU consolidated itself by establishing a permanent office with a small staff in Kingston, Jamaica. Regional seminars are held annually at different places. Topics dealt with at these seminars have included the following: The organisational strengthening of party work; the building up of party youth organisations; OECS unity; media policy; and 'Communist infiltration'. The CDU also supports its member-parties in holding their own

[343] *Caribbean Democrat Union Monthly Newsletter* 1.1 (July, 1986).

seminars. Its member-parties' leaders' conference, as its highest body, meets biennially on a rotating basis. At the first such conference in Grenada, in February, 1986, the CDU Chairman was able to obtain the participation of then President Reagan, who made effective use of his visit, from a public relations point of view.

Links within the CDU have survived the electoral defeats by its member-parties in Belize, Montserrat, Grenada and Jamaica which thereafter became the Opposition in each case. When the NNP in Grenada split, the CDU stood by the duly elected party leadership and supported it in the 1990 election campaign. A new CDU Chairman — namely, James Mitchell, Prime Minister of St. Vincent and the Grenadines — was elected in September, 1991, to succeed Edward Seaga, who demitted office.[344]

The *Caribbean Institute for Democratic Youth* was founded in March, 1990, by representatives of the youth organisations of eight CDU member-parties as well as those of the Antigua Labour Party with the aim of 'promoting the democratic ideal amongst the youth of the Caribbean and to promote friendship and Caribbean integration' (*CDU Quarterly Newsletter* 5.2., p. 6).

The ability of the CDU, as the first affiliation of political parties in the Commonwealth Caribbean, to influence the political fortunes of the region is clear not least of all from the reactions of its opponents. The collective membership of almost all OECS ruling parties affiliated to the CDU, which Prime Minister, James Mitchell, had referred to as being at a 'fortuitous time to unite' (1987b, p. 11) led to the creation of the Standing Conference of Popular Democratic Parties in East Caribbean States (SCOPE) with initially eleven parties as members. It accused the CDU of trying 'to subvert legitimate regional institutions such as CARICOM, in pursuit of their external directives and to perpetuate themselves in power'.[345]

From the very beginning the stigma of 'foreign determination' plagued the CDU. In particular, this working alliance has been accused of being directed politically by the Republican Party of the USA. Such charges have, however, always belonged to the political armoury, in terms of the vocabulary, of that sort of confrontation in the Commonwealth Caribbean. Thus, for instance, the Socialist parties were constantly accused of being financially and ideologically dependent on Cuba, the then USSR, other East European States, Libya and North Korea.

In point of fact, as was confirmed by the Chairman of the US Republican Party at the meeting founding the CDU, in Kingston (Jamaica) the CDU was supported financially by the US National Republican Institute of International Affairs (*CDU Monthly Newsletter*, 1.4., p. 3). The financial support ended in 1992. The Republican Institute receives its funding partly through the National Endowment for Democracy from the Budget of the US House of Representatives. Having regard to the fact that most regional, non-commercial institutions in the Caribbean survive, only thanks to external financing, the question of external dependence is properly posed elsewhere.

---

[344] Deputy Chairmen are Dr. Kennedy Simmonds, Manuel Esquivel and Keith Mitchell, with John Compton as Treasurer; the Executive Secretary is Hector Wynter; and the regional office remains in Kingston.

[345] SCOPE Communiqué dated 28.2.1988.

The Roseau/Dominica-based Eastern Caribbean Institute for Democracy (ECID)[346] was founded there by eight parties from that sub-region in September, 1985, and has the following main aims:

'- to promote and foster the teaching of the principles of freedom and democracy in all their forms,

- to promote, establish and support democratic institutions within the member states,

- to undertake research in and to publish the findings of all aspects of the social, political and economic life of peoples in the Eastern Caribbean,

- to provide facilities for the advancement of knowledge and understanding in the principles and practices of democratic institutions' (*Caribbean Media Directory*, p. 60). [347]

The ECID membership is, excepting the Antigua Labour Party, identical with the CDU member-parties in the Eastern Caribbean.[348] The establishment of the Caribbean Institute for Democratic Youth emanated from the ECID. Both these Institutes are funded by the Konrad-Adenauer-Stiftung, which is close to the German Christian Democrats.

The Caribbean Youth Conference (CYC) had also received help from this Foundation, welcomed the establishment of the CDU and invited the ECID to its annual assemblies as an observer.

The links between the CYC and the Jamaica-based Bustamante Institute of Public and International Affairs (BIPIA) were close. In September, 1990, the CYC for the first time held a Caribbean Youth Festival with the BIPIA at its annual meeting. At the festival, 200 young persons, mainly sent by youth groups of political parties from seventeen countries, discussed in a UN General Assembly-type Parliament, Caribbean integration and drug problems. The Festival succeeded in bringing to one table for three days, young politicians from Socialist and conservative youth organisations which, at home, fight each other fiercely (*Democracy Today* 6.5, pp. 2-5).[349]

The BIPIA was created in 1984 on the occasion of the centenary of the birth of a National Hero of Jamaica, Sir Alexander Bustamante, the founder of the Bustamante Industrial Trade Union (BITU) and later, the Jamaica Labour Party (JLP). Among its objectives is that of studying, among as many participants as possible, contemporary problems and their solutions from a Jamaican and Caribbean perspective. This Institute, despite its closeness to the JLP and the BITU sympathetic to the latter, succeeded in being completely independent from them organisationally and also in involving political forces of every type of ideology and social origin in the treatment of subjects such as the role of trade unions, drug abuse, Communism and reforms in the then Soviet Union, the status of women, youth problems, journalism and freedom of the Press. Youth conferences were held after 1987. Unfortunately, the BIPIA has now virtually ceased functioning.

---

[346] Sometimes called the East Caribbean Institute for Democracy

[347] See also Konrad-Adenauer-Stiftung 1993, pp. 7-10.

[348] The participants at its founding meeting advocated the creation of the Caribbean Democrat Union.

[349] Please see chapter 2.3.4.4.

The *Caribbean Women for Democracy* (CWD) which came into existence in the 1980s as a political organisation not linked to any specific political party, has worked closely with the BIPIA. The CWD has been composed overwhelmingly of committed women of the region not in the socialist camp.

To create an opportunity for ordinary people to 'speak to our common concerns and aspirations and focus our energies on a common agenda', are the aims and objectives of the *Assembly of Caribbean People*, initiated in 1992 by the Oilfields Workers Trade Union in Trinidad. Some 30 Caribbean territories are involved. Local Assemblies are to be set up in each territory. In August 1994 the *Assembly* is to be held in Trinidad (*DG* 30.7.1993, p.28).

Differing views exist about the effect of party political formations in the Caribbean on political integration in the region. Groups, such as the CDU and SCOPE, can be accused of polarising political forces, instead of promoting political consensus. On the other hand, without the formation of regional political parties, which can survive internal power struggles and electoral defeats, a future pan-Caribbean Parliament within the framework of a democratic political structure would not manage to survive. The pre-condition here is that the parties, at all levels, grow together through frequent inter-action and the practice of conflict resolution, with the progress of integration.

Institutes of political education, which overlap normal party boundaries, may help to establish an ethical code of behaviour between the politically and socially leading forces in the region. That code would make possible a peaceful balance of interests and, therefore, create the basis for confidence, which, for the first time, make possible the transfer of sovereignty and power necessary for political unity.

2.7.3.4 Socio-cultural Links through Religion

'Religion', the Jamaican social scientist, Rex Nettleford, has declared, 'is a cultural index of the greatest importance to Caribbean civilisation' (1987b, p. 28). Religion is, in fact, an important part of the social, political and cultural life of people in the Caribbean. Indeed as the Barbadian novelist, George Lamming (1984, p. 49), has put it: 'Any man who thinks that he can gain political leverage in this part of the world without paying attention how he speaks about God is very remote from the realities of the region.'

The predominant portion of the population of the Commonwealth Caribbean professes its adherence to the Christian Faith. But only 55% of that population is registered in Christian Church communities in the region.[350]

In point of fact, Hinduism and Islam have been able to hold their own as religions in countries of the region with a large East Indian population segment, such as Guyana and Trinidad and Tobago. Thus, in 1982, Hindus accounted for 24% of the latter's population; and 40% of the former — as against 6% and 10%, respectively, for Muslims.[351]

On the other hand, no representative figures or estimations exist concerning the number of adherents of the other non-Christian religions and folk religions, e.g. animism. Within the denominations of the Christian religion in the

[350] *cf.* Robert Cuthbert, 1986, pp. 23-25.
[351] *World Christian Encyclopedia*, 1982; quoted in Cuthbert, *op.cit.*, p. 25.

Caribbean, Cuthbert (*op. cit.*, pp. 16-18) distinguishes between the ancient established religions (e.g. Anglicans, Roman Catholics and Protestants) the 'non-conformist sects' (e.g. Quakers, Moravians, Methodists, Baptists, Presbyterians, and Congregationalists the last two now forming the United Church, emanating from German Pietism, the English Revivalist Movement and the Protestant Reformation) the evangelical sects originating mainly in the USA, and the folk religions of which *Rastafarianism* is the best-known.

Within the religious denominations themselves, views differ on politics and theological questions. Local Church leaders tend as little as politicians do to share their influence on their communities with regional groupings. This, in Cuthbert's view (*op. cit.*, p. 107) casts doubt on the 'transformative capacity' of religion in the genesis of Caribbean society. 'Ecumenism and regionalism appear to be difficult concepts for Caribbean church leaders to accept.'

The contribution made to Caribbean integration by the folk religions is even more difficult to assess than is that of both the established churches and the evangelical sects. The folk religions are, in the first place, the expression of a search for African identity and self-worth. In some of the Caribbean countries with a marked Roman Catholic presence, statues of the Saints rub shoulders with those of African animist gods; and the rituals of the Mass are intermingled with African religious ceremonies. This also occurs in, say, Brazil. On the other hand, in Caribbean areas with a marked Protestant presence, indigenous preachers have adopted the disposition of Caucasian evangelists and founded spiritualistic groups, such as the numerous Church of God and Pentecostal communities. The religious communities with African characteristics have stood in opposition to the orthodoxy of the established churches to which the plantocracy belonged.

Institutional regional links between the folk religions have been developed only weakly. Such religions came into existence independently of each other. Common traits in worship and rites repose rather on their common ethnic roots than on their intra-regional inter-action.

Nonetheless, the Rastafarian, without regional groupings, have had a dramatic influence on the Caribbean region (Wiltshire-Brodber, 1984, pp. 191ff). Indeed, they have succeeded in linking certain elements of the masses in the Caribbean by means of music, language and ethnicity as well as religious and political doctrine. The adherents of Rastafarianism have spread from Jamaica, through the entire Caribbean, and to North America and the United Kingdom. Internationally, they have become known especially through Reggae music, their braided hair and their form of speech. Among the black youth in the UK, Rastafarianism has gained so much influence that the Catholic Commission for Racial Justice has had to deal with the matter.

Rastafarians do not consider themselves to be Christians, although a large number of them have been baptised as Christians or come from Christian families (Barrett, 1977, XIII and p.3). Rastafarianism is a Messianic movement. Its adherents believe that Ethiopian Emperor, Haile Selassie I, is the Black Messiah in the flesh, who will free all black people living in exile in the world of the white oppressor. Ultra-orthodox members of this sect believe that the Emperor is still alive. The promised land is Ethiopia or Africa, to which the black population should be repatriated from all countries West of the Atlantic, where they have lived in slavery.

This sect goes back to the thought and teaching of Marcus Garvey (1887-1940) and his Back to Africa Movement. Garvey preached about the upliftment of the black people and demanded their return to their home in Africa. His followers took up this idea at the start of the 1930s.

The Rastafarians did not develop any ecclesiastical structures, although some beginnings exist in Jamaica, where, in 1970, the Ethiopian Orthodox Church was established. At first, this new Church was very popular. Owing to its strange ritual, but Christian character, however, it lost many adherents (Barrett, 1977, pp. 201ff; Blake Hanna, 1984). Nonetheless, prominent Rastas, such as Bob and Rita Marley and Peter Tosh, have been among its members.

On the other hand, fundamentalist Rasta groups seem to be coming closer to Christian theology. Thus, for instance, in 1983, the World Council of Churches' journal, *One Word*, reported that the largest Rastafarian group in Jamaica — namely, the Twelve Tribes of Israel — categorically rejected its pristine doctrine of the superiority of black people. It no longer claimed that the black population would rule civilisation, when its kingdom was created. The Rastafarian group recognises the Holy Scriptures and Jesus of Nazareth as Saviour. The Jamaica Council of Churches follows this development with great interest. Indeed, it conducted an official investigation into complaints by a Rasta group of religious discrimination and harassment by the security forces (*Catholic Standard* 26.6.1983, p. 4).

Rastafarianism, whose adherents initially came from the lower socio-economic class, gained considerably in importance and dissemination by means of the entry in its ranks of middle-class people. Having members of world-wide prominence also helped. Rastafarianism manifested itself as a resistance movement against influences of white, industrialised states on Afro-Caribbean culture as the basis for artistic creation in music, wood-carving and painting, but also as a vehicle for commerce, pure and simple.

Up to the present time, both Islam and Hinduism have had little significance for the integration movement in the Caribbean. But these two religions have not been militant. Unlike the situation in Africa and the USA, Islam has hardly been able to get a toe-hold among the black population in the Caribbean, because it is regarded as an 'East Indian' religion there (Mazrui, 1990).

Religion, despite all its efforts, has played a small role up to now, in bringing Caribbean societies together into a social unit. On the contrary, Robert Cuthbert holds that religion has contributed more to the separation, which marks the current situation (*op. cit.*, p. 107).

2.7.3.5 Regional Institutions of the Churches

The former established churches and most of the 'non-conformist sects' emanating from them belong to the Caribbean Council of Churches (CCC), an ecclesiastical integration movement representing some 33% of the population of the Commonwealth Caribbean (excluding non-Anglophone CCC members). The Barbados-based CCC, which is the first regional ecumenical conference that has included the Roman Catholic Church among its founding denominations, has additional secretariats in both Jamaica and Trinidad.

Caribbean integration has been among the principal objectives of the Caribbean Conference of Churches (CCC) ever since it came into existence. One of its predecessors was the Caribbean Committee on Joint Christian Action (CCJCA) which had been founded in 1957 in Puerto Rico. Consequently, in November, 1984, at an assembly in Georgetown (Guyana) eighty heads of religious denominations affiliated to the CCC confirmed their view of the role of the Churches in promoting the regional integration process in the following terms: Their Churches should drive forward the unity aimed at among the peoples of the region and attempt to oppose the fragmentation and manipulation — no matter from whichever quarter.

The heads of the Churches spoke out in favour of closer links to CARICOM and also for the abolition of travel and work restrictions in the Caribbean. 'The CCC's primordial commitment to regional integration as a *sine qua non* for the realisation of genuine development in the region remains unchanged. We view the Caribbean region as one,' in the words of CCC General Secretary, Rev. Allan Kirton, to the press in Barbados in January, 1986 (*CC* February, 1986, p. 3).

The CCC affiliated member-churches have individually come out repeatedly in favour of political integration. Thus, on November 19-20, 1987, five based in the OECS Member States discussed the proposals for the political unity of the region. Their collective communiqué published after their meeting unreservedly supported the initiative for political integration, and even ascribed to it a transcendental character. Thus, the Roman Catholic Bishop of Bridgetown (Barbados) Bishop Anthony Dickson, declared: 'We feel strongly that the unity of Caribbean people is part of God's overall plan for the unity of the entire human family. The Catholic Church promotes and supports efforts to overcome the fragmentation and isolation of our Caribbean peoples and to bring about the unity of peoples, which is God's plan for us. It is our hope as well that political integration would promote the moral, spiritual and cultural development of our people'. The unity of the OECS Member States should be the stimulus for closer collaboration within the CARICOM countries (*CC* January, 1988, p. 8).

OECS political unification efforts received a positive reaction from the Methodist church in the Caribbean at its May, 1988, annual meeting in Barbados. But it also showed consideration for the reservations of some territories concerning their feared threat to their sovereignty. The meeting recommended, instead of a unitary State in the Eastern Caribbean, rather efforts for strengthening and expanding common institutions (*CC* June, 1988, p. 3).

In 1969, then CCJCA General Secretary, David Mitchell, began a youth development programme for the social and economic development of the Leeward and Windward Islands as well as Barbados. That programme, the Christian Action for Development in the Eastern Caribbean (CADEC) received high praise and currently supports small development projects well beyond the Eastern Caribbean. CADEC has succeeded in channelling funds from a number of donors from industrialised countries into small projects, development research and documentation as well as the co-ordination of ecumenical programmes. In 1971, the aid agency organised the Caribbean Ecumenical Consultation for Development (CECD) from which the CCC emanated and also obtained its current ideological orientation towards 'Justice and Liberation' closely following the United Nations, the World Council of Churches and Vatican Council II (Cuthbert, *op. cit.*, p. 57).

The CCC leaders endorsed the demands, which have been popular since the 1970s, by Heads of Government, writers and social scientists for a New International Economic Order, a New International Communication Order, change of the capitalist market structure, collective self-reliance of poor countries *vis-à-vis* the rich industrialised states, the conversion of the Caribbean into a Zone of Peace and, finally, the broad collaboration of the population in the fashioning of their own future. The Churches did not wish to be in the position of being the last bastion of colonialism (Watty, 1992). The CCC supported in a sustained way, movements and theologies, which had dedicated themselves to the fight against oppression — meaning, first of all, political combat. Caribbean theologians deduced from the pointers in the Liberation Theology they adopted from Latin America, their *modus operandi* for practical political work, which did not deny the roots they shared in common with Marxism-Leninism. The Anglican priest, Leslie Lett, as co-ordinator of the Church and Society Division of the CCC, demanded the 'building of a truly Caribbean Church with a strong anti-imperialist stance.' He accused the United States of promoting, for reasons of foreign policy, 'the gradual religious re-colinisation of the Region,' by supporting American religious sects in the Caribbean (Lett and Harvey, 1984, pp. 6-8).

Lett himself and leading CCC staff-members strengthened this posture by means of numerous publications. *Caribbean Contact*, the newsmagazine, was the most important publication of the CCC. For a long time, it was the only such publication, which was distributed throughout the Caribbean, that contained political information and analyses from the entire region including the non-Anglophone areas.

Under the umbrella of the *Action for the Renewal of the Church Commission*, the CCC started, in 1971, programmes for women, the youth, religious formation, family life and to support territorial church councils. In August, 1974, the CCC founded the Cedar Press.[352] CADEC has created an audio-visual service and a documentation and research centre.

In 1981, the CCC introduced, under the motto, 'Fashion Me A People', a sessions syllabus for Church-run schools linking the thinking of Caribbean and Christian unity. 'The sessions deal with concerns of our identity and development as Caribbean people and as Christians,' wrote then CCC General Secretary, Roy Neehall, in a preface (1981). The widely-drawn curriculum, dealing with six age levels from small child to adult stage, with several introductory guidance books for each stage, did not have the sweeping success hoped for by the initiators. The work had to leap over the territorial and denominational fragmentation and also group self-interest from which the guardians of the Christian communities are not quite free themselves. Moreover,

[352] Cedar is the acronym for 'Christian Engagement in Development and Renewal'.

larger Faith communities had long had their own religious instruction programmes.

Also the call for a 'Caribbean Theology', which repeatedly sounded from the pages of the CCC publications, found little echo.[353] For most religious bodies, belief is not linked to a territory or a region, but is, instead, universal.

Some of the evangelical Churches in the Caribbean have come together in the Caribbean Association of Evangelicals and the Caribbean Association of Bible Colleges (Evangelicals). A conference of evangelical groups in Amsterdam in 1983 preceded their founding. At that conference, preachers and evangelists from the Caribbean found, to their shame, that they did not know each other (*SG* 9.10.1983, p. 4c). Since 1983, the journal, *Caribbean Evangelical Communicator*, has tried to maintain contacts between the evangelical groups, with the objective of being a sort of counterweight to the rather left-wing-oriented *Caribbean Contact* published by the Caribbean Conference of Churches.

All of the larger religious communities have formed Caribbean-wide associations. For example, the Seventh Day Adventists have a Caribbean Union Conference of Seventh Day Adventists with head office in Barbados; the Church of God, from the USA, also has its Caribbean Atlantic Assembly of the Church of God in Barbados; and the Baptists hold their annual Caribbean Baptists Fellowship at different locations.

[353] *cf* remarks by, William Watty, then UTCWI President, for instance, in: *Castries Catholic Chronicle*, 15.8.1982, p.9. For him, this theology is not something abstract and found in books — but rather the more devoted dedication of the Churches in the Caribbean to the specific problems of people living in the region, which in its general validity, certainly demands no separate theology.

3. Special Aspects of the Effect of External Factors on Caribbean Integration

3.1 Significance of External and Internal Factors

Opponents of Caribbean unity as well as sceptics are often heard making the reproach that politicians preparing for this unity are merely obeying whispered promptings from abroad, especially from the USA. 'I would be the last person in this region to seek motivation from abroad,' assured St. Vincent and the Grenadine's Prime Minister, James Mitchell, after allegations in the press that his initiative for Unity of the Eastern Caribbean was determined by the concern of foreign powers for their security (1987, p.23).

Both theoreticians and practitioners of Caribbean integration agree that external conditioning plays an important role. The coming into existence of the Caribbean Community as a step on the way to political unity was possible only through the formal Independence of the then British colonies in the Caribbean. Indeed, looking further back in history, the adventitious results of British colonial conquests also determined this. On the other hand, the break-up of the 1958-62 West Indies Federation is an example of the failure of externally imposed 'unity' through federal structures.

The external dependence of the Caribbean in the post-colonial period has changed, especially under the influence of the East-West confrontation and also during the period of the escalation of that confrontation and its subsequent de-escalation. Economic dependence has begun to overlay ideological links.

Small Caribbean States lose their pawn in the sense of their submissiveness to the USA in exchange for economic aid and benefits in terms of security policy. The coming into being of the single market of the European Union, NAFTA and the Asia-Pacific Economic Cooperation (APEC) the economic and power centre in the Pacific between Australia, the bordering Pacific States and Japan, marginalise countries on the periphery. In the shadow of the global economic and power centres, medium-sized powers, such as Brazil, Mexico, Colombia and Venezuela increase their influence.

The Caribbean Community came into existence without direct external influence. Shortly after the solemn signing of the Treaty of Chaguaramas in 1973, Dr. Eric Williams, then Prime Minister of Trinidad and Tobago, declared that the great achievement of the Treaty on the creation of the Caribbean Community was that, at any rate so far as he knew, it had been brought about by West Indians without any interference (1973a, p. 13).

William Demas (1987, pp. 11f), who had closely observed West Indian integration from the very beginning spoke in these terms:

'The movement for economic integration, functional co-operation and co-ordination of foreign policies — embodied in the OECS and wider CARICOM Treaties — has been entirely of indigenous West Indian origin'. There have been a number of initiatives and treaties, he declared, 'all of them emerging from West Indians, all of whom no one can allege to be subject to dictation or influence by middle and great powers outside the region.'

Opinions differ as to whether the international environment has exerted a marginal influence on Caribbean integration. Compton Bourne, (he did a comprehensive study on Caribbean development to the year 2000 for CARICOM) has stated that the international environment 'although providing sources of support and opportunities for growth as well as constraints on the nature and pace of development, need not be the dominant influence' (*Caribbean Development*, p. 123).

No one believes, however, that a unified Caribbean market is an alternative to trading relationships with countries outside the region or that the Caribbean Community could pursue its own security interests without external participation. Regional economic integration could prove to be one of the most practical means for creating a New International Economic Order, according to the Economic Policy Committee, chaired by Michael Manley, of the Socialist International (*Global Challenge*, p. 124).

In the wake of the post 1989 developments in Eastern Europe and the threatening political marginalization of the Commonwealth Caribbean, the idea of political unity has again gained ground. A new multilateralism seems to be replacing the hitherto preferred bilateralism in the external relationships of the CARICOM Member States. In 1985, then Barbadian Prime Minister, Bernard St. John, had warned against the latter at the CARICOM Summit held in his country (*CP*, Supplement, p. 4). A year earlier, the foreign policy expert, Anthony Bryan (1984, pp. 88ff) had attested to the fact that it did have occasionally a centrifugal effect, whether intended or not, on the collaborative efforts of the Community.

3.2 Marginalization of the Commonwealth Caribbean

Integration in the Commonwealth Caribbean is accomplished without external pressure — but not without the particular involvement of the power centres that are both the USA and Europe. St. Vincent and the Grenadines's Prime Minister, James Mitchell, has declared that the Caribbean needed unity not to survive, but to be heard (*WG* 28.11.1989, p. 20). Political realists such as Mitchell have repeatedly called attention to this lack of particular interest on the part of the external power centres. Indeed, European unity and German unification are internationally more important than the hobbling and dragging efforts at unity in the Caribbean (Fauriol, 1990, pp. 64-65). In the new, global cut-and-thrust order the Commonwealth Caribbean is threatened with marginalization.

Immediately following the start of new political orientation in Eastern Europe, fears were expressed in the Caribbean that the industrialised states could invest in Eastern Europe and push the Caribbean on to the periphery. Optimists envisage a new market in Eastern Europe for tropical products and produce from the Caribbean (*CI* December, 1989; *CR* 21.6.1990, p. 1). But they are outnumbered by critical voices, that fear that the economic development programmes in Eastern Europe could drastically alter the priorities for the flood of funds as aid and investment from the industrialised states[354].

The new foreign policy realities have intensified the pressure on the Caribbean Community to give up its stagnation (Vaughan Lewis, 1990, p. 32) and to decide in favour of greater integration in the direction of political unity. The acceptance by the European Union of Haiti and the Dominican Republic in the ACP group forces the Community, in the opinion of OECS Secretary-General, Vaughan Lewis, to re-examine its geographical and geopolitical focus. New initiatives concerning trade between North America and South America have had similar effects (Vaughan Lewis, *op cit*, 1990, p. 32). As then ACP and now CARICOM Secretary-General, Edwin Carrington, has found (1989, p. 4), the Caribbean, with mainly unilateral trade preferences for countries having a total population of 600 million inhabitants, belongs to the most privileged regions of the world, its own people having grown up, while being nourished on a 'diet of protection'.

On the other hand, however, the customs and trade preferences enjoyed thus far by the CARICOM Member States *vis-à-vis* the UK can clearly not survive forever, now that the single market of the European Union has come into existence. Edwin Carrington (1990, p. 3) has expressed fears that the entire system of preferences — from the old Imperial system through the Commonwealth system, to Lomé — is, with the coming into being of that single European market, on its death-bed. Only limited time extensions are granted to special arrangements, for instance, for the protection of rum and banana exports to the EU.

[354] For instance, Sir Neville Nicholls, CDB President, has expressed this view (*CDB News* October-December, 1989, pp. 1-2).

Existing trade preferences of the Caribbean States in the North American market are also threatened. The protectionist trade policies of both the USA and Canada have already throttled the importation into those countries, of important produce, such as sugar, as well as finished textiles and leather products. NAFTA may further limit the access to the most attractive market for many CARICOM Member States.

Shridath Ramphal, when he was Commonwealth Secretary-General, had warned that 'friendship' between a superpower and a small country could not hinder the 'friend' from being passed over when bilateral aid was to be granted (1985, p. 18). Shortly after the start of the post-1989 change in Eastern Europe, the USA switched to Poland US $ 25 million, which had been initially meant for Jamaica (*WG* 15.5.1990, p.11). Jamaica's then Prime Minister, Michael Manley, who, in the 1970s, had been anything but a friend of the White House, travelled twice to meet US President Bush. Manley's objective was to obtain assurances that the US Government would not cut its aid to Jamaica and the other CARICOM Member States in favour of Eastern Europe.

With the change in Eastern Europe and the abatement of East-West tension, security policy in the Caribbean has also received a new character. In April, 1989, then Prime Minister of Trinidad and Tobago, A.N.R. Robinson, acknowledged, shortly after the visit to Cuba of then USSR President Mikhail Gorbachev, that the real threat to the security of the Commonwealth Caribbean was posed internally. It was, he recognised, social instability, the migration of skills and expertise, the debilitating effects of unaided long-term structural adjustment and diversification programmes, natural disasters, pollution and spoilage of the environment, and the plague of illegal drug trafficking (*CI* May, 1989, p. 5).

As the July, 1990, attempted *coup d'état* by Muslim fanatics in Port-of-Spain showed, Robinson's words had a thoroughly prophetic character. The then Leader of the Opposition in Barbados, Henry Forde (1991) saw, as future potential centres of conflict, ethnic confrontation, religious intolerance[355] and the fight over resources (e.g. between Barbados and Trinidad and Tobago over fishing rights).

[355] Role of the muslim faith of the *coup* leaders (see Sitahal 1994).

3.3 Dependence Versus Self-determination: International Financial and Development Agencies

'The first thing you have to do; if you want to be independent is to stop begging, the second thing you have to do is to stop borrowing,' advised then Barbadian Opposition Leader, Errol Barrow, in a newspaper interview in 1985.

He criticised CARICOM Governments, which turned to USAID when they needed money — without considering how else they could get funds needed. Barrow, as Prime Minister, was proud that he had never asked the USA for cash. But his Government did accept money from international agencies or 'friendly Governments', which offered their services and, like the Canadian Government, displayed no colonial or Imperialist ambitions (*Barbados Advocate* 26.11.1985, p. 2).

The Caribbean belongs to the regions in the world, which, on per head basis, receive the most development aid[356]. The Caribbean Group for Co-operation in Economic Development (CGCED), headed by the World Bank and consisting of development agencies active in the region, co-ordinates economic co-operation. The World Bank prepares most of the technical analysis and proposals for the annual CGCED meeting (*Cf.* Pastor and Fletcher, 1992, p. 79).

With particular emphasis, the Commonwealth Caribbean States have tried to get the particular favourable IDA credits — even when they do not fulfill the criteria of Least Developed Countries to which IDA assistance is bound[357]. In other development banks, such as the Inter-American Development Bank (IDB) and the Caribbean Development Bank(CDB), which pay attention to the special concerns of Latin America and the Caribbean, CARICOM Governments have more influence — but the *quantum* of credit is less.

Practically all special CARICOM initiatives are financed by UNDP, the Commonwealth Fund for Technical Co-operation (CFTC) and the Swedish Government (*CR* 29.1.1990, p. 4). The expenses of the West Indian Commission established under Sir Shridath Ramphal in 1989 were paid by several agencies. The future CARICOM Commissioner, it was proposed, should be paid by the future European Union (*CI* December, 1990, p. 15) — a suggestion Lloyd Best, the Trinidadian economist and politician, roundly dismissed as 'wholly ludicrous' (*CP* 49, p. 39).

Similar dependence also exists in the OECS[358]. Effective aid is not merely a question of the amount of money made available thereby. On the contrary, even small sums often suffice to provide effective help. James Mitchell has pointed out that the sum spent by the US Government for one of thousands of new bridges or streets in the USA suffices to format anew the economy of an entire country in the Caribbean. Indeed, one can accomplish much with little — but

[356] 1991 official development aid for all CARICOM member-States has been estimated at US$1.2 billion, putting it at third place on a per head basis after Israel and Egypt (Tony Best, 1992).

[357] *Cf.*, for instance, the 1985 Barbados CARICOM Summit communiqué against 'graduation' meaning the exclusion of CARICOM member-States from IDA soft loans; or then Bahamian Prime Minister, Lynden Pindling's, remarks at the 1986 World Bank meeting in Washington, D.C. (*CDB News* 4.4, p. 5).

[358] *Cf.* Demas, 1982, pp. 5 and 13-14; *Bulletin of Eastern Caribbean Affairs* 7.6 (January-February, 1982), several contributions.

also, as the case of Jamaica in the 1980s showed, little can be done with a lot (Brana-Shute, 1985, p. 28).

External financial help often runs parallel with the sending of foreign experts to advise on projects. Such advisers on many occasions constitute a parallel bureaucracy feared by Carl Stone (1986c, p. 135) to lead to 'denationalisation', in the case of Jamaica. Edwin Jones warned of national decision-making shifting to the hands of expatriates. The most important development agencies, which operate in the CARICOM area, include the following: USAID; Canadian International Development Agency CIDA; UNDP; United Nations Industrial Development Organisation (UNIDO); FAO; PAHO; the European Development Fund (EDF); the Inter-American Development Bank, the German Agency for Technical Co-operation (GTZ), the Commonwealth Fund for Technical Co-operation (CFTC) and the German Credit Bank for Reconstruction (GCBR/KFW). Aid also comes from numerous other extra-regional state, partly state-controlled and private institutions and organisations.

The power of the financial and development agencies extends far beyond the money they make available to recipient countries. These agencies have, since the 1960s financed most of the infrastructural projects in the Commonwealth Caribbean. Two thirds of the foreign debt of the CARICOM Member States is, therefore, with such official agencies; and only one third is with commercial banks. In 1986, debt repayments of the CARICOM Member States already exceeded by US $ 97 million, the money they received as aid (Clive Thomas, 1989, p. 33).

The influence of external aid organisations on Caribbean integration has rarely been examined. Within the Caribbean Community, hardly a State body exists and — apart from the commercial sector — scarcely a non-State institution, which is not totally or partly financed from external sources. The Jamaican columnist, Dawn Ritch, complained in 1991 that this part of the world has very little respect for regional institutions; its politicians are repeatedly enthusiastic about funding — but never about paying for them. In reality, the CARICOM Secretariat in Georgetown (Guyana) would hardly exist, were it dependent totally on the payment of the contributions of the Member States of the Community[359]. The renowned UWI has been in a financial crisis, owing to the payment arrears of the participating territories, which amounted in 1992 to some US$125 million (*CI* May/June, 1992, p. 6).

The political and economic dependence of the Commomwealth Caribbean had its origin in the colonial past of the region. The UK market determined Caribbean production and plantation cultivation, namely, a few profitable crops, especially sugar, for export to the 'mother country', whence finished products had to be imported. Their monoculture forced Caribbean States, given their rising population, to import increasing quantities of food, which, with finished goods and crude oil imports, contribute still considerably to the balance of payments deficit.

---

[359] At the end of 1991 32.2% of the budgeted contribution of Member States was outstanding (Caribbean Community, 1992, p. 63). Nye has, not without reason, included development aid among the catalysts promoting integration (1965, p. 348).

3. Special Aspects of the Effect of External Factors on Caribbean Integration

The policy of 'incentive industrialisation' or 'industrialisation by invitation', which sought to industrialise the Caribbean with the help of foreign capital, increased the external economic dependence of the region in the 1950s and 1960s. By this means, having regard to the rapid growth of the population and the limited possibilities for expansion of the agricultural sector, urgently needed jobs were supposed to be created. Additionally, technology would be transferred, top executives trained for the private sector, exportable products produced to improve the foreign currency balance, savings made by employees and, on the whole, development promoted.

Nonetheless, the usefulness of this Puerto Rico-oriented model did not meet expectations. It clearly mattered to foreign investors to make use of cheap labour in the Caribbean. On the other hand, however, they also tried to get by with using as few workers as possible. There came into existence capital-intensive small and medium-sized enterprises employing few workers. Profits were, as a rule, transferred abroad, and re-invested only to a small extent. Hardly any transfer of technology or training of indigenous experts and executives took place. Moreover, enterprises financed with foreign capital were usually integrated vertically in the economic structure of exporting countries — thereby contributing little to intra-Caribbean integration and, instead, promoting the integration in the international economic system (*Cf.* Dennis Benn, 1984, p. 30; Axline, 1979, pp. 20ff).

Nonetheless, no alternative seems to exist to 'industrialisation by invitation'. The efforts by the CARICOM Member States to woo investors were also a reflection of their disappointment over the development of the Caribbean Community. The often arbitrary protectionism, the spectacular devaluations in Jamaica, Guyana and Trinidad and Tobago, as well as inadequate consultations of the Governments of the region among themselves prior to rather important decisions on economic policy, left practically no other choice open to Caribbean Governments, constantly under pressure to succeed, to compete against each other for foreign aid.

On extended trips through the Far East, West Europe and North America, their representatives kept a look-out for potential foreign investors[360]. Indeed, both Belize and Dominica even offered citizenship to foreigners investing certain sums of money in the country (*CI* August 1989, p. 11; March, 1992, p. 9; September 1994, p.6; *CC* July-August, 1992, pp. 5 and 8). Opponents of the Puerto Rican model and 'industrialisation by invitation' came together, at the start of the 1960s, around the UWI/Mona 'New World Group' of economists to which C.Y. Thomas and Alister McIntyre belonged. Out of their analyses of the dependence of the Caribbean economy, there developed a whole school of thought, which constructed the theory of the plantation economy on the work of Lloyd Best of Trinidad and the Canadian economist, Kari Levitt.

This theory is predicated on the assumption that the institutional structures and dependency of the plantation economy have continued from the beginning up to the present time and have been consolidated by the metropolitan powers. Payne (1984b) distinguishes a 'structuralist' school around the old 'New World

---

[360] *Cf.* 'Barbados Government looks to the Far East' in: *Caribbean Insight* 9.2 (February, 1968), p. 3).

Group', which seeks to define dependency under specific Caribbean conditions, and a 'neo-Marxist' school, which views the underdevelopment in Third World societies as a dialectic process of the internationalisation of the capitalist system. The latter group includes people like Trevor Munroe and Ralph Gonsalves, who have remained opposed to the ruling system. The 'structuralists', including Norman Girvan, Owen Jefferson, Sir Alister McIntyre, Havelock Brewster, Lloyd Best and Courtney Blackman have, according to Payne, integrated themselves, as technocrats, in the capitalist-influenced State system of the Commonwealth Caribbean.

In the CARICOM Member States' on-going balance of payments difficulties, the International Monetary Fund (IMF) in particular, has repeatedly become the centre of interest. This is, on one hand, as the body solving their problems. More often, on the other hand, however, it is as the scapegoat for the consequences of the structural adjustment measures ordered.

Adherents of the dependence school of thought belong to the harshest critics of the IMF/World Bank/US AID-imposed export-led, trade liberalisation economic strategies. Carl Stone (1990d), challenged the legitimacy of this criticism[361]. The concept of this school of thought has, according to Stone, led to the collapse of the Jamaican economy in 1972-80 — as, indeed, in many other countries — and made the call to the IMF necessary, in the first place. He ascribes responsibility for the plight of the countries affected by the IMF-imposed austerity measures mainly to internal policy reasons, in addition to the protectionist trade policies of the industrialised countries.

The Minister of Finance of Trinidad and Tobago, Selby Wilson (*WG* 25.12.1990, p. 17) has also come to the defence of the IMF against its critics. No country has recourse to the IMF, he has declared, if its economy is not in serious difficulties. The IMF programmes, although economically reasonable, often fail, because of the social reaction against a fiscal policy perceived as unfeeling. The Government of which he was a part had implemented the IMF-recommended measures, he said, even if not explicitly imposed. The Government's economy measures have had good effects, he added.

The CARICOM Member States' high foreign debt[362], which, at the end of 1992, amounted to US$9.3 billion[363], is one reason why these Governments have finally had to submit to the dictates of the IMF. Jamaica, Trinidad and Tobago, Barbados and Guyana accounted for 91.6% of the 1992 figure (Caribbean Community, 1993, pp. 16f).

Guyana, with a foreign debt of US$1.924 billion in November, 1992, and a debt servicing- to -exports earnings ratio of 40.4 % (*CI* December, 1992, p. 8), is one of the most indebted developing countries in the world (*CI* January, 1990, p. 2) on a per head basis. Antigua and Barbuda has a much higher *per capita* debt load[364] than Guyana, but is economically better suited to service it. Jamaica had to use 40% of its exports earnings, amounting to US$1.6 billion, to meet

[361] *Cf.* also the defence of CDB President, Sir Neville Nicholls, of the IMF in his address to trade unionists in Antigua in November, 1992 (*CDB News* 11 1 and 2 (January-June, 1993), pp. 20-23).

[362] For a comprehensive account, please see Bernal (1991).

[363] In 1991, this amounted to US$ 9.7, in 1990 to 10.3 billion.

[364] US$ 400 million for 64,000 people. *Associated Press* in a report from St.John's, undated in *WG* 22.3.1994, p.26.

debt repayment and servicing, in 1989 (Pastor and Fletcher, *op cit.*, p. 79). Without IMF agreements, regarded by international financial creditors as attesting to the creditworthiness of the debtor country, countries, such as Guyana, could hardly hope for further credits from commercial banks or the international financial agencies (*Cf.*, for many others, Tetzlaff, 1988).

The IMF, however, also shares indirectly some of the blame for the heavy indebtedness of the CARICOM Member States. This is because it has infringed the requirement postulated on the adaptation-of-financing criterion. This agency often is satisfied with mere declarations of intent to adapt their economics by debtor countries, instead of insisting on the measures agreed. The assumption underlying this is that, the higher the amount involved in financing, the better are the prospects for the successful, long-term adaptation to the demands of balance of payments equilibrium and the acceleration of the speed of the growth of economic development in the Third World (Schüller, 1988).

3.4 External Political Counselling

So far, the influence on the socio-political factors of Caribbean integration by extra-regional States—controlled, in whole or in part, and private agencies and organisations, has been little studied. The reason for this situation may well be that foreign influences on political and pre-political matters conflict most markedly with the postulates of self-determination and sovereignty. The participating external and internal actors do not exactly seek publicity, when it is a matter of elucidating the network of relationship and possible dependence.

At the peak of the East-West confrontation, the relationships with US agencies, on the one hand, and, on the other hand, with the then USSR and their Caribbean allies, reposed on particular discretion. Reproaches to opponents that they have been 'bought' by foreign intelligence services—to wit, the CIA and the KGB—belonged to the standard vocabulary of political confrontation.

Only a few Heads of Government went as far as did the Prime Minister of Dominica, Eugenia Charles, when, in 1986, she demanded 'an evaluation of the role of foreign aid agencies operating in the Caribbean' (*Barbados Advocate*, 27.8.1986, p. 6)[365]. She asked the participants of the assembly of the Caribbean Youth Conference to ponder whether the role of these agencies 'that had come to take part in building our lives in this community' were in the region 'merely to assist our people to a better life' or if 'they are carrying out the nefarious task for the purpose of bringing in abhorrent ideologies which the majority of people in our area do not want to have.'

Ms Charles did not name any of the agencies she was referring to, but told participants, 'you are closer to their actions than any of us and you can judge for yourselves and weigh the things that they do ... the way in which they do it ... and the servants whom they choose to do it—to know whether they are being honest, whether they are being democratic, and whether they really want these countries to remain on the democratic path.'

She said the Caribbean operations of some foreign agencies was something that had engaged her attention and about which she had been concerned for some years now. She urged the young people to evaluate what is happening to be able to take what they want, and to 'throw overboard', what they wanted to reject from the agencies. 'Let us decide that when agencies are bringing in assistance, they are not bringing in assistance that is meant and planned to undermine the things we cherish most in these countries,' the Prime Minister said.

Two years earlier, at a regional seminar on Caribbean sovereignty, sponsored by the *Friedrich-Ebert-Stiftung* which is close to the Social Democratic Party in Germany, Tony Bogues, the Jamaican journalist and PNP activist, had warned against new foundations, which were the deliverers of a certain ideology. He named specifically the then newly established Bustamante Institute of Public and International Affairs, which, in the course of later years, would be recognised throughout the Caribbean owing to its pluralistic posture. The funds

[365]She made these remarks at a conference largely financed by the *Konrad-Adenauer-Stiftung* of Germany, towards which she evidently did not direct that warning.

for this Institute came from private donors in the USA, Canada and the Caribbean, as far as is known.

The Konrad-Adenauer-Stiftung[366]— which is close to the Christian Democratic Party in Germany, was not only present at the birth of the Caribbean Youth Conference. It also gives financial support to the East Caribbean Institute for Democracy (ECID) of which several Eastern Caribbean parties are members, as well as helping indirectly, the Caribbean Democrat Union (CDU)[367]. Moreover, the Konrad-Adenauer-Stiftung promotes Caribbean trade unions affiliated to the Christian Latin American trade union movement, CLAT[368].

While the Konrad-Adenauer-Stiftung was first represented in the Commonwealth Caribbean in 1981, the involvement there of the Friedrich-Ebert-Stiftung began at the start of the 1970s. The list of Caribbean institutions whose work is promoted by this foundation is truly impressive.

It has been for a long time among the most important financial backers of the Caribbean Congress of Labour (CCL) and the Caribbean Broadcasting Union (CBU). It also made a significant contribution to the coming into existence of the Caribbean Institute of Mass Communication (CARIMAC) at the Mona campus in Kingston, Jamaica, of the UWI[369]. The Friedrich-Ebert-Stiftung also sponsors seminars of the Association of Caribbean Economists, to which numerous leading University lecturers and technocrats of the region belong. Additionally, it is much more involved than the Konrad-Adenauer-Stiftung in the exchange of ideas and information with Latin America, e.g. through the journal, *Nueva Sociedad*, in Caracas, Venezuela, and in supporting the Caribbean activities of Socialist International.

The work outside of Germany by both the Konrad-Adenauer and Friedrich-Ebert-Stiftung is almost entirely financed from the budgets of the German Government. From the same source, routed through UNESCO, the Caribbean News Agency (CANA) was able to expand its news network, modernise it and establish a radio service. Through the German Protestant Central Office for Development Aid, mostly again from the Budgets of the German Government, projects of the Caribbean Conference of Churches (CCC) were promoted as well. *Caribbean Contact*, the CCC newsmagazine, 'survived for twenty-one years because it was funded by agencies external to the Caribbean,' the editors have admitted. 'Even though proposals were made to break this dependency and bring about viability of the publication, a clear policy about how those proposals could be implemented was never devised and worse was a sad lack of will even to try. ' The 'inability and unwillingness of Caribbean societies to free themselves of their dependency syndrome' had brought the magazine to its end (*CC* August 1994, p. 2).

---

[366] *cf* Konrad-Adenauer-Stiftung 1993.

[367] Please see Chapter 2.7.3.3 on this.

[368] Please see Chapter 2.3.4.9, on the Commonwealth Caribbean work of the Konrad-Adenauer-Stiftung; please see as well *Caribbean Insight*, September, 1984, pp. 1-2, and *The Democrat* (Kingston, Jamaica) 4.3 (December, 1986).

[369] Please see the 1986 *Annual Report* of the Friedrich-Ebert-Stiftung (Bonn: Freidrich-Ebert-stiftung, 1987, pp. 85 and 87.

US reaction to the Caribbean activities of German foundations took the form of the National Endowment for Democracy (NED) which, on the initiative of then President Reagan, was launched in November, 1983, with the mission of supporting democratic institutions world-wide.

US organisations, under a host of flags and organisational structures, have always taken an interest in the internal affairs of other countries. American missionaries, who wanted to improve the world, were, in certain regions, more numerous than the US traders and representatives of industry.

Only in the NED, do the foreign institutes of the Democratic and Republican parties as well as the AFL-CIO and the US Chamber of Commerce all came together, with funds from the US House of Representatives and private donors, in order to promote similarly postured organisations, installations and initiatives in the Caribbean.

Under the auspices of the NED, the Center for International Private Enterprise (CIPE) was able to promote Chambers of Commerce, employers' organisations and other private sector bodies in the region; the American Institute for Free Labor Development (AIFLD) was enabled to strengthen its influence on the trade union movement in the Caribbean[370]; the Republican National Institute for International Affairs was in a position to foster the work of like-minded parties and institutions, e.g. the Caribbean Democrat Union (CDU); and, finally, the National Democratic Institute for International Affairs promoted, together with CIPE, seminars, such as the much-appreciated Conference on Democracy in the English-speaking Caribbean in 1985. The NED received an amount (*CR* 26.7.1990, p. 8) of US$ 3.0 million approved by the US House of Representatives in May, 1990, to support free and fair elections all over the world.

After tough negotiations, former US President, Jimmy Carter, and his group of observers from the Carter Center in Atlanta, Georgia, succeeded in helping to bring about in Guyana the electoral reforms long demanded by the Opposition — and thereby to prepare for the first free and fair elections in that country, since 1964 (*Cf. CI* November, 1990, pp. 1-2; *CR* 1990, p. 3). The NED-supported Electoral Assistance Bureau there helped in the mobilization of national support for the reforms (*CI* July, 1992, p. 8).

[370] Please see as well Clive Thomas, 1988, p. 347, and Chapter 2.3.4.9.

3.5 Socio-cultural Foreign Influences

The differentials of the 'West Indian personality' have been dealt with earlier in this book[371]. Hence, the following remains to be dealt with: What external socio-cultural factors affecting this fictitious concept had an influence on Caribbean integration concept, i.e. what influences — simply put — give the people of the Commonwealth Caribbean a collective feeling of oneness; and what binds them rather to the culture and way-of-life of extra-territorial societies. Somewhat along the lines of the position adopted by the UWI *dependence* school in the debate concerning the economic dependence of the Caribbean, representatives of this school have called foreign socio-cultural influences on the region 'Cultural Imperialism' (Mike Richards, 1987). The most prominent advocates of this point of view are the Jamaican artiste and social scientist, Rex Nettleford and the Barbadian novelist, George Lamming.

According to Ernest Duff[372], 'cultural imperialism' displays similar characteristics all over the world. Among the foreign socio-cultural influences, dominate the following:

- Dress: The professionally successful dress in US style;
- eating habits: Fast food developed abroad pushes out indigenous fare;
- the educational system: This is still too much oriented towards the former colonial power, Great Britain, even though the successful introduction of the CXC and the significance gained by the UWI seem to have reduced the size of the problem, with the sensitive reaction of Caribbean academics to influence at University level, as shown by the general criticism of the penetration in the region of US off-shore Universities (*Cf.* J. Edward Greene, 1985);
- Tourism: The demonstration, a million times over, of the metropolitan ways-of-life does not remain without imitators, especially since, on many Caribbean islands, up to 40% of the labour force works in this sector, as much as 85% of which is controlled by foreign financial backers — giving rise to excessive foreign influence from which arise problems, such as servility *vis-à-vis* foreigners, adjustment to the behaviour of tourists, homosexuality, including lesbianism, sexually transmitted diseases, AIDS and drug addiction (*Cf.* *CC* February, 1988, p. 16).
- the language used in the region: Most recognised creative writers of the Commonwealth Caribbean write in English. Professional success depends on complete linguistic mastery with English or US pronunciation.

The denounced foreign influences enter Caribbean living rooms first of all through the media. US TV soap operas transport the materialistic values of the North American middle class into the skulls of Caribbean people, who will probably never be in a position to have that standard of living.

Radio programmes promote acculturation through North American music. Most magazines distributed regionally come from the USA containing the Caribbean as a travel destination or crisis flash-point at most. The rather

---

[371] *Cf.* Chapter 2.7.1, *ante*.

[372] He is an economist lecturing at the Randolph-Macon Woman's College, Lynchburg, Virginia, USA.

condescending reporting on the Caribbean directed to the majority of the readers is hardly suitable to strengthen the self-esteem of the inhabitants of the region.

Only few extra-territorial media organs keep regular correspondents in the Commonwealth Caribbean. On the contrary, most of them deal with special events only by means of reporters and TV teams travelling through the region — thereby encouraging distorted and superficial reporting[373].

The Trinidadian, V.S. Naipaul, one of the most prominent novelists produced by the Caribbean, has observed a tendency of his countrymen to regard everything foreign as superior and everything local as inferior. Indeed, in Jamaican English, the very word, 'local', normally has an underlying connotation of inferiority, for instance. In Naipaul's view, this is an 'old West Indian problem'. Imported food is preferred to locally grown or locally produced food, even when the latter is cheaper and of superior quality. The latter, given a foreign label, however, reportedly sells well in the local market. Conversely, there have been reports of foreign labels being sewn on textiles made or finished in Free Zones in Jamaica for export to foreign markets.

Hong Kong plastic furniture is rated more highly than is elegant locally-made wooden furniture, Naipaul has pointed out. Similarly, in his view, only foreign fashion is regarded as stylish. 'Modernity in Trinidad, then,' he writes in *The Middle Passage*, 'turns out to be the extreme susceptibility of people who are unsure of themselves and, having no taste or style of their own, are eager for instruction' (p. 50).

Awareness of this feeling of inferiority as one of the reasons for imitating foreign socio-cultural influences lies at the base of many calls by Nettleford, Lamming, Demas, Barrow and others for corrective action. They have taken a stand against cultural dependence. Instead, they have stood for the contemplation and reflection on historical experience, cultural dynamics and the creativity specific to the people of the Caribbean (*Cf.*, *inter alios*, Rickey Singh, 1985b).

'But we are so busy Westminsterising ourselves into becoming a clone of the Anglo-Saxon world and its American extension that we forget that we have a life and history of our own to be examined, dealt with and used as a source of energy for the development of this nation/region and the shaping of a civilised society,' Nettleford has complained (*CC* July, 1987, p. 8)[374].

The people currently living in the Caribbean — like large sections of the very flora and fauna themselves — did not have their origins there. Hence their somewhat schizophrenic attitude towards the 'Discovery' of the region for the later European colonial powers by Christopher Columbus, on the occasion of its 500th anniversary in 1992. That anniversary was labelled as the 'Encounter Between Two Worlds' and observed, at least in the Commonwealth Caribbean, as an occasion for regional co-operation and integration[375].

[373] In April, 1985, the then JLP Jamaican Government had first-hand experience of this, when only rather insignificant footage of opponents and violent confrontations between a few delegates to a massively mounted International Youth Conference were shown to the U.S. public by the media.

[374] Quoted by Errol Barrow, 1983.

[375] *Cf.* the communiqué of the 11th meeting of the CARICOM Heads of Government in Kingston, Jamaica, in July-August, 1990

3. Special Aspects of the Effect of External Factors on Caribbean Integration

Columbus and his followers have given names to almost all territories of the Commonwealth Caribbean, numerous cities, communities, rivers and other geographical locations. The ethnic variety and the different origins of the people of the Commonwealth Caribbean clearly make it difficult for them to contemplate and reflect on their common historical roots[376]. Since the end of the 1980s, a change has been occurring in the assessment of socio-cultural influences on the Caribbean. A contribution may well have been made to this change by the realisation that the people of the area have adapted voluntarily the externally-imposed culture and that it would hardly be possible to impose on them a way-of-life defined arbitrarily as 'Caribbean' by their own *élites*.

Cuba, formerly the model for a country whose people have completely turned away from US acculturation, now stands alone as an outsider (*Cf.* Duff, 1990, p. 46).

Conversely, enough examples exist of cultural influences emanating from the Caribbean. Reggae, soca and calypso participate audibly in the development of music as a global manifestation of culture. Trinidad's steel drum is, as already mentioned, one of the few really new musical instruments of the twentieth century. The exporting and re-importing of types of music lead to further development and the creation of variants[377].

The Jamaican media specialist, Professor Aggrey Brown (1990, pp. 61ff) who is also the Head of the renowned Caribbean Institute of Mass Communication (CARIMAC) has demanded a re-thinking of the concept of 'cultural imperialism'. The Caribbean Community possesses, he has argued, adequate technical competence and creativity to collaborate in the development, production and distribution of visual media software. Nonetheless, regional co-operation calls for full freedom of movement of personnel, equipment and supplies. Caribbean tourism could also benefit from developments, according to him, in the fields of information and communication.

---

[376] St. Lucia renamed the Columbus Square in central Castries, the capital, in honour of its Nobel Literature Laureate, Derek Walcott, at the end of that year, whereas Trinidad and Tobago has long replaced Discovery Day with another holiday.

[377] Reggae bands exist even in Japan; and reggae rhythms are used by many Rock bands all over the world.

3.6 Migration

'Today we live a global inequality which drives men and women from the soil that gave them birth, the immediate landscape that shaped their childhood, across oceans, since any dream that they may have of rescuing life in dignity from poverty, that dream is elsewhere, it is not in the landscape where they were born.'

That was how the Barbadian novelist, George Lamming, in an address to the Press Association of Jamaica[378] described a phenomenon — i.e. migration — which exerts direct effects on the economic and political development of the Commonwealth Caribbean and, finally, also, on the integration of the region. Lamming, in that speech, complained that most emigrants knew little about their new host countries; moreover, their fellow citizens, still at home, did not believe the emigrants' reports of the latters' difficult living conditions abroad.

'This deceptive magic of the dream of milk and honey, to the ones who have not visited Canaan, makes for a tremendous resistance to any sane perception of the world in which we live.'

Accurate figures on emigration do not exist. In 1980, it was estimated that 20-30% of the population of Caribbean islands lived in Europe and North America — as many Jamaicans live abroad as those residing at home. Between five and ten per cent of each Caribbean country's population emigrated between 1950 and 1980, the highest rate of out-migration of any region in the world. The USA counted 747,000 official immigrants from the Commonwealth Caribbean during that period (Carlson 1994, 143). In 1991 an estimated 1.74 million West Indians lived in the USA, with 800,000 in New York City (*Time for Action* p. 412).

The rate of returnees from among the emigrants is also not known, nor is the rate of internal migration within the region. This is because there were no standardised and regular censuses (Conway, 1990, pp. 73-75)[379]. Thirty-nine percent of the population of Barbados, 40% of that in Nevis, 45% of that in St. Vincent and the Grenadines and 54% of that in St. Kitts reportedly wished to emigrate, according to a study cited at a family planning conference in Barbados in 1985 (*DG* 23.5.1985, p. 13).

The 'loss' of experts through the brain drain has been quite considerable. Thus, between 1977 and 1980, Jamaica suffered the loss of 9,500 University graduates and other leading personnel by emigration — or over 50% of those who graduated during that period from the country's tertiary institutions (*CP* 29, p. 26). In the industrialised countries, which are far superior in terms of their number of trained experts and other leading personnel to the developing countries, the emigrants falling in these categories offer their services as cheap labour, often below the cost and value of their education. At the same time, however, they are urgently needed at home and they burden the scant

[378] Printed in the *Sunday Sun* (Kingston, Jamaica) 20.12.1981, p. 9.

[379] Thus, the 1991 Antigua and Barbuda census counted only 63,880 of an estimated 80,000 residents, the rest having apparently emigrated (*CI* March, 1992, p. 6) thereby showing the inaccuracy of estimates and extrapolations. In 1990 and 1991 censuses took place in almost all of the Commonwealth Caribbean states and territories. The Statistical Departments are sharing their information and expertise and support each other also technically (*cf* Caribbean Community, 1992, p.52). There is also a Regional Census Office in Trinidad to direct the management of the census in the various CARICOM countries (*CP* 61 and 62, p. 69).

educational and training opportunities of their home countries, where they are more urgently needed than abroad, as bad investments.

The economic decline of their home countries, low salaries, limited prospects for further professional development and disadvantages for ethnic or political reasons — all these have been responsible for this situation. Guyana, where all the aforementioned factors play a role, now hardly possesses the technical personnel necessary to bring that country to the level of development, under its own steam, of the other member-countries of the Caribbean Community.

Conversely, hardly anyone from that area is willing to work in Guyana under such conditions. Filling posts with qualified personnel becomes, therefore, the biggest single problem — even for the Guyana-based CARICOM Secretariat. Enticements also come from millions of tourists, who, in the special situation of their vacation, seem to have unlimited supplies of money and stimulate desires to emigrate[380]. Emigrants also contribute to further emigration. On travelling back to their home countries, they give the often erroneous impression of being prosperous and successful, looking down on their fellow countrymen who have stayed home. Successful emigrants or their successful offspring — such as Harry Belafonte, retired Chairman of the US Joint Chiefs of Staff, General Colin Powell, Ben Johnson, the disgraced sprinter, and less well-known artistes, actors and politicians of Caribbean origin — let emigrants from the region hope for a better future, at least for their children and grandchildren.

In view of the high mobility, however, the decision to leave their native lands need not be definitive. Returning to their homelands by trained Caribbean persons does contain some advantages for the region, according to Carl Stone (1989b, pp. 74ff). Their return, in his view, should be facilitated by lifting exaggerated foreign currency control.

Caribbean integration is no longer a problem in the main metropolitan centres of high migration from the region, such as Brooklyn, the Bronx and Queens in New York; Hartford, Connecticut; Toronto; Brixton in London; or Handsworth in Birmingham (UK). Caribbean emigrants, while keeping their national identity, work closely together politically, socially and culturally; and distinguish themselves markedly from other groups of emigrants of the same skin colour. The election in June, 1987, to the British House of Commons of Guyana-born Bernie Grant and a woman candidate with Jamaican connections accounted for two of the three black MPs who won such seats for the first time in history (*CC* July, 1987, p. 11). Trinidad-born Lord Learie Constantine and Grenada-born Lord David Pitt[381] had been members of the House of Lords for years before that.

The UK, the USA and Canada allow professionally qualified Caribbean persons to immigrate to their countries; but, in the last few years, have been adopting an increasingly restrictive immigration policy to the professionally unqualified. In this, the island Caribbean States have been losing an outlet

[380] Hence the following dialogue noted in Small, 1982, p. 22: *Tourists*: 'A pretty island you've got here — hot sunshine, friendly people, beautiful sand, liquor's so cheap !' *We*: 'Of course', we reply, but we really want to say this instead: 'Hell man ! You stay here and let *me* go to your America for you'.

[381] Baron of Hamstead, died in December, 1994.

through which they had been previously — and especially in the 1960s — able to siphon off a portion of the excessive population pressure.

This could increase social tension and lead to open conflict, with unforeseen effects on tourism and other sectors of the economy. Guyana, under better economic and political conditions, could by all means become a host country for migrants from the Commonwealth Caribbean islands. In Belize, a considerable change has already taken place in the demographic composition of the population, owing to immigration. That country, with about 180,000 inhabitants, absorbed some 50,000 refugees and emigrants from neighbouring Central American countries in the last few years, even while segments of its own black population emigrated to the USA. The 'Hispanics', who are mostly less educated, have been changing the social and ethnic structure of the nation[382]. This could lead to a new orientation of the country away from the Caribbean Community (Tony Best, 1987).

---

[382] Provisional evaluation of the 1991 census, (as against the 1980 census) showed the *mestizos* increasing to 43.6% (from 33.4%) and a decline in the *Creoles* to 29.8% (from 40.0%), the Latin Americans having a considerably higher fertility rate than the Afro-Belizeans (*CI* October, 1992, p. 5).

3.7 External Factors Influencing Federation

The external factors described in the previous Chapters of this book must be favourable to the integration of the Commonwealth Caribbean — and, hence, work as *federators* — should it be the objective of these Governments to limit their countries' loss of significance as a result of the geopolitical changes in Europe since 1989.

The reasons for this are as follows:

1. Threatening marginalization in both political and economic terms, in the absence of a collective foreign policy and the gradual realisation of political unity: The USA no longer has any direct use, in terms of its security policy, for the vassal-like allegiance of — and, therefore, has correspondingly less obligations to — its Caribbean friends; a united Caribbean would have greater weight in the United Nations and other international fora, where real influence is more important than the mere counting of delegates' votes; CARICOM could also become a successful mediator in the region, especially if it were in a position to act in a neutral way — thereby somewhat removing itself from the direct security interests of the one remaining superpower;

2. Unburdening the international system weighted down by new small states resulting from the recent disintegration of formal Federations, such as the ex-USSR and then Yugoslavia: That disintegration may weaken the significance of international bodies and lead to the creation of exclusive club-like groupings of industrialised medium-sized and large states — thereby excluding small countries;

3. Better prospects of getting aid from the large international financial institutions, which prefer projects of a certain size, owing to the proportionally smaller portion of that sum allocated to administrative costs;

4. Concentration of competence and jurisdiction facilitating the more cost-effective use of scarce human resources of experts and senior staff, who thereby have a greater incentive to remain in the region, instead of making their careers abroad; the qualitative improvement of staff-members may possibly result from organisationally tightening the administrative network — with a few dozen Ministries and State agencies replacing hundreds of them and being staffed with qualified personnel;

5. Promotion of the return migration of indigenous experts with specialist knowledge obtained in the industrialised countries, owing to the now improved economic situation at home;

6. Break-down of social tensions resulting from full freedom of movement of people, goods and services, as well as of capital within the Community, facilitating the free exchange of ideas and entrepreneurial initiative, and reducing population pressure; a prospering Guyana could feed far more people than its current population;

7. Sharing of economic risks, thereby flattening the prosperity gradient within the Community and removing arrogance towards the LDCs — which, as the recent course of the economy of Trinidad and Tobago and Barbados has shown, is totally unjustified;

8. A sovereign currency policy: Free convertibility of currency and its movement within the region are the necessary conditions for internal free trade;

9. Trade creation by the Community, e.g. in Eastern Europe and in a Cuba opening itself to its Caribbean neighbours. Anthony Bryan (1990, p. 5) has recommended to the Caribbean Community intensifying South-South co-operation. Good prospects exist for small Third World regional groups, he holds, with the Non-Aligned Movement and the Group of 77 offering no alternative, for their members are more disunited than ever before.

4. Caribbean Integration and Integration Theories

4.1 Research Pointers on Caribbean Integration

Integration is basically the creation of a totality out of different members; it is the joining together under a unified *system*, to form a whole. In Sociology, the term is used in connection with the creation and internal strengthening of a social unit. Kaplan (1957, p. 98) defines integration as a *process* through which the separate systems develop a common framework, which makes possible the collective pursuit of objectives and unified implementation of policies.

This book deals with *regional political integration* understood as a process in the course of which two or more *actors* transfer political *values* with a certain commitment to a new actor. In this sense, political actors are states and societies of different *nationalities*, including territories with limited sovereignty. Political values in this context are defined as political decisions as well as the means and authority necessary for their implementation. The transfer of these values takes place through the formation of collective institutions and processes. Feelings, expectations, economic exchange and freedom of movement flow into political integration, if, out of common obligations, regulated and on-going decision-making occurs. (*cf.* on this, Lindberg, 1970).

Political integration is not linked to the voluntariness of the actors. The number of voluntary integration efforts of independent nations has, however, increased since World War II. With the radical political changes in Eastern Europe since 1989, numerous forced integration structures have come unstuck.

Integration is useful and sensible, if certain objectives and goals can be better attained collectively. These objectives can be classified, depending on whether they serve, as a matter of priority, to meet the needs for improvement of the general living conditions, internal and external security, as well as the ideological, socio-cultural or personal extension of power of *élites*. When the reasons for integration no longer apply, or the cost-benefit parameters change, then the integration structures can again fall apart.

The reasons for integration efforts in many regions are similar. The structures of regional problems and decision-making fall apart; the problems are regional, decision-making is national. Integration can provide the conditions for international ability to act and the opportunity to form social integration politically. Mutual dependence increases and demands a framework for political order (*cf.* Weidenfeld, 1987, p. 13).

Political integration is determined by both *internal* and *external* factors. The former are forces working from within the integrative area: e.g. geographical proximity of the units; common ethnic, linguistic, cultural, ideological, social and historical links (*cf.*, *inter alios*, Cantori and Spiegel, 1970, p. 6) security interests (*cf. inter alios*, Deutsch, 1972, pp. 72-93) or economic ones. *External* factors are forces operating from the outside on the forces working on the integrative area — e.g. economic, social, cultural and security-policy influences. Internal and external factors are only partly capable of being shaped. *Objective* factors, such as geography and the environment, condition the frame within which political integration can be effective.

Internal and external factors may together combine forces, which can start, co-ordinate and give powerful impulses to integration processes — and thereby act as *federators* (*cf.* Schwarz, 1971, p. 383).

Under the influence of such agents, directed both internally and externally, co-operation between states occurs in certain areas. The number of examples of formal and informal co-operation at international level between states is really quite countless. At the world level, the UN is certainly the most prominent model of *functional co-operation*. Particularly at the regional level, frequent examples of such co-operation are as follows: The regulation of trade, industrial collaboration; common research, as well as youth and cultural exchange. Functional co-operation may lead to integration, if the participating actors or units transfer *sovereignty* to common central institutions exercising on their behalf, and autonomously, previously agreed responsibilities (*cf.* Haas, 1973, p. 105).

The integration potential of a region is determined by a series of variables, which could be as follows:[383]

- The behavioural compatibility of the actors.
- The interchangeability of the groups.
- Convergence in critical areas.
- Equilibrium of the transactions.
- Reciprocity of benefits arising from integration and the confidence of the actors in their impartial distribution.
- Equality in the developmental level of communications and frequency of transactions.
- The speed of transactions in relation to population size.
- The accuracy of communications.
- The equality of the effect of transactions.
- Equilibrium of initiative in transactions.
- A similar degree of openness in transactions.
- Ability of adjustment to external factors.
- Low or exportable costs of integration.

At all events, the integration potential of a region should not be regarded as static. Indeed, changed parameters influence the variables and, therefore, the stability of the process of unification. Drastically changed cost-benefit economic ratios place high demands on the firmness of the links at other levels of integration — as well as on the application of the intervention mechanisms limiting the disadvantages both quantitatively and in terms of time.

Thus, for instance, Guyana's extensive use of the CMCF, at the expense principally of Barbados and Trinidad and Tobago, has seriously impaired the economic integration of CARICOM. Guyana's settlement of these debts is one of the conditions for the further integration of that country in the Common Market and the re-activation of the CMCF.

---

[383] *cf* Karl Deutsch, 1954, p. 64; Nye, 1971, pp. 77-86

The integration potential determines the *integration area*, which should be defined in terms of behavioural orientation, following identification with a certain region or objective, rather than legally (Cooper, 1968, pp. 8-9). From the identification with that area, the convergence of the units in external relations and the level of inter-action and co-operation, the area in question gains, in the international system, the qualities of a *sub-system*.[384]

Integration is also conceivable between unequal states, if a core area exists from which certain payoffs (e.g. of a military or economic nature) emanate (Haas, 1973, pp. 108ff). But small countries will avoid this, merely if what it involves is exchanging sovereignty against exploitation by larger states, which are partners in the process. Therefore, current theoretical constructs, such as great power orbits, have limited prospects of being realised in praxis. That particular construct adduces a planetary model of a regional group of small states orbiting a relevant and larger state in a system providing them with collective military, economic and other resources in both peace and war. Yalem (1973, p. 223) regards this construct as realisable only if the larger state in the region is able to guarantee the security of the others and shows restraint with regard to them, and the interests of all these countries are compatible.

Hence, Lewis' thesis (1984 a) that an integration area is more stable in the presence of a leading state with enough financial and other resources to extend its internal structure, as a sort of starting-up investment, to the other states involved in the integration process, does not apply to the Commonwealth Caribbean. The Government of a hegemonic state must get economic and power benefits from its involvement and determine the direction of the integration process, if it is to keep popular consensus.

On the other hand, domination by the hegemonic partner in the integration process arouses the suspicions of its weaker partners. The involvement of the Government of Trinidad and Tobago under Dr. Eric Williams was, in fact, an exemplary illustration of Lewis' postulate. Williams' embittered successor, George Chambers, terminated the attempt.[385] Since 1962, Barbados has not succeeded in bringing together seven Eastern Caribbean small states in a new Federation. Indeed, the unification of the Windward Islands may be successfully completed, because there has been similar structure and size of the individual units and the absence of any leading power.

In point of fact, the regional claims for leadership by Trinidad and Tobago stimulated Jamaica's rejection of the deepening of the integration process. But the former's Eastern Caribbean neighbours, which benefited directly from its economic strength, were also opposed to its hegemonic aspirations. The most economically sensible solution — namely, the coming together of the Windward Islands with Trinidad and Tobago — failed repeatedly. The latter's Prime Minister, Dr. Williams, procrastinated, because he would have had to fear the verdict of his own people — especially the poorer population segments, whom he would have exposed to the tougher competition of migrant workers from the less developed neighbouring islands.

---

[384] *cf* Mols (1982, pp. 192-194) on Latin America as a sub-system.

[385] *cf* Chamber's speech at the 1984 CARICOM summit (Chambers, 1984)

The transfer of sovereignty from the independent Member States to a common central body as well as formation of a unitary state can take place at the end of the process of political integration. In praxis, the voluntary creation of such associations occurs rarely. The Executive branch of Government is the principal source and object of such a transfer of power. But, depending on the type and progress of the integration, the Legislative and Judicial branches as well as NGOs may also be involved. Little significance was initially ascribed to the latter in integration research. But it was recognised early that, say, the course of West European integration did not begin with the state actors (i.e. Schuman, De Gasperi and Adenauer). On the contrary, those actors were able to build on an *integration movement* the idealistic efforts of which were successful after the disastrous consequences of the two Europe-centred world wars of the twentieth century.

Integration is possible in many state and governmental systems and ideologies. But it has differing manifestations and stability on different political parameters. Dictatorships are only apparently more successful than pluralistic democracies in integration efforts, as a result of 'directed transformation' (Harrison, 1974, p. 116-119). Planning and direction, which are immanent in dictatorships, fail in the long run owing to insufficient authority to formulate and implement political goals.

Harrison regards a mixture of dirigism and consensus as more effective. In his view, the stronger the links and bindings, the better are the prospects for arriving at a consensus among the participating units. In this context, it does not depend on Governments, *élites* and other segments of society having the same objectives and priorities. Thus, for instance, a regime could have, as its most important aim, that of staying in power; the population of the country in question could be focused on improving its living conditions; and sections of the *élites* could have ideological motives, as, for example, the lessening of *dependence* on principle. If the wishes come closer to being realised through political integration, it is then easier to come to a consensus on this matter.[386]

Democratic consensus on integration is, however, definitely difficult to arrive at, because majorities in favour of the transfer of sovereign rights must be found. Opponents of change vociferously express their opposition; but supporters, in order not to lose voter support, give it only lukewarm backing — until they are sure that the changes are both lasting and advantageous. This explains, according to Schwarz (1971, pp. 308ff) why Federations occur more frequently under hegemonic force than voluntarily. But democratic structures are a condition for the durability of Federations. That much is clear, in a positive sense, from the studies of the USA, Australia, Germany, Canada or Switzerland; and, *a contrario*, from the failure of the Habsburg Empire, the ex-USSR and former Yugoslavia — all multi-ethnic states threatened with dissolution (*cf.* Schwarz, *op. it.*, p. 433).

New developing states face significantly greater hurdles to integration than do industrialised countries (*cf.* Sloan, 1971, pp. 153ff) because they try to find their national identity. They are sensitive to being disadvantaged and also to

[386] Rosenbaum and Tyler (1975) have adduced similar arguments in considering transnational South-South relationships

structures perceived as *neo-colonial*. The uneven distribution of economic benefits has made many integration efforts, accompanied by high hopes, collapse in the Third World.[387]

The condition of 'underdevelopment' — that is, poverty; shortage of capital; the unequal distribution of income and real property, an entrepreneurial sector that is little developed; the one-sided structure of exports based on raw materials as well as growing foreign debt — often lead to unstable Governments. These lack both legitimacy and the will for long-term planning. Often, too, corrupt, ineffective bureaucracies result. Rapid population growth, tribal, ethnic and class conflicts as well as illiteracy all prevent the improvement of living conditions. In such situations, it is difficult to convince the people involved that they could improve their condition by working with neighbours having similar problems. Agreement on, and the implementation of, mechanisms for the just distribution of the benefits of integration are, therefore, important (*cf.* Sloan, 1971, pp. 151ff).

Integration does not automatically mean *distributive justice per se*. Indeed, it may intensify unequal economic growth within a region, as Axline has warned (1979, p. 15). A Common Market may be more susceptible to crises than are smaller, national markets. Gonzales (1984b, p. 9) has pointed out that the worldwide economic recession of the 1970s would have affected CARICOM much worse, if the Treaty of Chaguaramas had actually been implemented. Governance has been more flexible; and the crisis has been overcome by the individual efforts of each country involved, he has argued. On the other hand, however, the crisis has also increased the heterogeneity of the participating states, and thereby intensified the conflict potential.

The successes of integration take years to become visible. But Governments, especially in the Third World, are hardly able to wait that long. This is because they are exposed to the pressure of high, self-set expectations as well as — in pluralistic democracies — to the pressure of time imposed by the date of the next general elections. Hence, the Opposition can easily castigate the putative sell-out of the countries' vital interests and politically exploit popular resentment, indifference or misunderstanding for its own electoral purposes. This is precisely what occurred in Jamaica in 1960-61 and climaxed inevitably in the referendum that, in retrospect, though not inevitably, sealed the fate of the 1958-62 West Indies Federation.

In developing countries, obstacles to integration between the political units involved in such a process of integration come about through deficient transportation, communication and finance. The underdeveloped condition of the industrial sector, balance of payments problems and inadequate confidence in the prospects of South-South trade are further obstacles.

The bottom line in economic co-operation between developing countries is, quite simply, the following: The situation in which the advantages of the Common Market can be reasonably expected to outweigh its disadvantages, occurs only in markets of certain size (*economy of scale*) with the deployment of

[387] The failure of integration between states at different stages of economic development in Africa is described particularly clearly in Robson (1968).

sufficient human and material resources, enhanced by both geographical location and access to markets in developed countries.

Directing the flow of trade plays a significant role in the technical discussion of the economic integration of developing countries. As a rule such states are at a disadvantage, owing to their one-sided economic structure. Their historical function in the world economy has traditionally been that of supplying raw materials and other primary products and produce to the industrialised countries from which they, in turn, imported finished goods. But this traditional pattern of international trade need not inevitably be a form of manipulated dependence that the neo-colonial school of thought claims it to be.

On the contrary, dependence rather comes about instead, when the population in developing countries prefers foreign goods and services, which are technologically superior or qualitatively better processed, to those produced locally. This thoroughly understandable consumer behaviour inhibits indigenous economic development in the Third World, because it makes it more difficult to build up viable local production.

This situation is rendered acute by the fact that the different Third World suppliers of raw materials and other primary products and produce undercut each other's prices — and thereby always obtain lower prices for their exports, when compared with their imports of finished goods. Consequently, an obstacle arises to the equilibrium of trade between the poorer (i.e. undeveloped) and the richer (i.e. developed) nations.

Directing trade regionally, constitutes one of the ways out of this dilemma. Viner (1950) and many others distinguish between *trade diversion* and *trade creation*. In the former situation, cheaper imports are artificially made more expensive — e.g. by taxation, customs duties or quota restrictions. Indigenous products and produce thereby become marketable. In the latter situation, on the other hand, goods and services capable of standing up to international competition are produced. The market then decides on their marketability.

In order to start up *import substitution*, intra-regional trade and the production of goods and services, which are, at first, less competitive, common customs barriers (e.g. a common external tariff) must be created. Conversely, intra-regional barriers must be dismantled. Even where, however, indigenous goods and services are more expensive than their imported counterparts, they are better than none at all. This, from quite early on, has been the justification adduced, for example, by William Demas (1965, p. 87). GDP can, he argued, be increased by job creation.

Additionally, the domestic markets of many developing countries are too small, even if those countries actually have large populations. This is because of the small purchasing power of their inhabitants. The existence of regional markets improves the prospects for marketing their goods and services. It also makes economic growth possible, with a rise in income and higher employment levels for their people. Additionally, it becomes possible to have the *complementarity of production* — i.e. different countries specialising in different products — instead of maintaining costly parallel industries in the individual countries. Competition can develop by means of the larger trading area, which had hitherto been dominated by local monopolies. Indeed, it is rather possible so to raise standards, that products and produce from that trading area can be sold even in industrialised countries — thereby improving the foreign trade balance. Both the dependence of developing countries on industrialised states and their vulnerability by external influences can be lessened. Rising income levels of the indigenous population increase internal demand, and they may also set in motion a dynamic process of self-sustaining economic growth. The bargaining power of such a region *vis-à-vis* the industrialised countries may, therefore, increase, as a result of its greater economic power.

Despite such efforts, however, economic growth caused by integration, often measured against the GNP, may not be all that great. This is precisely what has happened in CARICOM, for instance. But even modest net profits do exert an influence on the dynamics of the economy. And *dynamic* profits from the community are much larger than are *static* ones (Jaber, 1970, pp. 262-267).

When the 'critical mass' is reached, at which the cost-benefit ratio changes, depends on the effectiveness defined by the actors and the time-frame for achieving it. Thus, for instance, the Common Market (CARICOM) would be faced with excessive demands, if its total and most significant effectiveness were supposed to reside in its net returns from intra-regional exports. This would, at any rate, be unrealistic: After all, intra-regional imports accounted in 1991 for some 6.5% — and exports, for 10.8% — of the total volume of trade in the region.[388]

The smaller East Caribbean Common Market has a common currency, which offers more advantages to the relevant actors than would separate currencies for the individual Member States. The extension of the common currency area to include Guyana or Trinidad and Tobago would, however, reverse the cost-benefit ratio. This is because the structural deficits in the newly-added countries would lead to the instability of the common currency.

Centrifugal forces permanently call into question the very existence of communities. In keeping with the scapegoat syndrome, common institutions run the risk of being held responsible for all failures in the units. Indeed, it is more difficult for the individual citizen to ascertain guilt ascribed to far-distant actors. Friedrich (1972, pp. 35ff) has also regarded the conscious fanning of the flames of envy by the actors, or by the certain classes or population segments, owing to alleged cheating, as possibly exerting a centrifugal effect. Haas, for his part, has observed (1970, pp. 614ff) a particular susceptibility of the population of LDCs for feeling disadvantaged.[389]

Consciously giving preferential treatment to any one actor by allocating certain means of production in the course of a complementary economic order and simultaneous waiving by the other actors of their rights to production, can hardly be done in the Third World. There, national interests are still being placed — and that, in a myopic way — above those of all the units, taken together (*cf.* Belassa and Stoutjesdijk, 1975).

---

388 Caribbean Development Bank, 1994, p. 18).

389 Please see also Sloan (1971) and Belassa and Stoutjesdijk (1975, p. 43), where the latter have termed the expectation of unjustified allocation of benefits and costs as the most important reason for the limited success of integration in LDCs.

4.2 The Theory and Integration Praxis of Small Developing Island States

The integration movement in the Commonwealth Caribbean differs from other such movements in that some of the most important regional theoreticians on the subject, have had the opportunity to put their theories into praxis, while occupying leading political posts in the region. The Caribbean community has been thereby possibly made into the most stable integration movement—and the one most advanced on the way to political union—in the Third World.

Studies by indigenous social scientists, such as Brewster and Thomas (1967) even before the creation of CARICOM, provided important building blocks for it—namely, the concepts of *self-reliance* and the *integration of production*. UWI academics have produced brilliant accounts of the contemporary state of the development of the region.

The search for new forms of integration seems to the observer, however, like fleeing from one's own past. Terms, such as *federation* and *confederation*, are carefully omitted from any political and scientific discussion of the form and organisation of a future Caribbean nation, although these types of political organisation are usually what are meant, when one speaks evasively of a union or *unification*.

The obfuscation of the objectives of Caribbean integration—namely, the formation of a confederation of sovereign states, which transfer certain functions to a central and common Government—weakens the integration movement. Additionally, it puts the adherents of integration in a state of uncertainty. Obviously out of fear of the effects of the traumatic experience with the West Indies Federation, both the CARIFTA and CARICOM treaties and all official communiques of CARICOM summits have avoided references to a possibly too highly-placed—but still desirable—aim of Caribbean integration: namely, political unity.

Effective economic integration cannot be separated from this aim. This is because a Common Market requires the transfer of loyalty to common actors, which may not take place only at the technocratic level of *low politics*. Haas (1976, p. 199) has regarded economic integration as only a 'half-way house' to political union. Vaughan Lewis (1984, p. 30) has termed the separation of political integration from economic integration, as attempted in the formation of both CARIFTA and CARICOM, as a misunderstanding of the development of the system of the European Union, the example of which was the force behind the creation of the Caribbean Community.

For integration to succeed, at least in developing countries, the final objective should not, in Axline's view (1979, pp. 57ff) be set too low. The higher the level of integration which is aimed at from the very beginning, the more certain is it to be achieved, according to this viewpoint. Conversely, integration has less prospects of success, the lower the expectations placed in it. But false starts at a lower integration level do not necessarily exclude subsequent new starts at a higher level with a smaller number of actors.

The Commonwealth Caribbean, like hardly any other integration area, has had primary experience with almost all forms of integration: Incorporation by force of arms in the British Empire; then, the looser collaboration of the Leeward and Windward Islands under one Governor; the 1958-62 West Indies Federation; then, the St. Kitts and Nevis Confederation; finally the unitary states of the island groups of Antigua and Barbuda, Trinidad and Tobago, the Bahamas, Grenada and St. Vincent and the Grenadines. The Caribbean Community, the OECS and the mooted state form of the Windward Islands are only the more recent results of integration attempts going back over centuries.

Only rarely have the processes of integration and disintegration in the Commonwealth Caribbean been analysed by indigenous authors, by using integration theories. Studies by Vaughan Lewis, Hugh Springer and William Demas have been exceptions. Other authors (e.g. Sherlock and Augier) have studied Caribbean integration from a historical and descriptive point of view, or from one of interdependence and dependence, to a great extent. Numerous analysts within and outside the Caribbean have treated this region as the backyard of the United States. Additionally, they have regarded the dependence on the big neighbour to the North as the main obstacle to the collective and autonomous development of Commonwealth Caribbean States.[390] The geopolitical changes towards the end of the 1980s made such analyses and prognoses quickly obsolete. Neither had they foreseen the failure of the Cuban model nor the marginalization of this region, owing to the changed economic interests of the industrialised states.

In view of the failure of central economic planning in Trinidad and Tobago, Jamaica and Guyana, even Marxists, such as C.Y. Thomas, came to have an understanding of an opening towards the market economy and structural adjustment. But they did not become supporters of CARICOM in its contemporary form. On the other hand, conservative adherents of Commonwealth Caribbean integration, such as James Mitchell, who had repeatedly warned against the threatened loss of significance of the fragmented world of small island states of the Commonwealth Caribbean and, therefore, urgently demanded their political union, were able to stay in the right. In this, however, knowledge gleaned from integration theory played so negligible a role as to be virtually non-existent.

The predictability of the theoretical constructs of, *inter alios*, Deutsch, Friedrich, Nye, Haas and Harrison ends where phenomena — such as small size, insularity, underdevelopment, lack of ethnic homogeneity, colonial bureaucracy and the two-party system — clash as determinants combined in the integration process. The focus of integration research on large continental states or islands of considerable size does not reduce the applicability to the Caribbean on general principles. But it does make it necessary to add supplements to those principles.

The insularity of the small Caribbean states is more than merely geographical. Indeed, their 'almost inevitable consequence' (Lowenthal and Clarke, 1982, p. 235) is particularism. While political reason demands the collaboration of small states, which are both weak economically and exposed from the viewpoint of security policy, with larger units, the democratic structures that

[390] For several other authors in the region: e.g. Beckford, Girvan, Munroe, Gordon K. Lewis, Kari Levitt, Nettleford and Clive Thomas

replaced the colonial era of imposed rule, favour the striving of individuals for autonomy and freedom. Such persons fear — reinforced by historical experience — heteronomy and non-transparent structures. This posture is aided and abetted by the water separating the units and also by the great distances between them. The largest common unit in which the residents were prepared to submit themselves to Governments resulting from elected Parliaments, was their own island of residence. This is confirmed by the secessionist efforts to which Caribbean archipelagic states have been repeatedly exposed.

Insularity is, in fact, the decisive factor separating the Commonwealth Caribbean States and territories. As Hugh Springer observed (1962, pp. 46ff), following the failure of the West Indies Federation of 1958-62, Caribbean unity would not have needed a federation, had the states and territories involved not been divided by the Caribbean Sea. The integration potential defined by Deutsch (1954) and Nye (1971) is sufficiently present in the states of the Commonwealth Caribbean. Indeed, it exists there in greater measure than in the European Union. The *compatibility of the behaviour* of the actors and the *interchangeability of the groups* exist, as a result of common language, education, training and uniform professional qualifications, even while maintaining variety. *Convergence in critical areas* also exists — thanks to the ability to create consensus in ideological positions and the marginalization of extreme ideologies.

An *equilibrium of transactions* exists only in part owing to the differing development, resources and differences in geographical size of the various units. The *reciprocity of benefits* is also objectively in place; but, subjectively, is not assessed uniformly; certainly there is not sufficient *confidence of the actors in the impartiality of distribution. Equality in the developmental level of communications* exists. *Frequency of transactions* changes with geographical proximity. The *speed of transactions* is being improved in the course of technical progress, so is the *accuracy of communications,* but also require some change of mentality. The *equality of the effect of transactions* and the *equilibrium of initiative in transactions* exist as well, though also varying with the geographical position of the actors. The *degree of openness in transactions* varies from high (in the Eastern Caribbean) to rather low (on the periphery). Finally, the postulate of *low or exportable costs* of integration is satisfied in the Caribbean Community only in the sense that liabilities are borne by external donors. A common adjustment to *external factors* takes place to a high degree and very flexibly.

The Commonwealth Caribbean has qualities which allow it to be considered as a *sub-system* (*cf.* Mols, 1982; and Lewis and Singham, 1967). The region has established itself, in Vaughan Lewis' terms (1984a, pp. 38-41) as a *diplomatic zone* or *diplomatic theatre.* It has not yet, however, become an autonomous integration area — i.e. a substantially self-sustaining area, such as Vaughan Lewis has himself demanded; but it has nonetheless developed into an area which accepts certain common norms of behaviour in the definition and the solution of conflicts. In the entire Caribbean, no other of such *diplomatic theatre* is visible, but perhaps the new Association of Caribbean States could develop into one. The deepening of integration in the Commonwealth Caribbean ranks, however, ahead of expanding the integration area, which would be tantamount to merely pursuing just the concept of a Common Market (*cf.* Axline, 1979, p. 201).

In a certain sense, Commonwealth Caribbean immigrant communities (e.g. in New York, Toronto or London) are a mirror image of what the Caribbean Community could be. Certainly, there, too, tensions handed down between various nationalities can be seen. But, on the other hand, a higher sense of community can also be observed. This is expressed in both cultural events and common political lobbying.

The insular situation is the main reason why conventional integration theories can be applied only with difficulty to the Commonwealth Caribbean. All theses on integration and disintegration obtained deductively from observing the development of other integration areas are conditioned by the differing quality of the geographical neighbourhood (*cf.* Springer, *op. cit.* p. 46). The 1958-62 West Indies Federation developed, in Springer's view, its own dynamics, which, after overcoming structural weaknesses in a more favourable geographical constellation, would certainly have been able to save that federation. In the early 1990s, however, the Caribbean integration movement, despite the most favourable combination of external pro-federal factors since the creation of the Community, was in a state of integration and resignation.[391]

The advocates of integration (*cf.* Vaughan Lewis, 1984a; Wiltshire-Brodber, 1983; and Demas, 1990) have tried to overcome the geographical obstacles by defining various integration areas. The following seven such regions can be distinguished:

- an external integration area comprising all states and territories of the Caribbean Basin, including those on the mainland;
- a circle of selected Caribbean states and territories in direct relationship with the Caribbean Community (CARICOM) and, therefore, including, in addition to the latter, Venezuela, Colombia, Mexico, the Dominican Republic, Puerto Rico, the Netherlands Antilles, Suriname and the USVI;
- both, full and associated Member States and territories of the Caribbean Community (CARICOM);
- the OECS Member States and territories;
- the Leeward Islands states and territories of Antigua and Barbuda, Montserrat and St. Kitts and Nevis;
- the Windward Islands states and territories of Dominica, Grenada, St. Lucia and St. Vincent and the Grenadines;
- the States of the Manning Initiative, Barbados, Guyana and Trinidad and Tobago.

The development of integration in these areas depends on the future shaping of internal and external pro-federal factors and the answer to this question: Does a combination of the two forces succeed in achieving a binding transfer of values to new actors of a common government, legislative and judiciary — despite the geographical conditions and the centrifugal tendencies resulting from this?

---

[391] See Press commentaries on the July, 1992, CARICOM Summit in *CR* 23.7.1992, p. 2.

4.3 The Participation Factor in the Integration Movement

Commonwealth Caribbean integrationists do not constitute a mass movement. In Demas' words (1987, p. 33), 'It is totally unrealistic and indeed romantic that by some spontaneous process the people would arise one day and demand political union. In a democratic society, political leaders, by definition, always have to be somewhat ahead of the people — but of course not too far ahead.' Political union of the Commonwealth Caribbean is, in fact, rather the concern of the *élites*. By means of their education and frequent interaction, they have come to know international models — especially the European Union and integration associations in Latin America; and they have always worked together supra-regionally. In contrast, as Nadir (1989, p. 74)[392] has observed, the majority of the population has rather a nationalistic orientation. Indeed, even in the Eastern Caribbean, that majority is only half-heartedly in favour of efforts at unity.

The risks of failed integration are also disproportionately larger for that population segment than they are for the *élites* whose members are more flexible professionally and, because of their technical competence and linguistic knowledge, less tied to any one place. They have better prospects to migrate. Conversely, they are less exposed than members of the lower population segments to the pressure of competition from immigrants, who take advantage of the freedom of movement made available in the integration area. Intra-Caribbean collaboration, as measured by election manifestos and slogans used by political parties to obtain Parliamentary majorities, has an extremely low priority. Indeed, James Mitchell is one of the few leaders of such parties who have dared to take Caribbean political unity as an election slogan and have been elected. Thus, in an interview in the weekly, *The Island Sun* (1987c, p. 11) he pointed out that Caribbean political union was one of the 'fundamental principles' of his New Democratic Party; and that each new NDP member and prospective election candidate must support this position. 'All my life,' he declared, 'I have campaigned for this issue. We had a by-election recently in which I articulated [our pro-unity position] and we increased the majority.'[393]

It is, in fact, difficult to propagate views about surrendering certain areas of national sovereignty in countries which have fought for decades for their independence and have paid the price in blood for this. As Mitchell has put it (1987b, p. 21) 'The ordinary man in the street who is beginning to learn his new anthem, identify with the flag, and who has settled into his particular ambience, may not understand why we Prime Ministers are anxious for another kind of change.'

Most spectacularly, N.W. Manley experienced this reality — but not first in 1962, when he had to surrender political power to the JLP Opposition, after the latter's massive anti-Federation campaign. Indeed, in the first and last elections to the Federal Parliament in 1957, the anti-Federal forces in Jamaica won more Parliamentary seats than did the ihtegrationists. In Trinidad and Tobago, the

---

[392] Manzoor Nadir, a Guyanese, was for some time General Secretary of the St. Lucia-based Caribbean Youth Conference and serves now in the same capacity with the Caribbean Youth Institute in Georgetown/Guyana, where he is the Leader of the United Force Party and a Member of Parliament.

[393] The 1989 and 1994 general elections in St. Vincent and the Grenadines again confirmed this

People's National Movement, under the federalist, Dr. Eric Williams, lost votes. In 1962, then Grenadian Opposition Leader, Herbert Blaize successfully fought an election on the theme of Grenada leaving the 'Little Eight' truncated rump of the 1958-62 West Indies Federation.

St. Vincent and the Grenadines' Prime Minister, James Mitchell, knows only too well why he cannot risk holding alone in his country a referendum on political union and, therefore, has urged simultaneous referenda in all participating OECS Member States and territories. Two Opposition parties in his country are members of SCOPE.[394] *Standing Conference of Popular Democratic Parties in East Caribbean States.* In the event of separate days for the referenda, united efforts could well be made by all SCOPE-affiliated parties to obtain a negative result ('No' or 'Not like that' or 'Not yet') in St. Vincent and the Grenadines. Such a result would send a clear signal to the other interested countries. Mitchell and Demas (1987, pp. 31ff) posit that the opposition parties would cautiously recommend a 'yes' vote in simultaneously-held referenda, in order to benefit from a positive result.

Only the actual behaviour of the people enables one to discover whether the thought of Caribbean unity and consciousness has penetrated the population of the CARICOM Member States and territories. Electoral and voting patterns yield important circumstantial evidence.

Other indicators are as follows:

a) *The link of one's personal life plans with living in the Caribbean*

In 1980, Morissey conducted a study of 781 15-year-old secondary school students from seven English-speaking Caribbean countries[395], who were asked to rate forty countries in their order of preference and rejection as places of residence, giving reasons for their first-placed and last-placed choices.

The United States topped their list, followed by Canada, Barbados, Great Britain, Trinidad and Tobago, Australia and Mexico. Iran was at the bottom of the list, with Jamaica ranked 38th; and the then USSR, Saudi Arabia, South Africa and Indonesia on the other lowest ranks.

The 105 young Jamaicans rated their country third, after the USA and Canada, followed by Panama, the UK, France, Barbados and Australia.

It would obviously be rather difficult to get such young people to work for the long-term improvement of living conditions in their home countries.

The larger CARICOM Member States are exposed to an influx of untrained or only semi-skilled workers from the smaller island states. Their own skilled labour force, however, migrates to the industrialised countries — that is, increasingly to the USA and Canada, in view of the restrictive immigration policy of the UK since 1960. Jamaica, Trinidad and Tobago, Guyana and Grenada have had the biggest losses.[396]

At the start of the 1980s[397], the Jamaican social scientist Professor Carl Stone (1982a, p. 78) put to a representative sample of adult Jamaicans the following question: 'Do you think Jamaica would be better off if we gave up our independence to become a state of the United States?' Forty-three percent of the

---

[394] Please see chapter 2.2.8.

[395] That is, Barbados, Belize, Grenada, Guyana, Jamaica, Montserrat and Trinidad and Tobago

[396] *cf Caribbean Development*, 7 and 52

[397] Precise dates, in terms of the year of the poll, were not published.

sample replied, 'Yes, [we] would be better off', as against 53% who answered in the negative: 'No, [we] would not be better off.' The 'don't knows' accounted for 4%. A somewhat different picture emerged, when the replies were evaluated according to party preference. Thus, 57% of the pro-US Jamaica Labour Party supporters gave a positive reply; 65% of the People's National Party supporters, however, were opposed; and 52% of the politically uncommitted also gave a negative reply. The results for the Jamaica Labour Party showed that the supporters of then Prime Minister Edward Seaga, at least at the time of the poll, gave a markedly lower preference to national sovereignty than to integration with the near-by super-power. In this context, the example of Puerto Rico may well have been the force behind their posture. Puerto Rico, it will be remembered, receives significant US subventions and privileges from its special Commonwealth status.

b) *Political Socialisation*

In December, 1981, Carl Stone (*ibid.*, pp. 38ff) put to 1,000 Jamaican nationals over eighteen years old and to 500 14-17 year-olds the following question in a representative public opinion poll: 'What things can we be proud of?' Forty-eight percent of the adherents of the then ruling JLP replied 'Not sure' or 'Nothing' — as against 50% of the then opposition PNP and 60% of the politically uncommitted. Of those in the three groups who gave positive replies, 23%, 14% and 11% indicated the 'right to vote'; 'good leaders': 8%, 2% and 2%; 'freedom of speech': 3%, 3% and 2%; 'people benefit': 4%, 2% and 1%; and 'stable Government': 4%, 1% and 2% respectively. The pollster regarded these results as a sign of an inadequate political learning process or political socialisation and 'reflecting more than just an under-current of cynicism', given the high level of voter participation and party activity, and since 48-60% of those who replied could find nothing to be proud of in Jamaican politics.

c) *Integration of the Races*

Especially in Trinidad and Guyana, tensions exist between the large Indian population and the African population that has long been politically dominant. In 1962, the Indian minority in Trinidad suspected, behind Dr. Eric Williams' unitary state plans, a plot of the African population to stabilise its majority rule permanently by the massive influx of blacks from neighbouring states (*cf.* Payne, 1980, p. 34). Similar reasons were suspected in Guyana behind Forbes Burnham's invitation to the Caribbean population to migrate to his thinly-settled country (*ibid.*, p. 73). Fr. Ron Peters, Jesuit, summarised his experiences in Guyana as follows: 'Indians, Africans, Portuguese, Chinese and Amerindians, living together for 150 years, have not learned to love and respect each other' (*Catholic Standard*, Guyana, 29.7.1984, p. 2).

d) *Views on Integration*

Broad foundations for Caribbean integration can come about, in Stone's view (1989c) only if the political leaders are convinced that political unity can solve the region's problems: Beyond all rhetoric, he held, there are not many signs of real conviction that regionalism can bring any long-term solutions. Many leaders, who play prominent roles in small states, are not qualified to hold corresponding posts in larger countries. Regional integration, for them, would, therefore, mean a loss — or, at least, a sharing — of power and prestige. Consequently, such political integration has greater prospects of being implemented, if those holding power are certain of at least being able to retain their previous power, after the transfer of functions to the new central authority. This would be possible, with many participating states, only in a rather loose confederation with a weak central Government — or in a federation of a few neighbouring units of roughly equal demographic and geographical size and similar in economic terms.

In the past, Caribbean politicians repeatedly took the worsening of relationships with other states of the Caribbean Community in their stride for the sake of keeping popular support (*cf.* Vaughan A. Lewis, 1984b, p.68). An impression of instability of intra-regional relationships is thereby created. The long-term interests of the political actors, however, see to it that the integration process is not interrupted or even broken off permanently.

Commonwealth Caribbean politicians are in the habit of making their tiny states out to be the centre of the universe for the favours of which world leaders, transnational firms and the international financial agencies allegedly tear themselves apart. This myth may also have contributed to the disorientation of the local population. On the other hand, advocates of integration point to the condescending behaviour characterising the relationship.[398] France's President General Charles de Gaulle is said to have scathingly referred to the 'specks of dust' in the Caribbean Sea, as a way of indicating the insignificance of regional states. Terms, such as the US 'soft underbelly', 'backyard' or 'front garden', reportedly come from the US Government.

Opposition to integration does not become more credible, if integration efforts are misrepresented as being a plot of profit-addicted power politicians — or even as a conspiracy directed from abroad.[399] Stone (1989b, pp. 73ff) found that only some 5% of the Jamaican voters understood the economic realities and political options of their country. How much more difficult, he extrapolated from this, must it be to make Caribbean public opinion understand the questions facing the region at the start of the twenty-first century. Conspiracy theories had to serve as a model for explaining economic decline. Stone hoped that the educational system would provide Caribbean people with energy, the motivation and the dynamism to bring about solutions forcibly.

e) *The Attitude of NGOs, Interest Groups and Functional Institutions*

As long ago as in 1971, Shridath Ramphal (p. 24) found that the non-government organisations had undertaken an initiative to involve broad population segments in integration, in a process of natural and almost spontaneous co-operation:

> 'Our trade unions were perhaps the pioneers in this pursuit of strength through regional action. Today, they have been joined by many others — by our commercial and manufacturing communities, by our teachers, by our public servants, by our engineers, by our lawyers, by our nurses, by our cane farmers, by our clergymen, by our musicians, by our sportsmen, by our writers, by our broadcasters, and now, in the year of 'Women's Lib', by our women. And this is by no means an exhaustive

[398] *cf* Mitchell, in: Brana-Shute.

[399] *cf* for instance, the attacks by SCOPE (in chapter 2.2.8).

> catalogue, for no list has yet been compiled, so natural and uncontrived has been the growth. No less significant, on the other side of Governments, our radical, reformist and protest groups have themselves sought co-ordination and joint action in pursuit of their 'new world'. The foundations of nationhood are truly being laid by the people of the West Indies themselves; they have much to contribute to the building of the mansion in which we must all dwell.'

The Group of Caribbean Experts pointed to the significance of NGOs, which are important for the creation of an environment, a consciousness and interest, which facilitates the successful working of the rather conventional state integration organisations (*The Caribbean Community in the 1980s*, p. 98).

f) *Intensity of Informal Relationship of the Caribbean Population*

The *élites* of the Commonwealth Caribbean recognised quite early that, seen objectively, good pre-conditions do exist for regional states and their populations to work together. Most of these geographical areas, despite their insularity, are linked with one another by historical, ethnic, cultural, linguistic and political commonalties. Indeed, their small size is, in this regard, an advantage (*cf. inter alios*, Lewis and Singham, 1967). The existence of a common cultural foundation in the units participating in the integration process (Gordon K. Lewis, 1984, p. 52) is the pre-condition for the coming into being of the voluntary integration of a region. This foundation must be laid with the ordinary people. Regional feelings cannot be created by ideological statements; nor does unity repose on a constitution or wishful thinking. Popular institutions — especially churches and cults in the Commonwealth Caribbean — are important aids in forming consciousness.

Regional integration can hardly become a reality, as long as it is striven for by a small group of political enthusiasts or liberal technocrats — and does not have the broad approval of the population. Indeed, then Caribbean Community (CARICOM) Secretary General, Roderick Rainford (1984, p. 17) has found an 'inner instinctive drive' and a 'social and psychological imperative' to collaborate, which predates institutional co-operation, among the people of the Anglophone Caribbean.

Alister McIntyre, on the other hand, has regarded all Third World integration movements as suffering from not obtaining the support of their people for the objective of integration (1984b, p. 25). But, if self-reliance is the main objective of the integration movement, then rather large population segments including the private sector must be involved in the process. Supranational integration movements must also, he has held, proceed more from the bottom towards the top; and from within (i.e. the national level) outwards, towards the regional level, and not conversely.

The 'integration movement', properly speaking, takes place in migration and trade. Errol Barrow (*CC* July, 1987, p. 8) opined that, even when the population did not sometimes understand the nature of regional integration, the latter had long been a reality with the people. Thus, in Barbados, families, judging by their origins, were no longer exclusively Barbadian, Barrow pointed out: 'We have Barbadian children of Jamaican mothers, Barbadian children of

Antiguan and St. Lucian fathers, and there is no need to mention Trinidad and Tobago who have always been tied to us not only by the inestimable bonds of consanguinity, but by the burgeoning cross-fertilisation of cultural art forms.'

Wiltshire-Brodber (1984, pp. 192ff) found a 'strong integration movement' in Caribbean countries, the population of which was integrated with one another by close political, economic and social bonds. Indeed, massive population movements took place in an inner core centring on Trinidad and Tobago, St. Vincent and the Grenadines and Grenada. Around that inner core, the immigration state, Guyana, and the emigration target Barbados stood, in a way, as the next ring. The colonial office had repeatedly canvassed the idea of promoting emigration from the rest of the Commonwealth Caribbean to Guyana — and this was discussed after the country's independence in 1966 by then Prime Minister and later President Linden Forbes Burnham (*cf.* Payne, 1980, pp. 73-74).[400]

With increasing distance from that core, the bonds of integration have weakened. Thus, both Barbados and Guyana have less bonds to the core; and the weakest links are in the external areas (e.g. Jamaica, the Bahamas and Belize).

On the periphery, links exist to extra-regional neighbouring states (e.g. Trinidad with Venezuela; Guyana and Suriname with Brazil; Brazil and Venezuela; Dominica and St. Lucia with the French *départments* of Guadeloupe and Martinique; Jamaica with Panama, Cuba and Costa Rica; the Bahamas with the USA; and, finally, Belize with Mexico and Central America).

Wiltshire-Brodber (*op. cit.*, p. 194) has represented the *strength of the bonds*, along the lines of the centre-periphery model in six concentric circles around that inner core; on a scale of one (the strongest) to six (the weakest bond to the centre). The OECS and Guyana have a reading of one to four; Jamaica, one of five, with the Bahamas, Belize and the Virgin Islands at six.

The strength of these bonds (*loc. cit.*) is determined by the following:

- Multiple loyalties;
- the Free Movement of Labour and Capital;
- Strong Trade Ties;
- Shared Services;
- High Level of Political Participation;
- Common Language, Culture and History.

Using Jamaica as an example, this author (*ibid.*, p. 198) showed that a country can be integrated by means of administrative functionalism. In that context, Jamaica was seen as linked with the rest of the region by means of CARICOM mechanisms, an economic *élite* with trans-national interests, an intellectual élite, Rastafarianism and sport. The two last-named factors had, on this view, the character of involving the masses of the people. Jamaica's integration in the Caribbean Community was seen as a slow, reversible process. This was because the basic fundamentals were too weak to absorb the inevitable conflict of the *élite*.

[400] Other Guyanese politicians — e.g Eusi Kwayana (1970) — have also suggested balancing out the high population density of numerous Caribbean islands by transferring some of their people to thinly-populated Guyana.

In 1980, the Group of Caribbean Experts that has already been referred to, urged the fuller involvement of the people of the region in the integration process by means, *inter alia*, of the following steps:

- encouragement of the press and other media to devote more attention to deeper and more extensive coverage of regional integration, development and other related issues;
- measures to encourage more intraregional travel;
- the bringing together of young people from different parts of the region to enable them to get to know and understand each other better;
- the establishment of a Standing Committee of Ministers of Information as an institution of the Community;
- the continuation and strengthening of the general policy of giving West Indians more favourable access to employment in both the public and private sectors over nationals of third countries;
- where applicable, the introduction of dual citizenship as between CARICOM States and making it easier for nationals of other CARICOM Member States to become residents of a CARICOM country than for nationals of third countries;
- organisation by the Secretariat, with the agreement of Member States, of a series of public forums in Member Countries for the purpose of giving information about CARICOM and obtaining 'feedback' views from the public;
- greater support should be given to the intellectual and artistic community in the region who have through their work contributed much to a sense of Caribbean consciousness. (*The Caribbean Community in the 1980s*, pp. 124-125).

Political integration — and this is not only the view of Demas (1987, pp. 32ff) — cannot arise merely from functional co-operation or the Caribbean-friendly consciousness of the population. Certain far-reaching decisions by the leadership are needed here.

Without a strong central Government, the West Indian nations would, after centuries of insular isolation, never come together, according to the political scientist and historian, Professor Gordon K. Lewis (1968, p. 370), in discussing the failure of the 1958-62 West Indies Federation. In Lewis's view, the collective revolt against the Imperial power, which aroused integrative forces in other countries, was absent in the West Indies. Only collective efforts in areas of perceptible common interest led to unity. Public education campaigns were of little use. In contrast, central economic planning and inter-dependence could make one nation out of the West Indies, he claimed.

On the other hand, Lewis's thesis, adduced (1968) in the same context, that federal consciousness is the result and, hence, not the starting point of creating a Federation, is not shared by other authors. It is really to be seen in the context of the period of its creation at the end of the 1960s, when the integration movement seemed actually to sink in the waves of isolationist efforts at political independence.

4.4 Integration and the Democratic System

Broad consensus is one pre-condition for achieving political unity. Democratic states ensure the stability of integration by means of legitimacy obtained by the approval of the population. For this reason, the process of integration is particularly difficult in democracies.

Politicians in such states are obliged to obtain popularity by measures which must show positive results after only a short time.[401] But political integration demands measures whose results can be seen only in the long-term — which is not the time-frame for their decisions whose results keep them in power. Politicians face the risk that their decisions must prove able to give them victory at the polls in four to five years. Indeed, the time-frame for achieving such results is usually shorter. This is because of the differing term limits and Parliamentary legitimacy of Governments in several countries which have to take the decisions involved in the unification process. Those decisions, too, stand under the pressure of the polarising two-party system and a first-past-the-post election system oriented more to personalities than to statements of facts and to programmes.

Democratic structures are, on the one hand, the pre-condition for the durability of integration movements. On the other hand, however, popular acceptance is the biggest obstacle on the way from the *low* politics of integration to the levels of *high* politics.[402] Functional co-operation can also be implemented in the existence of a majority of the population that is less ready for integration, if many people can immediately benefit directly from it. Here, too, it has had the best results in the CARICOM region, e.g. in health, education, prevention and dealing with natural catastrophes — services affecting everybody, without affecting the freedom of making political decisions here. The *spill-over* (Schmitter, 1970) from co-operation to the formation of common institutions is the most advanced, and the barriers of even an integration area extending beyond the CARICOM region are the easiest to surmount.

Integration sections with current costs but only future, long-term benefits, requiring even initial sacrifice[403] and the 'strategy of the long-distance runner', behave differently. Karl Theodore (1988, p. 27)[404] has pointed out the risks posed to the readiness for integration by removing all trade barriers within the Caribbean Community, if the population is not made to understand the possible meaning of such a measure. How would some countries react, if unemployment or a worsening of the foreign trade balance resulted directly from this? Indeed, do the countries of the region remain fully responsible for their foreign debts, even when the removal of trade barriers led to a fall in the foreign currency reserves of some of them?

The expectations of the Caribbean population with respect to the justice of allocation of benefits are marked by personal experiences. In small states, in which everybody knows everybody else, impartial behaviour is possible only

---

[401] Thus, the following question, at the start of the 1970s, by then St. Kitt's Premier (and ex-Federal Minister) Robert Bradshaw. 'Son, do you know our West Indian people like to sow today, and reap yesterday?' (Mitchell, 1987b, p. 22).

[402] 'High' and 'low' (*cf.* Nye, 1968, p. 335) denote the level of irreversibility in political integration.

[403] Please see, on this, Augier, 1989, p. 22.

[404] He is a Lecturer in the Department of Economics, UWI, St. Augustine.

with great difficulty, as was stated in the author's preface to this work. The acting persons are evaluated more according to feelings and personal esteem than on the facts (*cf.* Neish, 1991). Nonetheless, confidence in the equal allocation of the costs and benefits of integration is one of the pre-conditions for popular approval and consensus.

A five-year election cycle has little prospects of convincing low-income population segments of improvements expected in the future. Vaughan Lewis (1984a, p. 30) has also pointed out this drawback. Since governmental programmes at national level focus on visible, short-term benefits, democracy is rather an obstacle in the integration process for Axline as well (1979, p. 202). Only the absence of a strong Opposition enabled Dr. Eric Williams in Trinidad and Tobago and President Forbes Burnham in Guyana to play a less nationalistic role. In Jamaica, owing to the strong anti-regional Opposition to pro-regional PNP Governments under both N.W. and Michael Manley, such a role was not granted to them. If the integration movement is to convince the population of the necessity of political union, then links have to be forged between the economic and political effectiveness of the total Community obtained by creating a larger central unit, on the one hand, and, on the other, the desire of the residents for greater participation in the formation of their direct living space (*cf.* Vaughan Lewis, 1989, p. 17). Here, opponents of integration easily hit the weakest point of the unity movement: Namely, that the population is not willing to let itself become legally incapacitated by distant central Governments, on account of long-term and, moreover, still clearly unproved economic, foreign and security policy benefits. An area of conflict arises between integration and insularism on which the integration movement of the small island states of the Commonwealth Caribbean could be thwarted.

As Karl Theodore (1988, p. 29) has put it, the residents of the Caribbean Community are by no means faced with the alternative of 'integrate or die'. In reality, it is so, Theodore has held, that 'each country actually believes that with a little help now and then from the USA, or the EEC, or from some export commodity cartel, it can really make it without coming together with other countries in the region.'[405] For many, the choice taken with or without integration is rather an abstract one. The task of the integration movement, according to Theodore, is to make integration appear to be the more attractive choice. And this is possible only with facts.

Theodore (*op. cit.* pp. 28ff) has proposed that the education of the Caribbean residents on integration should begin with a subject affecting everybody: Namely, the security of regional food supply. The problem, he has stated, would be clearer, if it were made plain to the people that they spend about one billion US dollars yearly on food imports. The people could be made to understand that it is important to produce more of the food they need to eat, to arrange to import collectively and on a regional basis — and thereby save invaluable foreign currency.

[405] Similarly, Vaughan Lewis (1984a, p 31) has claimed that small countries await a free ride through the international system in which the larger countries meet the costs of bilateral economic co-operation, thereby making insular independence possible.

Carl Stone (1989a, pp. 31-34) warned against over-estimating the economic benefits of Caribbean integration. The regional market, he claimed, was quite small; and a whole range of goods, which the Member States and territories could offer each other, had already been produced there anyway. Economic benefits reside at most in competition, which could lead to the improved quality of the goods supplied.

Stone regarded the political advantages as more important. A larger state could dissolve the authoritarian power structures which had been created in the small units, and contribute to the maturation of Caribbean democracy. But this very division of power is one of the reasons why, in his view, Caribbean political unity has not yet come about. Those holding power just did not want to lose it.

5. Future Prospects for Caribbean Integration

In 1972, the year preceding the creation of the Caribbean Community, then CARIFTA Secretary-General, William Demas (1974, p. 47) addressed trade unionists in Guyana in the following terms:

> 'On the purely economic side it is often argued that if the West Indian countries move steadily along the road to closer economic integration, they will wake up one morning and find that they are politically united. This may well be so. But the relationship may also work in the opposite way! We will probably not get very far along the road to purely economic integration unless we are conscious that the ultimate goal is political union.'

Almost twenty years later, however, the prospects of political union did not seem more favourable. Demas's countryman, the Trinidadian born sportsman, jurist and writer, Ian McDonald[406] (1990, p. 116) then stated as follows:

> 'I am cynical in the extreme about any possibility of political integration. The rolling periods of fine rhetoric will continue to flow at convenient times, such as at CARICOM Summits, but nothing practical will happen. There is no chance whatsoever of political power in the individual states being ceded to a federal West Indian authority. For decades one has heard, like an oft-repeated mantra, politicians speak of the absolute need, in a ruthless world, for West Indian political unity. But nothing has happened and nothing will happen.'

McDonald's evaluation of the Common Market (*ibid.*, p. 118) was equally merciless:

> 'I am only fractionally less cynical about making real progress towards a West Indian common market. It is like a mirage on a desert path. A green oasis with flowering trees and splendid battlements beckon you, only to shimmer in the ever-riding hot air and disappear completely as you get near enough to touch reality. Our leaders continuously stress 'the cardinal importance of re-vitalising intra-regional trade and payments and of achieving greater co-operation and co-ordination of efforts in the field of production'. Word-smoke, I fear, mere word-smoke. Good intentions and splendidly worded minutes dissolve in the face of hard reality.'

External factors at least do not stand in the way of the region growing together both economically and politically, and are beneficial in many cases. *Internal factors*, however, inhibit rather strong economic and political integration — as, indeed, the Group of Caribbean Experts who studied the projected development of the Caribbean Community in the 1980s, found. 'Weaknesses at the national level' were the main reason for CARICOM not exerting greater influence on regional development. In their view, the community, through its mere existence, could not — and here was one of the principal misunderstandings of the role of

[406]Former Secretary and President of the *West Indian Society*, now living in Guyana.

Caribbean integration — cure the 'economic ills of the region' and create immediate prosperity for its Member States and territories. Integration, in fact, merely helped to increase the prospects of development and the bargaining power of the region (*The Caribbean Community in the 1980s*, p. 2).

It is doubtful if a line can be drawn between political union and economic integration, as urged by, *inter alios*, Payne (1980, p. 269). He has himself argued that the Caribbean Community can do no more than co-ordinate governmental policy on a regional basis. Such limitation to a co-ordinating function is certainly true of CARICOM in its condition in the mid-1990s — but is also a weakness! A Community, from which any member can opt out as it wishes, if it no longer wishes to be 'co-ordinated' in the event of a disagreement, can, in the long-run, exert a positive influence on neither a greater bargaining power nor the development prospects, as already mentioned in the report of the Group of Caribbean Experts. Such a loosely-constituted working association, without binding commitment, can most certainly not deal with economic crises, social unrest or acute problems of internal or external security; which, owing to their very nature, puts the readiness for solidarity of its participating Member States, particularly severely to the test. No such Member States will, unless forced by contractual obligations, take risks for the other Member States; at most, extra-ordinary political personalities will, for altruistic objectives, put their careers at risk. Only within the framework of a proper political union on a continuing basis could the Community exercise regulatory functions, with individual Member States or sectors of the economy being temporarily disadvantaged or burdened.

As the above-mentioned Group of Caribbean Experts pointed out, the insularity of the region 'is ever in danger of becoming more than a geographical expression' (*op. cit*., p. 7). That insularity — involving, as it does, psychological resistance to every act of heteronomy, the drive for independence, mistrust of politicians and experts of all types — makes Caribbean integration, without further ado, into a fragile structure. This is quite independent of how close political union may have been welded together. The secessionist efforts of Nevis, Tobago, Barbuda, Union Island and Anguilla clearly show this. Without a firm political structure, CARICOM, as a non-binding co-ordinating instrument, is really tantamount to a superfluous commitment of human and material resources. The tasks could well be co-ordinated by Governments of Member States on a rotating base. Functional co-operation could be performed by means of contracts between interested Governments within and outside the region, through the instrumentality of largely independent institutions.

Despite the stagnation of the integration process, the importance of CARICOM has recently increased. A rapprochement has occurred between the pure South-South co-operation 'self-sufficiency' school of thought and that of a Puerto Rico-type of extreme export orientation. The former has had to understand that even a unified Caribbean market could offer no alternative to the expansion of extra-regional trade and the boosting of exports. The regional market is simply just too small for self-sustained economic growth. Such small markets neither themselves develop nor produce capital goods, machines, transportation equipment and technologies. These small markets remain import-dependent and must export, merely to obtain the foreign currency necessary for this (Carl Stone, 1990d). On the other hand, the export or die school has now realised that production oriented purely towards exports can swiftly collapse. This is partly because of growing protectionism in the larger export markets despite the signing in Marrakech, Morocco, on April 15, 1994, of the Uruguay Round of the General Agreement of Tariffs and Trade (GATT) with the prospects of substantial liberalisation of international trade. Competition with other Third World countries producing similar goods, and development opportunities calculable only over the short-term, are further reasons for this situation. These countries do not push for an expansion of the regional market, though, which they perceive as being too small. The reason for this is that potential additional CARICOM Member States (e.g. the Dominican Republic, Haiti and Cuba) have marketing problems similar to those of the existing Member States and could, in turn, penetrate the market of the Commonwealth Caribbean.

It would be unreasonable to be satisfied with the current state of co-operation in CARICOM. This is provided that the following view, expressed in this book by the author, is correct: Namely, that the improvement of living conditions in the Commonwealth Caribbean can be better achieved by any form of political integration. Postulates for achieving political integration, that can be deduced from the previous chapters of this book and which, with certain reservations, apply also to the OECS and smaller integration areas are as follows:

1. The population of the Commonwealth Caribbean must become confident that general living conditions will improve by means of a political and/or economic union with other Caribbean states rather than through the system existing heretofore of territorial sovereignty. Only in this way can sacrifices be justified. The experience of the past has taught Caribbean people that integration, in contrast to erroneous pronouncements, is not a recipe for automatic economic success. The Caribbean Community (CARICOM) was founded at an extremely inpropitious time — namely during a world economic crisis. It, therefore, had a difficult beginning. The year 1973 marked the start of the first oil price shock of 1973-74, with sharply increasing crude oil prices.

Structural deficits in the industrialised countries led to rising unemployment and heightened protectionist tendencies both among themselves and *vis-à-vis* the Third World. The instruments of collective foreign policy and integrated production contained in the Treaty of Chaguaramas were not implemented. The Community was not able to prove its value in difficult times.

More understanding for the integration process and its conditions must be aroused in the population. At the 1985 CARICOM Summit in Barbados, then Grenadian Prime Minister, Herbert Blaize, who has since died, warned that the Community could have not only advantages, but also its disadvantages (*CP* 32, Supplement, p. 10). Should the regional market contract, and, therefore, put dismissals of workers on the agenda, then that could fan the flames of resentment in the population against the Common Market.

People in the Commonwealth Caribbean know little about the functioning of the Common Market (*cf.* Archibald Moore in: *CP* 15, p. 16). They are, therefore, all ears, when doubts are expressed about the sense of integration.

Scepticism about the latter must be cleared up beforehand, for it could later lead to the renewed break-up of the Community. An advance contribution of confidence is, therefore, necessary, because CARICOM could easily be made later into the scape-goat for all ills. A continuous dispute over the allocation of real or putative benefits derived from the Common Market is, even now, foreseeable.

CARICOM means little to most people living in the region (*cf.* Payne, 1985, p. 226). Indeed, many of them are not even aware that the integration process takes place through the sphere of economics. Former CARICOM Secretary-General, Roderick Rainford, at the end of his tenure, said that, the absence of a living community of West Indians had cemented itself in the consciousness of the people as the biggest failure of CARICOM (*CP* 54 and 55 (January-June, 1992), pp. 8 and 34). Errol Barrow again called attention to the fact that the cultural history common to the people of the region, and their shared experiences, are much older than CARICOM and the trade agreements. In his last CARICOM Summit address, he accused the Governments of the region of not being able to convey to their people the nature and cultural infrastructure of the integration movement, or to arouse their 'collective understanding'. The media, the University, the churches and all institutions bearing the designation, 'Caribbean', should, in Barrow's view, be used to disseminate the message that their region was more than mere trade — and that even trade agreements could be positively influenced by the collective understanding of the Caribbean 'masses'.

According to former Secretary-General of the Caribbean Youth Conference, Manzoor Nadir, the call for a West Indian nation emanated especially from academics, politicians and economists (1989, p. 74). Creativity concerning political integration, Shridath Ramphal has said, should come from the bottom (1985, p.30) and impose itself on the political leadership, which must be part of the movement — but not the movement itself.

The Group of Caribbean Experts already referred to on several occasions, who examined the prospects of CARICOM for the 1980s, concluded that this Community had to 'draw up a fresh affirmation of political and popular will for development'. Indeed, a 'new public dialogue' within and between the countries of the region was, in the view of these experts, necessary (*The Caribbean Community in the 1980s*, pp. 2-3).

2. The Caribbean Member States must be ready to sacrifice at least a part of their sovereignty and national interests. For decades now, their political striving had been for independence from the colonial 'mother country'. In order to cement this, they put everything on promoting national pride with their own flag, national anthem and other signs of formal political independence. It would be difficult for these new nations to surrender these insignia, even if their standard of living was improved by surrendering certain sovereign rights or executive powers. The journalist, Arthur Gay (1985) put it this way: 'No Government is going to do anything which remotely looks like forsaking its national identity, for the sake of such a cumbersome idea as Caribbean unity.'

Regional integration is quite impossible, if national interests are always given priority over the collective concerns of the region. Nor is such integration reconcilable with the principle of unanimity, which obtains in all important decision-making bodies of CARICOM. In fact, the very founding of the OECS was, despite the accompanying rhetoric, a vote of no confidence of the LDCs against the Caribbean Community. One of its main difficulties, as another former CARICOM Secretary-General, Kurleigh King, put it, was to bring both long-term and short-term developmental stages into accord with each other.

3. Both politicians and bureaucrats just cannot avoid surrendering a part of their power for the general good. The 1958-62 West Indies Federation failed, according to Roderick Rainford, because the Caribbean leaders wanted to remain as big fish in a small pond (1986, p. 7). The local kinglets do not wish to share their petty kingdoms with others, at most in subordinate areas.[407] Who, then, will willingly waive his right to the title of Prime Minister (or even of an ordinary Minister of Government) even if he has only a tiny budget and a few employees and the entire population of his tiny country could comfortably fill a rather large football stadium? Otherwise as in, say, Latin America, such Commonwealth Caribbean Heads of Government can be re-elected to office, through repeated electoral victories of their political parties. Even Guyana's Presidential system, which is patterned on Latin American models, has no term limits.[408] Public officers remain in their posts, as a rule, after a change of Government. Thus, neither the Government nor the Civil Service shows a tendency to make itself prematurely redundant.

Carl Stone (1991b) has described the region as easily the most expensively administered group of states in the Third World, with more politicians and bureaucrats per head of the population than anywhere else. Hence, more (not less) politicians and functionaries would result, in his view, from a new West Indies Federation, should politicians in office allow such a structure to come into existence. Not every good idea, Alister McIntyre has warned (1984b, p. 20), immediately gets its own and appropriate institution. Recurringly, CARICOM has over the years become surrounded and bloated by committees and special bodies, which have bureaucratised the integration development in a negative sense, instead of making it progress. It is better, he has claimed, to fall back on available facilities. The region needs a strong Federal Government equipped with a mandate to remodel its economy, thereby making it more competitive and more powerful in an increasingly more competitive world market, according to Stone (1991b).

4. The convention of Commonwealth Caribbean politics should include a self-denying ordinance, preventing national and ethnic prejudices from being used as a weapon against integration. Alexander Bustamante, for instance, built his anti-Federation campaign of the late 1950s on the resentment of Jamaicans against the small islands of the Eastern Caribbean, which allegedly wanted to be fed at Jamaica's expense. Hence, for example, the JLP's logo then of Jamaica as a milch cow, with each of the small islands as a calf drinking milk from its teats. Over three decades later, it would be easy to pit Jamaicans against Antiguans, Trinidadians or Bahamians; and, conversely, Guyana against Trinidad and Tobago, or the latter against Barbados. Similarly, it would also be child's play to

[407] *cf Time for Action*, pp. 77ff.

[408] Such limits are under discussion. For other reasons, considerations exist that the Prime Minister of Antigua and Barbuda is limited to two terms of office and MPs, to three Parliamentary terms.

convince Guyanese or Trinidadian East Indians that they would lose political and economic influence in any scheme involving them working with the other Caribbean states, in view of the latter's African majority.

5. The CARICOM Secretariat must receive Executive power and, financially, have a sound base. Pan-Caribbean Legislative and Judicial branches of Government must be set up. In the long-term, the loose, amorphous structures of the Community strengthen centrifugal tendencies. The CARICOM Secretariat must be put in the position to act as an independent unit and be able to take over the function of creating consensus (*cf.* Gonzales, 1984b, p. 8). Instead, however, its work has been impaired by powerlessness, underfinancing, poor equipment and, consequently, a shortage of suitable personnel. Attention was called to this by the 1990 Report of the Commission headed by then UWI Professor, Gladstone Mills, of Jamaica, which had been established by the CARICOM Heads of Government to evaluate the programmes, institutions and organisations of the Community (*cf.* Mills *et al.*, 1990). Constitutionally, this Secretariat is unable to compel the Member States to implement the decisions agreed on together by their Heads of Government at the CARICOM Summits though Executive Power is vested in the Secretary-General. Nor is it able, owing to human resources deficiencies, to ensure the surveillance of those decisions.

True, many efforts are made to improve the situation of the Secretariat and to follow up the proposals made in the Mills Report and by the West Indian Commission. Its reorganisation is in full gear. However, the very location of the CARICOM Secretariat in Georgetown, Guyana at the southern tip of the region constitutes a significant obstacle to its effectiveness. Economically, Guyana is still the weakest member-state of the Caribbean Community, with an underdeveloped infrastructure, a small, continuously decreasing supply of qualified and trained employees and a certain level of political instability. The CARICOM Heads of Government's demand, on several occasions, for the relocation of this Secretariat has foundered on both the opposition of the Guyanese Government and rivalry of the other participants. The application of the unanimity rule clearly ensures the continuation, therefore, of the *status quo* with this Secretariat remaining on the periphery of the itinerary of visiting politicians and experts. Besides, conditions for holding meetings in Guyana are anything but attractive. Communications there are among the most unreliable in the Commonwealth Caribbean; transportation links are among the worst. The generally poor quality of life and security problems offer little inducements to potential staff-members. Indeed, Guyana has been called a non-developing country (NDC).

Almost all the other related Caribbean institutions and organisations with which this Secretariat must work closely have had to be sited elsewhere — preferably in Barbados — thereby necessitating continual travel by the leading staff-members, in order to meet those bodies personally. The reduced presence of these persons in Georgetown arising from this situation does, however, constitute one of the most important reasons why many CARICOM initiatives do not proceed beyond the stage of being well-meant declarations of intention. The shortage of funds and personnel already alluded to merely exacerbates this.

CARICOM Heads of Government decisions are further delayed in their implementation by the dependence of the Community on extra-regional financial support. Thus, for almost each new measure they decide on, and whose immediate realisation they often announce prematurely, donors have to be sought by the Secretariat. Such donors, as a rule, exert influence on the implementation of the CARICOM Heads of Government decisions — thereby reducing the importance of not only this Secretariat, but also of the Caribbean Community as a whole (*cf.* Nunes, 1986).

The planned — but later renounced — appointment of a CARICOM Commissioner to oversee the carrying out of decisions taken by the Heads of Government was characteristic of the much-used praxis in the Community, whereby new authorities are established when discontentment arises — instead of improving existing ones or giving them plenipotentiary powers. The Commission suggested by the West Indian Commission did, in fact, include the Secretary-General of CARICOM and was supposed to have real executive powers. But it hardly improved the position of the Secretary-General or Secretariat.

In the Commonwealth Caribbean, a strong Executive branch of Government requires, for its legitimacy, a Legislative branch. In this context, the memory of the failed attempts of West Indian Parliamentarism during the existence of the 1958-62 Federation appears to be a principal obstacle. Indeed, a Parliament without influence, with a weak Executive branch, would be really nothing more than an expensive talk shop, with second-class representatives of the people, devoid of a local electoral base, attempting to celebrate national particularism and fan the flames of popular resentment, in order to get the attention of the disinterested local public and not quite totally lose contact with home.

The expanded responsibilities of the CARICOM Secretariat and of a Commission could be initially put in supplementary treaties subject to ratification by the Parliament of each participating member-State. Nonetheless, this would leave both the initiating and controlling functions in the hands of the Heads of Government — and, therefore, in a body, which is by no means representative and has too little democratic legitimacy. These Heads of Government, excepting that of Barbados, reacted with reserve to the proposal of their Barbadian colleague, Erskine Sandiford, for establishing a Caribbean Assembly of Parliamentarians. This was because they would have had to face the possibility of, over time, losing some power themselves.

The establishment of a Caribbean Court of Appeal, as the final judicial instance in the region, has continued to be the subject of controversy. Some demand this step as an expression of real sovereignty; but others see in it no improvement on the system, kept since political Independence, of using for this purpose the Judicial Committee of the UK Privy Council — so long as the individual territories are not even able to satisfy the demands of a national and local jurisdiction. Without this third branch of regional power, however, no political union can exist over time.

6. Caribbean integration must be given a higher priority rating at the level of national policy. At the national level, the implementation of decisions taken at CARICOM Summits is the responsibility of several Ministries of Government or, is better left to their discretion. Often owing to their heavy work load and

limited authority, they follow them up sluggishly or not at all. For this very reason alone, CARICOM Heads of Government deadlines set, cannot be met. Thus, for instance, it took four years merely to work out the new Rules of Origin for finished goods produced in the CARICOM Member States, which was done by the relevant technical Ministries of the latter, following the proposal by the CARICOM Secretariat. Only in Trinidad and Tobago has there existed — and that just at times — a Ministry for West Indian Affairs specifically responsible for, *inter alia*, co-ordinating the preparation and carrying out CARICOM decisions at national level (*CP* 19, p. 9). In 1992, each member agreed to designate a Minister responsible for CARICOM-Caribbean Affairs. The convergence of the economic and developmental policies of the various CARICOM Member States is one of the conditions for economic integration. In the overwhelming majority of cases, regional integration is mentioned only in passing in national development plans, however — to say nothing of specifically including it in the formulation of sectoral programmes and projects (McIntyre, 1984b, p. 8).

7. The private sector must develop larger production and trade units. But, in the Commonwealth Caribbean, it focuses on small and very small firms, apart from a few multinational corporations. Those larger production and trade blocs, involving the merging of capital, knowledge-basis and experts, are indispensable, if CARICOM Member States are to play an appropriate role in world markets. Carl Stone (1991b) pointed to the significant ethnic food market in the UK, Canada and the USA, which has not even manifested the first signs of being taken over by Caribbean interests. Similarly, he argued, the opening up of markets in important regional centres for finished goods, such as Brazil, Mexico, Venezuela and Colombia, has got stuck in isolated arrangements. Indeed, he accused the Commonwealth Caribbean private sector of too much awaiting initiatives from the USA and the helpless and money-less Governments of the region — instead of becoming active themselves.

8. The sale of products and produce from CARICOM must also be promoted within the Community itself. In fact, however, the private sector and its customers prefer those from the industrialised world to ones from their own region. In this context, bad experience by Caribbean consumers with the latter may well have played a secondary role. Contrary to this, the omnipresent consumer-goods advertisements from the USA and the region's underdeveloped self-confidence in its own ability to produce adequate quantities of high-quality goods, make Caribbean consumers turn to even food imported from the USA, Canada or Europe. In actual fact, however, Belize, for example, could supply meat to the entire Community; instead, though, CARICOM Member States, such as Antigua and Barbuda as well as Barbados continue, as before, to buy US beef and pork. This is because, as then foreign Minister of Belize, Eduardo Juan, has complained, his country allegedly cannot satisfy the necessary health and hygienic requirements (*WG* 12.5.1987, p. 14). Belize would also willingly export more citrus to the rest of the Community, but could find a market only in Trinidad and Tobago. Entrepreneurs in Belize are turned against CARICOM, owing to the dearth of markets in that region, he claimed. On the other hand, he pointed out, his country imports paint, etc. from Jamaica, even though it could purchase it considerably cheaper in the USA.

9. Technical and professional experts must be rated more highly in the preparation and implementation of political decisions concerning the realisation of Commonwealth Caribbean integration. The UNDP expert, Frederick E. Nunes, found that the policy pursued in the region, however, tended rather to be driven by ideas than to be fuelled by reliable information: 'The cart has often been ahead of the horse' (1986, p. 26).

Carl Stone (1991b) accused CARICOM of missing the opportunity to develop a think-tank of economists and other experts, who would indicate the options available to the region and point to the direction for productive energy in the activation of trade in the Western hemisphere. Compton Bourne's study on the development of the Caribbean to the year 2000 does provide Stone admitted, a framework for regional political thought. More concrete and specific proposals for production and trade initiatives were needed, however. In this, the University of West Indies in particular was challenged. Others have also issued a challenge for such studies to involve the local University. Thus, then UWI/Mona Institute of Social and Economic Research (ISER) Director, J. Edward Greene, took up an earlier idea of his colleagues from the UWI Cave Hill (Barbados) campus: He proposed a study on the future of the Caribbean, which would reflect the current situation and make concrete proposals. The study would have to go beyond the dependence model, with which Raúl Prebisch analysed Latin American development in the 1960s, thereby producing objective — but not value-free — projections on the future.

Such studies, however, make sense, only when commissioned by CARICOM Heads of Government and have prospects of being implemented. There was no shortage of intelligent studies by Caribbean experts on all sectors of the economy, complained Errol Barrow (*CC* July, 1987, pp. 8-9). But the studies were hardly more taken into account by more persons than from the specialists for — or by — whom they had been written. The problem, in Barrow's view, was this: 'There was no link between that great storehouse of knowledge and the toiling masses of workers who are the motor-force of any society.' Early proponents of South-South co-operation — i.e. the concept of *self-reliance* — such as Clive Thomas, Havelock Brewster, Norman Girvan, and Owen Jefferson, have theoretically prepared the model of the Caribbean Community — but against the backdrop of the hegemony of 'neo-colonialist' powers and marked anti-capitalistic signs. 'A lot of the things made sense on paper, but sufficient attention was not directed towards the mechanism for converting the paper formulation to actual and sustainable programmes,' Thomas (*CP* 30, p.25) has admitted.

In particular, the belief in the superiority of a centrally-oriented state economy, as against initiative of the private sector, was shattered by State misuse in Guyana, gigantic bad investments in prestigious State projects in Trinidad and Tobago, as well as the failure of the Jamaican developmental model under the PNP Government, led by Michael Manley, in 1977-80. Finally, Cuba did not prove to be the ideal developmental model, either; especially since its economic dependence on the previous hegemonic super-power, that is, the then-USSR, became all too clear.

Fauriol (1990, p. 59) criticised the fact that the Anglophone Caribbean interminably discusses its collective future — even while important questions must be swiftly answered about the binding of this region to an environment in which European and US strategy is changing rapidly. The setting up of commissions is a well-loved habit — and that, not only in the Caribbean — as a means of avoiding sustained action, even while simulating deeds. The most striking example in the recent past has been the West Indian Commission set up under Sir Shridath Ramphal, which Stone (1991b) excoriated as a 'colossal waste of time and money; another useless political circus which will produce yet another irrelevant report.' However, neither this report nor others were 'useless' by themselves. They were simply not dealt with honestly and taken seriously.

10. Agreements made must be binding and lasting. Political debates in the institutions of the Caribbean Community are characterised by, as a rule, brutal frankness — but with cheerfulness and readiness to compromise. Only rarely are decisions made by formally voting. In such cases, they are also unanimous, despite reservations — with the consequence that their non-binding nature is clear in the minutes; alternatively, participants at the meeting will seek to explain away, in relativistic terms, the way they voted. Opposition to apparently unanimous decisions also takes the form of voting abstentions, or sudden absence at the very meeting itself. This manner of voting with deviations, satisfies a certain need for harmony felt by politicians and officials, who know each other, are sometimes friends, but do not want to appear to be sabotaging the initiatives of their partners.

This informal manner does give the Commonwealth Caribbean decision-making process a more relaxed character. But, it also means that the decision-makers regard the agreement reached as non-binding, as renegotiable at any time (*cf.* Kurleigh King, 1984, p. 10). This non-binding nature is hidden behind terms, such as the following: Accords; understandings; talks of harmonisation; promises of renewed commitment; assurances of further compliance; or affirmations of conformity (Nunes, 1986, p. 25). The West Indian Commission, in its Report, complained of the absence of the possibilities for sanctions for not honouring agreements made. No institutions existed, it said, which implemented CARICOM laws, ordinances and regulations for carrying them out. Parliaments in the region rarely dealt with CARICOM matters. Governments were not put under Parliamentary or popular pressure in favoür of the Community. No regional political parties existed. Additionally, there was insufficient administrative capacity for implementing decisions at national level (*Time for Action*, pp. 54ff).

Consequently, lip service was paid on all suitable occasions; and decisions were formally agreed on, concerning measures for regional integration, towards which few of those taking those decisions really oriented themselves. Rainford (1990b, p. 7) has identified three types of such decisions: The ritualistic, the perfunctory and real decision. 'It is a pity', complained Arthur Gay in 1985, for many others, 'that people can come together, at such high-powered levels, talk through their problems, in a spirit of understanding, and then walk away from those meetings without the slightest intention of carrying out the noble actions which they said they would.'

Not altogether unsurprisingly, therefore, important agreements in the *Treaty of Chaguaramas* remained unimplemented over two decades later. Although dates for the removal of trade barriers were set on several occasions, no great penchant exists really to expand intra-regional trade, to re-activate the CMCF, which is necessary for this purpose, and to harmonise the national currencies of the various CARICOM Member States.[409] The integration of production has scarcely taken place. But efforts to achieve this are still continuing.

To a great extent, the collective foreign policy has remained largely rudimentary. According to Vaughan Lewis (1989, pp. 7-9), this was clear especially in the 1983 Grenada crisis and the developments in Haiti in 1988. Similarly, collective extra-regional economic negotiations were not continued in a sustained way, after initial successes. Examples of deficient co-ordination include the following: The various Lomé Treaties; CBI-I and II; and CARIBCAN. Consultations of the Governments of CARICOM Member States on a common economic policy have, as Lewis has found, lessened in all. The success of intra-regional trade agreements is, he argued, left to the discretion of unilaterally pursued fiscal and monetary policies of each CARICOM Member State.

With such arbitrary behaviour, the Caribbean Community is deformed into a type of self-service grocery, where a broad range of goods must be on display. Only those on special, at bargain prices, are taken by the customers, however — and on credit, at that. Instead, they buy elsewhere the really profit-making items.

The non-binding nature of CARICOM decisions has its counterpart at the national level. There, after bombastic announcements and ground-breaking ceremonies marked by great pomp and circumstance, large development projects all too often get stuck in their initial phases. Such empty promises, at both national and regional level, result in the loss of political credibility. Moreover, the people, firms and institutions concerned, become oriented extra-regionally. No one reposes any further confidence in declarations of intention meant so honestly, however. The preparations necessary for implementation cease in the relevant state and private sectors. This, in turn, means even well-thought-out and feasible decisions cannot be implemented on a timely basis.

Kurleigh King (1984, p. 11) has pointed to another facet of Commonwealth Caribbean political culture, which makes it difficult to honour agreements: These people, while law-abiding, do not stick to the letter of the law. This has, on the one hand, the advantage of greater flexibility, he has argued; in discussions, one comes swiftly to the point, without caring too much for previous deliberations and agreements or prepared concepts. On the other hand, however, this greater flexibility may lead to a sort of anarchy — to over-hasty decisions, instead of strategies resulting from deliberation and reflection, and also to legal complications.

'On the whole, though,' King has hastened to add, 'it seems to me that our easy, flexible approach has served us well; that is, combined with our small size, it has led to an intimacy or at least a general cordiality, that enhances our

[409] But, at the 1991 CARICOM Summit, the Finance Ministers agreed to conduct intra-regional trade largely in those currencies, instead of on the basis of US dollars — yet another declaration of intention!

progress towards consensus and facilitates a sympathetic understanding of one another's point of view.'

11. Within the Caribbean Community, there must be complete freedom of movement of CARICOM Member States' nationals, best of all by introducing a common CARICOM citizenship. The West-Indian Commission rightly points to the anomaly, whereby foreign tourists were allowed to travel freely throughout the region — sometimes even without passports, one may add — whereas Caribbean people are subjected to all possible humiliations, when travelling there and receive work permits only at a snail's pace (*Time for Action*, pp. 53 and 79). Freedom of movement means being able to travel everywhere within the CARICOM area without a passport; settle; open a business; purchase property (including land); and, after a certain period of residence, to have the same rights and obligations as the nationals of the country of residence. In the mid-1990s, only certain specialist employees, media workers, artists and artistes are accorded this facility.

But freedom of movement also means that many Caribbean people must also be technically given the opportunity to move freely, in a physical sense. Hence, sea and air transport systems must be expanded to make this possible. Instead of numerous, expensive national airlines, one single airline should be maintained — and, where necessary, subsidised. This would make it possible for less profitable air routes to be flown at acceptable fares as well.

12. CARICOM Member States must put a brake on their massive population growth in order to increase their real, per head income and reverse the trend which is clear from the following facts: In 1988, real, per head income in seven of thirteen of these countries was less than that in 1980; and it was in the process of falling in the other six. Instead, the Compton Bourne Report has argued, an annual growth rate of at least 6% must be achieved in real terms in income, in order to meet the problem of unemployment caused by the growth of the population. Up to the year 2000, the 25-49 year-olds — the segment of the labour force most suitable for employment — will increase by 100% in some CARICOM countries; and, even if one makes minimalist assumptions, will grow by an average of 23-54% (*Caribbean Development to the Year 2000*, p. XV). At the same time, the possibilities for emigration will be restricted with increasing severity. The biggest population growth is moreover in the population segments with the least likelihood of being able to migrate to the industrialised countries, even with the most generous and liberal immigration regulations.

The need to satisfy the growing population creates serious balance of payments problems for the CARICOM countries. The costs of developmental planning and internal security rise. True, the number of consumers grows with that of the population. But only someone participating in the production process and earning an income can buy anything (*cf.* Vaughan Lewis, 1984a, pp. 33ff).

Social conflicts arising from the sequelae of over-population could prevent the region from growing together. The more prosperous CARICOM Member States will fight against the influx of neighbouring have-nots. Within the Commonwealth Caribbean, sub-groups of states will probably be formed, which are more easily able to overcome the obstacles on the way to political integration by working together than by collaborating with the rest of the

Community. Thus for example, in the sense of Wiltshire-Brodber's model (1984, p. 194) the inner core should be provided by a Community consisting of the four Windward Island groups, possibly with the addition of Trinidad and Tobago. At a later stage, concentric circles could be constituted by Barbados, Antigua and Barbuda, Montserrat and St. Kitts and Nevis. According to Demas (1988, p. 51) new attempts at integration would occur a few years later, even if the current efforts at achieving political unity in the OECS were unsuccessful. 'The way how I interpret West Indian history is: There'll always be attempts at political unity.'

13. The inclusion of Suriname, Guyana, Jamaica, Belize and the Bahamas in a political union is less likely. Indeed, Jamaica has always had closer relationships with the Dominican Republic, Haiti, Puerto Rico and Cuba.[410] Jamaica, owing to its wide regional and international interests, had always regarded CARICOM as a marginal structure left to itself (Gonzales, 1984b, p.10).

The Bahamas, as already pointed out, is not a member of the Common Market. Indeed, it follows the activity of the Community from a geographical distance as well. The fixation of the Bahamian economy on its neighbour, the USA, and especially on tourism, does not make the Caribbean region either economically or politically interesting for it.

The main interest of Belize in remaining in CARICOM has been the menacing loss of identity, which a rather strong integration in Central America could bring to the creole population. For the *élite* in the latter group, a rather strong Latinisation signifies the loss of power and having minority status. As in some near-by countries, a fall into second-class status and discrimination threatens the black portion of the population. For its dispute with Guatemala, owing to the latter's still existing territorial claim against it, Belize needs, in addition to British protection, the solidarity of CARICOM.

Belize will, however, orient itself rather more towards the neighbouring markets and the USA. This geographical imperative can, even now, be foreseen. The permanent displacement of that country's demographic pattern in favour of Latin American immigrants provides for this process as well.

The Virgin Islands as well as the Turks and Caicos Islands and Anguilla will soon exchange their current associated status for that of full membership in the Caribbean Community. Montserrat, on becoming independent, will be admitted to full participation in the foreign and security policy discussions of the Community. In contrast, the Cayman Islands will remain a British colony with increased internal self-Government; and, as such, will not seek closer links with CARICOM.

The relocation to, for example, Barbados of the CARICOM Secretariat has theoretically become easier, following the coming to power in the autumn of 1992 of an East Indian-centred Government in Guyana. That Government may well throttle the previous pro-Caribbean involvement of the country and strike out on its own developmental path, with good contacts with its South American neighbours. In all probability, however, both Barbados and Trinidad and

[410] Some leading Jamaican hoteliers have invested in Cuba since the post-1989 political changes in Eastern Europe.

Tobago will insist that Guyana should pay its debts arising from extensive use of the CMCF.

It is possible that the existing CARICOM Member States will decide to expand the Community by admitting non-Anglophone Caribbean countries. Suriname has used its chance, after ridding itself of the military dictatorship. They will admit other such states only under great external pressure, or if they become convinced that expanding the Community brings more advantages than disadvantages.

'CARICOM is now simply a fact of Caribbean political and economic life which nobody seems to want to destroy but nobody seems able to rescue.' That was Payne's view of the prospects of the Community in the 1980s (1985, p. 228). Barbados's previous Prime Minister, Bernard St. John (*CI* July, 1985, p. 12) regarded the Community as indispensable. 'Were we to allow CARICOM to collapse, there would be set in train an uncontrollable ripple effect that would have disastrous consequences for the institutions of functional co-operation.' Former CARICOM Secretary-General, Roderick Rainford (1990, p. 20) hoped for the self-dynamism of the integration process in the sense of a *spill-over* effect. Effective political and functional co-operation would lead generally to the creation of a favourable psychological environment, which would maintain the process of economic collaboration. At both the beginning and end of economic solidarity, political agreement must exist, he argued.

James Mitchell, Prime Minister of St. Vincent and the Grenadines, seems to be pessimistic. 'The political union in which we had so much faith in the East Caribbean and which was conceptualised on many principles, but always with the one enduring hope — that of sustaining the confidence for our continued progress — is quickly slipping into oblivion,' he said at the 14th CARICOM Summit in July, 1993 ('Communique and Speeches', p. 18).

'We in the Caribbean are already integrated. It is only the Governments who didn't know it,' remarked the late Professor George Beckford of the UWI Mona campus.[411] William Demas' dream may, therefore, yet come true: After persistent efforts on the way to integration, the West Indian population wakes up one fine morning and finds that it is united!

---

[411] This economist was quoted by Lamming (1992, p 31)

One attempt to bring young politicians from the Caribbean together was the Caribbean Youth Conference. Shown are delegates at the Annual Assembly of the Caribbean Youth Conference, 1988 in Castries, St. Lucia.

Photo: Muellerleile

Appendices

Appendix 1: Map of the Organisation of Eastern Caribbean States

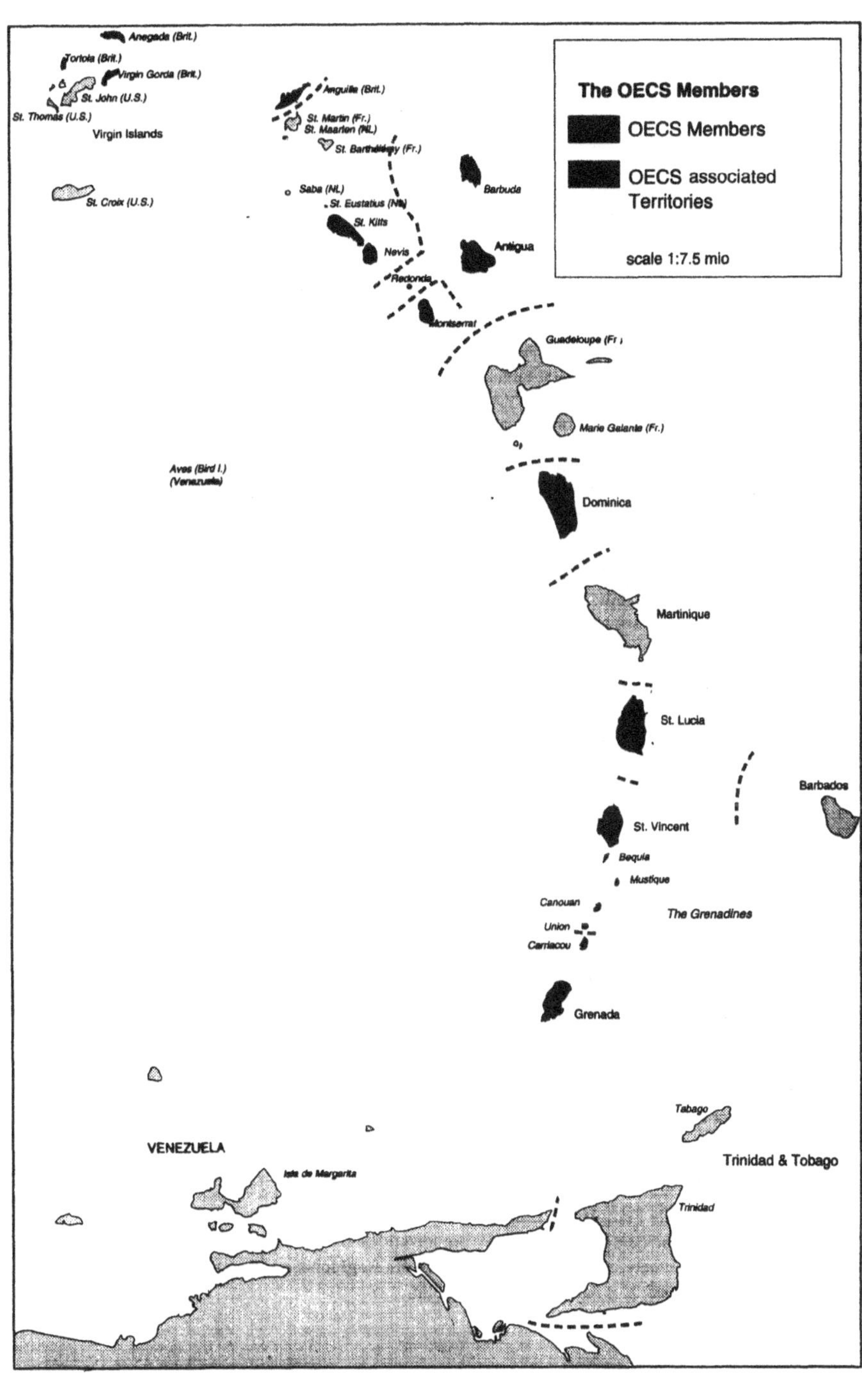

Appendix 2: Selected Organisations and Institutions of Integration in the Commonwealth Caribbean

Y = year of establishment;
A = aims and objectives;
M = member-bodies;
CC= Commonwealth Caribbean;
H = location of head office;
Af = affiliated to;
R= responsible to;

Caribbean Agricultural and Rural Development Advisory and Training Service (CARDATS)
Y = 1973; A = Support of agriculture in the Eastern Caribbean LDCs; R = CARICOM; H = Grenada; Af = CARICOM project.

Caribbean Agricultural Research and Development Institute (CARDI)
Y = 1975; A = Research in agriculture; R = CARICOM; Af. = CARICOM project.

Caribbean Association for Industry and Commerce (CAIC)
Y = 1955; A = training, lobbying and co-ordination for the Caribbean private sector; M = Chambers of Commerce and producers associations of the Anglophone, Francophone and Dutch-speaking Caribbean; H = Barbados; Af. = consultative status with CARICOM.

Caribbean Broadcasting Union (CBU)
Y = 1970; A = promotion of co-operation in the fields of radio and television in the Anglophone and Dutch-speaking Caribbean; M = radio and television stations in the Anglophone Caribbean, the Dutch and French-speaking Antilles, Bermuda, Cuba, Canada, Germany, the Netherlands, United Kingdom, and the USA; H = Barbados.

Caribbean Conference of Churches (CCC)
Y = 1973; A = renewal of the Christian community at regional level and co-ordination of ecumenical projects for developing the region; M = regional organisations of Christian Churches in the Caribbean; H = Barbados; Af. = the World Council of Churches.

Caribbean Congress of Labour (CCL)
Y = 1960; A = representing and co-ordinating the work of affiliated trade unions; M = trade unions in the Anglophone and Dutch-speaking Caribbean; H = Barbados; Af. = consultative status with CARICOM and member of the ICFTU.

Caribbean Development Bank (CDB)
Y = 1970; A = promotion of the economic development and co-operation of Caribbean Member States; M = all Commonwealth Caribbean States and territories, Colombia, Mexico. Venezuela, Canada, France, Germany, Italy and the UK; H = Barbados; Af = associated status with CARICOM.

Caribbean Development and Co-operation Committee (CDCC)
Y = 1966; A = Implementation of ECOSOC programmes in the Caribbean; M = all UN Member States in the Caribbean; H = Port-of-Spain, Trinidad and Tobago; Af = ECLAC / CEPALC and ECOSOC.

Caribbean Economic Development Corporation (CODECA)
Y = 1965; A = promotion of the social and economic co-operation of all the islands of the Caribbean; H = Puerto Rico; R = Government of Puerto Rico.

Caribbean Examinations Council (CXC)
Y= 1973; A = organising internationally recognised Caribbean examinations in high schools; M = CARICOM Member States, the BVI and the Turks and Caicos Islands; H = Barbados; Af = associate status with CARICOM.

Caribbean Family Planning Affiliation (CFPA)
Y = 1971; A = advising national sister organisations in preparing family planning programmes; M = twenty-one sub-organisations in the Anglophone, Francophone and Dutch-speaking Caribbean; H = Antigua; Af. = the IPPF.

Caribbean Festival of Arts (CARIFESTA)
Y = 1972; A = promotion of cultural exchange and Caribbean identity in the arts; Participants: States and territories from the entire Caribbean; Organiser = CARICOM Governments on a rotation basis; Af = CARICOM project.
Caribbean Group for Co-operation and Development (CGCD)
Y = 1977; A = the co-ordination of technical and financial assistance for the region: M = some forty donor and beneficiary countries and about twenty international and regional organisations; H = Washington, D.C.; Af = the IBRD (the World Bank).
Caribbean Human Rights Network (Caribbean Rights)
Y = 1987, A = co-ordinating human rights activities in the Caribbean; M = national human rights organisations in the Caribbean. H = Barbados.
Caribbean Manufacturers Council (CMC)
Y = 1983; A = forum and lobbying body for national producers' associations; M = Commonwealth Caribbean national producers' associations; H = Barbados.
Caribbean Meteorological Council (CMC)
Y = 1962; A = co-ordination of meteorological services and promotion of training and research by the Caribbean Meteorological Institute; R= CARICOM Member States, the BVI and the Cayman Islands; H = Trinidad; Af. = associated status with CARICOM.
Caribbean News Agency (CANA)
Y = 1976; A = private sector news agency providing written and audio news, reports and features; owners = Commonwealth Caribbean media houses; H = Barbados.
Caribbean Publishing and Broadcasting Association (CPBA)
Y = in the 1960s; A = Lobbying for the owners of newspapers, news agencies, radio and TV stations. M = Media houses in the Commonwealth Caribbean and beyond; H = Barbados.
Caribbean Telecommunications Union (CTU)
Y = 1990; A = co-ordinating CARICOM telecommunications activities; R = CARICOM Member States; H = Trinidad; Af. = CARICOM project.
Caribbean Tourism Organisation (CTO)
Y = 1951; A = exchange of information; market research; training; marketing; advertising and co-ordination in promoting tourism in the Caribbean; M = thirty-two states of the Caribbean; M(allied) = about 400 private firms and tourism experts; H = Curaçao, with its main once in New York; Af = the *Caribbean Hotel Association* (CHA) and *Caribbean Tourism Research and Development Centre* (CTRDC) (*Barbados*).
CARICOM Export Development Council (CEDC)
Y = 1986; A = Advisory role to the CARICOM Council of Ministers in promoting exports and supervising the *CARICOM Export Development Project (CEDP)*; M = export-promoting institutions of CARICOM Member States as well as representatives of the private sector and trade unions; H = Barbados; Af = CARICOM project.
CARICOM Industrial Programming Scheme (CIPS)
Y = 1988; A = promoting industrial development by integrating production; R = CARICOM; Af. = CARICOM project.
CARICOM Investment Fund (CIF)
Y = 1991; A = promoting investment by firms in the entire CARICOM area; R = CARICOM; Af. = CARICOM project.
Council of Legal Education
Y = 1971; A = co-ordinates the training of lawyers; R = CARICOM Member States, the BVI and the Cayman Islands; H = Jamaica and Barbados; Af. = associated status with CARICOM.
East(ern) Caribbean Common Market (ECCM)Y = 1968; A = promoting economic co-operation in the Eastern Caribbean; R = OECS members; H = Antigua; Af. = OECS Body.
Eastern Caribbean Central Bank (ECCB)
Y = 1983; A = currency authority of the OECS and control of the money supply; M = OECS members and Anguilla; H = St. Kitts; Af. = associated status with the OECS.
Eastern Caribbean Supreme Court (ECSC)
Y = 1967; A = Court of Appeal for OECS Courts; R = OECS members; Af = associated status with the OECS.

Leeward Islands Air Transport Company LIAT **(1974) Ltd**
Y - 1974; A - air transportation for the Eastern Caribbean; R - CARICOM Member States, excluding Belize; privatisation is being processed; H - Antigua; Af - CARICOM project.
Organisation of Eastern Caribbean States (OECS)
Y - 1981; A - strengthening the Member States in the common use of resources, external representation and protection against foreign and internal dangers; M - Antigua and Barbuda, Dominica, Grenada, Montserrat, St. Kitts and Nevis, St. Lucia and St. Vincent and the Grenadines; H - St. Lucia (central Secretariat) and Antigua (Department of Economics).
University of Guyana (UG)
Y - 1963; A - University education and training; R - the Government of Guyana; H - Georgetown, Guyana; Af. - associated status with CARICOM.
University of the West Indies (UWI)
Y - 1948; A - University education and training; R - CARICOM Member States (except Guyana, participates in legal training), the BVI and the Cayman Islands, H - campuses in Barbados, Jamaica and Trinidad, with centres in all contributing states; Af. associated status with CARICOM
West Indies Shipping Corporation (WISCO)
Y - 1961; wound up in 1992, A - regional shipping service, R - CARICOM Member States, H - Trinidad; Af - CARICOM project.
Women and Development (WAND)
Y - 1978: A - Scientific research on the role of women in the Caribbean, H - Barbados; Af. - UWI.

Appendix 3: Brief Presentation and Chronology of the CARIBBEAN Community

CARICOM (the Caribbean Community and Common Market) was founded by the Treaty of Chaguaramas (Trinidad) of July 4, 1973.

Predecessors of CARICOM

17th Century: Antigua, Barbados, Nevis, Montserrat and St. Kitts were administered by British colonial officials based in Barbados, then, 1671, without Barbados, from Nevis; and, later, from Antigua.

1816: Anguilla, Nevis; St. Kitts and the Virgin Islands formed one British colonial administrative unit; Antigua, Barbuda and Montserrat, another.

1832: Antigua, Dominica, Montserrat, Nevis and St. Kitts were administratively united as the British colony of the Leeward Islands.

1832-1884: British Honduras administered by British colonial officials based in Jamaica. The Cayman Islands and the Turks and Caicos Islands were similarly administered up to 1962.

1833-1885: Barbados, Grenada, St. Vincent and Tobago formed one British colonial administrative unit; St. Lucia and Trinidad were added in 1838; the latter being separated in 1840.

1871-1956: Antigua, Dominica, Montserrat, Nevis and St. Kitts formed the *Leeward Islands Federal Colony.*

1958-1962: *Federation of the West Indies,* with its capital temporarily sited in Port-of-Spain (and its formal capital at Chaguaramas, then occupied by the USA under the 1941 US-UK destroyers-for-bases agreement). Members of the Federation were the members of CARICOM in 1994, except the Bahamas, Belize and Guyana.

1965-1973: *The Caribbean Free Trade Association* (CARIFTA) created in 1968 with headquarters in Georgetown, Guyana, its members were the CARICOM Member States of 1994, except the Bahamas.

The Secretariat

Georgetown, Guyana and has had the following Secretaries-General:
CARIFTA 1968-1970: Fred Cozier (Barbados); CARIFTA/CARICOM 1970-1974: William Demas (Trinidad and Tobago); 1974-1977· Alister McIntyre (Grenada); 1977-1978: Joseph Tyndall (Guyana) (acted); 1978-1983: Kurleigh King (Barbados); 1983-1992: Roderick Rainford (Jamaica); 1992 to date: Dr. Edwin Carrington (Trinidad and Tobago).

Organs of CARICOM

The Conference of Heads of Government, consisting of the Heads of Government of the Member States, is the highest instance. It can legally make binding decisions as well as conclude Treaties between CARICOM and other states or international organisations. The *Bureau of Heads of Government,* consisting of the present, immediately past and next CARICOM Heads of Government Chairmen and the Secretary-General of CARICOM, initiates proposals, updates consensus, mobilises action and secures implementation of CARICOM decisions.

The *Caribbean Community Council of Ministers,* consisting of Ministers responsible for CARICOM Affairs, sent by the Governments, is the second highest organ of the Community, responsible for the on-going business of the *Secretariat* and the functioning of the *Common Market.* The *Joint Consultative Group,* consisting of the Council of Ministers and representatives from NGOs (e.g. the CCL and CAIC) makes CARICOM and important regional NGOs keep in touch.

Conference of Ministers responsible for Health, Standing Committees of Ministers responsible for: Agriculture; Education; Energy; Mines and Natural Resources; Finance; Foreign Affairs; Information; Industry; Labour; Legal Affairs; Science and Technology; Tourism; and Transportation .

CARICOM's Flag

Blue background—the upper part being of a light blue representing the sky and the lower part of a dark blue representing the Caribbean Sea. A yellow circle in the centre of the flag represents the sun. It is surrounded by a green circle representing vegetation. Within the yellow surface two black rings of a broken chain forming the letters 'CC'.

The Members of CARICOM

Full members: **Antigua and Barbuda, The Bahamas (in the Caribbean Community only), Barbados, Belize, Dominica, Grenada, Guyana, Jamaica, Montserrat, St. Kitts and Nevis, St. Lucia, St. Vincent and The Grenadines, Suriname and Trinidad and Tobago.**

Associate members: **The British Virgin Islands and The Turks and Caicos Islands.**

Observer status: **Anguilla, Aruba, Bermuda, Cayman Islands, Colombia, Dominican Republic, Haiti, Mexico, Federation of the Netherlands Antilles, Puerto Rico, Venezuela.**

Participation in functional co-operation: **Cayman Islands.**

Surface and Inhabitants

434,929 km², 6 million inhabitants, GDP 1993 ca. US$13 billion.

Aims and Objectives of CARICOM

Economic co-operation through the Common Market; Creation of common services and functional co-operation; Foreign policy co-ordination.

Associated Institutions

The Organisation of Eastern Caribbean States (OECS); the Caribbean Development Bank (CDB); the Caribbean Meterological Council (CMC); the Caribbean Examinations Council (CXC); the Council of Legal Education (CLE); the University of the West Indies (UWI) and the University of Guyana (UG).

Chronology of the Caribbean Community

1962 (July): *Common Services Conference* in Trinidad held to deal with the redundancy of Civil Servants of the failed West Indies Federation.

1963 (January): The *Caribbean Meterological Service* started working in Trinidad. In July the First *Heads of Government Conference* was held in Trinidad and was attended by Trinidad and Tobago, Jamaica, Barbados and then British Guiana. Informal discussions were held on trade questions.

1964: (January): The Second *Heads of Government Conference* was held in Jamaica with the same participating countries and territories as at the first such conference. Informal discussions were held on trade and then British Guiana's striving for Independence.

1965 (March): The Third *Heads of Government Conference* was held in Jamaica with the same participating countries and territories as at the first such conference. Informal discussions were held on trade, emigration to the UK, entry in the OAS and the establishment of a Permanent Secretariat.

1965 (December): Antigua, Barbados and Guyana sign in Antigua the *Agreement of Dickenson Bay,* establishing CARIFTA.

1967 (October): The Fourth *Heads of Government Conference* was held in Barbados. For the first time, all Commonwealth Caribbean States and territories participated and agreed to expand CARIFTA as well as establishing the *Caribbean Development Bank.* Subjects discussed included the following: Regional air transportation; a *Bureau of Standards;* a regional news agency and the establishment of the *Commonwealth Caribbean Regional Secretariat.* Georgetown, Guyana, was proposed as the latter's location by then Prime Minister of Trinidad and Tobago, Dr. Eric Williams.

1968 (May): The CARIFTA-Agreements entered into force, with the following founding members: Antigua, Barbados, Guyana, and Trinidad and Tobago. In July, Dominica, Grendad, St. Kitts-Nevis-Anguilla, St. Lucia and St. Vincent joined CARIFTA; Jamaica and Montserrat, in August.

1968 (June): The *East Caribbean Common Market* (ECCM) was founded with its Secretariat in Antigua.

1969 (February): The Fifth *Heads of Government Conference* was held in Trinidad. Topics discussed included the UWI and BWIA as a regional airline.

1969 (October): In Kingston/Jamaica the *Caribbean Development Bank* was founded by representatives of 18 states and territories.

1970 (April): The Sixth *Heads of Government Conference* was held in Jamaica. Discussions were held on a Common External Tariff (CET) and the deepening of the integration process.

1971: Belize joined CARIFTA.

1971 (June): A special meetingwas held in St. Lucia by the Heads of Government concerning the estblishment of the *Caribbean Development Bank.*

1972 (October): The Seventh *Heads of Government Conference* was held in Trinidad and agreed to change CARIFTA into CARICOM as of May 1, 1973. The *Caribbean Community* was created with a *Caribbean Common Market*, the co-ordination of foreign policy and functional co-operation.

1973 (April): The Eighth *Heads of Government Conference* was held in Guyana. The Georgetown Accord was agreed upon. The establishment of CARICOM was postponed to August 1, 1973. The relationship of the MDCs to the LDCs was defined.

1973 (July): In Chaguaramas, Trinidad, the *Treaty of Chaguaramas* was signed for the establishment of the Caribbean Community and the Common Market by Barbados, Guyana, Jamaica and Trinidad and Tobago.

1974 (April): Belize, Dominica, Grenada, Montserrat, St. Lucia and St. Vincent also signed the Treaty of Chaguaramas.

1974 (July): The Ninth *Heads of Government Conference*, and the First CARICOM Heads of Government Conference, met in St. Lucia. Decisions were taken on the integration of production and freedom of movement. Relations were begun with the Central American Common Market and the *Junta* of the Treaty of Cartagena (Andean Pact).

1975 (December): The Second CARICOM *Heads of Government Conference* was held in St. Kitts. Topics discussed included the following: The co-ordination of foreign policy; the fight against inflation; regional food production; transportation; special measures for the LDCs. The UK was urged to end the status of Associated Statehood. The UN was asked to protect the territorial integrity of Belize.

1976 (March): A Special *Heads of Government Conference* was held in Trinidad on the restructuring of the UWI.

1977 (June): The CARICOM *Multilateral Clearing Facility* (CMCF) between participating countries, up to a fixed *quantum*, replaces the bilateral clearing accords thereto existing between the relevant central banks and monetary authorities. Foreign trade surpluses with one participating country could be set off against a deficit with another participating country.

1980 (March): The CARICOM Council of Ministers commissioned a *Group of Caribbean Experts* to audit the Community; pending receipt of the experts' report, the next scheduled CARICOM *Heads of Government Conference* was postponed.

1981 (June): At a meeting in Grenada, the Heads of Government of Antigua and Barbuda, Dominica, Grenada, Montserrat, St. Kitts and Nevis, St. Lucia, as well as St. Vincent and the Grenadines signed the *Treaty establishing the Organisation of Eastern Caribbean States* (OECS), which has included the East Caribbean Common Market.

1982 : The OECS — except Montserrat — founded, with Barbados, the *Regional Defence and Security System* (RSS) to protect the participating states and territories against internal subversion and external attacks.

1982 (November): At the Third CARICOM *Heads of Government Conference*, held at Ocho Rios, Jamaica, the *Ocho Rios Declaration* confirmed the political, civic, economic and cultural rights of the population; and also accepted the ideological pluralism of the CARICOM countries. Haiti and Suriname were granted observer status in some ministerial committees.

1983 (January): The introduction, in Jamaica, of the parallel foreign exchange market signified a considerable set-back for intra-regional trade.

1983 (March): The CARICOM *Multilateral Clearing Facility*, CMCF, having reached its agreed liabilities ceiling of US$ 100 million, owing to Guyana's payment arrears, was suspended.

1983 (May): At the Fourth CARICOM *Heads of Government Conference in* Trinidad, the Bahamas was admitted as the thirteenth member of the Community — but did not join the Common Market. The *Regional Energy Action Plan* was adopted. And the *Civil Aviation Consultative Committee* was established.

1983 (October): An emergency meeting of the CARICOM *Heads of Government* took place in Trinidad, following the overthrow of the Bishop Government in Grenada; diplomatic and trade sanctions were decided upon against the spice island, where a US-led military-intervention, with Caribbean support, occurred.

1984 (July): At the Fifth CARICOM *Heads of Government Conference* in the Bahamas, the *Nassau Understanding* for structural adjustment and the revival of intra-regional trade was adopted. New deadlines were laid down for the introduction of the CET. The Dominican Republic, and again Haiti and Suriname, were granted observer status in some ministerial committees.

1985 (July): At the Sixth CARICOM *Heads of Government Conference* in Barbados, the *Barbados Consensus* for developing local and regional entrepreneurship and training skilled workers was adopted, once again, the implementation of the *Common External Tariff* (CET) was called to mind. CARIMEX '85, first CARICOM-wide trade fair for the promotion of the intra-regional trade, in Barbados.

1985 (December): The Trinidad and Tobago dollar was devalued by about 33 3%, thereby impairing intra-regional trade, in which that country was the most important partner.

1986 (July): At the Seventh CARICOM *Heads of Government Conference* in Guyana, the creation of the *Export Credit Facility* with the CDB, to support local producers in exporting non-traditional products and produce, was decided upon. The *Georgetown Declaration* called to mind the implementation of the 1973 Treaty in foreign trade, industrial policy and the use in common of regional resources. The inadequacy of the CBI was criticised.

1986 (October): At the OECS *Heads of Government Conference* in St. Lucia, James Mitchell, the Prime Minister of St. Vincent and the Grenadines, puts forward a detailed plan for building the nation of the *East Caribbean* in the year 1988.

1987 (May) Prime Minister Mitchell, at the OECS *Heads of Government Conference* in Tortola, in the BVI, makes an impassioned appeal for political unity, to his colleagues

1987 (June/July). The eighth CARICOM *Heads of Government Conference* in St Lucia agreed to remove all intra-regional trade barriers by September 30, 1988. Barbados suggested the establishment of a CARICOM Parliament, a human rights commission and an appeal court for the CARICOM region.

1988 (January): At a meeting in Barbados of CARICOM and other Caribbean Leaders (including those from the Netherlands Antilles, Aruba and France) on Haiti, CARICOM Heads of Government were not united in their position on the Haitian military regime and its scheduled Presidential elections.

1988 (July)· A stormy debate on Haiti's observer status, at the Ninth CARICOM *Heads of Government Conference* in Antigua, did not lead to a common CARICOM position. The expert's Report, 'Caribbean Development to the Year 2000', and especially the implications of the rapid population growth, were discussed The establishment of a *Caribbean Court of Appeal* was approved in principle The Summit issued a protest against operations by the US DEA in Caribbean States and territories It also expressed concern at the effects of the Single Market of the future European Union The *Order of the Caribbean Community* (OCC) for honouring personalities of merit was established The Netherlands Antilles were granted observer status

1989 (June). The *Port-of-Spain Accord on the Management and Conservation of the Caribbean Environment* was adopted by the CARICOM Ministers with responsibility for the Environment at their meeting in Trinidad

1989 (July): At the Tenth CARICOM *Heads of Government Conference* in Grenada, the *Grand Anse Declaration* was adopted under the pressure of the then pending creation of the single market of the future European Union and threatening marginalization. The aim of Commonwealth Caribbean integration was changed to a *Single* (instead of a common) market — and a single (instead of a common) economy. New deadlines for implementing the Treaty of Chaguaramas were promulgated. The establishment of an *Assembly of Caribbean Community Parliamentarians* without legislative function was approved. An independent *West Indian Commission for Advancing the Goals of the Treaty of Chaguaramas,* headed by Sir Shridath Ramphal, was commissioned to prepare a status report on the Community.

1990 (July/August): The *Kingston Declaration* was adopted at the Eleventh CARICOM *Heads of Government Conference* in Kingston, Jamaica, which was overshadowed by the attempted *coup d'état* of the Jamaat-al-Muslimeen in Port-of-Spain. Agreement was reached to establish a regional security mechanism for enforcing maritime rights and combating the illegal narcotics trade. The following new deadlines were set· *1 1 1991*: The creation of a *Caribbean Stock Exchange* as part of a regional capital market; the relevant Central Bank Governors were instructed to undertake preparatory work for a common currency; *1 1 1991*: Re-activation of the CMCF; *1 1 1991*: CET for the MDCs; *1992.* CET for the LDCs except Montserrat (1.1 1994) and the Bahamas (excluded). Mexico, Venezuela and Puerto Rico were granted observer status in some ministerial committees. A decision on the application of the Dominican Republic for full CARICOM membership was postponed

1991 (January): The first meeting was held in Kingstown, St Vincent, of the *Regional Constituent Assembly of the Windward Islands* (RCA) to prepare the political unity of Grenada, Dominica, St. Lucia and St. Vincent and the Grenadines.

1991 (February) Inter-Sessional Meeting of the CARICOM *Heads of Government Conference* in Trinidad dealt with certain organisational questions of the Community.

1991 (February/March). The first *Caribbean Regional Economic Conference* was held in Port-of-Spain, Trinidad, with private sector representatives, officials, trade unionists and financial experts from the CARICOM region as well as observers from six non-CARICOM countries. Following discussion on the sustainable development of the region, the conference adopted the *Port-of-Spain Consensus — Securing Caribbean Development to the Year 2000 and Beyond*. This conference, it was decided, should be held triennially.

1991 (July): The Twelfth CARICOM *Heads of Government Conference decided* in St.Kitts to establish a joint *CARICOM-US Council* for trade and investment questions, especially those in connection with the EAI, the Uruguay Round of the GATT and NAFTA. The introduction of the CET was postponed to October 1, 1991. The preliminary report and recommendations of the *West Indian Commission* were received. Five of the Heads of Government personally accepted individual responsibilities (e.g. to work on the *Caribbean Investment Fund* or freedom of movement) arising from those recommendations. Venezuela's offer of one-way free trade was accepted; and that country applied for full CARICOM membership. The British Virgin Islands and the Turks and Caicos Islands were admitted as associate members of CARICOM. Anguilla was granted observer status Colombia, aiming at full membership of CARICOM, was admitted as an observer in some ministerial committees. A Caribbean satellite network is to be established within one year.

1991 (December): Travel without passports became possible in the OECS by its nationals

1992 (January): The first ever *CARICOM/Central America Ministerial Conference* was held in San Pedro Sula/Honduras, and agreement reached on the establishment of a *CARICOM/Central America Consultative Forum* to pursue co-operation between the two regions

1992 (February)· The Inter-Sessional Meeting of the CARICOM Heads of Government Conference in Kingston/Jamaica adopted a work programme in the *Single Market and Economy for Caricom*. Establishment of the Regional *Tourism Marketing Programme* for North America.

In the same month Grenada, Guyana, St Kitts and Nevis, St. Lucia and Trinidad and Tobago introduced travel without passports for CARICOM nationals. Guyana and Jamaica exempted UWI graduates automatically from the need to get work permits; Jamaica also exempted artistes and media practitioners.

1992 (April): *CARICOM/United States Council on Trade and Investment* inaugurated in Washington and signed in July; provides forum for the discussion and resolution of trade and investment problems between the Parties.

1992 (June): The *West Indian Commission* published its final Report, *Time for Action*, proposing, *inter alia*, the creation of a *CARICOM Commission*, as of January 1, 1993, to oversee the implementation of Summit decisions, to promote integration and co-ordinate negotiations with international bodies. The *CARICOM Supreme Court* — another recommendation — was to be both a *Court of Appeal* and a *Court for Regional Affairs* The *CARICOM Assembly* — yet another recommendation — was to be an 'Assembly of the People' without legislative function. CARICOM, it was also recommended, should remain a Community of sovereign states, without federal character. The *Association of Caribbean States*, which was to be established, should extend the integration process to other parts of the Caribbean.

1992 (June/July): Differences of opinion developed at the Thirteenth CARICOM *Heads of Government Conference* in Port-of-Spain, Trinidad, over the levels and led to the appointment of a Working Group of Experts to study the matter. A three-phase plan was proposed to achieve a common currency by the year 2000. The *Order of the Caribbean Community* was awarded for the first time, to William Demas, Sir Shridath Ramphal and Derek Walcott. Aruba was granted observer status in certain ministerial committees.

1992 (October): The Report of the *West Indian Commission* and also that of the Working Group of Experts on the CET were studied at a Special Meeting of the CARICOM Heads *of Government Conference* in Port-of-Spain It was decided to establish, as of January 1, 1993, a *Bureau of Heads of Government* consisting of the present, immediate past and next Chairmen of the CARICOM *Heads of Government Conference* as well as the CARICOM Secretary-General. This Bureau should make proposals, implement decisions, and adapt them to topical developments. Restructuring of the CARICOM Secretariat with executive authority to the Secretary-General. The CET was now fixed at 5-20% up to January 1, 1998, with special arrangements for the LDCs.

Establishment of the *Caribbean Community Council of Ministers*, comprising the Ministers responsible for CARICOM Affairs in each country, replacing the *Common Market Council* as second highest Organ of the Community. Readiness was expressed to set up common representation abroad. The Summit confirmed that it was prepared to establish the *Assembly of Caribbean Community Parliamentarians* after ratification of the agreement by at least seven CARICOM members. The preparation of the *CARICOM Charter of Civil Society* for formulating common political, economic, social and cultural bases was agreed to It was decided to hold consultations with other Caribbean States on establishing the *Association of Caribbean States* proposed by the West Indian Commission. Finally, the transportation of nuclear material and the holding of nuclear tests in the Caribbean were opposed.

In the same month in Caracas the *CARICOM/Venezuela Trade and Investment Agreement* was signed.

1993 (March): At an Inter-Sessional Meeting of the CARICOM Heads of Government in Dominica, the following topics were discussed: The possible affects of NAFTA; the economic policy of US President, Bill Clinton; and the restructuring of the CARICOM Secretariat.

1993 (June): Special meeting of the CARICOM Heads of Government in St. Lucia. Common landing tax for cruise ship passengers discussed.

1993 (July): At the Fourteenth CARICOM *Heads of Government Conference* in the Bahamas, no agreement was reached on the unified landing tax for cruise ship passengers. Agreement was reached in principle on establishing a *Regional Air Carrier* by January 1, 1995. A common foreign policy and integration in NAFTA were discussed. The intention to establish a *CARICOM-Cuba Joint Commission,* despite US opposition, was confirmed, and a *Joint Technical Group* for co-operation with the French Overseas Departments in the Caribbean agreed to. The *Caribbean Investment Fund* was established.

1993 (October): Special Meeting of the CARICOM *Heads of Government Conference* with the Presidents of the *Group of Three,* Colombia, Mexico and Venezuela, and with the Vice-President of Suriname, in Port-of-Spain. Signing of an *Action Plan for Co-operation among the Caribbean Community, Suriname and the Group of Three,* to co-operate in the fields of business opportunities, tourism, transport, hemispheric trade, co-ordination of multilateral financial institutions, agriculture, environment, fight against drug and crime, science and technology, culture, information, human development; monitored by a commission.

1994 (March): Inter-Sessional Meeting of the CARICOM *Heads of Government* in St.Vincent. Decisions: CARICOM seeks early inclusion in the list of countries eligible for negotiating early entry to the NAFTA, sets up working group under Sir Alister McIntyre to assist regional private sector investment and promote the development of a regional capital market. No common regional tax for cruise ship passengers. Call for establishment of a *New Global Humanitarian Order* to respond to the widening gap between the rich in the North and the poor in the South.

1994 (July): The Fifteenth CARICOM Heads of Government Conference in Barbados confirmed that the Agreement establishing the *Assembly of Caribbean Community Parliamentarians* would come into force on 3rd August 1994 following the ratification by Antigua and Barbuda, the Bahamas, Barbados, Grenada, Guyana, Jamaica and Trinidad and Tobago. Date and venue for the First Session not determined. The management of LIAT was turned over to the Governments of Antigua and Barbuda and Trinidad and Tobago as of August, 1994, pending privatisation in 1995

On 24th July in Cartagena/Colombia the Convention of the *Association of Caribbean States* (ACS) was signed by representatives from 25 countries.

On the same occasion an *Agreement on Trade, Economic and Technical Co-operation* was signed between CARICOM and Colombia, opening additional avenues for business people and investors from the Region, providing special conditions for LDCs.

1994 (September) Sunrise, then Carib Express, a new airline, was scheduled to start operating by Christmas 1994, backed by the governments of Barbados, Dominica, Grenada, St. Lucia and St. Vincent and the Grenadines.

On September 19, US troops began to occupy Haiti, backed by most of the CARICOM states. Some CARICOM heads of government met in Kingston, Jamaica, with US officials to discuss common action.

1994 (October), after heavy lobbying by the US administration, a 266-man CARICOM contingent consisting of soldiers and policemen from Antigua and Barbuda, Barbados, Belize, Guyana, Jamaica and Trinidad and Tobago became part of a 24-nation strong peace keeping force in Haiti.

1995 (February): The Inter-Sessional Meeting of the Conference of Heads of Government in Belize approved the application by Suriname for membership in the Caribbean Community and the Common Market with effect from the 16th Meeting of the Conference to be held in July, 1995, in Guyana. The Heads of Government agreed in principle to a joint proposal of the governments of Antigua and Barbuda and Trinidad and Tobago for the privatisation of LIAT.

Appendix 3

1995 (July) Suriname accepted as the fourteenth menber of CARICOM.

Sources: Murray, pp. 165ff; *Caribbean Review* 13.4. (Fall 1984), pp. 11 and 40; Payne, 1980; CARICOM PERSPECTIVE, *Caribbean Insight* and *Caribbean Report*.

Appendix 4: Leading Executives of the CARICOM Secretariat (1995)

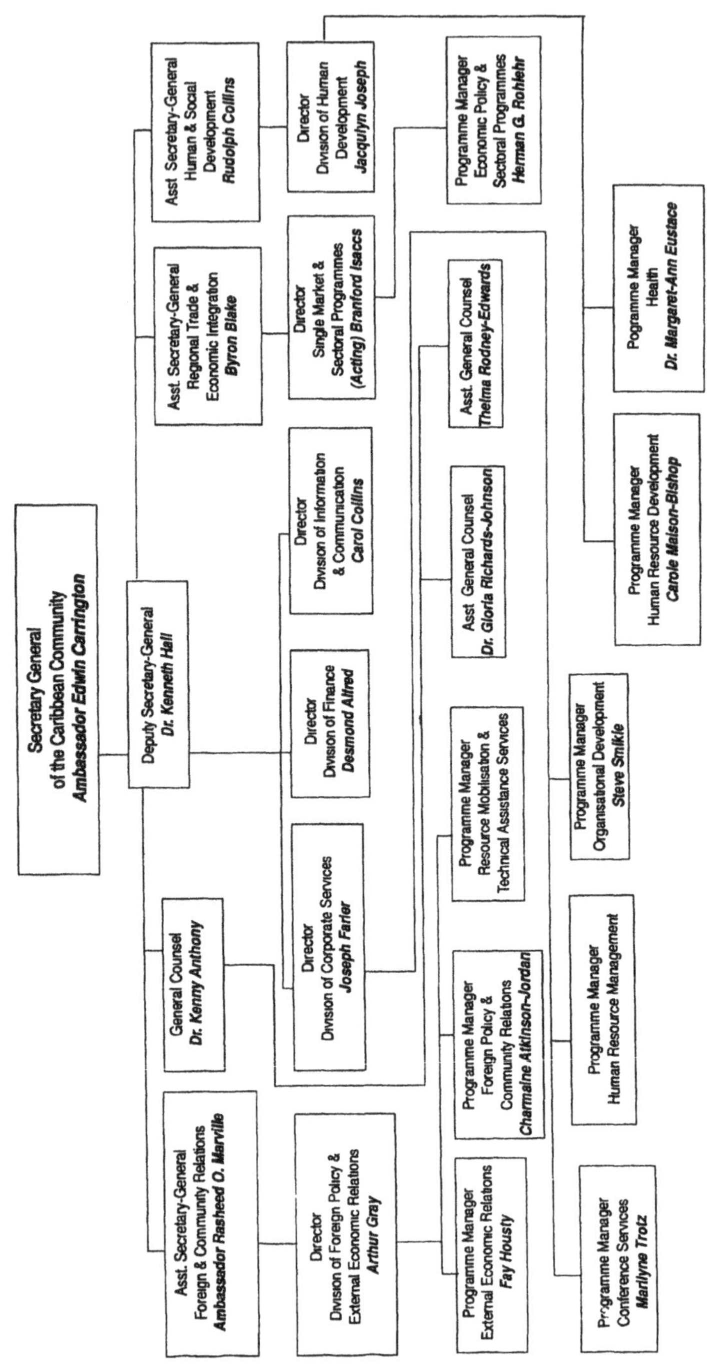

Appendix 5: Table of Organisation of the CARICOM Secretariat in Georgetown, Guyana (1995)

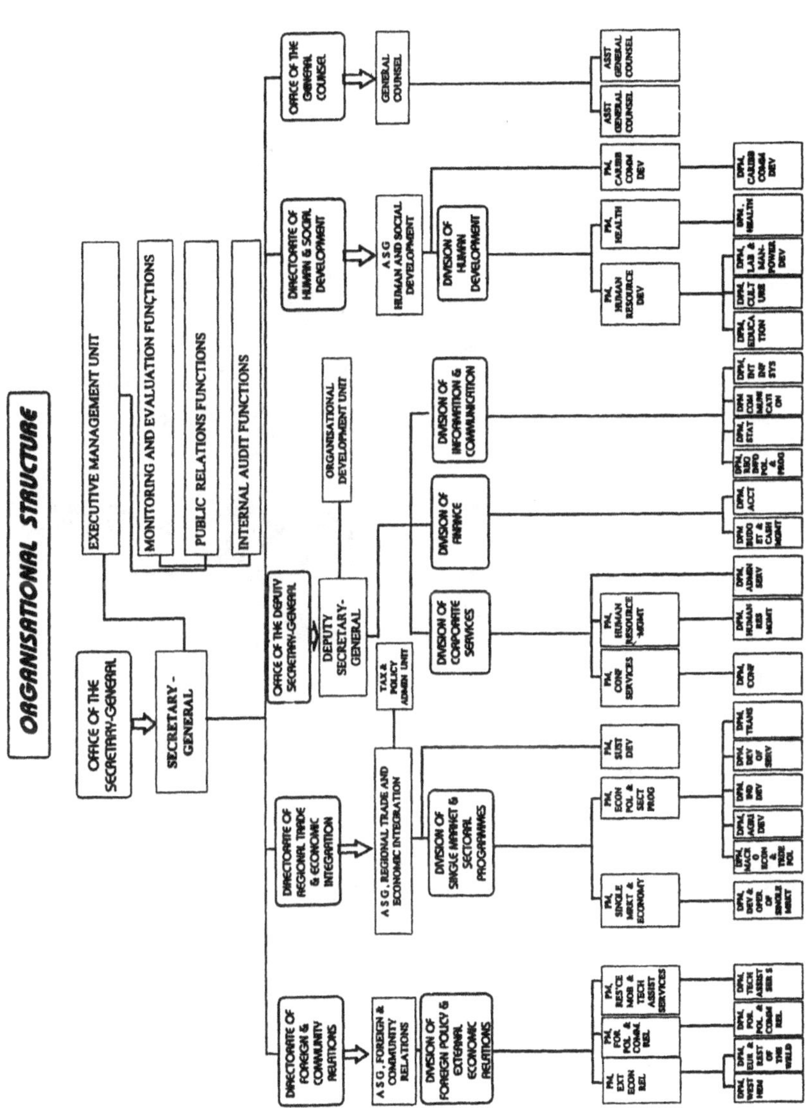

Appendix 6: 'CARICOM' Cartoon

From: *EC News* (Barbados), 26.8.1988, p. 7.

Select Bibliography

Abend, Michael. Trincom 90. Panel Discussion: 'Cultural Penetration and the Loss of Identity through News, Advertisements and Entertainment', Typescript. Christ Church, Barbados: Caribbean Broadcasting Union, (30.11.)1989[a].

— International Conference of Journalists, December 6-9, 1989, Kingston Jamaica. Panel Presentation. Typescript. Christ Church, Barbados: Caribbean Broadcasting Union, (9.12.)1989[b].

— *Television in Paradise. The Caribbean Experience*. Bonn, Germany: Friedrich-Ebert-Stiftung, 1992.

— Medienszene 1993 in der Karibik. *M & K—Informationsblatt des Referats Medien und Kommunikation* (Bonn, Germany: Friedrich-Ebert-Stiftung) [Media Scene in the Caribbean. *M & K—Information Bulletin of the Media and Communicahons Department*], October 1993, pp. 8-9.

Action Plan for Co-operation among the Caribbean Community, Suriname and the Group of Three. Supplement to *CARICOM PERSPECTIVE* 61 and 62 (July-December 1993).

Adams, Tom. Welcoming Address. *Ten Years of CARICOM*. Papers presented at a seminar sponsored by the Inter-American Development Bank, July 1983. Washington, D.C., Inter-American Development Bank, 1984. pp. 3-7.

Agreement Establishing the East Caribbean Common Market. *Treaty Establishing the Organisation of Eastern Caribbean States*. Appendix A. (Castries, St Lucia: OECS Secretariat), n.d., pp. 37-48.

Ahyoung, Selwyn Ellore. *Soca Fever! Change in the Calypso Music Tradition of Trinidad &Tobago, 1970—1980*. Indiana University, Thesis, 1981.

Aide Mémoire on a Proposal for an Alliance of Solidarity, Co-operation and Mutual Assistance amongst the Parliamentary Democratic Parties in the Caribbean Typescript, Kingston, Jamaica, 1980.

Alford, Jonathan. Security Dilemmas of Small States. *The Round Table* 292 (1984), pp. 377-382.

Allahar, Anton L. Caribbean Cultural Community: Myth or Reality. *Caribbean Affairs* 5.3 (July-Sept. 1992) pp. 21-32.

Alleyne, George A.O., and Halmond C. Dyer. Cooperation in Health in the Commonwealth Caribbean. *Caribbean Affairs* 3.2 (April-June 1990), pp. 135-150.

Alleyne, Mervyn. Creole Language and the Caribbean Community. *CARICOM PERSPECTIVE* (Georgetown, Guyana) 37 (January-March 1987) pp. 24-26.

Ambursley, Fitzroy. Grenada: the New Jewel Revolution. *Crisis in the Caribbean*. In: (Eds.) Fitzroy Ambursley and Robin Cohen. 2nd ed. London: Heinemann Education Books, 1984, pp.191-222 .

Anderson, Patricia. The Demographic Basis of Social Instability in the Caribbean of the Eighties. *Peace, Development and Security in the Caribbean. Perspectives to the Year 2000*. In: (Eds.) Anthony T. Bryan, J. Edward Greene and Timothy M. Shaw. Houndmills and London: Macmillan Press, 1990, pp. 160-179.

Anderson, Thomas A. *Geopolitics of the Caribbean Ministates in a Wider World*. Praeger Special Studies. New York: Praeger, 1984.

Andic, Fuat, Suphan Andic and Douglas Dosser. *A Theory of Economic Integration for Developing Countries. Illustrated by Caribbean Countries*. London: George Allen and Unwin, 1971.

Anduze, Madeleine. The CBI and the US Hegemony: Something Old or Something New?. *Caribbean Affairs* (Port-of-Spain, Trinidad) 3.4 (October—December 1990) pp. 182-203.

Anglin, Douglas C. *The Political Development of the West Indies. The West Indies Federation. Perspectives on a New Nation*. (Eds.) David Lowenthal. American Geographical Research Series 23. New York: Columbia University Press; London: Oxford University Press, 1961, pp. 35-62.

Annamunthodo, Walter, (Ed.) 1972 *Calypsoes*. Pleasantville, San Femando, Trinidad and Tobago: Unique Services, 1972.

Antilles Radio Corporation. *1986/1987 Audience Survey for Radio Antilles and BBC. Prepared by Antilles Radio Corporation and Mandra/SBRA*. Montserrat and London, 1987.

Ashley, Paul. The Commonwealth Caribbean and the Contemporary World Order: The Case of Jamaica and Trinidad. *The Newer Caribbean—Decolonization, Democracy and Development*. In: (Eds.) Paget Henry and Carl Stone. Philadelphia: Institute for the Study of Human Issues, 1983,pp.59-176.

Augier, Fitzroy Richard *et.al. The Making of the West Indies, Trinidad and Jamaica*. London: Longmans, 1974.

— Federations: Then and Now. *Caribbean Quarterly* (Kingston, Jamaica) 35.3 (September 1989), pp.16-23.

Avery, William P. The Extraregional Transfer of Integrative Behavior. *International Organization* 27.4 (Autumn 1973), pp. 549-556.

Axline, Andrew. Underdevelopment, Dependency and Integration: the Politics of Regionalism in the Third World. *International Organization* 31, 1977, pp. 83-105.

— *Caribbean Integration. The Politics of Regionalism*. London: Frances Pinter, 1979

— *Agricultural Policy and Collective Self-Reliance in the Caribbean*. Boulder, Colorado, and London: Westview Press, 1986.

— Lessons for the Caribbean from Small States of Other Regions. *Peace, Development and Security in the Caribbean. Perspectives to the Year 2000*. In: (Eds.) Anthony T. Bryan, J. Edward Greene and Timothy M. Shaw. Houndmills and London: Macmillan Press, 1990, pp. 299-320.

Bahadoorsingh, Krishna. The East Caribbean Federation Attempts. *Regionalism and the Commonwealth Caribbean*. In: (Ed.) Roy Preiswerk. Special Lecture Series 2. St. Augustine, Trinidad: University of the West Indies, Institute of International Relations, 1969, pp.157-169.

Ballantyne, Maralyn. Meeting on Mustique. Interview with Prime Minister James Mitchell. *CARICOM PERSPECTIVE* 34 (January-March 1986), pp. 10-11.

Bank for all Seasons. *CDB News* (Wildey, Barbados) 7.3 (July-September 1989) pp. 8-10.

Baranyi, Steven, and Edgar Dosman. Canada and the Security of the Commonwealth Caribbean. *Peace, Development and Security in the Caribbean, Perspectives to the Year 2000*. In: (Eds.) Anthony T. Bryan, J. Edward Greene and Timothy M. Shaw. Houndmills and London: Macmillan Press, 1990, pp. 102-125.

The Barbados Consensus on Development of Local and Regional Entrepreneurship and Skills in the Member States of the Caribbean Community. Supplement to *CARICOM PERSPECTIVE* 32 (July-October 1985).

Barrett, Leonard E. *The Rastafarians—Dreadlocks of Jamaica*. Kingston, Jamaica: Sangster's Book Stores, 1977.

Barrow, Errol. The Danger of Rescue Operations. *Caribbean Review*, 12.4 (Fall 1983), pp. 3-4.

Barry, Tom *et. al. The Other Side of the Paradise. Foreign Control in the Caribbean. New York:* Grove Press, 1984.

Basdeo, Sahadeo. Caribbean Media and Telecommunication in the Information Age *Caribbean Affairs* 2.2 (April-June 1989) pp. 44-52.

—Cuba in Transition: Socialist Order Under Siege. *Caribbean Affairs* 5.4 (October December 1992) pp.91-117.

Beck, Robert J. *The Grenada Invasion: Politics, Law, and Foreign Policy Decisionmaking* Boulder, Colorado: Westview Press, 1993.

Beckford, George *Cultural Sovereignty and Economic Development*. I Caribbea Conference of Intellectual Workers, Grenada, November 20-22, 1982. Typescript n.d

— Sovereignty and Self-Reliance: The Economic Implications *Mobilization for Developme and Self-reliance: The Tasks of Political Education*. Kingston, jamaica: People National Party, 1984, pp.51-76.

— and Michael Witter. *Small Garden...bitter Weed, The Political Economy of Struggle a Change in Jamaica*. Morant Bay, Jamaica: Maroon Publishing House; London: Z Press, January 1982 Beckles, Hilary. In Support of West Indian Women Crickete Caribbean Contact, October 1993, p.6.

Belassa, Bela, and Ardy Stoutjesdijk. Economic Integration among Developing Countri *Journal of Common Market Studies* 14, 1975, pp. 37-55.

Bellers, Jürgen. Integration. *Handwödrterbuch Internationaler Politik [Small Dictionary International Politics*. In· (Ed) Richard Woyke]. Leverkusen, Germany: Leske, 19 pp. 201-206.

Select Bibliography

Benn, Denis. The Caribbean Community: The Internal Environment. The Geographical, Economic and Political Legacy. *Ten Years of CARICOM*. Papers presented at a seminar sponsored by the Inter-American Development Bank, July 1983. Washington, D.C: Inter-American Development Bank, 1984, pp. 27-38

Bennett, Karl M. A Note on Exchange Rate Policy and Caribbean Integration. *Social and Economic Studies* 34.4, December 1985, pp. 35-43.

Bennett, Olivia. *Festival! Carnival.* Houndmills and London: Macmillan Education, 1986.

Bernal, Richard. Caribbean Debt: Possible Solutions. *Caribbean Affairs* 4.2 (April-June 1991), pp. 45-58.

Best, Lloyd. A Model of Pure Plantation Economy. *Social and Economic Studies*, September 1968, in: George Beckford 1986, pp. 53-55.

— The February Revolution in Trinidad and Tobago, 1970. *Readings in Government and Politics of the West Indies*. Eds. Trevor Munroe and Rupert Lewis. Kingston, Jamaica: University of the West Indies, Department of Government, 1 97 1, pp. 2 1 0-2 1 4 .

Best, Tony. A CARICOM or Central American Nation. *Caribbean Contact* November 1987, p. 8.

— Caribbean can Benefit from more Aid. *Caribbean Contact*, May/June 1992, p 4.

Bird Pleads for Better US Deal. *Barbados Advocate*, 12 November 1985, p. 2.

Bishop, Keith. UWI Students Face Grim Year. *The Sunday Gleaner* 9 July 1989.[1]

Bishop, Maurice. *Address by Maurice Bishop at the Opening of the Caribbean Conference of Intellectual Workers*. Grenada, 20 November 1982, n.d.

— *Maurice Bishop Speaks. The Grenada Revolution 1979-1983*. New York: Pathfinder Press, 1983.

Blackman, Courtney N. Sir Arthur Lewis and the Agony of the Little Eight Revisited. *Caribbean Affairs* 2.3 (July-September 1989) pp. 62-72.

— Two Lost Decades in Caribbean Economic History· 'Retrospect and Prospect'. *Caribbean Affairs* 2.4 (October—December 1989b) pp. 92-108.

— The Economic Management of Small Island Developing Countries *Caribbean Affairs* 4.4 (October -December 1 99 1) pp. 1-1 2 .

Blake, Byron W. Production Integration: Scope, Limitation and Prospects in CARICOM. *Ten Years of CARICOM*. Washington, D.C.: Inter-American Development Bank, 1984, pp 118-130.

Blake Hanna, Barbara Abuna Yesehaq looks back on 14 years of ministry in Jamaica *The Sunday Gleaner Magazine* 25 November 1984, pp. 2,3 and 11.

Bogues, Tony. Ideology, Nationalism and Political Education. *Mobilization for Development and Self-reliance. The Tasks of Political Education*. Kingston, Jamaica: People's National Party, 1 986, pp. 1 3-27.

Borchard, Ralf Der ungeliebte Nachbar ist zum umworbenen Partner avanciert [Unloved Neighbour Becomes Courted Partner.] *Frankfurter Rundschau* 21 May 1992, p. 19.

Bosshard, Peter. Endlich haben wir eine Regierung der Liebe! Demokratischer Sozialismus in Jamaica unter Michael Manley (1972-1980) [Finally We Have a Government of Love. Socialism in Jamaica under Michael Manley 1972-1980.] Basel, Switzerland: Z-Verlag, 1987.

Bousquet, Earl Success in Belize. *Caribbean Contact*, July 1986, p. 6.

Brana-Shute, Gary Interviewing James F. 'Son' Mitchell. *Caribbean Review* (Miami, FL) 12 March [1983], pp. 10-12.

— An Eastern Caribbean Centrist. Interviewing Prime Minister James F. 'Son' Mitchell *Caribbean Review* 14.4. (Fall 1985), pp. 27-29.

Brathwaite, Kamau. Dedicated to Quality and Experimentation. *CARICOM PERSPECTIVE* 33 (November-December 1985), pp. 24-26.

Braveboy-Wagner, Jacqueline A *The Venezuela-Guyana Border Dispute: Britain's Colonial Legacy in Latin America*. Boulder, Colorado: Westview Press, 1984

[1] *Gleaner* quotations are from *The Daily Gleaner* (Kingston, Jamaica), *The Sunday Gleaner* (Kingston, Jamaica), *The Weekly Gleaner* (Birmingham, UK) up to 10 November 1987, *The Weekly Gleaner, Midland and Northern Edition* (Birmingham, UK) up to March 1988. *The Weekly Gleaner, London and Southern Edition* (London, UK) from April 1988

— *The Caribbean in World Affairs: Foreign Policies of the English-speaking Caribbean*. Boulder, Colorado Westview Press, 1988.

Brewster, Havelock, and Clive Y[olande] Thomas. *The Dynamic of West Indian Economic Integration*. 1st edn. 1967, 2nd edn. Kingston, Jamaica: Institute of Social and Economic Research, University of the West Indies, 1973.

— The Report of the West Indian Commission. *Time for Action*—Critique and Agenda for Further Work. *Caribbean Affairs* 6.1 (Jan.-March 1993), pp. 56-72.

Brown, Aggrey. The West Indies and the New International Information Order. *Media in Latin America and the Caribbean: Domestic and International Perspectives*. Eds. Walter C. Soderlund and Stuart H. Surlin. Windsor, Ontario: University of Windsor, 1985a, pp. 12-19.

— Geopolitics and the Role of Caribbean Media. *CARICOM PERSPECTIVE* 33 (November-December 1985b), p. 13.

— Caribbean Cultures and Mass Communication Technology in the 21st Century. *Caribbean Affairs* 4.3 (October-December 1990), pp. 49-64.

Bryan, Anthony T. The CARICOM and Latin American Integration Experience. *Ten Years of CARICOM*. Washington, D.C.: Inter-American Development Bank, 1984, pp. 71-94. Cuba's impact in the Caribbean. International Journal, 11.2 (Spring 1985) pp. 331-347.

— A Tropical Perestroika? Cuba, the Soviet Union and the Caribbean. *Caribbean Affairs* 2.2 (April-June 1989a), pp. 92-103.

— The New International Relations Agenda: Is the Commonwealth Caribbean Ready for the 1990s? *Caribbean Affairs*, 2.4 (October-December 1989b), pp. 49-54.

— International Relations of the Caribbean towards the Year 2000. *Caribbean Affairs* 3.4 (October-December 1990), pp. 13-34.

— (Ed.) *The Caribbean. New Dynamics in Trade and Political Economy*. New Brunswick, N.J.:Transaction Books, 1994.

Burnham, Linden Forbes. *To Build a New World*. Speech by Comrade L.F.S. Burnham [...] at the Sixth Conference of Non-aligned Countries in Havana, Cuba [...] Complete off-print. Georgetown, Guyana: Ministry of Information, 1981.

Bustamante, Alexander. *The Best of Bustamante: Selected Quotations 1935-74*. Red Hills, Jamaica: Twin Guinep, 1977.

Butler, David. Variants of the Westminster Model. *Democracy and Elections. Electoral Systems and their Political Consequences*. In: (Eds.) Vernon Bogdanor and David Butler. Cambridge *et.al.*, Cambridge University Press, 1983, pp. 46-61.

Campbell, Frank A. *The New International Information and Communication Order. A Caribbean Perspective*. Georgetown, Guyana: Ministry of Information, February 1980.

Cantori, Louis J., and Steven L. Spiegel. *The International Politics of Regions*. Englewood Cliffs, N.J.: Prentice-Hall, 1970.

Caporaso, James A. Theory and Method in the Study of International Integration. *International Organization* 25, 1971, pp. 228-253.

Carew, Jan. *Grenada: The Hour will Strike Again*. Chicago: Imported Publications, 1986.

Caribbean after Grenada: Revolution, Conflict and Democracy. In: (Eds) Scott B. MacDonald, Harold M. Sandstrom and Paul B. Goodwin. New York: Praeger, 1988.

Caribbean Basin Initiative. Reprint of President Ronald Reagan's OAS Speech on 24 February 1982 in Washington. *Bulletin of Eastern Caribbean Affairs* (Cave Hill, Barbados) 8.1 (March/April 1982), pp. 23-30.

Caribbean Basin Initiative, Hearings and Markup before the Committee on Foreign Affairs and its Subcommittees on International Economic Policy and Trade and on Inter-American Affairs, House of Representatives, Ninety-Seventh Congress, Second Session on H.R.5900, March 23,25,30, April 1 ,27,29, May 11, July 1 5, 1982. Printed for the use of the Committee on Foreign Affairs. Washington, D.C.: US Government Printing Office, 1982.

Caribbean Broadcasting Union. *Constitution*. April, 1979. Christ Church, Barbados: CBU, n.d.

Caribbean Catholic Directory1980. Kingston, Jamaica: Caribbean Catholic Directory, 1980.

Caribbean Community. *Report of the Secretary-General of the Caribbean Community 1988*. Georgetown, Guyana: Caribbean Community Secretariat, 1989.

Caribbean Community. *Annual Report of the Caribbean Community 1989*. Georgetown, Guyana: CARICOM Secretariat, 1990.

Caribbean Community. *Annual Report of the Secretary General of the Caribbean Community 1991*. Georgetown, Guyana: CARICOM Secretariat, 1992.

Caribbean Community. *Annual Report of the Secretary General of the Caribbean Community 1992*. Georgetown, Guyana: CARICOM Secretariat, 1993.

Caribbean Community In the 1980s. Report by a Group of Caribbean Experts. Appointed by the Caribbean Community Market Council of Ministers. Ed. Caribbean Community Secretariat. Georgetown, Guyana 1981.

Caribbean Community 1985, Report of the Secretary-General. Ed. Caribbean Community Secretariat. Georgetown, Guyana: Caribbean Community Secretariat, 1986.

Caribbean Community 1986, Report of the Secretary-General. Ed. Caribbean Community Secretariat. Georgetown, Guyana: Caribbean Community Secretariat, 1987.

Caribbean Community 1987. Report of the Secretary-General. Ed. Caribbean Community Secretariat. Georgetown, Guyana: Caribbean Community Secretariat, 1988.

Caribbean Community Secretariat. History of CARICOM. June 1982 Typescript

Caribbean Conference of Churches. *Annual Report 1984.* Bridgetown, Barbados: Caribbean Conference of Churches, February 1985.

Caribbean Congress of Labour. *Twenty-fifth Anniversary Celebrations 1960—1985.* Bridgetown, Barbados: Caribbean Congress of Labour, 1985.

Caribbean Conservation Association. *Action Programme 1988 —1991.* Savannah Lodge, The Garrison, Barbados: Caribbean Conservation Association, n.d.1988.

Caribbean Development Bank. *Making CDB More Effective.* Statement by the President, Mr. William G.Demas, to the Board of Governors at the Thirteenth Annual Meeting, held at Cartagena, Colombia May 11 & 12, 1983. Wildey, St. Michael, Barbados: Caribbean Development Bank, 1983.

Caribbean Development Bank—Its Purpose, Role and Functions. Twenty Questions and Answers. Wildey, St. Michael, Barbados, Caribbean Development Bank, 30 April 1985a.

— *Financial Policies.* Wildey, St. Michael, Barbados: Caribbean Development Bank, 30 April 1985.

— *Annual Report 1990.* Wildey, St. Michael, Barbados, 1991.

— *Annual Report 1991.* Wildey, St. Michael, Barbados, 1992.

— *Annual Report 1992.* Wildey, St. Michael, Barbados, 1993.

— *Annual Report 1993.* Wildey, St. Michael, Barbados, 1994.

Caribbean Development to the Year 2000. Challenges, Prospects and Policies. In: (Eds.) Commonwealth Secretariat and Caribbean Community Secretariat. London: Commonwealth Secretariat; Georgetown, Guyana: Caribbean Community Secretariat, June 1988.

Caribbean Free Trade Association. Consolidated Text of the Principal, Supplementary Agreement, Subsidiary Agreement and Protocols. Georgetown, Guyana: Government Printery, 1987.

Caribbean Governments to Sign Environmental Protection Pact'. United Nations Information Centre for the Caribbean Area. Feature (Port-of-Spain, Trinidad) No. 3(17 March 1983.)

Caribbean Handbook 1988, Ed. Jeremy Taylor. St. John's, Antigua: FT Caribbean, 1988.

Caribbean Handbook 1993/94, Ed. Lindsay Maxwell. Tortola, Jungferninseln: FT Caribbean, 1 993.

Caribbean Media Directory. In: (Eds.) Jamaica Institute of Political Education and Eastern Caribbean Institute for Democracy. Kingston, Jamaica, and Roseau, Commonwealth of Dominica: Jamaica Institute of Political Education and Eastern Caribbean Institute for Democracy, November 1986.

Caribbean News Agency. Owned by the Media—Operated for the Media. Leaflet. June 1983.

Caribbean Organization—The First Three Years, Hato Rey, Puerto Rico, Central Secretariat, 1 964

Caribbean Press Council. Articles of Constitution. 23 May 1980 with amendments dated 9 September 1981. Typescript.

Background Paper-CPC...Whence?...Whither. By Alister Hughes, Executive Secretary. September 1982. Typescript.

Caribbean Publishing and Broadcasting Association, Rules of the... Amended at a Meeting of the Association November 14 and 15, 1974. n.d.

Caribbean and World Politics. Cross Currents and Cleavages, The. In: (Eds.) Jorge Heine and Leslie Manigat. New York and London: Holmes & Meier, 1988.

CARICOM/Suriname/Group of Three: Joint Communique and Speeches, Port-of-Spain, Trinidad and Tobago, 12-13 October, 1993. Supplement to *CARICOM PERSPECTIVE* 32 (July-December 1993).

Carifesta Forum. An Anthology of 20 Caribbean Voices. Ed. and introduced by John Hearne Kingston, Jamaica: Institute of Jamaica and Jamaica Journal, 1976

Carimac — Emphasis on Development Communication *The Daily Gleaner* 3 January 1982, p. 13.

Carimex '85 — A Caribbean Manufacturers Exhibition Barbados: Caribbean Association of Industry and Commerce, 1985.

Carlson, Alvar W., Caribbean Immigration to the US 1965-1989, *Caribbean Affairs* 7.1 (March-April 1994), pp. 142-160.

Carlucci, Frank C. US Defence Policy and Latin America. Remarks prepared for delivery by the Honourable Frank C. Carlucci, Deputy Secretary of Defense, to the Council of the Americas, Washington, D.C. Monday, June, 1982. Typescript Washington: Office of Assistant Secretary of Defense (Public Affairs) No.271-82.

Carrington, Edwin. The Record of CARICOM/ACP-EEC Relations. *Ten Years of CARICOM.* Washington, D.C.: Inter-American Development Bank, 1984, pp. 175-182.

Towards a Single Market 1992 *CARICOM PERSPECTIVE* 46 and 47 (July-December 1989, January-March 1990), pp. 3, 4 and 28.

Carter, Samuel. The Development of Peoples: Twenty Years Later. A Pastoral Letter from Archbishop Samuel E. Carter S J.' Kingston, Jamaica, Pentecost, 1987. Supplement to *Catholic Opinion* (Kingston, Jamaica).

Chambers, George. Statement by the Honourable George Chambers, Prime Minister of the Republic of Trinidad and Tobago, at the Formal Opening Ceremony of the 5th Conference of Heads of Government of the Caribbean Community. Nassau, Bahamas 4, July 1984. Trinidad and Tobago: Ministry of Information, Press Release No.453, 1984, Typescript.

Clarke, Colin. *Sovereignty, Dependency and Social Change In the Caribbean 1986* London: Europa Publications, 1985.

Clarke, Edith. *My Mother Who Fathered Me* 1 August 1957. 6th edn. London *et.al.*.: Allen & Unwin, 1979.

Closing the Skills Gap. *CARICOM PERSPECTIVE* 29 (January-February 1985), pp. 26-27

Cobham, Rhonda. The Background. *West Indian Literature.* Ed. Bruce King. London and Basingstoke: Macmillan, 1979, pp. 9-29

Coldrick, A. P., and Philip Jones. *The International Directory of the Trade Union Movement* London and Basingstoke, Macmillan, 1979.

Commonwealth and the Caribbean Community. PERSPECTIVE interviews Shridath Ramphal. *CARICOM PERSPECTIVE* 32 (July-October 1985), pp. 29-30.

Communique and Speeches. 14th Meeting of the Conference of Heads of Government of The Caribbean Community, Nassau, The Bahamas 5—8 July, 1993. Supplement *CARICOM PERSPECTIVE* 61 and 62 (July — December 1993).

Compton, John. Interview with the Rt. Hon. John Compton, Prime Minister of St.Lucia, August 26, 1988 in Castries St.Lucia. Questions asked by Christoph Müllerleile. *Reflections* (Kingston, Jamaica) July 1988 [*sic*], pp. 18-22.

Constitution of The Caribbean Youth Conference, Unity, Freedom, Democracy Castries, St. Lucia: Caribbean Youth Conference, 1987.

Constitution of the Co-operative Republic of Guyana Georgetown, Guyana, 1980

Conway, Dennis. Migration and Urbanisation Policies. Immediate Needs for the 21st Century. *Caribbean Affairs* 4 3 (October-December 1990), pp. 64-86

Cooper, Richard N. *The Economics of Interdependence Economic Policy in The Atlantic Community.* New York *et al* · McGraw-Hill, 1968.

Corsbie, Ken. *Theatre in the Caribbean* London *et al* Hodder and Stoughton, 1984.

Crassweller, Robert D *The Caribbean Community Changing Societies and US Policy* Published for the Council on Foreign Relations. New York, Washington and London. Praeger, 1972.

Cummings, Christine. Why Sports: The Relevance of a Co-ordinated Sports Policy to National Development in Jamaica. *The Money Index* (Kingston, Jamaica) 179 (11 July 1989), pp. 4-7 and 13.

Curtin, Philip. *The Atlantic Slavetrade: A Census.* Madison, Wisconsin: University of Wisconsin Press, 1969

Cuthbert, Marlene Lillian. The Caribbean News Agency, Genesis of an Indigenous News Agency in a Developing Region. Typescript, Diss. Syracuse University, 1979.

Cuthbert, Robert W.M. *Ecumenism and Development. A Socio-Historical Analysis of the Caribbean Conference of Churches.* Bridgetown, Barbados: Caribbean Conference of Churches, 1986.

DaBreo, D. Sinclair. *Of Men and Politics —The Agony of St. Lucia.* Castries, St. Lucia: Commonwealth Publishers International, 1981.

Dabydeen, David, and Brinsley Samaroo, (Eds.) *India in the Caribbean.* London: Hansib, 1987.

Dahlberg, Kenneth A. Regional Integration: The Neo-Functional Versus a Configurative Approach'. *International Organization* 24, 1970, pp. 122-128.

Danns, George K. The Role of the Entrepreneur in the Development Strategy of the Caribbean. *Caribbean Affairs* 2.3 (July-September 1989), pp. 152-160.

Davis, Stephen, and Peter Simon. *Reggae International.* New York: Alfred A. Knopf/ Rogner and Bernard, 1983.

Demas, William G. *The Economics of Development in Small Countries with Special Reference to the Caribbean.* Montreal: McGill University Press, 1965.

West Indian Nationhood and Caribbean Integration. Barbados: CCC Publishing House, 1974.

Change and Renewal in the Caribbean. Challenges in the New Caribbean No.2. Ed. David I. Mitchell. Barbados: CCC Publishing House, 1975.

Essays on Caribbean Integration and Development. With an introduction by Alister McIntyre. Kingston, Jamaica: Institute of Social and Economic Research, University of the West Indies, 1976.

The Viability of the Organisation of East [*sic*] Caribbean States. *Bulletin of Eastern Caribbean Affairs* (Cave Hill, Barbados) 8.1 (March/April 1982), pp. 5-23.

Making CDB More Effective. Statement to the Board of Governors, Cartagena, Colombia May 11 & 12, 1983. Wildey, St.Michael, Barbados: Caribbean Development Bank, 1983.

Consolidating Our Independence. The Major Challenge for the West Indies. Institute of International Relations. Distinguished Lecturer Series. St. Augustine, Trinidad and Tobago, University of the West Indies, Institute of International Relations, 1986. Shortened version in: *Caribbean Contact* August 1986, pp. 8-9.

Seize the Time. Towards OECS Political Union. Based on an Address at the Inauguration of the National Advisory Committee of St.Vincent and the Grenadines on Political Unity in the Eastern Caribbean on Monday, 20 July, 1987. St. Michael, Barbados: [Caribbean Development Bank] 26.8.1987.

Political Unity in Perspective. *CARICOM PERSPECTIVE* 41 (January-March 1988), pp. 37 and 51.

Towards West Indian Survival An Essay by William Demas. Black Rock, St James, Barbados: The West Indian Commission Secretariat, 1990

Dennils, Colin. *The Road not Taken. Memoirs of a Relucant Guerrilla.* Kingston, Jamaica: Kingston Publishers, 1985

Deosaran, Ramesh. The wounded state of Caribbean patriotism. *The Sunday Gleaner* 27 March 1983, pp. 13 and 26.

Nationalism vs. CARICOM. *Caribbean Contact,* April 1984, p. 7.

Role of the Press in the Caribbean. *Caribbean Review* 13.4 (Fall 1984b), pp. 16-19, 45-46.

dePestre, René. Problems of Identity for the Black Man in the Caribbean. *Carifesta Forum. An Anthology of 20 Caribbean Voices.* Edited and introduced by John Hearne. Kingston, Jamaica: Institute of Jamaica and Jamaica Journal, 1976, pp. 1 -67.

Depestre dePestre, René. Aus dem Kreolismus entstand die Neue Welt der Antillen [The New World of the Caribbean has Arisen from Creolism]. *UNESCO-Kurier* 22.12 (1981), pp. 16-17.

Deutsch, Karl W. *Political Community at the International Level* New York: Doubleday, 1954.

Nationenbildung — Nationalstaat — Integration [Nation-building — the Nation State — Integration.] In: (Eds.) A. Ashkenasi and P. Schulze. Dusseldorf, Germany: Bertelsmann, 1972.

Devonish, Hubert. *Language and Liberation—Creole Language Politics.* London· Karia Press. 1986.

DeVree, Johan K. *Political Integration: The Formation of Theory and its Problems.* The Hague and Paris: Mouton, 1972.

Diner, Dan. Internationales Seerecht [International Maritime Law]. *Pipers Wörerbuch zur Politik. [Piper's Political Dictionary.]* Ed. Dieter Nohlen. Vol. 5. Munich and Zürich: Piper, 1984, pp. 260-267.

Documents on the Invasion of Grenada. *Caribbean Monthly Bulletin*. Supplement No. 1. Rio Piedras, Puerto Rico: University of Puerto Rico, October 1983.

Dominguez, Jorge I., and DeLisle R. Worrell (Eds.). *Democracy in the Caribbean. Political, Economic and Social Perspectives*. Baltimore and London: Johns Hopkins University Press, 1993.

Dookhan, Isaac. *A Post-Emancipation History of the West Indies*. 2nd edn , London: Collins, 1977.

Doyle-Marshall, William. Regional Governments Urged to Save LIAT. *Weekly Gleaner* 15 November 1994, p. 11.

Drayton, Kathleen. UWI at the Cross Roads. *Caribbean Contact*, August 1981, pp. 8-9.

Duff, Ernest A. Cultural Imperialism in the Caribbean: The Challenge in the 90s. *Caribbean Affairs* 3.1 (Jan.-March 1990), pp. 38-48.

Duncan, Neville. Caribbean Security. *CARICOM PERSPECTIVE* 37 (January-March 1987), pp. 2, 5 and 6.

Dymally, Mervyn. Irrational Passions Underlie US-Carib Policies: Dymally. *Caribbean Contact* December 1985, pp. 8-9.

East Caribbean Common Market Agreement. Castries, St. Lucia: Attorney General's Chambers, Government Buildings, 9th June 1968.

Eaton, George E. *Alexander Bustamante and Modern Jamaica*. Kingston, Jamaica: Kingston Publishers, 1975.

Eckenstein, Christopher. The Rationale and Obstacles of Regional Integration among Developing Countries. *Regionalism and the Commonwealth Caribbean*. Ed. Roy Preiswerk. Special Lecture Series No. 2. St. Augustine, Trinidad: University of the West Indies, Institute of International Relations, 1969, pp. 25-32 .

Regional Integration among Unequally Developed Countries. *Regionalism and the Commonwealth Caribbean*. Ed. Roy Preiswerk. Special Lecture Series No. 2. St. Augustine,Trinidad: University of the West Indies, Institute of International Relations, 1969, pp. 41-55.

Economic Integration. The OECS Experience. Castries, St. Lucia: OECS Central Secretariat, March 1988.

The EEC and the Caribbean. *Europe Information, Development*. Commission of the European Communities, Director General of Information. X/188/1981. Brussels, June 1981.

Emmanuel, Patrick, Vaughan A. Lewis and Alister McIntyre. The Political Economy of : Independence for the Leeward and Windward Islands. Typescript Barbados 23 February 1975.

— Farley Brathwaite and Eudine Barriteau. *Political Change and Public Opinion in Grenada 1979-1984*. Occasional Paper No. 19. Cave Hill, Barbados: Institute of Social and Economic Research (Eastern Caribbean), University of the West Indies, 1986.

— *Approaches to Caribbean Political Integration*. Occasional Paper No. 21. Barbados: Institute of Social and Economic Research (Eastern Caribbean), University of the West Indies, Cave Hill, 1987.

Emtage, Steve E. Notes on the Role of Financial Cooperation in the Integration Process. *Ten Years of CARICOM*. Washington, D.C.: Inter-American Development Bank, 1984, pp. 131-141.

Entwicklungen im karibischen Raum 1980-1985. Ed. Wolfgang Binder. Erlanger Forschungen, Reihe A Geisteswissenschaften, Bd.37. Erlangen: Universitätsbund Erlangen-Nürnberg [*1980-85 Caribbean Area Developments*. (Ed.) Wolfgang Binder. Erlangen Research Series A, Humanities No. 37. Erlangen: Erlangen-Nuremberg University Union], 1985.

Erisman, H. Michael. *Pursuing Postdependency Politics. South-South Relations in the Caribbean*. Boulder, Colorado: Lynne Rienner, 1993.

— and John D. Mantz, (Eds.) *Colossus Challenged: The Struggle for Caribbean Influence*. Boulder, Colorado: Westview Press, 1982.

— (Eds.) *The Caribbean Challenge. US Policy in a Volatile Region*. Boulder, Colorado: Westview Press, 1984.

Espeut, Audley A. The Long Term Effects of Under-Capitalisation of a Small Airline. *CDB News* 9.1-2 (January-June 1991), pp. 5-7.

Etzioni. Amitai. *Die aktive Cesellschaft. Eine Theorie gesellschaftlicher und politischer Prozesse*. Translated by Sylvia and Wolfgang Streeck. Orig. *The Active Society,* 1968. Opladen, Germany: Westdeutscher Verlag, 1975.

Europa Yearbook 1989, A World Survey. 2 volumes. London: Europa Publications, 1989.

Fanger, Ulrich. Problems of Public Administration in a Small State Setting: Conclusions from the Caribbean Experience of the Past Two Decades. *Problems of Caribbean Development. Regional Interaction, International Relations, and the Constraints of Small Size.* Ed. Ulrich Fanger *et.al.* Contributions to the Sociology and Social Information on Latin America, Vol.21; Ed. Hanns-Albert Steger. Munich: Wilhelm Fink, 1982, pp. 187-200.

Farrell, Terrence W. The Political Economy of Caribbean Monetary and Financial Integration. *Caribbean Affairs* 4.4 (October-December, 1991), pp. 20-29.

Farrell, Trevor M. The Caribbean State and its Role in Economic Management. The State in Caribbean Society. Ed. Omar Davies. Kingston, Jamaica: University of the West Indies, Department of Economics, 1986, pp. 6-27.

— Oil and Political Economy in the Commonwealth Caribbean. *The Caribbean and World Politics. Cross Currents and Cleavages.* In: (Eds.) Jorge Heine and Leslie Manigat. New York and London: Holmes & Meier, 1988, pp. 112-129.

Fashion Me A People. A Curriculum for Church Schools. Youth. Year One. (Bridgetown, Barbados) Caribbean Conference of Churches, 1981.

Fauriol, Georges. US Caribbean Policy in the 1990s. *USA, USSR and the Caribbean—The New Realities.* Kingston, Jamaica: Bustamante Institute of Public and International Affairs, 1990, pp.58-65 .

Feinberg, Richard E.*et.al.* The Battle Over the CBI. *Caribbean Review* 2.12 (Spring 1983), pp. 15-1 8, 47

Fergus, Howard A. Cultural Survival & Development. *CARICOM PERSPECTIVE* 41 (January-March 1988), pp. 15 and 18.

— Constitutional Downgrading for Montserrat—Tampering with the Constitution? *Caribbean Affairs* 3.2 (April-June 1990), pp. 56-67.

— Machinery for Implementation: Response to the Report of the West Indian Commission. *Caribbean Affairs* 5.4 (October-December 1992), pp. 138-147.

Figueroa, John J. *Society, Schools and Progress in the West Indies*. Oxford *et.al* : Pergamon Press, 1 971 .

Der Fischer Weltalmanach 1988 [The Fischer World Almanach 1988]. Frankfurt/Main, Germany:Fischer Taschenbuch Verlag, *1987.*

Der Fischer Weltalmanach 1994. [The Fischer World Almanach 1994]. Frankfurt/Main, Germany:Fischer Taschenbuch Verlag, 1993.

Forde, Henry. Security of Small States. A Caribbean Perspective. *Democracy Today* January/February 1991, pp. 3 and 5.

Forging a New Democracy — Beyond the Post-Colonial Aera Ed. Raphael Sebastien. Trinidad and Tobago: Office of the Leader of the Opposition, (March 1985).

Fourth and Final Report of the Regional Constituent Assembly of the Windward Islands. The Windwards Way to Union. (St. Lucia:1992).

Francis, Fitzgerald. The Caribbean Development Bank. *Regionalism and the Commonwealth Caribbean.* Ed. Roy Preiswerk. Special Lecture Series No.2. St. Augustine, Trinidad: University of the West Indies, Institute of International Relations, 1969, pp. 80-107.

Freymond, *Jean F. Political Integration in the Commonwealth Caribbean. A Survey of Recent Attempts with Special Reference to the Associated States(1967-1974).* Serie Études et travaux de l'Institut Universitaire de Hautes Études Internationales [Studies and Papers of the Graduate School of International Affairs] No. 17. Geneva: Institut Universitaire de Hautes Études Internationales [Graduate School of International Affairs], 1980.

Friedrich, Carl Joachim. *Europa—Nation im Werden? [Europe—Becoming a Nation?]*. Bonn, Germany: Europa Union Verlag, 1972.

— Politik als Prozeß der Gemeinschaftswerdung. Eine empirische Theorie [*Politics as the Process of Becoming a Society: An Empirical Theory*]. Köln and Opladen, Germany: Westdeutscher Verlag, 1970.

Furtak, Robert K. Die Lateinamerika-Politik der Sowjetunion. *Aus Politik und Zeitgeschichte.* Beilage zur Wochenzeitung *Das Parlament* [The Latin American Foreign Policy of the Soviet

Union in: *Politics and Contemporary History*. Supplement to the weekly, *Parliament*] B9/86, 1 March 1986, pp. 43-54.

Garvey Jr., Marcus. I Simply Told the Truth. *The Weekly Gleaner* 24 November 1987, p. 20.

Gasiorowski, Mark J. The Structure of Third World Economic Interdependence. *International Organization* 39 (Spring 1985), pp. 331-342.

Gastil, Raymond D. The Comparative Survey of Freedom 1987. *Freedom at Issue* 94 (January-February 1987), pp. 19-34.

Gay, Arthur. Accord Heavier than Paper it is on. *Daily Nation*, Barbados 11 November 1985, p. 4.

Gehren, Georg von. Das britische Commonwealth heute. Ein bedeutsames Forum für internationale politische Diskussionen . *Das Parlament* [The British Commonwealth Today: a significant Forum for International Political Discussions' in: *Parliament*] 1987 8 (21.February), p. 9.

Geiser, Hans J., Pamela Alleyne and Carroll Gajraj. *Legal Problems of Caribbean Integration* St. Augustine, Trinidad: Sijthoff-Leyden and Institute of International Relations, 1976.

The Georgetown Declaration. Supplement to *CARICOM PERSPECTIVE* 36 (July-December 1986).

Gewecke, Frauke. *Die Karibik Zu Geschichte, Politik und Kultur einer Region* [*The Caribbean. its History, Politics and Culture*] 2nd Edn. Frankfurt/Main, Germany: Vervuert, 1988.

Ghany, Hamid. The Myth of the Westminster Model *Caribbean Affairs* 7 3 (July/August 1994), pp. 62-82.

Girvan, Norman, and Owen Jefferson, (Eds.) *Readings in the Political Economy of the Caribbean*. Reprint. Kingston, Jamaica: New World Group, 1974

Global Challenge. From Crisis to Co-operation. Breaking the North-South Stalemate. The Report of the Socialist International Committee on Economic Policy chaired by Michael Manley. London and Sydney: Pan Books, 1985.

Gloudon, Barbara, *vide* 'Stella'.

Götz, Nicola. *Familie und Matrifokalitat in der Karibik.* [*Family and Matrifocality in the Caribbean*]. Saarbrücken, Germany: Breitenbach, 1986.

Gonzales, Anthony P. ACP/EEC Negotiations: Onward Never, Backward Ever? The Setting: Striking a New Regional/Global Balance. *CARICOM PERSPECTIVE* 24 (March-April 1984a), pp. 10, 11, 17 and 23.

— The Future of CARICOM Collective Self-Reliance in Decline? *Caribbean Review* 13.4 (Fall 1984b), pp. 8-11 and 40.

— The End of ACP/EEC Negotiations, Lomé Cooperation Rides Again. *CARICOM PERSPECTIVE* 29 (January-February 1985), pp. 16-17.

— Lomé and Structural Transformation in the Region. *CARICOM PERSPECTIVE* 42 (April-June 1988), pp. 4 and 7.

— CARICOM: Back to Square One — with Experience. *CARICOM PERSPECTIVE* 36 (April-June 1986), pp. 2 and 27.

— Caribbean External Strategy and the Changing International System. *CARICOM PERSPECTIVE* 46 & 47 (July-December 1989 — January-March 1990), pp. 12 and 39.

— NAFTA and the Caribbean: Weighing the Options. *CARICOM PERSPECTIVE* 56 and 57 (July-December 1992), pp 5-7.

Goodwin, Clayton. *West Indians at the Wicket*. London and Basingstoke· Macmillan,1986.

Gordon, Ernle P. In Defence of Communism. Letter to the Editor in *The Daily Gleaner* 22 August 1983, p. 3

— Christianity — A Religion of the Poor. *Caribbean Contact* September 1984, p. 12.

Gramckow, Heike. Die Drogenpolitik der Bush-Administration and die Entwicklung des Drogenproblems in den USA. *Aus Politik und Zeitgeschichte*. Beilage zur Wochenzeitung *Das Parlament*. [The Anti-Narcotics Policy of the Bush Administration and the Development of the US Drug Problems' in: *Politics and Contemporary History*. Supplement to the weekly, *Parliament*] B42/90 (12.10.1990), pp. 28-39).

Grand Anse Declaration and Work Programme for the Advancement of the Integration Movement. Issued at the Tenth Meeting of the Conference of Heads of Government of the Caribbean Community (Off-print. Georgetown, Guyana: Caribbean Community Secretariat, 1989).

Granger, David A Regional Security Regime for the Caribbean? *CARICOM PERSPECTIVE* 56 & 57 /July-December 1992), pp. 76, 77 and 79.

Grant, Rudolph W., and Una M. Paul. Perceptions of Caribbean Regional Integration: A Comparative Study of the Perceptions of Caribbean Teacher Trainees. *Social and Economic Studies* 34.1 (1985),pp. 1-26.

Grayson, George W. The Joint Oil Facility. *Caribbean Review* 12.2 (Spring 1983), pp. 19-21 and 49.

Green, Andrew Wilson. Review Article. Mitrany Reread with the Help of Haas and Sewell. *Journal of Common Market Studies* 8.1 (1969), pp. 50-69.

Greene, J. Edward. *Race vs. Politics in Guyana*. Kingston, Jamaica: Institute of Social and Economic Relations, 1974.

— Towards Finding Solutions. *CARICOM PERSPECTIVE* 31 (May-June 1985), p. 37.

Greene, James R., and Brent Scowcroft, (Eds.) *Western Interests and US Policy Options in the Caribbean Basin. Report of the Atlantic Council's Working Group on the Caribbean Basin*. Boston, Mass.: Oelschlager, Gunn & Hain for The Atlantic Council of the United States, 1984.

Greenidge, Carl. 1992 and the Caribbean Part 1. *CARICOM PERSPECTIVE* 43 (July-December 1988), p. 9.

Greenleaf, W.H. *The Ideological Heritage*. The British Political Tradition, Vol.2. London and New York: Methuen, 1983.

Gregg, Robert W. The UN Regional Economic Commissions and Integration in the Underdeveloped Regions. *Regional Politics and World Order*. In. (Eds.) Richard A. Falk and Saul H. Mendlovitz. San Francisco: W.H. Freeman, 1973, pp. 308-327.

The Grenada Declaration 1971. *Caribbean Quarterly* 18.2 (June 1972), pp. 48-50.

Grenada Papers, In: (Eds.) Paul Seabury and Walter A.McDougall. San Francisco: Institute for Contemporary Studies, 1984.

Griffith, Ivelaw L. The Regional Security System —A Decade of Caribbean Collective Security. *Caribbean Affairs* 5.3 (July-September 1992), pp. 179-191.

Grigsby, Daryl Russell. *For the People. Black Socialists in the United States, Africa and the Caribbean*. San Diego, CA: Asante Publications, 1987.

Guyana Fraudulent Revolution London: Latin-America Bureau, 1984

Haas, Ernst B. The Study of Regional Integration: Reflections on the Joy and Anguish of Pretheorizing Richard A. Falk and Saul H. Mendlovitz (Eds.) *Regional Politics and World Order*. San Francisco: W.H.Freeman, 1973. 103-132. *International Organization* 24.4 (Autumn 1970), pp. 607-646.

— Turbulent Fields and the Theory of Regional Integration. *International Organization* 30 2 (Spring 1976), pp. 173-212.

— and Philippe C. Schmitter. Economics and Differential Patterns of Political Integration. *International Political Communities*. New York: Doubleday Anchor, 1966, pp. 259-299.

Hall, Kenneth O The Management of External Political Relations and Its Effect on the Integration Process. *Ten Years of CARICOM* Washington, D.C.. Inter-American Development Bank, 1984, pp. 167-174.

Hamilton, Beverly. Caribbean Culture—Frank Pilgrim Reminisces. *Caribbean Contact*, February 1987, p. 13

Harker, Peter Winds of Change — Moving towards an Integrated Subregion. *CARICOM PERSPECTIVE* 37 (January-March 1987), pp. 19 and 27.

Harris, Allan, and Michael Harris. The Westminster Model — Can We Work It Better? *Forging a New Democracy — Beyond the Post-Colonial Aera*. Ed Raphael Sebastien Trinidad and Tobago: Office of the Leader of the Opposition, March 1985.

Harrison, Reginald J. *Europe in Question. Theories of Regional International Integration*. London: George Allen & Unwin, 1974.

Hasters, Rainer. Putschversuch in Trinidad — Hintergründe und Ausblick. *KAS-Auslandsinformationen* ['The Attempted Coup d'État in Trinidad: Background and Prospects'. Konrad-Adenauer-Stiftung Information from Abroad] 1990. 11 (November 1990), pp. 7-15.

— Karibik vor neuen Herausforderungen. *KAS-Auslandsinformationen* [New Challenges Facing the Caribbean] Konrad-Adenauer-Stiftung Information from Abroad 1993.1 (January 1993), pp. 2 1 -24.

Hearne, John. Identity. A Further View. The Dai/y Gleaner February 23 1984, p. 8.

— Last Chance for W. I Integration. *Democracy Today* (Kingston, Jamaica) 6.1 (January 1990), pp. 2.

Heberle, Rudolf. *Hauptprobleme der politischen Soziologie.* [*Main Problems of Political Sociology*] Stuttgart, Germany: Enke, 1967.

Hector, Tim. *The Media and the Caribbean State.* First Caribbean Conference of Intellectual Workers, Grenada. November 20-22, 1982. Address by Tim Hector, Antigua. Typescript n.d.

— Shell Shield without Shell. *CARICOM PERSPECTIVE* 37 (January-March 1987), pp. 29 and 47.

Heine, Jorge, Ed. *A Revolution Aborted. The Lessons of Grenada.* Pittsburgh, Pennsylvania: University of Pennsylvania Press, 1990.

Hellinger, Marlis. The Heritage of Colonialism: Bilingualism in the English-speaking Caribbean. *El Caribe y América Latina — The Caribbean and Latin America.* In: (Eds.) Ulrich Fleischmann and Ineke Phaf. Frankfurt/Main, Germany: Vervuert, 1987, pp. 245-252.

Henry, Mike. Whither the Small Publisher. *CARICOM PERSPECTIVE* 33 (November-December 1985), pp. 26-28.

Hippolyte-Manigat, Mirlande. *Haiti and the Caribbean Community. Profile of an Applicant and the Problematique of Widening the Integration Movement.* Kingston, Jamaica: University of the West Indies, Institute of Social and Economic Research, 1980.

— What Happened in Ocho Rios. Last Chance for CARICOM? *Caribbean Review* 12.2 (Spring 1983), pp. 10-14.

Hodge, Merle. The Caribbean Crisis of Marriage — An Analysis. *Caribbean Contact* April 1985, pp. 17-18.

— West Indian Literature and its Political Context. *Caribbean Contact,* June 1987, pp. 9-10.

Hope, C.M. Charles Understands Thatcher on South Africa. *Caribbean Contact,* November 1985, pp. 1 and 5.

— Barbados Revolution. *Caribbean Contact,* July 1986, p. 7.

— Class and Racial Antagonisms Defeat Sandiford. *Caribbean Contact,* August 1994, p. 4f.

Horowitz, Irving Louis. Democracy and Development. *The Newer Caribbean — Decolonization, Democracy and Development.* In: (Eds.) Paget Henry and Carl Stone. Philiadelphia: Institute for the Study of Human Issues, 1983, pp. 221-233.

Hoyos, F.A. *Barbados. A History from the Amerindians to Independence.* London and Basingstoke: Macmillan Education, 1978.

Hoyte, Desmond. Making the Quantum Leap: Imperatives, Opportunities and Challenges for CARICOM. *Caribbean Affairs* 2.2 (April-June 1989a), pp. 51-72.

— Growth, Development and the Environment in the Caribbean Community. *Caribbean Affairs* 2.4 (October-December 1989b), pp. 63-70.

Huber Stephens, Evelyne, and John D. Stephens. *Democratic Socialism in Jamaica. The Political Movement and Social Transformation in Dependent Capitalism.* Houndmills and London: Macmillan, 1986.

Hudson-Phillips, Karl. Flying Together. *CARICOM PERSPECTIVE* 48 (April-June 1990), pp. 46 and 51.

Hurley, Sharon. 15 Years of the CXC's Achievements. *Caribbean Contact* November 1988, p. 8.

Husbands, Avril. CXC — Its Role and Contribution to Regional Integration. *CARICOM PERSPECTIVE* 31 (May-June 1985), p. 42.

Inglehart, Ronald. Public Opinion and Regional Integration. *International Organization* 24.4 (Autumn 1970), pp. 764-795.

Irish Slaves in the West Indies. *Catholic News* (Trinidad) 19. and 26 February 1910. Reprinted *Catholic News* 6 March 1983, pp. 9-10.

Jaber, Tayseer A. The Relevance of Traditional Integration Theory to Less Developed Countries. *Journal of Common Market Studies* 9 (1970), pp. 254-267.

Jacob, Debbie. CAREC: Achievement through Cooperation. *Caribbean Affairs* 4.2 (April-June 1991), pp. 162-166.

Jacobs, Cecil. The Eastern Caribbean Central Bank. *OECS in PERSPECTIVE 1987.* Castries, St. Lucia, and St. John's, Antigua: Organisation of Eastern Caribbean States, May 1987, pp. 39-40.

Jacobs, W. Richard, and Ian Jacobs. *Grenada. The Route to Revolution.* Havana, Cuba: Casa de las Américas, 1980.

Jäger, Hermann. Deutsches Radio in der Karibischen See [German Radio in the Caribbean Sea]. *Neue Zürcher Zeitung* 17 August 1977.

Jagan, Cheddi. *The West on Trial. The Fight for Guyana's Freedom.* Revised version 1972, Reprinted Berlin: Seven Seas Publishers, 1980.

— The Caribbean Community: Crossroads to the Future. *Caribbean Affairs* 7.3 (July/August 1994), pp. 18 — 37.

Jagdeo, Tirbani P. *Teenage Pregnancy in the Caribbean.* New York and Antigua: International Planned Parenthood Federation, Western Hemisphere Region, and Caribbean Family Planning Affiliation, 1984.

Jain, Ajit. Hinduism is on a March. *The Star* (Kingston, Jamaica) 4 August 1984, p. 8.

— *Caribbean Youth and the International Year.* Kingston, Jamaica: Bustamante Institute of Public and International Affairs, January, 1986.

Jamadar, Peter A. *The Mechanics of Democracy. Proportional Representation vs. First Past the Post.* Port-of-Spain, Trinidad: Inprint Caribbean, 1989.

Jamaica All-Media Survey 1984. Kingston, Jamaica: Market Research Ltd, 1984.

James, Mike. Challenges to Caribbean Theology. *Caribbean Contact* April 1984, p. 13.

James, W.A. *Love is All I Bring. A Critical Analysis of Democratic Socialism in Jamaica 1972-1980.* London 1982.

Januszczah, Waldemar. Walcott — The Longing on St. Lucia. *Cannelles.* Supplement to *Weekend Voice* (St. Lucia). 20 August 1988, p. 2.

Jeffrey, Henry B., and Colin Baber. *Guyana. Politics, Economics and Society.* London: Frances Pinter, and Boulder, Colorado: Lynne Rienner, 1986.

Jennings, Ivor W., and Gerhard A. Ritter. *Das britische Regierungssystem. Leitfaden und Quellenbuch* [The English System of Government: Guide and Sourcebook]. 2nd revised and expanded edition. Cologne and Opladen, Germany: Westdeutscher Verlag, 1970.

JLP 1943 — 1978. 35 Years Ringing the Freedom Bell for Equal Rights and Justice. Kingston, Jamaica: Jamaica Labour Party, 1978.

Joint Opposition Statement on Grenada Declaration. Typescript, 13 November 1971.

Jones, Edwin. Comments on Stone. *The State in Caribbean Society.* Ed. Omar Davies. Kingston, Jamaica: University of the West Indies, Department of Economics, September 1986, pp. 145-154.

Jones-Hendrickson, S.B. Rational Expectations, Causality and Integrative Fiscal-monetary Policy in the Caribbean. *Social and Economic Studies* 34.4 (December 1985), pp. 111-138.

Kambon, Khafra. The Political System and its Constraints on Cultural Sovereignty. *Independence and Cultural Sovereignty.* First Caribbean Conference of Intellectual Workers, Grenada. November 20-22, 1982. Typescript 1984, pp. 3-27.

Kamenev, Konstantin. The Regional Foreign Policy of the United States. USSR in the Caribbean. USA, *USSR and the Caribbean — The New Realities.* Kingston, Jamaica: Bustamante Institute of Public and International Affairs, 1990, pp. 46-49.

Kaplan, Morton A. *System and Process in International Politics.* New York: John Wiley, 1957.

Katzenstein, Peter J. Hare and Tortoise: The Race toward Integration. *International Organization* 25 (1971), pp. 290-295.

Kaufman, Michael. *Jamaica under Manley. Dilemmas of Socialism and Democracy.* London: Zed Books, 1985.

Keohane, Robert O., and Joseph S. Nye. *Power and Interdependence.* Boston: Little, Brown & Company, 1977.

Kiderlen, Hans-Joachim. Das vorbereitende Tiefseebergbauregime unter 'Resolution II' [The Preparatory Deep Sea Mining Regime under 'Resolution II']. *Vereinte Nationen* 1/1990, pp. 7-11.

King, Kurleigh. Opening Address. *Ten Years of CARICOM.* Washington, D.C.: Inter-American Development Bank, 1984, pp. 8-13.

Kingston Declaration, Kingston, Jamaica, 2 August 1990. Supplement to *CARICOM PERSPECTIVE* 49 (July-December 1990).

Kirton, Allan. A Theology to Serve the Powerless. *Caribbean Contact,* October 1984, p. 4.

— Bringing the Caribbean on Board CARICOM. *Caribbean Contact,* August 1983, p. 3.

— Give We Back One Nation? *Caribbean Contact,* March 1986, p. 3.

Knaack, Kristian. Foreign Media vs Caribbean Culture. Lecture for the Caribbean Broadcasting Union. Typescript, Montserrat, 4 October 1987.

Knight, Franklin W. *The Caribbean. The Genesis of a Fragmented Nationalism.* New York: Oxford University Press, 1978

Knowles, Yereth Kahn. *Beyond the Caribbean States: A History of Regional Cooperation in the Commonwealth Caribbean* Doctoral Thesis, Geneva University, 1972 San German, Puerto Rico: Caribbean Institute and Study Center for Latin America, 1972.

Kohut, Karl. Rasse als Problem der Karibikforschung. Ed. *Rasse, Klasse und Kultur in der Karibik* Publikationen des Zentralinstituts für Lateinamerika-Studien der Katholischen Universität Eichstätt, Serie A, Kongreßakten, 5. ['Race as Problem in Caribbean Research' in: (Ed.) *Race, Class and Culture in the Caribbean*: Publications of the Central Institute for Latin-American Studies of the Catholic University of Eichstätt, Series A. Proceedings of the 5th Congress] Frankfurt/Main, Germany: Vervuert, 1989, pp. 7-20.

Konrad-Adenauer-Stiftung (ed.). *Partner Organisations in the English-speaking Caribbean.* Kingston, Jamaica: Jamaica Institute of Political Education, 1993.

Krämer, Raimund. Kuba: Das Ende des 'karibischen Sozialismus'. *Aus Politik und Zeitgeschichte* Beilage zur Wochenzeitung *Das Parlament* Cuba: The end of Caribbean Socialism in: *Politics and Contemporary History* Supplement to the weekly, *Parliament* B39/91 (20 September 1991), pp 19-28.

Krosigk, Friedrich von Entwicklungsprobleme und Uberlebensperspektiven kleiner Staaten: Karibik und Südpazifik im Vergleich. *Entwicklungen im karibischen Raum 1980-1985* Ed Wolfgang Binder Erlanger Forschungen, Reihe A Geisteswissenschaften, Vol 37 Erlangen Universitätsbund Erlangen-Numberg ['Developmental Problems and Survival Prospects of Small States: the Caribbean Compared with the South Pacific', in: *1980-85 Caribbean Area Developments.* (Ed.) Wolfgang Binder. Erlangen Research Series A, Humanities No 37 Erlangen: Erlangen-Nuremberg University Union], 1985, pp 237-258

Krumwiede, Heinrich W. Militärherrschaft und (Re-)Demokratisierung in Zentralamerika. *Aus Politik und Zeitgeschichte* Beilage zur Wochenzeitung *Das Parlament* [Military Rule and (Re)-democratization in Central America, in: *Politics and Contemporary History.* Supplement to the weekly, *Parliament*] B9/86 (1 3.1986), pp 17-29

Kwayana, Eusi. Economic Relations in Pre-Republican Guyana. *Co-operative Republic Guyana 1970 — A Study of Aspects of a Way of Life* Georgetown, Guyana, June 1970, pp 21-36.

Lamming, George Sovereignty, Mobilization and Popular Consciousness. *Mobilization for Development and Self-reliance The Tasks of Political Education* Kingston, Jamaica People's National Party, 1984, pp. 37-50

— Most Sacred of Human Creations. *CARICOM PERSPECTIVE* 56 and 57 (July-December 1992), pp. 31

Lashley, Lynette. The Impact of American Television on the Youth of Trinidad and Tobago. *Caribbean Affairs* 4.4 (October-December 1991), pp 121-128.

Layne, Anthony. *Education, Inequality and Development in the Commonwealth Caribbean* Werkstattberichte zur vergleichenden Bildungsforschung [Workshop Reports in Comparative Training Research] Vol.1. Frankfurt/Main, Germany: Deutsches Institut für Internationale Pädagogische Forschung [The German Institute for International Pedagogic Research], 1982.

Leary, Paul M. and Klaus de Albuquerque The Other Side of Paradise: Race and Class in the 1986 Virgin Islands Election'. *Caribbean Affairs* 2.1 (January-March 1989), pp 51-63

Lebourne, Darnley WINFA Points the Way for Bananas. *CARICOM PERSPECTIVE* 56 and 57 (July-December 1992), pp 80-81.

Lennert, Gernot. *Die Außenbeziehungen der CARICOM-Staaten* Politikwissenschaftliche Perspektiven 2 [*The External Relations of the CARICOM States* Perspectives in Political Science No 2] Münster and Hamburg, Germany LIT, 1991.

Lent, John A. Communication Technology in the Caribbean The Ever-Increasing Dependency *Caribbean Affairs* 2 1 (January-March 1989), pp 155-179

— *Mass Communications in the Caribbean.* Ames, Iowa: Iowa State University Press, 1990.

— Who Owns Caribbean Mass Media? Foreign Domination — A Passing Phase. *Caribbean Affairs* 1.4 (January-March 1991), pp. 117-141.

Lestrade, Swinburne. The Special Regime for the OECS States. *CARICOM PERSPECTIVE* 36 (July-December 1986), pp. 22

Lett, Leslie [A.] Third World Theology: Why it is Political. *Caribbean Contact* March 1984, pp. 6.

— and Clyde Harvey *The Church and Caribbean Sovereignty.* II Caribbean Conference of Intellectual Workers. Mount St Benedict, Trinidad, January 13-14, 1984. Typescript n.d.

Levine, Barry B. Geopolitical and Cultural Competition in the Caribbean — An Introduction: Cuba versus the United States' In: (Ed.) *The New Cuban Presence in the Caribbean.* Boulder, Colorado: Westview Press, 1983, pp. 1-18.

Levitt, Kari. Canada and the Caribbean. *The Caribbean and World Politics. Cross Currents and Cleavages* In: (Eds.) Jorge Heine and Leslie Manigat. New York and London: Holmes & Meier, 1988, pp. 225-247.

Lewis, David The North American Free Trade Agreement· Its Impact on Caribbean Basin Economies *Caribbean Affairs* 4.4 (October-December 1991), pp. 56-67

Lewis, Gordon K. *The Growth of the Modern West Indies* New York and London. Modern Reader Paperbacks, 1968

— *Gather with the Saints at the River The Jonestown Guyana Holocaust of 1978.* Rio Pedras, Puerto Rico: University of Puerto Rico, 1979.

— *Main Currents in Caribbean Thought The Historical Evolution of Caribbean Society and Its Ideological Aspects, 1492 — 1900.* Baltimore and London: Johns Hopkins University Press, 1983.

— The Caribbean Community (CARICOM) Integration Experience: The Historical and Cultural Background. *Ten Years of CARICOM.* Washington, D.C.: Inter-American Development Bank, 1984, pp 39-53.

— *Grenada. The Jewel Despoiled.* Baltimore and London: Johns Hopkins University Press, 1987.

Lewis, James O'Neil. Reflections on Early Integration Efforts. *CARICOM PERSPECTIVE* 44 & 45 (January-June 1989a), p. 64

— Some Thoughts on Caribbean Integration *Caribbean Affairs* 2.3 (July-September 1989b), pp. 42-61

Lewis, Vaughan A. *The Idea of a Caribbean Community.* New World, Pamphlet No.9 Tunapuna, Trinidad: New World Publishing Co., April 1974

— *Size, Self-Determination and International Relations. The Caribbean* Kingston, Jamaica: Institute of Social and Economic Research, University of the West Indies, 1976.

— Regional Integration and Theories of Regionalism in the Commonwealth Caribbean. *The Economic Integration Process of Latin America in the 1980's. Papers presented at a seminar sponsored by the Inter-American Development Bank September 22-23, 1982* In: (Eds.) José Nuñez del Arco, Eduardo Margain and Rachelle Cherol. Washington, D.C.: Inter-American Development Bank, January 1984a, pp. 27-52.

— Geopolitical Realities in the Caribbean, with Special Reference to the Anglophone Caribbean. *Ten Years of CARICOM.* Washington, D C.: Inter-American Development Bank, 1984b, pp. 54-70.

— The Organisation's Mission *OECS in PERSPECTIVE* Castries, St. Lucia, and St John's, Antigua: OECS Secretariat, May 1987, pp. 5-6.

— Then and Now: Future Relations among the States of the Caribbean Community. *Caribbean Affairs* 2.2 (April -June 1989), pp. 1-17

— Caribbean Perspectives of the US-USSR Relationship. *USA, USSR and the Caribbean — New Realities* Kingston, Jamaica: Bustamante Institute of Public and International Affairs, 1990, pp. 22-34.

— and A.W.Singham. Integration, Domination and the Small-State System· The Caribbean. *Caribbean Integration.* Papers on Social, Political, and Economic Integration. Third Caribbean Scholars' Conference, Georgetown, Guyana, April 4-9, 1966. In: (Eds.) S.Lewis and T.G.Mathews. Rio Piedras, Puerto Rico· Institute of Caribbean Studies, University of Puerto Rico, 1967, pp. 119-140.

Lewis, William Arthur. The Industrialization of the British West Indies. *Caribbean Economic Review* 2 (1950).

— *The Agony of the Eight* Barbados: Advocate Commercial Printery, 1965.

— *Labour in the West Indies* London: New Beacon Books, 1977.

— Striving to be West Indian. *West Indian Law Journal* (Kingston, Jamaica· University of the West Indies, Council of Legal Education) Reprinted in· *The Daily Gleaner* 20 February 1983, p 18

Lijpart, Arend. Size, Pluralism, and the Westminster-Model of Democracy. Implications for the Eastern Caribbean. *A Revolution Aborted The Lessons of Grenada* Ed. Jorge Heine. Pittsburgh, Pennsylvania: University of Pennsylvania Press, 1990. pp. 321-340.

Lindberg, Leon N. Political Integration as a Multidemensional Phenomenon Requiring Multivariate Measurements. *International Organization* 24.4 (Autumn 1970), pp. 649-731.

Loewenstein, Karl. *Der Britische Parlamentarismus. Entstehung und Gestalt.* [*British Parliamentarism: Emergence and Form*] Reinbek, Germany: Rowohlt, 1964.

Lowenthal, David. The Social Background of the West Indies Federation. *The West Indies Federation. Perspectives on a New Nation.* In: (Ed.). American Geographical Research Series No.23. New York: Columbia University Press; London: Oxford University Press, 1961, pp. 63-99.

— and Colin G. Clarke. Caribbean Small Island Sovereignty: Chimera or Convention? *Problems of Caribbean Development. Regional Interaction, International Relations, and the Constraints of Small Size.* In: (Eds.) Ulrich Fanger *et.al.* Munich, Wilhelm Fink, 1982, pp. 223-242.

Lutchman, Harold A. Political Developments in Guyana and the Influence of the Small Political System. *Problems of Caribbean Development. Regional Interaction, International Relations, and the Constraints of Small Size.* In: (Eds.) Ulrich Fanger *et.al.* Munich: Wilhelm Fink, 1982, pp. 201-222.

MacDonald, Scott B. The Future of Foreign Aid in the Caribbean after Grenada: Finlandization and Confrontation in the Eastern Tier. *Inter-American Economic* Affairs (Washington) Vol.38. 4 (Spring) 1985, pp. 59-74.

— Harold M. Sandstrom and Paul B.Goodwin, (Eds.) *The Caribbean After Grenada: Revolution, Conflict and Democracy.* New York: Praeger, 1988.

Maingot, Anthony P. Reflections on a Caribbean Conference. *Express* (Trinidad) *Sunday Digest* 26 October 1980, p. 3.

— The Falklands for the Falklanders. *The Miami Herald* 25 April 1982, p. 3E.

— Cuba and the Commonwealth Caribbean: Playing the Cuban Card. *The New Cuban Presence in the Caribbean.* In: Ed. Barry B.Levine. Boulder, Colorado: Westview Press 1983a, pp. 1942.

— Ideology and Business in the Caribbean. Lecture to the Caribbean Central-American Action Conference on the Caribbean 30 November 1983b. Typescript.

— The United States and the Caribbean: Geopolitics and the Bargaining Capacity of Small States'. *Peace, Development and Security in the Caribbean. Perspectives to the Year 2000.* In: (Eds.) Anthony T.Bryan, J.Edward Greene and Timothy M.Shaw. Houndmills and London: Macmillan, 1990, pp. 57-84.

— *The United States and the Caribbean* . Boulder, Colorado: Westview Press, 1994.

Mandle, Jay R. *Big Revolution, Small Country: The Rise and Fall of the Grenada Revolution* Lanham: North-South Publishing, 1985.

Manigat, Leslie F. Is there a Common Caribbean Identity? *Problems of Caribbean Development. Regional Interaction, International Relations, and the Constraints of Small Size.* In: (Eds.) Ulrich Fanger *et.al.* Beiträge zur Soziologie and Sozialkunde Lateinamerikas [Contributions to the Sociology and Social Studies of Latin-America], Vol.21; Ed. Hanns-Albert Steger. Munich: Wilhelm Fink, 1982, pp. 11-34.

— Grenada. Revolutionary Shockwave, Crisis and Intervention. *The Caribbean and World Politics. Cross Currents and Cleavages.* In: (Eds.) Jorge Heine and Leslie Manigat. New York and London: Holmes & Meier, 1988, pp. 179-221.

Manigat, Mirlande. CARICOM at Ten. *The Caribbean and World Politics. Cross Currents and Cleavages.* In: (Eds.) Jorge Heine and Leslie Manigat. New York and London: Holmes & Meier, 1988, pp. 94-111.

Manley, Michael. Grenada in the Context of History. *Caribbean Review* 12.4 (Fall 1983), pp. 7-9, 45-47.

— *Up the Down Escalator.* Washington, D.C.: Howard University Press, 1987.

— *A History of West Indies Cricket.* London: André Deutsch, 1988

Manning, Patrick. Prospects for the Manning Initiative. *Prospects for the Manning Initiative: The Report.* Ed. Caribbean Youth Institute. February 1993. [Georgetown, Guyana, 1993], pp. 15-20.

Martini, Jürgen (Eds .) *Gesellschaft und Kultur in der Karibik.* Beiträge zur 1. interdisziplinären Karibik-Tagung an der Universität Bremen [*Society and Culture in the Caribbean.* Papers Read at the First Inter-disciplinary Caribbean Conference at the University of Bremen] (1981). Bremen, Germany: Universität Bremen, 1982.

Massiah, Joycelin. *Women as Heads of Households in the Caribbean: Family Structure and Feminine Status.* Paris: UNESCO, 1983.

— The UN Decade for Women: Perspectives from the Commonwealth Caribbean. *Bulletin of Eastern Caribbean Affairs, Special Issue, End of the UN Decade for Women 1975-1985* 11.2 (May/June 1985), pp. 1-9.

Maxwell, Neville. *The Power of Negro Action*. London: Self-print, 1965.

Mayers, Harry. Caribbean News Agency (CANA) Moves Forward. CANA-Feature. *The Sunday Gleaner* 3 February 1985, p. 21.

Mazrui, Ali A. Religious Alternatives in the Black Diaspora: From Malcolm X to the Rastatari. *Caribbean Affairs* 3.1 (January-March 1990),pp. 157-160.

McClean, Maxine. The 'New Venture Capitalists': The Caribbean Credit Union Movement in the Year 2000. *Caribbean Affairs* 4.3 (October-December 1990), pp. 137-149.

McDonald, Ian. To Be a West Indian: A Personal View of the Integration Movement. *Caribbean Affairs* 3 .3 (J ul y-September 1 990), pp. 113-133 .

McIntyre, Sir Alister. Caribbean Economic Community. Some Issues of Trade Policy in the West Indies. *New World Quarterly*. Croptime 1966.

— *The Caribbean after Grenada: Four Challenges Facing the Regional Movement*. Institute of International Relations Distinguished Lecturer Series. St. Augustine, Trinidad: University of the West Indies, 1984.

— Review of Integration Movements. *Ten Years of CARICOM*. Washington, D C · Inter-American Development Bank, 1984, pp. 14-26.

— The UWI Revisited. *CARICOM PERSPECTIVE* 43 (July-December 1988), pp. 5 and 8.

The Media and the Caribbean State. I Caribbean Conference of Intellectual Workers, Grenada November 20-22, 1982. Address by Tim Hector, Antigua. Typescript n.d..

Midgett, Douglas. *Eastern Caribbean Elections* 1950-1982. Iowa City, Iowa: University of Iowa, n.d.

Mills, Gladstone E., Sir Carlisle Burton, J.O'Neil Lewis and Crispin Sorhaindo. *Report on a Comprehensive Review of the Programmes, Institutions and Organizations of the Caribbean Community*. Georgetown, Guyana: Caribbean Community Secretariat, 1990.

Milne, Anthony. CARICOM's Ninth Heads of Government Conference: A Time for every Purpose under Heaven. *Caribbean Affairs* 2.1 (January-March 1989), pp. 64-85.

Mitchell, James F. *The Caribbean Mini State—The Exquisite Isles. Address to the World Affairs Council Northern California*. San Francisco 21st November 1973. [Kingstown, St. Vincent and the Grenadines] n.d.

— *East Caribbean Unity. Speeches Delivered by Rt. Hon. J F ('Son') Mitchell in Tortola and St. Kitts*. Kingstown, St.Vincent and the Grenadines: Government Printing Office, 1987.

Two Decades of Caribbean Unity. Kingstown, St.Vincent and the Grenadines· Government Printing Office, 1987b.

— ...I know that unity will deliver results to the people better... Elihu Rhymer: ...Only if there is a commitment to enforce the integrity of the union... An exclusive joint interview with Prime Minister James Mitchell of St.Vincent and the Grenadines, and Elihu Rhymer. *The Island Sun* (Tortola, B.V.I.), 6 June 1987c, pp. 10-11.

— To Be or Not to Be a Single Nation: That is the Question. *The Island Sun* (Tortola. B.V.I.) 6 June 1987d, pp. 16-17, and in: James Mitchell. *East Caribbean Unity. Speeches Delivered by Rt. Hon. J. F. (Son) Mitchell in Tortola and St Kitts*. Kingstown, St. Vincent and the Grenadines: Government Printing Office, 1987a.

— Time to Reflect: Time to Re-evaluate. Speech at the Miami Conference on the Caribbean in November 1986. Printed in: *Caribbean Democrat Union Monthly Newsletter* 2.5 (June 1987f), pp. 2-3.

Mitrany, David. *A Working Peace System*. Chicago: Quadrangle Books, 1966.

Mols, Manfred, Ed. *Integration und Kooperation in Latelnamerika*. Internationale Gegenwart I [*Integration and Co-operation in Latin America*. International Current Affairs, Vol. I] Paderbom *et.al*., Germany: Ferdinand Schöningh, 1981.

— Entstehungs- und Funktionsbedingungen eines lateinamerikanischen regionalen Subsystems. *Lateinamerika: Herrschaft, Gewalt und Internationale Abhängigkei* [Creation and Functional Conditionalities of a Regional Latin-American Sub-system *Latin America: Governance, Force and International Dependence*]. In: Ed. Klaus Lindberg. Off-print. Bonn, Germany: Verlag Neue Gesellschaft, 1982, pp. 191-216.

— SELA *Pipers Wörterbuch zur Politik.* [*Piper's Political Dictionary*] Ed Dieter Nohlen Vol 5 Munich and Zürich: Piper 1984, pp 449-451.

Moreno Fraginals, Manuel. Kultur zwischen Sklaverei und Plantagenwirtschaft [Culture Between Slavery and the Plantation Economy]. *Unesco-Kurier* 22 December 1981, pp 10-14

Morissey, M.P. The Country Preferences of School Children in Seven Caribbean Territories, 1982. *The Sunday Gleaner* 20 March 1983, pp 11.

Morrison, Herbert. *Regierung und Parlament in England. Government and Parliament in England.* Munich: C.H.Beck, 1956

Müllerleile [Muellerleile], Christoph Falkland-Konflikt löste Befürchtungen aus' *IIS-Auslandsiniormaionen* [Fear From the Falklands War *IIS Foreign Reports*] (St Augustin, Germany) 7 September 1982, pp. 15-18.

— Treffen der Regierungschefs der CARICOM-Staaten in Jamaica. *IIS-Auslandsinformationen* [CARICOM Heads Meet in Jamaica *IIS Foreign Reports*] (St Augustin, Germany) 18 February 1983a, pp.1-11.

— Intervention auf Grenada. *IIS-Auslandsinformationen* [The Intervention in Grenada *IIS Foreign Reports*] (St. Augustin, Germany) 28 November 1983b, pp 1-13

— Die internationalen Beziehungen Jamaicas *IIS-Auslandsinformationen* [The International Relations of Jamaica. *IIS Foreign Reports*] (St Augustin, Germany) 20 December 1983c, pp. 1-14.

— Die politische Entwicklung in Jamaica und der Karibik. *Konrad-Adenauer-Stiftung. Mitarbeiterkonferenz Lateinamerika 1983. Protokoll* [Political Development in Jamaica and the Caribbean. *Konrad-Adenauer-Stiftung. 1983 Staff Conference on Latin America.* Minutes] Sankt Augusin, Germany: Konrad-Adenauer-Stiftung, Institut für Internationale Solidarität; 1984, pp.277-26.

— Die Rolle der Blockfreien Staaten am Beispiel Mittelamerika und Karibik. *KAS Auslandsinformationen* [The Role of Non-Aligned States· Central America and the Caribbean *Konrad-Adenauer-Stiftung Reports from Abroad*] (St Augustin, Germany) September 1985, pp 24-60

— Attacke auf die kleinen Königreiche [Attack on Small Kingdoms] *Die Entscheidung* 37.3 (March 1989), pp. 22-24

Munroe, Trevor Comments on Thomas *The State in the Caribbean Society* In Ed Omar Davies. Kingston, Jamaica: University of the West Indies, Department of Economics, 1986, pp. 84-89.

— *Jamaican Politics· A Marxist Perspective in Transition.* Kingston, Jamaica. Heinemann (Caribbean); Boulder, Colorado: Lynne Rienner, 1990.

— and Rupert Lewis, (Eds.) *Readings in Government and Politics of the West Indies.* Kingston, Jamaica: University of the West Indies, Department of Government, 1 971.

Murray, R.N. *Nelson's West Indian History.* London *et.al.*: Nelson, 1971.

Nadir, Manzoor. *Economic and Political Problems in the Regional Integration of Small Caribbean States* Typescript, M A Thesis Manchester, University of Manchester, Faculty of Economic and Social Studies, September, 1989.

Naipaul, V[idiadhar] S[urajprasad]. *The Overcrowded Barracoon.* With Cricket 17-22; Power? 246-254 London· André Deutsch, 1972.

— Guerrillas. London: André Deutsch, 1975.

— *The Middle Passage Impressions of Five Societies — British, French and Dutch— in the West Indies and South America* André Deutsch 1962 Reprint· Harmondsworth, Middlesex *et. al.*· Penguin Books, 1985.

Nascimento, Christopher A. *The World Communication Environment Conflict or a Free and Open Encounter* A Collection of His Own Speeches Georgetown, Guyana: Ministry of Information, August 1981.

Nassau Understanding, The. Structural Adjustment and Closer Integration for Accelerated Development in the Caribbean Community. Nassau, Bahamas 7 July 1984. Supplement to *CARICOM PERSPECTIVE* 26 (July-August 1984).

Neal & Massy Holdings Limited *Annual Report & Accounts* 1988 Port-of-Spain, Trinidad, 1989

Neish, Robert Democracy and Security in the Caribbean *Democracy Today* (Kingston, Jamaica) 7 3 (May, June 1991), pp 2-3.

Nettleford, Rex M. *Caribbean Cultural Identity. The Case of Jamaica* Kingston, Jamaica Institute of Jamaica, 1978.

— Dance and Survival. *CARICOM PERSPECTIVE* 33 (November-December 1985), pp. 2 and 12.

— Restructuring of the UWI *CARICOM PERSPECTIVE* 38 (April-June 1987a), pp. 36.

— Cultivating a Caribbean Sensibility. Media, Education and Culture. *Caribbean Review* 15.3 (Winter 1987b), pp. 4-8 and 28.

— The Caribbean: The Cultural Imperative and the Fight Against Folksy Exotic Tastes. *Caribbean Affairs* 2.2 (April-June 1989), pp. 18-30.

New Cuban Presence in the Caribbean, Ed. Barry B. Levine. Boulder, Colorado: Westview Press, 1983 .

Newell, Granville. Caribbean Family Planning. *Caribbean Conact* March 1982, p. 12.

Newfarmer, Richard S. Economic Policy toward the Caribbean Basin: The Balance Sheet. *Journal of Interamerican Studies and World Affairs* 1.27 (February 1985), pp. 63-89.

Newton, Velma. *Commonwealth Caribbean Legal Systems: A Study of Small Jurisdictions*. Bridgetown, Barbados: Triumph Publications, 1988.

Nicholls, Neville. *The Caribbean at another Crossroads*. His Presidential Statement at the 22nd Annual Meeting of the Board of Governors, Radisson Resort Hotel, George Town, Grand Cayman, Cayman Islands, May 20 and 21, 1992. [Wildey, St. Michael, Barbados: Caribbean Development Bank, 1992].

— *Sustaining Development in the Commonwealth Caribbean*. His Presidential Statement at the 23rd Annual Meeting of the Board of Governors, Marriott's Sam Lord's Castle, St. Philip, Barbados, West Indies, May 12 and 13, 1993. [Wildey, St. Michael, Barbados: Caribbean Development Bank, 1993].

Nitoburg, Eduard Lwowitsch, Alexander Stepanowitsch Fetissow and Pjotr Pawlowitsch Jakowlew. *Licht und Schatten über Grenada. Hintergründe der USA-Agression*. [*Light and Shadows over Grenada. Background to the US Aggression*] Berlin, Germany: Militärverlag der DDR, 1987.

Nohlen, Dieter *et. al.*, (Eds.) *Mittelamerika und Karibik: Unterentwicklung und Entwicklung. Handbuch der Dritten Welt* [*Central America and the Caribbean: Under-development and Development*. Third World Handbook]. Vol. 3. 2nd revised Edn. Hamburg, Germany: Hoffmann and Campe, 1982

Mehr Demokratie in der Dritten Welt? *Aus Politik und Zeitgeschichte* Beilage zur Wochenzeitung *Das Parlament*. [More Democracy in the Third World? in: *Politics and Contemporary History*. Supplement to the weekly, Parliament] B 25-26/88 (17 June 1988), pp. 3-18.

Norton, Philip. The Norton View. *The Politics of Parliamentary Reform*. Ed. David Judge. London and Exeter: Heinemann Educational Books, 1983, pp. 54-69.

Nunes, Frederick E. The Nassau Understanding: From Agreement to Action *CARICOM PERSPECTIVE* 36 (July-December 1986), pp. 24-27.

Nurse, Lawrence. Organised Labour in the Commonwealth Caribbean. *A Caribbean Reader on Development*. Ed. Judith Wedderburn. Kingston, Jamaica: Friedrich-Ebert-Stiftung, 1986,1987, pp. 119-151.

Nye, Joseph Samuel. Patterns and Catalysts in Regional Integration. *International Organisation* 19.4 (Autumn 1965), pp. 870-884. International Regionalism. Readings. Boston: Little, Brown & Co, 1968, pp. 333-349.

— *Peace in Parts: Integration and Conflict in International Organizations*. Boston: Little, Brown & Co, 1971.

The Ocho Rios Declaration 18.11.1982. Caribbean Community Secretariat [Georgetown, Guyana] *News Release* No. 52/1982, 22 November 1982.

OECS in PERSPECTIVE 1987 Castries, St. Lucia, and St. John's, Antigua. Organisation of Eastern Caribbean States, May 1987.

OECS. Forms of Political Union. A Discussion Paper on A Union To Suit Our Needs. Federation? Confederation? Unitary State? Another Form? St. Lucia· OECS Secretariat, April 1988a.

OECS Secretariat. *Why a Political Union of OECS Countries? The Background and the Issues*. Castries, St. Lucia: OECS Secretariat, July 1988b.

Osborn, André. As I See It—The Caribbean Community. *Nation's Voice* (Antigua) 7 June 1985, p. 5.

O'Shaughnessy, Hugh. *Grenada: Revolution, Invasion and Aftermath*. London: Sphere Books, 1984

Oxaal, Ivar. *Race and Revolutionary Consciousness. A Documentary Interpretation of the 1970 Black Power Revolt in Trinidad*. Cambridge, Mass. and London: Schenkman, 1971.

Oxford Universal Dictionary Illustrated, (Eds.) William Little *et al.*, 3rd revised edn., 2 vols. Oxford *et.al.*, Oxford University Press, 1970.

Palmer, Ransford W. *Problems of Development in Beautiful Countries*. Lanham, Maryland: North South Publishing Company, 1984.

Pantin, Dennis. CARICOM Intraregional Trade Not Enough. *Caribbean Contact* July 1987 pp. 1 and 12.

Pantin, Raoul. Black Power on the Road: Portrait of A Revolution. *Caribbean Affairs* 3.1 (January-March 1990), pp. 171-185.

Pastor, Robert, and Richard Fletcher The Caribbean in the 21 st Century—A US Perspective. *The Courier* 132(March-April 1992), pp. 76-81.

Patmos, Jane [Pseud. for Aimée Webster]. CARICOM: Who Created this Whimsy? *The Sunday Gleaner* 17 June 1984, pp. 13 and 24.

Patterson, Orlando. The Ritual of Cricket. *Caribbean Essays—An Anthology*. Ed. Andrew Salkey. London: Evans, 1983, pp. 108-118.

Paxton, Jon, Ed. *The Statesman's Year-Book 1981 - 82*. New York. St. Martin's Press,1981.

Payne, Anthony. *The Politics of the Caribbean Community 1961-1979: Regional Integration among the States*. New York: St. Martin's Press, 1980.

— *Change in the Commonwealth Caribbean*. Chatham House Papers No. 12. London: The Royal Institute of International Affairs, 1 98 1.

— *The International Crisis in the Caribbean*. Baltimore: Johns Hopkins University Press, 1984a.

— Whither CARICOM? The Performance and Prospects of Caribbean Integration in the 1980s. *International Journal* (Toronto, Canada) 40 (Spring 1985), pp. 207-228.

— The Belize Triangle: Relations with Britain, Guatemala and the United States. *Journal of Interamerican Studies and World Affairs*, Coral Gables, Fla. 32.1 (1990), pp. 119-135.

— . and Paul Sutton, (Eds.) *Dependency under Challenge — The Political Economy of the Commonwealth Caribbean*. Manchester: Manchester University Press, 1984.

— ,Paul Sutton and Tony Thorndike. *Grenada—Revolution and Invasion* London and Sydney: Croom Helm, 1984.

— . and Paul Sutton, (Eds.) *Modern Caribbean Politics*. Baltimore and London· Johns Hopkins University Press, 1993 .

Pereira, Joseph R. The Function of a People's Regional University. *The University and the People*. Second Caribbean Conference of Intellectual Workers, Mount St. Benedict, Trinidad, January 13-14, 1984. Typescript n.d., pp. 3-17.

Petty, Colville L. *Anguilla: Where There's a Will There's a Way*. Anguilla: self published, 1984.

Phillips, Douglas Leopold. The DLP Philosophy. *Sunday Advocate* (Barbados) 1 December 1985, p. 4.

Phillips, Sir Fred. *Caribbean Life and Culture: A Citizen Reflects*. Kingston, Jamaica: Heinemann (Caribbean), 1991.

Plischke, Elmer. *Microstates in World Affairs: Policy Problems and Options*. Washington, D.C.: American Enterprise Institute for Public Policy Research, 1977.

Polanyi-Levitt. The Origins and Implications of the Caribbean Basin Initiative: Mortgaging Sovereignty? *International Journal* (Toronto) 2.4 (Spring 1985), pp. 37-281.

Political Parties of the Americas, Canada, Latin America and the West Indies. Ed. Robert J. Alexander. 2 Vol. Westport, Conn., and London: Greenwood Press, 1982.

Poon, Auliana. The Future of Tourism. *CARICOM PERSPECTIVE* 44 and 45 (Jan.-June 1989), pp. 51 and 52; 46 and 47 (July-December 1989, January-March 1990), p. 53.

Port-of-Spain Accord on the Management and Conservation of the Caribbean Environment, The. Issued by The First CARICOM Ministerial Conference on the Environment, Port-of-Spain, Trinidad and Tobago, 31 May-2 June, 1989. Georgetown, Guyana: CARICOM Secretariat, 1989.

Port-of-Spain Consensus of the Caribbean Regional Economic Conference. Port-of-Spain, Trinidad and Tobago I March, 1991. Supplement to *CARICOM PERSPECTI VE* 50 and 51 (January-June 1991).

Preiswerk, Roy, Ed. *Regionalism in the Commonwealth Caribbean*. Port-of-Spain: Institute of International Relations, 1969.

Premdass, Ralph R. Guyana: The Critical Elections of 1992 and a Regime Change. *Caribbean Affairs* 6.1 (January-March 1993),pp. 111-140.

Problems in Writing a General History of the Caribbean. *The Sunday Gleaner* (Kingston, Jamaica) 29 May 1983, p. 8.

Profile. The Organisation of Eastern Caribbean States, A. *CARIMEX '85 — A Caribbean Manufacturers Exhibition.* [Barbados: Caribbean Manufacturers Association, 1985].

Puchala, Donald J. International Transactions and Regional Integration. *International Organization* 24.4 (Autumn 1970), pp. 732-763.

Punnett, R. M. *British Government and Politics.* 4th Edn. Brookfield: Gower, 1984

Radio Antilles. 25 *Years 1963 — 1988.* Plymouth, Montserrat: Antilles Radio Corporation, 1988.

Rainford, Roderick. The Decision-making Process and the Institutional Fabric of CARICOM. *Ten Years of CARICOM.* Washington, D.C.: Inter-American Development Bank, 1984, pp. 217-232.

— The Caribbean Today: Perspective in the Caribbean Community. Address delivered at the Norman Bethune Conference, York University, Toronto, Canada, March 3, 1986. *CC Press Feature* 1/1986.

— 1992 and Beyond. *CARICOM PERSPECTIVE* 46 and 47 (July-Dec.1989/Jan.-March 1990), pp. 14-15.

— Some Implications for the Caribbean in 1991: The Single European Market. *Caribbean Affairs* 2.3 (July-Sept. 1990a), p. 14.

— Reflections on the Lessons to be Learnt from the Caribbean Community. *Caribbean Affairs,* 2.4 (October-December 1990b), pp. 6-20.

Rampersad, A.J. India's Imperialism and its Implication for St.Lucia and the Caribbean. Typescript n.d..

Ramphal, Shridath S. *West Indian Nationhood — Myth, Mirage or Mandate?* Opening Address in a series on 'Caribbean Perspectives' sponsored by the Institute of International Relations UWI delivered at the Public Library, Port-of-Spain, Trinidad, May 26, 1971, by the Honourable S.S.Ramphal, S.C. Attorney General and Minister of State. Georgetown, Guyana: Ministry of External Affairs, June 1971.

— *To Care for CARICOM. The Need for an Ethos of the Community.* Speech delivered by His Excellency Shridath S.Ramphal, Secretary General of the Commonwealth, at a dinner held in his honour by the CARICOM Council of Ministers, Montego Bay 5 July 1975. (Georgetown, Guyana) n.d.

— *Options for the Caribbean. The Lure of Real Politik.* Institute of International Relations, Distinguished Lecturer Series, St. Augustine, Trinidad and Tobago: University of the West Indies, Institute of International Relations, 1985.

— The University in the 90s: Finding Ways to Reduce the Knowledge Gap. *Caribbean Affairs* 3.1 (January-March 1990), pp. 109-113.

Rastafarians in Jamaica and Britain. Report of the Catholic Commission for Racial Justice. *Everybody's Magazine* (New York) 6.3 and 4 (1982).

Ratcliff, William E. Guyana'. *Communism in Central America and the Caribbean.* Ed. Robert Wesson. Stanford, California: Hoover Institution Press, 1982, pp. 143-158.

Regional Food and Nutrition Strategy, Supplement to *CARICOM PERSPECTIVE* 33 (November-December 1985).

Regional Integration and Theories of Regionalism in the Commonwealth Caribbean. *The Economic Integration Process of Latin America in the 1980s.* Papers Read at an Inter-American Development Bank Seminar 22.-23. September 1982. In: (Eds.) José Nuñez del Arco, Eduardo Margain and Rachelle Cherol. Washington, D.C.: Inter-American Development Bank, (January 1984).

Regionalism and the Commonwealth Caribbean. Ed. Roy Preiswerk. Special Lecture Series No.2. St. Augustine, Trinidad: University of the West Indies, Institute of International Relations, 1969.

Regis, Humphrey A. The Theoretical Framework for the Study of Cultural Domination by Re-exportation. *Caribbean Affairs* 1.4 (January-March 1991), pp. 106-116.

Report by the Hon. E.F.L.Wood, M.P., on His Visit to the West Indies and British Guiana, December 1921 to February 1922. *Cmd. 1679,* London 1922.

Report of the Caribbean Task Force. Part 1 *Overview and Recommendations.* Part 2 *Main Report and Appendices.* Trinidad and Tobago: Government Printery, February 1974.

Report of the Constitution Commission on the West Indies Associated States and Montserrat. Typescript Barbados 1976.

Ritch, Dawn. Abolishing Our Rights of Appeal. *Weekly Gleaner* 30 April 1991, p 25.

Richards, Mike. A Counter to Cultural Imperialism. *Caribbean Contact* February 1987, p. 13.

Richards, Viv. Mastering the Masters' Game. *CARICOM PERSPECTIVE* 44 and 45 (January-June 1989), pp. 20-21.

Rickey Singh and the Caribbean Media. Caribbean Conference of Intellectual Workers (I & II). Lectures. Grenada November 20-22, 1982, and Mount St. Benedict, Trinidad, January 13-14, 1984. Typescript n.d..

Roaring Lion, The. Calypso — from France to Trinidad. 800 Years of History San Juan, Trinidad: General Printers, 1987.

Robinson, A[rthur] N[apoleon] R[aymond]. Freedom of Our Own Creation. *CARICOM PERSPECTIVE* 37 (January-March 1987), pp. 4 and 36.

— *Transition and Reconstruction in Independence. Trinidad and Tobago A Third World Challenge* Fourth of the Distinguished Lecture Series of the Institute of International Relations, Trinidad Hilton, May 11, 1987. (Port-of-Spain, Trinidad and Tobago) Office of the Prime Minister (Information Division), n.d.

— *International Relations — Selected Addresses* (Port-of-Spain, Trinidad and Tobago) Office of the Prime Minister, August 1988a.

— *25th Independence Anniversary.* Port-of-Spain Trinidad and Tobago Office of the Prime Minister (Information Division) 1988b.

— The Future of the Caribbean. Address to the Royal Institute of International Affairs — Chatham House, 5 October 1988. Ed. Office of the Prime Minister (Information Division) (Port-of-Spain, Trinidad and Tobago). *News Release* No.1368, 25 October 1988c.

Robson, Peter. *Economic Integration in Africa.* London: Allen & Unwin, 1968.

Rodney, Walter. *The Groundings with my Brothers* London: Bogle L'Ouverture Publications, 1970.

Romero, Carlos A. Pragmatic Democracy. *Caribbean Affairs* 2 1 (January-March 1989), pp. 9-18.

Rosenbaum, H. Jon, and William G.Tyler. South-South Relations. the Economic and Political Content of Interactions among Developing Countries. *International Organization* Summer 1975, pp 243-274.

Royer, John. This Restless World. *The Daily Gleaner* 20 April 1983, p. 6

Rudder, Michael. Broadcasting in the Caribbean — A Unique Experience. Typescript. Christ Church, Barbados: Caribbean Broadcasting Union, 20 May 1985.

Russia in the Caribbean Special Report Series No.13. Washington, D.C.: Georgetown University, The Center for Strategic and International Studies, 1973.

Ryan, Selwyn. Ideology and Leadership in Trinidad and Tobago. *Caribbean Issues* (Trinidad and Tobago) 4.2 (August 1978), pp. 30-52.

— The Muslimeen Grab for Power: The Quaddafi Connection. *Caribbean Affairs* 4.2 (April-June 1991), pp. 69-80.

Salkey, Andrew *Georgetown Journal. A Caribbean Writer's Journey from London via Port-of-Spain to Georgetown, Guyana, 1970.* London: New Beacon Books, 1972.

Samuel, Wendell An Assessment of the CARICOM Integration Experience. *Development in Suspense* In: (Eds.) Norman Girvan and George Beckford. Kingston, Jamaica· Friedrich-Ebert-Stiftung and Association of Caribbean Economists, March 1989

Sanatan, Roderick. The Poor and the Powerless. Part 2 of an interview with Clive Thomas. *CARICOM PERSPECTIVE* 43 (July-December 1988), pp. 16-19

Sanders, Ron. Indian Indentureship in West Indies Marked. *Caribbean Contact* May 1988, pp. 8 and 12.

— Political Union in the OECS: An Opportunity Squandered? *Caribbean Affairs* 2.2 (April-June 1989), pp. 114-124.

— Narcotics, Corruption and Development: The Problems in the Smaller Islands. *Caribbean Affairs* 3.1 (January-March 1990), pp. 79-92.

Sandner, Gerhard. Antillen-Westindien-Karibischer Raum. Begriffe, Abgrenzungen, inhaltliche Definition. *Der Karibische Raum. Selbstbestimmung und Außenabhangigkeit* Ed. Institut für Iberoamerika-Kunde. Aktueller Informationsdienst Lateinamerika [The Antilles — West Indies — Caribbean Region: Terms, Delimitations, Definition of Content. in: *The Caribbean Area Self-determined and External Dependence.* (Ed.) Institute for Latin-American Information.

Topical Latin-American Information Service Special Issue] No.3. Hamburg, Germany: Inst. für Iberoamerika-Kunde, 1980, pp. 41-60.

Sandoval, José Miguel. State Capitalism in a Petroleum-Based Economy: the Case of Trinidad and Tobago. *Crisis in the Caribbean*. In: (Eds.) Fitzroy Ambursley and Robin Cohen. Revised Edition. Kingston, Port-of-Spain and London. Heinemann, 1984, pp. 247-268.

Scheman, L.Ronald. OAS gets a Surprising Overhaul at Cartagena *The Times of the Americas* 18 December 1985, pp. 1 and 12.

Schmitter, Philippe C. Central American Integration: Spill Over, Spill-Around or Encapsulation? *Journal of Common Market Studies* 9 (September 1970), pp 1-48

— *Autonomy or Dependence as Regional Integration Outcomes Central America* Berkeley: University of California, Institute of International Studies, 1972.

Schüller, Alfred. Die Verschuldungskrise als Ordnungsproblem. *Neue Zürcher Zeitung* 11 July 1988.

Schwarz, Hans Peter. Europa föderieren — aber wie? Eine Methodenkritik der europäischen Integration. *Demokratisches System und Politische Praxis in der Bundesrepublik.* [A Federation of Europe — How? A Methodological Critique of European Integration. *The Democratic System and Political Parties in the Federal Republic of Germany*] In: (Eds.) Gerhard Lehmbruch, Klaus von Beyme and Iring Fetscher. Munich: Piper, 1971, pp. 377-443.

Seaga, Edward. *Parliamentary Democracy in the Caribbean* (Kingston, Jamaica): API Press, May 1981

— *A Development Plan for the Caribbean. Address to the CARICOM Foreign Ministers Conference*, Kingston, 4th September 1981. Kingston, Jamaica: API [1981].

— Revival Cults in Jamaica — Notes Towards a Sociology of Religion. *Jamaica Journal* 3.2 (June 1969). Reprint Kingston, Jamaica. Institute of Jamaica, 1982.

— Major Issues in the Contemporary Caribbean Address by Prime Minister Edward Seaga to Harvard Centre for International Affairs. 9 March 1984 Typescript.

— The Caribbean and the Cuban Bombshell. *The Daily Gleaner* 10 March 1991. Quoted in: Rainer Hasters. Momentaufnahme Kuba Frühjahr 1991 Ausbau des Tourismus soll reduzierte Sowjethilfe ausgleichen [Cuba in Spring, 1991: Tourism to Make Up for Cut in Soviet Aid]. *KAS-Auslandsinformationen* Konrad-Adenauer-Stiftung Information from Abroad June 1991, pp. 1-9.

Sealey, John, and Krister Malm. *Music in the Caribbean* London *et al* : Hodder and Stoughton, 1982.

Searwar, Lloyd. Joint Conduct of External Political Relations and Its Effect on the Integration Process. *Ten Years of CARICOM* Washington, D C Inter-American Development Bank, 1984, pp. 156-166.

— Dominant Issues in the Role and Responses of Caribbean Small States *Peace, Development and Security in the Caribbean Perspectives to the Year 2000.* In· (Eds.) Anthony T. Bryan, J. Edward Greene and Timothy M. Shaw. Houndmills and London: Macmillan Press, 1990, pp 3-33.

Segal, Aaron *The Politics of Caribbean Economic Integration* Rio Piedras, Puerto Rico: Institute of Caribbean Studies, University of Puerto Rico, 1968.

Senghaas, Dieter. Einleitung. Regionalkonflikte in der internationalen Politik *Regionalkonflikte in der Dritten Welt: Autonomie und Fremdbestimmung.* [Introduction· Regional Conflicts in International Politics In: *Regional Conflicts in the Third World Autonomy and Heteronomy*]. In this author's Current Papers on International Politics. Vol.21. Baden-Baden, Germany: Nomos, 1989, pp. 11-28.

Serbín, Andrés. La izquierda caribeña antes y despues de Grenada, The Caribbean Left before and after Grenada *El Caribe contemporáneo*, Mexico 1986, No.12, pp. 37-58.

— *Etnicidad, clase y nación en la cultura política del Caribe de habla inglesa* Biblioteca de la Academia Nacional de la Historia [*Ethnicity, Class and the Nation in Anglophone Caribbean Political Culture*. Library of the National Academy for History] Vol 93. Caracas, Venezuela· Academia Nacional de la Historia, 1987.

— Race and Politics. Relations between the English-speaking Caribbean and Latin America. *Caribbean Affairs* 2.4 (October-December 1989), pp. 146-171.

— The CARICOM States and the Group of the Three: A new partnership between Latin America and the non-Hispanic Caribbean? *Journal of Interamerican Studies and World Affairs*, Coral Gables, Fla. 33.2 (1991), pp. 53-80.

Shah, Raffique. The Military Crisis in Triniad and Tobago During 1970. *Readings in Government and Politics of the West Indies.* In: (Eds.) Trevor Munroe and Rupert Lewis. Kingston, Jamaica: University of the West Indies, Department of Government, 1971, pp. 215-221.

Shearman, Peter. The Soviet Union and Grenada under the New Jewel Movement. *International Affairs* 61.4 (Autumn 1985), pp. 661-673.

Shelton, Sally A. Testimony of Sally A. Shelton before the Sub-Committee on Inter-American Affairs, US House of Representatives 15 June 1982. *Bulletin of Eastern Caribbean Affairs* 8.5 (November — December 1982), pp. 12-17.

Sherlock, Philip. Authentic West Indian Voices: Changing Perspectives on the West Indian Past. *CARICOM PERSPECTIVE* 35 (April-June 1986), p. 12.

— . and Rex Nettleford. *The University of the West Indies. A Caribbean Response to Challenge of Change.* London and Basingstoke: Macmillan Caribbean, 1990.

Shorey-Brian, Norma. The Making of Male/Female Relationship in the Caribbean. *Bulletin of Eastern Caribbean Affairs, Special Issue, End of the UN Decade for Women 1975 — 1985* 11.2 (May — June 1985), pp. 34-38.

Simpson, George Eaton. Religion and Justice: Some Reflections on the Ras Tafari Movement. *Journal of Caribbean Studies.* 5.3 (Fall 1986), pp. 145-154.

Singh, Rickey. Progress and Failure of the Hilton Summit. *Caribbean Contact* August 1983, p. 8.

— *Rickey Singh and the Caribbean Media.* Caribbean Conference of Intellectual Workers (I & II). Lectures. Grenada November 20-22, 1982, and Mount St.Benedict, Trinidad, January 13-14, 1984a. Typescript n.d..

— Peace in the Caribbean. *Weekend Nation*, 5 October 1984b, p. 7.

— Caribbean Sovereignty Jeopardised. *Caribbean Contact*, January 1985a, pp. 4 and 6.

— A Word to the Wise. *The Daily Gleaner*, 15 January 1985b, p. 8.

— Foreign TV — What We Say and Do. *Weekend Nation*, (Barbados) 8 November 1985c, pp. 8 and 13.

— Drugs — the Challenge that we Face. *Weekend Nation*, 19 November 1985d, p. 8.

— CARICOM's Human Rights Agenda'. *Weekend Nation*, 20 December 1985e, p. 8.

— CARICOM on 'Solid Ground'? *The Sunday Gleaner*, 11 August 1985f

— Barbados — US Relations. *Caribbean Contact*, 14 February (July 1986), pp. 4-5.

— Caribbean Year in Review. *Weekly Gleaner*, 9 January 1990, p. 22.

— The Windwards March to Political Union. *Weekly Gleaner*, 10 March 1992, p. 17.

Sitahal, Harold. Religion, Culture and Resistance. *Caribbean Contact*, March/April 1994, p. 18.

Sloan, John W. The Strategy of Developmental Regionalism: Benefits, Distribution, Obstacles, and Capabilities. *Journal of Common Market Studies* 10 February (December1971), pp. 138-163.

Small, Augustus C. Studying in the States. *Caribbean Review* (Miami, FL) 11April (Fall 1982), p. 22.

Small is Dangerous: Micro States in a Macro World· Report of a Study Group of The David Davies Memorial Institute of International Studies. Ed. Sheila Harden. London: Frances Pinter, 1985.

Smith, M.G. *Culture, Race and Class in the Commonwealth Caribbean.* Kingston, Mona, Jamaica: Department of Extra-Mural-Studies, University of the West Indies, 1984.

Sosoe, Lukas K. Die Sozialphilosophie Marcus Garvey: Nur eine Antwort auf eine Rassenfrage? *Rasse, Klasse und Kultur in der Karibik.* Ed. Karl Kohut. Publikationen des Zentralinstituts für Lateinamerika-Studien der Katholischen Universität Eichstätt, Serie A, Kongreßakten, 5 [The Social Philosophy of Marcus Garvey: only a Reaction on the Race Question? in: (Ed.) Karl Kohut *Race, Class and Culture in the Caribbean.* Publications of the Central Institute for Latin-American Studies of the Catholic University of Eichstätt, Series A. Proceedings of the 5th Congress]. Frankfurt/Main, Germany: Vervuert, 1989, pp. 63-71.

Sontheimer, Kurt. *Das politische System Großbritanniens.* [*The Political System of Great Britain*]. Munich: Piper, 1972.

Soviet Seapower in the Caribbean: Political and Strategic Implications. Ed. James D.Theberge. New York, Washington, London: Praeger, 1972.

Spence, Ermine. *Social and Political Communication through Popular Music in Jamaica.* M.A. Thesis, Dept. of Government, University of the West Indies, Mona. Kingston, Jamaica, October 1978.

Springer, Hugh W. *Reflections on the Failure of the First West Indian Federation.* Occasional Papers in International Affairs 4. Harvard University, Center for International Affairs, July 1962.

State in Caribbean Society, Ed. Omar Davies. Kingston, Jamaica: University of the West Indies, Department of Economics, September 1986.

Stella (Pen-name for Barbara Gloudon). Near and Yet So Far. *The Daily News* (Jamaica) 26 January 1982, p. 6.

Stone, Carl. *Democracy and Clientelism in Jamaica.* New Brunswick, N.J.: Transaction Books, 1980.

— Democracy and Socialism in Jamaica, 1962 — 1979. *The Journal of Commonwealth & Comparative Politics.* 19 February (July 1981), pp. 115-133.

— *The Political Opinions of the Jamaican People (1976-81).* Kingston, Jamaica: Blackett Publishers, 1982a.

— Poverty and Communism. *The Daily Gleaner* 10 March 1982b, p. 15.

— *Work Attitude Survey. A Report to the Jamaican Government.* St.Ann, Jamaica: Earle Publishers, 1982c.

— The Jamaican Reaction. Grenada and the Political Stalemate. *Caribbean Review,* 12.4 (Fall 1983 a), pp. 31,32, 60-63.

— Democracy and Socialism in Jamaica: 1972 — 1979. *The Newer Caribbean — Decolonization, Democracy and Development.* In: (Eds.) Paget Henry and Carl Stone. Philadelphia: Institute for the Study of Human Issues, 1983b, pp. 235-256.

— Decolonization and the Caribbean State System. *The Newer Caribbean — Decolonization, Democracy and Development.* In: (Eds.) Paget Henry and Carl Stone. Philiadelphia: Institute for the Study of Human Issues, 1983c, pp. 37-62.

— Caribbean Publications. *The Daily Gleaner* 7 December 1984, p. 10.

— Jamaica in Crisis: from Socialist to Capitalist Management. *International Journal* (Toronto, Canada) 40 (Spring 1985), pp. 282-311.

— *Power in the Caribbean Basin — A Comparative Study of Political Economy.* Philadelphia: Institute for the Study of Human Issues, 1986a

— A Political Profile of the Caribbean. *CARICOM PERSPECTIVE* 34 (January-March 1986b), p. 28.

— Democracy and the State. *The State in Caribbean Society.* Ed. Omar Davies. Kingston, Jamaica: University of the West Indies, Department of Economics, Sept.1986c, pp. 90-144.

— Buying Power. *Weekly Gleaner,* 28 April 1987a, p. 18.

— Lundstrom's 'Invasion Crusade'. *Weekly Gleaner,* 7 July 1987b, p. 18.

— Garvey Junior Returns. *Weekly Gleaner,* 8 December 1987c, p. 21.

— Black Racial Attitudes. *Weekly Gleaner,* 24 November 1987d, p. 21.

— Shut Up or Stay Home. *Weekly Gleaner,* 12 May 1987e, p. 16.

— Race and Economic Power in Jamaica: Toward the Creation of a Black Bourgeoisie. *Caribbean Review* 16.1 (Spring 1988), pp. 10-12.

— *On Jamaican Politics, Economics & Society. Columns from the Gleaner 1987 — 88.* Kingston, Jamaica: Gleaner Company, 1989a.

— Caribbean Development in the Year 2000: A Review of the Bourne Report. *Caribbean Affairs* 2.4 (October-December 1989b), pp. 71-79.

— Revival of Regionalism. *Weekly Gleaner,* 25 July 1989c, p. 15.

— The New Appeal Court. *Weekly Gleaner,* 18 July 1989d, p. 15.

— The Stench of Corruption. *Weekly Gleaner,* 1 August 1989e, p. 15.

— *Politics versus Economics.. The 1989 Elections in Jamaica.* Kingston, Jamaica: Heinemann Publishers (Caribbean), 1989f.

— Genuine Democracy Bastardised'. *Weekly Gleaner,* 1 May 1990a, p. 21.

— The Politics of Backwardness. *Weekly Gleaner,* 26 June 1990b, p. 21.

—Race and Leadership — The Hidden Agenda. *Weekly Gleaner,* 3 July 1990c, p. 21.

— Penetrating the Single Market. *Europe 1992 — The Single Market and its Implications for Labor.* Kingston, Jamaica: Bustamante Institute of Public and International Affairs, 1990d, pp 15-24.

— Bashing the IMF. *Weekly Gleaner*, 16 October 1990e, p 21.

— Soca Kill (*sic*) Reggae? Absolute Rubbish. *Weekly Gleaner*, 16 April 1991a, p. 21.

— Integration Talk *Weekly Gleaner*, 16 July 1991b, p. 33.

— Hard Drugs Use in a Black Island Society. *Caribbean Affairs*,4.2 (April-June 1991c), p. 142-161.

— Democracy in Haiti. *Weekly Gleaner*, 15 October 1991d, p. 21.

Strong, C.F. *Modern Political Constitutions — An Introduction to the Comparative Study of their History and Existing Form* Sixth Edn. (revised and expanded). London: Sidgwick and Jackson, 1963.

Sunshine, Catherine. CDU's Roots in Washington. *Caribbean Contact*, August 1986, p. 13.

Sutton, Paul. The Future of Relations between the European Community and the Caribbean. *The Courier* 132 (March-April 1992), pp. 56-58.

— . and Anthony Payne, (Eds.) *Size and Survival. The Politics of Security in the Small Island and Enclave Developing States of the Caribbean and the Pacific.* Portland, Oregon: International Specialized Book Service, 1993.

Taylor, Frank. Militarisation of the Caribbean Basin. *Caribbean Contact*, March 1984, pp. 14 and 16.

Taylor, Lloyd. The Grenada Crisis — The Barebones of an Analysis. *Forging a New Democracy — Beyond the Post-Colonial Aera* Ed. Raphael Sebastien. Trinidad and Tobago: Office of the Leader of the Opposition, (March 1985), pp. 75-83.

Ten Years of CARICOM Papers presented at a seminar sponsored by the Inter-American Development Bank July 1983. Washington, D.C.: Inter-American Development Bank, 1984.

Tetzlaff, Rainer. Weltbank und Währungsfonds als umstrittene 'Krisenmanager' in den Nord-Süd-Beziehungen. *Aus Politik und Zeitgeschichte* Beilage zur Wochenzeitung *Das Parlament* [The IMF and the World Bank: Controversioal 'Crisis Managers' in the North-South Relationship in. *Politics and Contemporary History.* Supplement to the weekly, *Parliament*]. B33-34/88 (12 August 1988), pp. 36-46

Tewarie, Bhoendradatt Understanding our Political Party System *Forging a New Democracy — Beyond the Post-Colonial Aera* Ed. Raphael Sebastien. Trinidad and Tobago. Office of the Leader of the Opposition, (March 1985), pp. 189-197.

Theodore, Karl. Pragmatism and Integration — Prospects and Possibilities for the Caribbean. *CARICOM PERSPECTIVE* 43 (July-December 1988), pp. 26-29.

Thinking Things Over. The Constitution Commission (1987) of the Republic of Trinidad and Tobago. (Port-of-Spain) Government Printery, 1988.

Third ACP-EEC Convention, Signed at Lomé on 8 December 1984. Complete Text. *The Courier Africa-Caribbean-Pacific — European Community.* Special Issue. 89 (January-February 1985).

Thomas, Clive Y[olande]. Neo-Colonialism and Caribbean Integration *Rattoon* (Georgetown, Guyana) April 1975, pp. 1-28.

— *From Colony to State Capitalism· Alternative Paths of Development in the Caribbean* Paramaribo: Foundation of the Arts and Sciences, 1982.

— *The Rise of the Authoritarian State in Periphal Societies* New York and London Monthly Review Press, 1984a

— State Capitalism in Guyana: An Assessment of Burnham's Co-operative Socialist Republic' *Crisis in the Caribbean.* In. (Eds) Fitzroy Amburseley and Robin Cohen. First Ed.1983, reprinted 1984 (with additions). Kingston, Port-of-Spain and London. Heinemann [b], pp 27-48

— The Authoritarian State in Caribbean Societies. *The State in Caribbean Society.* Ed. Omar Davies. Kingston, Jamaica: University of the West Indies. Department of Economics, September 1986, pp. 62-83.

— *The Poor and the Powerless Economic Policy and Change in the Caribbean.* New York: Monthly Review Press, 1988.

— Economic Crisis and the Commonwealth Caribbean: Impact and Response. *Caribbean Affairs* 2.4 (October-December 1989), pp. 21-48.

Thompson, L.O'Brien. How Cricket Is West Indian Cricket? Class, Racial and Color Conflict. *Caribbean Review* 12.2 (Spring 1983), pp. 22 and 53.

Thompson, P.A. A Strategy of Economic Development and the Integration Process. *Ten Years of CARICOM.* Washington, D.C.: Inter-American Development Bank, 1984, pp. 142-155.

Thorndike, Tony [Anthony E.]. The Politics of Inadequacy. A Study of the Associated Statehood Negotiations and Constitutional Arrangements for the Eastern Caribbean 1965-67. *Social and Economic Studies* (Kingston, Jamaica) 28.3 (1979), pp. 597-617.

— The Conundrum of Belize. An Anatomy of a Dispute. *Social and Economic Studies* (Kingston, Jamaica) 32.2 (1983), pp. 65-102.

— The Future of the British Caribbean Dependencies. *Journal of Interamerican Studies and World Affairs*, Coral Gables, Fla. 31.3 (1989), pp. 117-140.

Europe and the Caribbean: Threat or Opportunity. *Caribbean Affairs* 4.3 (October-December 1990), pp. 35-47.

Thoughts of Some OECS Leaders on Political Union for the OECS. Ed. Alvin Knight. Roseau, Dominica: East Caribbean Institute for Democracy, 1988.

Time for Action: The Report of the West Indian Commission. Black Rock, Barbados: The West Indian Commission, 1992.

Tobago Declaration, 1972, Towards an Eastern Caribbean Federation. Group of West Indians meeting in Tobago, June 10-11, 1972. Port-of-Spain, Trinidad: Busby's Printery, n.d.

Tracey, Lolita. CARIMAC Celebrates 10 Years of Progress. *Sunday Gleaner Magazine* 3 March 1985, pp. 4-5.

Trade Union Programme for the Structural Transformation of the Caribbean, A. ICFTU/CCL Conference and Special Session of the General Council, BWU Labour College, Barbados 9-11 April 1986. n.d.

Treaty Establishing the Caribbean Community: Chaguaramas, 4th July 1973. Caribbean Community Secretariat, November 1982.

Treaty Establishing the Organisation of Eastern Caribbean States. OECS Secretariat, n.d.

Trotman, Donald A.B. 'The European Convention on Human Rights: Its Relevance to the Commonwealth Caribbean'. *Caribbean Affairs* 2.1 (January-March 1989), pp. 141-154.

Troubles in a Pauper's Paradise. The Caribbean Archipelago of Tiny Democracies Faces Economic Woes. *Time Magazine.* Nachdr. *The Sunday Gleaner*, 16 January 1983, p. 11.

True Freedom and Development in the Caribbean. A Christian Perspective. A Joint Pastoral Letter of the Bishops of the Antilles Episcopal Conference. Commonwealth of Dominica 2 February 1982.

Tulloch, Vincent. Consolidating the Left in the Caribbean. *The Daily Gleaner* 8 July 84, p. 10.

Unity and Action for Democratic and Revolutionary Change in the Regional Youth Movement. Addresses by Cheddi Jagan and Earl Bousquet to the 13th Congress of the Progressive Youth Organisation (July 5-7, 1986, Enmore, East Coast Demerara, Guyana). Georgetown, Guyana: Progressive Youth Organisation, n.d.

USA, USSR and the Caribbean — The New Realities. Kingston, Jamaica: Bustamante Institute of Public and International Affairs, 1990.

UWI Under New Management. *Pelican* Cave Hill, Barbados: University of the West Indies, 1985, pp. 4-5.

UWIDITE — Reaching Out by Satellite. *Pelican.* Cave Hill, Barbados: University of the West Indies, 1985, pp. 10, 11 and 18.

Venner, Dwight, Vaughan A.Lewis, and Swinburne Lestrade. Statement on the Grenada Declaration. *Caribbean Quarterly* 18.2 (June 1972).

Viner, Jacob. *The Customs Union Issue.* New York: Carnegie Endowment for International Peace, 1950.

Vitalis, David. Drugs: Shake-Up Major Institutions. *Weekend Voice* (St. Lucia) 20 August 1988, p. 11.

Vitzthum, Wolfgang Graf. Seerecht. Staatslexikon. Ed. Görres-Gesellschaft. [Maritime Law. *State Lexicon.* (Ed.) Görres Society] Vol.4, 7th edn. Freiburg, Basel, and Vienna: Herder, 1988, pp. 1142-1144.

Vulnerability: Small States in the Global Society. Report of a Commonwealth Consultative Group. London: Commonwealth Secretariat 1985.

Walcott, Clyde. Steering from Behind. Sir Clyde Walcott interviewed by Hilary Beckles. *CARICOM PERSPECTIVE* 61 and 62 (July-December 1993), pp. 57 — 60.

Warner, Keith. *Kaiso! The Trinidad Calypso. A Study of the Calypso as Oral Literature.* Washington, D.C.: Three Continents Press, 1982.

Watty, William W. What is Caribbean Theology? *Castries Catholic Chronicle* (St.Lucia) 15 August 1982, p. 9.

— The Past, The Present and The Future of CCC. *Caribbean Contact* May/June 1992, pp. 13-14.

Weidenfeld, Werner. *30 Jahre EG. Bilanz der Europäischen Integration.* [*The European Community Thirty Years On. European Integration . A Balance Sheet*]. Bonn, Germany: Europa Union Verlag, 1987.

— Die Bilanz der Europäischen Integration 1988/89. *Jahrbuch der Europäischen Integration 1988/89.* [The 1988 — 89 Balance Sheet of European Integration. *European Integration Year Book for 1988-89*]. In: (Eds.) Werner Weidenfeld and Wolfgang Wessels. Bonn: Europa Union Verlag, 1989, pp. 13-24.

Wentzlaff-Eggebert, Harald. Auf der Suche nach karibischer Identität. Zum dichterischen Selbstverständnis von Gabriel García Márquez. *Entwicklungen im karibischen Raum 1980 — 1985* Ed. Wolfgang Binder. Erlanger Forschungen, Reihe A Geisteswissenschaften 37. Erlangen: Universitätsbund Erlangen-Nürnberg [Searching for Caribbean Identity on the Poetic Self-Perception of Gabriel García Márquez. *1980-85 Caribbean Area Developments.* (Ed.) Wolfgang Binder. Erlangen Research Series A, Humanities No.37. Erlangen: Erlangen-Nuremberg University Union], 1985, pp. 43-63.

Wenzel, Jörg. 'Filme aus der Karibik. Bilder aus dem Mittelmeer der neuen Welt'. *10.Französische Filmtage Tübingen 16.-23.6.93.* Tübingen: Verein zur Förderung der deutsch-französischen Filmkultur e.V. ['Caribbean Films — Pictures from the Mediterrenium of the New World'. *10th Tübingen French Film Festival.* 16. — 23 June 1993. Tübingen, Germany: Franco-German Film Promotion Society, Inc.], 1993. pp. 154-155.

West Indian Socialist Tradition. Educo Series 1, Political Philosophy. Ed. Anthony Mark Jones. Port-of-Spain, Trinidad: Educo Press, n.d.

Western Interests and US Policy Options in the Caribbean Basin. The Policy Paper. Atlantic Council's Working Group on the Caribbean Basin. *Western Interests and US Policy Options in The Caribbean Basin.* In: (Eds.) James R.Greene and Brent Scowcroft. Boston, Mass: Gunn & Hain, 1984.

Wheare, K[enneth] C[linton]. *Föderative Regierung* [*Federal* Government] Munich: C.H.Beck, 1959.

Whither Caribbean Health. Authored by Sir George Alleyne and Dr. Karen A. Sealey. West Indian Commission Occasional Paper 5. Black Rock, St. Michael, Barbados: The West Indian Commission Secretariat, May 1992.

Whitney, Peter. President Bush's New Enterprise for America's (*sic*) Initiative. *USA, USSR and the Caribbean — The New Realities.* Kingston, Jamaica: Bustamante Institute of Public and International Affairs, 1990, pp. 67-72.

Williams, Eric. *Inward Hunger. The Education of a Prime Minister.* London: André Deutsch, 1969.

— *The Caribbean Community Treaty. Speech by the Prime Minister of Trinidad and Tobago, Dr. Eric Williams in the House of Representatives on Friday, 15 June, 1973.* Port-of-Spain Public Relations Division, Office of the Prime Minister 1973a.

A New Federation for the Commonwealth-Caribbean? Port-of-Spain: PNM Publishing Company, 1973b. Reprinted from the *Political Quarterly* (London.) 44.3 (July-Sept.1973), pp. 242-256.

Capitalism and Slavery 1944 (University of North Carolina) Press. Reprinted. London: André Deutsch, 1974.

Forged from the Love of Liberty Selected Speeches of Dr. Eric Williams. Ed. Paul Sutton. Trinidad and Jamaica: Longman Caribbean, 1981.

Williams, Marion. An Analysis of Regional Trade and Payment Arrangements in CARICOM: 1971 — 82. *Social and Economic Studies* 34.4 (December 1985), pp. 3-33.

Wiltshire-Brodber. What Role Do the Caribbean People Play in Promoting Regional Integration? Towards a Wholistic [*sic*] Theory of Regional Integration. *Ten Years of CARICOM.* Washington, D.C.: Inter-American Development Bank, 1984. 183-200. *Ex parte* as The Caribbean Integration Movement: An Alternative Prospective. *CARICOM PERSPECTIVE* 21 (September-October 1983), pp. 10-12.

Wint, Carl. Local TV Programming — a Fair Job. *Weekly Gleaner*, 2 June 1987, p. 13.

Wöhlcke, Manfred. *Die Karibik im Konflikt entwicklungspolitischer und hegemonialer Interessen. Sozio-ökonomische Struktur, politischer Wandel und Stabilitätsprobleme.* Internationale Politik und Sicherheit 7. Ed. Stiftung Wissenschaft und Politik, Ebenhausen [*The Caribbean Caught Between Developmental and Hegemonic Interests Socio-economic Structure, Political Change and Stability Problems.* International Politics and Security No.7. (Ed.) The Foundation for Science and Politics, Ebenhausen]. Baden-Baden, Germany: Nomos, 1982.

— *Die Intervention in Grenada.* [*The Grenada Intervention.*] Ebenhausen, Germany: Stiftung Wissenschaft und Politik, 1984.

— Die Ursache der anhaltenden Unterentwicklung. *Aus Politik und Zeitgeschehen* Beilage zur Wochenzeitung *Das Parlament* [The Cause of Sustained Under-development in. *Politics and Contemporary History.* Supplement to the weekly, *Parliament*] B46/91 (8 November 1991), pp. 15-22.

Wood, E.F.L. Report by the Hon. E.F.L.Wood, M.P., on his Visit to the West Indies and British Guiana, December 1921 to February 1922. *Cmd. 1679,* London, 1922.

Woodward, Bob. *Geheimcode VEIL. Reagan und die geheimen Kriege der CIA.* [*Secret Code VEIL. Reagan and the Secret Wars of the CIA.*] Munich: Droemer/Knaur, 1987.

Working for Justice in the Hope for Peace. *CARICOM PERSPECTIVE* 41 (January-March 1988), pp. 32 and 35.

Worrell, DeLisle. Small Island Economies. Structure and Performance in the English-speaking Caribbean since 1970. New York, Westport, Connecticut, and London: Praeger, 1987.

— *A Common Currency for the Caribbean.* Black Rock, St. Michael, Barbados: West Indian Commission, 1992.

Worrell, Keith. Some Lessons from the Economic Integration of Very Small Economies: The Case of CARICOM. *Problems of Caribbean Development. Regional Interaction, International Relations, and the Constraints of Small Size.* In: (Eds.) Ulrich Fanger *et. al.* Beiträge zur Soziologie and Sozialkunde Lateinamerikas [Contributions to the Sociology and Social Studies of Latin-America], Vol. 21; Ed. Hanns-Albert Steger. Munich: Wilhelm Fink, 1982, pp. 155-173.

Yalem, Ronald. Theories of Regionalism. In: (Eds.) Richard A. Falk and Saul H. Mendlovitz. *Regional Politics and World Order.* San Francisco: W. H. Freeman, 1973, pp. 218-231.

Yelvington, Kevin A. Vote Dem Out. The Demise of PNM in Trinidad and Tobago. *Caribbean Review* 15.4 (Spring 1987), pp. 8-12, 29-33.

Young, Colville. Popular Cultures of the Caribbean. *CARICOM PERSPECTIVE* 44 and 45 (January-June 1989), p. 19.

Youth, Drugs and Morality Report of the Proceedings of the Second Youth Conference. Held at Government Conference Centre August 11-12, 1988 by The Bustamante Institute of Public and International Affairs. [Kingston, Jamaica]: Bustamante Institute of Public and International Affairs, October 1988.

The Author

Christoph Müllerleile's intimate relationship with the Caribbean reached its first apogee in 1981-85. That was when he was based in Kingston, Jamaica, as the Regional Observer of the International Institute of the Konrad-Adenauer-Stiftung. His main responsibilities included economic and social policy analysis, as well as cultivating contacts with relevant bodies in nineteen Caribbean States, territories and dependencies. Advising local entities on the creation and financing of institutions for political education in the Caribbean as well as for its political integration also formed part of his brief at that time. He has travelled widely throughout the Caribbean and still maintains several close contacts there.

Since his return to Germany, he has obtained his doctorate in Political Science at the Johannes Gutenberg University of Mainz and has continued being employed in the private sector. Distance and time have allowed him to reflect further and also more deeply in an internationally comparative context, on the Caribbean — besides, of course, keeping abreast of subsequent, relevant developments in this geopolitically strategic area.

His last post in his homeland, before first coming to the Caribbean, had been that of Deputy Press Spokesman for the Federal Christian Democratic Union in the German capital (1977-81). Prior to occupying that post, the author had, after completing his compulsory two-year German Army service in 1968, been, *inter alia*, a staff member in the Institute of Journalism (his major with minors in Political Science and Book Studies) at the Johannes Gutenberg University, and obtained his Master's degree in May, 1976. He also worked as a journalist with various German media houses since 1962.

Born in 1946 in Diez-on-Lahn, Dr. Müllerleile, married to Elisabeth, is the father of three children.

The Translator

Fitzroy Fraser was well known to the world of Caribbean letters and political studies. His satirical first novel, *Wounds in the Flesh* (1962) was favourably compared, in the English Quality Press, to the work of Sir Kingsley Amis and Evelyn Waugh. His 1968 study of political pathology of the West Indies Federation *(Centrifugalism in British Caribbean Federalism)* gave both historical depth and an international framework to that largely gratuitous fiasco.

Born in Kingston, Jamaica, in 1936 and educated there privately as well as in Basle, Madrid and Paris, he held an honours degree in History and Political Science from the University of London (1958) as well as a doctorate *(summa cum laude)* in Political Science (with minors in English and History) from the University of Heidelberg (1968) where he also studied Economics and Linguistics. In addition to lecturing at Geneva University and in Eastern Europe he was a sessional lecturer at the University of the West Indies. He had some twenty-seven years professional experience as a technical and general translator into English from Italian, German, French, Polish, Russian and Spanish. He returned to Jamaica in the early 1980s, planning to spend a mere few months, after living in Switzerland for almost two decades, but remained there, on and off, ever since. Before that, he also worked with international organisations in information and technology, besides being a marketing and information executive with several European multi-national corporations. Since returning to the Caribbean, he was also a political and economic consultant specialising in risk analysis and foreign exchange strategy and operation. He travelled extensively both within the CARICOM region and outside it.

Besides writing for the print and electronic media since 1956, his radio plays, short stories and poems have been broadcast regularly (including on the British Broadcasting Corporation, where he was trained in the Midlands Service in 1963). From 1989, Dr Fraser edited and published *Caribbean Spectrum*. A novel, a third collection of poems and a study on Jamaican politics as a Third World paradigm were his works in progress.

The father of two children, he enjoyed gardening, offshore sailing and Alpine skiing.

Dr. Fraser died in early 1996.

Index

C

D

H

I

J

K

L

M

N

O

U

V

Y

Z

www.ingramcontent.com/pod-product-compliance
Lightning Source LLC
Chambersburg PA
CBHW022346280326
41935CB00007B/92
* 9 7 8 9 7 6 8 1 8 4 6 1 0 *